WRITING BY STUDENTS IN *BACK TO THE LAKE*

5th Edition

Back to the Lake

A Reader & Guide for Writers

THOMAS COOLEY

BACK
TO THE
LAKE

A READER
& GUIDE FOR
WRITERS

Thomas
Cooley

FIFTH EDITION

W · W · NORTON & COMPANY · NEW YORK · LONDON

W. W. Norton & Company has been independent since its founding in 1923, when William Warder Norton and Mary D. Herter Norton first published lectures delivered at the People's Institute, the adult education division of New York City's Cooper Union. The firm soon expanded its program beyond the Institute, publishing books by celebrated academics from America and abroad. By midcentury, the two major pillars of Norton's publishing program—trade books and college texts—were firmly established. In the 1950s, the Norton family transferred control of the company to its employees, and today—with a staff of five hundred and hundreds of trade, college, and professional titles published each year—W. W. Norton & Company stands as the largest and oldest publishing house owned wholly by its employees.

Editor: Erica Wnek
Project Editors: Laura Dragonette and Diane Cipollone
Developmental Editor: Alice Vigliani
Assistant Editor: Serin Lee
Managing Editor, College: Marian Johnson
Managing Editor, College Digital Media: Kim Yi
Production Manager: Karen Romano
Media Editor: Joy Cranshaw
Media Project Editor: Diane Cipollone
Media Editorial Assistant: Juliet Godwin

Ebook Producer: Emily Schwoyer
Marketing Manager, Composition: Michele Dobbins
Design Director: Rubina Yeh
Text Design: Jo Anne Metsch
Director of College Permissions: Megan Schindel
College Permissions Editor: Patricia Wong
Photo Editor: Ted Szczepanski
Photo Research: Lynn Gadson
Composition: Westchester Publishing Services
Manufacturing: TC-Transcontinental Printing

Permission to use copyrighted material is included in the credits section of this book, which begins on p. 827.

Library of Congress Control Number: 2023947551
ISBN: 978-1-324-04680-6

W. W. Norton & Company, Inc., 500 Fifth Avenue, New York, NY 10110
wwnorton.com
W. W. Norton & Company Ltd., 15 Carlisle Street, London W1D 3BS
1 2 3 4 5 6 7 8 9 0

Preface

Back to the Lake takes its title from E. B. White's classic essay "Once More to the Lake," which I first read with awe and wonder as a student in a beginning writing course. Over the years since then, I have learned that the writing process, like the lake in White's essay, remains pretty much as it has always been—for humans, that is. (If you are a robot using AI to write, you're not exactly writing; you are combining phrases and sentences that have been written by humans who understand, as bots do not, that words stand for ideas.) Consequently, this book focuses on those timeless strategies of thinking and writing—particularly as they pertain to the traditional rhetorical modes of narration, description, exposition, and argument—to which even accomplished writers like White commonly turn (and return) in their work.

What *has* changed dramatically since White banged out his great *New Yorker* essays on a manual typewriter—and since the talented spider in *Charlotte's Web* used her early web skills to save Wilbur the pig from being turned into bacon—is not the process of writing itself but our *understanding* of the process. We now take it for granted, for instance, that the writing process is one we can untangle, decipher, and eventually master. This was not the case in White's day, as I discovered when, as a young associate professor of English, I rashly fired off a letter asking him to explain how he had composed "Once More to the Lake." To my astonishment, White not only responded in thoughtful detail to my inquiry, but he also said he didn't really know how he wrote anything. "The 'process' is probably every bit as mysterious to me," he confided, "as it is to some of your students—if that will make them feel any better."

Fortunately for today's students and teachers, the scene has changed; we now know a lot more than we once did about how the writing process works and how to teach it. *Back to the Lake* applies this understanding of the process to show students how to make the basic moves that seasoned writers make, whether consciously or otherwise, in their writing.

An Overview of the Book

Back to the Lake is a reader and guide for writers. It contains eighty readings—from the classic ("Shooting an Elephant") to the most current ("Why People Are So Awful Online")—all demonstrating basic, fundamental strategies of thinking and writing that all good writers use. Each method is illustrated by five to eight readings (including at least one annotated student example) that show how the modes are used both in general writing and in common academic genres such as reports, arguments, and analyses. And substantial writing guidance appears in chapters covering the writing process, the parts of the essay, writing sentences and paragraphs, using sources, and more.

Chapter 1 introduces students to the steps for reading actively (previewing, annotating, summarizing, and responding) and provides templates and examples.

Chapter 2 covers the basic moves of academic writing, helping students research a topic, synthesize ideas, respond with ideas of their own, consider counterarguments, and explain why their ideas matter.

Chapter 3 offers guidance on the elements that make up an essay: topic, thesis, coherence, tone, and style.

Chapter 4 gives an overview of the writing process, preparing students to analyze assignments, come up with topics and generate ideas, draft and revise an essay with a particular audience and purpose in mind, and edit and proofread.

Chapter 5 helps students craft clear and effective sentences by giving advice on identifying and editing common sentence-level issues, including sentence fragments, comma splices, and the passive voice.

Chapter 6 provides guidance on writing paragraphs, with an in-depth discussion of topic sentences, transitions, and parallel structures—and how to use the modes to develop coherent paragraphs, including introductory and concluding paragraphs.

Chapters 7 through 15 each focus on one of the rhetorical modes as a basic strategy of discovery and development. Practical guidelines lead students through the process of composing a text using that mode: generating ideas, organizing and drafting, getting feedback, and revising and editing a final draft.

Chapter 16 demonstrates how real-world writing combines these strategies.

Chapter 17 offers guidance in finding, incorporating, and documenting sources using MLA style, with a complete color-coded documentation guide—and includes an annotated student research paper. Guides for APA, Chicago, and CSE styles are available in the accompanying *Little Seagull Handbook* ebook at digital.wwnorton.com/backtothelake5.

A glossary / index completes the book, providing definitions of all the key terms along with a list of the pages where they are covered in detail. In the ebook, pop-up definitions define key terms right where they appear. And an index of templates for writing makes it easy to find and use these tools for getting started.

Highlights

The perfect mix of model essays: classic and contemporary, long and short, by students and professional writers. From classic ("Ain't I a Woman?") to current ("Dear Ijeawele") to humorous ("Types of Women in Romantic Comedies Who Are Not Real"), all selections demonstrate the patterns taught in this book. Each chapter includes an annotated student essay.

A complete writing guide, with advice intuitively organized into three parts: the writing process, essays and approaches, and using sources in your writing.

Readings and writing instruction are explicitly linked with notes in the margins that make this book work well in courses taking an *integrated reading-writing approach*. See pp. 110 and 142 for two examples.

Everyday examples show that the methods taught in this book are familiar ones—and that they are not used just in first-year writing: that crossing a street, for example, relies on process analysis; and that advertisements are carefully constructed arguments.

Templates for drafting provide language to help students get started with the fundamental moves of describing, comparing, defining, and so on. An index of templates begins on p. 871.

Practical editing tips help students check for the kinds of errors that frequently occur with each of the rhetorical methods taught in this book; and a chapter on writing and editing sentences offers guidance on fixing common issues.

Help for students who can use more support, including glosses for unfamiliar terms and cultural allusions, templates for getting started, and advice for writing paragraphs and catching common sentence-level issues. Adaptive activities in InQuizitive also help students practice their writing, editing, and research skills.

Access to *The Little Seagull Handbook*, the #1 best-selling handbook. Students who purchase *Back to the Lake* get four-year ebook access to the *Little Seagull*—no special package or extra cost required. Visit digital.wwnorton.com/backtothelake5.

The Norton Illumine Ebook includes low-stakes, auto-graded Check Your Understanding questions for every chapter and reading in the text, helping students gauge their comprehension as they read and providing personalized feedback.

Resources for your LMS include integrated links for your online, hybrid, or lecture courses. The Norton Illumine Ebook, InQuizitive for Writers, *The Little Seagull Handbook* ebook, Norton's animated composition videos, and the plagiarism tutorial can all be accessed from within your learning management system. Graded activities can be configured to report to the LMS course gradebook.

What's New

Half of the readings (forty-one) are new, including Michelle Zauner's descriptive essay about Korean food and culture, Trevor Noah's narrative about attending school in apartheid South Africa, and Roxane Gay's argument about why people are so awful online. The classics are refreshed, too, with additions such as George Orwell's "Shooting an Elephant" and Louise Erdrich's "Two Languages in Mind, but Just One in the Heart."

A new chapter, "Elements of the Essay: Topic, Thesis, and Style," offers guidance on the main elements to consider when crafting an academic essay.

Expanded coverage of analytical writing guides students in composing analyses of texts and visuals in addition to writing process analysis essays.

Two new topics of debate appear in the Argument chapter: "Debating the Effects of Living Online and on Our Devices," with selections by Roxane Gay, Sherry Turkle, Jonathan Haidt and Jean M. Twenge, and Andrea Lunsford; and "Debating the Ethics of Banning Books and Canceling People and Ideas," with selections by Viet Thanh Nguyen, Shannon Palus, David French, and Robert DesJarlait.

New InQuizitive for Writers activities on Rhetorical Situations, Elements of Argument, Thesis Statements, Critical Reading Strategies, and Paragraph Development complement the classic research and sentence-editing activities.

A new collection of animated videos offers students extra help with rhetorical concepts and processes, from recognizing and developing thesis statements to understanding citation practices to organizing and synthesizing ideas—and more. The videos are brief—less than three minutes—and can be used in your online, hybrid, or classroom-based course.

A new Norton Teaching Tools website includes both the updated Instructor's Guide, now easily searchable and filterable, and a new comprehensive guide to teaching first-year writing that covers everything from designing a course to responding to student writing to engaging in difficult conversations in the classroom. You will also find tips and best practices for assigning InQuizitive for Writers, *The Little Seagull Handbook* ebook, Norton's animated composition videos, and other digital resources.

Find all of the digital resources at <u>digital.wwnorton.com/backtothelake5</u>.

Acknowledgments

For their generous assistance with this Fifth Edition of *Back to the Lake*, I wish to thank a number of people. As always, I am most grateful to Barbara Cooley, whose work as an editor and science writer has long helped reduce pollution not only in my prose but in the Florida Everglades and beyond. To Erica Wnek and Claire Wallace, my general editors at Norton, thank you yet again for holding this sprawling project together and guiding it steadily forward at every stage of a busy period for us all. Thanks to Alice Vigliani for her expert line editing and other hands-on work and to Serin Lee for her nimble editorial assistance and good cheer. For research assistance, especially with the new essays, I thank Olivia Cooley. I wish to also thank Joy Cranshaw and Juliet Godwin for their work on the fine digital resources that support this book, including the Check Your Understanding questions for the Norton Illumine Ebook and the revised Instructor's Guide for the Norton Teaching Tools site created by Michal Brody, Cheryl Smart, Aaron Cloyd, and Frances Johannsen. In addition, I am grateful to Laura Dragonette for expertly managing this project; Ted Szczepanski for handling the many photos; Patricia Wong for clearing the numerous permissions; Karen Romano for getting the book produced in good form despite the many deadlines some of us missed; and Marilyn Moller, Marian Johnson, and Julia Reidhead for their support of this ambitious project all along the way. Finally, thanks to marketing manager Michele Dobbins and the indomitable army of Norton travelers and sales specialists who spread the word.

Thanks go as well to the following teachers who reviewed the Fourth Edition: Judith P. Broadbent, Columbia State Community College; Matt Byars, Lubbock Christian University; Patrick Callan, Monroe Community College; Jennifer Collar, Paris Junior College; Anne L. Dearing, Hudson Valley Community College; Darren DeFrain, Wichita State University; Jennifer Eble, Cleveland State Community College; Carey Gable, Paris Junior College; Nay S. Heng, East Los Angeles College and Rio Hondo College; Edwina Howard-Jack, Pierpont Community & Technical

College; Stephen Hoyle, Dabney S. Lancaster Community College; Ronette Jacobs, Paul D. Camp Community College; Alice Justice, Paul D. Camp Community College; Kateema Lee, Montgomery College; Claire Lutkewitte, Nova Southeastern University; Jose Rene Martinez, South Texas College; Eleni Mylonas, Fairleigh Dickinson University; Deborah Muse, Crowder College; Anthony Romano, Fairleigh Dickinson University; Elizabeth Ruleman, Tennessee Wesleyan University; Cheryl Smart, Southwest Tennessee Community College; Rachel G. Wall, Georgia Highlands College; and Jason Walter, East Georgia State College.

I am grateful as well to the instructors who took time to share their thoughts on the new readings: Joyce Choi, Crescenta Valley High School; Claire Lutkewitte, Nova Southeastern University; Shaun Morgan, Ball State University; Deborah Muse, Crowder College; Christina Nalbandian, Chaminade College Preparatory; Leah Sneider, Montgomery College; and Brian Stepanic, Newark High School.

Thanks also to the many teachers across the country who have reviewed various previous editions and offered valuable input and encouragement: Heidi Ajrami, Victoria College; Shenai Alonge, Lubbock Christian University; Camila Alvarez, Indian River State College; Kellee Barbour, Virginia Western Community College; Andrea Bates, Coastal Carolina Community College; Judy Bello, Lander University; Debra Benedetti, Pierpont Community and Technical College; Dawn Marie Bergeron, St. Johns River State College; Mark Bernier, Blinn College—Brenham Campus; Kathleen Collins Beyer, Framingham State College; Don Boes, Bluegrass Community and Technical College; Patricia Bostian, Central Piedmont Community College; Jonathan Bradley, Concord University; Elizabeth Broadwell, Eastside High School; Mary Jane Brown, Miami University Middletown; Jennifer Browne, Frostburg State University; Sarah Burns, Virginia Western Community College; Marian Carcache, Auburn University; Darci Cather, South Texas College; Amy (Cooper) Suchon, St. Cloud State University; Lily Corwin, Kutztown University; Sara Danielson, Lincoln Southeast High School; Larry O. Dean, Northeastern Illinois University; Kathleen Dixon, University of North Dakota; MaryBeth Drake, Virginia Western Community College; Justin Eatmon, Coastal Carolina Community College; George Edwards, Tarrant County College–Northwest Campus; Jennifer Eimers, Missouri Valley College; Christine N. Ethier, Camden County College and Community College of Philadelphia; Jean M. Evans, Norwalk, Connecticut, Public Schools; Lynn Ezzell, Cape Fear Community College; Richard Farias, San Antonio College; Adam Fischer, Bowie State University; Adam Floridia, Middlesex Community College; Gabriel Ford, Penn State–University Park; Kerry L. Frabrizio, Warren County Community College; Kelley D. McKay Fuemmeler, Missouri Valley College; Curtis Fukuchi, Tarrant County College–Northwest Campus; Hannah Furrow, University of Michigan–Flint; Bill Gahan, Rockford College; Margaret V. Gardineer, Felician University; Judy Gardner, University of Texas at San Antonio; Mary Ellen Ginnetti,

Hillsborough Community College; Loren C. Gruber, Missouri Valley College; Peggy Hach, SUNY New Paltz; Monica Hatchett, Virginia Western Community College; Catherine F. Heath, Victoria College; Beth Heim de Bera, Rochester Community and Technical College; Christa Higgins Raney, University of North Alabama; James M. Hilgartner, Huntingdon College; Gina L. Hochhalter, Clovis Community College; Sylvia Holladay, Hillsborough Community College; Jo Ann Horneker, Arkansas State University; Stephen A. Housenick, Luzerne County Community College; Tina Hultgren, Kishwaukee College; Elizabeth Huston, Eastfield College; Donald Hutchinson, Arkansas State University Mid-South; Laura Jensen, University of Nebraska; Sandra Kelly, Virginia Western Community College; Aaron Kimmel, Penn State; Malvina King, Hillsborough Community College; Katie Kozak, Marysville High School; Anne M. Kuhta, Northern Virginia Community College; Jim LaBate, Hudson Valley Community College; Jill A. Lahnstein, Cape Fear Community College; Mary E. Lounsbury, Tarrant County College–Northwest Campus; Henry Marchand, Monterey Peninsula College; Matthew Masucci, State College of Florida; Howard Mayer, University of Hartford; Sean McAuley, North Georgia Technical College; Mary Murray McDonald, Cleveland State University; Scott Moncrieff, Andrews University; Stephen Monroe, University of Mississippi; Bryan Moore, Arkansas State University; Steve Moore, Arizona Western College; Jeanne-Marie Morrissey, Castleton State College; Angela Mustapha, Penn State; Daniel Olson, North Harris College; Joyce O'Shea, Wharton County Junior College; Michelle Paulsen, Victoria College; Betty J. Perkinson, Tidewater Community College; Jacklyn R. Pierce, Lake-Sumter State College; Jeffrey Powers-Beck, East Tennessee State University; Gregg Pratt, North Country Community College / SUNY Adirondack; Rodney Rather, Tarrant County College–Northwest Campus; James Rawlins, Sussex County Community College; Lisa Riggs, Oklahoma Wesleyan University; Louis Riggs, Hannibal LaGrange University; Jacquelyn Robinson, Victoria College; Cheryl Saba, Cape Fear Community College; Craig-Ellis Sasser, Northeast Mississippi Community College; Lori Svatora, Lincoln North Star High School; Alex Tavares, Hillsborough Community College; Anne Taylor, North Dakota State College of Science; Kelly Terzaken, Coastal Carolina Community College; Julian Thornton, Gadsden State Community College; Nann Tucker, Hillsborough Community College; Anita Tully, Nicholls State University; April Van Camp, Indian River State College; Julie Vega, Sul Ross State University; Maryann Vivolo-Sclafani, Felician University; Karina Westra, Point Loma Nazarene University; Lea Williams, Norwich University; Mark Williams, California State University, Long Beach; Stephanie Witcher, Crowder College; Glen Young, Petoskey High School; Daniel Zimmerman, Middlesex County College; and Jamie L. Zorigian, Lehman College.

It is a great pleasure to name the teachers of writing and experts in the field of composition and rhetoric who have given advice, or otherwise assisted me, at various stages in the evolution of this book. They include my colleagues at Ohio State, particularly Beverly Moss, Sara Garnes, and the late Edward P. J. Corbett; the late Dean McWilliams of Ohio University; Roy Rosenstein of the American University of Paris; and, for his great generosity in allowing me to use the fruit of his research and experience in the appendix, Richard Bullock of Wright State University. For a clean, well-lighted place to write away from home, thanks to Ron and Elisabeth Beckman of Syracuse University and Paris.

Finally, I say a big thank you to Gerald Graff and Cathy Birkenstein for showing me—particularly in *"They Say / I Say": The Moves That Matter in Academic Writing*—how to represent sophisticated intellectual and rhetorical strategies in a shorthand, generative way that teachers can actually use to help students make those moves in their own writing. I believe, with them, that writing and reading are "deeply reciprocal activities" and that "imitating established models" is one of the best ways to learn how to write.

Contents

• Student writing

"In real life, my parents had bypassed that kind of irresistible attraction with almost three decades of houses, children, and pets. In real life, their marriage had proved to be a patchwork of incongruities, the kind that were bound to exist between a cosmopolitan girl from Bombay and a small-town boy from outside Madras."

"I put my 1983 Nikes on . . . and my denim jacket with the Michael Jackson button, and of course, my headscarf."

◆ Student writing

8 Description 179

9 Example 249

◆ Student writing

◆ **ANA PACHECO,** *Street Vendors: Harvest of Dreams* 261

EVERYDAY EXAMPLE / Food Fakes 268

THE ONION, *All Seven Deadly Sins Committed at Church Bake Sale* 271
"In total, 347 individual acts of sin were committed at the bake sale, with nearly every
attendee committing at least one of the seven deadly sins as outlined by Gregory the
Great in the Fifth Century."

CHIMAMANDA NGOZI ADICHIE, *Dear Ijeawele* 275
"At the checkout counter, the cashier said mine was the perfect present for the new boy.
I said it was for a baby girl. She looked horrified. 'Blue for a girl?' I cannot help but
wonder about the clever marketing person who invented this pink-blue binary."

PETE BUTTIGIEG, *On Suicide Circle* 281
"As the seconds passed, I had a choice: I could *trust* that the man had good intentions, or
I could jump out of the lightly armored SUV in the middle of a traffic jam and level my
M4 at him until he retreated."

ASHLEY PELDON, *My Scream Is Famous* 286
"We do a wide variety of screams as actors, and there's a difference between what we do in
reality and what we expect to see on screen. In real life, a lot of people would just suck in
their breath and not release any noise when they are frightened, but that's not as dramatic
when it's shown on screen."

10 Analysis 291

PHILIP WEISS, *How to Get Out of a Locked Trunk* 321
"Every culture comes up with tests of a person's ability to get out of a sticky situation. . . . When they slam the [car] trunk, though, you're helpless unless someone finds you. You would think that such a common worry should have a ready fix, and that the secret of getting out of a locked trunk is something we should all know about."

ANNIE DILLARD, *How I Wrote the Moth Essay—and Why* 328
"Walking back to my desk, where I had been answering letters, I realized that the burning moth was a dandy visual focus for all my recent thoughts about an empty, dedicated life. Perhaps I'd try to write a short narrative about it."

MAGDALENA OSTAS, *Emily Dickinson and the Space Within* 337
"Isolation proved a guard against rigid social expectations, especially those imposed on women, which would likely have restrained her poetic craft. Alone with herself, and her boundless creative explorations, she found a world in inner space."

DAN REDDING, *What Does the Nike Logo Mean?* 343
"To say that the Nike Swoosh represents motion and speed is only to inspect the surface of the design. The Nike logo meaning is imbued with the results of long-term, multi-billion-dollar branding efforts."

11 Cause and Effect 349

◆ Student writing

◆ Student writing

16 Combining the Methods 733

PART III: Using Sources in Your Writing

◆ Student writing

Guide to the Readings by Theme

Family and Home

Gender

History

Humor and Satire

Identity

Language

Life, Death, and Health

Media and Popular Culture

Overcoming Adversity

Public Policy

Sports and Leisure

Student Writing

Technology

Work and Business

Writers and Writing

Guide to the Readings by Academic Genre

Evaluations

Literacy Narratives

Memoirs and Personal Narratives

Profiles

Reflections

Reports Based on Research

Rhetorical Analyses

Textual Analyses

1

The Reading Process: Good Writers Are Good Readers

The more that you read, the more things you will know. The more that you learn, the more places you'll go.

—Dr. Seuss, *I Can Read with My Eyes Shut!*

Let's start with the alphabet. By the time you learned the alphabet song, you were already proficient at what linguists call *first order* language skills—listening and speaking. We pick up these skills naturally as young children simply by hearing other people talk and by imitating the sounds we hear. The *second order* language skills, reading and writing, take much longer to learn, and they require more formal instruction—just as it took you more time and study to learn the written (as opposed to spoken or sung) alphabet. This is especially true if we are to achieve real competence with the written word. To a degree, however, we learn to write as we first learned to speak—by imitating the words of others.

Consequently, good writers are usually good readers. They may not read every book in the library; but they read critically, or mindfully—paying close attention to the strategies and techniques that accomplished writers use all the time for presenting their ideas. They also read critically by questioning the accuracy and validity of what they read, a vital skill for intellectual survival in the age of digital technology and the internet. This chapter focuses on how to engage in such close reading and provides some guidelines to help you read the essays in this book with an eye for what they can teach you about your own writing.

Reading as a Writer

Like writing, reading is an active process. Even when you take a thriller to the beach and read for fun, your brain is at work translating words into mental images and ideas. When you read more purposefully, as with the essays in this book, your brain will get even more of a workout. In both instances, however, the words on the page form a text that can be analyzed and interpreted. The word "text," like the word "textile," derives from the Latin word for weaving. A text is a written fabric of words. When you read a text with a critical eye, you unravel that fabric, looking at how the words fit together to make meaning. You also question what you're reading and think more deeply about your own ideas on the subject.

Reading a text critically doesn't mean that you have to be judgmental. Instead, it means that you analyze the text as carefully and objectively as you can. This is why critical reading will be defined in this book as *close* reading: it sticks to the text as closely as possible and avoids reading too much (or too little) into the text.

Reading critically is also a little like investigating a crime scene. You're looking for the writer's motives. The clues lie mainly in the text itself—the words on the page or screen before you. You're also looking for the writer's methods. You want to know not only *why* the text was committed but also *how*. With a crime scene investigation, the goal is to identify the perpetrators and bring them to justice.

Your ultimate goal in reading a text—and exactly how you go about achieving it—will depend on your PURPOSE for reading—on *why* you're examining the text in the first place.

Considering Your Purpose

Consider the words of a great essayist:

> Some books are to be tasted, others to be swallowed, and some few to be chewed and digested; that is, some books are to be read only in parts; others to be read, but not curiously; and some few are to be read wholly, and with diligence and attention.
>
> —Francis Bacon, "On Studies" (1597)

Why would anyone read a book or essay "wholly, and with diligence and attention"? One reason would be if you were assigned a reading in a course and expected to be tested on the material in it. Another would be if you were writing a paper, and your research indicated that a particular article was essential reading in the field. Or you might read a book wholly and with attention (but not necessarily so much diligence) if you were reading it—a novel, say—largely for pleasure, for what Bacon called "delight."

When your purpose is to read for pleasure, read any way you like. But when you're reading to gather information and develop ideas, there is no better way than by "chewing and digesting"—that is, by thinking carefully and critically ("with diligence and attention") about the meat of what you're reading as you read it. Before you consume an entire text, however, there is a proven way—like a taste before swallowing—to see whether or not a particular text will fit your purpose: you can *preview* it.

Previewing a Text

Before you delve "wholly" into a text only to discover that you're totally on the wrong track, take a few minutes to survey the territory. Previewing a text will give you a rough idea of what the text is about and where it's going. It's your chance to anticipate, to make educated guesses—perhaps a false start or two. So let yourself be surprised; no harm will come of a little early exploration. You can always change your mind when you have more information—and are sure you're on the right track now because you've gotten your bearings before you start.

Here are some tips for previewing before reading:

- *Think about your purpose for reading.* Is it to verify facts, obtain basic information on a subject, look for ideas, investigate a CLAIM? Will you be citing (or even directly responding to) the text in your own writing? Are you hoping the text will lead you to other sources you can use? Whatever it may be, your purpose in reading will affect what you look for and focus on as you read.

- *Consider the context.* Before you dig deeply into the text, read any prefatory material that accompanies it, such as a headnote or ABSTRACT. Who is the author (or authors)? Do they appear to have an agenda—or an ax to grind? When and where (an academic journal, a magazine or newspaper, a blog) was the text originally published, and what do these facts suggest about the text?

- *Think about the title.* What does it reveal about the TOPIC and TONE of the text? Does the title make a direct statement or CLAIM? Is it intended to provoke the reader? poke fun at its subject? something else?

- *Skim the text for other design elements* that may help guide your reading. Note headings, boldfaced words, lists, and other features that highlight important information and suggest how the text is organized.

- *Read the introductory paragraph(s) and the conclusion.* What do they imply (or tell you directly) about the topic, purpose, and main message of the text?

- *Think about the overall form and method of the text.* Does the writer seem mainly to be giving an EXPLANATION, conducting an ANALYSIS, drawing COMPARISONS, constructing an ARGUMENT, telling a story? How might this strategy offer clues to what the writer has to say?

TEMPLATES FOR PREVIEWING A TEXT

Every text is different, and no piece of writing that is worth reading can be reduced to a simple formula. However, the following templates can help you apply these strategies of prereading as you survey almost any text:

▸ My ultimate purpose in reading X is _____.

▸ Judging from the context and title, I would say the main subject of X is _____.

▸ Skimming the headings and other design elements in X, I see that it is organized by / as / into _____, perhaps indicating _____.

▸ About the general subject of X, the introductory and concluding paragraphs suggest that the writer is saying, specifically, _____ and/but _____.

▸ This reading is supported by the overall form and method of the text, which appears to be basically a _____ developed largely by _____.

To see how these templates can help you preview a specific text, let's apply them to a classic American essay, "Once More to the Lake" by E. B. White. The full text of White's essay begins on p. 215. Turn to it now, and read the introductory note for information about the circumstances, or CONTEXT, in which the essay was written. Then preview the text itself, using the templates above—and the advice on which they're based—as your guide. Hopefully, they'll lead you to something like this:

▸ My ultimate purpose in reading "Once More to the Lake" is to understand the essay and learn more about the reading process.

▸ Judging from the context and title, I would say the main subject of the essay is a fishing trip the writer takes with his young son to a remote lake in Maine where he himself vacationed as a boy.

▸ Skimming the headings and other design elements, I see that it is organized as a single essay—perhaps indicating a sharp focus on the scene at the lake.

▸ About the general subject of "Once More to the Lake," the introductory and concluding paragraphs suggest that White is saying, specifically, that everything seems the same at first but this sense of timelessness turns out to be an illusion.

▸ This reading is supported by the overall form and method of the text, which appears to be basically a personal narrative developed largely by comparing and contrasting the scene now with how it was in the past.

Reading a Text Closely and Critically

Once you've previewed a text and have a general idea of what you think it's about, the next step is to probe more deeply into the meaning of the text—and how the author gets that meaning across to the reader.

Whether you're reading just a few paragraphs or an entire book, the key to understanding what any text has to say (and how) is to "interrogate" the text by asking—and jotting down your answers to—certain leading questions along the way. (You can record your responses on a separate page or directly in the margins as you read.) Here are some fundamental questions to ask (and respond to) as you interrogate a text:

- *What is the writer's main point (or thesis)?* Is it clearly stated? If so, where? If the main point is not stated directly, where is it most clearly implied?

- *Where and how does the text support its main point?* Look for specific details, facts, examples, expert testimony, and other forms of evidence.

- *Is the evidence sufficient?* Or does it fail to convince you? Why? Are sources clearly identified so you can tell where cited material is coming from?

- *Does the text introduce opposing points of view?* What are they? Are they represented fairly and accurately? Where and how?

- *What seems to be the main purpose of the text?* To provide information? Describe something or someone? Tell a story? Argue a point of view?

- *What is the general tone of the text?* Serious? Informal? Inspirational? Which specific passages illustrate this tone of voice most clearly?

- *Who is the intended audience?* Readers who are familiar with the topic? Those who know little about it? People who are inclined to agree—or disagree? How can you tell?

TEMPLATES FOR QUESTIONING A TEXT

Again, every text is different, and no piece of writing that is worth reading can be reduced to a simple formula. However, the following templates can help you answer these fundamental questions as you probe more deeply into the meaning and form of any text:

▶ On the general subject of _____, the main point of this text seems to be that _____.

▶ The text supports this thesis mainly through _____ and _____.

▶ As further evidence for this view, the text also offers _____.

▶ The ultimate purpose of the text would seem to be _____.

▶ The overall tone of the text can be described as _____.

▶ The intended audience for the text is apparently _____.

Turn again to White's "Once More to the Lake" (pp. 215–20), and read it closely from beginning to end, using these templates to question the text as you go. Plunging more deeply into White's essay with these templates in mind, we might come up with something like the following:

▶ On the general subject of <u>time and change</u>, the main point of this text seems to be that <u>both are inevitable in human life</u>.

▶ The text supports this thesis mainly through <u>a detailed description of the altered scene</u> and <u>a narrative of the events that lead the writer to feel his own mortality</u>.

▶ As further evidence for this view, the text also offers <u>a comparison and contrast between the place as it seems and as it actually is</u>.

▶ The ultimate purpose of the text would seem to be <u>showing the folly of believing that time can stand still</u>.

▶ The overall tone of the text can be described as <u>nostalgic</u>.

▶ The intended audience for the text is apparently <u>readers whose dreams of a more innocent time are soon to be clouded by war</u>.

APPLYING THE "QUESTIONING" TEMPLATES TO AN ACADEMIC ESSAY

In the following passage from a *Wikipedia* article, the authors (including the Oxford University philosopher Martin Poulter) examine the origins of a new area of study within the field of psychology. The marginal comments show how the "questioning" templates can be used to probe an example of more formal academic writing:

On the general subject of heuristics, the main point of the text seems to be that heuristics are strategies for making judgments and decisions.

The text supports this thesis mainly through references to the work of two psychologists named Tversky and Kahneman and . . .

. . . by giving the specific example of statements about a person called "Linda."

As further evidence for this view, the text also offers a basic rule of logic having to do with "conjunction."

The ultimate purpose of the text would seem to be explaining that heuristics can often be linked to cognitive biases.

The overall tone of the text can be described as critical yet sympathetic, toward both the subjects and the experimenters.

The intended audience for the text is apparently people whose intuitive judgments don't always follow the rules of logic.

Heuristics in Judgment and Decision-Making

"Heuristics" are simple strategies to form judgments and make decisions by focusing on the most relevant aspects of a complex problem. . . . In the early 1970s, psychologists Amos Tversky and Daniel Kahneman linked heuristics to cognitive biases. Their typical experimental setup consisted of a rule of logic or probability, embedded in a verbal description of a judgment problem, and demonstrated that people's intuitive judgment deviated from the rule. The "Linda problem" is an example.

Tversky and Kahneman gave subjects a short character sketch of a woman called Linda, describing her as "31 years old, single, outspoken, and very bright. She majored in philosophy. As a student, she was deeply concerned with issues of discrimination and social justice, and also participated in anti-nuclear demonstrations." People reading this description then ranked the likelihood of different statements about Linda.

Among others, these included "Linda is a bank teller" and "Linda is a bank teller and is active in the feminist movement." People showed a strong tendency to rate the latter, more specific statement as more likely, even though a conjunction of the form "Linda is both X and Y" can never be more probable than the more general statement "Linda is X." The explanation in terms of heuristics is that the judgment was distorted because, for the readers, the character sketch was representative of the sort of person who might be an active feminist but not of someone who works in a bank.

Annotating a Text: The "Says" / "Does" Approach

By asking leading questions of a text and then using the "questioning" templates to help you find answers, you open a sort of dialogue with the text. That dialogue is ongoing because each time you revisit the text (or a part of it), you may think of new questions to ask—or additional answers to your original questions. How do you keep track of this "conversation"—your observations, reactions, and ideas in response to a reading? You do it by *annotating* the text.

When you ANNOTATE a text you mark it up, either by hand or by using digital annotation tools, in order to note your immediate reactions to the text and any further questions it raises in your mind as you read. In much academic writing, the writer makes a point by stating it directly and then doing something to back up that statement, such as giving EXAMPLES, making COMPARISONS, or offering logical reasons. One useful way to annotate a text, in part, therefore, is by following the "says/does" approach.

With the says/does approach, you mark the text to indicate when and where the writer makes a significant statement or CLAIM, either direct or implied. You also mark the text in some way to indicate each time the writer does something to support this statement or claim. One benefit of annotating a text by using this approach is that it helps you distinguish what a writer has to say (the "content" of the text) from how the writer says it (the "form" of the text). The ultimate purpose of the approach is to enable you to recognize the basic patterns of writing outlined in this book so that you can use them in your own writing.

So, beginning with the says/does approach, here are some tips for annotating a text as you read.

TIPS FOR ANNOTATING A TEXT

- **Mark what the text says.** Underline or otherwise indicate THESIS STATEMENTS, TOPIC SENTENCES, RHETORICAL QUESTIONS (questions that are actually statements), key terms, and other places in the text where the writer says, or directly implies, what the text is about. You can even tag these elements by writing "says" in the margin next to them. This practice will help you identify the main claims and other "content" of what you're reading—focusing your attention more on *what* the text says than *how* it says it. Wherever you make a "says" notation, try restating the passage in your own words in the margin to make sure you understand it. If time permits, you might try reading through the entire text and concentrate on making "says" annotations alone.

- **Mark what the text does.** Underline or otherwise indicate where the writer introduces facts, figures, logical reasoning (including FALLACIES in logic), claims of special knowledge or authority, ANECDOTES (or longer stories), physical DESCRIPTIONS, COMPARISONS, analyses of CAUSE AND EFFECT, and FIGURES OF SPEECH—or uses any other rhetorical strategies—as a way of giving proof or support for what the text has to say. Tag these elements by writing "does" in the margin next to them. This practice will help you identify the specific rhetorical strategies and patterns of organization that shape the "form" of whatever you're reading—focusing your attention more on *how* the text works than *what* it says. If feasible, try reading through the entire text again, concentrating this time on "does" annotations.

- **Jot down your immediate reactions.** Mark places in the text where you agree, disagree—or both—with the author(s), and note why. If you have an emotional reaction to the text, or it reminds you of a personal experience, indicate that and describe your feelings or recollections. Log any COUNTERARGUMENTS or related sources that you want to check out.

- **Tag passages you find confusing or hard to understand.** Circle or underline unfamiliar words and phrases, and write down what they mean in your own words after you've looked them up. Use question marks to indicate difficult passages, and ask specific leading questions of your own about the text as you go. Be persistent when reading a difficult passage. Simply noting tough spots and admitting that they're difficult can help you deal with them later.

Here's how a deeply engaged reader might annotate a page from "Once More to the Lake" by following these tips and procedures:

We went fishing the first morning. I felt the same damp moss covering the worms in the bait can, and saw the dragonfly alight on the
tip of my rod as it hovered a few inches from the surface of the water.
It was the arrival of this fly that convinced me beyond any doubt
that everything was as it always had been, that the years were a
mirage and that there had been no years. The small waves were the same,
chucking the rowboat under the chin as we fished at anchor, and the
boat was the same boat, the same color green and the ribs broken
in the same places, and under the floorboards the same freshwater
leavings and débris—the dead helgramite, the wisps of moss, the
rusty discarded fishhook, the dried blood from yesterday's catch. We
stared silently at the tips of our rods, at the dragonflies that came
and went. I lowered the tip of mine into the water, tentatively, pensively dislodging the fly, which darted two feet away, poised, darted
two feet back, and came to rest again a little farther up the rod.
There had been no years between the ducking of this dragonfly and
the other one—the one that was part of memory. I looked at the boy,
who was silently watching his fly, and it was my hands that held his
rod, my eyes watching. I felt dizzy and didn't know which rod I was
at the end of.

Annotations:
- DOES: tells a story
- SAYS: nothing has changed here since he was a boy
- Figuratively—like with a child
- Great bait for bass!
- DOES: describes the scene in minute detail
- What helgramite worm turns into: a transformation
- DOES: com-pares the lake now with the lake as it was
- SAYS: the essay is about a state of mind

Responding to a Text

After you have read and reread a text closely, "re-view" it once more: think about
your general experience in reading the text, and record your response in writing,
perhaps in a notebook or file set aside for that purpose. This step in the reading process will serve you well when it comes time to recall what you've learned and put it
to use on an exam, in a paper, or in other critical reading that you do. Here are a few
tips for reflecting on and responding to a text as you review it.

TIPS FOR RESPONDING TO A TEXT

- **Answer, alter, or add to your earlier annotations.** If you've found an answer to a question you posed when reading the text earlier, jot it down now. If you misunderstood something before, correct yourself; but don't erase your original thought—your annotations are like a diary of your travels back and forth through the text.

- **Summarize what you've read in your own words.** If you can write a brief, accurate SUMMARY of a writer's main points, you probably have a good grasp of what you read. Looking back at your notes on previewing, questioning, and annotating the text may help.

- **Think about and record your lasting impressions of the text.** After reading the text in full, where are you most inclined to accept the writer's ideas? Least inclined? Aren't sure?

- **Consider what you've learned about writing.** Looking back at your annotations—particularly those indicating what the writer "does"—ask yourself which methods, devices, and patterns you most want to try in your own writing. Also, consider which ones you think didn't work so well and that, consequently, you want to avoid.

Identifying Common Patterns

How a writer structures a piece of writing is often your best clue to what the writer has to say. Consider the following passage from a language experiment:

> The procedure is actually quite simple. First you arrange things into different groups. Of course, one pile may be sufficient depending on how much there is to do. If you have to go somewhere else due to lack of facilities, that is the next step. Otherwise you are pretty well set. . . . After the procedure is completed, one arranges the materials into different groups again. Then they can be put into their appropriate places. Eventually they will be used once more, and the whole cycle will then have to be repeated. However, that is part of life.
> —JOHN D. BRANSFORD AND MARCIA K. JOHNS, "Contextual Prerequisites for Understanding"

Although the authors of this little passage never utter the words "doing the laundry," that is clearly (or at least dimly) what it is about. We know this because the passage has the overall form of a **PROCESS ANALYSIS**. In other words, this would seem to be a set of instructions for doing something. We may not be told what that something is at first; but by the time we get to the end of the "procedure" and learn that the "cycle" starts over again once the things are "used," we can likely guess just what the writers are asking us to sort out.

> Annie Dillard (p. 328) writes a process analysis of her own writing process.

When you read a text for meaning (what the text says), sometimes your best guide is the form, structure, or underlying pattern of the text (how the text says it) rather than any direct statement of meaning within the text itself. In the case of our laundry example, the authors deliberately relied on the form of the passage to convey its meaning because it was part of a study about how learning is affected by using **ABSTRACT** language—"things," "lack of facilities," "part of life"—instead of more **CONCRETE** words like "jeans," "socks," and "dirty towels." Sorting your laundry, it would seem, is good practice for other, more stubborn forms of analysis because they, too, require putting "things into different groups."

Four Basic Types of Writing

All the essays you'll read in this collection can be divided into four fundamental types of writing: narration, description, exposition, and argument. These basic writing strategies can be defined as follows:

- **NARRATION** is storytelling. Narrative writing focuses on events; it tells what happened ("pitched tent, launched canoe, caught two bass"). Patterns and methods of narration are discussed in Chapter 7.

- **DESCRIPTION** appeals to the reader's senses. Descriptive writing tells what something looks, feels, sounds, smells, or tastes like ("nice here but buggy"). Patterns and methods of description are discussed in Chapter 8.

- **EXPOSITION** is informative writing ("the fish are bigger this year than they were last year"). It is the form of writing you use when you give examples (Chapter 9), analyze a subject and its causes and effects (Chapters 10 and 11), compare and contrast things (Chapter 12), classify them (Chapter 13), or construct definitions (Chapter 14). Exams, research papers, job applications, sales reports, insurance claims—in fact, almost every kind of practical writing you do over a lifetime, including your last will and testament—will require expository skills.

- **ARGUMENT** is persuasive writing. It makes a claim and offers evidence that the writer hopes will be sufficient to convince the reader to accept that claim—and perhaps even to act on it ("it's very relaxing here; you should come"). Patterns, methods, and strategies of argument are discussed in detail in Chapter 15.

IDENTIFYING COMMON PATTERNS OF WRITING IN E. B. WHITE'S "ONCE MORE TO THE LAKE"

Assuming that you've read "Once More to the Lake" carefully now—using the various reading strategies discussed in this chapter—let's return yet again to White's essay for a final read. This time our focus is on how a great writer like White weaves together, in a single essay, strands from the four most basic forms of writing. If you can see how White uses these common patterns even in such a finely textured piece of work, you'll be on your way to using them in your own writing.

RECOGNIZING NARRATION. White begins his essay with a phrase pertaining to time: "One summer along about 1904." He might as well have written "Once upon a time," as the opening paragraph takes place long ago and is almost pure narrative. **NARRATIVE** writing tells what happened to someone or something. You can recognize a narrative because it deals with events, such as:

- taking the family to a camp on a lake in Maine
- getting ringworm and having to apply Pond's Extract
- rolling over in a canoe with clothes on
- returning year after year

White's essay focuses on a particular occasion "a few weeks ago" when he took his young son to fish for the first time on the freshwater lake in Maine where White himself vacationed when he was a boy (1). What follows is an account of the ordinary events that take place during that brief visit, leading to a **CLIMAX** in the **PLOT** at the end of the week when a storm gathers over the lake and the writer suddenly feels older as his son pulls on his wet bathing suit.

RECOGNIZING DESCRIPTION. "Once More to the Lake" is a superb piece of **DESCRIPTIVE** writing. You can recognize description because it focuses on aspects of people, places, and things that appeal directly to the five senses. For example, White writes about:

- "the fearful cold of the sea water" (1)
- "the wet woods whose scent entered through the screen" (2)
- "the first glimpse of the smiling farmer" (9)
- "[t]he shouts and cries of the other campers" (9)
- "the pop [that] would backfire up our noses and hurt" (11)

White describes the lake itself as "fairly large and undisturbed" (3). Its shores are "heavily wooded," and the whole place feels remote, despite some cottages "sprinkled around" the water (3). When White goes fishing the first morning, he pictures the boat in vivid, CONCRETE detail: "the dead helgramite, the wisps of moss, the rusty discarded fishhook, the dried blood from yesterday's catch" (5). And, of course, there are the dragonflies: "We stared silently at the tips of our rods, at the dragonflies that came and went" (5). The DOMINANT IMPRESSION we get of the lake and its surroundings here is one of tranquility and timelessness— at first.

RECOGNIZING EXPOSITION. White is not only telling a story about what happened at the lake and giving a description of the place, but he is also explaining the meaning and significance of those events and that setting. Writing that explains is called EXPOSITION; expository writing makes direct statements about the nature and significance of its subject, such as:

- "This was the American family at play" (8).
- "[T]hose times and those summers had been infinitely precious and worth saving" (9).
- "I had trouble making out which was I, the one walking at my side, the one walking in my pants" (11).

Among the many strategies of exposition that writers draw on to support statements like these, one of the main methods that White uses is COMPARISON AND CONTRAST. In particular, White is comparing his perceptions of the lake in the present with his memories of it in the past. At first, everything seems "pretty much the same as it had been before" (4). The water is still "cool and motionless"; the bedroom still smells "of the lumber it was made of" (2); and the rowboat is "the same boat, the same color green and the ribs broken in the same places" (5). White's comparison shades into contrast, however, as the tranquil scene is interrupted by the "unfamiliar nervous sound of the outboard motors" (10). In the past, White explains, the sound of the motors was peaceful. Now, however, the boats are more powerful and "whine . . . like mosquitoes" in the night (10). At the end of the essay, the peace and tranquility of the lake are interrupted by a thunderstorm.

Using various SIMILES and METAPHORS, White likens the gathering storm to a scene in a drama: the thunder sounds at first like a "kettle drum"; then comes "the snare, then the bass drum and cymbals"; lightning flashes against the dark sky; and, as in a Greek tragedy, "the gods" grin from "the hills" (12). Why this sudden turn of events in an otherwise tranquil scene from the life of the American family on vacation? Are the gods grinning, perhaps, at the swimmers' sense of security?

RECOGNIZING ARGUMENT. By comparing his past and present experiences at the lake, White is constructing an ARGUMENT about time and change. Arguments make claims that require discussion and further proof. For instance:

It was the arrival of this fly that convinced me beyond any doubt that every-thing was as it always had been, that the years were a mirage and that there had been no years. (5)

"Once More to the Lake" was published just a few months before the United States entered World War II, and in the idyllic background of his essay lurks the author's nagging suspicion that the world is about to change forever. As the boy prepares to go swimming in the lake in the rain, White cannot escape the realiza-tion that a number of years have actually passed since he last visited this place. As he feels suddenly older (and war lies just around the corner), White concludes that the generations are bound not only by the "return of light and hope and spirits" after a storm but also by the reality of change and "the chill of death" (12, 13). The dream of "summer without end," no matter how warmly inspired by nature and fond memories of childhood, White concludes, is just that—a dream (8).

White makes this key point by weaving together various strands of narrative, description, exposition, and argument. When you compose a text, let yourself be guided by the work of the great writers you have read. In the end, however, you must plunge in and choose the techniques and patterns of development (or likely a single pattern) that best fit your specific topic and the particular point you want to make about it—as well as your singular audience and purpose in writing.

Reading the Essays in This Book

In *Back to the Lake*, you will be reading and analyzing numerous essays by many different writers on a variety of topics. The essays are grouped into chapters accord-ing to the principal methods of development they use: NARRATION, DESCRIPTION, EXAMPLE, ANALYSIS, CAUSE AND EFFECT, COMPARISON AND CONTRAST, CLASSIFICATION, DEFINITION, and ARGUMENT. Experienced writers often employ more than one method in the same essay, so there is also a final chapter called "Combining the Methods."

The essays in *Back to the Lake* are introduced with a headnote—like the one before White's "Once More to the Lake" in Chapter 8—that provides information about the author of the text and its historical, social, or cultural CONTEXT. In addi-tion, each selection is followed by study questions and writing prompts. Far from being mere afterthoughts, these are the teaching heart of the book, and they ask you to approach the readings in the following ways:

• *For Close Reading.* These questions are intended to help you look at the text as an exchange of ideas between a writer and a reader. They prompt you to read in order to understand *what* the text is saying and to discover your own views on the subject under discussion. In other words, these are questions that will help you think about what the author is saying and then consider what you think and why.

- *Strategies and Structures.* Focusing on the common patterns and techniques by which the writer's ideas are organized and presented to an audience, these questions should help you understand *how* the text is constructed—and how to make these basic moves in your own writing.

- *Thinking about Language.* These questions focus on the language and style of the text. They're designed to help you think about both the literal and figurative meanings of specific words and phrases.

- *For Writing.* These prompts can get you started with your own writing by suggesting topics to write on or by asking you to think about and respond to key ideas or issues in the text.

The reading process can take you so many places, as Dr. Seuss noted, that it's useful to have guidelines like these. Hopefully, by following them as you read the sample essays in this book, you won't get lost—and you'll pick up lots of strategies and techniques along the way that you can use in your own writing. These should include large-scale, fundamental methods for organizing an entire text—and also smaller ways of beginning, of using TRANSITIONS to move a text along, of presenting certain kinds of information in lists or charts, of incorporating words and ideas from trustworthy sources, and more.

2

Learning the Basic Moves of Academic Writing: Putting in Your Oar

You listen for a while, until you decide that you have caught the tenor of the argument; then you put in your oar.
—KENNETH BURKE, *The Philosophy of Literary Form*

You come late to a party. A lively conversation is going on around you. You aren't sure what it's about at first—a class, a movie, the rivalry of two teams? Academic writing is like this, except the discussion began long ago, and—as suggested by philosopher Kenneth Burke in a comparison that has become famous among academics—it never ends. Here's the scene as Burke describes it:

> Imagine that you enter a parlor. You come late. When you arrive, others have long preceded you, and they are engaged in a heated discussion, a discussion too heated for them to pause and tell you exactly what it is about. You listen for a while, until you decide that you have caught the tenor of the argument; then you put in your oar. Someone answers; you answer him; another comes to your defense; another aligns himself against you. . . . The hour grows late, you must depart. And you do depart, with the discussion still vigorously in progress.

Like Burke's parlor, academic writing is the site of an ongoing conversation—about ideas. The ultimate purpose of that conversation is the advancement of human knowledge. More immediately, you can learn a lot about any field of study that interests you, from physics to dance, just by listening to what knowledgeable people in that field have to say.

Academic writing, like other social activities and forms of conversation, has its own rules and generally accepted customs, called conventions. Don't leave a party without properly thanking the hosts; don't turn in a paper without properly citing your sources. This chapter covers some of the basic conventions and strategies (or "moves") of academic writing:

- researching what's been said about your topic
- synthesizing the ideas you find with your own ideas
- presenting your ideas as a response to the ideas of others
- considering other views
- saying why your ideas matter
- using description, comparison, and the other methods taught in this book

Finding Out What's Been Said about Your Topic

Before you put in your oar, you need to get your bearings. So before you leap into a discussion on a topic that's new to you, test the waters by attending lectures, talking with your teachers and fellow students, and reading and thinking about what others have written on the topic under discussion. In short, you need to do some preliminary research.

With many kinds of academic writing—a brief answer on an essay exam, for example—your research will consist mostly of thinking about your topic and figuring out what you want to emphasize. For a research paper, however, you will need to find out what experts in the field are saying. So you'll need to look for authoritative written sources of information, such as academic books and articles that have been peer reviewed—evaluated by scholars in the appropriate field of study. Remember that all the sources you consult when writing a research paper should be identified in a reference list at the end of your paper—and you'll also name many of your most important sources as you go along.

See Ch. 17 (p. 771) for information on finding, evaluating, and citing sources.

Academic writing is about much more than amassing sources, however. With even the most informal research paper, you'll be expected to show what you've learned and even to contribute ideas of your own to the discussion. Coming up with ideas, in fact, is the main reason you join in the give-and-take of an academic conversation in the first place.

In some cultures, it is impolite to disagree directly and openly with others, especially if they're older than you are or if they're your hosts at a social event. But imagine a conversation in which every assertion ("the earth is flat," "printing new money will ease the financial crisis") is always met with polite assent ("I agree"; "yes, that's right"). Academic discourse should always be courteous, but in most US academic contexts, the conversation goes more like this: "I see what you're saying, but what about . . . ?" "No, that's not my point. My point is . . ." In other words, this tradition of academic discourse is based on a synthesis, or blend, of different—even conflicting—ideas and viewpoints.

Synthesizing Ideas

Suppose you're writing a paper on how the internet impacts our lives. You've begun to do your research, and you're finding lots of useful ideas, some of which you plan to weave into your paper—with full attribution, of course. You don't want to simply repeat what others have said on your topic, however. You want to synthesize their ideas and come up with some new ones of your own.

Here's how that process might work. As you read through your many sources, you keep running into various arguments to the following effect: "The internet is making us stupid." You don't agree with this view, but you find it thought-provoking. You may even mention it in your paper as an idea that helped nudge you into taking a different (more positive) position on your topic.

As you mull over such negative statements about the effect of the internet on the human brain, you come upon others that are virtually the antithesis of the first.

They run, more or less, as follows: "The internet is making us all smarter because it places more information at our fingertips more quickly than ever before."

You don't agree entirely with these ideas either, but by bringing them together—which is what "synthesis" means—with other, opposing ideas on your topic, a spark is struck in your mind. You now have a clearer conception of what you want to say.

You jot down some notes before you forget: "Both of these positions have problems. The internet's not really making us smarter or dumber. Just speeding up our access to information. Conclusion: the internet is not fundamentally changing how we think; it's simply making us more efficient."

This last statement is a synthesis of the opposing views you've encountered in your research. It will make a great THESIS, or main point, for the paper you want to write about the internet. And it came to you out of the intellectual give-and-take that is the heart—or rather, the brain—of academic writing. As you present this proposition to your readers, you may also want to explain some of the other, contrasting ideas that inspired it.

Presenting Your Ideas as a Response to Those of Others

In "Why Are Textbooks So Expensive?" (p. 375), Henry Roediger III summarizes others' opinions before presenting his own.

Starting with the ideas of others is so basic to academic writing that some of those who teach and study writing consider it *the* underlying pattern of much academic prose, cutting across all disciplines and majors. The following is an elegant statement of this view:

> For us, the underlying structure of effective academic writing . . . resides not just in stating our own ideas, but in listening closely to others around us, summarizing their views in a way that they will recognize, and responding with our own ideas in kind. Broadly speaking, academic writing is argumentative writing, and . . . to argue well you need to do more than assert your own ideas. You need to enter a conversation, using what others say (or might say) as a launching pad . . . for your own ideas.
>
> —Gerald Graff and Cathy Birkenstein,
> *"They Say / I Say": The Moves That Matter in Academic Writing**

In the following passage from an opinion piece in the *New York Times*, for example, a psychology professor starts by summarizing the views of other writers—and then disagrees, advancing his own view.

---

*In fact, the work of Graff and Birkenstein in demystifying the argumentative aspect of academic writing has served not only as a launching pad for this chapter but for the templates throughout the book. As these scholars demonstrate, such templates "do more than organize students' ideas; they help bring those ideas into existence."

Media critics write as if the brain takes on the qualities of whatever it consumes, the informational equivalent of "you are what you eat." As with primitive peoples who believe that eating fierce animals will make them fierce, they assume that watching quick cuts in rock videos turns your mental life into quick cuts or that reading bullet points and Twitter postings turns your thoughts into bullet points and Twitter postings. . . . Far from making us stupid, these technologies are the only things that will keep us smart.

—STEVEN PINKER, "Mind over Mass Media"

Although Pinker disagrees completely with those who say digital media are making us stupid, he nonetheless puts forth his own views as a response to their views. In particular, he does so by COMPARING—a common pattern in academic writing—their ideas with those of "primitive peoples."

Andrea Lunsford (p. 702) also disagrees, reporting on trends in undergraduate writing and thinking.

In any academic writing you do, there are many ways of introducing the ideas of others. Three of the most common ones are:

- *Quoting another writer's exact words.* "Media critics," says Steven Pinker, "write as if the brain takes on the qualities of whatever it consumes, the informational equivalent of 'you are what you eat.'"

- *Paraphrasing another writer's ideas.* According to Steven Pinker, critics of the new media have a faulty view of the human brain as an organ that must be fed a constant diet of intellectual red meat.

- *Summarizing another writer's ideas.* Steven Pinker attacks the views of media critics as a primitive form of superstition.

Now let's look at a more complicated example. In the following passage, a student writer both summarizes and quotes from the work of writers with whom she agrees:

Pioneering evolutionary psychologist Robert L. Trivers has observed that having and rearing children requires women to invest far more resources than men do because of the length of pregnancy, the dangers of childbirth, and the duration of infants' dependence on their mothers (145). According to Helen Fisher, one of the leading advocates of this theory, finding a capable mate was a huge preoccupation of all prehistoric reproductive women, and for good reason: "A female couldn't carry a baby in one arm and sticks and stones in the other arm and still feed and protect herself on the very dangerous open grasslands, so she began to need a mate to help her rear her young" (Frank 85). . . . [T]hese are the bases upon which modern mate selection is founded, and there are many examples of this phenomenon to be found in our own society.

—CAROLYN STONEHILL, "Modern Dating, Prehistoric Style"

In this passage, Stonehill is not simply reporting what she learned about human mating behavior by reading the work of experts in the field of evolutionary biology, such as Trivers and Fisher. Having synthesized their views in her own mind, she uses them as a framework to support *her* thesis, stated in the previous paragraph, about the origins of "modern mate selection": "Driven by the need to reproduce and propagate the species, these ancestors of ours formed patterns of mate selection so effective in providing for their needs and those of their offspring that they are mimicked even in today's society."

For tips on determining when to quote, paraphrase, or summarize, see pp. 784–85.

As you introduce the ideas of others into your writing, you can present your own ideas by responding to theirs in many different ways. These three are the most common: agree with what they say (as Stonehill did), disagree (like Pinker), or both. The templates on p. 25 suggest some ways to structure your response.

Considering Other Views

Read the complete version of Dzubay's paper on p. 27.

Even when citing the views of others with whom you generally agree, don't forget to acknowledge opposing views. In "An Outbreak of the Irrational," for example, the writer, a student at the University of Notre Dame, argues against the choice by some parents not to have their children vaccinated against measles and other childhood diseases:

> The movement to opt out of vaccination, in fact, is irrational and dangerous. Advocating the right of personal choice above all, it looks in the wrong places for justification and ignores the clear threat it presents to society as a whole.
> —Sarah Dzubay, "An Outbreak of the Irrational"

To support her position, Dzubay cites a number of other writers who advocate broad-scale vaccinations, but she also summarizes and responds to arguments from the other side: "The fear of vaccines," she admits, "is not unwarranted—the idea of injecting your child with some foreign substance, whose purpose, origins, and side effects you may not be educated about, is a frightening concept."

Introducing an opposing point of view like this shows readers that you've considered others' views and taken a particular position only after reflecting carefully on the issues under debate. It's also a good way of setting up a COUNTERARGUMENT.

After acknowledging that parents have every right to question the purpose and possible side effects of any vaccine proposed for their children, Dzubay adds: "As with many aspects of medicine, though, the costs must be weighed against the benefits. The fact of the matter is that without vaccines, our globe would be ravaged by disease." Introducing an opposing point of view for the express purpose of refuting it, by the way, is a rhetorical move known as *planting a naysayer*.

TIPS AND TEMPLATES FOR RESPONDING TO OTHERS

Agree. When you agree with others, do more than just echo their arguments—also point out unnoticed implications in what they say, or explain a concept that you think needs to be better understood.

▶ One of the most respected experts in the field is X, who says essentially that _____.

▶ Advocates of this view are Y and Z, who also argue that _____.

▶ Persuaded by these arguments, I agree with those who say _____.

Disagree. Don't just contradict the views of others: offer persuasive reasons why you disagree. Justify your reason for writing, and move the conversation forward.

▶ In my view, these objections do not hold up because _____.

▶ Like some critics of these ideas, particularly X and Y, I would argue instead that _____.

▶ Z's focus on _____ obscures the underlying issue of _____.

Both agree and disagree. This approach works well when your topic is complex. It avoids a yes/no standoff and displays your thorough understanding of the issues. You don't have to give equal weight to all aspects of the topic—just the main points under debate. This approach invites COMPARISON, for example, when you want to list pros and cons.

▶ Although I concede that _____, I still maintain that _____.

▶ Whereas X and Y make good points about _____, I have to agree with Z that _____.

▶ X may be wrong about _____, but the rest of their argument is persuasive.

Saying Why Your Ideas Matter

Who cares? Why does it matter? Whatever you're writing about, you also need to explain the *significance* of your ideas to the reader. Sarah Dzubay does this in her essay "An Outbreak of the Irrational" when she explains why she advocates universal vaccinations: "Vaccines have helped us overcome diseases that have haunted civilizations since the dawn of humanity. . . . Vaccines are some of the most important medical discoveries in history." The following templates suggest some other ways of saying why your ideas matter:

> ▸ The prevailing view has long been _____; but now, because of _____, we can see that _____.
>
> ▸ Looking at _____ in this light is important because _____.
>
> ▸ Other reasons this view is significant include _____ and _____.
>
> ▸ These findings should be of particular interest to those who _____ and _____.

Using the Rhetorical Methods in Academic Writing

The basic purpose of most academic writing is to prove a point. The writer makes a claim in the form of a thesis and then supports that claim throughout the rest of their paper. The basic strategies and methods of ARGUMENT are, therefore, particularly useful in academic writing.

Chapter 16 presents several essays that skillfully combine some of these methods. In addition to argument, however, the other basic methods of development taught in this book—NARRATION, DESCRIPTION, EXAMPLE, ANALYSIS, CAUSE AND EFFECT, COMPARISON AND CONTRAST, CLASSIFICATION, and DEFINITION—can also help you figure out and present what you have to say in any piece of academic writing. Useful as these methods of development are for presenting your ideas in an academic paper, they can also serve as ways of discovering what you have to say in the first place—as you do research and begin to write. Much of the rest of this book, in fact, is about that process of discovery and the use of these methods as ways of thinking as well as strategies for writing.

A Sample Academic Essay

In "An Outbreak of the Irrational," Sarah Dzubay draws on research to argue against opting out of vaccination against measles, mumps, and other infectious childhood diseases. An undergraduate biology major considering medical school, Dzubay uses ANALYSIS (particularly of CAUSE AND EFFECT), among other methods, to explain why she thinks parents who fail to get their children vaccinated are being "irrational." Dzubay's essay was written on the eve of the COVID-19 pandemic. What constitutes rational behavior during a full-blown pandemic, rather than a mere outbreak, may be harder to define. Dzubay's basic logic, however, is as valid as ever. Because Dzubay wrote her essay for a first-year composition class, she uses MLA style to cite her sources.

An Outbreak of the Irrational

In the spring of 2015, a number of families who visited Disneyland in the hopes of enjoying "the happiest place on Earth" returned home only to discover that the children had contracted measles. Measles, as well as diseases like polio and pertussis (whooping cough), is generally believed by the public to be a plague of the past. These diseases were effectively eradicated through the discovery of vaccines. So why have they reemerged in some of the most developed, wealthy, and educated countries in the world?

Before the vaccine for measles was created in the 1960s, this disease had killed hundreds of millions of people throughout history. Measles wiped out any population who had not developed some form of resistance to it, especially native populations who came into contact with the foreign illness because of the arrival of Europeans and their domesticated animals. After the vaccine was produced and the majority of developed countries were inoculated with it, rates of infection for measles were reduced to almost nothing.

Now, after generations have lived with no contact with anyone who has had measles, some people are starting to lose their awareness of the severity of the disease. Parents who no longer fear measles and are more concerned with the possible effects (other than disease prevention) of the Measles, Mumps, and Rubella (MMR) vaccine itself are opting out of vaccinating their children with it (Lin and McGreevy). It is because of these misinformed choices that outbreaks of measles and other diseases preventable by vaccines are becoming more and more common around the United States and in other countries as well.

The fear of vaccines is not unwarranted—the idea of injecting your child with a foreign substance, whose purpose, origins, and side effects you may not be educated about, is a frightening concept. As with many aspects of medicine, though, the costs must be weighed against the benefits. The fact of the matter is that without vaccines, our globe would be ravaged by disease. Vaccines have helped us

1 A one-sentence NARRATIVE introduces the general subject of the essay—infectious childhood diseases.

2 ANALYZES the EFFECTS of the disease before the invention of vaccines.

ANALYZES original CAUSES of outbreaks and of their eventual eradication.

3 Identifies a recent side EFFECT of the invention of vaccines.

4 Recognizes an opposing POINT OF VIEW.

overcome diseases that have haunted civilizations since the dawn of humanity; they protect us from the pathogens that fill our environments—deadly killers we now are able to live with because of modern medical achievements. Vaccines are some of the most important medical discoveries in history.

Why does it matter? This passage explains why the issue is important.

With life expectancies vastly lengthened and our daily lives less affected by sickness than in earlier centuries, however, citizens of developed countries can sometimes overlook the importance of getting their children vaccinated. The movement to opt out of vaccination, in fact, is irrational and dangerous. Advocating the right of personal choice above all, it looks in the wrong places for justification and ignores the clear threat it presents to society as a whole.

States the main point, or THESIS: the anti-vaccine movement is "irrational" and "dangerous."

During the COVID-19 pandemic, Dzubay might argue, the threat has only gotten clearer.

One of the most important concepts behind the effectiveness of inoculation is that of herd immunity. This term refers to the idea that if a majority of a given population are vaccinated, the minority who cannot be vaccinated for medical reasons, such as infants, elderly people, or those with compromised immune systems, will still be protected from the disease. Epidemiologists, who study the way that diseases spread, try to determine a basic "reproduction number" for any disease, which is the number of people to whom one infected individual can likely spread it (Sadava). This number then helps to determine the percentage of the population who must be vaccinated in order to protect those who cannot be, a number called the immunity threshold (Willingham and Helft). At this level, the general population is safe because those who have had their vaccinations are not only directly protecting themselves, but also indirectly aiding those who have not been vaccinated. However, when the levels of vaccination drop below this threshold, diseases can come back with a vengeance, just as measles has begun to do.

DEFINES key terms that may be unfamiliar to Dzubay's AUDIENCE.

Families opting out of the MMR and other vaccines solely on the basis of personal choice are a threat to the protection that we, as a national and international community, have built against disease. By refusing the vaccine, they become free riders in a vaccinated

Develops the THESIS by identifying who, in Dzubay's view, is the cause of the problem—and how.

5

6

7

community whose herd immunity they are counting on to protect them. Vaccine refusal is dangerous because it puts herd immunity at risk by lowering the number of vaccinated individuals below the immunity threshold.

Who are these people, and why are they choosing to threaten the safety of the greater population? Perhaps surprisingly, the people in developed countries who are refusing to have their children vaccinated are not the underprivileged or uneducated, but rather the opposite. Faced with the decision of whether or not to vaccinate their kids, some middle- and upper-class families are finding various reasons to say no. Questioning what doctors recommend, they do their own research, mostly online, and are confident in their findings and beliefs.

Being curious and asking questions about the effectiveness or safety of a vaccine is not the issue; these precautions are, in fact, prudent and advisable. Often, however, the sources that people are consulting for information are not reputable and have little scientific validity. One of the biggest concerns today about vaccinations, for example, is that they may cause autism. The root of this fear is a paper published in 1998 by Andrew Wakefield that has been completely invalidated by follow-up research ("Case").

Another, more complex issue raised by anti-vaccine advocates involves the belief that vaccines cause children to have seizures, along with other dangerous reactions that result in long-term disabilities. One couple, featured in a NOVA television episode about the vaccine controversy, were horrified when their infant son began to have violent seizures only hours after he received his first round of vaccines (*Vaccines*). At first, like a number of other parents who have had similar experiences, they blamed the vaccines. However, as they delved deeper into the issue and consulted more medical professionals and researchers, they discovered that their son's epilepsy had not been caused by a vaccine but instead had been *triggered* by it. While watching their child have seizures was a terrible experience, they came to understand that an underlying

8

9
Offers sympathy for opposing views, but ...

... refutes a common objection raised by opponents.

10
Acknowledges an opposing CLAIM that is more difficult to refute.

genetic problem would have resulted in his eventually having them anyway.

Identifies a weak spot in the opposing claim.

Herein lies the difficulty with the argument that negative reactions to vaccines cause children to have life-long health problems: often the reaction is the result of a previously unobserved problem that the child has suffered from birth ("Infant"). Because babies get their first vaccines so quickly after birth, it can be exceedingly difficult to differentiate between a vaccine-related issue and underlying health problems. Vaccines can sometimes cause unpleasant reactions or even illness, but this fact does not justify choosing to avoid them altogether. Rather, for the benefit of all, those who suffer a negative experience with a vaccine should advocate for improvement in that particular type of inoculation.   11

Introduces a new line of ARGUMENT about the causes of the anti-vaccine movement.

With Operation Warp Speed in 2021, however, the pressure (and the profits) flowed in the other direction.

Political values and distrust of doctors or drug manufacturers can also play a role in deciding not to vaccinate. Some parents who are libertarians or home-school their children object to vaccines out of general hostility to government requirements (Lin and McGreevy). In addition, some people fear that pharmaceutical companies are hoping to profit from the vaccines they produce and are pressuring regulatory agencies to approve vaccines before they are truly effective or safe (Fadda et al.). Some anti-vaccine activists even argue that vaccines are not really necessary but are the result of payoffs to doctors by these corporations in order to force families to use their products.   12

Gives economic reasons for Dzubay's position.

Besides being scientifically incorrect, these arguments also fall short because vaccines are not a profitable investment for companies. At most, this type of vaccine against childhood diseases is administered only three times to any individual, not two or three times daily like some heart or pain medications. Without subsidies or other incentives from the government, companies would not be able to make any money from vaccines, and there would simply be no economic reason for them to manufacture these products ("Key Concepts").   13

SUMMARY of Dzubay's position suggests what should be done about the issue.

Research and debate are vital to society. Relying on outdated and unfounded "evidence," however, only promotes paranoia and   14 does not make a useful contribution to public discourse on the subject of medicinal standards and patient-physician relations. It is time for anti-vaccination advocates not only to discuss their fears with the medical community but also to listen to the hard evidence. We must all claim our roles as responsible protectors of our nation's health.

Works Cited

"A Case of Junk Science, Conflict, and Hype." Editorial. *Nature Immunology*, vol. 9, no. 12, 1 Dec. 2008, p. 1317, www.nature.com /articles/ni1208–1317.

Fadda, Marta, et al. "Addressing Issues of Vaccination Literacy and Psychological Empowerment in the Measles-Mumps-Rubella (MMR) Vaccine Decision-Making: A Qualitative Study." *BMC Public Health*, vol. 15, no. 1, 2015, p. 836.

"Infant Immunizations FAQs." Centers for Disease Control and Prevention, 2016, www.cdc.gov/vaccines/parents/parent-questions .html.

"Key Concepts: Economics of Vaccine Production." World Health Organization, www.who.int/immunization/programmes _systems/financing/analyses/en. Accessed 22 Apr. 2016.

Lin, Rong-Gong, II, and Patrick McGreevy. "California's Measles Outbreak Is Over, but Vaccine Fight Continues." *Los Angeles Times*, 17 Apr. 2015, www.latimes.com/local/california/la-me -measles-20150418-story.html.

Sadava, David E. *Life: The Science of Biology.* 10th ed., W. H. Freeman, 2013.

Vaccines—Calling the Shots. Directed by Sonya Pemberton, WGBH, 26 Aug. 2015, www.pbs.org/wgbh/nova/body/vaccines-calling -shots.html.

Willingham, Emily, and Laura Helft, writers. "What Is Herd Immunity?" *Nova*, WGBH, 5 Sept. 2014, www.pbs.org/wgbh/nova /body/herd-immunity.html.

3 | Elements of the Essay: Topic, Thesis, Coherence, Tone, and Style

> There is a big difference between a coherent passage of writing and a flaunting of one's erudition, a running journal of one's thoughts, or a published version of one's notes.
>
> —STEVEN PINKER, *The Sense of Style*

Like many other things, an essay is composed of certain fundamental elements. Works of art, for example, have form, line, color, space, and texture; musical compositions are made up of rhythm, pitch, tempo, and volume; and in the field of chemistry, a compound like water (H_2O) is a combination of such physical elements as hydrogen and oxygen.

Essays are made up of ideas, and ideas are not substances in the same sense as those that make up chemical compounds. With any essay you write, however, we can speak of both its content (what you have to say) and its form (how you say it). Most essays have an introduction, a body, and a conclusion as part of their basic form. In this chapter, we'll focus on the elements of the essay that will be most important for communicating what you have to say, whether you're telling a story, drawing comparisons, analyzing a process, making an argument, or doing something else.

There are no simple formulas for writing a good essay. Fortunately, however, the basic elements that you can use to make meaning in an essay are far fewer than the 118 chemical elements in the standard periodic table. In this chapter, we'll boil them down to just five: topic, thesis, coherence, tone, and style.

Topic

Although we often lump the two together, the TOPIC of an essay is not the same as the subject. A subject is a broad field of inquiry; a topic is a specific area within that field. For example, if you're writing about the use of drugs in professional baseball, "baseball" is your subject and "the use of drugs in baseball" is your topic. The following subjects, for instance, are too broad to be manageable topics in an essay: education, college sports, science, pets.

A strong topic focuses on a particular aspect of your general subject. It is your subject narrowed down to a manageable scope and size for the length of the composition you're writing. The following are more specific areas within general fields and would make more manageable topics for an essay:

• the advantages of attending a community college rather than a university
• the rewards of college sports
• studying science as a profession
• choosing a pet

Here's a template that can help you get started as you look for a meaningful topic to write about in an essay:

▶ Within the general subject of _____, what I want to write about specifically is _____.

Here's just one way you might fill in the blanks, for example:

> ▶ Within the general subject of <u>higher education</u>, what I want to write about specifically is <u>the advantage of attending a community college</u>.

Thesis

In any essay you write, your topic is the specific aspect of your subject you plan to focus on. Your **THESIS** is what you have to say about that topic—the main point you want to make about it. That point is usually set forth in a thesis statement. Here are some examples taken from essays in this book:

> So even if you disdain young people who can't find the will or time to vote . . . you should want to fix this problem.
> —JAMELLE BOUIE, "Why Don't Young People Vote?"

> Books can indeed be dangerous. . . . They are not inert tools of pedagogy. They are mind-changing, world-changing.
> —VIET THANH NGUYEN, "My Young Mind Was Disturbed by a Book"

> Increasingly, I've felt that online engagement is fueled by the hopelessness many people feel when we consider the state of the world and the challenges we deal with in our day-to-day lives.
> —ROXANE GAY, "Why People Are So Awful Online"

The following template can help get you started as you figure out the main point you want to make (the thesis) about your topic in an essay:

> ▶ The main point I want to make about _____ is that _____.

You might fill in the blanks like this:

> ▶ The main point I want to make about <u>competitive college sports</u> is that <u>the players should be paid</u>.

Once you've come up with a thesis that makes a particular point about a specific topic, you may need to limit it further by using such qualifiers as "possibly," "may be," "often," "for most people," and "in this situation." Roxane Gay, for example, qualifies her thesis about online discourtesy by saying "increasingly" and "I've felt." If she had written "since the beginning" and "I've observed," her thesis would be wider in scope but harder to defend—a proclamation rather than an opinion.

Where to Position a Thesis Statement

THESIS STATEMENT AT OR NEAR THE BEGINNING OF THE ESSAY

Jack Horner does this in "The Extraordinary Characteristics of Dyslexia" (p. 565).

A direct statement of your thesis can appear anywhere in your essay. Most often, however, it should come near the beginning to help set up the rest of what you have to say. In this example from the beginning of a humorous piece on the English language, the thesis statement appears at the start of the second paragraph:

> English is the most widely spoken language in the history of our planet, used in some way by at least one out of every seven human beings around the globe. Half of the world's books are written in English, and the majority of international phone calls are made in English. . . .
> Nonetheless, it is now time to face the fact that English is a crazy language.
> —Richard Lederer, "English Is a Crazy Language"

From this statement, in order to support his claim, Lederer goes on to provide one example after another of linguistic "craziness": "no egg in eggplant, no grape in grapefruit . . . and no ham in hamburger."

THESIS STATEMENT IN THE BODY OF THE ESSAY

Building up to a thesis is almost as common a pattern in essay writing as building down from one. Consider the following thesis statement from an essay on reading (and writing) PERSONAL NARRATIVES:

> But perhaps the deepest challenge in articulating and considering the stories of our lives is not that they force us to admit our privileges but that they force us to admit our suffering. Some realities hurt to look at. Therefore, our harshest critics are often those with whom we share the most common ground.
> —Sarah Smarsh, "Believe It"

This statement about the pain of telling (and hearing) the stories of our lives comes more than two-thirds of the way into Smarsh's essay. To lead up to it, she cites the personal narratives of Sojourner Truth and Harriet Jacobs, two writers who not only endured the evils of slavery—from which they escaped—but who also suffered the indignity of defending themselves to White readers as credible witnesses of their own experience. The harsh critic of her personal story that Smarsh anticipates here is her grandmother.

THESIS STATEMENT AT THE END OF THE ESSAY

When your thesis statement comes at the end of an essay, it can both sum up what you have to say and also give your reader a satisfying sense of closure. See how a professional mortician (and humor writer) soothes the reader's fears of premature burial:

> But I feel confident saying that this is not going to happen to you. On your list of "Freaky Ways to Die" you can move "buried alive—coma" down to just below "terrible gopher accident."
>
> —CAITLIN DOUGHTY, "What If They Bury Me When I'm Just in a Coma?"

Deborah Tannen (p. 495) does this at the end of her essay on ways in which men and women miscommunicate in the workplace.

How likely is a terrible gopher accident that would be fatal to anyone but the gopher? That's Doughty's point: coroners and morticians really know when people are dead—or not.

IMPLIED THESIS

In the following passage, by a physician and writer, the message is only implied rather than stated explicitly. The writer, who died in 2015 at age eighty-two, is speaking about a chemical element on his desk:

> Bismuth is element 83. I do not think I will see my 83rd birthday, but I feel there is something hopeful, something encouraging, about having "83" around. Moreover, I have a soft spot for bismuth, a modest gray metal, often unregarded, ignored, even by metal lovers. My feeling as a doctor for the mistreated or marginalized extends into the inorganic world and finds a parallel in my feeling for bismuth.
>
> —OLIVER SACKS, "My Periodic Table"

Sacks is writing about bismuth most explicitly, but he is also making a larger point about the importance of passion in the pursuit of science and medicine.

However you choose to develop your thesis, it's probably always a good idea to restate it at the end of an essay. Sacks himself did this in an essay he wrote at the end of his life when he noted that it "has been an enormous privilege and adventure" to be "a sentient being, a thinking animal, on this beautiful planet" ("My Own Life," 2015).

Coherence

COHERENCE in writing has to mainly do with meaning, with what you have to say. A piece of writing is coherent when every idea in the text is clear—and clearly related to every other idea.

Consider the following example from one student's response to a writing prompt that "the best way for a society to prepare its young people for leadership in government, industry, or other fields is by instilling in them a sense of cooperation, not competition":

> Some may argue that competition is not needed. That those that are meant to be leaders will not become complacent, because they have their own internal drive to lead. If there was no competition, there would be no world records. Michael Phelps may not be a leader of government or industry, but he is certainly educated on the technique of swimming, and a leader in his field. Would he be as good as he is today if there was not competition? Would the leaders of Microsoft have been motivated to create Bing if there was no Google?
>
> —EDUCATIONAL TESTING SERVICE,
> GRE Practice General Test in Analytical Writing

Although the ideas expressed in this passage may be related in the writer's mind, the passage lacks coherence because those ideas are not clearly and explicitly tied together in ways that are immediately evident to a reader.

See how this passage can be edited to be more coherent:

> Some may argue that competition is not needed and that those of us who ~~that~~ are meant to be leaders in any field will not become complacent, because ~~they~~ we have ~~their~~ our own internal drive to lead. If there was no competition, however, there would be, for example, no world records in athletics. The Olympic swimmer Michael Phelps may not be a leader of government or industry, but he is certainly ~~educated on the technique of swimming, and~~ a leader in ~~his field~~ the pool. Would he be as good a swimmer as he is today if there was not competition from other world-class swimmers? Or, to take an example from the field of business, would the leaders of Microsoft have been motivated to create Bing if there was no Google?

This edited version is hardly perfect, but it is more coherent than the original. Simply adding the word "however" in the second sentence, for instance, makes it clear that the example of Michael Phelps is intended to challenge the idea of cooperation, not uphold it. And by indicating that the writer is talking about leadership in "other fields" besides industry and government, the new language helps justify comparing an athlete with "the leaders of Microsoft." (In case you're interested, Phelps—the most decorated Olympic athlete ever—won twenty-eight medals across five Olympics and retired in 2016.)

Adding connecting words and phrases like "because," "however," and "for example" is one of the best ways to make your writing more coherent; but be careful to choose TRANSITIONS that actually lend unity to your paragraph. Otherwise, your paragraph is just longer and more wordy. (See Chapter 6 for more on tying sentences together into coherent paragraphs and tying paragraphs together into coherent essays.)

Chimamanda Ngozi Adichie uses "but," "instead," and other transition words throughout her essay, p. 275.

Using Rhetorical Patterns to Make Your Ideas Coherent

You can use any of the rhetorical patterns discussed in this book—description, narrative, example, and so on—to help you achieve COHERENCE in an essay. Here are five examples of how these patterns can help you tie your ideas together into a coherent whole and make clear what you have to say:

Using DESCRIPTION *to show how physical characteristics are related*

> These steep, verdant hills carved out of prehistoric violence have had an eternity to become smooth. They roll and undulate like fairy-tale landscapes. The homes sit far apart, isolated. A church stands alone on a hill.
> —EDWARD LEE, "Slaw Dogs and Pepperoni Rolls"

Lee is a chef, and a key idea in his essay is that even in the most apparently isolated places, food brings people together to celebrate a common culture.

Using NARRATIVE *to show how events are related in time*

> *Iron Chef* was my jam. By the time I was eight, the original Japanese version had just begun airing in America. I followed the epic battles of crustaceans and butternut squash like it was March Madness, year round.
> —KWAME ONWUACHI, "Angles"

For some chefs, preparing food is not so much a way of bringing people together as a form of competition. By going back in time in a personal narrative, Onwuachi shows how a *Top Chef* contestant came to see cooking as "a blood sport."

Using COMPARISON AND CONTRAST *to show similarities and differences*

> This is the story of two boys living in Baltimore with similar histories and an identical name: Wes Moore. One of us is free and has experienced things that he never even knew to dream about as a kid. The other will spend every day until his death behind bars. . . .
>
> —WES MOORE, "The Other Wes Moore"

In an essay about the importance of making good decisions at critical "inflection points" in life, Wes Moore compares and contrasts his own fate with that of a man who has the same name and a similar background but is serving a life sentence in prison.

Using CAUSE AND EFFECT *to explore consequences*

> Much attention has been given to a "rural brain drain" . . . and all the reasons young people leave rural communities. But our research shows some of the characteristics of rural communities that have been associated with a return home.
>
> —STEPHANIE SOWL,
> "Three Reasons College Graduates Return to Rural Areas"

In this conclusion to her essay, Sowl returns to the main effect of the various causes "associated with" a new trend that she and her colleagues have been studying: instead of staying in urban environments, some recent college graduates are finding greener pastures back in their hometowns and rural areas.

Using ARGUMENT *to make logical connections among ideas*

> Across generations, technology is implicated in this assault on empathy. We've gotten used to being connected all the time, but we have found ways around conversation—at least from conversation that is open-ended and spontaneous, in which we play with ideas and allow ourselves to be fully present and vulnerable.
>
> —SHERRY TURKLE, "Stop Googling. Let's Talk."

Technology, particularly the almost universal use of cell phones during face-to-face conversation, is not only making us less empathetic toward each other, Turkle argues; it is also changing the nature of conversation.

Tone and Style

The ideas you express in an essay can be meaningful and logically coherent; yet readers still may not fully understand what you have to say, or accept your conclusions, if your ideas do not reflect a clear and consistent POINT OF VIEW. The elements of writing that most directly convey your stance toward your topic are TONE and style. Tone may be defined as your attitude toward your subject or audience. Style refers to the kind of language you use to present yourself in a piece of writing. In practice, tone and style are closely intertwined because both are directly affected by your **AUDIENCE** and **PURPOSE** in writing.

Tone

Let's suppose you have an essay due before noon. You've been working on it for days, and you've gotten up at 6:45 a.m. to add the finishing touches. In your neighborhood, local ordinances prohibit excessive noise before 8:00 a.m. As you begin to write, however, a jackhammer starts up outside your window, making it impossible for you to concentrate. Exasperated, you text the following message to a friend who lives in the same building:

> wow these ppl drilling outside really don't care huh? ugh

In this example, your audience is your friend, and your purpose is to express your frustration. Your tone here is one of annoyance, suggesting a certain animosity toward your subject—those who persist in disturbing the peace when you have an assignment to complete. As for your style of writing: it might be called informal and personal ("wow," "ppl," "ugh"), as befits one aggrieved friend texting another.

Now assume a different audience for your grievances and a different purpose in writing. Logging on to your city's official website, you discover a suggestion form and file the following complaint:

> As a concerned citizen, I would like to report a violation of the city noise ordinance this morning at 7:00 a.m. outside 907 Whitehead Street. I found it impossible to concentrate when, as I sat down to finish an important writing assignment . . .

Writing to a different audience (city officials) with a different purpose in mind (to inform them of a violation of a law) so that they can address the problem, you have changed your tone and style considerably. Your tone is now more measured and detached; your style is more formal and impersonal (with terms like "violation" and "ordinance") in keeping with the role (concerned citizen) that you've adopted in your text.

The range of tones you have to choose from as a writer is virtually limitless—for example, you can sound annoyed and angry, patient and rational, or sympathetic and enthusiastic. Since tone is a reflection of your attitude toward your subject, a useful way to think about the tone you might adopt in an essay is simply to consider whether you want to sound largely positive, neutral, or negative toward your subject and then to choose words to suit your audience and purpose.

In its trademark satirical style, *The Onion* takes a humorous tone in "All Seven Deadly Sins Committed at Church Bake Sale" (p. 271).

In our jackhammer examples, the indignant text to a friend clearly adopts a negative tone toward the noisemakers. The message to city hall, on the other hand, is more neutral in tone. You can probably imagine a written message that would be positive in its attitude toward construction noise, and thus more enthusiastic in tone, but that would require a different audience, perhaps the readers of a trade publication for paving companies, and a different purpose, let's say to sell jackhammers or other equipment.

As you look for the right tone to use in an essay, try the following template to help you get started:

> ► On the topic of _____, my attitude is _____; my purpose in writing is _____ to an audience of _____. My tone, therefore, should be _____.

You might fill in the blanks this way:

> ► On the topic of <u>why young people sometimes don't vote</u>, my attitude is <u>there's no excuse</u>; my purpose in writing is <u>to explain the importance of voting</u> to an audience of <u>fellow students, some of whom have had trouble with the voting system</u>. My tone, therefore, should be <u>understanding</u>.

Style

As with tone, there are almost as many possible variations in style as there are writers. As in our jackhammer examples, however, a useful way to think about the style you want to adopt in a particular piece of writing is to consider whether you want to come across as formal or informal, personal or impersonal—or something else. Let's look at two examples from the work of Ernest Hemingway. In the following passage from his novel *A Farewell to Arms,* the narrator comes across as impersonal, a detached observer.

In the late summer of that year we lived in a house in a village that looked across the river and the plain to the mountains. In the bed of the river there were pebbles and boulders, dry and white in the sun, and the water was clear and swiftly moving and blue in the channels. Troops went by the house and down the road and the dust they raised powdered the leaves of the trees.

—ERNEST HEMINGWAY, *A Farewell to Arms*

Contrast this style of writing with the style in the next passage, which includes part of a letter that Hemingway wrote for *Esquire* magazine when the town of Key West, where he was living at the time, went bankrupt. To deal with this economic crisis, the authorities introduced tourism as the main industry in the town and published a tourist guide that included Hemingway's house.

> The house at present occupied by your correspondent is listed as number eighteen in a compilation of the forty-eight things for a tourist to see in Key West. So there will be no difficulty in a tourist finding it or any other of the sights of the city, a map has been prepared by the local . . . authorities to be presented to each arriving visitor. Your correspondent is a modest and retiring chap with no desire to compete with the Sponge Lofts (number 13 of the sights), the Turtle Crawl (number 3 on the map), the Ice Factory (number 4), the Tropical Open Air Aquarium containing the 627 pound jewfish (number 9), or the Monroe County Courthouse (number 14). . . . Yet there your correspondent is at number 18 between Johnson's Tropical Grove (number 17) and Lighthouse and Aviaries (number 19). This is all very flattering to the easily bloated ego of your correspondent but very hard on production.
>
> —ERNEST HEMINGWAY, "The Sights of Whitehead Street:
> A Key West Letter"

In this journalistic passage, Hemingway adopts a writing style that is different from the celebrated "plain style" of his fiction. In much of Hemingway's fiction, the language is informal; yet the plain-speaking narrator comes across as impersonal, a detached observer. In his letter, the style is the reverse. The language of the passage is deferential and formal: "modest and retiring chap"; "your correspondent" (as opposed to "this reporter"); "no desire to compete"; "all very flattering." And the implied author is a self-consciously personable "chap" who claims to have an "easily bloated ego." This difference in style suggests a difference in audience and purpose.

As a famous writer living in a small town, Hemingway may well have felt overwhelmed and annoyed by the hordes of tourists at his door. His purpose in writing here, however, is not to produce great literature or even to register a complaint about a public nuisance that, in this case, has been officially promoted by the authorities. His main purpose is to entertain the knowing and sophisticated readers of *Esquire*, a men's general interest magazine. For this audience, Hemingway the journalist adopts a different style of writing from that of Hemingway the novelist and short-story writer.

Stephanie Sowl (p. 383) uses accessible language to explain complex scientific research findings to the general public.

The point of this example, however, is not that you should write like Hemingway or any other particular writer, though imitating the various styles of writers whose work you admire is a helpful way of developing a style of your own. The point, rather, is that your writing style—how you present yourself through the kind of language you use—will depend not only on who you are but also on your **AUDIENCE** and your specific **PURPOSE** in writing.

As you think about the most appropriate writing style to use in an essay, try this template to help you get started:

> ▶ In this essay on _____, I want to present myself as _____; my purpose in writing is _____ to an audience of _____. My style of writing, therefore, should be _____.

Here's one way to fill in the blanks:

> ▶ In this essay on <u>Hemingway's journalism of the 1930s</u>, I want to present myself as <u>an informed reader</u>; my purpose in writing is <u>to explain the novelist's role as a reporter</u> to an audience of <u>my classmates and teacher</u>. My style of writing, therefore, should be <u>formal enough for an academic paper but still fun to read</u>.

Putting It All Together

Here's a template you can use to check that any essay you write includes all the basic elements outlined in this chapter:

> ▶ Within the general subject of _____, I focus in this essay on the specific **TOPIC** of _____.
>
> ▶ My **THESIS** is that _____.
>
> ▶ To present what I have to say as **COHERENTLY** as I can, I have used the following rhetorical strategies: _____, _____, and _____.
>
> ▶ My general attitude toward this subject is _____, so my **TONE**, overall, is _____.
>
> ▶ Since I am writing largely to an audience of _____ with the purpose of _____, my style is _____.

When Sarah Dzubay, for example, was writing "An Outbreak of the Irrational" (pp. 27–31), here's one way that she might have filled in the blanks in this template:

- ▶ Within the general subject of <u>public health</u>, I focus in this essay on the specific **TOPIC** of <u>vaccines for preventing common communicable diseases</u>.
- ▶ My **THESIS** is that <u>vaccine refusal is dangerous because it puts herd immunity at risk</u>.
- ▶ To present what I have to say as **COHERENTLY** as I can, I have used the following rhetorical strategies: <u>giving examples, such as measles and a child with seizures; defining key concepts like herd immunity; and logical argument</u>.
- ▶ My general attitude toward this subject is <u>deep concern</u>, so my **TONE**, overall, is <u>critical but respectful</u>.
- ▶ Since I am writing largely to an audience of <u>anti-vaccine advocates</u> with the purpose of <u>convincing them to accept vaccines,</u> my style is <u>impersonal and factual</u>.

With any essay you write, if you can't fill in all the blanks, consider the possibility that some important element may be missing.

4 | The Writing Process

I think I did pretty well, considering I started out with nothing but a bunch of blank paper.

—STEVE MARTIN

To learn to do anything well, from baking bread to programming a computer, we usually break it down into a series of operations. Writing is no exception. This chapter introduces all the steps of the writing process that will take you from a blank page to a final draft: planning; generating ideas; organizing and drafting; revising your draft as it progresses, both on your own and with the help of others; and editing and proofreading your work into its final form.

Keep in mind, however, that writing is a recursive process—that is, it involves a certain amount of repetition. We plan, we draft, we revise; we plan, we draft, we revise again. Also, we tend to skip around as we write. For example, if we suddenly think of a great new idea, we may go back and redraft what we've already written, perhaps revising it completely. Often, in fact, we engage in the various activities of writing more or less at the same time—and many times we perform these activities in **COLLABORATION** with others.

Planning

Most of the writing we do—and not just in school—starts with an assignment. An English teacher asks you to analyze a poem. A college application includes an essay question, asking you to explain why you want to go to that school. A prospective employer wants to know, on a job application form, why they should hire you. Before you plunge headlong into any writing assignment, however, you need to think about where you're going. You need to plan.

To plan any piece of writing effectively, think about your purpose in writing, the audience you're writing for, and the nature and scope of your topic. If a topic hasn't already been suggested or assigned to you, of course, you'll have to find one. You'll also need to budget your time.

Managing Your Time

When is the assignment due? As soon as you get a writing assignment, make a note of the deadline. Some teachers deduct points for late papers; some don't accept them at all. Even if your instructor is lenient, learning to meet deadlines is part of surviving in college—and beyond. And remember that it's hard to plan well if you begin an assignment the night before it's due. Especially with research papers and other long-range projects, you should begin early so you have plenty of time to do everything the assignment requires.

What kind of research will you need to do? If you're writing a personal narrative or analyzing a process you know well (such as teaching an Irish setter to catch a Frisbee), you may not need to do much research before you begin to write. On the other hand, if you're preparing a full-scale research paper on climate change or the fiction of Henry James, the research may take longer than the actual writing. Most college assignments require at least some research. So as you plan any piece of writing, think about how much and what kind of research you will need to do, and allow plenty of time for that research.

Finding a Topic

Though we often use the words interchangeably, a "subject," strictly speaking, is a broad field of study or inquiry, whereas a "topic" is a specific area within that field. If you are writing a paper for an ecology class, the subject of your paper is likely to be ecology. However, if your teacher asks what you're planning to write on and you reply simply, "ecology," be prepared for a few more questions.

Even if you said "climate change," your teacher would still want to know just what approach you planned to take. A strong topic not only narrows down a general subject to a specific area within that field, but it also addresses a particular aspect of that more limited area—such as what climate change is, or what causes climate change, or what effects climate change has on the environment, or how to slow down climate change.

> Jonathan Haidt and Jean M. Twenge (p. 696) take the general subject of excessive smartphone use, narrow it to its effects on teenagers' mental health, and address ways of reducing overuse.

With many writing assignments, you may be given a specific topic or a choice of specific topics. For example, an essay exam in Ecology 101 might ask, "Can climate change be stopped? How? Or why not?" Or it might say, more specifically, "Describe the key principles of the Kyoto Protocol." In a literature course, you might get a topic like this: "The narrator of Henry James's *The Turn of the Screw:* heroine or hysteric?" Or in a political science course, you might be asked to compare Marx's theory of revolution with Lenin's.

When you're given such a specific topic, make sure you read the assignment carefully and know just what you are being asked to do. Pay close attention to how the assignment is worded. Look for key terms like "describe," "define," "analyze," "compare and contrast," "evaluate," "argue." Be aware that even short assignments may include more than one of these directives. For example, the same assignment may ask you not only to define climate change but also to analyze its causes and effects or to compare and contrast present-day climate conditions with those of an earlier time or to construct an argument about what should be done to slow down climate change.

Many teachers provide lists of possible topics. With longer assignments, however, you may have to work out a topic yourself, perhaps after meeting with your teacher. Start the conversation as soon as you get the assignment. Let your instructor know if there are any areas within your field of study that you find particularly interesting or would like to learn more about. Ask for guidance and suggestions—and start looking on your own. If your school has a writing center, it might be useful to discuss possible topics with someone there.

Thinking about Purpose and Audience

We write for many reasons: to organize and clarify our thoughts, express our feelings, remember people and events, solve problems, persuade others to act or believe as we think they should.

For example, let's look at a passage from a recent government report on climate change:

> Climate change, once considered an issue for a distant future, has moved firmly into the present. Corn producers in Iowa, oyster growers in Washington State, and maple syrup producers in Vermont are all observing climate-related changes that are outside of recent experience. So, too, are coastal planners in Florida, water managers in the arid Southwest, city dwellers from Phoenix to New York, and Native Peoples on tribal lands from Louisiana to Alaska. This National Climate Assessment concludes that the evidence of human-induced climate change continues to strengthen and that impacts are increasing across the country.
>
> —US GLOBAL CHANGE RESEARCH PROGRAM,
> *Climate Change Impacts in the United States: Highlights*

The main PURPOSE of this passage, and the report it introduces, is to persuade the reader that serious climate change, far from an issue to be addressed in the distant future, has already occurred.

As you think about *why* you're writing, however, you also need to consider *who* your readers are. In this report on climate change, for example, the authors speak directly to their intended audience:

> Climate change presents a major challenge for society. This report advances our understanding of that challenge and the need for the American people to prepare for and respond to its far-reaching implications.

The intended audience here is ordinary citizens in communities across the country. Your intended AUDIENCE can be yourself; someone you know, such as your roommate or your teacher; or someone you can't know immediately and directly, such as "the American people." These different audiences have different needs, which you'll want to take into account as you write. If *you* are the intended audience—as when you write in a diary or journal, or jot down a reminder for yourself—you can be as cryptic as you like:

> CC lecture tonight @ 8 in Denney.
> Joy @ Blue Dube, get notes, ask her to feed cat.

QUESTIONS ABOUT PURPOSE AND AUDIENCE

What is the occasion for writing? Are you writing a research paper? Applying for a job? Responding to an email? Commenting on a blog? Planning a wedding toast?

What is your purpose? Do you want to tell your readers something they may not know? entertain them? convince them to do something? change their minds?

Who is going to read (or hear) what you write? Your classmates? Your teacher? Your followers on *Instagram*? Guests at a wedding?

What do you know about your audience's background? For example, if you're writing an argument on how to slow down climate change, you can expect readers who come from coal-mining regions to be more sympathetic if you suggest reducing carbon emissions than if you propose shutting down all coal-burning power plants.

How much does your audience already know about your subject? If you're writing for a general audience, you may need to provide some background information and explain terminology that may be unfamiliar. For example, if you're writing about climate change for a newsmagazine, you might note that sequestration is one way to reduce carbon emissions—and then define "sequestration" for those who don't already know. If you're writing for an audience of environmental scientists, though, you may be able to assume that they are familiar with carbon sequestration and you don't have to define it.

What should you keep in mind about the demographics of your audience? Does the gender of your audience matter? How about their age, level of education, economic status, or religion? Once you have sized up your audience, you're in a better position to generate ideas and evidence that will support what you have to say *and* appeal to that audience.

Who do you want your audience to be? The language you use can let your readers know that you are writing to them—or not. In particular, be careful how you use the personal pronouns "we," "us," and "our." For instance, if you write, "As Christians, we need to have compassion for others," be sure you want to limit your audience to Christians, for this language excludes anyone who is not.

Once you plan to address someone else in writing, no matter what your purpose, you'll need to fill in more blanks for the reader, even if you know that person well and are simply, as in the following example, leaving an informal message:

> Joy,
>
> I have to go to a lecture on climate change tonight in Denney. Meet you at the Blue Danube at 6. May I borrow your ecology notes? Please feed Gen. Burnsides for me. Friskies in cabinet above fridge. Half a can. Thanks!
>
> Fred

Obviously, the writer of this message is familiar with his audience. He can assume, for example, that she knows Denney is the name of a building on campus and that General Burnsides is the name of a cat—but even Joy has to be told where the cat food is stashed and how much to serve. When you don't know your audience, or when you can't be sure they know what you're talking about, you need to supply them with even more information.

In each chapter that follows, you'll find a section that will help you think about purpose and audience as you write. For now, refer to the checklist of general guidelines on p. 51 to help you think about your intended audience and your purpose.

Collaborating with Others

Listen to Wiley's "Last Kind Words Blues" at digital .wwnorton.com /links-backtothe lake5.

From a brief post on *Instagram* or *Twitter* ("Listening to an *amaazzing* tune by Geeshie Wiley. Who was she?") to a full-scale research project on, for example, early black female blues singers—most of the writing you do in the digital age invites collaboration with others. Whether you're working online or face-to-face, follow these general guidelines:

Set clear goals and deadlines. One way to do this is to draw up a "contract" that spells out the purpose, scope, and schedule of the project—and have everyone sign it. Update this document periodically.

Be flexible and open minded. The whole point of collaboration is to encourage everyone to contribute. Listen carefully, and be respectful of other people's ideas. You're working for consensus, not total agreement.

Appoint a group manager. Although everyone needs to take responsibility for the efforts of the group, one well-organized person should be chosen to coordinate those efforts and be in charge of communication within the group. Otherwise, deadlines will be missed and potholes will go unfilled.

Appoint a chief editor. This may or may not be the same person as the group manager, but it should be someone who writes well. Without a general editor, collaborative writing becomes writing by committee.

Assign specific tasks to each member. These should include all aspects of research, writing, editing, and distribution. Tasks should be assigned according to the skills and preferences of each member of the group, and everyone should willingly agree to accept their assignment. No (heavy) arm-twisting.

Confer regularly, and do periodic progress checks. In addition to talking things over throughout the writing process, this is best done by scheduling regular meetings, whether online or in person, and by requiring (and sharing) written samples of everyone's work.

ADDITIONAL TIPS FOR COLLABORATING FACE-TO-FACE

Sit in a circle or around a table. Collaboration is a form of conversation, and most people converse best when speaking face-to-face.

Appoint a discussion leader. Someone needs to be in charge of moving the discussion along, while keeping it on point and making sure that everyone participates. Unlike that of group manager or chief editor, however, this job can be assigned to different members of the group at different meetings, or as the topic of discussion changes.

Appoint a scribe. Someone else should take notes and write a SUMMARY of the proceedings.

ADDITIONAL TIPS FOR COLLABORATING ONLINE

Decide on a method of exchange. For example, you can agree to cut and paste contributions directly into emails, or send them as attachments, or post them to an online discussion board inside or outside of your course's learning management system.

Name files clearly and consistently. You need to be able to find one another's work and know what you're looking at.

Be polite; proof before you send. Collaboration should always be synonymous with courtesy. But remember: anything you post to the internet could end up being read by your grandmother or a potential employer.

THE HUNT FOR A LOST BLUES SINGER

Aside from the internet itself, one of the most comprehensive sites for the collaborative exchange of ideas in human history is *Wikipedia,* the online universal encyclopedia. As an example of how collaboration, particularly online collaboration, can shed light on the most elusive of topics, consider the brief *Wikipedia* entry for the early blues singer Geeshie Wiley—and its sequel.

When accessed in November 2018, Wiley's sketchy biography included the line, "Little is known of her life, and there are no known photographs of her." As early as 2007, however, a researcher identified as "John" had made the following appeal in the TALK thread accompanying the Wiley article: "Help me Geeshie Wiley Fans! I have undertaken an impossible research project: find out more about Geeshie Wiley." Over the following decade, numerous blues fans and other researchers responded to this appeal. Thanks to their collaborative effort, we now know that Lillie Mae ("Geeshie") Wiley—also known as Lillie Mae Scott—was born in 1908 ("possibly" in Louisiana, according to the *Wikipedia* entry) and died in 1950 ("possibly" in Texas). We also know why Wiley stopped performing and disappeared for a time.

The key to the mystery came in an online exchange between the musicologist John Jeremiah Sullivan—likely the initiator of the *Wikipedia* thread on Wiley—and his research assistant Caitlin Love, at the time an undergraduate at a university in Arkansas. Here's how Sullivan, in a *New York Times* article in 2014, describes what his collaborator had just found in a Houston archive:

> I opened the message and the attachment. It was an official form, like a birth certificate. No, a death certificate. State of Texas. Thornton Wiley. Not that exciting. Not "!!!!!!!" Of course he died. Wait, though—it was from 1931, just a year after she was living with him on Saulnier Street in the Fourth Ward. Not long after they made the records. He died young. That was sad. . . . Maybe she is thinking of him in "Last Kind Words" when she sings, "What you do to me, baby, it never gets out of me / I believe I'll see you after I cross the deep blue sea."
>
> I'm reading down through the crowded handwriting. "Inquest." "Homicide." He had been murdered.
>
> Manner of injury: "Stab wound in between collarbone and neck. . . ."
>
> Then the form got to the cause of death. "Knife wound inflicted by Lillie Mae Scott."
>
> —John Jeremiah Sullivan and others,
> "The Ballad of Geeshie and Elvie"

Generating Ideas

Once you have a topic, purpose, and audience clearly in mind, it's time to start generating ideas. Where do you look for ideas? How do you go from nothing to something in a systematic way?

Over the years, writing teachers have developed a number of techniques to help writers find ideas. FREEWRITING, LOOPING, LISTING, and BRAINSTORMING are ways to probe what you already know; CLUSTERING can help you connect ideas and begin organizing a text around them; questioning can be particularly useful when you're trying to make a topic more specific; and keeping a journal can be helpful at any stage. All these techniques, in fact, may come in handy at various points in the writing process, not just at the outset.

Freewriting

When you freewrite, you simply put pen to paper (or fingers to keyboard) and force yourself to jot down whatever pops into your head. Here are some tips for freewriting:

1. Write nonstop for a short period of time, say five or ten minutes. If nothing comes to mind at first, just write: "Nothing. I'm getting nothing. The words aren't coming." Eventually, the words *will* come—if you keep writing and don't stop until time runs out.
2. This is freewriting—so skip around freely and don't get bogged down.
3. Circle, underline, or highlight words and ideas that you might want to revisit, but don't stop freewriting until your time is up. Then go back over what you've written, and mark any passages that stand out as promising.
4. Freewrite again, using something you marked in the previous session as your starting point. Do this over and over until you find an idea you want to explore further.

Here's an example of a five-minute freewriting session by a (then) high school senior, Zoe Shewer, as she was beginning to work on the college application essay that eventually helped put her in the freshman class at Vanderbilt University. The assigned topic for the essay was: "Write about an experience that has taught you something new about yourself."

Write write write. Five minutes. Okay, something I learned about myself. Yikes, what a question. I'm me. Blond, not too tall—okay, looks really aren't the point here. I'm a pretty good athlete, love riding horses. I have a brother named Max and 2 dogs named Oz and Jazz. I tutor kids in Harlem—I like volunteering. I had a great time at Camp Robin Hood last summer. Working with all those different nonprofits was great. But did I learn anything about myself? I learned how to clean gutters, some American Sign Language, how to make spaghetti sauce. I learned that I'm not a good cook. Time.

Freewriting like this is more than a stretching exercise. It can lead to many new ideas if you take something you've just said as the point of departure for more probing. Shewer's freewriting session led her to a possible source for an essay topic: her volunteer work.

Looping

To narrow down the subject you're exploring, try the more directed form of freewriting called *looping*. Looping not only helps you turn up a specific topic, it also nudges you into writing sentences about it. Later on, you may want to use some of these sentences in your essay.

1. Freewrite for five or ten minutes, focusing on a single subject or idea and putting down everything about that subject that you can think of.
2. When you've finished that first loop, look over what you've written and summarize the most important part in a sentence: "I learned a lot volunteering last summer."
3. Use this summary sentence as the point of departure for your next loop. Write for another five or ten minutes without stopping. Then reflect on what you've just written, and compose another sentence summing it up: "Volunteering taught me that I have a lot to learn."
4. Do as many loops as necessary until you have a direction in mind. If you already know the final destination of your essay, so much the better; but for now you're mainly looking for ways of refining your topic along the way.

Looping can be especially useful when you are trying to make an **ABSTRACT** subject more **CONCRETE**. Shewer summed up her freewriting exercise with the sentence "I learned a lot volunteering last summer" and used that sentence as the starting point for a new loop that helped her explore what she learned about herself.

Summary sentence from freewriting: I learned a lot volunteering last summer.

Loop 1: I learned a lot volunteering last summer through Camp Robin Hood. At Ready, Willing & Able, Seymour taught me to clean gutters. At ABC, I learned some American Sign Language, and I learned how strong those kids were. Every day, they came in determined to do everything. At the homeless shelter, I learned so much from Elsie about the city and how to survive in it. But did I learn anything about *myself?* At the end of the summer I had more admiration for Seymour, Elsie, and the kids at ABC. They all had so much more experience with life—even the kids. They had a lot of hard knocks and kept getting back up. Maybe I learned just how lucky I've been. But I think I already knew that. Maybe it was mostly that I learned that I really haven't experienced all that much.

Summary sentence: Volunteering taught me that I have a lot to learn.

Loop 2: Volunteering taught me that I have a lot to learn. Seymour told me a lot of stuff that I didn't know before, not just how to drain gutters but what his life was like. Elsie didn't talk much about her personal life, but she did tell me a lot about being homeless. And just being with the kids at ABC gave me insight into what it's like to be disadvantaged. They had to have so much determination. So did Seymour and Elsie. I don't have that kind of determination.

Summary sentence: Volunteering taught me to admire the determination of Seymour, the children at ABC, and Elsie.

As these excerpts show, looping brings ideas into sharper focus. By writing out her thoughts and looping back over them several times, Shewer was able to come up with concrete ideas about what she'd learned through volunteering.

Listing

Most writing is better and clearer if it is detailed and specific instead of general and abstract. Keeping lists is a useful way to generate ideas—and to illustrate those ideas with interesting examples and specific details.

1. A list can be written anywhere: on paper, on a smartphone, in a notebook, on a napkin. Apps for keeping digital lists and notes abound, but always keep a pencil handy. Keep your lists handy, too, so you can add to them at any time.
2. Don't worry about the form of your lists. But if the lists start to get long, group related items into piles, as you would if you were sorting your laundry.
3. Look for relationships not only *within* those piles but *among* them. Later, if you decide to construct a formal outline for your essay, you can build on the loosely arranged lists you already have.

Brainstorming

Brainstorming is a form of listing, but in this approach you write down words and ideas in one sitting rather than over time.

1. If you are brainstorming by yourself, first jot down a topic at the top of your page or screen. Then make a list of every idea or word that comes to mind.
2. Brainstorming is often more effective when you do it collaboratively, as part of a team, with everyone throwing out ideas and one person acting as scribe.

3. If you brainstorm with others, make sure everyone contributes. If one person monopolizes the session, the purpose of brainstorming is lost.

Clustering

Clustering helps you make connections among ideas.

1. Write down your topic in the center of the page, and circle it.
2. Outside this nucleus, jot down related topics and ideas, and circle each one. Draw a line from each of these satellite ideas to the central topic.
3. As you think of additional ideas, phrases, facts, or examples, group them in clusters and connect them to one another.

Zoe Shewer created the following cluster to group her ideas.

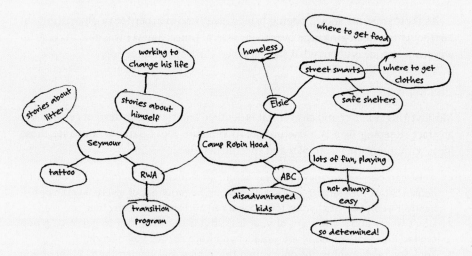

Questioning "Who," "What," "Where," "When," "Why," and "How"

Journalists ask "who," "what," "where," "when," "why," and "how" to uncover the basic information that readers look for in a news story. These standard journalistic questions can be useful for all kinds of writing. Here is how you might use them in an essay about a car accident involving a member of your family:

1. *Who* was involved in the accident? What should I say about my sister (the driver)? about the passengers in the car (including the dog)? the police officer who investigated? the witnesses on the sidewalk?

2. *What* happened? What were the main events leading up to the crash? What did my sister do to avoid hitting the other car head-on? Should I mention that the dog got out of the car first?
3. *Where* did the accident occur? How much of the scene should I describe? The intersection itself? The hill leading up to it?
4. *When* did the accident take place? What time did my sister leave the party? Was it still raining?
5. *Why* did the accident happen? Did the other car swerve into her lane?
6. *How* could it have been avoided? Would my sister have reacted sooner if she hadn't been on her cell phone? Should I write about cell phone usage as a contributing cause in traffic accidents?

Asking key questions like these early in the writing process will help you turn up ideas and figure out which aspects of your subject you want to write about. Later on, the questions you choose to answer will determine, in part, the methods you use to organize your essay. For example, if you decided to explain in detail what happened on the day of your sister's accident, you would draw extensively on the techniques of **NARRATION**. Or if you decided to focus on the scene of the accident, you would write a largely **DESCRIPTIVE** essay.

Keeping a Journal

A personal journal can be a great source of raw material for your writing. Here, for example, is part of a journal entry that Annie Dillard kept when she went on a camping trip in Virginia:

> Last night moths kept flying into the candle. They would hiss & spatter & recoil, lost upside down & flopping in the shadows among the pans on the table. Or—and this happened often, & again tonight—they'd burn their wings, & then their wings would stick to the next thing they'd touch—the edge of a pan, a lid. . . . These I could free with a quick flip with a spoon or something.

Two years after she made this journal entry, Dillard used some of those same details in an essay titled "The Death of a Moth." In the published essay, the moth-drawn-to-the-flame becomes a vivid image of the dedicated writer who devotes all her energy to her work. Obviously, however, Dillard didn't begin the writing process with a big idea like this in mind, and neither should you. She started with the homely details of pots and pans and ordinary moths as recorded in her journal. If you keep a journal regularly, as many writers do, you'll have at your fingertips a world of concrete details to think and write about.

Look for the text of Dillard's essay on p. 767.

You can learn a lot about keeping a journal from an entry like Dillard's:

1. Write down your observations as close to the time of the event as possible; don't wait until you get home from a camping trip to note what happened while you were camping.
2. The observations in a journal don't have to deal with momentous events; record your everyday experiences.
3. Make each journal entry as detailed and specific as possible; don't just write "the bugs were bad" or "another beautiful day."
4. The entries don't have to be long or formally composed; they are for your eyes alone, so be as informal as you like.
5. You may not know the significance of a particular entry until months, even years, after you've written it.

Organizing and Drafting

First drafts can be messy—especially if they are handwritten (p. 330).

Once you accumulate enough facts, details, and other raw material, your next job is to organize that material and develop it into a draft. The method (or methods) of development that you use will be determined by the main point you want your draft to make.

Stating Your Point

As you begin gathering materials for an essay, you probably won't know exactly what your THESIS—your main point—is going to be (unless, of course, you've been given a specific one as part of your assignment). Before you begin writing, however, try to state your thesis in one sentence. You may find as you go along that you need to revise it, but you should start with a thesis in mind.

What makes a strong thesis statement? First, let's consider what a thesis statement is not. A general announcement of your topic—"In this paper I plan to write about how you can fight climate change"—is *not* a thesis statement. A thesis statement tells the reader what your topic is, and it makes an interesting CLAIM *about* your topic, one that is open to further discussion. This is why statements of fact aren't thesis statements either: "The effects of climate change were first predicted in the 1890s by a little-known Swedish chemist." Historical and scientific facts may help support your thesis, but the thesis itself should say something about your subject that requires further discussion. For example:

The best way you can fight climate change is by reducing your personal carbon footprint.

The fight against climate change will be won or lost in developing nations such as India and China.

The United States is still the biggest energy hog on the planet.

When drafting an essay, make sure to state your thesis clearly and directly, usually near the beginning. The following templates can help serve as starting points for drafting a thesis:

> ▸ The main point of this paper is that _____, which is significant because _____.
>
> ▸ As this paper will show, recent studies in the field demonstrate not only _____ but also, and more important, _____.
>
> ▸ According to the latest evidence, it no longer seems to be the case that _____.

Making an Outline

An informal outline is simply a list of your main points in the order they might appear in your draft. For example, after grouping her ideas into clusters, Zoe Shewer created this informal outline for her essay on an unexpected lesson:

Volunteering
    three nonprofits
    learned about myself
Ready, Willing & Able
    Seymour
    draining gutters
    telling stories
    his plans
Association to Benefit Children
    disadvantaged kids
    loved to play
    persevered
Homeless shelter
    Elsie
    street smarts
Learned that I have a lot to learn

For longer projects, such as a research paper, you may need a more detailed outline, indicating the order of both the main ideas and the less important ones. When you make a formal outline, you also show—by indenting and using letters and numbers—how all your ideas fit together to support your thesis.

Thesis statement: Volunteering taught me to admire the determination of Seymour, the children at ABC, and Elsie.

   I. Camp Robin Hood
      A. Crash course in volunteering
      B. Ready, Willing & Able
      C. Association to Benefit Children
      D. Homeless shelter
  II. Ready, Willing & Able
      A. Seymour worked with me
      B. Taught me to drain gutters
      C. Told me about his own life
 III. Association to Benefit Children (ABC)
      A. Played with disadvantaged kids
      B. Read to them
      C. Admired their determination
 IV. Homeless shelter
      A. Elsie talked with me
      B. Depended on handouts and shelters
      C. Had figured out the system
  V. Conclusion
      A. Wanted to give something back
      B. Hope I helped others
      C. Sure I learned a lot myself

When you construct a formal outline like this, try to keep items that are at the same level in more or less the same grammatical form. Also, include at least two items for each level; otherwise, you don't need to subdivide. Whatever kind of outline you make, however, change it as necessary as you write and revise.

Using the Basic Methods of Development

Once you've accumulated enough material to write about, have narrowed your subject down to a manageable topic, and have identified a workable thesis, you should choose one or more methods of development.

Zoe Shewer ultimately chose to develop her topic by writing a narrative that shows what she learned from doing volunteer work over the summer. Within a narrative framework, however, she also incorporated some description and analyzed cause and effect. Whatever you're writing about, you can draw on the following methods, as Shewer did, to help develop your topic:

- *Tell a story.* NARRATION (Chapter 7) is one of the oldest ways of making a point.

- *Help the reader see, hear, feel, smell, or taste* what you're writing about. Good DESCRIPTIONS (Chapter 8) include specific details that appeal to the senses and help create some dominant impression in the reader's mind.

- *Give a "for instance."* Giving EXAMPLES (Chapter 9) is one of the best ways to make general statements more specific and abstract statements more concrete.

- *Break a subject into its parts* in order to show how they fit together to make the whole. If your subject is a written text, the primary purpose of your ANALYSIS (Chapter 10) is to help the reader understand what the text means.

- *Trace causes and effects.* This method of development is a fundamental way of understanding and explaining relationships among actions and events. How to analyze CAUSE AND EFFECT is examined in Chapter 11.

- *Trace similarities and differences.* As a method of development, COMPARISON AND CONTRAST (Chapter 12) tells readers how two subjects are alike or different or both.

- *Divide a subject into types or kinds.* CLASSIFICATION (Chapter 13) helps explain a complex subject by breaking it down into basic categories.

- *Identify the main characteristics of your subject.* DEFINITION (Chapter 14) tells the reader what something is (or is not) by identifying the particular qualities and attributes that set it apart from others like it.

- *Make a claim and give evidence to support it.* How to state a claim, choose the best evidence you can find to support it, and present that evidence in a logical way are all discussed in ARGUMENT (Chapter 15).

The methods you choose for developing your essay will depend on the nature of your topic and your purpose in writing. If your purpose is simple—to give someone written directions for finding the nearest grocery store, for example—a single method may suffice. Often, however, you will want to use several methods together, as bestselling author Michael Lewis does in *Liar's Poker,* which we will examine part by part, method by method in Chapter 16 ("Combining the Methods").

The Parts of an Essay

No matter what methods of development you use, any essay you write should have a beginning, a middle, and an end. These three basic parts are usually referred to as the introduction, the body, and the conclusion.

In the introduction, you introduce the topic and state your thesis. That is, you tell the reader exactly what you're writing about and what your main point is. In the body—which may run anywhere from a few sentences or paragraphs to many pages—you offer evidence in support of your thesis. In the conclusion, you wrap up what you have to say, often by restating the thesis—but with some variation based on the evidence you've just cited.

For example, here is a brief essay about alligators with its parts indicated in the margins. The author states her thesis in the first two paragraphs. In the middle paragraph—the body of her essay—she cites facts and figures to support her thesis. And in the final paragraph, she concludes by restating that thesis—with a twist.

Introduction States the THESIS.

At the Congregational Church, Pastor John puts on puppet shows for the children. One of the star characters is Chompers, a crocodile who talks, attends church, and could go to City Hall if he wanted to.

In the real world, however, the alligators on this sanctuary island can't speak for themselves. So maybe it's time for the rest of us to do it for them and ask if we should reevaluate our alligator policy.

Body Supports the thesis with facts, figures, and other evidence.

In 2004, responding to two fatal attacks, the city changed how it deals with alligator complaints. Under that policy, not only nuisance alligators can be destroyed but *any* alligator in the area that exceeds four feet in length. More than 200 alligators have been killed since the 2004 policy was initiated.

Since alligators don't breed until they're about six feet long, we could be on our way to eliminating these reptiles from the island and dramatically altering the natural balance among its wildlife. Fewer alligators mean more raccoons, snakes, and other natural prey left to feed on birds' eggs and hatchlings. Is that what we want?

Conclusion Restates the thesis with a twist.

Now that the alligator population on the island is clearly under control, perhaps even threatened, let's ask City Hall to reconsider its "targeted harvest" policy. Attend Tuesday's Council meeting and speak up for the alligators. Tell 'em Chompers sent you.

—BARBARA JOY WHITE, "Speaking Up for Alligators"

As in this reptilian example, any essay you write should have an introduction and a conclusion that state and restate your main point. In addition, you'll want to include, in the main body of the essay, at least one paragraph for each supporting point you make. If you're writing about how individuals can combat climate change, for example, you might include a body paragraph for each way of reducing carbon consumption that you propose, such as recycling old clothes, eating less red meat, planning a green wedding, and making fewer left turns when driving.

More tips for writing effective introductory, body, and concluding paragraphs can be found on pp. 100–106.

Using Visuals

In addition to giving your essay a clear beginning, middle, and ending, you may want to consider using visuals. Illustrations such as graphs and charts can be especially effective for presenting or comparing data, and photographs can help readers see things you describe in your written text.

Visuals should never be mere decoration or clip art, however. Any visuals should be directly relevant to your topic and must support your thesis in some way. For example, if you are writing about conserving energy by carrying a reusable shopping bag, you might include an illustration showing the kind of bag you have in mind.

As with a written text, any visual material you include should be appropriate for your audience and purpose. A picture of a raven, for example, wouldn't add much to an essay for a literature class on Edgar Allan Poe's famous poem—but it might be appropriate, if properly labeled, for a biology paper or a field guide to birds.

This reusable bag lets you avoid using plastic shopping bags, thereby conserving energy and reducing landfill waste.

If you do decide that a visual will genuinely enhance your argument, be sure to refer to it in your text and number it, if necessary, so that readers can find it ("see fig. 1"). Position the visual as close as possible to the part of your text that it illustrates, and provide a caption that identifies and explains its point. If you found the visual in another source, identify the source and provide documentation in a list of works cited or references.

To cite visual sources in MLA STYLE, see p. 809.

Revising

Revising is a process of "re-vision," of looking again at your draft and making necessary changes in content, organization, or emphasis. Occasionally when you revise, you discover only a few minor scrapes and bruises that need your attention. More often, however, revising requires some major surgery: adding new evidence, narrowing a thesis, cutting out paragraphs or entire sections, rewriting the beginning to appeal better to your audience, and so on.

For advice on editing common sentence errors, see Ch. 5 (p. 79).

Revising is not generally the time to focus on words or sentences, though you may change some words and smooth out awkward or unclear sentences as you go. Nor is revising a matter of correcting errors, but rather of more general shaping and reshaping. Many writers try to revise far too soon. To avoid this pitfall, put aside your draft for a few hours—or better still, for a few days—before revising.

Reading a Draft with a Critical Eye

Start by reading the draft yourself, and then try to get someone else to look it over—a classmate, a writing tutor, your roommate, your grandmother. Whoever it is, be sure that person is aware of your intended audience and purpose. Here's what you and the person with fresh eyes should look for as you read:

AN EFFECTIVE TITLE. Is the title more than a label? How does it pique the reader's interest? Does it indicate the point of the essay—and if not, should it?

A CLEAR FOCUS. What is the main point? Is it clearly stated in a THESIS statement—and if not, should it be? Is the thesis too broad? too narrow?

SUFFICIENT INFORMATION FOR YOUR AUDIENCE. How familiar is the topic likely to be to your readers? Is there sufficient background information? Are there clear definitions for any terms and concepts readers might not know? Will readers find it interesting?

ADEQUATE SUPPORT FOR THE THESIS. What EVIDENCE supports the thesis? Is the evidence convincing and the reasoning logical? Could the draft be strengthened by adding more facts or specific details?

ORGANIZATION. Is the draft well organized? Does it have a clear beginning, middle, and ending? Are paragraphs related to each other by clear TRANSITIONS? Does each paragraph contribute to the main point, or are some paragraphs off the topic? Does the ending give a sense of closure?

METHODS OF DEVELOPMENT. What is the main method of development—is the draft primarily a **NARRATIVE**? a **DESCRIPTION**? an **ARGUMENT**? Is this method effective? If not, which other methods might be introduced? For instance, would more **EXAMPLES**, or **DEFINITIONS**, or a discussion of **CAUSES** be beneficial?

SOURCES. Is there material from other sources? Did you confirm the sources are trustworthy and accurate? If so, how are those sources incorporated—are they quoted? paraphrased? summarized? How are they acknowledged? In other words, is it clear to the reader whose words or ideas are being used? How does the source material support the main point? Have all source materials been properly cited and documented? If you aren't sure about any aspect of finding, evaluating, citing, documenting, or otherwise using sources in your writing, consult the guidelines in Chapter 17.

PARAGRAPHS. Does each paragraph focus on one main idea and have a clear topic sentence? Does the structure of paragraphs vary, or are they too much alike? If they all begin with a topic sentence, should you consider rewriting some paragraphs to lead up to the topic sentence instead of down from it? Does every sentence in a paragraph support the point that the rest of the paragraph is making? Are there any long or complex paragraphs that should be subdivided?

> For more on writing paragraphs, see Ch. 6 (p. 89).

    The more common problem, however, is that paragraphs are too short. Are there paragraphs that should be combined with other paragraphs or developed more fully? How well does the draft flow from one paragraph to the next? If any paragraphs seem to break the flow, look to see if you need to add transitions or to use repetition to help the reader follow the text.

SENTENCE LENGTH AND VARIETY. Check the length of your sentences. If they are all approximately the same length, try varying them. A short sentence among long sentences can provide emphasis. However, too many short sentences, one after another, can sound choppy. Try combining some of them.

VISUALS. Does the draft include any visuals? If not, is there any material in the text that would be easier to understand as a chart or table? Are there descriptive passages where a photo might help readers see what you're talking about? If there are visuals, are they relevant to the topic? How do they support your thesis?

A Sample Student Essay

Here is Zoe Shewer's first draft of an essay—written as a high school student for her college applications—on what she learned about herself from a summer program. It's based on her formal outline on p. 62.

FIRST DRAFT

How should I spend my summer vacation? Many students have internships or summer jobs. Some travel. I spent last summer volunteering with three nonprofits through Camp Robin Hood.

Camp Robin Hood is a hands-on summer crash course in New York City nonprofit organizations. Every week, I worked at a different nonprofit: a day care center, a homeless shelter, and a transitional lifestyle program for ex-convicts and former addicts. At every organization, I learned something about working with the underprivileged, but at the end of the summer, I realized that I had also learned something about myself.

I began by working at Ready, Willing & Able, where ex-convicts and former addicts clean streets as part of a transitional lifestyle program. I'll never forget the street cleaning attendant I worked with there. Seymour was tall, tattooed, and a former addict. He was also calm and completely at ease in his RWA jumpsuit, sweeping the sidewalks and wheeling a huge blue trash can through the streets. Seymour taught me how to drain gutters by diverting the flow of water with a rolled-up towel. He also taught me to "read" the back stories in the litter. It was like he saw a story in every piece of trash: a schoolgirl who discarded a bracelet in a temper tantrum, a closet eater who ate Twinkies in the street. He talked about his family, too, and his dreams and plans. I grew to respect him and admire his perseverance and determination, despite all the setbacks in his life.

That respect and admiration was something I would come to feel at each of the nonprofits. At the Association to Benefit Children, an organization that provides services to underprivileged children, I played with and taught children who had many challenges. Like any kids, they loved singing, finger painting, and playing with toys. But there was no escaping the fact that these activities didn't always come easily to them. They worked hard for what they wanted. It was impossible not to admire their determination.

At a homeless shelter, where I handed out clean clothes and tickets for showers, I met people from every walk of life. Some had addiction problems or other illnesses, but many had simply fallen on hard times. The loss of a job or an unexpected medical problem ended up costing them their homes, and they had nowhere else to go. I spent many evenings talking to one woman in particular, Elsie. She had been homeless for several years and knew the streets of New York better than anyone I've ever met. She knew which restaurants would give out their leftover food and when you should appear at their back door for dinner. She knew which churches had the best soup kitchens, and which shelters were safest, and where to find the best cast-off clothing. I never found out how she'd become homeless, but she'd figured out the system and made it work for her. Although I grew up in New York City, her street smarts made me feel like I'd never really known the city.

I volunteered for Camp Robin Hood because I wanted to give something back. I know that my upbringing has been privileged, and I've been lucky to have never gone without. I wanted to do something for those who weren't so lucky. But I discovered that while I may have more tangible goods than those I was volunteering to help, they had a lot to teach me about the intangible: qualities like perseverance, determination, optimism, and cheerfulness no matter what the circumstances. They taught me that I have a lot to learn.

Getting Response before Revising

After finishing her first draft, Shewer set it aside for a few hours and then reread it, using the guidelines for reading a draft with a critical eye (pp. 66–67). She also asked a classmate to read it, and he offered the following comments:

I really like the topic of your essay, and I think it meets the prompt well. But maybe it would be more effective if you picked one of the three places you worked to focus on, so that you could talk about it more in depth. I'd like to know more about them.

You kind of state a thesis—"At every organization, I learned something about working with the underprivileged, but at the end of the summer, I realized that I had also learned something about myself"—but then you state it more directly at the end of the paper—"They taught me that I have a lot to learn." That works pretty well, and the body paragraphs do support this idea.

You describe the people you met, but it might be more interesting if there was more of a story.

Shewer agreed with her classmate's suggestions to focus on just one of the places she worked and to incorporate more narration. She chose to write about her experience at Ready, Willing & Able and to focus on her day working with Seymour. After some **BRAINSTORMING** about that day, she decided to add a **NARRATIVE** about one incident in particular. She then revised her **THESIS** to reflect her narrower focus on that specific day. She also added a title, which she hadn't included in her first draft.

SECOND DRAFT

Ready, Willing, and Able

July is stifling in New York City, and I was not looking forward to   1
wearing an oversized jumpsuit in ninety-degree heat. I was suited up to
clean streets as part of the Camp Robin Hood program. I was at the headquarters of Ready, Willing & Able. Most RWA employees are ex-convicts
or former addicts for whom street cleaning is both a job and part of a
transitional lifestyle program.

The program coordinator waved me toward a tall man who had   2
apparently been waiting for me. His name was Seymour, and he was
the street cleaning attendant I would be working with all day. As he
reached out to shake my hand, I noticed that he had a tattoo on his
forearm.

We headed out to the street, and while I fidgeted with the broom I   3
carried, Seymour calmly wheeled a bright blue trash can behind him. As

we began sweeping the sidewalks, Seymour not only showed me how to drain the gutters, he talked about who might have dropped certain kinds of trash and why and told me about his family and his desire to get his life back on track. Though I had lived in the city my entire life, I began to see things in a new light. I became so absorbed in Seymour's stories that I heard some girls laughing and almost didn't realize they were laughing at me. "I wonder what *she* did to deserve *that!*"

I looked up and saw a group of girls about my age laughing at me as they walked past. They obviously thought I was serving a juvenile court sentence. Ordinarily I may have laughed at the idea that I could be mistaken for a juvenile delinquent, but on this day I felt butterflies in my stomach. 4

What if Seymour thought I was just like those other girls? What if he thought I didn't want to be there and was counting down the minutes until the day would be over? I wanted to tell him that I had a lot of respect for his work and that I knew I couldn't possibly understand what he does just by shadowing him for a day. I wanted to tell him that I was not simply doing a day of community service so I could include it on a résumé. 5

But Seymour broke the silence, saying, "Put some muscle in it, Goldilocks." 6

Revising a Second Draft

After setting her revision aside for a day, Shewer came back to her essay and reread it, again following the questions for revision on pp. 66–67. She liked the story of her day working with Seymour, but she thought that now there was too much narration and she needed to have more **DESCRIPTIVE** details. She also decided that she needed to explain more about the incident with the girls—how she felt and how that moment taught her something. Finally, she revised some of her sentences to keep them from being the same length and tried to make some of her language more precise.

FINAL DRAFT

Ready, Willing, and Able

Introduction ······• Wearing a canvas jumpsuit zipped up to my neck, I must have   1
looked as though I was stepping onto the set of *ET: The Extra-
Terrestrial,* but my actual destination was Madison Avenue, home to
some of the fanciest boutiques in New York City. The bright blue
jumpsuit I wore was far from high fashion: it was sized for a full-
grown man, and it ballooned about my slender frame. My blond hair
was pulled back in a ponytail, and the only label I displayed was the
bold-lettered logo on my back: Ready, Willing & Able. I was suited up
to collect trash from the sidewalks of New York.

Beginning of
NARRATIVE: the ······• July is stifling in New York City, and I was not looking forward   2
first day   to wearing the oversized jumpsuit in ninety-degree heat. As I made
my way through the Ready, Willing & Able (RWA) headquarters, I
passed colorfully decorated bulletin boards bearing smiley-faced
reminders: "Drug testing is on Monday!" "Curfew is midnight!" Most
fulltime employees of RWA are ex-convicts or former addicts for
whom street cleaning is the work-for-housing component of a transitional lifestyle program. For me, street cleaning was day one of Camp
Robin Hood, a hands-on summer crash course in New York nonprofit
organizations. As I selected a broom from the supply closet, I
reminded myself that I had volunteered to do this. Feeling like a new
kid on the first day of school, I stood nervously next to the program
supervisor who would introduce me to the street cleaning attendant
I would be helping.

If I was the awkward new kid, the street cleaning attendant   3
to whom I was assigned, a tall man named Seymour, was undoubt-
Description of
key character, ······• edly the Big Man on Campus. Seymour wore his RWA cap slightly
with CONCRETE   askew, and, as he reached out to shake my hand, I caught a glimpse
details   of a tattoo under his sleeve. We headed out to the street together,
and, while I nervously fidgeted with the broom I carried, he calmly
wheeled a bright blue trash can behind him. Seymour began sweep-

ing the sidewalks, and I followed his lead. He not only showed me how to drain the gutters by diverting the flow of water with a rolled-up towel, he also taught me how to "read" the back stories in the litter. To Seymour, a torn hemp bracelet on the curb was a schoolgirl's temper tantrum; a Twinkie wrapper in the street was a closet eater's discarded evidence. Though I have lived in New York my entire life, I began to see my surroundings in a new light. The streets that had always felt so familiar seemed full of surprises. As our afternoon continued, Seymour also told me stories about his sister, his desire to get his life back on track after some time on the wrong side of the law, his love of Central Park, and his aspiration to travel across the country.

After several hours, I had more or less forgotten about my tent-sized RWA jumpsuit when suddenly I heard someone laughing at me: "I wonder what *she* did to deserve *that*?!" [4] *PROLOGUE and CLIMAX of narrative*

I looked up and saw a group of girls my age looking in my direction and laughing as they walked past. My stomach tightened. They obviously thought I was being punished, perhaps serving a juvenile court sentence. Ordinarily I might have laughed at the idea that I could be mistaken for a juvenile delinquent, but on this day I felt a jumble of feelings—panic, shame, sadness, and admiration for a man whose history is suggested by his jumpsuit and the logo on his back. I will admit that a few hours earlier I was embarrassed about my ill-fitting uniform. Halfway through the workday, however, the girls' rude comments caused an entirely different kind of shame: What if Seymour thought *I* was anything like those girls? What if he thought that I was faking a smile and counting down the minutes until the day was over? [5] *Effect of incident* *THESIS indicated indirectly*

I suddenly wanted to thank Seymour for this experience. I wanted to tell him that he was probably the best guide through these streets I had ever had, and that I knew I could not possibly understand what he does by shadowing him for a day in a borrowed uniform. I wanted to explain to him that I volunteer regularly in New York: I am committed to working with at-risk children, and have [6] *Significance of narrative* done so for years at an after-school program in Harlem. I wanted to share how much I relate to his closeness with his family, his desire to travel, and his love of Strawberry Fields in Central Park. But the girls' mocking comments and laughter had left us in an uncomfortable silence, and I felt that anything I might say would make us feel even more awkward.

It was Seymour who broke this silence. As I stood next to the trash can and tried to avoid staring off in the direction of the latte-carrying girls, Seymour caught my eye, smiled, and nodded toward my broom with one excellent piece of advice: "Put some muscle in it, Goldilocks."

7

Conclusion with dialogue

This final draft, Shewer felt, better blended the modes of narration and description, and it fulfilled the assignment to write about an experience that taught her something new about herself. She especially liked the concrete details she included and the dialogue that ended the essay.

Editing and Proofreading

When you finish revising your essay, you're still not quite done. You've put the icing on the cake, but you need to make sure all the candles are straight and wipe the edge of the plate. That is, you need to edit and proofread your final draft before presenting it to the reader.

For more on editing sentences, see Ch. 5 (p. 79).

When you edit, you add finishing touches and correct errors in grammar, sentence structure, punctuation, and word choice that affect the sense and meaning of your text. When you proofread, you take care of misspellings, typos, problems with your margins and format, and other minor blemishes in the appearance of your document.

Certain types of problems are common to certain types of writing. Chapters 7–15 include sections on "Editing for Common Errors"—the kinds that are likely with the method being discussed. Here are some tips that can help you check your drafts for some common mistakes.

TIPS FOR EDITING SENTENCES

Check to be sure that each sentence expresses a complete thought—that it has a subject (someone or something) and verb performing an action or indicating a state of being. Watch out for SENTENCE FRAGMENTS, RUN-ONS, and COMMA SPLICES.

Check capitalization and end punctuation. Be sure that each sentence begins with a capital letter and ends with a period, a question mark, or an exclamation point.

Look for sentences that begin with "it" or "there." Often such sentences are vague or boring, and they are usually easy to edit. For example, if you've written "There is a doctor on call at every hospital," you could edit it to read "A doctor is on call at every hospital."

Check for parallelism. All items in a list or series should have parallel forms—all nouns ("Lincoln, Grant, Lee"), all verbs ("dedicate," "consecrate," "hallow"), all phrases ("of the people," "by the people," "for the people").

Check adjective order. Adjectives usually go in the following order: number, size, shape, age, color, nationality ("a pair of small round hand-me-down navy earrings").

Consider the stylistic issues—such as using strong verbs and avoiding PASSIVE VOICE—discussed in the next chapter.

TIPS FOR EDITING WORDS

"There," "their." Use "there" to refer to place or direction or to introduce a sentence: "Who was there? There was no answer." Use "their" as a possessive: "Their intentions were good."

"It's," "its." Use "it's" to mean "it is": "It's difficult to say what causes dyslexia." Use "its" to mean "belonging to it": "Each car has its unique features."

"Lie," "lay." Use "lie" when you mean "recline": "She's lying down because she's tired." Use "lay" when you mean "put" or "place": "Lay the book on the table."

TIPS FOR EDITING PUNCTUATION

Check for commas after introductory elements in a sentence.

Internally, of course, where the cameras couldn't see, I was just as terrified as I'm sure the other contestants were.

—Kwame Onwuachi, "Angles"

Check for commas before "and," "but," "or," "nor," "so," or "yet" in compound sentences.

My father often brought his work home, and Mia was one of many commercial-art images I saw him work on in his studio.

—Robert Desjarlait, "They Got Rid of the Indian and Kept the Land"

Check for commas in a series.

Inside an H Mart complex, there will be some kind of food court, an appliance shop, and a pharmacy. . . . There will usually be a pseudo-French bakery with weak coffee, bubble tea, and an array of glowing pastries that always look much better than they taste.

—Michelle Zauner, "Crying in H Mart"

When you quote other people's words, be sure to put quotation marks at the beginning and end of the quotation.

It tends to be the passion part of grit that people need more help with. "I find that people's passion scores are lower than their perseverance scores," Duckworth said.

—Melissa Dahl, "Don't Believe the Hype about Grit"

Check to be sure that you've put commas and periods inside quotation marks.

"Put some muscle in it, Goldilocks."

—Zoe Shewer, "Ready, Willing, and Able"

"Come to me, that I may give your flesh to the birds of the heavens and the beasts of the field," the giant cried out when he saw his opponent approach.

—Malcolm Gladwell, "David and Goliath"

Check your use of apostrophes with possessives. Singular nouns should end in 's, whereas plural nouns should end in s'. The possessive pronouns "hers," "his," "its," "ours," "yours," and "theirs," should not have apostrophes.

> Both sides of my family, my mother's and father's, have lived there for generations.
> —JESMYN WARD, "Tulane Commencement Address"

> Some agree with The Slants' approach and some disagree, as is normal in a robust artistic marketplace.
> —ILYA SHAPIRO and THOMAS A. BERRY,
> "Does the Government Get to Decide What's a Slur?"

> Theirs was the life I dreamt about during my vacations in eastern North Carolina.
> —DAVID SEDARIS, "Remembering My Childhood
> on the Continent of Africa"

Proofreading and Final Formatting

Proofreading is the only stage in the writing process where you are *not* primarily concerned with meaning. Of course you should correct any substantive errors you discover, but your main concerns when proofreading are small technicalities and the appearance of your text. Misspellings, margins that are too narrow or too wide, unindented paragraphs, missing page numbers—these are the kinds of imperfections you're looking for as you put the final touch on your document.

Such minor blemishes are especially hard to see when you're looking at your own work. So slow down as you proofread, and view your document more as a picture than as a written text. Use a ruler or piece of paper to guide your eye line by line as you scan the page; or read your entire text backward a sentence at a time; or read it out loud word by word. Use a spellchecker, too, but don't rely on it: a spellchecker doesn't know the difference, for example, between "spackling" and "spacing" or "Greek philosophy" and "Geek philosophy."

After you've proofread your document word for word, check the overall format to make sure it follows any specific instructions that you may have been given. If your instructor doesn't have formatting requirements, follow these tips based on the Modern Language Association guidelines.

TIPS FOR FORMATTING AN ESSAY IN MLA STYLE

Heading and title. Put your name, your instructor's name, the name and number of the course, and the date on separate lines in the upper-left-hand corner of your first page. Center your title on the next line, but do not underline it or put it in quotation marks. Begin your first paragraph on the line that follows.

Typeface and size. Use ten-, eleven-, or twelve-point type in an easy-to-read typeface, such as Times New Roman, **Arial**, or Cambria.

Spacing. Double-space your document, including your heading and title.

Margins. Set one-inch margins at the top, bottom, and sides of your text.

Paragraph indentation. Indent the first line of each paragraph one-half inch.

Page numbers. Number your pages consecutively in the upper-right-hand corner of the page, and include your last name with each page number. This information should be set one-half inch from the top of the page.

Long quotations. When quoting more than three lines of poetry, more than four lines of prose, or dialogue between characters in a drama, set off the quotation from the rest of your text, indenting it one-half inch (or five spaces) from the left margin. Do not use quotation marks, and put any parenthetical documentation *after* the final punctuation.

Turn to pp. 814–25 to see a model MLA-style essay.

5 Writing and Editing Sentences

All you have to do is write one true sentence.

—ERNEST HEMINGWAY

It all starts with a sentence.

—JUDITH C. HOCHMAN

Consider your feet: each one contains twenty-six bones, thirty-three joints, and more than one hundred muscles, tendons, and ligaments. When you walk, however, you don't have to think about what every piece is doing; you just need to know your right foot from your left foot—and how to put one in front of the other.

Likewise when you write: writing, after all, is basically the act of putting one sentence after another—and another and another. But fortunately, the bare bones of sentence structure aren't as complex as the anatomy of the human foot. And understanding those basics will help you not just start off your writing on the right foot, by writing strong sentences, but also regain your footing when you stumble, by revising to clear up confusing sentences and grammatical errors.

What Makes a Sentence?

Throughout this chapter, you'll find opportunities for online editing practice in InQuizitive. To get started, ask your instructor how they want you to access InQuizitive.

A sentence is a group of words expressing a complete thought and falling into one of four basic categories: DECLARATIVE ("This is a sentence."); INTERROGATORY ("Is that a sentence?"); IMPERATIVE ("Write better sentences."); and EXCLAMATORY ("That's quite a sentence!"). The main purpose of writing sentences, of course, is to express thoughts and ideas. For the moment, however, let's concentrate on the skeleton of sentences rather than their meat.

What constitutes the basic anatomy of a sentence? If you can order a pizza with pepperoni but without onions, you already know enough to understand, more or less intuitively, how sentences work. In fact, most well-constructed sentences simply combine the following four elements in various orders:

subject + verb + object + modifier

There are a few more possible parts, but these are the four fundamental elements—what some might call the earth, air, fire, and water—of basic sentence writing. The following exchange illustrates all of them:

Who did this virtuous deed? I did it.

Most sentences tell who or what does something (the SUBJECT), what is done (the VERB), and to whom or what it is done (the OBJECT). The example "I did it" follows this most fundamental of sentence patterns:

I *(subject)* + did *(verb)* + it *(object)*.

On this three-legged stool rests many a sturdy English sentence. We can add a fourth leg to the structure by introducing MODIFIERS (words that change or limit the meaning of other words in the sentence), as in the question we started with:

Who *(subject)* + did *(verb)* + this virtuous *(modifiers)* + deed *(object)*?

In this construction, "this" and "virtuous" are called modifiers because they modify—that is, they change or limit—the meaning of the word "deed." We're not talking about just any old deed here, but *this* particular one—and it's "virtuous."

Watching Out for Sentence Fragments

Complete sentences don't have to include all four basic elements, but they do need a SUBJECT and a VERB. Otherwise, you've got a SENTENCE FRAGMENT, such as:

> Two turtle doves and a partridge in a pear tree.

This is only a fragment of a sentence because it includes subjects ("doves," "partridge") and modifiers ("two," "turtle," "a," "in a pear tree") but no verb. What did the doves and the partridge do? We don't know. Other kinds of fragments include a verb but no subject, include neither a subject nor a verb, or include both a subject and a verb but depend on another sentence for their meaning. (Imperatives, by the way, are always considered complete sentences rather than fragments because the subject, "you," is understood even if not stated: "[You] ask your teacher.")

You should avoid sentence fragments in academic writing because they leave the reader up in the air. The student who included the following paragraph in a term paper probably didn't realize that it leaves the reader hanging because the last "sentence" is actually a sentence fragment:

> Polls now indicate that fewer Americans feel they are better off today than they were five years ago. A public-opinion analysis group has found that large numbers of Americans now see themselves as standing lower on the economic ladder. <u>With worsening living conditions and the anticipation of further decline over the next five years.</u>

Fragments are useful in certain circumstances; see how Amy Tan uses them in "Mother Tongue" to represent her mother's speech (p. 483, par. 6).

Even if you do your best to avoid fragments in your academic writing, they can easily slip in and confuse your readers. In revising, there are several ways to fix an unintentional sentence fragment like this.

ATTACH THE FRAGMENT TO ANOTHER SENTENCE

> A public-opinion analysis group has found that large numbers of Americans now see themselves as standing lower on the economic ladder, <u>with worsening living conditions and the anticipation of further decline over the next five years.</u>

Attached to the sentence before it, the modifying phrase specifies the current and future economic challenges that some Americans face.

SUPPLY THE MISSING PART(S) OF THE FRAGMENT

A public-opinion analysis group has found that large numbers of Americans now see themselves as standing lower on the economic ladder. <u>These Americans face</u> worsening living conditions and the anticipation of further decline over the next five years.

Adding a subject ("these Americans") and a verb ("face") to the fragment makes it a complete sentence about current and future challenges.

REWRITE THE FRAGMENT AND ITS CONTEXT

<u>Seeing their living conditions worsen and anticipating further decline over the next five years,</u> large numbers of Americans see themselves as standing lower on the economic ladder, according to a public-opinion analysis group.

Rewritten to be part of the subject of the sentence, the modifying phrase now describes what some Americans are experiencing and thinking.

Are Sentence Fragments Ever Okay?

In 1890, a Texas railway agent, aptly named William Crush, arranged to crash two thirty-five-ton locomotives head on as a publicity stunt. A local newspaper reported the spectacle as follows:

A crash, sound of timbers rent and torn, and then a shower of splinters.

The reporter who composed this sentence fragment surely knew what a complete sentence is. "There was just a swift instant of silence," he wrote elsewhere in the article, "and then . . . the air was filled with flying missiles of iron and steel." Yet he deliberately chose to begin his piece with just a piece of a sentence. Why?

For dramatic effect. A sentence fragment stops the forward motion of a passage of writing dead in its tracks. Especially in academic writing, though, it may have unintended consequences. (As did the physical fragments from Crush's train crash: it attracted national attention, but two spectators were killed, and the photographer hired for the occasion lost an eye). Sentence fragments can confuse your readers or put off those who expect a more formal tone.

So should you ever use them? Depends. Or it depends. Ask your teacher.

For more practice, complete the InQuizitive activity on sentence fragments.

Fixing Fused and Other Run-On Sentences

If a sentence fragment is a disconnected scrap, a **RUN-ON SENTENCE** is a grammatical pileup, in which two or more sentences get jammed together without sufficient punctuation or other separation between them.

Sometimes a run-on is called a **FUSED SENTENCE**. In this case, two or more sentences are written as if they were one, with no separation at all. The following example is adapted from an essay written for an ACT exam:

> Machines are useful but they take people's jobs like if they don't know how to use them they get fired.

If you find run-ons when proofreading your writing, there are several strategies for fixing them so that your train of thought becomes clear. First, try separating the ideas that a run-on is expressing into basic "kernel" sentences:

> Machines are useful.
> Machines can take people's jobs.
> People don't know how to use the machines.
> People get fired.

You can always correct run-ons by separating them into shorter sentences as in this example. But this strategy doesn't always make your point clearer, and (as the example shows) may result in choppy sentences that don't follow along a clear track. To avoid running sentences together (or setting them apart) in a way that confuses readers, think about how the basic ideas they express can fit together clearly to form more complex ideas.

There are multiple ways to join basic kernel sentences into more complex sentences, but most of them use either *coordination* or *subordination*. Coordinate ideas are *independent* of each other; each one can stand on its own ("Machines are useful" and "My uncle is a mechanic"). Subordinate ideas don't make sense by themselves; their meaning is *dependent on* another idea in the sentence ("that are useful" and "If they don't know how to use the machines"). To repair run-on sentences in your writing, then, you can use either **COORDINATING WORDS** or **SUBORDINATING WORDS**. Or if the ideas are coordinate, you can use a semicolon and, if appropriate, a transitional word or phrase between them.

Here are a few helpful strategies for fixing run-on sentences by combining kernel sentences clearly.

USE A COORDINATING WORD SUCH AS "AND," "OR," "BUT," "FOR," "YET," AND "SO"

Machines are useful, <u>but</u> they can take people's jobs.

Here the idea that machines are useful is just as important as the idea that they can take away jobs. The two parts of the sentence that express these ideas are also *independent* of each other; each is an **INDEPENDENT CLAUSE**, a group of words with a subject and a verb that can stand alone as a sentence. When they link independent clauses, coordinating words like "but" are usually preceded by a comma.

USE A SUBORDINATING WORD SUCH AS "IF," "BECAUSE," "ALTHOUGH," AND "SINCE" OR "WHO," "THAT," AND "WHICH"

<u>If</u> people don't know how to use the machines, they get fired.

Because of the subordinating "If," the first part of this sentence is a **DEPENDENT CLAUSE**—a group of words that has a subject and a verb but that doesn't express a complete thought by itself. Consequently, this part of the sentence is logically and grammatically *dependent on* the second part—the independent clause. People being fired is the main idea, and not knowing how to use the machines is less important—it's just the *reason* for the firing. When the dependent clause comes at the beginning of the sentence, as it does here, it is usually followed by a comma.

Here's another way to join these two ideas using a subordinating word and a dependent clause:

People <u>who don't know how to use the machines</u> get fired.

USE A SEMICOLON WITH A TRANSITIONAL WORD OR PHRASE

Machines are useful<u>; however,</u> they can take people's jobs.

The semicolon clearly separates the two coordinate ideas in the independent clauses, and the transitional word makes clear the logical relation
between them. The transitional word or phrase is usually followed by a
comma, as it is in the example above and the one below.

> For more
> practice,
> complete the
> InQuizitive
> activity on
> run-on
> sentences.

Machines are useful<u>; on the other hand,</u> they can take people's jobs.

Correcting Comma Splices

Run-ons aren't all head-on collisions between clauses; sometimes they're more like fender-benders, with a bumper—in the form of a comma—to soften the blow.

In the following sentence, for example, the reader confronts a small internal problem:

> The surgeon did his work thoroughly, he turned the patient's colon into a semicolon.

Although the comma in the middle signals the transition to a new idea, alone it isn't strong enough to separate two independent clauses. This is still a run-on sentence—in this case, a COMMA SPLICE. Though readers can usually figure out what a comma splice is trying to say, it can also lead to reader confusion. So look out for—and correct—comma splices in your own writing. To fix a comma splice, you can use the same methods you can to fix a fused sentence, including these:

USE A SEMICOLON INSTEAD OF A COMMA

> The surgeon did his work <u>thoroughly; he</u> turned the patient's colon into a semicolon.

A semicolon signals a break not as strong as the full stop of a period but stronger than the mere pause of a comma—and strong enough to separate two independent clauses. After the semicolon, you can also include a transitional word or phrase, if appropriate, usually followed by a comma.

> The surgeon did his work <u>thoroughly; in fact, he</u> turned the patient's colon into a semicolon.

ADD AN APPROPRIATE COORDINATING WORD

> The surgeon did his work thoroughly<u>, and</u> he turned the patient's colon into a semicolon.

A coordinating word like "and" or "but" makes a stronger separation than a comma does. Without the comma, however, the dividing line between the clauses might not always be clear. So use both the comma *and* the conjunction.

USE A PERIOD TO CREATE SEPARATE SENTENCES

> The surgeon did his work thoroughly. He turned the patient's colon into a semicolon.

The added period prevents these brief trains of thought from colliding by signaling a full stop at the end of the first one.

For more practice, complete the InQuizitive activity on comma splices.

Choosing Strong Verbs

Verbs are the action words in a sentence; so if you want your sentences to have punch, you need to use strong verbs. But what makes a verb strong or weak?

Suppose you're writing about buffalo moving across a plain. You could choose to say, simply:

The buffalo move across the plain.

To signify the group behavior of large animals, however, "move" is a pretty wimpy verb. Not only does it suggest little in the way of power and energy, but it's also overly ABSTRACT, telling the reader nothing specific about *how* the animals move. Strong verbs, by contrast, are CONCRETE: they capture precisely what your subject does, whether that action is heavy and lumbering (buffalo) or light and quick (hummingbirds).

The verbs in the following list are strong not only because they express forceful actions, but also because they specify particular ways of moving—mostly on foot (or hoof):

> *tramp, trudge, slog, trek, march, stride, run, race, stampede*

No matter what action you're depicting, you can find lists of synonyms like these in almost any dictionary or thesaurus.

For sheer energy and force in a verb with "buffalo" as the subject, you can't go wrong with

The buffalo <u>stampede</u> across the plain.

But suppose the buffalo are actually moving at a more leisurely pace. In that case, you'd need a kinder, gentler verb like one of the following:

> *walk, stroll, amble, saunter, wander, ramble, mosey, roam*

Although they signify less strenuous actions, any of the verbs in this list can be as "strong" a choice as "stampede" if it captures precisely what your subject is doing.

And furthermore, a carefully chosen verb often tells the reader not only how the subject acted but, to a degree, *why*. Why do buffalo "ramble," "roam," or "stampede"? Most of the verbs we've been considering for their movement imply a lack of a reason: aimlessness. If, however, you want to convey a sense of motivated purpose behind *human* locomotion, you might try a verb like "march," "stalk," or "stride."

Edward Lee (p. 226) uses strong verbs such as "<u>breathe in the view</u>," "her short hair <u>hugs</u> the curves of her temples," "yellow mustard is <u>slathered</u> on."

Avoiding Passive Voice—Most of the Time

In most academic writing, you should avoid the passive voice like you would a stampeding herd. An important reason is that even strong verbs generally end up sounding weaker when they're cast in the passive voice. Consider this example:

> The chicken crossed the road.
> The road was crossed by the chicken.

In the English language, a sentence is usually written as in the first example above, with the subject ("chicken") first, followed by the verb ("crossed"), followed by the object ("road"). This sentence is said to be in the **ACTIVE VOICE** because the subject is doing the action specified by the verb. In sentences that use the **PASSIVE VOICE**, by contrast, like the second example, the subject is acted on. That is, the object of the sentence in the active voice ("road") becomes the subject in the passive voice; the verb changes, typically by adding a form of "be" ("was crossed"); and the original subject drops out of the kernel sentence, often to land in a modifying phrase ("by the chicken").

"The road was crossed by the chicken" sounds wrong because the emphasis is wrong. Using the passive voice is not an error in grammar; often, though, it's a slip in style—and an obstacle to clarity.

When Is Passive Voice a Better Choice?

Occasionally, however, passive voice might actually be the better choice in a sentence. Here are some examples of situations when you might consider using it.

WHEN THE RECEIVER OR RESULT OF AN ACTION IS MORE SIGNIFICANT THAN THE DOER

> Vagility is defined by biologists as the ability of wild animals to roam freely.

The term being defined is more important than who defines it.

> The vagility of wild animals is threatened when humans put up obstacles in the natural landscape.

What happens to the animals is the key point here, not what causes that result.

WHEN THE DOER OF AN ACTION IS UNKNOWN OR YOU DON'T WANT THE DOER TO BE KNOWN

> The money has been stolen.
> Mistakes were made.

By turning the object or the result of an action into the subject, each of these sentences avoids assigning responsibility for the deed.

WHEN A CHANGE IN VOICE CHANGES THE FOCUS

> *Active:* Brewster M. Higley wrote the lyrics to "Home on the Range."
> *Active:* Daniel E. Kelley composed the tune.

The focus is on the identity of the composers, Higley and Kelley.

> *Passive:* The lyrics to "Home on the Range" were written by Brewster M. Higley.
> *Passive:* The tune was composed by Daniel E. Kelley.

The emphasis is on the different aspects (lyrics and tune) of the song.

WHEN YOU WANT TO LAY CLAIM TO OBJECTIVITY, AS IN A LAB REPORT OR OTHER SCIENTIFIC WRITING

> DNA was extracted from the subject's mouth.
> The DNA was then subjected to qPCR analysis.

Use of the passive voice implies that these procedures were carried out in an impersonal, purely scientific manner.

Sometimes, however, the passive voice in scientific writing can get out of hand. For example:

> After the analysis was performed on the data, the results were sent to the lab.

For a list of common sentence issues to check when proofreading, see p. 75.

There is a missing person, or more than one, in this sentence. Who performed the analysis? Who sent the results to the lab? The passive voice doesn't tell us. Most of the sentences you write should include a clear subject as well as a strong verb.

In this chapter, we've seen that sentences are strings of words that, in part, make coherent statements because of how (and how well) they're tied together. In the next chapter, we'll see that much the same can be said about meaning and coherence in paragraphs.

6 | Writing Paragraphs

Maybe it's the first really good paragraph you ever wrote, something so fragile and yet full of possibility that you are frightened. You feel as Victor Frankenstein must have when the dead conglomeration of sewn-together spare parts suddenly opened its watery yellow eyes.

—STEPHEN KING, *On Writing*

Just as an essay is made up of a number of related paragraphs, a paragraph is made up of a number of related sentences on the same topic. In any piece of writing longer than a few sentences, paragraphs are necessary to indicate when the discussion shifts from one topic to another. Just because a group of sentences is on the same topic, however, doesn't mean they're all closely related. All the following sentences, for example, are about snakes:

> There are no snakes in Ireland. Ounce for ounce, the most deadly snake in North America is the coral snake. Snakes are our friends; never kill a snake. North America is teeming with snakes, including four poisonous species. Snakes also eat insects.

Although they make statements about the same topic, these sentences do not form a coherent paragraph because they're not closely related to one another: each one snakes off in a different direction. In a coherent paragraph, all the sentences work together to support the main point.

Supporting the Main Point

Suppose the main point you wanted to make in a paragraph about snakes was that despite their reputation for evil, snakes should be protected. You could still mention snakes in North America, even the deadly coral snake. You could say that snakes eat insects. But the sentence about snakes in Ireland would have to go. Of course, you could introduce additional facts and figures about snakes and snakebites—so long as you made sure that every statement in your paragraph worked together to support the idea of conservation. For example, you might write:

> Snakes do far more good than harm, so the best thing to do if you encounter a snake is to leave it alone. North America is teeming with snakes, including four poisonous species. (Ounce for ounce, the most deadly snake in North America is the coral snake.) The chances of dying from any variety of snakebite, however, are slim—less than 1:25,000,000 per year in the United States. Snakes, moreover, contribute to a healthy ecosystem. They help control the rodent population, and they eat insects. (Far more people die each year from the complications of insect bites than from snakebites.) Snakes are our friends and should be protected; never kill a snake.

This is a coherent paragraph because every sentence contributes to the main point, which is that snakes should be protected.

Don't Go Off on a Tangent

Anytime the subject of snakes comes up, it's tempting to recall the legend of Saint Patrick, the patron saint of Ireland who, in the second half of the fifth century, is said to have driven the snakes from the land with his walking stick. Beware, however, of straying too far from the main point of your paragraph, no matter how interesting the digression may be. That is, be careful not to go off on a tangent. The term "tangent," by the way, comes from geometry and refers to a line that touches a circle at only one point—on the periphery, not the center.

And, incidentally, did you know that St. Patrick used a three-leaf clover to explain the Christian doctrine of the Trinity to the Irish people? Which is why shamrocks are associated with St. Patrick's Day. Also, there's another really interesting legend about St. Patrick's walking stick. . . . But we digress.

Writing Topic Sentences

To stay on track in a paragraph, state your main point in a **TOPIC SENTENCE** that identifies your subject (snakes) and makes a clear statement about it ("should be protected"). Most of the time your topic sentence will come at the beginning, as in this paragraph from an essay about the benefits of working at McDonald's:

> Working at McDonald's has taught me a lot. The most important thing I've learned is that you have to start at the bottom and work your way up. I've learned to take this seriously—if you're going to run a business, you need to know how to do all the other jobs. I also have more patience than ever and have learned how to control my emotions. I've learned how to get along with all different kinds of people. I'd like to have my own business someday, and working at McDonald's is what showed me I could do that.
> —MARISSA NUÑEZ, "Climbing the Golden Arches"

When you put the topic sentence at the beginning of a paragraph like this, every other sentence in the paragraph should follow from it.

Sometimes you may put your topic sentence at the end of the paragraph. Then every other sentence in the paragraph should lead up to the topic sentence. Consider this example from an essay on hummingbirds that ultimately makes a statement about all living things:

> Mammals and birds have hearts with four chambers. Reptiles and turtles have hearts with three chambers. Fish have hearts with two chambers. Insects and mollusks have hearts with one chamber. Worms have hearts with one chamber, although they may have as many as eleven single-chambered hearts.

Unicellular bacteria have no hearts at all, but even they have fluid eternally in motion, washing from one side of the cell to the other, swirling and whirling. No living being is without interior liquid motion. We all churn inside.

—BRIAN DOYLE, "Joyas Voladoras"

All the statements in this paragraph are about hearts, or otherwise pertain to the circulation of fluid ("liquid motion") within the bodies of living creatures. Thus they all contribute to the topic sentence at the end: "We all churn inside."

Sometimes the main point of a paragraph will be implied from the context, and you won't need to state it explicitly in a topic sentence. This is especially true when you're making a point by telling a story. In both of the following paragraphs from her essay about working at McDonald's, Marissa Nuñez explains how she got the job in the first place:

> Two years ago, while my cousin Susie and I were doing our Christmas shopping on Fourteenth Street, we decided to have lunch at McDonald's.
>
> "Yo, check it out," Susie said. "They're hiring. Let's give it a try." I looked at her and said, "Are you serious?" She gave me this look that made it clear that she was.

Nuñez doesn't have to tell the reader that she is explaining how she came to work for McDonald's because that point is clear. (Also, she later writes that "finally one day the manager came out and said we had the job.")

Topic sentences not only tell your reader what the rest of a paragraph is about; they also help, collectively, to tie all your ideas together in support of the essay's main point. In Nuñez's case, the main point is what she learned about people, business, and herself from working at a fast-food restaurant, as she states clearly at the beginning: "Working at McDonald's has taught me a lot."

Using Parallel Structures

See how parallel structure is used in "Grant and Lee" (p. 441).

Another way of tying ideas together in a paragraph is by using parallel structures. Brian Doyle does this in his paragraph about hearts and liquid motion: "Reptiles and turtles have hearts with three chambers. Fish have hearts with two chambers. Insects and mollusks have hearts with one chamber." The similarities in form among these sentences (subject + verb + phrase) tie them together in support of the topic sentence about churning inside with liquid motion.

Parallel structures indicate key elements in a paragraph or even in an entire essay. They do not, however, tell the reader exactly how those pieces of the puzzle fit together. For this, we need transitions.

Using Transitions

Paragraphs are all about connections. The following words and phrases can help you make **TRANSITIONS** that clearly connect one statement to another—within a paragraph and also between paragraphs.

- **When describing place or direction**: across, across from, at, along, away, behind, close, down, distant, far, here, in between, in front of, inside, left, near, next to, north, outside, right, south, there, toward, up

- **When narrating events in time**: at the same time, during, frequently, from time to time, in 2030, in the future, now, never, often, meanwhile, occasionally, soon, then, until, when

- **When giving examples**: for example, for instance, in fact, in particular, namely, specifically, that is

- **When comparing**: also, as, in a similar way, in comparison, like, likewise

- **When contrasting**: although, but, by contrast, however, on the contrary, on the other hand

- **When analyzing cause and effect**: as a result, because, because of, consequently, so, then

- **When using logical reasoning**: accordingly, hence, it follows, therefore, thus, since, so

- **When tracing sequence or continuation**: also, and, after, before, earlier, finally, first, furthermore, in addition, last, later, next

- **When summarizing**: in conclusion, in summary, in the end, consequently, so, therefore, thus, to conclude

In comparing his childhood with his partner's, David Sedaris (p. 433) uses transitional phrases such as "When Hugh was in the fifth grade" and "About the same time I was frightening my grandmother."

Consider how transitional words and phrases like these work together in the following paragraph about perpetuating a family tradition; the transitions are indicated in **bold**:

One summer, **along about 1904**, my father rented a camp on a lake in Maine and took us all there for the month of August. We all got ringworm from some kittens and had to rub Pond's Extract on our arms and legs night and morning, and my father rolled over in a canoe with all his clothes on; **but outside of** that the vacation was a success and **from then on** none of us ever thought there was any place in the world like that lake in Maine. We returned summer after summer—**always on** August 1 for one month. I have **since** become a salt-water man, but **sometimes** in summer there are days **when** the restlessness of the tides and the fearful cold of the sea water and the incessant wind that blows across the afternoon and into the evening make me wish for the placidity of a lake in the woods. **A few weeks ago** this feeling got so strong I bought myself a couple of bass hooks and a spinner and returned to the lake **where** we used to go, for a week's fishing and to revisit old haunts.

—E. B. WHITE, "Once More to the Lake"

Without transitions, the statements in this paragraph would fall apart like beads on a broken string. Transitions indicate relationships: they help tie the writer's ideas together—in this case, by showing how they are related in time, the passage of which is the grand theme of White's essay.

Developing Paragraphs

There are many ways—in addition to supporting a topic sentence and using parallel structures and transitions—to develop coherent paragraphs. In fact, all the basic patterns of writing discussed in this book work just as well for organizing paragraphs as they do for organizing entire essays. Here are some examples, with explanations of how they draw on the various modes of writing.

Narration

One of the oldest and most common ways of developing a paragraph on almost any subject is by narrating a story about it. When you construct a NARRATIVE (Chapter 7), you focus on events: you tell what happened. In the following paragraph, a writer tells what happened on the day she returned to her hometown in Kentucky soon after publishing her first novel:

In November 1988, bookstoreless though it was, my hometown hosted a big event. Paper banners announced it, and stores closed in honor of it. A crowd assembled in the town's largest public space—the railroad depot. The line went out the door and away down the tracks. At the front of the line they were plunking down $16.95 for copies of a certain book.

—BARBARA KINGSOLVER, "In Case You Ever Want to Go Home Again"

<table>
<tr>
<td>

Joan Didion tells a classic story on this theme in "On Going Home" (p. 745).

</td>
<td>

Narratives are organized by time, and they usually present events in CHRONO-LOGICAL ORDER. In this narrative, the time is a particular day in 1988 when the triumphant young author returns to her hometown for a booksigning. The events of the day ("banners announced," "stores closed," "crowd assembled,"

</td>
</tr>
</table>

"line went out the door") are presented in chronological order—all leading up to the climactic event ("plunking down" the money to buy the book) at the end of the paragraph.

Description

A common way of developing a paragraph, especially when you're writing about a physical object or place, is to give a detailed **DESCRIPTION** (Chapter 8) of your subject. When you describe something, you show the reader how it looks, sounds, feels, smells, or tastes, as in the following description of her grandmother's house (or *casa*) in Puerto Rico as the author remembers it:

> Edward Lee writes a mouth-watering description of West Virginia hot dogs (p. 227, par. 9).

> I remember how in my childhood it sat on stilts; this was before it had a downstairs. It rested on its perch like a great blue bird, not a flying sort of bird, more like a nesting hen, but with spread wings. Grandfather had built it soon after their marriage. He was a painter and housebuilder by trade, a poet and meditative man by nature. As each of their eight children were born, new rooms were added. After a few years, the paint did not exactly match, nor the materials, so that there was a chronology to it, like the rings of a tree, and Mamá could tell you the history of each room in her *casa*, and thus the gene-alogy of the family along with it.
>
> —JUDITH ORTIZ COFER, "More Room"

Descriptions of physical objects are often organized by the configuration of the object. Here the object is a house, and the writer develops this descriptive para-graph by moving from one part of the house to another ("stilts," "new rooms," "mis-matched paint and materials"), ending up with an overall sense of the family's history as chronicled in the physical attributes of the house.

Example

When you use **EXAMPLES** (Chapter 9) to develop a paragraph, you give specific instances of the point you're making. In the following tongue-in-cheek paragraph, a linguist uses multiple examples to show how "unreliable" the English language can be:

> In this unreliable English tongue, greyhounds aren't always grey (or gray); panda bears and koala bears aren't bears (they're marsupials); a woodchuck is a groundhog, which is not a hog; a horned toad is a lizard; glowworms are fireflies, but fireflies are not flies (they're beetles); ladybugs and lightning bugs are also beetles (and to propagate, a significant proportion of ladybugs must be male); a guinea pig is neither a pig nor from Guinea (it's a South American rodent); and a titmouse is neither mammal nor mammaried.
>
> —RICHARD LEDERER, "English Is a Crazy Language"

Although the language and punctuation of this paragraph are playfully complex, the organization is simple: it is a series, or list, of brief examples in more or less random order.

In addition to using multiple examples to develop a paragraph, you can focus on a single example, as in this paragraph from an essay on the limits of dictionary definitions:

> Definitions are especially unhelpful to children. There's an oft-cited 1987 study in which fifth graders were given dictionary definitions and asked to write their own sentences using the words defined. The results were discouraging. One child, given the word *erode*, wrote, "Our family erodes a lot," because the definition given was "eat out, eat away."
>
> —ERIN MCKEAN, "Redefining Definition"

Here the writer states the point to be exemplified, identifies the source of the example she is going to use, comments on the significance of that source, and then gives the example: an exemplary use of example to develop a paragraph.

Analysis

When you develop a paragraph by using ANALYSIS (Chapter 10), you identify the basic constituents of the topic being discussed and explain how they work together in a meaningful way. In the following paragraph, a former art teacher analyzes a famous graphic design:

> The Nike logo—known as the "Swoosh"—is the simplest logo imaginable, consisting of only two lines. And yet this remarkable logo represents billions of dollars' worth of accumulated branding and marketing associations. But what does it *mean*?
>
> —DAN REDDING, "What Does the Nike Logo Mean?"

This paragraph not only breaks the Nike logo into its most basic components, but it also uses analysis to move the discussion from the simple to the complex by identifying additional, more complicated elements of the subject, including its meaning.

Cause and Effect

One of the most fundamental ways of developing a paragraph is to examine what CAUSED your subject or what EFFECTS it may have (Chapter 11). In the following paragraph, a science writer analyzes why young boys are more often diagnosed with behavioral disorders than girls are:

Lest males of all ages feel unfairly picked upon, researchers point out that boys may be diagnosed with behavioral syndromes and disorders more often than girls for a very good reason: their brains may be more vulnerable. As a boy is developing in the womb, the male hormones released by his tiny testes accelerate the maturation of his brain, locking a lot of the wiring in place early on; a girl's hormonal bath keeps her brain supple far longer. The result is that the infant male brain is a bit less flexible, less able to repair itself after slight injury that might come, for example, during the arduous trek down the birth canal. Hence, boys may well suffer disproportionately from behavioral disorders for reasons unrelated to cultural expectations.

—Natalie Angier, "Intolerance of Boyish Behavior"

Here Natalie Angier begins with an effect (a frequent medical diagnosis in boys); she then introduces a possible immediate cause of this effect (a physical vulnerability), followed by a more remote cause (hormonal differences between boys and girls).

Elisa Gonzalez (p. 365) starts with an effect (her diagnosis of bipolar disorder) and then explores immediate and remote causes, as well as other effects.

Comparison and Contrast

With a **COMPARISON AND CONTRAST** (Chapter 12) of two or more subjects, you point out their similarities and differences. In the following paragraph, a historian compares two Civil War generals, Ulysses S. Grant and Robert E. Lee:

So Grant and Lee were in complete contrast, representing two diametrically opposed elements in American life. Grant was the modern man emerging; beyond him, ready to come on the stage, was the great age of steel and machinery, of crowded cities and a restless burgeoning vitality. Lee might have ridden down from the old age of chivalry, lance in hand, silken banner fluttering over his head. Each man was the perfect champion of his cause, drawing both his strengths and his weaknesses from the people he led.

—Bruce Catton, "Grant and Lee"

Here the writer examines both of the subjects he is comparing in a single paragraph, moving systematically from the characteristics of one to those of the other.

Often, when comparing or contrasting two subjects, you will focus first on one of them, in one paragraph; and then on the other, in another paragraph, as in this comparison of two monkeys, Canto and Owen, who are being fed different diets in order to see which one will live the longer (if not happier) life:

Canto looks drawn, weary, ashen and miserable in his thinness, mouth slightly agape, features pinched, eyes blank, his expression screaming, "Please, no, not another plateful of seeds!"

Well-fed Owen, by contrast, is a happy camper with a wry smile, every inch the laid-back simian, plump, eyes twinkling, full mouth relaxed, skin glowing, exuding wisdom as if he's just read Kierkegaard and concluded that "Life must be lived forward, but can only be understood backward."

—ROGER COHEN, "The Meaning of Life"

The author of this comparison doesn't really believe that monkeys can read philosophy, but he fancifully assigns that power to Owen in order to sharpen the contrast between the two simians. Owen's apparent wisdom is in opposition to Canto's despair ("not another plateful of seeds!"). So are the two monkeys' other traits, presented one by one in the same order from paragraph to paragraph.

Classification

With **CLASSIFICATION** (Chapter 13), you divide your subject into categories. In the following passage, a writer classifies the different kinds of English she uses:

Fortunately, for reasons I won't get into today, I later decided I should envision a reader for the stories I would write. And the reader I decided upon was my mother, because these were stories about mothers. So with this reader in mind—and in fact she did read my early drafts—I began to write stories using all the Englishes I grew up with: the English I spoke to my mother, which for lack of a better term might be described as "simple"; the English she used with me, which for lack of a better term might be described as "broken"; my translation of her Chinese, which could certainly be described as "watered down"; and what I imagined to be her translation of her Chinese if she could speak in perfect English, her internal language, and for that I sought to preserve the essence, but neither an English nor a Chinese structure. I wanted to capture what language ability tests can never reveal: her intent, her passion, her imagery, the rhythms of her speech and the nature of her thoughts.

—AMY TAN, "Mother Tongue"

Gloria Anzaldúa builds paragraphs around different types of Spanish (p. 755).

This is a complex paragraph, obviously; but the heart of it is the author's classification of her various "Englishes" into four specific types. The opening statements in the paragraph explain how this classification system came about, and the closing statement explains the purpose it serves.

Definition

A **DEFINITION** (Chapter 14) explains what something is—or is not. Is a good waitress, or other skilled blue-collar worker, merely physically competent; or is she intellectually smart as well? According to the author of this paragraph from an essay on the "brilliance" of blue-collar workers, how we define intelligence depends on a number of factors:

> I couldn't have put it in words when I was growing up, but what I observed in my mother's restaurant defined the world of adults, a place where competence was synonymous with physical work. I've since studied the working habits of blue-collar workers and have come to understand how much my mother's kind of work demands of both body and brain. A waitress acquires knowledge and intuition about the ways and the rhythms of the restaurant business. Waiting on seven to nine tables, each with two to six customers, Rosie devised memory strategies so that she could remember who ordered what. And because she knew the average time it took to prepare different dishes, she could monitor an order that was taking too long at the service station.
>
> —MIKE ROSE, "Blue-Collar Brilliance"

In this paragraph, the writer first presents an overly simplified definition of "competence" among "blue-collar workers" as the ability to do physical labor. He then redefines this key term to include a mental component ("knowledge and intuition"), concluding the paragraph by observing how his mother's work as a waitress demonstrates these defining traits.

For more paragraphs defining "Blue-Collar Brilliance," see p. 569.

Argument

When you ARGUE a point (Chapter 15), you make a claim and give evidence to support it. In the following paragraph, a conservationist takes exception to some of the best efforts in his field:

> There are, as nearly as I can make out, three kinds of conservation currently operating. The first is the preservation of places that are grandly wild or "scenic" or in some other way spectacular. The second is what is called "conservation of natural resources"—that is, of the things of nature that we intend to use: soil, water, timber, and minerals. The third is what you might call industrial troubleshooting: the attempt to limit or stop or remedy the most flagrant abuses of the industrial system. All three kinds of conservation are inadequate, both separately and together.
>
> —WENDELL BERRY, "Conservation Is Good Work"

The point Berry is arguing here is that even the most common forms of conservation in practice today are (in his view) "inadequate." Before stating that point at the end of the paragraph, however, he must first identify the different kinds of conservation and then devote a sentence to each one.

Introductory Paragraphs

As noted in Chapter 4, a well-constructed essay has a beginning, middle, and ending. Every paragraph plays an important role within this basic structure, but introductory and concluding paragraphs are particularly important because they represent your first and last chance to engage the reader.

In an introductory paragraph, you tell the reader what your essay is about—and otherwise seek to earn the reader's interest. The following famous introductory paragraph to an important document is as clear and stirring today as it was in 1776:

> When in the Course of human events, it becomes necessary for one people to dissolve the political bands which have connected them with another, and to assume among the powers of the earth, the separate and equal station to which the Laws of Nature and of Nature's God entitle them, a decent respect to the opinions of mankind requires that they should declare the causes which impel them to the separation.
>
> —THOMAS JEFFERSON, The Declaration of Independence

This paragraph tells the reader exactly what's coming in the text to follow: an inventory of the reasons for the colonies' rebellion. It also seeks to justify the writer's cause and win the sympathy of the reader by invoking a higher authority: the "Laws" of God and nature trump those of Britain's King George III. Here are a few other ways to construct an introductory paragraph that may entice the reader to read on.

Use an anecdote to lead into what you have to say. This introductory paragraph, from a report about research on technology and literacy, begins with a story (actually two of them) about how today's students read and write:

> Two stories about young people, and especially college-age students, are circulating widely today. One script sees a generation of twitterers and texters, awash in self-indulgence and narcissistic twaddle, most of it riddled with errors. The other script doesn't diminish the effects of technology, but it presents young people as running a rat race that is fueled by the internet and its toys, anxious kids who are inundated with mountains of indigestible information yet obsessed with making the grade, with success, with coming up with the "next big thing," but who lack the writing and speaking skills they need to do so.
>
> —ANDREA LUNSFORD, "Our Semi-literate Youth? Not So Fast"

See p. 682 for a cluster of stories on the effects of living online and on our devices. The author of this paragraph considers both of the stories she is reporting to be inaccurate; so after introducing them here, she goes on in the rest of the essay to construct "alternative narratives" that are based on her own research.

Ask a question—or questions. This strategy should be used sparingly, but it works especially well when you want to begin with a touch of humor—or otherwise suggest that you don't have all the answers. In this opening paragraph, a food critic explores new territory:

Vanessa Bohns (p. 448) also opens with a series of questions.

> I've always wondered about dog food. Is a Gaines-burger really like a hamburger? Can you fry it? Does dog food "cheese" taste like real cheese"? Does Gravy Train actually make gravy in the dog's bowl, or is that brown liquid just dissolved crumbs? And exactly what *are* by-products?
> —ANN HODGMAN, "No Wonder They Call Me a Bitch"

Sound appetizing? Even if your subject doesn't exactly appeal to everyone, a strong opening paragraph like this can leave readers eager for more—or at least willing to hear you out.

Start with a quotation or dialogue. In this example from *Outside* magazine, the author opens with an intriguing bit of dialogue, words that get the reader's interest and make a point about the beauty of nature:

> "The thing is, there's this red dot," says Beau Turner, standing quietly in a longleaf-pine forest on his Avalon Plantation, 25,000 red-clay acres half an hour south of Tallahassee. It's 6:30 on a late-spring morning, and the humidity is rolling in like a fog; already I regret the hot coffee in my hand. One of our chores today is to band some new woodpecker chicks with Avalon identification, but then the red dot came up and I was anxious to see it. Not much bigger than the head of a pin, the red dot is a nearly Zen idea of nature's beauty. It sits behind the ear of the male red-cockaded woodpecker, an endangered species that Turner has spent the last four years trying to reintroduce to this land.
> —JACK HITT, "One Nation, under Ted"

Place your subject in a historical context. In the essay from which this introduction is taken, an economist makes the point that the climate may be changing faster than originally estimated; but first he puts the issue in historical perspective:

> The 1995 consensus was convincing enough for Europe and Japan: the report's scientific findings were the basis for the Kyoto negotiations and the treaty they produced; those same findings also led most of the developed world to produce ambitious plans for reductions in carbon emissions. But the consensus didn't extend to Washington, and hence everyone else's efforts were deeply compromised by the American unwillingness to increase the price of energy.

Our emissions continued to soar, and the plans of many of the Kyoto countries in Western Europe to reduce emissions sputtered.

—WILLIAM MCKIBBEN, "Warning on Warming"

Shock or provoke the reader—mildly. You don't want to alarm your reader needlessly, but sometimes you may want to say "listen here" by being mildly provocative or controversial:

Let's use the F word here. People say it's inappropriate, offensive, that it puts people off. But it seems to me it's the best way to begin, when it's simultaneously devalued and invaluable.

Feminist. Feminist, feminist, feminist.

—ANNA QUINDLEN, "Still Needing the F Word"

Choose a Method (or Methods) of Development That Sets Up the Rest of Your Essay

The following paragraph is about the organizing power of paragraphs:

I can remember picking up my father's books before I could read. The words themselves were mostly foreign, but I still remember the exact moment when I first understood, with a sudden clarity, the purpose of a paragraph. I didn't have the vocabulary to say "paragraph," but I realized that a paragraph was a fence that held words. The words inside a paragraph worked together for a common purpose. They had some specific reason for being inside the same fence. This knowledge delighted me. I began to think of everything in terms of paragraphs. Our reservation was a small paragraph within the United States. My family's house was a paragraph, distinct from the other paragraphs of the LeBrets to the north, the Fords to our south and the Tribal School to the west. Inside our house, each family member existed as a separate paragraph but still had genetics and common experiences to link us. Now, using this logic, I can see my changed family as an essay of seven paragraphs: mother, father, older brother, the deceased sister, my younger twin sisters and our adopted little brother.

—SHERMAN ALEXIE, "Superman and Me"

Alexie uses several methods of development in this paragraph. First, he **NARRATES** the story of "the exact moment" he learned what a paragraph was. He then **DEFINES** what he means by "a paragraph" ("a fence that held words"). And, finally, he uses this definition to **CLASSIFY** people and places into "distinct" paragraphs that lead to an entire "essay of seven paragraphs." The following templates can help serve as starting points for drafting an introductory paragraph:

▸ The key points of this paper can be illustrated by a brief story about
_____. The story goes like this: _____.

▸ The usual definition of X is _____. The problem with such a definition, however, is that it ignores _____, _____, and
_____.

▸ What led up to X, historically, was _____. Recently, however, it has
become evident that _____ and _____.

Body Paragraphs

The body of your essay supports and develops your thesis; it is where you give the evidence for the main point you're making. Suppose you're making the point that avoiding left turns while driving is beneficial for the environment because it cuts down on carbon emissions. The various kinds of evidence you cite to support this thesis can provide useful ways of developing body paragraphs in your argument.

Facts and figures. According to its website, United Parcel Service used to plan truck routes "by hand"; now the company uses computers to minimize left turns because, it says, that saves energy. The following paragraph in support of this point is built around related facts and figures:

> Since the deployment of this route planning technology in 2004, UPS has eliminated millions of miles off delivery routes, taking already-expedient routes and giving them razor edge efficiency. As a result, UPS has saved ten million gallons of gas and reduced carbon dioxide emissions by 100,000 metric tons, the equivalent of taking 5,300 passenger cars off the road for an entire year.
>
> —UPS, "Saving Fuel"

Expert testimony. Why do you still see UPS drivers occasionally making left turns? In this body paragraph from a recent post on *priceonomics*, the author builds up to a quotation from a company executive:

> Since UPS uses software to map out routes, it can send drivers on right-turn heavy routes while making exceptions when a left turn is easier and faster. As an amicable senior VP of the company said in an interview about the rule, "That's why I love the engineers, they just love to continue to figure out how to make it better."
>
> —ALEX MAYYASI, "Why UPS Trucks Don't Turn Left"

Personal experience. Making left turns wastes time as well as energy. To develop this related point in the body of an essay about avoiding left turns, you might include a paragraph based on personal experience: "First I made the trip through the Chicago Loop taking nothing but right turns. I traveled down Columbus Drive, took a right on Congress Parkway, and then took another right turn to my destination, the Dirksen Federal Building at Dearborn and Adams Streets. Then I made the trip through the Loop to the Dirksen Building taking mostly left turns. The traffic was the same, but the left-turn trip took me three minutes and thirty seconds longer than the right-turn trip."

How Much Evidence Is Enough?

That depends in part on the scope of your topic. UPS's claim that avoiding left turns saves gas can be substantiated with a few facts and figures. A broader discussion on the need and means for combating climate change in general, however, might require more evidence. Ultimately, it's the reader who determines how much evidence is enough. If the reader is convinced, the evidence is sufficient. If the reader is still wavering, more (or different) evidence may be in order.

QUESTIONS ABOUT SUPPORTING EVIDENCE

Is your evidence concrete and specific? Have you provided details that will make your point clear and interesting to the reader?

Is your evidence relevant to the case? Will the reader understand immediately why you're citing particular facts, figures, personal experience, and other evidence? Do you need to explain further or choose other evidence?

Is your evidence sufficient to prove the case? Have you cited enough evidence, or is the reader likely to require additional—or better—support before becoming convinced?

Are your sources fully and adequately documented? Have you represented your sources fairly and accurately? Can readers locate them easily if they want to check your facts or interpretation? Have you scrupulously avoided representing the words or ideas of other writers as your own? (For specific guidelines on finding, evaluating, citing, documenting, and otherwise using documents in your writing, see Chapter 17.)

Concluding Paragraphs

The final paragraph of an essay should be just as satisfying as the opening paragraph. The conclusion of your essay is your last chance to drive home your point and to leave the reader with a sense of closure. Here are a few ways this is commonly done.

Restate your main point. But don't just repeat it; add a little something new. A recent government report about climate change, for example, adds the following:

> What is new over the last decade is that we know with increasing certainty that climate change is happening now. . . . Global climate is projected to continue to change over this century and beyond, but there is still time to act to limit the amount of change and the extent of damaging impacts.
>
> —US GLOBAL CHANGE RESEARCH PROGRAM,
> *Climate Change Impacts in the United States: Highlights*

Sometimes a grim conclusion has no hopeful sequel: "World ends tomorrow; get ready." When there is one, however, you're always well advised to end a negative conclusion on a positive note.

Show the broader significance of your subject. In an essay about protecting wolves, an advocate for one of nature's most fearsome predators ends her appeal with the following:

> Many biologists have warned that we are approaching another mass extinction. The wolf is still endangered and should be protected in its own right. But we should also recognize that bringing all the planet's threatened and endangered species back to healthy numbers—as well as mitigating the effects of climate change—means keeping top predators around.
>
> —MARY ELLEN HANNIBAL,
> "Why the Beaver Should Thank the Wolf"

Hannibal is aware that not everyone wants wolves in the backyard, but by linking this single threatened species to the mass extinction of other species and to climate change, she broadens a wooly subject into territory that even sheep farmers might be willing to consider.

End with a recommendation. This strategy is especially appropriate when you're winding up an argument. Before coming to the conclusion stated in the following paragraph, the author, a sportswriter, has made the claim that student athletes should be paid for their "work":

Jack Horner does this at the end of "The Extraordinary Characteristics of Dyslexia" (p. 565).

The republic will survive. Fans will still watch the NCAA tournament. Double-reverses will still be thrilling. Alabama will still hate Auburn. Everybody will still hate Duke. Let's do what's right and re-examine what we think is wrong.

—Michael Rosenberg, "Let Stars Get Paid"

Not only is he recommending pay for college athletes, but the author of this paragraph also asks the reader to rethink, and totally revise, the conventional wisdom that says paying them is morally wrong.

The following templates can help serve as starting points for drafting a concluding paragraph:

▶ The takeaway here is clearly _____; however, it is also important to remember that _____.

▶ Why did X have these effects on Y? The ultimate cause seems to have been _____.

▶ Given this state of affairs, the way forward would seem to be _____.

7 | Narration

Narrative is the oldest and most compelling method of holding someone's attention; everyone wants to be told a story.

—William Zinsser

Narration is the storytelling mode of writing. The minute you say to someone, "You won't believe what happened to me this morning," you have launched into a narrative. To understand how narration works, let's have a look at the story of a young man's arrival, after an arduous journey, in the city of Philadelphia:

> I walked up the street, gazing about till near the market-house I met a boy with bread. I had made many a meal on bread, and, inquiring where he got it, I went immediately to the baker's he directed me to, in Second-street, and ask'd for bisket, intending such as we had in Boston; but they, it seems, were not made in Philadelphia. Then I asked for a three-penny loaf, and was told they had none such. So not considering or knowing the difference of money, and the greater cheapness nor the names of his bread, I bade him give me three-penny worth of any sort. He gave me, accordingly, three great puffy rolls. I was surpriz'd at the quantity, but took it, and, having no room in my pockets, walk'd off with a roll under each arm, and eating the other. Thus I went up Market-street as far as Fourth-street, passing by the door of Mr. Read, my future wife's father; when she, standing at the door, saw me, and thought I made, as I certainly did, a most awkward, ridiculous appearance. Then I turned and went down Chestnut-street and part of Walnut-street, eating my roll all the way, and, coming round, found myself again at Market-street wharf, near the boat I came in, to which I went for a draught of the river water; and, being filled with one of my rolls, gave the other two to a woman and her child that came down the river in the boat with us, and were waiting to go farther.
>
> —BENJAMIN FRANKLIN, *Autobiography*

Telling What Happened

What makes Franklin's text a narrative? Like all narratives, the story of his arrival in Philadelphia is an account of events. It answers the question "What happened?"— to a particular person in a particular place and time. Young Franklin arrived in the city, shopped for bread, ate, gazed and strolled about, saw a young woman, performed an act of charity.

Narratives focus on events, but you don't have to live a life of high adventure or witness extraordinary acts in order to write a compelling narrative. The events in Franklin's story, you'll notice, are all perfectly ordinary; they could have happened to anybody. The interest, even the drama, that we all enjoy in a well-told story often comes not so much from the nature of the events themselves as from how they are presented.

"Thus I went up Market-street as far as Fourth-street, passing by the door of Mr. Read, my future wife's father; when she, standing at the door, saw me, and thought I made, as I certainly did, a most awkward, ridiculous appearance."

In this chapter, we will examine how to come up with the raw materials for a story, how to select details from those raw materials to suit your purpose and audience, and how to organize those details as a narrative—by the use of chronology, transitions, verb tenses, and plot. We'll also review the critical points to watch for as you read over a narrative, as well as common errors to avoid when you edit. But first, let's consider *why* we write narratives at all—and how they can help us make a point.

Why Do We Write Narratives?

Everybody likes a good story, and we tell stories for many reasons: to connect with other people, to entertain, to record what people said and did, to explain the significance of events, to persuade others to act in a certain way or to accept our point of view on an issue. Ben Franklin, for example, tells his famous story at the beginning of his *Autobiography* in order to capture the reader's attention right off the bat—and to set the scene for the rest of his life story.

Anecdotes support Mira Jacob's purpose in relating a love story about her parents (p. 135).

Brief illustrative narratives, or **ANECDOTES**, appear in all kinds of writing, often at the beginning. Writers typically use them to grab the reader's interest and then lead into their main points, much as a graduation speaker opens with a humorous story or poignant tale before getting down to the serious business of talking about life after college.

Franklin's great point in his *Autobiography* is to show readers how he succeeded in life, and so he begins with the story of his humble arrival in Philadelphia as a young man from out of town. That way, says Franklin, "you may in your mind compare such unlikely beginnings with the figure I have since made."

Marjane Satrapi's point in "Kim Wilde" (p. 142) is to show how her family resisted political oppression.

Notice that Franklin is not only telling a story here. He is **COMPARING AND CONTRASTING** different versions of himself, just as he does with the different currencies and kinds of bread he finds in Philadelphia after leaving Boston. He is also **DESCRIBING** the "most awkward, ridiculous appearance" that he makes upon arrival in the new city. Narratives often make use of other forms of writing and the rhetorical strategies they draw on.

The reverse is also true. Although a good story can be an end in itself, many of the narratives discussed in this chapter play supporting roles in other types of writing, where they give an example or help explain a point or support a claim.

Suppose you're a geneticist, and you're writing about mitochondrial DNA and how it can be used to study human evolution. (Mitochondrial DNA is passed down, unaltered, from generation to generation on the mother's side.) Suppose, further, that you've isolated seven strains of mitochondrial DNA and traced them back to the seven prehistoric female ancestors of all persons presently alive. How would you convey your exciting conclusions to a general audience?

THE SUCCESS STORY

One common narrative pattern, which Ben Franklin practically invented in his famous Autobiography, is the success story. As in many fairy tales, the central event of such a narrative is the transformation of the hero, often at some magical moment or turning point. In Franklin's case, we don't see the transformation at first; we see this instead:

> Thus I went up Market-street as far as Fourth-street, passing by the door of Mr. Read, my future wife's father; when she, standing at the door, saw me, and thought I made, as I certainly did, a most awkward, ridiculous appearance.

Young Franklin could not possibly have known what Miss Read was thinking as he passed her door on Market Street—much less that she would one day be his wife.

The elder Ben Franklin knew this, however, and he was not one to let the facts stand in the way of a good story. So, looking back on the scene, Franklin makes himself appear "ridiculous" in order, later in the book, to highlight the imposing, immensely successful figure he was to become.

To see how you can use the success-story pattern in your own writing—and how narratives differ from the actual events on which they are based—think of a successful person you might write about, and make a list of key events in that person's life. Then identify a "turning point"—a particular event or series of events that changed the fortunes of your hero or heroine forever. Divide the rest of the events on your list into "before" and "after." Imagine the story you might construct around this outline.

Now take the same person and life events and consider how you'd arrange them according to some other pattern, such as a journey or a fall from favor or from privilege. This time, instead of dividing your narrative into before and after, imagine a different storyline—a meandering path or a downward spiral. As you can see, you would end up telling a different story about the same person.

Bryan Sykes, a professor of genetics at the Institute of Molecular Medicine at Oxford University, had to solve this problem because his research team had isolated those seven separate lines of human descent. He decided to convey the findings by re-creating the story of each of these "seven daughters of Eve," whose DNA can be identified by modern research methods.

Here is how he concludes his narrative about one of them, a woman who lived 45,000 years ago:

> Ursula had no idea, of course, that both her daughters would give rise, through their children and grandchildren, to a continuous maternal line stretching to the present day. She had no idea she was to become the clan mother, the only woman of that time who could make that claim. Every single member of her clan can trace a direct and unbroken line back to Ursula. Her clan were the first modern humans successfully to colonize Europe. Within a comparatively short space of time they had spread across the whole continent, edging the Neanderthals into extinction. Today about 11 percent of modern Europeans are the direct maternal descendants of Ursula. They come from all parts of Europe, but the clan is particularly well represented in western Britain and Scandinavia.
>
> —BRYAN SYKES, *The Seven Daughters of Eve*

Sykes's story about Ursula efficiently explains a number of complicated points about genetic studies and human descent. By giving each of the maternal ancestors a story, Sykes makes his findings much easier to understand—and to remember. Sometimes there's no better way to make a point than by telling a good story—*if* it really fits the subject you are writing about and doesn't go off on a tangent.

Composing a Narrative

Let's go back to the adventures of Ben Franklin for a moment. How did Franklin know, on his initial stroll around the city, that the young woman he saw standing at Mr. Read's door would one day be his wife? Obviously, he couldn't know this when he first saw her. Franklin's reference to his future wife shows us not that young Franklin was psychic but that his narrative has been carefully composed—after the fact, as all narratives are.

As the author of a narrative, you know everything that's going to happen, so you can present events in any order you please. However, if you want anyone else to understand the point you're trying to make, you need to compose your narrative carefully. Consider, first of all, your AUDIENCE and your PURPOSE for writing. Then think about which details to include and how to organize them so that readers can follow your story and see your point in telling it. To make your story a compelling one, be sure to give it a PLOT and tell it from a consistent POINT OF VIEW.

Thinking about Purpose and Audience

The first thing to do as you compose a narrative is to think hard about the audience you want to reach and the purpose your narrative is intended to serve. Suppose you are texting a friend about a visit to Best Buy, and your purpose is simply to say what you did yesterday. In this case, your narrative can ramble on about how you got to the store, discovered it was much larger than you expected, went into the monitor section and looked around, then wandered over to the printers and couldn't get a salesperson's attention but eventually spoke to a very helpful manager, and so on. The story might end with your emerging triumphantly from the store with a good printer at a good price. It wouldn't matter much that your story goes on and on because you're writing to a friendly reader who is interested in everything you do and has time to listen.

Now suppose you're writing an advertisement, the purpose of which is to sell printers to the general public. You could still write about your visit to a store, but you would tell your story differently because you now have a different purpose and audience: "When I walked into Best Buy, I couldn't believe my eyes. So many printer options! And such low prices! Plus my local store gives you a ream of paper absolutely free! I went home with a printer under each arm." Or suppose you're writing a column in a technology magazine, and your purpose is to show readers how to shop for a printer by telling them about the problems you dealt with as you shopped. You might write, "The first hurdle I encountered was the mind-numbing variety of brands and models."

Whatever your purpose, you'll want to think about how much your audience is likely to already know about your subject—computers, for instance—so you can judge how much background information to give, how much technical language to use, what terms to DEFINE, and so on. If you're writing for an audience that knows little about computers, for instance, you might have to explain what cloud-based storage space is before you tell your readers how to buy or use it.

The purpose of Lynda Barry's narrative about her early school days (p. 165) is to share her discovery about the therapeutic value of art.

Generating Ideas:
Asking What Happened—and Who, Where, When, How, and Why

Before you can tell a good story, you have to have a story to tell. How do you come up with the raw materials for a narrative in the first place? BRAINSTORMING, CLUSTERING, and other methods can help you generate ideas. But a narrative isn't just a kind of writing; it's also a way of thinking, one that can help you find ideas to write about. How do you get started? Let's look at an example.

Consider the following passage in which Annie Dillard tells about something that happened while she was reading during a camping trip in the Blue Ridge Mountains of Virginia:

> One night a moth flew into the candle, was caught, burnt dry, and held. I must have been staring at the candle, or maybe I looked up when a shadow crossed my page; at any rate, I saw it all. A golden female moth, a biggish one with a two-inch wingspan, flapped into the fire, dropped her abdomen into the wet wax, stuck, flamed, frazzled and fried in a second. Her moving wings ignited like tissue paper, enlarging the circle of light in the clearing and creating out of the darkness the sudden blue sleeves of my sweater, the green leaves of jewelweed by my side, the ragged red trunk of a pine.
>
> —ANNIE DILLARD, "The Death of a Moth"

Dillard wrote this passage two years after the event, so she must have probed her memory to find many of the vivid details she recalls here. Perhaps she asked herself the questions that journalists typically ask when developing a story: who, what, where, when, how, and why. Certainly her narrative answers most of these questions: who (Dillard herself and a giant female moth), what (reading by candlelight on a camping trip; flying into the candle flame), where (in a clearing fringed with jewelweed and a pine tree), when ("One night"), and how ("I saw it"). What the passage doesn't say, however, is why: Why was Dillard camping by herself on a lonely mountainside, and why was she so fascinated by the death of a mere moth? Does her fascination perhaps have something to do with the proverbial moth drawn to the flame that consumes it?

When you're planning a narrative, then, ask yourself leading questions like "who," "what," "where," "when," and "how" ("why" can wait, if necessary, as you figure out where your story is going), and probe your memory and observations for specific sensory details, particularly visual and auditory ones. "To start a narrative," Dillard writes in "How I Wrote the Moth Essay—and Why" (pp. 328–34), "you need a batch of things . . . specific objects and events: a cat, a spider web, a mess of insect skeletons, a candle, a book about Rimbaud, a burning moth."

You can read Dillard's piece "How I Wrote the Moth Essay—And Why" in Ch. 10, p. 328.

"What do you do with these things?" Dillard asks. As we'll see when we discuss CRITICAL ANALYSIS of a text in Chapter 10, what you do with the basic ingredients of a narrative, according to Dillard, is "toss them around" until you begin to see the structure of your narrative and what it's about. "To begin," she writes, "you don't need a well defined point. You don't need 'something to say'—that will just lead you to reiterating clichés. . . . You start anywhere and join the bits into a pattern by your writing about them." In other words, you discover the organization and meaning of your narrative as you draft it.

Organizing and Drafting a Narrative

As you draft a narrative, your task is to turn the *facts* of what happened into a *story* of what happened. To do this, you will need to put the events in **CHRONOLOGICAL ORDER**, connect them with appropriate **TRANSITIONS** and **VERB TENSES**, give your narrative a **PLOT**—and somehow indicate the point, or **CLAIM**, you are making. The templates on p. 116 can help you get started.

STATING YOUR POINT

Most of the narrative writing you do as a student will be for the purpose of making some kind of point, and sometimes you'll want to state that point explicitly. If you are writing about information technology for an economics class, for example, you might tell your story about going to a computer store; and you would probably want to explain why you were telling about the experience in a **THESIS** statement like this: "Go into any computer store today, and you will discover that information technology is the main product of American business."

FOLLOWING CHRONOLOGICAL ORDER

In his arrival narrative, Ben Franklin's point is to show how far he's going to go from his humble beginnings. To this end, he arranges events in chronological order: first his arrival; then breakfast, followed by a stroll around the town; next comes the encounter with Miss Read; and, finally, the return to the wharf and the dispensing of the bread—all in the order in which they occurred *in time*. There is no law that says events in a narrative have to follow chronological order, and there are times when you will want to deviate from it. As a general rule, though, arrange events chronologically so your reader doesn't have to figure out what happened when.

DEVELOPING A PLOT

Connecting events in chronological order is always better than presenting them haphazardly. Chronology alone, however, no matter how faithfully followed, is insufficient for organizing a good narrative. A narrative, yes; a good narrative, no.

Suppose Ben Franklin returned for a visit to modern-day Philadelphia and filed the following account:

> I took 76 East (the Schuylkill Expressway) to 676 East, exited at Broad Street (the first exit), and continued straight on Vine Street to 12th Street. Then I turned right and proceeded two blocks to the Convention Center. There I

TEMPLATES FOR DRAFTING

When you begin to draft a narrative, you need to say who or what it's about, when and where it takes place, and what's happening as the story opens. See how Annie Dillard makes these basic moves near the beginning of her piece about writing the moth essay:

> Walking back to my desk, where I had been answering letters, I realized that the burning moth was a dandy visual focus for all my recent thoughts about an empty, dedicated life. Perhaps I'd try to write a short narrative about it.
>
> —ANNIE DILLARD, "How I Wrote the Moth Essay—and Why"

Dillard says who and what her narrative is about ("I"; "the burning moth"), when and where it takes place ("Walking back to my desk"), and what is happening as the narrative opens ("I realized"; "I'd try to write a short narrative"). Here are two more examples from this chapter:

> In reality, it is two o'clock in the afternoon, and Ms. Cochran is lying on a bed at St. Francis Hospital in Hartford.
>
> —SNEHA SAHA, "The Wedding Carriage"

> For relief, I used to sneak out the service elevator of the hotel and wander around the streets.
>
> —KWAME ONWUACHI, "Angles"

The following templates can help you make some of these basic moves in your own writing. But don't take these as formulas where you just fill in the blanks. There are no shortcuts to good writing; however, these templates can serve as starting points.

- ▸ This is a story about _____.
- ▸ The time and place of my story are _____ and _____.
- ▸ As the narrative opens, X is in the act of _____.
- ▸ What happened next was _____, followed by _____ and _____.
- ▸ At this point, _____.
- ▸ The climax of these events was _____.
- ▸ When X understood what had happened, he / she / they said, "_____."
- ▸ The last thing that happened to X was _____.
- ▸ My point in telling this story is to show that _____.

paused for lunch (a Caesar salad with three great puffy rolls), afterward continuing my journey down 12th and back to Vine. Proceeding east for some distance, I then rounded Franklin Square, crossed the Franklin Bridge, and entered into New Jersey.

This account is technically a narrative, and it follows chronological order. By comparison with the original, however, it's pretty dull. If it went on like this for another paragraph or two, most readers would give up long before Franklin got back to Boston. Little more than an itinerary, this narrative moves steadfastly from place to place, but it doesn't really get anywhere because it has no plot.

Whether we read about pirates on the high seas or hobbits and rings of power, one of the most important elements that can make or break the story is how well it is plotted. It's no different when you write narratives of your own—events need to be related in such a way that one leads directly to, or causes, another. Taken together, the events in your narrative should have a beginning, a middle, and an end. Then your narrative will form a complete action: a plot.

One of the best ways to plot a narrative is to set up a situation; introduce a conflict; build up the dramatic tension until it reaches a high point, or CLIMAX; then release the tension and resolve the conflict. Consider the following little horror story, complete with a giant insect. First we set up the situation:

> *Little Miss Muffet sat on a tuffet*
> *Eating her curds and whey.*

Now comes the conflict:

> *Along came a spider**

Then the climax:

> *Who sat down beside her*

And finally the resolution:

> *And frightened Miss Muffet away.*

You likely knew all along how it was going to end; but it's still a satisfying story because it's tightly plotted with a keen sense of completion at the close.

Back to Ben Franklin's narrative. One reason this story of starting out in Philadelphia is among the most famous personal narratives in American literature, even though it's just one paragraph, is that it has a carefully organized plot—a *beginning*

> Ocean Vuong enlivens his literacy narrative (p. 160) with tension between himself as a young student and his language arts teacher.

---

*Recognizing a good plot twist when he saw one, best-selling novelist James Patterson—whose thrillers have sold more copies than those of Stephen King, John Grisham, and Dan Brown combined—chose this line for the title of his first blockbuster, *Along Came a Spider* (1993).

action (the hero's arrival); a *middle* (the stroll), in which a complication is introduced and the tension rises as the young hero sees his future wife and appears ridiculous; and an *ending* (the return to the wharf), in which the narrative tension is resolved as the hero comes back to his starting point and dispenses bounty in the form of the bread.

ADDING TRANSITIONS

Notice the many direct references to time in Ben Franklin's narrative: "then," "immediately," "when," "again." No doubt, you can think of countless others: "first," "last," "not long after," "next," "while," "thereafter," "once upon a time." Such direct references to the order of time can be boring in a narrative if they become too predictable, as in "first," "second," "third." But used judiciously, such transitions provide smooth links from one event to another, as do other connecting words and phrases like "thus," "therefore," "consequently," "what happened next," "before I knew it," "as he came back to the dock."

USING APPROPRIATE VERB TENSES

In addition to clear transition words, your verb tenses, especially the sequence of tenses, can help connect events in time. To review for a moment: an action in the past perfect tense (he <u>had arrived</u>) occurs before an action in the past tense (he <u>arrived</u>), which occurs before an action in the present tense (he <u>arrives</u>), which occurs before an action in the future tense (he <u>will arrive</u>). Actions in the present perfect (he <u>has arrived</u>) may start in the past and continue in the present.

Many of the verbs in Franklin's narrative are in the simple past tense: "walked," "went," "ask'd," "thought," "found," "gave." "I had made many a meal on bread," however, is in the past perfect tense because the action had already occurred many times *before* young Franklin asked for directions to the bakery.

Tense sequences mark the time of actions in relation to one another. Thus all actions that happen more or less at the same time in your narrative should be in the same tense: "The young man got off the boat, went to the bakery, and walked around the town." Don't shift tenses needlessly; but when you *do* need to indicate that one action happened before another in time, be sure to change tenses accordingly—and accurately. Sometimes you may need to shift out of chronological order altogether. (It's called a FLASHBACK if you shift back in time, a FLASH-FORWARD if you shift into the future.) Most of the time, however, stick to chronology.

Notice how often Franklin uses *-ing* forms of verbs: "gazing," "inquiring," "intending," "considering," "knowing," "having," "eating," "passing," "standing," "eating" (again), "coming," "being," "waiting." Putting "-ing" on the end of a verb makes it a progressive form. If Franklin's writing seems especially vivid, part of his secret lies in those progressive verb forms, which show past actions as if they're still going on as we read about them more than two centuries later.

MAINTAINING A CONSISTENT POINT OF VIEW

Such is the difference between life and a *narrative* of life: life happens, often in disorderly fashion; but a narrative must be carefully composed—from a particular point of view, as when Annie Dillard writes, "I must have been staring at the candle, or maybe I looked up when a shadow crossed my page."

The point of view from which you report what happens in a narrative should be logical and consistent. Don't suggest that you or your NARRATOR can perceive things in a way that's physically impossible. Dillard, for example, can report that she sees a shadow cross the page of the book she's reading because the moth is in the act of flying between her and the candle flame. She cannot logically report that the sleeve of her sweater appears blue, however, until after the moth lands in the flame, catches fire, and enlarges its circle of light.

In a narrative written in the grammatical FIRST PERSON ("I" or "we"), like Dillard's, the speaker can be both an observer of the scene ("I must have been staring at the candle") *and* a participant in the action ("a shadow crossed my page"). In a narrative written in the grammatical THIRD PERSON ("he," "she," "it"), as is the case in many academic studies and history books (and in Bryan Sykes's narrative about Ursula, p. 112), however, the narrator is often merely an observer, though sometimes an all-knowing one.

> In Kwame Onwuachi's first-person narrative about being a contestant on *Top Chef* (p. 170), he is both a participant and an observer.

ADDING DIALOGUE

In contrast to narratives told in the third person—which can have unlimited points of view—first-person narratives are *always* limited to telling only what the narrator knows or imagines. There is a means, however, by which even first-person narrators can introduce the points of view of other people into a story. That is by the use of dialogue, or quoting their direct speech.

Suppose you witness an accident in which a pedestrian is hit by a turning car, and you want to tell what happened—in a police report, say. Your narrative might begin with an account of how you noticed a car stopped at a red light and then saw another car approach suddenly from the right and pause. After the light changed, the first car went straight ahead; then the second car turned left. At the same time, a pedestrian, who had been trying to cross behind the first car, moved into the middle of the street and was hit by the turning car.

Why did the pedestrian cross the street against traffic? Your narrative can't say for sure because you don't know what was going on in the pedestrian's mind. If, however, you (or the police) approached the man and started asking him questions as he pulled himself to his feet, his point of view might be revealed in the ensuing dialogue.

Then, if you incorporated that dialogue into your narrative, not only would you capture another person's motives and point of view, but your narrative would be more interesting and lively:

"Why did you cross the street?"
"The stoplight was red and the little man on the pedestrian sign was on."
"Did you see the car turning in your direction as you crossed?"
"No, the stopped car was blocking my view."
"After it started up, did you see the other car?"
"Yes."
"Why did you cross anyway?"
"The little man said I could."

You can *tell* the reader of your narrative that someone is delusional or means well or would never hurt a fly. But if you let people in your narrative speak for themselves and *show* what they're thinking, the reader gets to draw conclusions without your explicit direction. That way your story will seem more credible, your characters will come to life, and your whole narrative will have a greater dramatic impact.

USING OTHER METHODS

Narratives don't take place in a vacuum. As you tell what happens in your narrative, you'll likely need to draw on other methods of writing as well. For example, to show why your characters (the people in your narrative) do what they do, you may need to analyze the CAUSES AND EFFECTS of their actions. Or you may want to COMPARE AND CONTRAST one character with another. Almost certainly, you will want to DESCRIBE the characters and the physical setting in some detail.

Drew Hansen analyzes the effect a singer had on a famous speech (p. 154).

In Franklin's case, the description of his "awkward, ridiculous appearance" as he walks around the streets of Philadelphia "with a roll under each arm" is important to the story. The tattered young man may look foolish now—but not for long. This is an American success story, and already the new arrival is staking out his territory.

As with other kinds of writing, narration calls for distinctive patterns of language and punctuation—and thus invites certain kinds of errors. The following tips will help you check your writing for errors that often appear in narratives.

Check verb tenses to make sure they accurately indicate when actions occur

Because narrative writing focuses on actions or events—what happens or happened—it relies mightily on verbs. Some writers get confused about when to use the simple past tense (Ben <u>arrived</u>), the present perfect (Ben <u>has arrived</u>), and the past perfect (Ben <u>had arrived</u>).

Use the simple past to indicate actions completed at a specified time in the past.

> ▶ He ~~has~~ completed the assignment this morning.

Use the present perfect to indicate actions begun and completed at some unspecified time in the past, or actions begun in the past and continuing into the present.

> ▶ The war in the north ~~goes~~ <u>has gone on</u> for five years now.
> ▶ For five years now, the insurgents <u>have</u> fought in the north.

Use the past perfect to indicate actions completed *by* a specific time in the past or before another past action occurred.

> ▶ The bobcats arrived next, but by then the muskrats <u>had</u> moved out.

Check dialogue to be sure it's punctuated correctly

Narrative writing often includes the direct QUOTATION of what people say. This can be challenging because you have to deal with the punctuation in the dialogue itself and also with any punctuation necessary to integrate the dialogue into the text.

Commas and periods always go inside the quotation marks.

> ▶ "Perspective in painting is hard to <u>define,</u>" my art history professor said.
> ▶ She then noted that in a painting by Jacob Lawrence, "perspective means one <u>thing.</u>"

Semicolons and colons always go outside the quotation marks.

▸ But in a Cubist painting by Picasso, she said, "it means quite <u>another</u>"; then she went on to explain the differences.

▸ The painting presents the landscape "in <u>layers</u>": from the tops of mountains to the undersides of leaves in the same picture.

Question marks, exclamation points, and dashes go *inside* the quotation marks if they are part of the quoted text but *outside* if they are not part of the quoted text.

▸ The teacher asked, "Sam, how would you define perspective in <u>art?</u>"

▸ Did you say, "Divine <u>perspective</u>"?

Reading a Narrative with a Critical Eye

Once you have drafted a narrative, it's always a good idea to ask someone else to read it. And, of course, you yourself will want to review what you have written from the standpoint of a critical reader. Here are some questions to keep in mind when checking a narrative.

PURPOSE AND AUDIENCE. Does the narrative serve the purpose it is intended to serve? Is it appropriate for its intended audience? Does it need any additional background information or definitions?

THE STORY. Does it consist mainly of actions and events? Do they make up a plot with a clear beginning, middle, and end? Is every action in the narrative necessary to the plot? Have any essential actions been left out?

THE POINT. Does the narrative have a clear point to make? What is its claim? Is it stated explicitly in a thesis? If not, should it be?

ORGANIZATION. Is the storyline easy to follow? Are the events presented in chronological order? Are there any unintentional mistakes in chronology or verb tense? Are intentional deviations from chronology, such as flashbacks, clearly indicated? If there are intentional deviations, is their purpose clear?

TRANSITIONS. Are there clear transitions to help readers follow the sequence of events? Have you checked each transition to see that it logically connects the adjoining parts of the narrative?

DIALOGUE AND POINT OF VIEW. If there is no dialogue in the narrative, would some direct speech help bring it to life? If there is dialogue, does it sound like real people talking? Is the narrative told from a consistent, plausible point of view?

DETAILS. Does the narrative include lots of concrete details, especially visual and auditory ones? Does it show as well as tell?

THE BEGINNING. Will the beginning of the narrative capture the reader's attention? How? How well does it set up what follows? How else might the narrative begin?

THE ENDING. How satisfying is it? What does it leave the reader thinking or feeling? How else might the narrative end?

OTHER METHODS. Look again at the people and places in your narrative. Are people's motives clearly explained? Are physical characteristics of the setting clearly depicted? If not, use **CAUSE AND EFFECT**, **DESCRIPTION**, and other methods of development to fill in these gaps.

COMMON ERRORS. Are any verb tenses in the narrative needlessly complicated? For example, does the narrative use the past perfect (had been) when the simple past (was) will do? If so, change to the simpler form.

Student Example

Sneha Saha wrote "The Wedding Carriage" for a course in narrative essay writing at Johns Hopkins University. Narratives about elderly people who live in a reality of their own making can encourage writers to become sentimental or, worse, to look down on their subjects. Saha deftly avoids both as she simultaneously reports on and participates in her subject's visions. "As a reader," writes Professor Patricia Kain in a letter recommending Saha's essay for the Norton Writer's Prize, "I am never confused about where I am in the narrative." The author, she says, "makes excellent use of time cues and transitions to control the structure of the essay"; and she "skillfully interweaves the main elements" into "a rich narrative that draws readers in and demonstrates the power of empathy. She makes us feel it."

The Wedding Carriage

THIRD-PERSON point of view, with dialogue.

Ms. Cochran beckons to Karen, her twelve-year-old daughter, who has just come down from her bedroom. "Why aren't you wearing socks?" she chides her. "You're going to catch a cold if you leave the house like that. Go back to your room and put on some socks." Stubborn as she is, Karen does not budge. "I'm already wearing them, Mom. Look!" she insists, pointing down to her feet. In no mood for another one of her daughter's tantrums, Ms. Cochran calls out to her husband, "TOMMMM! Where are you? Get down here!" It appears to be an average morning in the Cochran household.

Point of view switches to FIRST PERSON.

Or at least that's how I imagine the scene plays out in Ms. Cochran's mind. In reality, it is two o'clock in the afternoon, and Ms. Cochran is lying on a bed at St. Francis Hospital in Hartford. There is no one else in the room besides me, a college student volunteering for the summer. I have just entered Ms. Cochran's room, and she is reprimanding me for not wearing my socks. My initial reaction is to look down and confirm that my shoes and socks are, in fact, still on my feet. This is my first time meeting Ms. Cochran, and it takes me several seconds to realize that she likely suffers from dementia and has mistaken me for someone named Karen. As a volunteer, I am not allowed to access a patient's records before visiting a room. The surprise of each encounter is one of the parts I enjoy most about my position. It is the reason I have been coming back to St. Francis for most summers since I was fifteen. And yet this is one of those moments when I desperately wish I had some prior knowledge of Ms. Cochran's history. I wonder who Karen and Tom are and whether Ms. Cochran ever experiences moments of clarity. How could I connect with someone who appeared to be in a world of her own?

Saha COMPARES Ms. Cochran's case with her grandfather's.

As a volunteer, I had no formal training in communicating with dementia patients. Until this point, my only experience with the disease came from interacting with my maternal grandfather in India, who suffered from dementia and had passed away when I was fifteen. Even then, I had communicated with him exclusively via Skype, exchanging a few words each week in broken Bengali. The last time I had seen him in person was seven years earlier, before his health had begun to deteriorate. In this moment at St. Francis, I find myself rummaging through vague memories of him in search of insight, anything really, to help me reach Ms. Cochran. Perhaps I could excuse myself and ask a nurse for assistance. But the nurses are already overloaded with work, and Ms. Cochran is becoming more and more impatient with me. It seems I will have to find a way to navigate this situation alone.

Naturally, I assume that the best approach is to reason with Ms. Cochran. Three years on the high school debate team taught me how to collect evidence, craft an argument, and persuade my listeners. Armed with these skills, I prepare to articulate my contentions and draw Ms. Cochran toward my point of view. Starting with the obvious, I point down and explain to her that I am wearing my shoes and socks. Though her gaze follows my finger, she seems to be looking past my feet at some distant object. At once, she resumes her tirade against my footwear, and I decide to shift gears. Perhaps I could convince Ms. Cochran that socks are not necessary because it is eighty-five degrees and sunny outside. I cross the room to the window and raise the blinds. As sunlight pours in, Ms. Cochran turns to me and scowls. "What do you think you're doing, young lady? You're not leaving this house until you clean your room." *At least it's not the socks this time*, I think, breathing a small sigh of relief. But I know I am still far from a breakthrough, and my powers of reasoned persuasion are failing me. While I have no doubt that Ms. Cochran can hear and see me, she appears to have conjured up a reality that only she is privy to—a reality in which my logic does not apply.

In this moment, I recall my grandfather, who during his early stages of dementia, held certain fixed beliefs about his own reality. Similar to Ms. Cochran, he would resist his family's attempts to reason with him, which further provoked him and made him cling more

4

The writer tries a new approach to a puzzling situation.

5

Returns to the comparison with the author's grandfather.

tightly to his delusions. For a long time, he was convinced that his two daughters were stealing from him and trusted only his caregivers. Ironically, as my aunt would later discover, there had been a caregiver who was caught stealing from the house. Despite this revelation, my grandfather continued to distrust my mother and aunt and remained loyal to his caregivers. Standing next to Ms. Cochran, I wonder how my mother managed to remain calm through her father's outbursts. How do you cope with a loved one who has seemingly turned his back on a forty-year relationship? I am barely ten minutes into meeting Ms. Cochran, and my frustration is already brewing. Back then, my mother told me that she understood the basis of my grandfather's delusion: she visited him once a year, whereas his caregivers took care of him every day. From this perspective, it made sense that my grandfather would trust them more than his family. While his caregivers were present in the moment, his family was fading into the past. Instead of denying my grandfather's accusations, my mother rationalized them, and in time she learned to accept his version of reality.

Perhaps it is time for me to try the same. Ms. Cochran calls again for Tom: "Come down, and look at this!" She is beaming, as if in preparation to reveal a surprise to her husband. "They're passing by again. It's so beautiful, don't you think?" I follow Ms. Cochran's gaze to the wall in front of her bed. At first, I see nothing but a TV, whiteboard, and hand sanitizer dispenser. "What is it? Who's passing by?" I begin to probe Ms. Cochran's visions. **6**

A climactic moment in the PLOT of Saha's narrative and in her subject's visions.

"It's the carriage! Just look at them. Aren't they gorgeous?" she asks. Against the backdrop of the wall, I build a window into Ms. Cochran's mind. Through it, I see a horse-drawn carriage carrying two people, a young Ms. Cochran and her husband. She appears as a young woman in her late twenties, dressed in a white, lace gown and surrounded by a crowd of people throwing kisses and flowers. Tom curls an arm around Ms. Cochran's shoulder, and the two exchange a kiss. Just then, the carriage is set in motion and drives off the screen. **7**

"They're beautiful," I reply, turning back to Ms. Cochran. "It's
like a scene straight out of a movie."   8

Whether or not Ms. Cochran was actually reliving her wedding   9
day is beyond my knowledge. Her descriptions of the scene were
vague, and at times I struggled to decipher her jumbled speech. The
most elegant interpretation, it seemed, was that Tom was Ms.
Cochran's deceased husband, whose memory she kept alive by living
in the past. However, it was entirely possible that Tom was a son or a
brother or a friend. Seeing the elation on Ms. Cochran's face, I realized that Tom's actual identity was not important. What mattered
was that this man, real or imagined, was very much a part of Ms.
Cochran's reality. By entering her world, I had finally found a way to
connect with her.

An apparent calm washes over Ms. Cochran as she leans back   10
against the headboard and loses herself in her visions. I take this as
my cue to excuse myself from the room. "Please let me know if
there's anything else you need today. It was very nice to meet you,
Ms. Cochran." I deliver the standard farewell, knowing full well that
she still doesn't know who I am.

> The theatrical term "cue" suggests the narrator is participating in a drama.

"You better be putting on those socks, missy!" she retorts.   11

"Yes, of course. I'm going to grab a pair from my room."   12
I smile and exit the room.

> Saha ends the narrative part of her essay with DIALOGUE.

As I would later learn, my acceptance of Ms. Cochran's real-   13
ity was actually the basis for validation therapy, a management
tool used by geriatric psychiatrists, social workers, and other
people who deal with dementia patients (Bursack). Historically, it
was believed that patients who lost touch with reality should be
"reoriented to the real world" (Bursack). In 1982, however, the
publication of Naomi Feil's book, *Validation: The Feil Method*, gave
rise to a new way of thinking, in which validating a patient's reality was found to "reduce stress and . . . [enhance] dignity by rein-
forcing self-esteem" (Bursack). This strategy has been shown to
foster trust and empathy between dementia patients and their
caretakers (Bursack).

> Time cue signals TRANSITION from actual narrative to the writer's commentary on it.

* * * * *

Although Feil's theory emphasizes the benefits of "therapeutic   14
fibbing" to patients, my own experience with Ms. Cochran—like my
mother's experience with her father—showed me how this method

Putting in her
oar: the writer
introduces a
key point of her
own into the
discussion.

·····• can offer relief to a caretaker as well (Bursack). By coming to terms
with her father's false accusations, my mother better understood the
nature of his illness and the ways in which it influenced his perception of the world. Her empathy helped her gain closure with him
toward the end of his life, when multiple strokes left him bedridden
and unable to speak. As for me, my initial frustration with Ms.
Cochran dissipated once I let go of the urge to prove to her that I was
correct. As it turned out, entering into Ms. Cochran's reality, a false
reality to us, was the key to establishing a real connection and ultimately calming her.

I wonder how things would have turned out if I were a physi-   15
cian or someone more familiar with Ms. Cochran's case. In some
sense, my inexperience proved to be an asset rather than a limitation.
It allowed me to overcome my early stubbornness and let go of the
need to "fix" Ms. Cochran's perceptions. By contrast, the field of
modern medicine is built on the principle of identifying a problem
and applying science to fix it. But what if the solution to some of
these apparent problems lies not in scientific rationality but in our
ability to redefine the issue? Instead of pathologizing a person's reality, what if we embraced it? Practicing empathy, I learned, does not
require special training or expertise. And yet with patience—and a
little bit of imagination—it can play a powerful role in a person's
healing process.

Work Cited

Bursack, Carol Bradley. "Validation Therapy for Dementia: Calming
    or Condescending?" *Aging Care*, 21 Feb. 2022, www.agingcare
    .com/articles/validation-therapy-for-dementia-166707.htm.

Analyzing a Student Narrative

In "The Wedding Carriage," Sneha Saha draws on rhetorical strategies and techniques that good writers use all the time when crafting a narrative. The following questions, in addition to focusing on particular aspects of Saha's text, will help you identify those common strategies and techniques so you can adapt them to your own writing. These questions will also help prepare you for the analytical questions—on content, structure, and language—that you'll find after all the other selections in this chapter, along with suggestions for writing on related topics.

FOR CLOSE READING

1. When Sneha Saha has her first encounter with Ms. Cochran, why doesn't she already know that the elderly patient is suffering from dementia? What is the nature of Saha's position at the hospital?

2. As it becomes apparent that Ms. Cochran is delusional, Saha tries unsuccessfully to reason with her. Why does this approach fail? How does Saha eventually manage to connect with her patient?

3. As she struggles to get through to Ms. Cochran, Saha recalls her experience with her grandfather in India, who "held certain fixed beliefs about his own reality" (5). How does Saha's (and her mother's) experience with the grandfather and his dementia help her meet the new challenge posed by Ms. Cochran?

4. "Tom" plays a central part in Ms. Cochran's delusions; Saha, however, says that "Tom's actual identity was not important" (9). Why not?

5. Saha later learns that her accepting attitude toward Ms. Cochran's view of reality is the basis of a now-standard form of treatment for patients with delusions. According to the experts cited at the end of Saha's essay, what is "validation therapy," and what benefits does it offer the patient (13)?

6. What key insight about the benefits of validation therapy for the "caretaker" does Saha herself contribute to the discussion (14)?

STRATEGIES AND STRUCTURES

1. Saha's NARRATIVE begins in the middle of one of Ms. Cochran's episodes. How effective is this way of getting the story started? Should Saha have grounded her narrative "in reality" before taking us into the unreality of her subject's mind (2)? Why or why not?

2. What is the climactic episode in Saha's narrative? How does she lead up to this CLIMAX, and how has her point of view as a narrator changed by then? *Why* has it changed?

3. The beginning of Saha's narrative focuses on Ms. Cochran's fixation with "Karen" and the socks. The middle section focuses on the patient's (or is it Saha's?) vision of the wedding carriage. How and where does the writer return to Ms. Cochran's original delusion to achieve a satisfying ending to the main part of her narrative?

4. What does the DIALOGUE in paragraphs 11 and 12 show about the part that the narrator herself has come to play in the story?

5. We often tell stories to make a point. How does the narrative of her adventures with Ms. Cochran support what Saha has to say, in the last three paragraphs of her essay, about treating patients with dementia? Explain.

6. *Other Methods.* The solutions to some medical problems, Saha concludes, might lie "in our ability to redefine the issue" (15). How does Saha use DEFINITION earlier in her essay to lead up to this conclusion?

THINKING ABOUT LANGUAGE

1. Saha refers to Ms. Cochran's fantasies as "visions" rather than delusions (6). What's the difference? How appropriate is Saha's choice of words in this case? Explain.

2. "The scene," says Saha, "plays out in Ms. Cochran's mind" (2). "It's like a scene straight out of a movie" (8). How does Saha's use of the language of theater and film help her present parts of Ms. Cochran's story?

3. If you're not familiar with it, look up the meaning of the Latin phrase "in medias res." How does it apply to Saha's narrative?

4. As a SYNONYM for the term "validation therapy," a serious method of treatment in the field of psychology and medicine, "therapeutic fibbing" might seem a bit disparaging (14). Saha and her sources use it nonetheless. Why?

FOR WRITING

1. Imagine and DESCRIBE, in a paragraph or two, an intense vision or scene that someone else has attempted to convey to you. Make it clear that you're piecing the situation together rather than actually reliving it.

2. Write a narrative about your experience with someone who lives (or lived) in a reality of their own making. Put yourself in the story, and include DIALOGUE that captures what you said to each other. Give your narrative a beginning, a middle, and an end.

3. Exchange stories with others in your class about people they know (or have heard about) who suffer from "reality problems." In a small group, identify and discuss the stories that might make particularly compelling case histories.

4. Either collectively or individually, write a brief narrative telling the story of one or more of the "cases" you and your classmates have identified. This time, keep yourself (or other narrators) largely out of the picture, but try to show both your sympathy for the subject and a degree of clinical detachment.

Signs on a Street Corner

A **NARRATIVE** is a story with a beginning, middle, and end. These signs mark a street corner in Fort Myers Beach, Florida. They also seem to tell a story, even if it's unintentional. Reading from top to bottom, we have a beginning (the lovers walk down the lane) and an end—a dead end (their romance goes nowhere). Why? What happened between the start and finish of this sad story? We don't know, because the middle part is missing—or displaced. Did one of the lovers depart from the scene, perhaps abruptly, like the striding figure on the bottom sign? How you begin and end a narrative is important, of course. But don't neglect the middle part of the **PLOT**. This is where you give a full accounting of the events, people, and motives that make up your main story. Also, unless you have a good reason for rearranging them, the beginning, middle, and end of your story should come in that order. Otherwise, your readers will feel they've been led down the garden path.

[FOR WRITING]..

Look for a street sign, billboard, or some other public inscription
or image that tells or suggests an incomplete story; then write a
brief narrative filling in the missing details. If the text or image
suggests more than one scenario, sketch out each alternative
beginning, middle, or ending the **PLOT** might have.

SUGGESTIONS FOR WRITING

1. In "Immigrating into English" (p. 160), Ocean Vuong tells the story of how he learned to write poetry in a strange new language (English). Read Vuong's essay and write a LITERACY NARRATIVE telling about your success (or difficulty) in coming to grips with the written word. Your narrative could focus, for example, on an early memory of reading a favorite childhood story. Or it might deal with a later experience, such as a writing assignment in school that you found particularly challenging or enlightening.

2. Write a RHETORICAL ANALYSIS of the role of the narrator (the person who tells the story) in "Kim Wilde" (p. 142), a chapter from Marjane Satrapi's graphic narrative *Persepolis*. Be sure to consider how the narrator is related to young Marjane and why the narrator's words appear mostly in boxes set off from the other images, like a voiceover in a movie.

3. In "Tell Them about the Dream, Martin!" (p. 154), Drew Hansen tells about the day the singer Mahalia Jackson, who was sitting nearby, shouted out to Martin Luther King Jr. to put the dream into his famous "I Have a Dream" speech. Read Hansen's narrative and King's speech (see digital .wwnorton.com/links-backtothelake5 for related links), and write a RHETORICAL ANALYSIS comparing the speech as delivered with the speech as it might have been without the dream reference.

4. In "Angles" (p. 170), Kwame Onwuachi tells the story of his appearance as a contestant on the reality television show *Top Chef* in 2015–16. This was the thirteenth season of the show, and Onwuachi was eliminated in episode 13. On *Hulu* or elsewhere, view this episode of *Top Chef* (or other episodes in which Onwuachi appeared). Then write a CRITICAL ANALYSIS that COMPARES AND CONTRASTS Onwuachi's television personality as depicted in "Angles" with his personality and performance as you interpret them on the show itself.

5. Drawing on several episodes from a show with which you are familiar, construct a carefully reasoned ARGUMENT in support of (or opposition to) the THESIS that reality television should be called "unreality television." Discuss how particular characters are exaggerated or flattened (or not), and also explain how the raw material of their experience or adventures is (or is not) shaped into a narrative form—epic battle, true crime, apprenticeship, coming-of-age or transformation story—that the audience may find entertaining or otherwise satisfying.

MIRA JACOB

The Arranged Marriage That Ended Happily Ever After: How My Parents Fell in Love, 30 Years Later

Mira Jacob (b. 1973) is a writer and illustrator and a founder of Pete's Reading Series, which brings writers and readers together every third Thursday of the month at a candy store in Brooklyn. The daughter of parents who emigrated from India in 1968, Jacob grew up in New Mexico, where there were so few Indians from Asia that she and her family were often mistaken for Mexicans or Native Americans. After graduating from Oberlin in 1996, Jacob moved to New York City, where she earned an MFA from the New School and where she now lives with her husband, the documentary filmmaker Jed Rothstein, and their son, Zakir. Young Zak, who asks his mother "difficult questions" about his mixed-race status as an Indian Jewish American, is the inspiration for Jacob's graphic memoir *Good Talk* (2018). Her debut novel, *The Sleepwalker's Guide to Dancing* (2014), about a father who talks to ghosts, was based on the stories and character of her father, the surgeon described in the narrative below.

  "The Arranged Marriage That Ended Happily Ever After: How My Parents Fell in Love, 30 Years Later" is a story of "Indian love" that turns into "American love" before a daughter's watchful (and disbelieving) eyes. As the plot thickens, however, she becomes more than a spectator. Jacob comes from a tradition that is neither Hindu nor Buddhist—her family belonged to an ancient Christian sect that developed in India—but her narrative ends with a "karmic trade-off" different from the one she had expected.

MLA CITATION: Jacob, Mira. "The Arranged Marriage That Ended Happily Ever After: How My Parents Fell in Love, 30 Years Later." *Back to the Lake: A Reader and Guide for Writers*, edited by Thomas Cooley, 5th ed., W. W. Norton, 2024, pp. 136–40.

THERE ARE THINGS YOU TELL YOURSELF when you realize your parents are not in love. Love probably isn't necessary past a certain age. Maybe the way your mother and father go about their daily routines like professional ice-skaters—a careful distance always held between them—is what real love looks like. Whose parents are really in love, anyway?

Growing up in New Mexico in the 1980s, I took it for granted that my parents' marriage, which was arranged by their families in India in 1968, would last forever. True, it lacked the palpable electricity I saw between some American couples, but so what? Who said all that hugging and kissing was a good thing? Too many of my friends' once-affectionate parents were splitting up. My parents, in contrast, were remarkably solid, a well-thought-through match of religion, goals, and socioeconomic standing, clearly in it for the long haul.

"The problem with the Americans is that they get so wrapped up in this who-I-chose business," my father, a surgeon and regular confidant of the OR nurses, told me when I was thirteen. "They will say, 'He has changed' or 'She isn't who I married.' Indians never say that. We have no idea who we married!"

His logic was simple: When you don't have passionate feelings to glaze over your partner's flaws in early marriage, you are less likely to be undone by inevitable disappointments later on. True, I'd never seen my parents look dreamily at each other, but I'd also never heard them threaten divorce.

It was a karmic trade-off that I planned to make myself someday. Never mind my habit of falling for brooding musicians. Whenever I imagined the future, I saw myself in a version of my parents' marriage—tied to someone I loved an acceptable-but-not-overwhelming amount, heat and heartbreak nowhere in sight.

By my mid-20s, I was well on my way, living in New York and dating a very lovely young man. We were kind and careful with each other in a way that felt grown up, if all too familiar. While we were still too young to discuss things like getting married without being tipsy or ironic, it seemed to be the end goal we were moving inevitably toward, like groceries down a conveyor belt. Then I went home to see my parents for a long weekend, and everything changed.

I was 24, and deeply absorbed in my own dramas. I barely noticed how close my mother was sitting to my father at dinner at our favorite restaurant. They watched me with giddy smiles. Poor parents, I thought. So lonely when I'm not here. Then I saw them playing footsie under the table.

For tips on punctuating dialogue, see p. 121.

That night, after we'd all gone to sleep, I woke up to the sound of them laughing. "You!" my mother squealed. "No, you!" my father insisted. I'd never heard them speak that way to each other in my life. Were they . . . flirting? The next morning, just as I was beginning to think it had all been a strange dream, I walked into the kitchen, and my parents sprang to opposite corners, blushing.

Something was definitely up. I called my brother, Arun, in a panic. Four years 9
older than me and deeply in love with an Indian woman, he was the closest thing we
had to a relationship expert in our family. "None of that is happening," my brother
replied calmly from Seattle. "You've lost your mind." His voice was full of the kind
of conviction I'd had myself just days before—a certainty about who our parents
were and what they were capable of.

"Come home!" I said. "You'll see!"   10

Arun was quiet for a long moment. Then he said, "Are you sure?" his voice edged 11
with wonder, and we were young suddenly, younger than we had been in years,
punted back to a time when our parents were larger than we could imagine, their
actions mysteries that could change the course of our entire lives. Forget that we
were grown-ups ourselves, that our lives were being lived elsewhere. This felt seismic, a shift so big it threatened to alter the way we looked at everything.

The night before I went back to New York, I came home to a sight so disquiet- 12
ing that I stood outside in the dark for a full five minutes, just watching. It was
late. The television was on in our living room. In front of it, my father sat on the
couch, my mother cradled in his arms. She was fast asleep, her cheek pressed to his
chest.

I went inside. Though I hardly made a sound, my mother woke up. She blinked 13
quietly, than sprang up with the realization that I was there. "I was asleep!" she
said, as if I'd accused her of something. Then she got up and took herself to bed,
disappearing down the hallway. My father gave me a funny grin and followed her. I
stood alone in front of the television clutching my heart, which I suddenly realized
was not a mere figure of speech.

Flying back to New York, I could not stop thinking one thing: Why now? Why 14
this sudden attraction to someone who had been there the whole time? Sure, it's
a plot staple in American movies, where clumsy, high-cheekboned beauties
regularly realize their "best friend" just happens to be Justin Timberlake, but in
real life? In real life, my parents had bypassed that kind of irresistible attraction
with almost three decades of houses, children, and pets. In real life, their marriage had proved to be a patchwork of incongruities, the kind that were bound to
exist between a cosmopolitan girl from Bombay and a small-town boy from outside
Madras.

If on the surface they had been well matched, temperamentally they
couldn't have been more different. My father was mercurial, charming,
intuitive, a man who liked to say "I am not sentimental" and then cry during commercials. He moved through the world with open arms, and for
good reason: He demanded love and gave it easily.

> Descriptions of the parents' conflicting temperaments build dramatic tension (p. 117).

Not true of my mother. I don't mean to make her sound cold or cruel. 16
She's the opposite: bright, engaging, and quick to laugh, a connoisseur of politics

and gossip. But she doesn't tolerate emotional scenes easily. When I was young, her deep reserve left me frustrated, and, as I grew older, occasionally furious. Later, once I realized she couldn't help it, it just made me sad. I worried for her and for my father, who sometimes seemed to want more of a connection than she could offer.

"Who knows what goes on inside her?" he had said once after a movie left him   17
teary-eyed and her shrugging, and though we all laughed at the time, there was a dart behind his words. My mother kept a wall up that no one could scale.

Until, of course, my father did. Somehow he had made it inside, past my mother's   18
carefully erected boundaries, past the cool remove, and in response, my mother loved him for it. And now, because of that, I knew what real love looked like. I also knew something else.

You are not in love like that, I thought as the plane touched down at Kennedy   19
airport.

It took me a few months to break up with my boyfriend. I won't pretend that I   20
handled things between us wisely or well. I could barely put together coherent sentences, much less make sense of the fact that I was acting on a vague hunch that even though we were pretty good together, we weren't great. It was an uneasy decision, one made more difficult by the fact that when I next visited home six months later, what I saw wasn't exactly inspiring.

My parents had gotten to the sticky, vulnerable part of being in love. If my earlier   21
visit back had caught them in the first flush of romance, this time I saw them in the middle of an awkward, transitional stage. Gone were the asymmetrical fights of my childhood, the shrugs of indifference, the wide berths, the gliding quietly to other rooms to regroup if anything got too intense.

My parents were now brazenly close. They laughed a lot, but they also fought   22
bitterly, sometimes bringing each other to tears, then promptly fumbling their way back to normal without apology or explanation because neither of them needed to be right as much as they needed to be together. Even mundane activities that were once simple—like going to parties, where they used to arrive in separate cars and leave at different times—became minefields of logistics and expectations. They wrestled over whose car to take, what time to go, how long to stay. It was as if, in deciding to be together, they had turned into one animal with two separate heads, each with distinct ideas about how to move through the world. Watching them became an exercise in worrying.

I couldn't help thinking that things would end badly. Pessimistic, yes, but when   23
you've grown up with the idea that Indian love leads to a rational, calm, reliable marriage and American love leads to a passionate, fragile marriage, then the fact that your Indian parents have fallen in American love is not good. I imagined the

worst, thinking I could prepare for it. Maybe someone would cheat, or lie, or double-mortgage the house to pay off a hidden gambling debt. I wasn't sure exactly how my parents would break each other's hearts, but I was on the lookout.

And then something happened that made me forget about my parents altogether: I fell in love. It happened quickly and without warning, the way flash floods hit the desert. Jed was a documentary filmmaker, a talker, a guy from back home, as it happened, and a person I could not remain coolly detached from, even though I tried pretty hard those first few months. It was one thing to want what my parents had, and another to actually try to get it. Pretty soon Jed and I started traveling together, then living together, then learning how to do things like run errands and cook meals together. Sometimes at night I would wake up and watch him, equally thrilled and unnerved by how much he was starting to matter to me.

> Transitional words and phrases (p. 118) help move a narrative smoothly from one event to another.

But being close to Jed didn't come easily. As a person who had long ago decided 25 that sleeping with someone automatically precluded showing them my flaws, I found vulnerability desperately uncomfortable. I'd take any issues or anxieties I had to my brother, or my close friends, or even strangers in bars before I would take them to Jed, something he picked up on quickly.

"Have you ever noticed that you only tell me things once you've figured them out 26 with someone else?" he asked one afternoon. "It's like you only want me to see the cleaned-up version of you." I smiled and shrugged, a fight-avoidance tactic that had worked well with my previous boyfriend. Jed frowned.

"It's weird," he said. 27

"You don't get to be everything to me," I said, escalating the conversation into a 28 fight so quickly that I thought to myself triumphantly that there was nothing for him to do but back down or break up. "Maybe find someone else if that's the kind of woman you need."

Before I knew what was happening, we went at it, exaggerating every slight 29 misunderstanding we'd had over the last few months. He said I was pushing him away. I said he was being too possessive. Just as things started to get really heated, Jed stood up and sang, "You're trying to stop yourself from loving me, but it's not going to work."

I stared at him like he had grown gills. He kept singing. He was just a normal guy 30 who wanted normal things, he sang. I was a mostly normal girl who didn't know how to let things be real.

Was it uncomfortable being sung the subtext of the undoing of every romantic 31 relationship I'd ever been in? Yes. But in that strange way that you don't know what you're looking for until you find it, I also knew he was giving me what I wanted most—a way to get over myself and start loving big.

Three years into our relationship, Jed went to shoot a film about political dissent 32
in Nigeria. We had made arrangements to talk every couple of days, so I didn't
panic with the first missed phone call, but as three days stretched into four, I went
into a sleepless frenzy. I knew there were plenty of reasons this might have happened (bad phone connections, long working hours), but another part of me feared
the worst. I wandered through our apartment alone and found things to organize—
bathroom drawers, spice cabinets. On the fifth day, I put on the last T-shirt he had
worn and lay in bed all day, terrified. When he finally called that night, a short
call full of echoes and blips, I started crying. He assured me he was OK, and I
assured him I was, too, but afterward, I still couldn't sleep. There was no undoing this kind of love, I realized, or the complications that came with it. Even after
he returned ten days later and I had him right next to me, I remained uneasy.
From that moment on, I understood that whatever happened to him would happen
to me, too.

Six months later, we got married. By then I knew that committing to each other 33
would not mean that I never felt scared again, or even that I was permanently safe
from heartbreak. But it would mean that for as long as we were together, I would
be part of something larger than myself. And I felt thankful then—truly thankful
that my parents had found each other, and given me a different idea of what marriage
could be, after nearly 30 years of living coolly side by side. ◆

FOR CLOSE READING

1. "How My Parents Fell in Love, 30 Years Later" is a love story. Whose?

2. What's the difference between "American love" and "Indian love" as Mira Jacob
   DEFINES them? Why is she so concerned that her "Indian parents have fallen in
   American love" (23)?

3. In her midtwenties and thinking about marriage, Jacob plans to follow the example
   her parents have set. Why does she fail to carry through on this plan?

4. In temperament, Jacob writes of her parents, "they couldn't have been more
   different" (15). What are the main differences between them, according to
   Jacob? Which one(s) does she resemble in her early relationship with Jed?
   Explain.

STRATEGIES AND STRUCTURES

1. Noticing that "something was definitely up" with her parents, Jacob calls her
   brother, Arun (9). Identify the paragraphs where their brief DIALOGUE occurs and
   explain how it contributes to a key FLASHBACK within the story.

2. Between the key scenes in Jacob's narrative, time passes. How much? Point out specific references to time and other **TRANSITIONS** through which Jacob manages the **CHRONOLOGY** of her story.

3. About two-thirds of the way through the narrative, "something happened" to send the **PLOT** in a new direction (24). What happened? How and how well does Jacob weave this new development into her original plotline before ending her story?

4. *Other Methods.* Jacob **COMPARES** her parents to "professional ice-skaters" (1). What are the implications of this comparison? of her comparison between herself moving "inevitably" toward marriage and groceries going "down a conveyor belt" (6)?

THINKING ABOUT LANGUAGE

1. "It was a karmic trade-off that I planned to make myself someday" (5). What trade-off is Jacob referring to here? Given the outcome of Jacob's narrative, is there **IRONY** in this statement? Explain.

2. Jacob and her brother are "punted" back in time by the sudden realization that their parents have fallen in love (11). Look up the meaning of the verb "punt" in relation to sports, and then explain the implications of this **METAPHOR**. Why might Jacob have used it instead of something softer?

3. Hyperbole is a **FIGURE OF SPEECH** that involves conscious exaggeration. For example, in paragraph 23 Jacob says, "Maybe someone would cheat, or lie, or double-mortgage the house to pay off a hidden gambling debt." Where else in her narrative does Jacob use hyperbole for (presumably) comic effect when describing the hazards of being in love?

FOR WRITING

1. Using the "simple logic" (4) of Jacob's father as a starting point for a **COMPARISON-AND-CONTRAST** essay of three to five paragraphs, outline the pros and cons of an arranged marriage versus those of "an American marriage." Be sure to address the proposition that having "no idea who we married" is an advantage (3).

2. Compose an **ARGUMENT** in defense of arranged marriages, or "marriages for love," or some combination of the two. Include a short narrative of at least one relationship you've experienced or observed in support of your **THESIS**.

3. Whether from the **POINT OF VIEW** of a participant, an observer, or both, write a personal narrative about a significant change in—or change in your perception of—a marriage, a friendship, or some other relationship. Include "before" and "after" scenes that use **DIALOGUE** to emphasize specific "seismic" events (11).

MARJANE SATRAPI

Kim Wilde

Marjane Satrapi (b. 1969) is a graphic novelist, film director, and author of children's books. Satrapi grew up in Tehran, the daughter of politically active parents who opposed the Iranian monarchy and favored more democratic policies. After the Shah of Iran was deposed in 1979, however, her parents grew even more alarmed by the repressive new regime of Islamic fundamentalists. (Satrapi later chronicled this period in her graphic narrative *Persepolis*, which was published in the United States in 2004.) As a teenager, Satrapi was sent to live and study at a French-speaking school in Austria. After high school, she returned to Iran and eventually earned a master's degree in visual communication from Islamic Azad University in Tehran. In 2008, the film version of *Persepolis* won a César Award for Best First Film.

As graphic narratives move from panel to panel, they are following chronological order (p. 115).

"Kim Wilde," a chapter from *Persepolis*, is named after the British pop singer who, along with Michael Jackson, was one of young Satrapi's cultural heroes as she and her family lived under the restrictions, both personal and political, of a rigid society whose arbitrary rules are captured in the stark blacks and whites of Satrapi's graphic style. Graphic narratives use the same elements and principles—such as point of view, chronology, and, especially, dialogue—as any other kind of narrative; they just add pictures to the words.

MLA CITATION: Satrapi, Marjane. "Kim Wilde." *Back to the Lake: A Reader and Guide for Writers*, edited by Thomas Cooley, 5th ed., W. W. Norton, 2024, pp. 142–51.

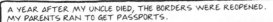

A YEAR AFTER MY UNCLE DIED, THE BORDERS WERE REOPENED. MY PARENTS RAN TO GET PASSPORTS.

LOOK AT THE LAST PAGE: "IT IS STRICTLY FORBIDDEN TO TRAVEL IN OCCUPIED PALESTINE WITH THIS DOCUMENT."

MY GOD. JUST LOOK AT ME IN THIS PICTURE, WITH THE SCARF ON MY HEAD.

CAN I SEE?

SHE SURE DIDN'T LOOK VERY HAPPY. IN FACT, SHE WAS UNRECOGNIZABLE.

NAME: CHALKH... TAJI
DATE OF BIRTH 12.03.1947
IRAN

AS SOON AS I GET MY PASSPORT, WE'LL GO ON A BIG TRIP!

WELL, ACTUALLY...

WE WANT TO SPEND SOME TIME TOGETHER, JUST THE TWO OF US, FOR A FEW DAYS.

WHERE?

TURKEY.

BAH...TURKEY'S FOR THE BIRDS. ONLY UNCOOL PEOPLE GO TO TURKEY. IF YOU'RE TAKING A TRIP, WHY NOT GO TO EUROPE OR THE UNITED STATES?!...

IF YOU WANT US TO BRING YOU BACK SOME PRESENTS, JUST ASK.

WHAT CAN YOU BRING ME BACK FROM TURKEY? SHISH-KEBABS?

LISTEN MARJI, WHERE DO YOU THINK ALL THE HIP STUFF YOU LIKE COMES FROM?

DURING THE WAR, THERE WERE NO IMPORTS FROM THE WEST.

A DENIM JACKET, CHOCOLATE, A POSTER, NO, TWO POSTERS. ONE OF KIM WILDE AND ONE OF IRON MAIDEN.

IRON MAIDEN? THOSE FOUR BRUTES?

THEY'RE NOT BRUTES. I REALLY LIKE WHAT THEY DO.

YOU LIKE THAT?

I LOVE IT.

SEE, MOM?

FIRST THING AFTER THEY GOT TO ISTANBUL, THEY WENT TO BUY THE POSTERS.

I'M GLAD WE FOUND JUST WHAT SHE WANTED!

ABSOLUTELY! IT'S SO HARD FOR KIDS IN IRAN. THE POOR THINGS.

TELL ME THE TRUTH, YOU REALLY LIKE IRON MAIDEN?

YOU HYPOCRITE!

ABSOLUTELY!

I WONDER HOW WE'RE GOING TO GET THEM PAST CUSTOMS!

I'VE BEEN WONDERING MYSELF. THEY'RE ENORMOUS.

AS SOON AS THEY WERE IN THE HOTEL, THEY SET TO FINDING A WAY.

WE COULD FOLD THEM AND HIDE THEM IN THE LINING OF THE SUITCASE!

FOLD THEM? THAT WILL LEAVE MARKS. SHE'LL BE DISAPPOINTED.

WE COULD JUST CARRY THEM UNDER OUR ARMS AND ACT NATURAL.

UNDER OUR ARMS? COME ON!

AND THEN MY MOTHER HAD A GREAT IDEA...

TAKE OFF YOUR COAT.

I PUT MY POSTERS UP IN MY ROOM.

IRON MAIDEN

KIM WILDE

I PUT MY 1983 NIKES ON...

...AND MY DENIM JACKET WITH THE MICHAEL JACKSON BUTTON, AND OF COURSE, MY HEADSCARF.

SO WHAT DO YOU THINK?

NICE! VERY CUTE!

OK, I'M GOING OUT.

WHERE?

TO BUY SOME TAPES.

WHERE?

NOT FAR. ON GANDHI AVENUE.

BE BACK IN AN HOUR!

I'LL BE BACK IN TWO HOURS.

FOR AN IRANIAN MOTHER, MY MOM WAS VERY PERMISSIVE. I ONLY KNEW TWO OR THREE OTHER GIRLS WHO COULD GO OUT ALONE AT THIRTEEN.

FOR A YEAR NOW, THE FOOD SHORTAGE HAD BEEN RESOLVED BY THE GROWTH OF THE BLACK MARKET. HOWEVER, FINDING TAPES WAS A LITTLE MORE COMPLICATED. ON GANDHI AVENUE YOU COULD FIND THEM SOMETIMES.

THEY WERE GUARDIANS OF THE REVOLUTION, THE WOMEN'S BRANCH. THIS GROUP HAD BEEN ADDED IN 1982, TO ARREST WOMEN WHO WERE IMPROPERLY VEILED. (LIKE ME, FOR EXAMPLE.)

THEIR JOB WAS TO PUT US BACK ON THE STRAIGHT AND NARROW BY EXPLAINING THE DUTIES OF MUSLIM WOMEN.

WHY ARE YOU WEARING THOSE "PUNK" SHOES?

WHAT PUNK SHOES?

THOSE!

BUT THESE ARE SNEAKERS!

SHUT UP! THEY'RE PUNK.

IT WAS OBVIOUS THAT SHE HAD NO IDEA WHAT PUNK WAS.

THERE WAS NO ALTERNATIVE. I HAD TO LIE.

I WEAR THESE BECAUSE I PLAY BASKETBALL.

I'M ON MY SCHOOL'S TEAM.

OH SURE. I CAN TELL BY YOUR HEIGHT!

AND YOU WEAR THIS JACKET FOR BASKETBALL TOO??

WHAT DO I SEE HERE? MICHAEL JACKSON! THAT SYMBOL OF DECADENCE?

NO, IT'S MALCOLM X, THE LEADER OF BLACK MUSLIMS IN AMERICA.

DON'T GIVE ME THAT! IT'S MICHAEL JACKSON!

WHO? I DON'T KNOW HIM.

BACK THEN, MICHAEL JACKSON WAS STILL BLACK.

LOWER YOUR SCARF, YOU LITTLE WHORE!

AREN'T YOU ASHAMED TO WEAR TIGHT JEANS LIKE THESE??

THEY SHRANK!!

GO ON, GET IN THE CAR. WE'RE TAKING YOU DOWN TO THE COMMITTEE.

THE COMMITTEE WAS THE HQ OF THE GUARDIANS OF THE REVOLUTION.

AT THE COMMITTEE, THEY DIDN'T HAVE TO INFORM MY PARENTS. THEY COULD DETAIN ME FOR HOURS, OR FOR DAYS. I COULD BE WHIPPED. IN SHORT, ANYTHING COULD HAPPEN TO ME. IT WAS TIME FOR ACTION.

I'M SORRY MA'AM! I'LL NEVER DO IT AGAIN...

GET IN THE CAR!

MA'AM, MY MOTHER'S DEAD. MY STEPMOTHER IS REALLY CRUEL AND IF I DON'T GO HOME RIGHT AWAY, SHE'LL KILL ME...

SHE'LL BURN ME WITH THE CLOTHES IRON!

SHE'LL MAKE MY FATHER PUT ME IN AN ORPHANAGE

MAYBE SHE BELIEVED ME, MAYBE SHE JUST PRETENDED TO. BUT, MIRACULOUSLY, SHE LET ME GO.

BACK HOME...

MARJI! WHAT HAPPENED? HAVE YOU BEEN CRYING?

NO MOM. I'M JUST TIRED. I'M GOING TO MY ROOM.

THERE WAS NO WAY I COULD TELL THE TRUTH. SHE NEVER WOULD HAVE LET ME GO OUT ALONE AGAIN.

I GOT OFF PRETTY EASY, CONSIDERING. THE GUARDIANS OF THE REVOLUTION DIDN'T FIND MY TAPES.

♫ WE'RE THE KIDS IN AMERICA WHOAO ♫

TO EACH HIS OWN WAY OF CALMING DOWN.

FOR CLOSE READING

1. Why are Marjane Satrapi's parents in such a hurry to get passports and go on a trip to Turkey? Why don't they take her with them?

2. What kind of "contraband" does Satrapi ask her parents to bring back to her? What do her requests suggest about society and popular culture in Iran—and America—in the early 2000s?

3. Given the dangers of getting caught, why don't Satrapi's parents refuse to bring back the things she wants? Are they justified in taking such risks to satisfy their daughter's demands? Why or why not?

4. On the streets of Tehran, Satrapi has no trouble buying Kim Wilde and Camel audiotapes. Why does Satrapi include this incident in her narrative? What does it tell the reader about the complexity of the city and its culture?

5. Why doesn't Satrapi tell her mother that she was stopped by the "Guardians of the Revolution, Women's Branch"? Should she have? Why or why not?

STRATEGIES AND STRUCTURES

1. Satrapi's aim in "Kim Wilde," as in the rest of *Persepolis*, is to depict what life was like for her and her family and friends under an authoritarian political and religious regime. How and how well does "Kim Wilde" accomplish this PURPOSE? Support your answer by pointing to specific events in the narrative.

2. In a narrative, events usually unfold one after another in linear or CHRONOLOGICAL fashion. Why? How does the sequence of panels in Satrapi's graphic narrative illustrate this linear principle of narrative in general? Explain by referring to several specific panels.

3. In "Kim Wilde," the beginning action of the PLOT takes place in five panels on the first page. What is the nature of that action, and where is it set? How do the plot and setting of Satrapi's narrative change on the next page?

4. After her parents purchase the forbidden items in Istanbul, the plot of Satrapi's narrative takes another turn, also depicted on a single page. What happens in *this* sequence of events? What other distinct twists and turns does the narrative take before ending in the last three panels with Satrapi "calming down" in her room?

5. A common element in narrative writing is suspense, which comes from the reader's not knowing what will happen next. How does Satrapi create suspense in her narrative? How and where does she temper that suspense with humor?

6. *Other Methods.* In addition to CHRONOLOGY, Satrapi uses CAUSE AND EFFECT to organize the events of her narrative. Having purchased the posters, for example, her parents must then hide them. Point out other examples of actions in the story that are linked by cause and effect; explain what they contribute to the plot and motivation of the characters.

THINKING ABOUT LANGUAGE

1. In "We're the Kids in America," Kim Wilde sings, "Outside a new day is dawning" and "There's a new wave coming, I warn ya." How does Satrapi's ALLUSION to this song help complicate the plot and enhance the significance of her narrative?

2. Graphic narratives are often called "comics." Both terms refer to a story told in words and pictures. How, if at all, do they differ in their CONNOTATIONS?

3. Some key terms in the vocabulary of graphic narratives are "panels," "gutters," "dialogue balloons," "thought balloons," "captions," and "sound effects." Point to several examples of Satrapi's use of these devices in "Kim Wilde."

4. What is the significance of the lightbulb in panel 15? Would the meaning of this figure be apparent in a graphic narrative written in some language other than English? Why or why not?

5. Graphic narratives are popular in Japan, where they're called "manga." Look up the translation of this word, and explain how its meaning compares with that of "comics."

FOR WRITING

1. In a graphic narrative, words and images work together to carry the storyline. Choose a panel (or sequence of panels) in "Kim Wilde" that you find particularly appealing. Then, in a paragraph or two, describe these images in some DETAIL; explain how they support what is being said—and vice versa.

2. Satrapi and her parents mostly wear dark clothes. Only in private, or when defying customary standards, are they depicted in lighter garb. Write an essay analyzing Satrapi's use of black and white as both a visual and a thematic element in "Kim Wilde." Be sure to say why such a stark color scheme is (or is not) more appropriate to her story than the full color range used by some graphic artists.

3. In collaboration with several of your classmates, look for examples of graphic narratives intended to be read in non-Western fashion, such as from right to left and back to front. (Japanese manga, in particular, can be found in English translation both on the internet and in print.) Have each member of the group report briefly in writing on their experience with reading at least one such text.

4. Write a brief ANALYSIS of "Kim Wilde" in which you evaluate the role of America in the narrative. Point to specific images and passages of dialogue to support your analysis.

5. In 2022, civil unrest broke out in Iran in protest of the suppression of free expression and women's rights—and the death of a young woman in the custody of the morality police. Suppose you were updating Kim Wilde's story to reflect conditions under an even more repressive regime. Starting from the point where she is threatened by the Guardians of the Revolution, write out the dialogue you would include to bring your narrative to a conclusion.

DREW HANSEN

"Tell Them about the Dream, Martin!"

Drew Hansen (b. 1972) is a member of the Washington State House of Representatives, where he works on issues of education, the environment, health care, jobs, and more. After graduating from Harvard, Hansen studied theology as a Rhodes Scholar at Oxford University and later earned a law degree from Yale. The author of *The Dream: Martin Luther King, Jr., and the Speech That Inspired a Nation* (2003), he has been invited to speak about civil rights issues at schools and colleges around the country.

Martin Luther King Jr. delivered his famous "I Have a Dream" speech at the Lincoln Memorial in Washington, DC, on August 28, 1963, before a crowd of about 250,000 people. It was one of the first mass demonstrations to be covered by television; and by late afternoon, according to Hansen, some speakers thought "the TV crews would leave to process their film for the evening news." This is why, vying for the spotlight, organizers of the event pushed King's speech to the end of a long day. In the version given to the press, King did not even include the "I have a dream" language; and before his time came to speak, the tired audience was packing up to go home.

According to Hansen's narrative of the lesser-known events of that day, these circumstances were altered—and history made—by the timely intervention of the great gospel singer Mahalia Jackson, who also had a late slot on the program. "Tell Them about the Dream, Martin!" (editor's title) appeared as an opinion piece in the *New York Times* on August 28, 2013, the fiftieth anniversary of the speech.

MLA CITATION: Hansen, Drew. "Tell Them about the Dream, Martin!" *Back to the Lake: A Reader and Guide for Writers*, edited by Thomas Cooley, 5th ed., W. W. Norton, 2024, pp. 155–57.

THE REV. DR. MARTIN LUTHER KING JR.'S SPEECH at the March on Washington   1
for Jobs and Freedom in 1963 was unusual among great American speeches in
that its most famous words—"I have a dream"—were improvised.

King had certainly thought about using the "dream" refrain in Washing-   2
ton. He had been fine-tuning it earlier that year. In April, in Birmingham,
Alabama, deputies of the public safety commissioner, Eugene Connor,
known as Bull, attended a mass meeting at the 16th Street Baptist Church,
where they reported that King "said that he had a dream of seeing little
Negro boys and girls walking to school with little white boys and girls, playing in the parks together and going swimming together."

> When you go back in time in a narrative, be sure to use appropriate verb tenses (p. 118).

And in June, King electrified an audience at Cobo Hall in Detroit, saying: "I have a   3
dream this afternoon that one day, right here in Detroit, Negroes will be able to buy a
house or rent a house anywhere that their money will carry them and they will be able
to get a job."

But King thought he wouldn't have time to use the "dream" language at the   4
March. He had asked his advisers to prepare drafts—an unusual move, as King typically didn't do more than jot down a few notes on the back of a church bulletin
before speaking—and he liked a "bad check" metaphor in one of the drafts, which
would support an argument that America had failed to fulfill its promises of liberty
and equality to black citizens. He didn't think he could fit both that and the "dream"
refrains into the five minutes allotted to each speaker. Walter E. Fauntroy, one of
King's advisers, counseled him not to worry about the time limits. "Look, Martin,"
he said, "you do what the spirit say do."

When King arrived at the Willard Hotel in Washington the night before the   5
march, he still didn't have a complete draft. King called his aides together in the
lobby, and they started arguing about what should go in the speech. One wanted
King to talk about jobs, another wanted him to talk about housing discrimination.
Finally King said: "My brothers, I understand. I appreciate all the suggestions. Now
let me go and counsel with the Lord."

King went up to his room and spent the night writing the speech in longhand.   6
Andrew Young stopped by and saw that King had crossed out words three and four
times, trying to find the right rhythm, as if he were writing poetry. King finished at
about 4 in the morning and handed the manuscript to his aides so it could be typed
up and distributed to the press. The speech did not include the words "I have a
dream."

King awoke the next morning to the disappointing news that the crowds at the   7
March were smaller than expected. "About 25,000," the television reporters were saying, as King left the hotel. Bayard Rustin, the march's chief organizer, was standing at
the Washington Monument, where reporters pressed him about why so few people
had shown up. Rustin looked intently at a yellow legal pad in his hand. "Gentlemen,"

he said, "everything is going exactly according to plan." One of Rustin's aides looked over his shoulder and saw that the pad Rustin was looking at was blank.

But at Union Station, buses and trains were coming in regularly, swelling crowds   8 that some onlookers compared to those that had gathered at the end of World War II. Train No. 42 of the Southern Railroad, which had carried Medgar Evers's body to Washington two months earlier, arrived full of marchers. A "Freedom Special," chartered from Florida, pulled in and discharged nearly 800 young people singing a massed chorus of "We Shall Overcome."

By late morning, the lawns around the Washington Monument were packed   9 with people, many of whom opened up the box lunches they had prepared (no mayonnaise, the march organizers had warned—it might spoil) and started to picnic. Then, around 11 a.m., some people began walking to the Lincoln Memorial, more followed, and soon most of the crowd was on its way. This surprised Rustin, who had planned for the leaders of the major civil rights groups to lead the way to the Memorial. "My God, they're going!" he shouted. "We're supposed to be leading them!" He hustled the leaders together, and they joined hands at a break in the middle of the crowd, with most of the marchers already far ahead.

There was a long afternoon program of songs and speeches at the Lincoln   10 Memorial. King had the last speaking slot—not just because he was a hard act to

Mahalia Jackson sings on the steps of the Lincoln Memorial during the March on Washington. (Martin Luther King Jr. is at the lower right-hand corner.)

follow, but because some other speakers thought they might get better coverage if they spoke earlier in the day. (By late afternoon, some leaders believed, the TV crews would leave to process their film for the evening news.) As the program went on, people packed up and started to walk away. Many had spent several days and nights on buses and trains to Washington, and they were tired and ready to head home.

Then A. Philip Randolph, the 74-year-old initiator of the march, who had   11
secured an executive order on nondiscrimination in defense-industry employment and contracts by pressuring President Franklin D. Roosevelt with a threat of a march on Washington in 1941, introduced the gospel singer Mahalia Jackson. She sang two spirituals, "I Been 'Buked and I Been Scorned" and "How I Got Over." King was seated nearby, clapping his hands on his knees and calling out to her as she sang. Roger Mudd, covering the event for CBS News, said after the first song: "Mahalia Jackson. And all the speeches in the world couldn't have brought the response that just came from the hymns she sang. Miss Mahalia Jackson." Then, after a speech by Rabbi Joachim Prinz, from the American Jewish Congress, it was King's turn to speak.

King read from his prepared text for most of his speech, which relied on the   12
Bible, the Constitution and the Declaration of Independence—just as President John F. Kennedy had a few months earlier, when he called for civil rights legislation in a nationally televised address: "We are confronted primarily with a moral issue. It is as old as the Scriptures and is as clear as the American Constitution."

As King neared the end, he came to a sentence that wasn't quite right. He had   13
planned to introduce his conclusion with a call to "go back to our communities as members of the international association for the advancement of creative dissatis-faction." He skipped that, read a few more lines, and then improvised: "Go back to Mississippi; go back to Alabama; go back to South Carolina; go back to Georgia; go back to Louisiana; go back to the slums and ghettos of our Northern cities, knowing that somehow this situation can and will be changed."

Nearby, off to one side, Mahalia Jackson shouted: "Tell them about the dream,   14
Martin!" King looked out over the crowd. As he later explained in an inter-view, "all of a sudden this thing came to me that I have used—I'd used many times before, that thing about 'I have a dream'—and I just felt that I wanted to use it here." He said, "I say to you today, my friends, so even though we face the difficulties of today and tomorrow, I still have a dream." And he was off, delivering some of the most beloved lines in American his-tory, a speech that he never intended to give and that some of the other civil rights leaders believed no one but the marchers would ever remember. ◆

See pp. 119–20 for tips on adding dia-logue to a narrative.

FOR CLOSE READING

1. What was "unusual," according to Drew Hansen, about the composition of Martin Luther King's "I Have a Dream" speech as he delivered it in Washington in 1963 (1)? In what ways was the process simply normal procedure for King himself?

2. Why would a singer, especially of blues and spirituals, be a likely collaborator for an orator on such an occasion as Hansen reconstructs in "Tell Them about the Dream, Martin!"?

3. In Hansen's account, Mahalia Jackson urges King forward in his performance by reminding him of "the dream" (14). Where and how did King support Jackson in *her* performance?

4. On the day that Hansen tells about, King's speech came last in the order of events, after people were getting "tired and ready to head home" (10). How else, besides reminding him of the dream, did Jackson help save the day for the reception of King's speech?

5. The 1963 marchers on Washington were advised not to use mayonnaise on their sandwiches because "it might spoil" (9). Is Hansen justified in reporting such a minor DETAIL in his narrative of such an important historical event? Why or why not?

STRATEGIES AND STRUCTURES

1. What is Hansen's main PURPOSE in retelling the story of the day King delivered his famous speech? What point is he making about the speech that can't be gleaned from simply watching a video of the event on *YouTube*? Where and how does he make that point most effectively?

2. King's usual method of composing a speech, according to Hansen, was to "jot down a few notes on the back of a church bulletin before speaking" (4). What are some of the advantages and disadvantages of this method of composition?

3. "Tell them about the dream, Martin!" is not the only direct quotation in Hansen's essay. Where else does Hansen incorporate bits of DIALOGUE, and what do they contribute to his narrative?

4. The March on Washington occurred on a single day in 1963. How and where does Hansen depart from the CHRONOLOGY of that day to bring ideas and events into his narrative from other times and places? Where and why does he stick closely to the order of events on August 28?

5. *Other Methods.* How, and how well, does Hansen DESCRIBE the physical setting and the people in his narrative? Point to specific details in the text that help capture the look and feel of the particular time and place he's writing about.

THINKING ABOUT LANGUAGE

1. In an earlier speech in Detroit, King's "dream" may have gotten a strong response from his audience, but they weren't literally "electrified" by it (3). Why are such **METAPHORS** nonetheless common in descriptions of speeches and other performances? Can you think of any circumstances when a reviewer might say that a performer "electrocuted" the audience?

2. Why does Hansen refer to the theme of racial equality in King's speeches as a "refrain" (2)? Where does the term come from, and how does it apply to writing speeches, especially when the writer has "crossed out words three and four times" (6)?

3. Why do you think King liked the "bad check" metaphor to which Hansen refers in paragraph 4? What does his including it in the speech suggest about King's sense of his audience?

4. Where and how does Hansen himself use the repetition and rhythms of music or poetry in the language of his narrative? Cite several specific examples from the text.

FOR WRITING

1. Videos of King's delivery of his speech on August 28, 1963, are all over the internet. Watch King's speech at digital.wwnorton.com/links-backtothelake5, and write an objective, **THIRD-PERSON** narrative of the event as if you were reporting it for a newspaper. Cite specific words and phrases (such as "I have a dream") in your report—as well as the speaker's key points and ideas.

2. In a brainstorming session with several of your classmates, list and discuss some of the differences—including the possibilities for improvisation—between *hearing* a text (as in a presented speech, lecture, or sermon) and *reading* a text. In a paragraph or two, present the conclusions of your discussion, perhaps using oral and written versions of King's (or someone else's) speech as an example.

3. In a journal or notebook, record your experiences, over time, in listening to a particular lecturer, speaker, or commentator—whether on campus or in the media—whom you find to be particularly effective (or ineffective). Write a narrative illustrating and commenting on that person's characteristic use of specific verbal techniques and devices.

4. In four or five paragraphs, write an **EVALUATION** of King's "I Have a Dream" speech in which you explain what makes it one of the "great American speeches" (1)—or, alternatively, why you think the speech is overrated.

5. Write a review of Drew Hansen's book, *The Dream: Martin Luther King, Jr., and the Speech That Inspired a Nation* (2003). Your review should focus on how and how well Hansen tells the story of King's speech—and **ARGUES** the case for its historic and literary significance.

OCEAN VUONG

Immigrating into English

Ocean Vuong (b. 1988) is a poet, essayist, and best-selling novelist. He was born in Ho Chi Minh City, Vietnam, and immigrated to the United States in 1990 after spending a year as a refugee in the Philippines. He is the first person in his family to learn how to read. A graduate of Brooklyn College, where he majored in British literature, Vuong earned an MFA from New York University and teaches creative writing at the University of Massachusetts-Amherst. His collection of poems, *Night Sky with Exit Wounds* (2016), won the T. S. Eliot Prize. In 2019, he received a MacArthur Fellows "Genius" Grant and published the best-selling novel *On Earth We're Briefly Gorgeous*. Vuong's latest poetry collection, *Time Is a Mother* (2022), explores his grief following his mother's death and his determination to appreciate life despite his loss. "Immigrating into English," first published in *New Yorker* magazine, is a literacy narrative that tells the story of Vuong's early experiences with learning English and writing one of his first poems.

READING AND WRITING, like any other crafts, come to the mind slowly, in pieces. But for me, as an E.S.L.[1] student from a family of illiterate rice farmers, who saw reading as snobby, or worse, the experience of working through a book, even one as simple as *Where the Wild Things Are*,[2] was akin to standing in quicksand, your loved ones corralled at its safe edges, their arms folded in suspicion and doubt as you sink.

MLA CITATION: Vuong, Ocean. "Immigrating into English." *Back to the Lake: A Reader and Guide for Writers*, edited by Thomas Cooley, 5th ed., W. W. Norton, 2024, pp. 160–62.

1 Refers to students learning English as a "second language," in addition to their own native language(s). Today, the acronym "ELL," short for "English Language Learner," is more commonly used.
2 Classic children's book by Maurice Sendak, first published in 1963.

My family immigrated to the U.S. from Vietnam in 1990, when I was two. We   2
lived, all seven of us, in a one-bedroom apartment in Hartford, Connecticut, and I
spent my first five years in America surrounded, inundated, by the Vietnamese language. When I entered kindergarten, I was, in a sense, immigrating all over again,
except this time into English. Like any American child, I quickly learned my ABCs,
thanks to the age-old melody (one I still sing rapidly to myself when I forget whether
"M" comes before "N"). Within a few years, I had become fluent—but only in speech,
not in the written word.

One early-spring afternoon, when I was in fourth grade, we got an assignment in   3
language-arts class: we had two weeks to write a poem in honor of National Poetry
Month. Normally, my poor writing abilities would excuse me from such
assignments, and I would instead spend the class mindlessly copying out
passages from books I'd retrieved from a blue plastic bin at the back of the
room. The task allowed me to camouflage myself; as long as I looked as
though I were doing something smart, my shame and failure were hidden.
The trouble began when I decided to be dangerously ambitious. Which is to
say, I decided to write a poem.

How to develop an interesting PLOT out of ordinary events is discussed on pp. 115, 117–18.

"Where is it?" the teacher asked. He held my poem up to the fluorescent   4
classroom lights and squinted, the way one might examine counterfeit money. I could
tell, by the slowly brightening room, that it had started to snow. I pointed to my work
dangling from his fingers. "No, where is the poem you plagiarized? How did you
even write something like this?" Then he tipped my desk toward me. The desk
had a cubby attached to its underside, and I watched as the contents spilled from the
cubby's mouth: rectangular pink erasers, crayons, yellow pencils, wrinkled worksheets
where dotted letters were filled in, a lime Dum Dum lollipop. But no poem. I stood
before the rubble at my feet. Little moments of ice hurled themselves against the
window as the boys and girls, my peers, stared, their faces as unconvinced as blank
sheets of paper.

Weeks earlier, I'd been in the library. It was where I would hide during recess.   5
Otherwise, because of my slight frame and soft voice, the boys would call me
"pansy" and "fairy" and pull my shorts around my ankles in the middle of
the schoolyard. I sat on the floor beside a tape player. From a box of cas-
settes, I chose one labeled "Great American Speeches." I picked it because
of the illustration, a microphone against a backdrop of the American flag.
I picked it because the American flag was one of the few symbols I
recognized.

Page 121 explains when to use the past perfect ("had been") instead of the simple past ("was").

Through the headset, a robust male voice surged forth, emptying into my body.   6
The man's inflections made me think of waves on a sea. Between his sentences, a
crowd—I imagined thousands—roared and applauded. I imagined their heads shifting in an endless flow. His voice must possess the power of a moon, I thought, some-

thing beyond my grasp, my little life. Then a narrator named the man as a Dr. Martin Luther King Jr. I nodded, not knowing why a doctor was speaking like this. But maybe these people were ill, and he was trying to cure them. There must have been medicine in his words—can there be medicine in words? "I have a dream," I mouthed to myself as the doctor spoke. It occurred to me that I had been mouthing my grandmother's stories as well, the ones she had been telling me ever since I was born. Of course, not being able to read does not mean that one is empty of stories.

My poem was called "If a Boy Could Dream." The phrases "promised land" and "mountaintop" sounded golden to me, and I saw an ochre-lit field, a lushness akin to a spring dusk. I imagined that the doctor was dreaming of springtime. So my poem was a sort of ode to spring. From the gardening shows my grandmother watched, I'd learned the words for flowers I had never seen in person: foxglove, lilac, lily, buttercup. "If a boy could dream of golden fields, full of lilacs, tulips, marigolds . . ."   7

I knew words like "if" and "boy," but others I had to look up. I sounded out the words in my head, a dictionary in my lap, and searched the letters. After a few days, the poem appeared as gray graphite words. The paper a white flag. I had surrendered, had written.   8

Looking back, I can see my teacher's problem. I was, after all, a poor student. "Where is it?" he said again.   9

"It's right here," I said, pointing to my poem pinched between his fingers.   10

I had read books that weren't books, and I had read them using everything but my eyes. From that invisible "reading," I had pressed my world onto paper. As such, I was a fraud in a field of language, which is to say, I was a writer. I have plagiarized my life to give you the best of me. ◆   11

FOR CLOSE READING

1. A quick preview of Ocean Vuong's essay would suggest that he is writing an immigration story. How does the NARRATIVE develop the basic idea of moving from one territory to another? Explain.

2. "Where is it?" asks Vuong's fourth-grade teacher (4). Vuong's teacher assumes that his pupil's poem is PLAGIARIZED and that he is hiding the source. Should the teacher have handled the situation differently? Why or why not?

3. "Reading and writing, like any other crafts, come to the mind slowly, in pieces" (1). Based on your experience, is Vuong right about this? What are some specific examples, in your own case, of the process of learning to read and write happening "slowly" and "in pieces"—or otherwise?

4. "Of course, not being able to read," says Vuong, "does not mean that one is empty of stories" (6). Writing is only about 5,000 years old. Do some research online to find out how long people have been telling stories. What kinds of stories?

5. As a child, Vuong was fluent in both Vietnamese and English—"but only in speech, not in the written word" (2). Why do you think learning to read and write a language takes children longer than learning to speak it?

STRATEGIES AND STRUCTURES

1. "Immigrating into English" is, in part, a **LITERACY NARRATIVE**, a personal story about coming to grips with language, either in written or spoken form. In Vuong's narrative, what specific aspects of language and literacy does the author find most challenging?

2. The **CLIMAX** of Vuong's story is not the moment of discovery, when the teacher accuses him of plagiarism; it is the act of writing the poem, which came earlier. The climax of a story usually comes near the end. How and how well does Vuong solve this problem of **CHRONOLOGY** in telling his story?

3. In Vuong's narrative, what event leads to the climactic writing of "If a Boy Could Dream"? How did Vuong's experience with his grandmother's stories prepare him (and his readers) for this sequence of events?

4. At the end of his narrative, Vuong speaks directly to his **AUDIENCE**. How effective is this strategy? Why might he use it, and who is his intended audience?

5. *Other Methods.* "I was a writer," says Vuong at the end of his narrative. By Vuong's **DEFINITION**, what makes a writer a writer? How and where does he indicate that defining the term is not an easy task?

THINKING ABOUT LANGUAGE

1. Vuong says his decision to write a poem was "dangerously ambitious" (3). Why was it ambitious? Why was it dangerous?

2. What is the function of the phrase "Weeks earlier" in Vuong's narrative (5)? How does it help him solve the problem of telling a story out of **CHRONOLOGICAL ORDER**?

3. Throughout his narrative, Vuong uses terms that are related to war and the military, for example: "camouflage" (3), "rubble" (4), "white flag" (8), "surrendered" (8). How appropriate is this language? What sort of battle is he telling about?

4. Point out places in his essay where Vuong uses **FIGURES OF SPEECH** such as **META-PHOR** ("moments of ice") and **SIMILE** ("as blank sheets of paper") in the last sentence in paragraph 4. How and how well does the use of such figurative language fit in with Vuong's account of the first poem he wrote?

5. **PLAGIARISM** is the use of another person's words or ideas without acknowledgment, as if they were one's own. Wrongly accused of plagiarism by his fourth-grade teacher, Vuong nevertheless says at the end of his essay that he has "plagiarized"

(11). What does he mean by this, and what is he implying about the nature of writing as he sees it?

FOR WRITING

1. Do some research on Vuong, and in a paragraph or two, tell the story of how he came to be called "Ocean."

2. If your dominant language isn't English, write a narrative of four to five paragraphs telling the story of how you "immigrated" into English. If immigration isn't the META-PHOR you would use for your English-learning process, how would you describe it instead? Why? Be sure to give EXAMPLES of particular words and phrases that inspired (or intimidated) you.

3. Whatever language(s) you consider your native language, you learned to think in that language before you learned to read and write it. Write a brief preliteracy narrative about some aspect of your early language acquisition or of that of somebody you know, such as a younger sibling. Again, cite specific examples of words and phrases that you (or they) learned—and how.

4. Although children all over the world learn to speak their native language(s) at about the same age, children generally take longer to learn to read and write in Chinese, which has a logographic writing system, than in English, which has an alphabetic writing system. Do some research on the differences between learning logographic and alphabetic writing systems, and write an essay explaining why one takes longer to learn than the other.

The Sanctuary of School

Lynda Barry (b. 1956) is a cartoonist, novelist, and teacher of writing. She was born in Wisconsin but spent most of her adolescence in Seattle, where she supported herself at age sixteen as a janitor. As a student at Evergreen State College in Olympia, Washington, Barry began drawing *Ernie Pook's Comeek*, the comic strip for which she is perhaps best known. Her first novel, *Cruddy* (2000), was about a teenager and her troubled family life "in the cruddiest part of town." In "The Sanctuary of School," which first appeared in the Education section of the *New York Times* in January 1992, Barry tells how she discovered the therapeutic value of art—and of good teachers. This narrative about her early school days also carries a pointed message for those who would cut costs in the public school system by eliminating art from the curriculum. In 2019, Barry was the recipient of a MacArthur Fellows "Genius" Grant.

I WAS SEVEN YEARS OLD the first time I snuck out of the house in the dark. It was 1 winter and my parents had been fighting all night. They were short on money and long on relatives who kept "temporarily" moving into our house because they had nowhere else to go.

My brother and I were used to giving up our bedroom. We slept on the couch, 2 something we actually liked because it put us that much closer to the light of our lives, our television.

At night when everyone was asleep, we lay on our pillows watching it with 3 the sound off. We watched Steve Allen's[1] mouth moving. We watched Johnny

MLA CITATION: Barry, Lynda. "The Sanctuary of School." *Back to the Lake: A Reader and Guide for Writers,* edited by Thomas Cooley, 5th ed., W. W. Norton, 2024, pp. 165–68.

1 American actor and musician (1921–2000) best known for his work on late-night television.

Carson's[2] mouth moving. We watched movies filled with gangsters shooting machine guns into packed rooms, dying soldiers hurling a last grenade, and beautiful women crying at windows. Then the sign-off finally came and we tried to sleep.

The morning I snuck out, I woke up filled with a panic about needing to get to school. The sun wasn't quite up yet but my anxiety was so fierce that I just got dressed, walked quietly across the kitchen and let myself out the back door. 4

It was quiet outside. Stars were still out. Nothing moved and no one was in the street. It was as if someone had turned the sound off on the world. 5

I walked the alley, breaking thin ice over the puddles with my shoes. I didn't know why I was walking to school in the dark. I didn't think about it. All I knew was a feeling of panic, like the panic that strikes kids when they realize they are lost. 6

That feeling eased the moment I turned the corner and saw the dark outline of my school at the top of the hill. My school was made up of about 15 nondescript portable classrooms set down on a fenced concrete lot in a rundown Seattle neighborhood, but it had the most beautiful view of the Cascade Mountains. You could see them from anywhere on the playfield and you could see them from the windows of my classroom—Room 2. 7

I walked over to the monkey bars and hooked my arms around the cold metal. I stood for a long time just looking across Rainier Valley. The sky was beginning to whiten and I could hear a few birds. 8

In a perfect world my absence at home would not have gone unnoticed. I would have had two parents in a panic to locate me, instead of two parents in a panic to locate an answer to the hard question of survival during a deep financial and emotional crisis. 9

But in an overcrowded and unhappy home, it's incredibly easy for any child to slip away. The high levels of frustration, depression, and anger in my house made my brother and me invisible. We were children with the sound turned off. And for us, as for the steadily increasing number of neglected children in this country, the only place where we could count on being noticed was at school. 10

> By adding DIALOGUE (pp. 119–20), you can introduce different POINTS OF VIEW into a narrative.

"Hey there, young lady. Did you forget to go home last night?" It was Mr. Gunderson, our janitor, whom we all loved. He was nice and he was funny and he was old with white hair, thick glasses and an unbelievable number of keys. I could hear them jingling as he walked across the playfield. I felt incredibly happy to see him. 11

He let me push his wheeled garbage can between the different portables as he unlocked each room. He let me turn on the lights and raise the window shades and I saw my school slowly come to life. I saw Mrs. Holman, our school secretary, walk into the office without her orange lipstick on yet. She waved. 12

---

2 American comedian and television personality (1924–2005) who hosted *The Tonight Show* for thirty years.

I saw the fifth-grade teacher, Mr. Cunningham, walking under the breezeway   13
eating a hard roll. He waved.

And I saw my teacher, Mrs. Claire LeSane, walking toward us in a red coat and   14
calling my name in a very happy and surprised way, and suddenly my throat got
tight and my eyes stung and I ran toward her crying. It was something that surprised us both.

It's only thinking about it now, 28 years later, that I realize I was crying from relief.   15
I was with my teacher, and in a while I was going to sit at my desk, with my crayons
and pencils and books and classmates all around me, and for the next six hours I was
going to enjoy a thoroughly secure, warm and stable world. It was a world I absolutely
relied on. Without it, I don't know where I would have gone that morning.

Mrs. LeSane asked me what was wrong and when I said "Nothing," she seem-   16
ingly left it at that. But she asked me if I would carry her purse for her, an honor
above all honors, and she asked if I wanted to come into Room 2 early and paint.

She believed in the natural healing power of painting and drawing for troubled   17
children. In the back of her room there was always a drawing table and an easel
with plenty of supplies, and sometimes during the day she would come up to you for
what seemed like no good reason and quietly ask if you wanted to go to the back
table and "make some pictures for Mrs. LeSane." We all had a chance at it—to sit
apart from the class for a while to paint, draw and silently work out impossible problems on 11 × 17 sheets of newsprint.

Drawing came to mean everything to me. At the back table in Room 2, I learned   18
to build myself a life preserver that I could carry into my home.

We all know that a good education system saves lives, but the people of this   19
country are still told that cutting the budget for public schools is necessary,
that poor salaries for teachers are all we can manage and that art, music
and all creative activities must be the first to go when times are lean.

> When you tell a story, it should have a point (p. 115).

Before- and after-school programs are cut and we are told that public schools are   20
not made for baby-sitting children. If parents are neglectful temporarily or permanently, for whatever reason, it's certainly sad, but their unlucky children must fend
for themselves. Or slip through the cracks. Or wander in a dark night alone.

We are told in a thousand ways that not only are public schools not important,   21
but that the children who attend them, the children who need them most, are not
important either. We leave them to learn from the blind eye of a television, or to the
mercy of "a thousand points of light"[3] that can be as far away as stars.

---

3 In his inaugural address on January 20, 1989, President George H. W. Bush used this phrase to refer to
"all the community organizations that are spread like stars throughout the Nation, doing good."

I was lucky. I had Mrs. LeSane. I had Mr. Gunderson. I had an abundance of art   22
supplies. And I had a particular brand of neglect in my home that allowed me to slip
away and get to them. But what about the rest of the kids who weren't as lucky?
What happened to them?

By the time the bell rang that morning I had finished my drawing and Mrs. LeSane   23
pinned it up on the special bulletin board she reserved for drawings from the back
table. It was the same picture I always drew—a sun in the corner of a blue sky over a
nice house with flowers all around it.

Mrs. LeSane asked us to please stand, face the flag, place our right hands over   24
our hearts and say the Pledge of Allegiance. Children across the country do it
faithfully. I wonder now when the country will face its children and say a pledge
right back. ◆

FOR CLOSE READING

1. As a seven-year-old leaving home in the dark in a fit of panic and anxiety, why did
   young Lynda Barry instinctively head for her school?

2. Why does Barry say, "We were children with the sound turned off" (10)? Who fails
   to hear them?

3. Barry always drew the same picture when she sat at the art table in the back of
   Mrs. LeSane's classroom. What's the significance of that picture? Explain.

4. Why does Barry refer to the Pledge of Allegiance in the last paragraph of her essay?

STRATEGIES AND STRUCTURES

1. Why does Barry begin her NARRATIVE with an account of watching television with
   her brother? Where else does she refer to watching TV? Why?

2. Most of Barry's narrative takes place at her school, which she pictures in some
   detail. Which of these physical DETAILS do you find most revealing, and how do
   they help present the place as a "sanctuary"?

3. Point out several places in her narrative where Barry characterizes Mrs. LeSane,
   Mr. Gunderson, and others through their gestures and bits of DIALOGUE. What do
   these small acts and brief words reveal about the people Barry is portraying?

4. What does young Barry's sense of panic and anxiety contribute to the PLOT of her
   narrative?

5. *Other Methods.* Where and how does Barry's narrative morph into an ARGUMENT
   about public schools in America? What's the point of that argument, and where
   does she state her CLAIM most directly?

THINKING ABOUT LANGUAGE

1. Is Barry speaking literally or metaphorically (or both) when she refers to children who "wander in a dark night alone" (20)? How and how well does she pave the way for this statement at the end of her narrative?

2. What does Barry mean when she says that the "points of light" in a child's life can be "as far away as stars" (21)? How and where does the idea of "light" take on different CONNOTATIONS during the course of her narrative?

3. Barry characterizes her old school as a "sanctuary" instead of, for example, a "haven" or "safehouse." Why do you think she chooses this term? Is it apt? Why or why not?

4. Why does Barry refer to the "blind eye" of television (21)? Is this an effective META-PHOR? Why or why not?

FOR WRITING

1. In a few paragraphs, tell about a time when you found school to be a sanctuary, or the opposite. Be sure to DESCRIBE the physical place and what people said and did there.

2. Following Barry's example in paragraph 12 and beyond ("I saw my school slowly come to life"), compose the beginning of a narrative about a school, business, or other place or institution as it comes to life after some period of darkness. Include DIALOGUE—and characters like Mr. Gunderson.

3. As you watch a film, sports event, news broadcast, or other show, turn off the sound on your device, and write a brief account of what you see. Be sure to describe the SETTING and maintain a consistent POINT OF VIEW, so that the reader gets the picture as you piece it together.

4. Write a short narrative essay in which you use your experience at school to make a point about the importance of some aspect of the school curriculum that you fear may be changed or lost. If you wish, you can expand your ARGUMENT to include schools in general, not just your own.

KWAME ONWUACHI

Angles

Kwame Onwuachi (b. 1989) is a chef, writer, and editor at *Food and Wine* magazine. Born on Long Island, he graduated from the Bronx Leadership Academy High School and the Culinary Institute of America. Beginning at age ten, Onwuachi lived with his grandfather in Nigeria, later joining his mother in Baton Rouge, Louisiana. Onwuachi also has family ties to Jamaica and Trinidad, and the cooking of all these regions has influenced his Afro-Cuban cuisine, for which he was named Rising Star Chef of the Year by the James Beard Foundation in 2019. The diversity of American food is a major theme in Onwuachi's memoir, *Notes from a Young Black Chef* (2019), and in his cookbook, *My America* (2022).

Before he opened the Shaw Bijou restaurant in Washington, DC, Onwuachi's highest position in the industry was line cook at the exclusive Eleven Madison Park (EMP) in New York City. To publicize his new venture, Onwuachi appeared as a contestant on the reality television series *Top Chef* in 2015. "I got eliminated in the thirteenth episode," he writes in "Angles," a chapter from his memoir that tells the story of how reality television made an aspiring chef a character in someone else's narrative—an experience that, he says, gave him valuable insights into how he saw himself. It also recounts how an eight-year-old boy was inspired to become a real chef, if not a celebrity one, by watching "hard-core" cooking competitions on television—and then pulling pots and pans from the shelf in his mother's kitchen.

MLA CITATION: Onwuachi, Kwame. "Angles." *Back to the Lake: A Reader and Guide for Writers*, edited by Thomas Cooley, 5th ed., W. W. Norton, 2024, pp. 171-75.

As LONG AS THE CAMERAS WERE ROLLING, you couldn't be sure of anyone, neither judges nor fellow contestants. Every interaction was a calculation, on my part and on theirs. Reality television distorts but does not fundamentally alter character. I was still Kwame, the Kwame I was when I woke up that morning, before the cameras came in. But superimposed over this was Kwame the character, the made-for-TV version of myself. He was less likable, perhaps, but acted more comfortable than I felt. He took my own confidence and exaggerated it to the point of arrogance. He was what I assumed the producers wanted. A perfectly three-dimensional person does not make for good television.

Internally, of course, where the cameras couldn't see, I was just as terrified as I'm sure the other contestants were. I was scared to make a mistake, scared to come off as a fool or an amateur, scared to be myself. To cope, as we all did, I had a strategy, one I'd honed for years: pack all that fear, all that self-doubt, all that weakness, tight into a box, close it, padlock it, and then put my head down and work. Don the mask of indifference and get on with it.

As for the other contestants, whether it was Jeremy Ford, who ultimately won the show, or Amar Santana, or anyone else, there was a similar dynamic at work. The characters we played for the cameras were heightened or flattened or distorted versions of our true selves. There was a real and a real plus. Jeremy *was* a laid-back dude, just not quite as laid back as he appeared. Amar *was* exuberant, though perhaps a bit more vivacious before the cameras. Isaac Toups really was a good ol' country boy from Louisiana, but he wasn't nearly as folksy after we wrapped. Each of us had a role to play, and as the show went on, by unspoken agreement with each other and the production team, we became our characters more and more.

And yet, I realized, this wasn't anything new, not to me and not to any other minority. In some ways I had prepared my whole life for reality television. Ever since I was born, I had been made aware that the world saw me in one way, thanks to the color of my skin, regardless of how I saw myself. This was a lesson learned on the streets of the Bronx and in the dining rooms of Baton Rouge and in the kitchens of Per Se and EMP. I would not survive if I didn't know how to play that game, to hustle to get ahead, to write my own story, and to manipulate, to the extent that I could, how I was seen.

But as I was coming to realize, that was only half of the battle. The other, and perhaps the more important part, was how I saw myself. When I closed my eyes, when the cameras were off, when there was no one but myself, who was I then, what Kwame did I want to be? The thing about filming *Top Chef* is that the production company basically quarantines you. Televisions are unplugged, cell phones confiscated, and computers removed. You're in a terrarium, unaware of the world outside.

For relief, I used to sneak out the service elevator of the hotel and wander around the streets. In Los Angeles, where we spent time at the beginning of the season, I walked up and down Hollywood Boulevard. What a bizarre feeling it was, as if I lived in another dimension than the people in their cars or streaming out of the gym or spilling out of bars. Who was real and who wasn't, I couldn't tell. Without cameras around, it felt like everything was a waste of time. Without cameras around, I struggled to know how to just be Kwame. It was unsettling. On those almost-delirious nocturnal wanderings—the only time I was alone for months—it occurred to me that perhaps it was precisely because I didn't know who I was when no one was watching that I sought the spotlight so hard, spending those early mornings in the green room at *Chopped*, fantasizing about becoming a star. When I got back to the hotel, I felt relief not only at not being caught, but also at returning to being seen, stepping back into a character I knew by heart.

You can read about flash-backs on p. 118. When I first got a call from a casting director asking whether I wanted to apply to be on *Top Chef*, I was conflicted. A few years earlier Liz Bacelar, who had been so supportive at Coterie, had set me up with a producer of hers. We were at Liz's weekend house upstate. I made a meal as elegant as the setting: Brussels sprouts petal salad, port-glazed quail with corn velouté, golden cauliflower polenta. The producer, a middle-aged white woman, loved the meal, putting her spoon to the side as she sucked down the velouté. As we sat around surrounded by empty plates, I expectantly awaited her judgment: Was I ready for TV?   7

"The dinner was amazing, absolutely amazing," she began. "It's clear you know how to cook." I waited as she paused for an uncomfortably long time, searching, it seemed, for what to say next. "The problem is, Kwame, and I hate to say it, but America isn't ready for a black chef who makes this kind of food."   8

"What kind?" I asked.   9

"Fine dining: velouté. What the world wants to see is a black chef making black food, you know. Fried chicken and corn-bread and collards."   10

And there it was, finally spoken aloud. I wasn't mad at this woman; she seemed apologetic enough. But as the evening stumbled on, now painfully awkward, I pondered my choice. Fame and maybe fortune dangled before me, but the cost would be my conforming to ignorant stereotypes of what a black chef "should" be. Or I could stay on my own path, applying all the technique I had gleaned to make the best food I knew how. Success, or at least exposure, was less certain. Just before she left, the producer handed me her card and told me to get in touch if I ever changed my mind. I thanked her, never changed my mind, and never called. If the price for being on TV was to become a caricature, I'd rather remain uncast. But because my first restaurant, the Shaw Bijou, was set to open that October in Washington, D.C., I needed all the help I could get. Win or lose, as long as I didn't bomb out in the first episode, *Top Chef* would hugely boost my exposure. As one of my partners put it, "Any press is good press," and so I agreed to appear on *Top Chef*.   11

A lot of chefs will tell you they grew up loving cooking shows. Julia Child. Jacques 12 Pépin. Ina Garten. I grew up loving cooking shows too, but those gentle chefs weren't for me. No, for as long as I can remember it has been the hard-core competitions, the shows that treated cooking as a blood sport (and along the way somehow made sous-viding pork loin seem heroic) that I loved. *Iron Chef* was my jam. By the time I was eight, the original Japanese version had just begun airing in America. I followed the epic battles of crustaceans and butternut squash like it was March Madness, year round. When my mom was out for her catering gigs at night, as she often was, I stayed home . . . sitting too close to the television tuned to Food Network. Everything about the show was amazing.

The whole thing was so over-the-top, it was like catnip for a food-obsessed young 13 boy. I followed the chefs as they moved with single-minded purpose under the bright lights of their kitchen stadium, heedless of the cameras shoved in their faces. They were so fearless, unhesitatingly wrenching octopuses from their tanks and twisting lobsters' bodies in two. Then it was a fury of chopping and blending, sautéing and flambéing. These Japanese men (and they were all men) in their shiny clothing and tall hats were my Power Rangers, my personal superheroes.

Sometimes I got so inspired, I headed into the kitchen, pulling down from their 14 high shelves my mother's pots, bowls, and sheet pans, grabbing from the pantry whatever ingredients I could find and from the refrigerator whatever I could reach. I imitated the techniques I saw on television, albeit with the skill of an eight-year-old. Not infrequently my mother came home late at night to a complete mess of a kitchen with me curled up asleep on the floor. To her credit, she never once yelled at me. She just scooped me up, dusted the flour from my clothes, and put me to bed.

In some circles there's still a stigma attached to reality television, a belief that 15 there are real chefs and TV chefs. The former climb up the ranks, unseen and unheard, in other people's kitchens. They pay their dues slowly and come to fame after years of toil, if at all. The latter, on the other hand, find fame first and figure out the particulars afterward. There are risks to both approaches, but by 2013 reality TV was clearly one of the best ways to build a brand.

With the Shaw Bijou, I was planning to open the most ambitious restaurant D.C. 16 had ever seen. Nonetheless, the highest position I had ever held in a restaurant was only as a line cook at EMP. I didn't have a fancy knife roll, packed with hard carbon steel, to unfurl on set. By this time, I had precisely two knives: a chef's knife and a tourné knife. The rest of my money back then went to rent. Now, if you know one thing about *Top Chef* you know the line delivered by Padma Lakshmi to the unlucky bastard being kicked off: "Pack your knives and go." I had heard it a hundred times as a viewer but hoped I would never hear it as a contestant. If I did, however, I at least needed knives to pack. As a parting gift before I went off to California to start filming that June, Kelly, one of my partners at the Shaw Bijou, handed me a thick roll of bills. "That's for you to get camera ready," he said with a grin. It was like some scene out of *Pretty Woman.* I took the cash and went on a shopping spree at Korin, a high-end Japanese knife shop in Tribeca. A good knife can run more than a grand, so after I bought my set I had only a few hundred dollars left over. Such was the pitiable state of my savings that I used the last of the money to finally replace my glasses, which I had worn crooked for years.

I got eliminated on the thirteenth episode. The elimination challenge was to create a   17 fast casual restaurant concept. The six of us were paired with six of the already elimi-nated contestants to act as our sous chefs. Marjorie Meek-Bradley, who won the Quickfire challenge, had earned the right to dictate the pairs. Since she saw me as a danger, she paired me with Philip Frankland Lee, who was as close to a villain as the season had. Philip and I didn't get along. In fact, no one got along with him. You can see it on the show; it wasn't clever editing. He was just a guy who refused to take responsibility for anything. But to be fair, it wasn't his fault I went home. It was mine.

> **Vivid details (p. 120) are effective seasoning for any description in a narrative.**

My restaurant concept was a bite-sized chicken-and-waffles stand called   18 Waffle Me. The idea was that you could customize your waffle from whole wheat to coriander to sweet potato, customize the level of spiciness on the chicken from mild to fiery, and you could add your own condiments. I'd had thirteen episodes to find my gimmick; now it was time to cash in. We were all in the same boat: Jeremy, a dude, did Taco Dudes. Isaac played up his Creole roots and did a gumbo shop called Gumbo for Y'all; I, the only black contestant, did chicken-and-waffles. It crossed my mind, of course, that I might be playing into age-old stereotypes of black folks' food. But fast-casual concepts have to be easy to grasp and delicious. There is nothing more comforting when done right than chicken and waffles. I was confident I'd walk away with the win.

Alas, I stumbled, fatally. Frozen waffles were my downfall. I get it now. I had two   19 things to make, the chicken and the waffles. The chicken I nailed, but as all the judges said, the waffles were a problem. I had planned to do my own and had asked the producers to procure a waffle iron for the challenge. This was according to the rules, but they hadn't gotten it until halfway through. By that time I had already made do with the frozen Eggo waffles I had bought as a contingency on our shop-ping run the day before. I knew it would be an issue, but I was hoping that griddling them with butter and ancho chili powder and adding a maple jus would be enough customization to compensate. I mean, maple jus, for Christ's sake.

I knew I was in trouble at the judges' table when Padma said, "I want to know how   20 you made your waffles." I waffled, naturally. I said I had griddled them in butter, but then, realizing that there was no way out, admitted I hadn't made them; they were frozen. Tom Colicchio fixed me with his blue eyes, and I could feel his dismayed incre-dulity bearing down on me. Padma gave me one of her sad, disappointed looks. Adam Fleischman, the guest judge and founder of Umami Burger, did a double-take.

After the challenge segment ended, we all headed into the stew room, where 21 contestants waited—fueled by ample booze—to learn our fates. I had a feeling I was going home, and I had plenty of time to rehearse what I wanted to say when Padma asked me to pack my knives. There were two things I wanted to be sure of. First, it was important to me to act with dignity in the last moments. Getting kicked off *Top Chef* is like a public execution. These were my last moments, the last image viewers might ever see of me, so I wanted to comport myself with grace. Second, I wanted to say something to Tom. I had never let on that I had worked at Craft, that I knew him from back in the day. That would be my final reveal.

In the end it was between Jeremy and his undercooked pork belly and me, with 22 my premade waffles. I felt exactly as uncomfortable as I appeared on TV, shifting from foot to foot with no idea what to do with my face or where to look.

When at last Padma spoke the words I had dreaded for so long, I turned to Jer- 23 emy for a hug. I had seen enough eliminations to know the rituals expected of us. I approached the judges' tables, said my piece to Tom, and headed out the door. And that was it. The bubble burst immediately and not without relief. After a brief exit interview, the mother of one of the PAs drove me to the elimination house.

Because there's such a long gap between filming and airing, eliminated contes- 24 tants are kept quarantined together in a house until the season finale is filmed. There was not much we could do but stew in a mixture of boredom and depression. During those blurry days and nights between elimination and the final, a week or so later, I thought a lot about what had happened. The show wouldn't air for months, and I wondered how I would be presented. I wondered how it would change my life. Would I be a hero or a villain? A celebrity or a failure? In the meantime, I had a restaurant to open. Once filming ended, I returned to D.C., to try to figure out who I was as a chef without a camera in my face. ◆

FOR CLOSE READING

1. Kwame Onwuachi says he agreed to appear on reality television in order to publicize the opening of his new restaurant. Why was he otherwise reluctant to do so?

2. To cope with the stress of being a contestant on *Top Chef*, Onwuachi followed a strategy he had "honed for years" (2). What was that strategy, and how did he develop it? How and how well did this "dynamic" work for him, according to his account of being on the show (3)?

3. In Onwuachi's struggle to become a celebrity chef—or rather, a celebrity *and* a chef—why is playing a part, or learning to manipulate how he is seen, "only half of the battle" (5)? What's the other half? Why is it "perhaps the more important part" (5)?

4. After being eliminated from *Top Chef*, Onwuachi wonders whether he will be perceived as "a hero or a villain," as "a celebrity or a failure" (24). If the author's **PURPOSE** in "Angles" is to tell his own side of the story, how well does he succeed in presenting himself to the reader in a favorable light? Explain.

STRATEGIES AND STRUCTURES

1. In a **MEMOIR** the writer looks back at the person they once were, often with **IRONIC** effect—as when Onwuachi says, "I was confident I would walk away with the win" (18). But was he truly confident during the entire experience of being filmed on *Top Chef*? Point out other places in "Angles" where the **NARRATOR** appears to be different from the character that was filmed for the show. How do these different **POINTS OF VIEW** contribute to (or take away from) the narrative's effectiveness?

2. In paragraphs 7–10, Onwuachi tells the story of what happened "a few years earlier" when he prepared a meal for a television producer. How does this change in **CHRONOLOGICAL ORDER** set the stage for the next episode in the story, in which the narrator ends up buying new glasses before setting off to California to compete on *Top Chef*?

3. Where else in his narrative does Onwuachi tell a story within a story? What do these minor episodes contribute, collectively, to the overall **PLOT** of the narrative?

4. A narrative about striving for celebrity, "Angles" might be seen as the opposite of a success story—except for the ending. How does Onwuachi save himself—if not his "reality" television self—from shame and defeat in paragraphs 21–24?

5. The linear nature of most narratives means they have a clear beginning, middle, and end. But might the ending of Onwuachi's story as a television celebrity serve as a new beginning for his continuing story of being a chef and restaurateur? Explain.

6. *Other Methods.* What aspects of reality television does Onwuachi find particularly distasteful and unnerving? Point to specific passages where he **DESCRIBES** them in greatest detail. What do these **DETAILS** contribute to the rest of his narrative?

THINKING ABOUT LANGUAGE

1. As described by Onwuachi in paragraph 1 and at other times in his essay, would you say that "reality" television is a misnomer? Why or why not? Why is it called that if it "distorts" a contestant's "character" and "superimposes" a "made-for TV version" (1)?

2. During the filming of *Top Chef*, Onwuachi felt that he was living in a "terrarium" (5). What are the **CONNOTATIONS** of this word as he uses it? of "quarantines" in the same paragraph? What would Onwuachi's **PURPOSE** be in choosing such words?

3. "Pack your knives and go" (16). With these "dreaded" words, host Padma Lakshmi informs *Top Chef* contestants that they have been eliminated (23). What's so significant about knives in Onwuachi's narrative?

4. Onwuachi refers to the set of *Iron Chef* as a "kitchen stadium" (13). Explain the dual implications of this term and the following terms: "stew room" (21), "public execution" (21), "hug...rituals" (23), "elimination house" (23).

5. Just before he is eliminated from the competition, Onwuachi says, "I waffled" (20). How appropriate is this PUN to the TONE and circumstances of his narrative? Incidentally, were the judges right to penalize him for not working totally "from scratch"? Look up the root meaning of this phrase as applied to cooking.

FOR WRITING

1. Suppose you accepted the challenge "to create a fast casual restaurant concept" (17). In a paragraph or two, outline what it would be and how the cuisine would reflect your "character."

2. In collaboration with a friend or classmate, write a brief PROPOSAL for a reality television show that you would like to produce. DESCRIBE some of the key people you would have on the show and what they would be doing. Include a brief scenario of a sample episode.

3. Write a narrative of three to five paragraphs about a childhood ambition that you (or someone you know) later tried to realize as an adult. Be careful to establish a consistent POINT OF VIEW, whether that of a child or of an adult looking back—or both, as Onwuachi does.

4. "A perfectly three-dimensional person," says Onwuachi, "does not make for good television" (1). In a well-reasoned ARGUMENT, challenge or defend this THESIS. Cite a number of specific shows and characters—and your own experience in watching them.

8 | Description

We went fishing the first morning. I felt the same damp moss covering the worms in the bait can, and saw the dragonfly alight on the tip of my rod as it hovered a few inches from the surface of the water.

—E. B. WHITE

In his classic essay "Once More to the Lake," E. B. White writes about going out early one morning in a rowboat with his young son:

> We went fishing the first morning. I felt the same damp moss covering the worms in the bait can, and saw the dragonfly alight on the tip of my rod as it hovered a few inches from the surface of the water. It was the arrival of this fly that convinced me beyond any doubt that everything was as it always had been, that the years were a mirage and that there had been no years. The small waves were the same, chucking the rowboat under the chin as we fished at anchor, and the boat was the same boat, the same color green and the ribs broken in the same places, and under the floorboards the same freshwater leavings and débris—the dead helgramite, the wisps of moss, the rusty discarded fishhook, the dried blood from yesterday's catch. We stared silently at the tips of our rods, at the dragonflies that came and went. I lowered the tip of mine into the water, tentatively, pensively dislodging the fly, which darted two feet away, poised, darted two feet back, and came to rest again a little farther up the rod.

You can picture the tranquil scene because this passage is a little masterpiece of descriptive writing with every detail carefully chosen to create the illusion of time standing still.

Telling How Something Looks, Sounds, Feels, Smells, or Tastes

Description appeals to the senses: it gives the reader something to look at ("the green boat," "the rusty fishhook," "the hovering dragonfly"); to feel ("the damp moss"); to hear ("the small waves"); and to smell ("the drying fish blood"). As for taste, White appeals more directly to that sense later in his essay, when he and his young son go to a nearby farmhouse for dinner ("fried chicken," "apple pie"). What does a subject look, sound, feel, smell, or taste like? These are the fundamental questions that descriptive writing addresses.

In this chapter we'll see where to fish for the specific physical DETAILS you need for building a good description. We'll examine how to select ones that best suit your PURPOSE and AUDIENCE and how to organize and present those details so they contribute directly to the DOMINANT IMPRESSION you want your description to make. Then we'll review the critical points to watch for as you read back over and revise your description, as well as common errors to avoid as you edit.

Why Do We Describe?

Description is a means of showing rather than telling. We describe something—a person, a lake, a memory, a chemical reaction—so that the reader can experience it directly as we do. Description makes anything we write less **ABSTRACT**, or general, and more **CONCRETE**, referring to specific characteristics we can perceive directly with the senses. White, for example, could simply tell us that time seemed to stand still on the lake, but he makes the abstract idea of timelessness much easier to grasp by showing us such specific details as the dragonfly hovering (like time) at the end of his fishing rod.

Composing a Description

Your reader will find almost anything you write easier to comprehend if you describe your subject in vivid detail. However, in a personal essay about your grandmother's cooking, you will probably describe things differently than in a lab report on dissecting a shark.

There are basically two ways of describing something—objectively or subjectively. An **OBJECTIVE DESCRIPTION** presents its subject impartially. Its purpose is to provide the reader with information, as in this description of a watershed in southern Alaska:

Paragraphs 10 and 11 of Edward Lee's essay give an objective description of the West Virginia hot dog and pepperoni roll (p. 228).

> Duck Creek is a small anadromous [running upriver from the sea] fish stream located in an old outwash channel of the Mendenhall Glacier in the center of the most populated residential area of Alaska's capital, Juneau. Duck Creek supports a large over-wintering population of coho salmon juveniles that migrate into the stream each fall from the estuarine wetlands.
>
> —ENVIRONMENTAL PROTECTION AGENCY,
> "Make Way for Salmon in Duck Creek"

The EPA's description is objective not only because it uses precise scientific terms ("anadromous," "estuarine") but because it is made up entirely of factual information about its subject—the size and age of the creek, where it's located, the type of fish that inhabit it, and so on.

USING DESCRIPTION IN AN ABSTRACT

The following is an abstract (or summary) that accompanied an article on the physical properties of tension springs in the *American Journal of Physics*. It uses description extensively:

A slinky is an example of a tension spring: in an un-stretched state a slinky is collapsed, with turns touching; and a finite tension is required to separate the turns from this state. If a slinky is suspended from its top and stretched under gravity and then released, the bottom of the slinky does not begin to fall until the top section of the slinky, which collapses turn by turn from the top, collides with the bottom. The total collapse time tc (typically ~0:3s for real slinkies) corresponds to the time required for a wave front to propagate down the slinky to communicate the release of the top end. We present a modification to an existing model for a falling tension spring [Calkin, Am. J. Phys. 61, 261–264 (1993)] and apply it to data from filmed drops of two real slinkies. The modification of the model is the inclusion of a finite time for collapse of the turns of the slinky behind the collapse front propagating down the slinky during the fall.

—R. C. CROSS and M. S. WHEATLAND,
"Modeling a Falling Slinky"

Description of a slinky in an "un-stretched state"

Description of a slinky in a "stretched" state

Description of a falling slinky released "under gravity"

Description of a falling (or fallen) slinky in its final state

Description is so basic to report writing that one type of summary, the *descriptive abstract*, attempts to capture an entire experiment or project in a single phrase. (The other two types are the *informative abstract*, like the one above, and the *proposal abstract*, which describes what a study is going to do.) Here, for example, are some brief descriptive abstracts that appeared along with the slinky study:

Video-based spatial portraits of a nonlinear vibrating string [Am. J. Phys. 80, 862 (2012)]

Exact non-Hookean scaling of cylindrically bent elastic sheets and the large-amplitude pendulum [Am. J. Phys. 79, 657 (2011)]

Strain in layered zinc blende and wurtzite semiconductor structures grown along arbitrary crystallographic directions [Am. J. Phys. 78, 589 (2010)]

A **SUBJECTIVE DESCRIPTION** provides information, too. But it also conveys the writer's personal response to the subject being described, as in this piece from an article about a visit to the Iowa State Fair:

> And then I wound up at an open-air brick pavilion for the llama judging. Llamas are gentle, dignified beasts, and here were four of them being shown by teenagers. The animals' military bearing, heads high, their stately gait, their dark soulful eyes—they looked as if they'd walked straight out of *Dr. Doolittle.* . . . According to a poster, they are raised for "fiber, showing, carting, guardians and companionship." One girl stood by her llama and blew gently on its nose, and he looked lovingly into her eyes. A sort of conversation. If every teenager had his or her own llama, this would be a very different country.
>
> —GARRISON KEILLOR, "A Sunday at the State Fair"

This is a subjective description: the author feels or imagines that the llamas are dignified and loving—and that one is having a "conversation" with his keeper.

However, many of the other details in Keillor's description—including the physical location, the number of llamas on display, the exhibitors' age, and the exact words of the poster explaining what llamas are raised for—are rendered objectively. Most descriptions include a combination of subjective and objective elements. And even the most subjective description should be grounded in the concrete physical features of the person, place, or thing it describes—which is why E. B. White's description of the lake is so effective.

Not all subjective descriptions are so successful, however. Consider the following passage, which refers to the same lake described by White. According to the region's official website, the area around that lake is "famous for its sparkling scenic streams and chain of seven lakes, its panoramic views of fields, hills and woodlands, its inviting towns and villages."

Sparkling streams, panoramic views. Sounds like a nice place. The same could be said, however, of a large car wash with a picture window in the waiting room. This subjective description offers no definite impression of the lakes because it merely names abstract qualities. So does the rest of the site, which says that the region is "picturesque and welcoming," providing "a retreat for peace and tranquility."

Picturesqueness and tranquility are difficult to smell or taste. The problem with this tourist-brochure prose is that it tells the reader what to think *about* the place; it doesn't capture the place itself. The fundamental purpose of descriptive writing, whether subjective or objective, is to re-create the characteristics of its subject so vividly that readers perceive it with their own eyes and ears—and mind.

Good descriptive writing is built on concrete particulars rather than abstract qualities. So don't just write, "It was a dark and stormy night"; try to make your reader see, hear, and feel the wind and rain.

Edward Lee switches to a subjective description of the West Virginia hot dog when he writes, "once you take a bite, you know you've touched the nirvana of hot dogs" (p. 227, par. 9).

Thinking about Purpose and Audience

Your purpose in describing something—whether to picture your subject as objectively as possible, capture it in a certain light or mood, express your feelings about it, persuade the reader to visit (or avoid) it, or merely to amuse the reader—will determine the details you'll want to include in your description. For example, the official Belgrade Lakes website promotes family vacations; like E. B. White, it dwells on the beauty, peace, and tranquility of the place, as well as the fishing and boating. Its slogan—"Where Memories Last a Lifetime"—might almost have been drawn from White's description. The website, however, aims to persuade the general public to visit the area and thus emphasizes "wholesome family fun" and "activities for all ages"—and leaves out the unsightly debris ("dead insects," "rusty fishhook," and "dried blood") in White's description.

Suppose you were describing Belgrade Lakes to friends who were thinking of going there and wanted information about the area. You might express your feelings toward the region, but your main purpose would be to inform your friends about it—as objectively as possible—so they could decide for themselves whether or not to go. You'd talk about the peace and quiet, of course; but you'd also include other aspects of the scene, such as the pebble beaches, touristy shops, and local restaurants—not to mention the night crawlers at the Pickled Trout Saloon.

PINE ISLAND, BELGRADE LAKES, ME.   51807

A postcard of Belgrade Lakes, Maine, c. 1914.

Instead of selecting details that presented only one aspect of the place, you'd choose representative details that painted a fair and accurate picture of what it was like as a whole.

Whatever your purpose, you need to take into account how much your audience already knows (or doesn't know) about the subject you're describing. For example, if you want to describe to someone who has never been on your campus the mad rush that takes place there when classes change, you're going to have to fill in the background for them: the main quad with its sun worshipers in bathing suits, the brick-and-stone classroom buildings on either side, the library looming at one end. In contrast, if you were to describe the same scene to fellow students who already know the territory well, you could skip the background description and go directly to the mob scene.

> Louise Erdrich's wide general audience is unlikely to know the Ojibwe language, so she carefully describes its history, structure, syntax, and the meaning of many words (p. 231).

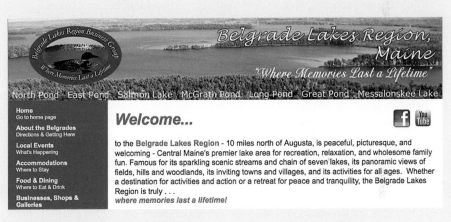

Three ways of looking at a lake. This website—like the old postcard on p. 184 and E. B. White's classic essay "Once More to the Lake" on p. 215—describes the Belgrade Lakes region of central Maine. All three capture the peace and tranquility of the place; but the two earlier "views" emphasize its remote, timeless qualities, while the website, which can be updated at any time, presents the region as an easily accessible tourist destination.

Generating Ideas: Asking How Something Looks, Sounds, Feels, Smells, or Tastes

Good descriptive writing begins and ends with the concrete physical characteristics of whatever you are describing. To gather those details, you need to ask what your subject looks, sounds, feels, smells, or tastes like. Methods like BRAINSTORMING and LISTING can help you probe for ideas as you run through each of the five senses.

Another resource for answering these questions is direct experience and observation. Even if you're describing a familiar subject—a lake you've often visited, your old neighborhood, a person from your hometown—go back to the source. Try to see your subject objectively as well as subjectively; take notes—much like a reporter on assignment or a traveler in an unfamiliar land.

Judith Ortiz Cofer (p. 209) draws on memories of her grandmother's house in Puerto Rico.

When you can't return to the source, you may have to rely on memory. Let's say you're describing your hometown but can't get back there to have a look around. In your mind's eye, pick a spot—maybe the main shopping street or town square. Ask yourself what it looked like, and try to see specific details: colors, landmarks, signs on the buildings, people's faces. Then try to recall sounds, smell, textures—and what you did there.

Sometimes you can release a flood of memories of things past by examining a material object associated with them, like the grandmother's old clothes in this example:

The saris, new and old, were stacked high in two columns of brilliant colors. . . .

As a child visiting India, I couldn't understand how she could sleep comfortably on sweltering nights wrapped in six yards of material, or how she could still look impeccable when she woke. . . .

The stains and scents were evidence of the life she had lived, so different from my own. Hers was a life of cooking curries, wearing turmeric, walking barefoot on dusty floors, participating in Hindu rituals, drinking milky coffee after afternoon naps, and clutching loved ones fiercely to her chest.

—Priya Chandrasekaran, "Cutting Our Grandmothers' Saris"

Even when you have no physical remnants of the past to cling to, the pond of memory is a rich reservoir of sensations for the writer of description. The process of recovering its treasures is a little like fishing: think back to the spots you knew well; bait the hook by asking the key sensory questions; weigh and measure everything you pull up. As you revise, you can always throw back the ones you can't use. Just the right details for capturing your subject on paper *are* lurking there, often in plain sight—or just below the surface. Your job as a writer is to bring those details to light, with the life still in them.

Organizing and Drafting a Description

Once you've gathered the specific details that capture your subject, you're ready to begin organizing and drafting. As you write, let those details speak for themselves. Give enough of them so that readers can picture your subject clearly, but select and arrange particular details so they contribute to the dominant impression you want your description to make. Maintain a consistent vantage point throughout, and, of course, let readers know the point of your description. The templates on p. 189 can help you get started with your draft.

STATING YOUR POINT

Description is seldom an end in itself. Ordinarily, we describe something to someone for a reason. Why are you describing a particular fishing trip, or a woman hanging out laundry, or bloody footprints in the snow? You need to let the reader know. It can be by way of an explicit THESIS statement: "This description of Washington's ragged army at Yorktown shows that the American general faced many of the same challenges as Napoleon in the winter battle for Moscow, but Washington turned them to his advantage."

Or your reasons can be stated less formally. Consider the following description of the streets of Havana, Cuba:

> Everywhere I went, there were men and women waiting in lines. There were lines to get water, lines to have cheap cigarette lighters repaired, lines to get into the city's lone merchandise store in Miramar where a simple sledgehammer costs fifty-six dollars. At the nationalized health care clinics, the lines wrapped away for blocks; the somber aged, the ill, the expectant young mothers, all waiting, patiently enduring.
>
> —RANDY WAYNE WHITE, *Last Flight Out*

The point of this description is to show that everyday life is difficult in a communist system where everything is centrally controlled, including simple consumer goods and services. Randy Wayne White is writing a descriptive travel essay, however, not a political treatise. So he states his point informally, as a personal observation: "A few weeks of living like that, and I myself—not the bravest of men—would consider worming into an inner tube and paddling north."

You don't always have to make a formal statement of your thesis— "Communism failed as a social system because it failed as an economic system"—when you write a description. But you *should* include a clear statement, however informal, of why you're writing the description.

See how E. B. White does this with a single chilling phrase (p. 220, par. 13).

BEGINNING WITH DETAILS

One way *not* to begin a description is to leap immediately into a general statement of the impression your subject is supposed to make. Instead, you should begin with specific descriptive details, and let your readers form that impression for themselves. The following statement, for example, wouldn't be the best way to begin a description of the Grand Canyon: "As the abyss yawned at my feet, I was swept away by the beauty and majesty of the scene."

Few writers have taught us this lesson better than Ernest Hemingway, whose stories and newspaper correspondence are full of powerful descriptions that show us a place or an object long before telling us what to think of it. Here's Hemingway's rendition of a father and son fishing on a lake early in the morning:

> They were seated in the boat, Nick in the stern, his father rowing. The sun was coming up over the hills. A bass jumped, making a circle in the water. Nick trailed his hand in the water. It felt warm in the sharp chill of the morning.
>
> —ERNEST HEMINGWAY, "Indian Camp"

The boy in the story, Nick Adams, has just witnessed a grisly suicide. As Nick and his father row home, the boy is soothed by the morning sun, the leaping bass, and the warm water. Nature seems kind, and the story ends with a direct statement of what the boy thinks about the scene: "In the early morning on the lake sitting in the stern of the boat with his father rowing, he felt quite sure that he would never die."

The purpose of Hemingway's description is to show us the boy's naivete. However, Hemingway doesn't deliver the punch line—the boy's stated feeling about the scene—until he has given us the physical details on which that feeling is based. You could organize an entire descriptive essay on this model: detail ("early morning"), detail ("lake"), detail ("boat"), detail ("boy sitting in the stern"), detail ("father rowing")—dominant impression ("boy feeling 'quite sure that he would never die'").

CREATING A DOMINANT IMPRESSION

Some descriptions, such as Hemingway's, appeal to several different senses—the sight of the rising sun, the sound of the jumping bass, the touch of the warm water in the chilled air. Don't feel that you have to give equal attention to all five senses when writing a description; but whether you appeal to a single sense or several, make sure they all contribute to the dominant impression you want your description to make on the reader.

"Cutting Our Grandmothers' Saris" (p. 223) conveys a dominant impression of nostalgia and pride in one's heritage.

The dominant impression conveyed by Hemingway's description of fishing on the lake, for example, is that of peace and calm—the soothing tranquility of nature. Now, suppose you were to describe a similar morning scene on a freshwater lake in a rowboat. But instead of bass and sunrise, you call the reader's attention to an ominous dark cloud in the distance, drawing nearer. The wind rises. The reader hears a nasty grating sound as the little boat scrapes over a sunken log in the fast-flowing current. Instead of gently chucking the boat under the chin, the waves, now grown to whitecaps, flip it over with a crash, throwing you into the icy water. Nature, the reader concludes as you disappear beneath the surface, is not kind. The reader is left with the dominant impression of danger because you've chosen to build your description on particular details (mostly sounds) that contribute to a sense of danger and foreboding.

TEMPLATES FOR DRAFTING

When you begin to draft a description, you need to identify who or what you're describing, say what your subject looks or feels like, and indicate the traits you plan to focus on—moves fundamental to any description. See how Judith Ortiz Cofer makes such moves in the beginning of her essay in this chapter:

> My grandmother's house is like a chambered nautilus; it has many rooms, yet it is not a mansion. Its proportions are small and its design simple.
>
> —JUDITH ORTIZ COFER, "More Room"

Ortiz Cofer identifies what she's describing ("my grandmother's house"); says something about what her subject looks like ("a chambered nautilus"); and indicates some of the physical characteristics (the proportions and design of the house) that she plans to discuss. Here is one more example from this chapter:

> Inside an H Mart complex, there will be some kind of food court, an appliance shop, and a pharmacy. Usually, there's a beauty counter where you can buy Korean makeup and skin-care products. . . . There will usually be a pseudo-French bakery with weak coffee, bubble tea, and an array of glowing pastries that always look much better than they taste.
>
> —MICHELLE ZAUNER, *Crying in H Mart*

The following templates can help you make some of these basic moves in your own writing. But don't take these as formulas where you just fill in the blanks. There are no shortcuts to good writing, but these templates can serve as starting points.

▶ X is like a _____; it has _____, _____, and _____.

▶ He / She / They looked a lot like _____, except for _____, which _____.

▶ From the perspective of _____, however, X could be described as _____.

▶ In some ways, namely _____, X resembles _____; but in other ways, X is more like _____.

▶ X is not at all like _____ because _____.

▶ Mainly because of _____ and _____, X gives the impression of being _____.

▶ From this description of X, you can see that _____.

ARRANGING THE DETAILS

While the events in a NARRATIVE are usually organized chronologically, the physical elements of a description are often organized according to their location.

So as you begin to get your description drafted, the physical configuration of whatever you're describing will often suggest a pattern of organization to you. Michelle Zauner's description (p. 245, paragraph 12) of the food court at her local H Mart, for example, starts by observing that the complex "has two stories; the grocery is on the first floor and the food court is above it." Then her description moves "upstairs" to focus on the stalls in the food court.

Descriptions of places are often organized, like Zauner's, by physical direction—around the block, north to south, front to back, left to right, inside to outside, near to far, top to bottom. If you were describing a room, for example, you might use an outside-to-inside order, starting with the door (don't forget the knob and other details). Next you could present the main physical features of the room as they might appear to someone just crossing the threshold (oak floors, high ceilings, ancient fireplace). Then would come the grand piano, the candle on a stand, the old lady mending a tapestry—just as these objects might appear to a person entering the room and adjusting their eyes to the light.

"More Room" (p. 209) traces several generations of a family by describing home renovations.

A particular object can suggest an order of arrangement as well as a place can. For instance, in the following description of a tarpon, addressed to a blind boy who has just caught it, the order of the details follows the anatomy of the fish.

> He's mostly silver, but the silver is somehow made up of *all* the colors. . . . He has all these big scales, like armor all over his body. They're silver too, and when he moves they sparkle. He has a strong body and a large powerful tail. He has big round eyes, bigger than a quarter, and a lower jaw that sticks out past the upper one and is very tough. His belly is almost white and his back is a gunmetal gray. When he jumped he came out of the water about six feet, and his scales caught the sun and flashed it all over the place.
> —CHEROKEE PAUL MCDONALD, "A View from the Bridge"

McDonald's description begins and ends with the colors of the fish, its most noticeable feature (to a sighted person) in the glinting sun. Most of his description, however, is organized according to the parts of the subject itself, moving from the body of the tarpon as a whole to the tail, eyes, belly, and back. From whole to parts, or parts to whole: you can go either way when constructing a description. Or you can describe the most important or unusual features of your subject first, then the least important or most familiar ones (or vice versa). Or you can go from the largest to smallest, or from specific to general, or from concrete to abstract—or vice versa—so long as you maintain a consistent VANTAGE POINT.

MAINTAINING A VANTAGE POINT

In McDonald's essay, as the title suggests, the vantage point is from the bridge. Here's the beginning of the essay, before the boy catches the tarpon:

> I was coming up on the little bridge in the Rio Vista neighborhood of Fort Lauderdale, deepening my stride and breathing to negotiate the slight incline without altering my pace. And then, as I neared the crest, I saw the kid.
>
> He was a lumpy little guy with baggy shorts, a faded T-shirt, and heavy sweat socks falling down over old sneakers.
>
> Partially covering his shaggy blond hair was one of those blue baseball caps with gold braid on the bill and a sailfish patch sewn onto the peak. Covering his eyes and part of his face was a pair of those stupid-looking '50s-style wrap-around sunglasses.

Like his description of the tarpon, McDonald's description of the boy moves from the whole ("lumpy little guy in shorts and T-shirt") to the parts ("hair," "cap," "patch," "eyes," "face," "glasses"). It also presents those details in the order in which the observer perceives them from his vantage point. That is, the reader of McDonald's essay sees only what the runner sees as he comes over the bridge. For example, at this point in his description, the runner doesn't yet know that the boy is blind, which is why he's wearing "stupid-looking . . . sunglasses." As you compose a description, be careful to maintain a consistent vantage point, as McDonald does.

USING FIGURATIVE LANGUAGE

Because descriptive writing presents the reader with images of the physical world, it lends itself to the use of figurative language. The three FIGURES OF SPEECH you are most likely to use in composing a description are similes, metaphors, and personification.

SIMILES tell the reader what something looks, sounds, or feels like, using "like" (or "as if"):

> She was like a pretty kite that floated above my head.
>
> —MAYA ANGELOU

In "Pressing" (p. 196), Charlotte Keathley uses similes to bring her subject to life.

> Suspicion climbed all over her face like a kitten, but not so playfully.
>
> —RAYMOND CHANDLER

Two policemen . . . were leaning into a third woman as if she were a stalled car.
—T. C. Boyle, *Talk, Talk*

METAPHORS make implicit comparisons, without "like" (or "as if"):

All the world's a stage.

You are my sunshine.

Papa was a rolling stone.

Metaphors have two parts: the subject of the description ("world," "you," "Papa"); and the thing ("stage," "sunshine," "rolling stone") to which that subject is being implicitly compared.

PERSONIFICATION assigns human qualities to inanimate objects, as in this poetic description of a mirror:

I am silver and exact.
I have no preconceptions.
Whatever I see I swallow immediately
Just as it is, unmisted by love or dislike.

—Sylvia Plath, "Mirror"

USING OTHER METHODS

Molly Case incorporates a historical NARRATIVE while describing her experience as a young nurse (p. 237).

When you describe something, you will often have reason to use other methods as well—to DEFINE it, analyze what CAUSED it, and so on. Especially if you're describing something that is unfamiliar to the reader—as in this description of a cemetery in rural El Salvador—consider COMPARING it with something the reader already knows about:

Plunged like daggers to the ground are the crosses, mainly a fabulous aqua color, though some are bleached white and some are unpainted. . . . It looks like the aftermath of a piñata party, with crepe-paper chains strewn like leis about the necks of the gravestone markers, plastic red roses wreathed at the feet, errant scraps of yellow paper and transparent cellophane trapped between the blades of grass.

—Beth Kephart, *Still Love in Strange Places*

"Daggers" imply violence, but the cemetery in this colorful description is far from somber. The dominant impression is a sense of festive disorder, as Kephart compares this strange scene to a more familiar one in which children have just left a party after hammering a piñata to release the candy and toys inside.

EDITING FOR COMMON ERRORS IN DESCRIPTIONS

Descriptive writing is often marred by qualifiers that are overly abstract, empty, or out of sequence. The following guidelines will help you check your description for these common problems and correct them.

Check your details to see if you can make them more concrete

▶ Great Pond is so ~~amazing and incredible~~ <u>clear and deep</u> that floating on it in a boat seems like floating on air.

"Amazing" and "incredible" are abstract terms; "clear" and "deep" describe the water in more concrete terms.

▶ The Belgrade region is famous for its ~~charming views~~ <u>panoramic views of fields, hills, and woodlands</u>.

The corrected sentence says more precisely what makes the views charming.

Check for filler words like "very," "quite," "really," and "truly"

▶ The lake was ~~very much secluded~~ <u>fifteen miles from the nearest village</u>.

If you've used several adjectives together, be sure they're in the right order

Subjective adjectives (those that reflect the writer's own opinion) go before objective adjectives (those that are strictly factual): write "fabulous four-door Chevrolet" rather than "four-door fabulous Chevrolet." Beyond that, adjectives usually go in the following order: number, size, shape, age, color, nationality.

▶ The streets of Havana were lined with many ~~old, big~~ <u>big, old</u> American cars.

Check for common usage errors

"Unique," "perfect"

Don't use "more" or "most," "less" or "least," or "very" before words like "unique," "equal," "perfect," or "infinite." Either something is unique or it isn't.

▶ Their house at the lake was a ~~very~~ unique place.

"Awesome," "cool"

Not only are these modifiers too abstract, but they're also overused. You probably should delete them or replace them with fresher words no matter how grand the scene you're describing.

▶ The Mississippi is ~~an awesome river~~ <u>the most extensive river system in the United States</u>.

Reading a Description with a Critical Eye

Once you have drafted a description, try it out on someone else to get a sense of what's working and what needs revision. Then read it over yourself with a critical eye. Here are some questions to keep in mind when reviewing descriptive writing.

PURPOSE AND AUDIENCE. Who is the intended audience, and why will they be reading this description? Does it tell them everything they'll need to know, or will they need more background information?

THE POINT. Does the description have a clear point? Is that point set out in a thesis statement? If not, should it be?

SPECIFIC DETAILS. Are there enough details to give the reader a vivid impression of the subject? To which senses in particular does the description appeal—sight? sound? smell? touch? taste?

OBJECTIVE OR SUBJECTIVE? Are the details of the description presented objectively, subjectively, or does it contain elements of both? Is the degree of objectivity appropriate for the overall purpose and audience of the description? If not, how can it be made more informative and less emotional (or vice versa)?

DOMINANT IMPRESSION. What overall impression does the description give? Does every detail contribute directly to that impression? What additional details would make the dominant impression clearer or stronger? Do any details detract from that impression?

ORGANIZATION. How are the details of the description presented—by moving from part to whole? whole to part? north to south? most important to least important? some other way?

VANTAGE POINT. From what perspective are the various aspects of the subject described? Near and intimate? Far and detached? Somewhere in between? Is that perspective maintained consistently throughout the description?

FIGURATIVE LANGUAGE. What figures of speech, such as metaphors, similes, or personification, does the description use? Are they appropriate for this purpose and audience?

OTHER METHODS. Has the description been expanded to include other methods of development—for example, by analyzing what caused something, or by comparing its attributes to those of other things with which the reader may already be familiar?

COMMON ERRORS. Check the adjective phrases in the description ("very beautiful," "quite tall," "really awesome"). Eliminate empty qualifiers like "very," "quite," and "really"; and substitute concrete terms for abstract ones. Instead of "awesome," for example, use the physical quality that inspired the awe ("clear," "bright," "deep").

Student Example

Charlotte Keathley wrote "Pressing" for her English class in personal writing at Yale University. The title refers to Keathley's memories of pressing apple cider as a child in rural Vermont. "Many writers recall only visual memories," observes Keathley's teacher, the writer Anne Fadiman, who recommended the essay for the Norton Writer's Prize. Keathley's description, however, is "multisensory," evoking what the child sees, hears, touches, smells, and, of course, tastes as the juice flows from the press and the conversation swirls around her. The result, as Fadiman says, is "a moving and evocative distillation of a rural ritual, like Sue Hubbell's writing on beekeeping or E. B. White's accounts of farm life."

Pressing

We moved to Vermont on the far side of my memory—my father, my mother, my older sister, me. We moved though we did not know anyone there, though we owned no appropriate coats. A few years later, when I was six or seven, Amy and Brad invited us over to press cider. They lived in an apple orchard just up the road with their daughter, Katherine, who was about a year younger than me. We went, and then we went back, each Friday in fall, for several years.

I had a strange passion at that age for repetitive, manual, seasonal work. I liked stacking wood, pitting cherries, shelling peas. I liked raking the cut grass into mounds and carting it to the goat pen in the wheelbarrow. I imagined the changing seasons looking over my shoulder, watching me work. I gained purpose, and thereby pleasure, from the piqued awareness of frost and rot that stacking, pitting, shelling, and raking provided. Still, these tasks and their associated joys felt like dregs, shards, brief shouts, in comparison to the pleasure of cider pressing.

On fewer than five acres, Amy and Brad grew almost a hundred varieties of apples. Many of the more obscure varieties had been planted or grafted by the country doctor who'd lived there before. He used to see his patients in the lofty, unpainted barn. When Amy and Brad bought the place they found a medical examination table among the ladders, crates, and cider press. Like the doctor, Brad had a day job. He was a chef. Like the doctor, Brad kept the orchard up, too: pruning, harvesting, pressing.

They fed us dinner in the house before pressing began, and dessert in the barn when the work was nearly done. Our hosts ate rather briskly, and they ate very, very well. All three of these habits, I now know, were picked up during years of eating on their feet in restaurant kitchens. On pressing nights, they would serve us less fussy versions of the food they'd learned to cook in Paris, Nantucket, Oaxaca. I learned to love several foods at that table—leeks, quince jam, smoked bluefish, Brussels sprouts done hot and fast in duck fat. I learned that you don't need a knife to cut a good biscuit. Simply hold the top and give it a little twist, like opening a jar, and the biscuit will split. There was a restless, dogged pace to those meals. All the food was laid on the table at once. We passed and poured with gusto, as there was rarely a table-cloth to worry about mussing. There was no clock-checking, as I recall, but there might as well have been foot-tapping, with the anxi-ety that the gesture evokes. Our work awaited. Periodically, this yawn of awareness would come over me. A light was on in the barn. Our boots were lined up in the hall.

On pressing nights, when the massive doors were flung wide, the barn seemed to have no front at all, like an open dollhouse. Approaching through the grass I could see the tall cider press at the center of the floor and all the other machinery at its hem. The whole tableau was brightly visible, and I see in pressing nights the initial stirrings of a joy which has stayed with me ever since, and which I imagine most people share: the pleasure of being able to see into well-lit rooms at night. Nested within this blinking realization a sec-ond one, equally universal: that yellow light is so much better than light of any other color. We stepped inside.

5   The scene of the pressing: a large, well-lit barn

I was often assigned to work the washtub, the first step of the pressing process. I understood my task there to be ritualistic, almost social. I would touch each apple that passed through, pay it heed, brush some debris from its cheek before tossing it into the mouth of the grinder. The water remembered each plunge of my hand. At any moment, it stirred in response to not only my most recent touch, but also to my contact two or three touches ago. This impelled the apples to rotate, so that each one was always turning its other face to me, the mass renewing itself constantly, like a crowd does. Seemingly red apples would show their green faces; seemingly green apples would show their pink spots; rotting apples blithely revealed their brown and puckering sides.

6

Next was the grinder, a long-necked, clamorous machine that chewed apples into pulp. We became so habituated to the machine's spluttering and stammering that a far greater disturbance was caused when the grinder was temporarily flicked off. First, in the initial

7   In the writer's memory, the machinery sounds almost human

trough of silence, someone would finish a sentence they had begun while the machine was still roaring, and they would finish it at unadjusted volume. *I mean, I hardly KNOW HER . . . Well, it'll TURN TO VINEGAR.* This was followed by a second silence, not really silent at all. There was the slow purr of a wasp trying to fight off the anesthesia of the season. There was the *plit, plit . . . plit* of water dashing against the sides of the washtub. And then there were all of us—we could not help ourselves—going *mmmmm.*

The doctor had left behind an old rack-and-cloth press, a tall machine that hazily resembled a printing press. One flat plane, above, strains to meet another, below. Layers of pulp, cloths, and racks are arranged between the two. I was not tall enough to lend my own hands to this task, but I liked to watch my father and Brad composing the layers: first, a bundle of pulp, swaddled neatly in cloth, then a "rack," a ridged rectangle of wood. They'd lay another bundle, another board, until the two men were tottering on their toes to fold the final cloth. There is a thrill to the rack-and-cloth press which those round, barrel-shaped presses lack. It has something to do with the evocation of the printing press: the folding, laying, stacking, the pleasing dissonance between paper and cider.

Near the base of the machine was a lever, low enough for me to reach. When pumped this lever would cause the top part of the press to descend, compacting the bundles of pulp. The cider would drip and collect in a stainless-steel drum below the press. When pressing proper was under way, we often suspended our work at other stations and gathered around the lever, taking turns sighing along with the joints of the machine. This process of composing and compressing the layers was repeated half-a-dozen times throughout the night. Among the sweeping, unidirectional arcs of the evening—the widening distance from dinner, the narrowing distance to dessert, the tightening shoulders, the tiring feet—was the cyclical drama of the press going up and up, then down.

We would taste the cider from a tap on the side of the stainless-steel drum. We'd fill small, fluttery paper cups that wilted if we didn't

For the young writer, the cider press evokes the production of written words via a printing press

Again, the machinery seems to echo what the people are doing

8

9

10

A traditional rack-and-cloth cider press with alternating layers.

down the cider immediately. When Brad wasn't looking, Katherine and I would fill our mouths directly. The tap was around thigh height, so drinking from it involved turning my head nearly upside down. Cider would spray into both my mouth and nose, and my senses of taste and smell would converge. There was the easy sweetness of September cider, composed of just a few early varieties of apples. There was the more acidic, considered taste of October cider, pleasantly brackish. And finally, there was the dozy flavor of late-November cider, which swept all the varieties of the preceding months under its opaque, milky-bronze cloak. Here, again, the rack-and-cloth press was so much better than a barrel-press because with

Smell and taste blend together in the writer's memory of the different "seasons" of harvest

the rack-and-cloth, you got to see the cider flowing twice: first, down the layers of the press, like strands of beads, and a second time, jetting from the spigot.

When the drum was full, my father and Brad would hoist it, 11 and as they did that would undergo that strange Frankensteining that comes from carrying a heavy load through a crowded space. Moving toward the bottling table, they would each develop a wild bulge in their eyes, a staggering gait, a tendency to bark at children underfoot. We would draw back and let them pass—our fathers, transformed!— and when they passed we could hear the cider swinging inside the drum: *gung, gung, gung.*

This brings us to the bottling table, long and orderly, its pha- 12 lanxes of plastic bottles lined up in rows. There were the small pint-sized bottles, which would be sold at market the next day in a metal tub filled with ice. There were the slim half gallons, probably my favorite size, which felt substantial but could still be lifted, one in each hand, with ease. And there were the stout full gallons. We would freeze a half dozen of these in the fall and thaw them throughout the winter. They reminded me of animals putting on winter weight, or fur, or down. We affixed a warning label to each bottle: *This product has not been pasteurized and may contain harmful bacteria that may cause serious illness in young children, the elderly, pregnant women, and people with weakened immune systems.* Of course, I did not count myself as a "young child"—what young child would?

Farthest from the rowdy grinder, the bottling table was the 13 only place in the barn where you could speak with any subtlety. I was not at ease with the roving exchanges that unfolded there. I preferred the noisy right-hand side of the barn, where you spoke only when you felt very strongly about what you had to say. The lurching, blurting talk of that region was more consistent with the way that children conducted conversation.

It was the women, my mother and Amy, who gravitated toward 14 the bottling table. In the final years of pressing, my sister began pre-

> Describes the end point of the cider pressing process

senting the earliest pangs of puberty. She and her friends would spend hours murmuring on the other side of her bedroom door. She would cry after getting a haircut or new pair of glasses. She would grow very loud, then very quiet, at the breakfast table. This transformation was largely illegible to me then, but I would have occasional flashes of lucidity when I observed her inclining toward the bottling table. I remember standing at the washtub, atop an apple crate, and seeing her across the room. She stood beyond the press, at the bottling table with my mother and Amy. I saw their lips moving, but could not hear them over the noise of the grinder. I did not so much wish I could hear them as I wished they would *stop*.

Near the end of the night, Amy would bring out a pie and place 15 it on the side table next to the grinder. Conversation would abandon the bottling table as the social weight of the room heaved toward the raucous right-hand side. This reminded me of a ship turning, the deck slanting, everyone reeling starboard. This feeling of barn as ship aligned with the evening's broader sense of nauticality. Damp air shaded with sugar is surprisingly similar to damp air shaded with salt. The slices of pie ticked away like a clock.

COMPARES a change in the tenor of the evening to the turning of a ship

At this point in the evening, Katherine and I liked to slip out, 16 away from the machines and into the orchard. The air there had a lighter touch. It seemed to place a cool hand on your forehead, like checking for a fever. From the back door of the barn, the orchard sloped downhill. I imagine the varieties of apples, though this cannot be true, descending into obscurity with the grade of the hill. At the top, nearest the barn, house, and road, lay a few rows of the varieties that everyone knows: Empire, McIntosh, Granny Smith, Golden Delicious. Down a little further, I picture the varieties of middling fame: Paula Red, Cortland, Northern Spy, Macoun. At the bottom of the hill, I imagine the varieties I've rarely seen since: Ida Red, Gravenstein, Tydeman's Red, Grenadine. Here, low, among the last of the mosquitoes, I imagine Roxbury Russet, Golden Russet, Windfall Golden, Early Joe. Of these obscure breeds, I loved the

gangly-named ones most of all: Belle de Boskoop, Hubbardton None-
such, and Tompkin's Country King, Esopus Spitzenberg, Sops-n-
Wine, and Westfield Seek-No-Further.

At night this heterogeneity was indistinguishable. We learned   17
that in the near-dark, your color vision goes before your vision goes
entirely. The difference between red and green collapses, as do the
differences between brown and tawny and yolk-yellow. In the near-
dark, you cannot tell if an apple is inchworm-green on the outside but
cuticle-pink when you bite into it. You wouldn't know if it's red on the
outside but enamel-white, or cream-colored, or honey-colored when
you bite into it. It all flattens into black. I remember holding an apple
up to the slate-gray sky. I could make out the fruit's contours: the
character of the curves, the apostrophe of the stem, the serration of
the leaf. A few minutes later, I could make out the hourglass of the
apple's core, but I could not see its color.

The same rules of vision applied to our bodies. Inside the barn,   18
Katherine and I would have occasional spells of shyness toward each
other. In the orchard, we studied each other's silhouettes. We adopted
a low-toned and affected mode of speech. We did not use contractions, and we did not use each other's names.

DIALOGUE shows
the girls' sudden ·····•
formality with
each other

"How are you."   19

"I am well."   20

"See this apple."   21

"Yes, I see."   22

If we ran off into the orchard, we discovered, we would remain 23
visible as long as we were standing. But if one of us dropped to the
ground and lay flat, it was nearly impossible for the other to find her.
I remember running off once, away from Katherine, and flattening
myself thus. While waiting for her to find me, I remember turning
my head, seeing the barn uphill, and encountering a thought. I
thought less often in language then, but the thought might be translated as "of course, of course." It might be translated into any number of repeated words: "well, well," "there, there," "hear, hear,"

"now, now." Any phrase brimming with self-evidence by way of doubling would do. I knew that inside the barn, Brad had uncoiled the hose and was washing the grinder, the floor, the press. The parents were having a drink. They were mixing cider with beer. It was always a dark beer, a porter, black as compost. As it mixed with the black beer, the chiffony cider turned to a silhouette in each glass. I have often felt that the difference between how you drink as a child and how you drink as an adult is less a matter of the drinks hardening than it is a matter of drinking at the ends of things—the work day, the pressing night, the year.

And then, people were calling out to me. I confess, I do not know if I am in my memory now or not, but I can hear them calling my name in the dark. I had flattened myself so well that the game was off. This dimension of hide-and-seek, that the game breaks if played too well, always fascinated me as a child. Katherine had run up to the barn and gotten one of our mothers, who was now standing at the back door, the light behind her. While playing hide-and-seek, I often thought that my breathing would give me away, so I'd try to smother the sound with my palm. The figure at the back door called; I did not respond. She was cupping her hands around her mouth, and I was covering my mouth with mine.

24

Ending suggests that remembering is perhaps a form of hide-and-seek

Analyzing a Student Description

In "Pressing," Charlotte Keathley draws on rhetorical strategies and techniques that good writers use all the time when they compose a description. The following questions, in addition to focusing on distinctive aspects of Keathley's text, will help you identify those common strategies and techniques so you can adapt them to your own writing. These examples will also help prepare you for the analytical questions—on content, structure, and language—that you'll find after the other selections in this chapter, along with suggestions for writing on related topics.

FOR CLOSE READING

1. As a child, Charlotte Keathley "had a strange passion...for repetitive, manual, seasonal work" (2). Why did this type of work appeal to her? Of all the tasks she remembers, which one was by far the most pleasing? Why?

2. How did the five-acre parcel owned by young Keathley's neighbors come to have so many unusual varieties of apples growing on it? Did the orchard actually contain all the varieties mentioned in paragraph 16, or might Keathley be imagining some of them? Explain.

3. The owners of the orchard did not make a living from growing apples and pressing cider. Why did they do it anyway? Point to specific paragraphs that convey possible reasons.

4. What was Keathley's job in the pressing barn? What part did she and Katherine play in the entire enterprise of gathering on "pressing nights" to produce the cider (5)?

5. "I thought less often in language then" (23). What might Keathley mean by this statement? As evidenced by her childhood memories, how *did* she think back then? Explain.

STRATEGIES AND STRUCTURES

1. "The whole tableau was brightly visible" (5). Keathley begins her description by focusing on what she sees in the barn while "approaching through the grass" (5). How and how well does this part of her essay set the stage for what follows? Does the vantage point change as the essay progresses?

2. Sight is important in Keathley's description, but so are the other senses. Point out specific passages throughout her essay where she captures other sensations as well, particularly sounds—and particularly the sounds of words.

3. Although Keathley's essay is an example of SUBJECTIVE DESCRIPTION, it successfully conveys the process of pressing cider. What else does it convey that an OBJECTIVE DESCRIPTION cannot?

4. The "old rack-and-cloth" cider press that Keathley describes in paragraph 8 reminds her of a printing press. How does this observation help set up the rest of her description? What is Keathley pressing from her memories here besides cider? Explain.

5. *Other Methods.* In addition to describing her cider-pressing memories from childhood, Keathley is analyzing the process of producing a farm product; it's a mini PROCESS ANALYSIS. What are some of the main steps in the process, and how and where does Keathley use them to help organize her essay?

THINKING ABOUT LANGUAGE

1. With the big doors open, the pressing barn, as Keathley remembers it, seemed to have no front, "like an open dollhouse" (5). Is the SIMILE appropriate? Find several other places where she uses this figure of speech.

2. How and how well does Keathley capture the change in volume of the conversation that she remembers in paragraph 7? Where else in her essay does she use the rhythms of the machinery to describe the rhythms of speech?

3. "I loved the gangly-named ones most of all," says Keathley of the rare varieties of apples that she identifies in paragraph 16. How do you suppose these varieties got such names, and what's "gangly" about them?

4. Keathley describes her job at the washtub as "ritualistic" (6). How might this term be applied to her entire description?

FOR WRITING

1. In a paragraph or two, describe the facade of a building or shop in such a way as to imply the nature of the business, or other activity, that takes place inside. Be sure to consider the DOMINANT IMPRESSION you want to convey.

2. In a few paragraphs, describe some repetitive task you performed as a child. Try to capture how it made you feel and what you learned from it.

3. Visit a farm, restaurant, or other small, family-owned business. Interview some of the people who work there, and then write a descriptive essay explaining not only how the business operates but also what each person does and how they feel about their jobs. Include lots of CONCRETE sensory details.

4. Write a descriptive essay that captures your earliest memories—or your memory of a particularly important or formative experience from childhood. Describe the physical setting and what you saw there, including colors and shapes, and other people; but also try to recapture particular sounds, smells, tastes, and textures.

A Social Media Post

Whether on social media or elsewhere, when you describe something, such as a house you once lived in, you tell what it looks (or looked) like and what characteristics distinguish it from other, similar objects. When the photographer and writer Tony Mendoza returned to his family's beach house in Cuba, it was "in perfect condition, just as I remembered it when I left in 1960"—unlike the house next door, which "had disappeared." The porch of the house overlooked the ocean, and there Mendoza found a young woman playing a saxophone, a "scene" he describes, along with a photo of the view from the porch, in a posting on his *Facebook* page. Like any form of memoir, Mendoza's posting is a means of capturing the past in writing (and images) in present consciousness: "I tried to remember those days when I was young and full of energy and very happy to be spending summers in our house by the sea."

[FOR WRITING]⋯⋯⋯⋯⋯⋯⋯⋯⋯⋯⋯⋯⋯⋯⋯⋯⋯⋯⋯⋯⋯⋯⋯⋯⋯⋯⋯

Write a 150-word description of the scene pictured in the photograph on the facing page. Consider which senses the photo appeals to and the dominant impression it creates. Also describe how the composition of the photo contributes to the dominant impression.

Tony Mendoza
April 24

I went back to Cuba in 1996. One of the first places I wanted to see was my family's house in Varadero Beach. As I got closer to the house, I expected to see a ruin, since all the houses I was walking by were gutted. I was pleasantly surprised—the house was in perfect condition, just as I remembered it when I left in 1960. It was a government guest house, impeccably maintained. The front door was open. I walked in and found a young woman, her eyes closed, playing a saxophone on the porch which overlooked the ocean. I liked the scene, it reminded me of a movie I had seen, and I liked the melody. When she opened her eyes, she found me there. We talked. I told her I grew up in the house, and she offered to give me a tour. Afterward, I went down to the water, put all my clothes in a pile with the camera on top, and went in. I was in the water for a while, looking towards the house. The house next to ours, the del Valle house, had disappeared. In its place there was a large pile of sand. I tried to remember those days when I was young and full of energy and very happy to be spending summers in our house by the sea.

SUGGESTIONS FOR WRITING

1. Go to the website of Belgrade Lakes, Maine, or some other resort that you have never visited. Based on the information you find on the website, write a vivid one-paragraph description of the place that you could text to a friend or relative in order to persuade them to join you there.

2. Old photographs can bring the past to life in present consciousness at the same time that they remind us of the gulf between past and present. In 150–200 words, describe what you see in the scene pictured on the old postcard on p. 184—or in some other old photo that you can find or remember. Be sure to describe the image itself in some detail as well as the **DOMINANT IMPRESSION**—such as familiarity or nostalgia—that it conveys. If it reminds you of another place or time, or a visit you once made, describe that scene as well.

3. Using the slinky example on p. 182 as a model, write an **ABSTRACT** of an experiment you've worked on or read about. Alternatively, write a **PROPOSAL** for an experiment that you would like to see conducted.

4. Write a description of these video frames illustrating the physicists' methodology as expressed in the abstract on p. 182. Be sure to explain how what you see in the frames corresponds to what the physicists report in their written description of the experiment.

5. "It seemed to me, as I kept remembering all this," writes E. B. White in "Once More to the Lake," "that those times and those summers had been infinitely precious and worth saving" (p. 218, paragraph 9). Using description as your basic method, write a **POSITION PAPER** about the value (or lack thereof) of remembering and writing about the past, whether in the form of a personal **MEMOIR** or as a more general history.

JUDITH ORTIZ COFER

More Room

Judith Ortiz Cofer (1952–2016) was born in Puerto Rico but moved to Paterson, New Jersey, as a small child. Though Ortiz Cofer grew up and went to school on the "mainland," she often returned for extended visits to her grandmother's home in Puerto Rico, the *casa de Mamá* described in "More Room." This bicultural experience was the basis of much of Ortiz Cofer's creative nonfiction writing, including *The Latin Deli* (1993), a collection of essays and poems that won the Anisfield-Wolf Book Award; the young-adult novel *The Meaning of Consuelo* (2003), which won the Americas Award; and *The Cruel Country* (2015), a memoir. Ortiz Cofer was the Regents' and Franklin Professor of English and Creative Writing, Emerita, at the University of Georgia.

"More Room" is from *Silent Dancing* (1990), a memoir of Ortiz Cofer's childhood in Puerto Rico and New Jersey. In this description, Ortiz Cofer shows how a few remembered details can bring back an entire scene and the people in it.

M Y GRANDMOTHER'S HOUSE is like a chambered nautilus; it has many rooms, yet it is not a mansion. Its proportions are small and its design simple. It is a house that has grown organically, according to the needs of its inhabitants. To all of us in the family it is known as *la casa de Mamá*. It is the place of our origin; the stage for our memories and dreams of Island life.

I remember how in my childhood it sat on stilts; this was before it had a downstairs. It rested on its perch like a great blue bird, not a flying sort of bird, more like

MLA CITATION: Ortiz Cofer, Judith. "More Room." *Back to the Lake: A Reader and Guide for Writers*, edited by Thomas Cooley, 5th ed., W. W. Norton, 2024, pp. 209–12.

Descriptive writing often includes figures of speech (p. 191). a nesting hen, but with spread wings. Grandfather had built it soon after their marriage. He was a painter and housebuilder by trade, a poet and meditative man by nature. As each of their eight children were born, new rooms were added. After a few years, the paint did not exactly match, nor the materials, so that there was a chronology to it, like the rings of a tree, and Mamá could tell you the history of each room in her *casa*, and thus the genealogy of the family along with it.

Her room is the heart of the house. Though I have seen it recently, and both woman and room have diminished in size, changed by the new perspective of my eyes, now capable of looking over countertops and tall beds, it is not this picture I carry in my memory of Mamá's *casa*. Instead, I see her room as a queen's chamber where a small woman loomed large, a throne-room with a massive four-poster bed in its center which stood taller than a child's head. It was on this bed where her own children had been born that the smallest grandchildren were allowed to take naps in the afternoons; here too was where Mamá secluded herself to dispense private advice to her daughters, sitting on the edge of the bed, looking down at whoever sat on the rocker where generations of babies had been sung to sleep. To me she looked like a wise empress right out of the fairy tales I was addicted to reading. 3

Though the room was dominated by the mahogany four-poster, it also contained all of Mamá's symbols of power. On her dresser instead of cosmetics there were jars filled with herbs: *yerba buena, yerba mala,*[1] the making of purgatives and teas to which we were all subjected during childhood crises. She had a steaming cup for anyone who could not, or would not, get up to face life on any given day. If the acrid aftertaste of her cures for malingering did not get you out of bed, then it was time to call *el doctor*. 4

And there was the monstrous chifforobe she kept locked with a little golden key she did not hide. This was a test of her dominion over us; though my cousins and I wanted a look inside that massive wardrobe more than anything, we never reached for that little key lying on top of her Bible on the dresser. This was also where she placed her earrings and rosary at night. God's word was her security system. This chifforobe was the place where I imagined she kept jewels, satin slippers, and elegant sequined, silk gowns of heartbreaking fineness. I lusted after those imaginary costumes. I had heard that Mamá had been a great beauty in her youth, and the belle of many balls. My cousins had other ideas as to what she kept in that wooden vault: its secret could be money (Mamá did not hand cash to strangers, banks were out of the question, so there were stories that her mattress was stuffed with dollar bills, and that she buried coins in jars in her garden under rosebushes, or kept them in her inviolate chifforobe); there might be that legendary gun salvaged from the Spanish-American 5

---

1 *Yerba buena, yerba mala:* Literally "good herb, bad herb." *Yerba buena* usually refers to a species of mint. *Yerba mala* could be almost any "bad herb."

conflict over the Island. We went wild over suspected treasures that we made up simply because children have to fill locked trunks with something wonderful.

On the wall above the bed hung a heavy silver crucifix. Christ's agonized head 6 hung directly over Mamá's pillow. I avoided looking at this weapon suspended over where her head would lay; and on the rare occasions when I was allowed to sleep on that bed, I scooted down to the safe middle of the mattress, where her body's impression took me in like a mother's lap. Having taken care of the obligatory religious decoration with a crucifix, Mamá covered the other walls with objects sent to her over the years by her children in the States. *Los Nueva Yores*[2] were represented by, among other things, a postcard of Niagara Falls from her son Hernán, postmarked, Buffalo, N.Y. In a conspicuous gold frame hung a large color photograph of her daughter Nena, her husband and their five children at the entrance to Disneyland in California. From us she had gotten a black lace fan. Father had brought it to her from a tour of duty with the Navy in Europe (on Sundays she would remove it from its hook on the wall to fan herself at mass). Each year more items were added as the family grew and dispersed, and every object in the room had a story attached to it, a *cuento* which Mamá would bestow on anyone who received the privilege of a day alone with her. It was almost worth pretending to be sick, though the bitter herb purgatives of the body were a big price to pay for the spirit revivals of her story-telling.

> Cofer's specific and vivid details contribute to the dominant impression of her subject (p. 188).

Mamá slept alone on her large bed, except for the times when a sick grandchild 7 warranted the privilege, or when a heartbroken daughter came home in need of more than herbal teas. In the family there is a story about how this came to be.

When one of the daughters, my mother or one of her sisters, tells the *cuento* of 8 how Mamá came to own her nights, it is usually preceded by the qualifications that Papá's exile from his wife's room was not a result of animosity between the couple, but that the act had been Mamá's famous bloodless coup for her personal freedom. Papá was the benevolent dictator of her body and her life who had had to be banished from her bed so that Mamá could better serve her family. Before the telling, we had to agree that the old man was not to blame. We all recognized that in the family Papá was as an *alma de Dios*, a saintly, soft-spoken presence whose main pleasures in life, such as writing poetry and reading the Spanish large-type editions of *Reader's Digest*, always took place outside the vortex of Mamá's crowded realm. It was not his fault, after all, that every year or so he planted a baby-seed in Mamá's fertile body, keeping her from leading the active life she needed and desired. He loved her and the babies. Papá composed odes and lyrics to celebrate births and anniversaries and hired musicians to accompany him in singing them to his family

2 *Los Nueva Yores*: The New Yorkers.

and friends at extravagant pig-roasts he threw yearly. Mamá and the oldest girls worked for days preparing the food. Papá sat for hours in his painter's shed, also his study and library, composing the songs. At these celebrations he was also known to give long speeches in praise of God, his fecund wife, and his beloved island. As a middle child, my mother remembers these occasions as a time when the women sat in the kitchen and lamented their burdens, while the men feasted out in the patio, their rum-thickened voices rising in song and praise for each other, *compañeros* all.

It was after the birth of her eighth child, after she had lost three at birth or in   9 infancy, that Mamá made her decision. They say that Mamá had had a special way of letting her husband know that they were expecting, one that had begun when, at the beginning of their marriage, he had built her a house too confining for her taste. So, when she discovered her first pregnancy, she supposedly drew plans for another room, which he dutifully executed. Every time a child was due, she would demand, *more space, more space.* Papá acceded to her wishes, child after child, since he had learned early that Mamá's renowned temper was a thing that grew like a monster along with a new belly. In this way Mamá got the house that she wanted, but with each child she lost in heart and energy. She had knowledge of her body and perceived that if she had any more children, her dreams and her plans would have to be permanently forgotten, because she would be a chronically ill woman, like Flora with her twelve children: asthma, no teeth, in bed more than on her feet.

And so, after my youngest uncle was born, she asked Papá to build a large room at   10 the back of the house. He did so in joyful anticipation. Mamá had asked him special things this time: shelves on the walls, a private entrance. He thought that she meant this room to be a nursery where several children could sleep. He thought it was a wonderful idea. He painted it his favorite color, sky blue, and made large windows looking out over a green hill and the church spires beyond. But nothing happened. Mamá's belly did not grow, yet she seemed in a frenzy of activity over the house. Finally, an anxious Papá approached his wife to tell her that the new room was finished and ready to be occupied. And Mamá, they say, replied: "Good, it's for *you.*"

And so it was that Mamá discovered the only means of birth control available to   11 a Catholic woman of her time: sacrifice. She gave up the comfort of Papá's sexual love for something she deemed greater: the right to own and control her body, so that she might live to meet her grandchildren—me among them—so that she could give more of herself to the ones already there, so that she could be more than a channel for other lives, so that even now that time has robbed her of the elasticity of her body and of her amazing reservoir of energy, she still emanates the kind of joy that can only be achieved by living according to the dictates of one's own heart. ◆

FOR CLOSE READING

1. Mamá's house in Puerto Rico was originally built on stilts to avoid high water, but the lower level got filled in when the family needed more room. How are these old additions different from the new room with shelves and a private entrance?

2. Mamá exercises "dominion" over all her house and family (5). Her grandchildren ascribe her power to the exotic items in her room, but what is its true source?

3. If Mamá is the "queen" (3) of the house and household that Judith Ortiz Cofer describes, what are some of Papá's other roles (besides that of prince consort)?

4. When Papá is preparing birthday odes and patriotic hymns to be sung at annual feasts, what are the women in the family doing? Why? What is Ortiz Cofer suggesting about the culture she is describing?

5. Why does Mamá need more room? What point is Ortiz Cofer making about women and families by describing her grandmother's home?

STRATEGIES AND STRUCTURES

1. Ortiz Cofer describes the outside of her grandmother's house before moving to the inside. What specific details does she focus on?

2. Once she moves inside the house, which room does Ortiz Cofer single out? Why? What does it contribute to her description of Mamá?

3. Ortiz Cofer is not so much describing her grandmother's house as it is today as the house as it exists in her memory. How is this "picture" (3) different from present-day reality? How does Ortiz Cofer capture the place from the viewpoint of a child?

4. Mamá's house is full of her "symbols of power" (4). What DOMINANT IMPRESSION of the place and of her do they help convey to the reader?

5. *Other Methods.* In addition to describing the author's grandmother's house and its contents, "More Room" tells the story of a "bloodless coup" (8). What coup? How does this NARRATIVE relate to Ortiz Cofer's description of the house?

THINKING ABOUT LANGUAGE

1. *Cuento* (6, 8) is the Spanish word for "story." Why does Ortiz Cofer mention the telling of stories in her description?

2. Mamá's room, says Ortiz Cofer, is the "heart" of the house (3). What are the implications of this METAPHOR?

3. A "monstrous chifforobe" ... a "little golden key" (5); "rum-thickened voices rising in song" (8)—these descriptive details appeal to the senses of sight and sound. Point to other phrases in the essay where the author's language evokes taste and texture.

4. Ortiz Cofer opens her essay with this line: "My grandmother's house is like a chambered nautilus; it has many rooms, yet it is not a mansion" (1). This is likely an

ALLUSION to the Oliver Wendell Holmes poem "The Chambered Nautilus" (1858) and the opening of its final stanza: "Build three more stately mansions, O my soul / As the swift seasons roll!" Do some research about this poem, and then explain how the allusion—and the image of the chambered nautilus in particular—relate to Ortiz Cofer's story.

FOR WRITING

1. Write a paragraph or two in which you **COMPARE** the present-day aspects of a house, room, or other place with those of the place as you picture it in memory.

2. Write a description of a house or other place that captures the tension (or harmony) among its inhabitants by highlighting the physical features of the place.

3. "More Room" is from Ortiz Cofer's memoir *Silent Dancing*. Read more from—or even better, all of—this richly descriptive exploration of growing up in two worlds. Keep notes of your reading in a reading **JOURNAL**.

4. Along with several others in your writing class, divide *Silent Dancing* into sections and assign each person in the group a different section to read and take notes on. Discuss the book together as a group, and share all notes.

5. In collaboration with several others in your class, do some research on the work of a famous architect, such as Frank Lloyd Wright, Zaha Hadid, Denise Scott Brown, or Frank Gehry. Choose a particular building or project designed by that person, and using description extensively, write a **CRITICAL ANALYSIS** of that structure or design. Be sure to say how the major components fit together (or don't) to serve their intended purpose.

E. B. WHITE

Once More to the Lake

Elwyn Brooks White (1899–1985) was born in Mount Vernon, New York. He graduated from Cornell University in 1921 and worked as a journalist and advertising copywriter before joining the staff of the *New Yorker* in 1926. From 1938 to 1943, he also wrote a regular column for *Harper's Magazine*. White's numerous books include the children's classic *Charlotte's Web* (1952) and his update of William Strunk's 1918 *Elements of Style* (1959), a guide to writing.

Written in August 1941 on the eve of World War II, "Once More to the Lake" originally appeared in *Harper's* and helped establish White's reputation as a leading essayist of his day. The lake described here is Great Pond in south-central Maine. As White returns to this familiar scene, it seems unchanged—at first.

ONE SUMMER, along about 1904, my father rented a camp on a lake in Maine and took us all there for the month of August. We all got ringworm from some kittens and had to rub Pond's Extract on our arms and legs night and morning, and my father rolled over in a canoe with all his clothes on; but outside of that the vacation was a success and from then on none of us ever thought there was any place in the world like that lake in Maine. We returned summer after summer—always on August 1 for one month. I have since become a salt-water man, but sometimes in summer there are days when the restlessness of the tides and the fearful cold of the sea water and the incessant wind that blows across the afternoon and into the evening make me wish for the placidity of a lake in the woods. A few weeks ago this feeling got so strong I bought myself a couple of bass hooks and a spinner and returned to the lake where we used to go, for a week's fishing and to revisit old haunts.

MLA CITATION: White, E. B. "Once More to the Lake." *Back to the Lake: A Reader and Guide for Writers*, edited by Thomas Cooley, 5th ed., W. W. Norton, 2024, pp. 215–20.

I took along my son, who had never had any fresh water up his nose and who had   2
seen lily pads only from train windows. On the journey over to the lake I began to
wonder what it would be like. I wondered how the time would have marred this
unique, this holy spot—the coves and streams, the hills that the sun set behind, the
camps and the paths behind the camps. I was sure that the tarred road would have
found it out, and I wondered in what other ways it would be desolated. It is strange
how much you can remember about places like that once you allow your mind to
return into the grooves that lead back. You remember one thing, and that suddenly
reminds you of another thing. I guess I remembered clearest of all the early mornings,
when the lake was cool and motionless, remembered how the bedroom smelled of the
lumber it was made of and of the wet woods whose scent entered through the screen.
The partitions in the camp were thin and did not extend clear to the top of the rooms,
and as I was always the first up I would dress softly so as not to wake the others, and
sneak out into the sweet outdoors and start out in the canoe, keeping close along the
shore in the long shadows of the pines. I remembered being very careful never to rub
my paddle against the gunwale for fear of disturbing the stillness of the cathedral.

The lake had never been what you would call a wild lake. There were cottages   3
sprinkled around the shores, and it was in farming country although the shores of
the lake were quite heavily wooded. Some of the cottages were owned by nearby
farmers, and you would live at the shore and eat your meals at the farmhouse. That's
what our family did. But although it wasn't wild, it was a fairly large and undisturbed lake and there were places in it that, to a child at least, seemed infinitely
remote and primeval.

I was right about the tar: it led to within half a mile of the shore. But when I got   4
back there, with my boy, and we settled into a camp near a farmhouse and into the
kind of summertime I had known, I could tell that it was going to be pretty much
the same as it had been before—I knew it, lying in bed the first morning, smelling
the bedroom and hearing the boy sneak quietly out and go off along the shore in a
boat. I began to sustain the illusion that he was I, and therefore, by simple transposition, that I was my father. This sensation persisted, kept cropping up all the time
we were there. It was not an entirely new feeling, but in this setting, it grew much
stronger. I seemed to be living a dual existence. I would be in the middle of some
simple act, I would be picking up a bait box or laying down a table fork, or I would
be saying something, and suddenly it would be not I but my father who was saying
the words or making the gesture. It gave me a creepy sensation.

We went fishing the first morning. I felt the same damp moss covering the worms   5
in the bait can, and saw the dragonfly alight on the tip of my rod as it hovered a few
inches from the surface of the water. It was the arrival of this fly that convinced me
beyond any doubt that everything was as it always had been, that the years were a
mirage and that there had been no years. The small waves were the same, chucking

the rowboat under the chin as we fished at anchor, and the boat was the same boat, the same color green and the ribs broken in the same places, and under the floorboards the same freshwater leavings and débris—the dead helgramite, the wisps of moss, the rusty discarded fishhook, the dried blood from yesterday's catch. We stared silently at the tips of our rods, at the dragonflies that came and went. I lowered the tip of mine into the water, tentatively, pensively dislodging the fly, which darted two feet away, poised, darted two feet back, and came to rest again a little farther up the rod. There had been no years between the ducking of this dragonfly and the other one—the one that was part of memory. I looked at the boy, who was silently watching his fly, and it was my hands that held his rod, my eyes watching. I felt dizzy and didn't know which rod I was at the end of.

We caught two bass, hauling them in briskly as though they were mackerel, pull- 6 ing them over the side of the boat in a businesslike manner without any landing net, and stunning them with a blow on the back of the head. When we got back for a swim before lunch, the lake was exactly where we had left it, the same number of inches from the dock, and there was only the merest suggestion of a breeze. This seemed an utterly enchanted sea, this lake you could leave to its own devices for a few hours and come back to, and find that it had not stirred, this constant and trustworthy body of water. In the shallows, the dark, water-soaked sticks and twigs, smooth and old, were undulating in clusters on the bottom against the clean ribbed sand, and the track of the mussel was plain. A school of minnows swam by, each minnow with its small individual shadow, doubling the attendance, so clear and sharp in the sunlight. Some of the other campers were in swimming, along the shore, one of them with a cake of soap, and the water felt thin and clear and unsubstantial. Over the years there had been this person with the cake of soap, this cultist, and here he was. There had been no years.

Up to the farmhouse to dinner through the teeming, dusty field, the road under 7 our sneakers was only a two-track road. The middle track was missing, the one with the marks of the hooves and the splotches of dried, flaky manure. There had always been three tracks to choose from in choosing which track to walk in; now the choice was narrowed down to two. For a moment I missed terribly the middle alternative. But the way led past the tennis court, and something about the way it lay there in the sun reassured me; the tape had loosened along the backline, the alleys were green with plantains and other weeds, and the net (installed in June and removed in September) sagged in the dry noon, and the whole place steamed with midday heat and hunger and emptiness. There was a choice of pie for dessert, and one was blueberry and one was apple, and the waitresses were the same country girls, there having been no passage of time, only the illusion of it as in a dropped curtain—the waitresses were still fifteen; their hair had been washed, that was the only difference— they had been to the movies and seen the pretty girls with the clean hair.

Summertime, oh, summertime, pattern of life indelible, the fade-proof lake, the   8
woods unshatterable, the pasture with the sweetfern and the juniper forever and
ever, summer without end; this was the background, and the life along the shore
was the design, the cottages with their innocent and tranquil design, their tiny
docks with the flagpole and the American flag floating against the white clouds in
the blue sky, the little paths over the roots of the trees leading from camp to camp
and the paths leading back to the outhouses and the can of lime for sprinkling, and
at the souvenir counters at the store the miniature birch-bark canoes and the post-
cards that showed things looking a little better than they looked. This was the
American family at play, escaping the city heat, wondering whether the newcomers
in the camp at the head of the cove were "common" or "nice," wondering whether it
was true that the people who drove up for Sunday dinner at the farmhouse were
turned away because there wasn't enough chicken.

<table>
<tr><td>Don't forget
to tell the
reader why
(p. 187) you're
describing
"all this."</td></tr>
</table>

It seemed to me, as I kept remembering all this, that those times and   9
those summers had been infinitely precious and worth saving. There had
been jollity and peace and goodness. The arriving (at the beginning of
August) had been so big a business in itself, at the railway station the farm
wagon drawn up, the first smell of the pine-laden air, the first glimpse of the
smiling farmer, and the great importance of the trunks and your father's
enormous authority in such matters, and the feel of the wagon under you for the long
ten-mile haul, and at the top of the last long hill catching the first view of the lake
after eleven months of not seeing this cherished body of water. The shouts and cries
of the other campers when they saw you, and the trunks to be unpacked, to give up
their rich burden. (Arriving was less exciting nowadays, when you sneaked up in
your car and parked it under a tree near the camp and took out the bags and in five
minutes it was all over, no fuss, no loud wonderful fuss about trunks.)

Peace and goodness and jollity. The only thing that was wrong now, really, was   10
the sound of the place, an unfamiliar nervous sound of the outboard motors. This
was the note that jarred, the one thing that would sometimes break the illusion and
set the years moving. In those other summertimes all motors were inboard; and
when they were at a little distance, the noise they made was a sedative, an ingredient of summer sleep. They were one-cylinder and two-cylinder engines, and some
were make-and-break and some were jump-spark, but they all made a sleepy sound
across the lake. The one-lungers throbbed and fluttered, and the twin-cylinder ones
purred, and purred, and that was a quiet sound, too. But now the campers all had
outboards. In the daytime, in the hot mornings, these motors made a petulant, irri-
table sound; at night, in the still evening when the afterglow lit the water, they
whined about one's ears like mosquitoes. My boy loved our rented outboard, and his
great desire was to achieve single-handed mastery over it, and authority, and he
soon learned the trick of choking it a little (but not too much), and the adjustment

of the needle valve. Watching him I would remember the things you could do with the old one-cylinder engine with the heavy flywheel, how you could have it eating out of your hand if you got really close to it spiritually. Motorboats in those days didn't have clutches, and you would make a landing by shutting off the motor at the proper time and coasting in with a dead rudder. But there was a way of reversing them, if you learned the trick, by cutting the switch and putting it on again exactly on the final dying revolution of the flywheel, so that it would kick back against compression and begin reversing. Approaching a dock in a strong following breeze, it was difficult to slow up sufficiently by the ordinary coasting method, and if a boy felt he had complete mastery over his motor, he was tempted to keep it running beyond its time and then reverse it a few feet from the dock. It took a cool nerve, because if you threw the switch a twentieth of a second too soon you would catch the flywheel when it still had speed enough to go up past center, and the boat would leap ahead, charging bull-fashion at the dock.

We had a good week at the camp. The bass were biting well and the sun shone endlessly, day after day. We would be tired at night and lie down in the accumulated heat of the little bedrooms after the long hot day and the breeze would stir almost imperceptibly outside and the smell of the swamp drift in through the rusty screens. Sleep would come easily and in the morning the red squirrel would be on the roof, tapping out his gay routine. I kept remembering everything, lying in bed in the mornings—the small steamboat that had a long rounded stern like the lip of a Ubangi, and how quietly she ran on the moonlight sails, when the older boys played their mandolins and the girls sang and we ate doughnuts dipped in sugar, and how sweet the music was on the water in the shining night, and what it had felt like to think about girls then. After breakfast, we would go up to the store and the things were in the same place—the minnows in a bottle, the plugs and spinners[1] disarranged and pawed over by the youngsters from the boys' camp, the Fig Newtons and the Beeman's gum. Outside, the road was tarred and cars stood in front of the store. Inside, all was just as it had always been, except there was more Coca-Cola and not so much Moxie and root beer and birch beer and sarsaparilla. We would walk out with the bottle of pop apiece and sometimes the pop would backfire up our noses and hurt. We explored the streams, quietly, where the turtles slid off logs and dug their way into the soft bottom; and we lay on the town wharf and fed worms to the tame bass. Everywhere we went I had trouble making out which was I, the one walking at my side, the one walking in my pants.

One afternoon while we were there at that lake a thunderstorm came up. It was like the revival of an old melodrama that I had seen long ago with childish awe. The second-act climax of the drama of the electrical

See p. 188 to read about dominant impressions.

---

1 *Plugs and spinners:* Types of fishing lures.

disturbance over a lake in America has not changed in any important respect. This was the big scene, still the big scene. The whole thing was so familiar, the first feeling of oppression and heat and a general air around camp of not wanting to go very far away. In midafternoon (it was all the same) a curious darkening of the sky, and a lull in everything that had made life tick; and then the way the boats suddenly swung the other way at their moorings with the coming of a breeze out of the new quarter, and the premonitory rumble. Then the kettle drum, then the snare, then the bass drum and cymbals, then crackling light against the dark, and the gods grinning and licking their chops in the hills. Afterward the calm, the rain steadily rustling in the calm lake, the return of light and hope and spirits, and the campers running out in joy and relief to go swimming in the rain, their bright cries perpetuating the deathless joke about how they were getting simply drenched, and the children screaming with delight at the new sensation of bathing in the rain, and the joke about getting drenched linking the generations in a strong indestructible chain. And the comedian who waded in carrying an umbrella.

When the others went swimming, my son said he was going in, too. He pulled his dripping trunks from the line where they had hung all through the shower and wrung them out. Languidly, and with no thought of going in, I watched him, his hard little body, skinny and bare, saw him wince slightly as he pulled up around his vitals the small, soggy, icy garment. As he buckled the swollen belt, suddenly my groin felt the chill of death. ◆   13

FOR CLOSE READING

1. When and with whom did E. B. White first visit the lake he describes so palpably? With whom—and in approximately what time period—does he return to the lake, as described in his essay?

2. What DOMINANT IMPRESSION of the lake and its surrounding do you take away from White's description? Explain.

3. In paragraph 2, is White describing the lake as it was in the past, or as it is in the present time of his essay? How about in paragraphs 4-6? And in paragraph 11? Explain.

4. In addition to his own adventures on the lake, White is also describing those of "the American family at play" (8). What sentiments and behaviors does he identify as particularly American?

5. Do American families still take summer vacations "at the lake"? How has the pattern of family play—on a lake or elsewhere—changed since White wrote his essay? How has it remained the same?

STRATEGIES AND STRUCTURES

1. In his description of the "primeval" lake, White stresses its qualities of calm and timelessness (3). What particular details contribute most effectively to this impression? What is his point in making it?

2. When he returned to the lake with his young son, the two of them went fishing, says White, "the first morning" (5). Point out other direct references to time in White's essay. How does he use CHRONOLOGY and the passing of time to organize his entire description?

3. One way in which the lake of his childhood has definitely changed, says White, is in its sounds. What new sounds does he describe? How does he incorporate this change into his description of the lake as a timeless place?

4. How would White's essay have been different without the last paragraph, in which he watches his young son get ready to go swimming?

5. *Other Methods.* As White describes the lake, he also tells a story about it. What's the plot of that story? How does White's NARRATIVE fit in with and support his description?

THINKING ABOUT LANGUAGE

1. What is the difference between an illusion and a "mirage" (5)? How and where do White's physical descriptions of the lake lead him to willful misinterpretations of the scene?

2. When he describes the lake as not only "constant" but "trustworthy" (6), White has PERSONIFIED the natural scene. When and where does it seem to take on a mind of its own in sharp contrast to his desires?

3. Why does White repeat the word "same" in paragraph 5?

4. When out in the boat alone as a boy, White did not want to disturb the "stillness of the cathedral" (2). What are the implications of this phrase? In what ways is White's son depicted as a chip off the old block?

5. The lake that White describes might be said to reside as much in memory as in the state of Maine. Why might fishing in a pond or lake provide an especially apt METAPHOR for probing memory—and writing about it?

FOR WRITING

1. Briefly describe a memorable family vacation or other outing. What do you remember most about it, and why? Try to recall the details that led you to this memory.

2. Recall a place that seemed "unique" or "holy" to you when you first visited it. Write a four- or five-paragraph essay describing how it has changed since then, and how it has remained the same. In choosing details to include, think about what DOMINANT IMPRESSION you want to give.

3. In a brief essay with CONCRETE details, describe how a familiar sight, taste, or sound sparks your remembrance of things past. Try to tie what you find back in with the present.

4. Write an essay-length MEMOIR recalling a place you once lived in or visited frequently. Describe the physical characteristics of the place in detail, but also capture the act of remembering it by describing how the sight of a particular object—or a particular taste, sound, smell, or texture—sparks your remembrance.

5. Time seems to stand still on the lake in White's essay. Study how he achieves this sensation—for example, note his use of the image of the dragonfly—and write an essay about a place (such as the interior of an old house, a museum, or a natural setting) that seems timeless or out of time. Be sure to explain why it gives this impression.

6. One of White's sources for "Once More to the Lake" is Henry David Thoreau's *Walden: Or Life in the Woods*. Do some research on *Walden*, and in particular read some passages of Thoreau's description of the pond itself. Then write a REPORT comparing White and Thoreau as nature writers.

PRIYA CHANDRASEKARAN

Cutting Our Grandmothers' Saris

Priya Chandrasekaran is an assistant professor of liberal arts and anthropology at the Juilliard School in New York City. She is a graduate of Cornell University and holds advanced degrees from the University of Mississippi, the New School, and the City University of New York, where she earned a PhD in cultural anthropology. Formerly a college writing teacher and a field researcher throughout the global South, she now focuses her research on environmental justice, globalization, and colonial histories, among other topics. In 2019, she was awarded a fellowship by the American Association of University Women.

"Cutting Our Grandmothers' Saris," written when Chandrasekaran was still in graduate school, describes not only the colorful, flowing saris—from the Sanskrit "strip of cloth"—that her grandmother bequeathed to her; it describes the dilemma that such an inheritance poses—and what the granddaughter made of it.

I'M NO SEAMSTRESS, but when my aunt showed me my grandmother's saris, I knew I was going to make something. The saris, new and old, were stacked high in two columns of brilliant colors. When I told my aunt of my intention to make a quilt, she was incredulous. These saris were valuable, meant to be worn, not cut.

Until then, I'd never seen my grandmother in anything but a sari. As a child visiting India, I couldn't understand how she could sleep comfortably on sweltering nights wrapped in six yards of material, or how she could still look impeccable when she woke. Now, bedridden and on oxygen, blind in one eye, and having recently had

MLA CITATION: Chandrasekaran, Priya. "Cutting Our Grandmothers' Saris." *Back to the Lake: A Reader and Guide for Writers*, edited by Thomas Cooley, 5th ed., W. W. Norton, 2024, pp. 223–24.

a stroke, she wore nothing but a loose nightshirt that flapped open, exposing a degree of nakedness I'd never imagined she had.

When I began the project well after her death, I didn't wash the saris. The stains and scents were evidence of the life she had lived, so different from my own. Hers was a life of cooking curries, wearing turmeric, walking barefoot on dusty floors, participating in Hindu rituals, drinking milky coffee after afternoon naps, and clutching loved ones fiercely to her chest.

But when it came time to cut the cloth, I found myself resistant. It wasn't my mother's allegations of blasphemy, so much as the fact that this fabric—so soft, so luxurious—had caressed my grandmother's skin, reflected her modesty, embodied her womanhood, shielded her from the sun, and made her feel beautiful. That her hand had pleated the folds of seamless silk countless times, and that my cut, once made, would forever alter that sari's potential to live a similar life.

"Do it," I finally commanded myself. So I did.

After that, the work became straightforward. When the quilt was finished, one could see that the edges of each panel didn't quite match, that the soft lavender and deep crimson from one sari clashed slightly with the brilliant yellow and green from another, that the stitches were crude and uneven. Yet beheld in unison, these imperfections fashioned something only I could have created, beautiful in its own way.

> **Parallel structures (p. 92) help to pull the writer's ideas together as she builds up to a conclusion.**

I believe we are entitled to cut our grandmothers' saris, that they were not meant to hang in dark closets collecting dust. I believe that what we create from them should make us proud, and also humble us. I believe that not every stain needs to be rubbed out, and that cutting the cloth can help maintain its integrity.

I believe that to love, and to bare the boundless depth of our love, we must have the courage to reshape what we inherit. ◆

FOR CLOSE READING

1. At first, Priya Chandrasekaran hesitates to cut up the colorful garments she has inherited from her grandmother simply for the purpose of making a quilt. Why is she so reluctant to do so?

2. Chandrasekaran decides to make the quilt anyway. Is she right to overcome her hesitation, or should she have listened to her aunt who thinks the saris are "to be worn, not cut" (1)? Why do you think so?

3. "I'm no seamstress," Chandrasekaran says at the beginning of her essay (1). Judging from her description of her work in paragraph 6, how accurate is this disclaimer, and why might she have included it?

4. In addition to being a writer and a writing teacher, Chandrasekaran was trained as a cultural anthropologist. How might her descriptive essay also be seen as a cultural study?

STRATEGIES AND STRUCTURES

1. Although she refers to "six yards of material," Chandrasekaran never actually says what a sari is (2). Should she have included a formal DEFINITION of this form of dress, or is she right just to let her description carry the weight? Explain.

2. In addition to DESCRIBING her grandmother's clothes, Chandrasekaran also describes her grandmother's life. Where and how does she do this most effectively?

3. In paragraph 6, Chandrasekaran describes the quilt she made. What specific qualities and characteristics does she ascribe to it? What does the quilt have in common with the other things she has been describing?

4. *Other Methods.* At the end of her description, Chandrasekaran makes a claim about the nature of inheritance. What's the point of this ARGUMENT, and how does she support it?

THINKING ABOUT LANGUAGE

1. When she proposes to make a quilt out of the saris, says Chandrasekaran, her aunt was "incredulous" (1). How does Chandrasekaran's use of this word, which means "disbelieving," help prepare for what comes later in her essay?

2. "Blasphemy" is speech that profanes something sacred (4). Why does Chandrasekaran's mother appropriate the term to describe what her daughter plans to do with the saris?

3. When Chandrasekaran first uses the word "stain," she is referring to literal stains in her grandmother's clothes (3). What is she talking about by the end of her essay when she says that "not every stain needs to be rubbed out" (7)? Explain the METAPHOR.

4. METONYMY is a figure of speech that identifies something by giving it the name of one of its parts or attributes—for example, calling a businessman a "suit." How might "seamstress" be considered an example of metonymy (1)? In "reshap[ing] what we inherit" (8), does Chandrasekaran go beyond being a mere seamstress?

FOR WRITING

1. In a paragraph, describe an article of clothing or other object that has been handed down to you or someone you know. Be sure to explain how and why the object is significant.

2. Write a brief essay that captures someone's character and personality by describing that person's clothes, car, truck, other valued possessions, workplace, or home. Include CONCRETE, physical details as well as more ABSTRACT qualities and traits.

3. Write an essay in which you argue that "we must have the courage to reshape what we inherit" (8). Describe in specific detail both something inherited and how it is to be reshaped—even if the inheritance is a general condition or way of thinking. Give particular reasons and examples to support your CLAIM.

EDWARD LEE

Slaw Dogs and Pepperoni Rolls

Edward Lee (b. 1972) is an award-winning chef, restaurant owner, and writer. The son of Korean parents, Lee was born and raised in Brooklyn, New York. He graduated from New York University with a degree in literature but began cooking professionally at age twenty-two. In 2002, Lee moved to Louisville, Kentucky, and opened several successful restaurants—including, in 2023, a steakhouse serving a mix of traditional and modern Korean dishes. Much of Lee's cuisine blends the flavors and ingredients of Korean food with those of the southern United States, such as sorghum, ham, and bourbon. His cookbook, *Smoke and Pickles* (2013), offers "Recipes and Stories from a New Southern Kitchen." In 2017, Lee founded an organization to promote diversity and growth in the restaurant industry.

"Slaw Dogs and Pepperoni Rolls" is a selection from Lee's 2018 book, *Buttermilk Graffiti: A Chef's Journey to Discover America's New Melting-Pot Cuisine*. This essay describes, in delicious detail, not only the local cuisine that Lee consumed on his travels in West Virginia but the landscape and culture of the region as well. Lee's traveling companion in this selection is the chef and cookbook writer—and West Virgina resident—Ronni Lundy.

I MEET RONNI at the Asheville airport. She is a small, sprightly woman in her sixties who glows with energy. The first thing I notice when I jump into her van is an oversize Rand McNally road atlas. It is so big that she is completely hidden behind it, except for her fingers curled around the edges of the cover. Her singsong voice echoes from the driver's seat. I start to laugh involuntarily. I ask her if she wants to use my GPS.

MLA CITATION: Lee, Edward. "Slaw Dogs and Pepperoni Rolls." *Back to the Lake: A Reader and Guide for Writers*, edited by Thomas Cooley, 5th ed., W. W. Norton, 2024, pp. 226–29.

"Mr. Lee, are you making fun of my maps?" 2

"No, ma'am." I snap back to attention. 3

And so begins our road trip through Appalachia. 4

The van sputters as we crest over a ridge. These steep, verdant hills carved out of 5
prehistoric violence have had an eternity to become smooth. They roll and undulate
like fairy-tale landscapes. The homes sit far apart, isolated. A church stands alone
on a hill. Through a clearing, we see an abandoned covered bridge spanning a shallow stream flanked by hulking limestone rocks. It is hard not to fall in love with this
land. It is hard to look at this place and not believe in God. The roads through the
valleys are lined with poplar and ash trees, dense and emerald green. You can drive
for miles without feeling sunlight on your cheeks. When we arrive at another vista,
Ronni slows the van to a crawl so we can breathe in the view. She points to
where the pasture meets the heavens. Her coral green eyes fall on me like
sunlight on a dewy morning. Her short white hair hugs the curves of her
temples. She starts every new sentence like the lyrics of a love song: "You are
never far from death and darkness even when you are standing in the light."

> Similes (here, using "like") can enliven descriptive writing; see p. 191.

For our first stop, we find a small roadside diner that sells sandwiches 6
and pies. Ronni talks to me about the pickles of this region, about bread and pigs
and why pork became the major source of protein—cattle were not a viable industry
in the steep landscape of Appalachia. I'm embarrassed to interrupt her discussion of
salt-risen bread with a request for a processed hot dog. I sheepishly ask her if we can
stop off at a few places if they're not too far out of the way.

"Well, buddy, why didn't you say so earlier? You're talking my language." 7

My heart nearly explodes. 8

A West Virginia hot dog is a regional specialty that starts with a soft commercial 9
hot dog bun. Yellow mustard is slathered on first. A boiled beef wiener is placed in
the bun next. Ground beef chili without beans is added to that. The kind of chili
will differ from place to place, but it is commonly a tomato-rich variety easy on the
spice. On top of the chili is placed chopped cabbage slaw held together with mayo
and vinegar, creamy and tart. Finally, a light smattering of finely chopped raw onion
gets put on top. You can find this dog almost everywhere in the region, from roadside diners to gas stations and local bars. In Virginia, it's called a slaw dog. In West
Virginia, it's simply a West Virginia hot dog, though in the northern parts, folks
tend to serve it without the coleslaw. At the famous Umberger's in Wytheville,
Virginia, they call them Skeeter Dogs and sell them for two bucks apiece, but at
most places, you can find them for two dollars for a pair. At first glance, there is
nothing about this hot dog that looks special, but once you take a bite, you know
you've touched the nirvana of hot dogs. That first bite tells you everything. The
structure of the chili is critical, because if it's too tight, it doesn't collapse in your
mouth with the other ingredients. Too loose, and the chili dog falls apart after the

first bite, dissolving into a sloppy mess in your hands. The same goes for the slaw. When it's done right, there is harmony and balance. I don't think Ronni truly trusted me as a person until she witnessed me take down two slaw dogs with a slug of hot black coffee before 8:00 a.m.

The West Virginia hot dog is a regional celebrity. There are websites devoted to it. Though the wiener and bun are almost always factory made, there is pride in the slaw and enough technique and variation in the chili that a lively debate rages about who makes it best. Skeenies or King Tut? Skeeter's or Buddy B's? No one knows the precise origin of this dog. Ronni traces it back to the chili buns served in the pool halls that littered the railroad towns of the region. Another plausible story tells of the struggling immigrant families, many of whom grew vegetables in their back-yards to supplement their humble diets. Cabbage was easy to grow, so families started to make slaw—lots of it. The slaw found its way into many dishes, including the hot dog. The first place to sell the slaw dog was the Stopette Drive-In in the 1920s, but many argue that home cooks in the region started eating their hot dogs with slaw well before that. One thing is for sure: the slaw dog is a celebration and a source of pride.

> Lee is using the subject-by-subject method of comparison and contrast (p. 406).

The slaw dog stands in stark contrast to West Virginia's other regional specialty: the pepperoni roll. A humble food of Italian origin, it was invented by immigrant Italian coal miners who needed a hearty snack that was both portable and easy to eat. D'Annunzio's, a landmark bakery in Clarks-burg, has been making it for decades. The preparation couldn't be simpler: pepperoni cut into sticks about four inches long and baked into a soft, sweet roll. Nothing else: just dough and pepperoni baked together.

I arrive at D'Annunzio's at 8:00 a.m., when the rolls are just coming out of the oven. I stand in a line of polite locals, many of whom are buying the rolls by the dozen. I take a bite of mine. The dough is soft and forgiving, the pepperoni luke-warm. All I taste is powdered paprika, dry and unbalanced. It takes a few chews to loosen the fat from the sausage and for flavors to develop in my mouth, but even then, it is bland and monotonous. I am underwhelmed, to say the least.

Ronni tells me that the pepperoni roll is the food of the working class. It is about making connections. When your entire day is spent deep in a coal mine, that little bit of pepperoni may be all that connects you to the sanity of family and your iden-tity and life aboveground.

I buy a dozen rolls and decide to carry them with me for the next few days.

> For tips on stating the point of your description, see p. 187.

So many of my assumptions about food come from a desire to tell a neatly packaged story, one that has a happy ending of climactic flavors and rewarded chefs. But that tidy story is rarely the case. Along my journey, through Appalachia or any of the small towns I've traveled to, the most insightful moments have been quiet and unseasoned. This has made me question myself and my expectations. I'm owed nothing by the people and the culture of this place. I have neither the right to judge nor the history to comment on them. If the pepperoni roll seems bland to me, it is a fault in my own palate, which is unable to detect the value of its plainness. I chew another bite and try to think of someone who has been working at a physically grueling job since dawn. This pepperoni roll is the one pleasure he may have been looking forward to all morning long. This pepperoni roll may be all he has to eat until he sits down to supper late in the evening. Slowly, I get it. The darkness of the room is suffocating, and I've been here only twenty minutes. The pepperoni roll suddenly tastes like the best thing I've ever eaten. ◆

FOR CLOSE READING

1. Edward Lee offers two explanations of the possible origins of the slaw in slaw dogs. What are they, and which one do you find more plausible? Why?

2. According to Lee, there seems to be little question about where pepperoni rolls came from. What is their origin story, according to him? How about the origin of the Appalachian Mountains, as Lee describes them at the beginning of his trip (5)?

3. From the first bite, Lee worships the slaw dog. The pepperoni roll, however, he finds bland at first. What changes his mind (or palate) about this "humble food" (11)? Where does he describe the change most fully—and how?

4. According to Lee, why does the cuisine of Appalachia often feature pork instead of beef? Why wasn't beef a "viable" alternative in the region (6)? Explain.

STRATEGIES AND STRUCTURES

1. When Lee first meets Ronni Lundy, she is "completely hidden" behind a book of maps (1). But by the end of paragraph 3, only two brief lines later, what have we learned about this traveling companion? How and how well does this opening set the stage for the road trip to follow?

2. As soon as the road trip starts, Lee describes the landscape he and Ronni will be traveling through. What DOMINANT IMPRESSION of the region does he convey? Point to specific details in the text that contribute to this impression.

3. Lee devotes two long paragraphs (9 and 10) to a detailed description of the West Virginia hot dog. What are the main distinguishing features of this "celebrity" dog (10)? According to Lee, which attribute in particular sets it apart from all other hot dogs?

4. By contrast with slaw dogs, says Lee, pepperoni rolls could not be "simpler" (11); yet he devotes about as much space to one as to the other. What exactly is Lee describing in the last third of his essay (11-13), if not the pepperoni rolls themselves? Explain.

5. *Other Methods.* Lee admits that he likes a "neatly packaged story," even if circumstances don't always provide "a happy ending" (15). Point out places throughout his description where Lee incorporates elements of **NARRATIVE**, such as dialogue and suspense, into his description.

THINKING ABOUT LANGUAGE

1. As they reach the mountains, Lee and Ronni stop to "breathe in the view" (5). Is this literally possible? As a chef, why might Lee be inclined to such blended impressions?

2. Lee asks "sheepishly" if they can stop the van and get a hot dog (6). What is "sheepish" about this request?

3. "My heart nearly explodes" (8). Why might Lee indulge in such **HYPERBOLE** here? Point out other places in his essay where he seems to be particularly enthusiastic about his subject.

4. After he eats the first slaw dog, Lee reaches "the nirvana of hot dogs" (9). What is nirvana, and how does applying this word fit in with the **TONE** and language of the rest of Lee's description, particularly of the "fairy-tale" landscape (5)?

5. On their road trip, says Lee, "the most insightful moments have been quiet and unseasoned" (15). What are the implications of this **METAPHOR** in an essay by a chef? How might this insight apply specifically to the writer's description of the pepperoni rolls at the end?

FOR WRITING

1. Write a paragraph describing a hot dog, burger, shake, candy bar, or other indulgent item of food in "delicious" detail.

2. When the last McDonald's closed in Iceland more than ten years ago, a local citizen purchased the final burger and fries to come off the line; a short time later, he donated them to the National Museum of Iceland. The original burger and fries are still being streamed "live" online. Do a little research on these national treasures, and write a three-to-five-paragraph description of their condition and history.

3. Write a review describing a meal you had recently. Focus on the food, but also try to convey a sense of the place itself and of the other people in it. Be sure to comment on the overall quality of the dining experience—and whether or not you would recommend it to the reader. A blend of **SUBJECTIVE** and **OBJECTIVE DESCRIPTION** will be useful in this review.

4. Give an account of a trip you have taken to an isolated (or other) region where the **DOMINANT IMPRESSION** you had was one of awe and wonder. Tell how the place affected you, but also describe what it looked, smelled, tasted, sounded, and felt like by referring to particular features of the place.

LOUISE ERDRICH

Two Languages in Mind,
but Just One in the Heart

Louise Erdrich (b. 1954) is an award-winning novelist, poet, short-story writer, and author of children's books. The oldest of seven children, Erdrich was born in Little Falls, Minnesota, and grew up in Wahpeton, North Dakota, where her parents taught at a boarding school sponsored by the Bureau of Indian Affairs. Erdrich attended Dartmouth College with a major in English (her "first love" language) and earned an MA in writing from Johns Hopkins University. Beginning with *Love Medicine* (1984), Erdrich wrote a series of novels set on and around a fictional reservation in North Dakota. These included *The Beet Queen* (1986) and *The Bingo Palace* (1994). *The Night Watchman* (2020), which won a Pulitzer Prize, was Erdrich's first novel to take place on the Turtle Mountain reservation, where her maternal grandfather, Patrick Gourneau, served as the longtime tribal chairman of a federally recognized Chippewa group known as the Turtle Mountain Band. Erdrich now lives in Minneapolis, where she owns a "teaching" bookstore, the setting for her 2021 novel *The Sentence*.

As a child, Erdrich often visited relatives on the Turtle Mountain reservation, but she was raised in town in the Catholic tradition of her German American father. Consequently, she did not learn the Ojibwe language of her maternal ancestors. "Two Languages in Mind, but Just One in the Heart" recounts Erdrich's struggle, which she describes as a belated "love affair," to acquire that language.

MLA CITATION: Erdrich, Louise. "Two Languages in Mind, but Just One in the Heart." *Back to the Lake: A Reader and Guide for Writers*, edited by Thomas Cooley, 5th ed., W. W. Norton, 2024, pp. 232–35.

F OR YEARS NOW I have been in love with a language other than the English in 1
which I write, and it is a rough affair. Every day I try to learn a little more
Ojibwe. I have taken to carrying verb conjugation charts in my purse, along with
the tiny notebook I've always kept for jotting down book ideas, overheard conversations, language detritus, phrases that pop into my head. Now that little notebook
includes an increasing volume of Ojibwe words. My English is jealous, my Ojibwe
elusive. Like a besieged unfaithful lover, I'm trying to appease them both.

Ojibwemowin, or Anishinabemowin, the Chippewa language, was last spoken in 2
our family by Patrick Gourneau, my maternal grandfather, a Turtle Mountain Ojibwe
who used it mainly in his prayers. Growing up off reservation, I thought Ojibwemowin
mainly was a language for prayers, like Latin in the Catholic liturgy. I was unaware
for many years that Ojibwemowin was spoken in Canada, Minnesota and Wisconsin, though by a dwindling number of people. By the time I began to study the language, I was living in New Hampshire, so for the first few years I used language tapes.

I never learned more than a few polite phrases that way, but the sound of the 3
language in the author Basil Johnson's calm and dignified Anishinabe voice sustained me through bouts of homesickness. I spoke basic Ojibwe in the isolation of
my car traveling here and there on twisting New England roads. Back then, as now,
I carried my tapes everywhere.

The language bit deep into my heart, but it was an unfulfilled longing. I had 4
nobody to speak it with, nobody who remembered my grandfather's standing with
his sacred pipe in the woods next to a box elder tree, talking to the spirits. Not until
I moved back to the Midwest and settled in Minneapolis did I find a fellow Ojibweg
to learn with, and a teacher.

Mille Lac's Ojibwe elder Jim Clark—Naawi-giizis, or Center of the Day—is a 5
magnetically pleasant, sunny, crew-cut World War II veteran with a mysterious
kindliness that shows in his slightest gesture. When he laughs, everything about
him laughs; and when he is serious, his eyes round like a boy's.

Naawi-giizis introduced me to the deep intelligence of the language and forever 6
set me on a quest to speak it for one reason: I want to get the jokes. I also want to
understand the prayers and the adisookaanug, the sacred stories, but the irresistible
part of language for me is the explosion of hilarity that attends every other minute
of an Ojibwe visit. As most speakers are now bilingual, the language is spiked with
puns on both English and Ojibwe, most playing on the oddness of gichi-mookomaan,
that is, big knife or American, habits and behavior.

This desire to deepen my alternate language puts me in an odd relationship to 7
my first love, English. It is, after all, the language stuffed into my mother's ancestors' mouths. English is the reason she didn't speak her native language and the
reason I can barely limp along in mine. English is an all-devouring language that
has moved across North America like the fabulous plagues of locusts that darkened

the sky and devoured even the handles of rakes and hoes. Yet the omnivorous nature of a colonial language is a writer's gift. Raised in the English language, I partake of a mongrel feast.

A hundred years ago most Ojibwe people spoke Ojibwemowin, but the Bureau of Indian Affairs and religious boarding schools punished and humiliated children who spoke native languages. The program worked, and there are now almost no fluent speakers of Ojibwe in the United States under the age of 30. Speakers like Naawi-giizis value the language partly because it has been physically beaten out of so many people. Fluent speakers have had to fight for the language with their own flesh, have endured ridicule, have resisted shame and stubbornly pledged themselves to keep on talking the talk.

Here, narrative adds historical context to the descriptive essay. See p. 192 to read about using other methods in a description.

My relationship is of course very different. How do you go back to a language you never had? Why should a writer who loves her first language find it necessary and essential to complicate her life with another? Simple reasons, personal and impersonal. In the past few years I've found that I can talk to God only in this language, that somehow my grandfather's use of the language penetrated. The sound comforts me. 9

What the Ojibwe call the Gizhe Manidoo, the great and kind spirit residing in all that lives, what the Lakota call the Great Mystery, is associated for me with the flow of Ojibwemowin. My Catholic training touched me intellectually and symbolically but apparently never engaged my heart. 10

There is also this: Ojibwemowin is one of the few surviving languages that evolved to the present here in North America. The intelligence of this language is adapted as no other to the philosophy bound up in northern land, lakes, rivers, forests, arid plains; to the animals and their particular habits; to the shades of meaning in the very placement of stones. As a North American writer it is essential to me that I try to understand our human relationship to place in the deepest way possible, using my favorite tool, language. 11

There are place names in Ojibwe and Dakota for every physical feature of Minnesota, including recent additions like city parks and dredged lakes. Ojibwemowin is not static, not confined to describing the world of some out-of-reach and sacred past. There are words for e-mail, computers, Internet, fax. For exotic animals in zoos. Anaamibiig gookoosh, the underwater pig, is a hippopotamus. Nandookomeshiinh, the lice hunter, is the monkey. 12

There are words for the serenity prayer used in 12-step programs and translations of nursery rhymes. The varieties of people other than Ojibwe or Anishinabe are also named: Aiibiishaabookewininiwag, the tea people, are Asians. Agongosininiwag, the chipmunk people, are Scandinavians. I'm still trying to find out why. 13

For years I saw only the surface of Ojibwemowin. With any study at all one looks deep into a stunning complex of verbs. Ojibwemowin is a language of verbs. All 14 action. Two-thirds of the words are verbs, and for each verb there are as many as 6,000 forms. The storm of verb forms makes it a wildly adaptive and powerfully precise language. Changite-ige describes the way a duck tips itself up in the water butt first. There is a word for what would happen if a man fell off a motorcycle with a pipe in his mouth and the stem of it went through the back of his head. There can be a verb for anything.

When it comes to nouns, there is some relief. There aren't many objects. With a 15 modest if inadvertent political correctness, there are no designations of gender in Ojibwemowin. There are no feminine or masculine possessives or articles.

Nouns are mainly designated as alive or dead, animate or inanimate. The word 16 for stone, asin, is animate. Stones are called grandfathers and grandmothers and are extremely important in Ojibwe philosophy. Once I began to think of stones as animate, I started to wonder whether I was picking up a stone or it was putting itself into my hand. Stones are not the same as they were to me in English. I can't write about a stone without considering it in Ojibwe and acknowledging that the Anishinabe universe began with a conversation between stones.

Ojibwemowin is also a language of emotions; shades of feeling can be mixed like 17 paints. There is a word for what occurs when your heart is silently shedding tears. Ojibwe is especially good at describing intellectual states and the fine points of moral responsibility.

Ozozamenimaa pertains to a misuse of one's talents getting out of control. Ozo- 18 zamichige implies you can still set things right. There are many more kinds of love than there are in English. There are myriad shades of emotional meaning to desig- nate various family and clan members. It is a language that also recognizes the humanity of a creaturely God, and the absurd and wondrous sexuality of even the most deeply religious beings.

Slowly the language has crept into my writing, replacing a word here, a concept 19 there, beginning to carry weight. I've thought of course of writing stories in Ojibwe, like a reverse Nabokov. With my Ojibwe at the level of a dreamy 4-year-old child's, I probably won't.

Though it was not originally a written language, people simply adapted the 20 English alphabet and wrote phonetically. During the Second World War, Naawi- giizis wrote Ojibwe letters to his uncle from Europe. He spoke freely about his movements, as no censor could understand his writing. Ojibwe orthography has recently been standardized. Even so, it is an all-day task for me to write even one paragraph using verbs in their correct arcane forms. And even then, there are so many dialects of Ojibwe that, for many speakers, I'll still have gotten it wrong.

As awful as my own Ojibwe must sound to a fluent speaker, I have never, ever, 21 been greeted with a moment of impatience or laughter. Perhaps people wait until I've left the room. But more likely, I think, there is an urgency about attempting to speak the language. To Ojibwe speakers the language is a deeply loved entity. There is a spirit or an originating genius belonging to each word.

Before attempting to speak this language, a learner must acknowledge these spirits with gifts of tobacco and food. Anyone who attempts Ojibwemowin is engaged in something more than learning tongue twisters. However awkward my nouns, unstable my verbs, however stumbling my delivery, to engage in the language is to engage the spirit. Perhaps that is what my teachers know, and what my English will forgive. ◆

Erdrich concludes with a statement of her thesis. Read about stating your point on p. 187.

FOR CLOSE READING

1. The Ojibwe language, as Louise Erdrich notes, was "not originally a written language" (20). How did it become one?

2. According to Erdrich, there are "almost no fluent speakers of Ojibwe in the United States under the age of 30" (8). Why not? Why is this situation a matter of concern to her?

3. Although her mother was of Ojibwe (and French) ancestry, Erdrich grew up speaking English. Why do you suppose she did not learn Ojibwe then as well?

4. What reasons, "personal and impersonal," does Erdrich give for wanting to acquire the Ojibwe language as an adult (9)? Why was that desire "unfulfilled" until she met Naawi-giizis (4–6)?

5. According to Erdrich, how does the history of the Ojibwe language make it "adapted as no other" to describing the lakes, rivers, forests, and even the stones of North America (11)? Why might a deep sense of place be an important attribute for a novelist to acquire?

STRATEGIES AND STRUCTURES

1. Erdrich describes her struggle to learn her "native" language as a love affair. How and how well does this extended **METAPHOR** serve to unify her entire essay?

2. Erdrich describes her belated love affair with the Ojibwe language as "rough" and herself as an "unfaithful lover" (1). What do these particular characteristics suggest about the nature of Erdrich's intended audience? Explain.

3. In paragraphs 14–18, Erdrich describes the Ojibwe language itself. According to her description, what are some of the main characteristics of its vocabulary and grammar? Point to some phrases in these paragraphs that reveal Erdrich's **VANTAGE POINT** as an English speaker learning—and learning about—this language.

4. When Erdrich describes herself as "a reverse Nabokov" (19), the reference is to the Russian American novelist Vladimir Nabokov (1899–1977). Do some research on Nabokov's background, and then explain what Erdrich means by "reverse" in this **ALLUSION**.

5. *Other Methods.* The Ojibwe language, says Erdrich, is "not static, not confined to describing the world of some out-of-reach and sacred past" (12). In her description, how and where does Erdrich use **EXAMPLES** to present an ancient tongue as a living language that is constantly adapting to fit the times?

THINKING ABOUT LANGUAGE

1. Before Erdrich translates an Ojibwe word or name (for example, "Center of the Day," 5), she typically offers a transliteration ("Naawi-giizis"; 5). What's the difference between translation and transliteration?

2. According to Erdrich, the word for American translates from Ojibwe into English as "big knife" (6). What aspects of Indigenous history does this meaning **CONNOTE**?

3. Why are "place names" so important in Erdrich's description of her love affair with the Ojibwe language (12)? Cite several examples from her essay.

4. "Slowly," says Erdrich, "the language has crept into my writing" (19). Point to specific places in her essay that illustrate (or fail to illustrate) this **CLAIM**. Be sure to consider the passage where she refers to a writer's need "to understand our human relationship to place" (11).

FOR WRITING

1. In a brief essay, describe your experience with learning a language other than your native language(s). Include a description of the "new" language and how specific aspects of it **COMPARE** with those of other languages you know.

2. Imagine a universe that began as "a conversation between stones" (16). In a descriptive essay, tell what that universe would look like—its landscapes, plants, animals, and other inhabitants. Include **DIALOGUE** from the original conversation out of which such a place would come into being.

3. As Erdrich describes it, Ojibwe is "a language of emotions" (17), while English, she implies, is better suited (or restricted) to matters of the intellect rather than the heart. Construct an **ARGUMENT** of 500 to 700 words supporting (or contesting) this claim. Give lots of examples, like those in paragraphs 17–18 of Erdrich's essay.

4. Read Erdrich's *The Night Watchman* (2020) and write a **CRITICAL ANALYSIS** of the novel, particularly as it pertains to the US government's "termination" policy from the 1940s to the 1960s. Be sure to describe, in some detail, the role of Thomas Wazhashk, the character based on Erdrich's grandfather.

MOLLY CASE

How to Treat People

Molly Case is a cardiac nurse at St. George's Hospital in London. Also a spoken word artist and a writer, she grew up just outside the city in the town of Bromley and earned a degree in creative writing from Bath Spa University. As an undergraduate, Case took a part-time job caring for people with dementia. Based on this experience, she decided to go to nursing school; and in 2013, while still a student nurse, she performed one of her poems before the Royal College of Nursing. "Nursing the Nation," a passionate defense of the British national health system, received a standing ovation and helped establish Case as a popular spokesperson for the medical profession in Britain. In an interview, she described a vital source of her inspiration, both as a nurse and as a writer: "I grew up on a smorgasbord of hip-hop and rappers.... I was hugely drawn to the literary devices and poetic techniques of these artists and the seductive quality of the way they rhyme."

The following selection is a chapter from *How to Treat People* (2019), Case's extended description of her experience as a young nurse. The perspective and language of the book were inspired in part, she says, by listening over and over to the mixtape album *Coloring Book* (2016) by Chicago artist Chance the Rapper and the Social Experiment. The rhythms she describes here are those of the human heart—and the cardiac ward of a big-city hospital.

D URING THE FIRST FEW WEEKS of my new job on the cardiothoracic ward, just six months into being qualified as a nurse, I was invited to watch my first cardiac bypass surgery. Most new starters are encouraged to witness an open-heart procedure

MLA CITATION: Case, Molly. "How to Treat People." *Back to the Lake: A Reader and Guide for Writers*, edited by Thomas Cooley, 5th ed., W. W. Norton, 2024, pp. 237–39.

The vantage point (p. 191) is that of a new nurse observing cardiac bypass surgery.

to better understand the patient's journey from outpatient clinic to surgery to recovery with the nurses back on the wards.

In the cool of the operating room I tentatively peered over the anaesthe- 2 tist's shoulder to watch the surgeon's blade make a clean, almost bloodless incision down the skin of a woman's chest. I watched as the surgeon and his registrar used heat to slice through the gelatinous layer of fat beneath, finally reaching the bone, which they proceeded to cut through with a saw. The smell of brazier smoke and fireworks nights momentarily distracted me from the surgery. When I looked back, they had already flayed the chest; the bone marrow was now visible, jam-colored and sponge-like. They worked quickly, with silver fingers, and with the chest cranked open they cut through the glistening pericardial sac to reveal the heart, the first I had ever seen.

My own heart leapt, but I tried to stay as still and quiet as possible, balancing on 3 tiptoes on a stool by the patient's head to get a better view. The team had inserted thick garden-hose tubes in the aorta and the atrium to attach the patient to the cardiopulmonary bypass machine—the heart-lung machine. They used clamps and silk sutures to ensure they could control the flow and that the tubes would remain fixed safely in place.

It was the perfusionist, sitting nearby, whose job it was to initiate the heart-lung 4 machine. The heart in front of me was emptied, the lungs deflated, no longer required to take breaths for themselves, since the machine would do it for them for the duration of the operation. The machine whirred to life, canisters filling up with blood, spooling it through tubes, arcing over spinning discs like a bloody rainbow bowing above a metallic sun, looping back again past pumps and filters, chrome panels, bags of fluid hooked high like Halloween piñatas waiting to be punctured. The patient could now not survive without the perfusionist's bypass machine oxygenating the body.

Three paragraphs of narration provide background information. See p. 192 for advice on using other methods in a description.

This machine was first successfully used on a human by John Gibbon, 5 who developed the earliest cardiopulmonary bypass machine in 1950s Philadelphia. His skill as a doctor had been handed down from his father, grandfather, great-grandfather and great-great-grandfather before him, and he had dedicated years of study to developing ways of enhancing cardiac surgery.

That morning he operated on a young woman who had an atrial sep- 6 tal defect . . . a hole in the heart that allowed blood to pass back and forth abnormally through the septum. The operation took twenty-six minutes; twenty-six minutes of her life spent beating and breathing through his new machine. It worked: she recovered uneventfully and went home, her heart fixed.

When Gibbon left Jefferson University Medical Center that afternoon, he 7 crossed the road and thought he could smell on the breeze the sweetness of bloodroot petals from the Catskill Mountains that had fallen and been carried all the way to Philadelphia by the Delaware River. He made his way home through Washington Square, the sycamore leaves green and vein-filled in the light. He walked the diagonal concrete paths of the park, his feet sore from standing, and stopped in the middle, where a fountain spurted. He closed his eyes and reflected on the operation, listening to the rush of the fountain as the water crashed to the ground and thinking back to how the heart had looked as it refilled with blood.

Back in the operating room in London, I watched as the senior house officer 8 extracted a suitable vein from the patient's leg to use as a graft in the heart. Her masked face was pressed close to the flesh, peering over her glasses to check she had removed the whole vessel, cutting it away from its branches. She carefully lifted it from its bed. With one hand she held the vessel; with the other she squirted water through its lumen to clean it and check its patency. It looked like the thorny stalk of a rose without its head. She passed the vein to the scrub nurse, who placed it safely in a sterile dish whilst the surgeons continued working on the heart. The SHO bowed her head once more, clamping the branch stumps and selecting sutures to tie them off at the root, before closing the leg and wrapping it in bandages.

The surgeons took the new vessel and planted it deep within the chest, sewing it to 9 the openings of the diseased arteries, using magnified lenses to inspect their work more closely. Blood flow was established to check the graft was working, and slowly the patient was weaned from the heart-lung machine as the operation came to an end.

The registrar inserted chest drains to remove any remaining fluid from the area, 10 and temporary pacing wires were positioned in the outer layer of the heart to provide electrical stimulation to manage the patient's heart rate and rhythm should it not be able to conduct for itself when they awoke.

Steel wires were used to close the sternum and the chest was sutured back 11 together. The patient was wheeled out to cardiac recovery, where they would remain breathing via a machine overnight. The nurses here would monitor vital signs closely, checking that blood pressure remained stable and the heart beat in a regular rhythm. They would use a variety of drugs to increase the strength of the heart's contractions and monitor the flow of blood, looking for early signs of bleeding. The location of the surgery, deep within the chest, meant that bleeding was often concealed, and nurses had to spot subtle signs before it was too late.

When I had more experience in cardiac nursing, I too would be able to work in 12 cardiac recovery, but in the meantime, I would start at the beginning of the patient's journey, on the cardiothoracic ward, getting them ready for their big operation. ♦

FOR CLOSE READING

1. As a newly qualified nurse in a London hospital, what is Molly Case's purpose in attending her first cardiac bypass surgery?

2. As the surgery begins, Case describes in detail what she sees—and smells. Why is she suddenly distracted by the memory of "brazier smoke and fireworks nights" (2)?

3. During the operation, Case describes the patient's blood flowing through the heart-lung machine like "a bloody rainbow" (4). Who invented the machine, how does it work, and what is its purpose?

4. As the inventor of the heart-lung machine strolled home after using it successfully for the first time, according to Case, he stopped in a park. What specific aspects of the scene does Case choose to describe here—and why?

5. Once the patient returns to the recovery room after surgery, what are the main duties of the attending nurses? What "signs" in particular are they looking for (11)?

STRATEGIES AND STRUCTURES

1. Case's description opens with the opening of the patient's chest cavity. How does it conclude? What does Case's watchful eye focus on in between? Does the sequence of her description follow an effective method of organization?

2. Case compares the vein harvested from the patient's leg to "the thorny stalk of a rose without its head" (8). Does this SIMILE surprise you, given Case's background as a writer? Why or why not?

3. Case says her writing has been influenced by hip-hop and rap. Point out phrases and sentences in her essay—for example, the looping description of the heart-lung machine in paragraph 4—that might be particularly effective if read aloud or even performed.

4. *Other Methods.* Paragraphs 1–4 and 8–12 of Case's essay describe steps in heart bypass surgery, but they are interrupted at paragraphs 5–7 by a NARRATIVE about the first successful use of a heart-lung machine. Is the switch in rhetorical mode effective at this point in the essay? Explain why or why not.

THINKING ABOUT LANGUAGE

1. "The surgeons took the new vessel and planted it deep within the chest" (9). Why do you think Case uses this METAPHOR to describe what the surgeons are doing instead of simply saying that they "placed" or "inserted" the vein into the patient's chest?

2. Case describes the patient's experience as a "journey" (1, 12). Who else is embarking on a journey in this essay? How appropriate is the metaphor in each case? Explain.

3. As Dr. Gibbon made his way home, Case notes, the leaves on the sycamore trees in Washington Square were "vein-filled" (7). How does this specific detail tie in

with the rest of her description? What about the "bloodroot pedals" that float down the river (7)?

4. Case's memoir, from which this chapter is taken, is titled *How to Treat People*. What are the implications of this title, especially for doctors and nurses? Might it imply a particular CLAIM? Keep in mind that Case is a passionate defender (and critic) of the National Health Service in Britain.

5. In Case's memoir, this selection is called "Circulation." How and how well does that title apply not only to the flow of blood in the patient's heart but to the other things Case describes here? Explain.

FOR WRITING

1. In a single long sentence, describe one of the following: an ice-skater's routine, a basketball player shooting a basket, a drummer moving around the drum set, a person chopping wood, the flow of a long sentence in English (or some other language). Use vivid, CONCRETE details.

2. Write a four-to-six-paragraph CRITICAL ANALYSIS of *How to Treat People* (either the book or the chapter presented here) in which you focus on the role and personal characteristics of the young nurse who is observing the hospital scene. Include a detailed description of her as both an individual and a representative of her profession.

3. Draft an essay in which you describe some important medical invention or discovery—for example, the microscope or the gene-editing technology CRISPR. Include details not only about the science but also about the people involved—and their personal reactions to their accomplishments. Keep your descriptions as OBJECTIVE as possible.

4. Watch Case reading one of her works on *YouTube*, and then write a CRITICAL ANALYSIS of her performance. Describe in some detail not only her delivery but also the basic elements of the text she is presenting.

MICHELLE ZAUNER

Crying in H Mart

Michelle Zauner (b. 1989) is a writer, music composer, and the lead vocalist of the alternative pop band Japanese Breakfast. Born in Seoul, South Korea, Zauner grew up in Eugene, Oregon, where her American father and Korean mother settled when she was nine months old. Although her command of the Korean language remains "elementary," Zauner has returned to Korea often over the years to visit family and is fluent in many aspects of Asian culture, particularly the food. At age fifteen, Zauner began to study guitar and was soon writing songs and playing at local venues under the name Little Girl, Big Spoon. Zauner is a 2011 graduate of Bryn Mawr College, where she earned a BA in creative writing.

Originally published as an essay in the *New Yorker* magazine, the following selection is the opening chapter of Zauner's best-selling memoir, *Crying in H Mart* (2021). H Mart is the largest grocery store chain in the United States devoted to Asian tastes, and young Zauner spent countless hours shopping and eating there with her mother, Chong Mi Zauner, who died of cancer in 2014. As Zauner describes it, level by level, the food court at her local H Mart is "a holy place" where a grieving daughter can savor a complicated relationship in all its sweet and sour aspects.

The essay's opening sentence lets readers know this will be a subjective description (see p. 183).

E VER SINCE MY MOM DIED, I cry in H Mart.   1

H Mart is a supermarket chain that specializes in Asian food. The *H* stands for han ah reum, a Korean phrase that roughly translates to "one arm full of groceries." H Mart is where parachute kids flock to find the brand of instant noodles that reminds them of home. It's where Korean

MLA CITATION: Zauner, Michelle. "Crying in H Mart." *Back to the Lake: A Reader and Guide for Writers*, edited by Thomas Cooley, 5th ed., W. W. Norton, 2024, pp. 242–47.

families buy rice cakes to make tteokguk, the beef and rice cake soup that brings in the New Year. It's the only place where you can find a giant vat of peeled garlic, because it's the only place that truly understands how much garlic you'll need for the kind of food your people eat. H Mart is freedom from the single-aisle "ethnic" section in regular grocery stores. They don't prop Goya beans next to bottles of sriracha here. Instead, you'll likely find me crying by the banchan refrigerators, remembering the taste of my mom's soy-sauce eggs and cold radish soup. Or in the freezer section, holding a stack of dumpling skins, thinking of all the hours that Mom and I spent at the kitchen table folding minced pork and chives into the thin dough. Sobbing near the dry goods, asking myself, Am I even Korean anymore if there's no one left to call and ask which brand of seaweed we used to buy?

Growing up in America with a Caucasian father and a Korean mother, I relied on my mom for access to our Korean heritage. While she never actually taught me how to cook (Korean people tend to disavow measurements and supply only cryptic instructions along the lines of "add sesame oil until it tastes like Mom's"), she did raise me with a distinctly Korean appetite. This meant a reverence for good food and a predisposition to emotional eating. We were particular about everything: kimchi had to be perfectly sour, samgyupsal perfectly crisped; stews had to be piping hot or they might as well have been inedible. The concept of prepping meals for the week was a ludicrous affront to our lifestyle. We chased our cravings daily. If we wanted the kimchi stew for three weeks straight, we relished it until a new craving emerged. We ate in accordance with the seasons and holidays.

When spring arrived and the weather turned, we'd bring our camp stove outdoors and fry up strips of fresh pork belly on the deck. On my birthday, we ate miyeokguk—a hearty seaweed soup full of nutrients that women are encouraged to eat postpartum and that Koreans traditionally eat on their birthdays to celebrate their mothers.

Food was how my mother expressed her love. No matter how critical or cruel she could seem—constantly pushing me to meet her intractable expectations—I could always feel her affection radiating from the lunches she packed and the meals she prepared for me just the way I liked them. I can hardly speak Korean, but in H Mart it feels like I'm fluent. I fondle the produce and say the words aloud—chamoe melon, danmuji. I fill my shopping cart with every snack that has glossy packaging decorated with a familiar cartoon. I think about the time Mom showed me how to fold the little plastic card that came inside bags of Jolly Pong, how to use it as a spoon to shovel caramel puffed rice into my mouth, and how it inevitably fell down my shirt and spread all over the car. I remember the snacks Mom told me she ate when she was a kid and how I tried to imagine her at my age. I wanted to like all the things she did, to embody her completely.

My grief comes in waves and is usually triggered by something arbitrary. I can 6
tell you with a straight face what it was like watching my mom's hair fall out in the
bathtub, or about the five weeks I spent sleeping in hospitals, but catch me at H
Mart when some kid runs up double-fisting plastic sleeves of ppeongtwigi
and I'll just lose it. Those little rice-cake Frisbees were my childhood, a happier time when Mom was there and we'd crunch away on the Styrofoam-
like disks after school, splitting them like packing peanuts that dissolved
like sugar on our tongues.

> Metaphors and similes can give depth to descriptive writing (see pp. 191–92).

I'll cry when I see a Korean grandmother eating seafood noodles in the 7
food court, discarding shrimp heads and mussel shells onto the lid of her daughter's
tin rice bowl. Her gray hair frizzy, cheekbones protruding like the tops of two
peaches, tattooed eyebrows rusting as the ink fades out. I'll wonder what my mom
would have looked like in her seventies, if she'd have wound up with the same perm
that every Korean grandma gets, as though it were a part of our race's evolution. I'll
imagine our arms linked, her small frame leaning against mine as we take the escalator up to the food court. The two of us in all black, "New York style," she'd say, her
image of New York still rooted in the era of *Breakfast at Tiffany's.* She would carry
the quilted-leather Chanel purse that she'd wanted her whole life, instead of the
fake ones that she bought on the back streets of Itaewon. Her hands and face would
be slightly sticky from QVC anti-aging creams. She'd wear some strange high-top
sneaker wedges that I'd disagree with. "Michelle, in Korea, every celebrity wears
this one." She'd pluck the lint off my coat and pick on me—how my shoulders
slumped, how I needed new shoes, how I should really start using that argan-oil
treatment she bought me—but we'd be together. . . .

Sometimes my grief feels as though I've been left alone in a room with no doors. 8
Every time I remember that my mother is dead, it feels like I'm colliding with a wall
that won't give. There's no escape, just a hard surface that I keep ramming into over
and over, a reminder of the immutable reality that I will never see her again.

H Marts are usually situated on the outskirts of the city and serve as a secondary 9
center for strip malls of Asian storefronts and restaurants that are always better
than the ones found closer to town. We're talking Korean restaurants that
pack the table so full of banchan side dishes that you're forced to play a
never-ending game of horizontal Jenga with twelve tiny plates of stir-fried
anchovies, stuffed cucumbers, and pickled everything. This isn't like the
sad Asian fusion joint by your work, where they serve bell peppers in their
bibimbap and give you the stink eye when you ask for another round of
wilted bean sprouts. This is the real deal.

> Zauner assumes her audience ("you") isn't likely to be familiar with the layout of an H Mart. See pp. 184–85 for tips on thinking about purpose and audience.

You'll know that you're headed the right way because there will be signs 10
to mark your path. As you go farther into your pilgrimage, the lettering on

the awnings slowly begins to turn into symbols that you may or may not be able to read. This is when my elementary-grade Korean skills are put to the test—how fast can I sound out the vowels in traffic? I spent more than six years going to Hangul Hakkyo every Friday, and this is all I have to show for it. I can read the signs for churches, for an optometrist's office, a bank. A couple more blocks in, and we're in the heart of it. Suddenly, it's another country. Everyone is Asian, a swarm of different dialects crisscross like invisible telephone wires, the only English words are HOT POT and LIQUORS, and they're all buried beneath an assortment of glyphs and graphemes, with an anime tiger or a hot dog dancing next to them.

Inside an H Mart complex, there will be some kind of food court, an appliance 11 shop, and a pharmacy. Usually, there's a beauty counter where you can buy Korean makeup and skin-care products with snail mucin or caviar oil, or a face mask that vaguely boasts "placenta." (Whose placenta? Who knows?) There will usually be a pseudo-French bakery with weak coffee, bubble tea, and an array of glowing pastries that always look much better than they taste.

My local H Mart these days is in Elkins Park, a town northeast of Philadelphia. 12 My routine is to drive in for lunch on the weekends, stock up on groceries for the week, and cook something for dinner with whatever fresh bounty inspires me. The H Mart in Elkins Park has two stories; the grocery is on the first floor and the food court is above it. Upstairs, there is an array of stalls serving different kinds of food. One is dedicated to sushi, one is strictly Chinese. Another is for traditional Korean jjigaes, bubbling soups served in traditional earthenware pots called ttukbaegis, which act as mini cauldrons to ensure that your soup is still bubbling a good ten minutes past arrival. There's a stall for Korean street food that serves up Korean ramen (basically just Shin Cup noodles with an egg cracked in); giant steamed dumplings full of pork and glass noodles housed in a thick, cakelike dough; and tteokbokki, chewy, bite-sized cylindrical rice cakes boiled in a stock with fish cakes, red pepper, and gochujang, a sweet-and-spicy paste that's one of the three mother sauces used in pretty much all Korean dishes. Last, there's my personal favorite: Korean-Chinese fusion, which serves tangsuyuk—a glossy, sweet-and-sour orange pork—seafood noodle soup, fried rice, and black bean noodles.

The food court is the perfect place to people-watch while sucking down salty, 13 fatty jjajangmyeon. I think about my family who lived in Korea, before most of them died, and how Korean-Chinese was always the first thing we'd eat when my mom and I arrived in Seoul after a fourteen-hour flight from America. Twenty minutes after my aunt would phone in our order, the apartment ringer would buzz "Für Elise" in MIDI, and up would come a helmeted man, fresh off his motorcycle, with a giant steel box. He'd slide open the metal door and deliver heaping bowls of noodles and deep-fried battered pork with its rich sauce on the side. The plastic wrap on top would be concave and sweating. We'd peel it off and dribble black, chunky goodness all over the noodles and pour the shiny, sticky, translucent orange sauce over the pork. We'd sit cross-legged on the cool marble floor, slurping and reaching over one another. My aunts and mom and grandmother would jabber on in Korean, and I would eat and listen, unable to comprehend, bothering my mom every so often, asking her to translate.

I wonder how many people at H Mart miss their families. How many are think- 14 ing of them as they bring their trays back from the different stalls. If they're eating to feel connected, to celebrate these people through food. Which ones weren't able to fly back home this year, or for the past ten years? Which ones are like me, missing the people who are gone from their lives forever? . . .

It's a beautiful, holy place. A cafeteria full of people from all over the world who 15 have been displaced in a foreign country, each with a different history. Where did they come from and how far did they travel? Why are they all here? . . .

We don't talk about it. There's never so much as a knowing look. We sit here in 16 silence, eating our lunch. But I know we are all here for the same reason. We're all searching for a piece of home, or a piece of ourselves. We look for a taste of it in the food we order and the ingredients we buy. Then we separate. We bring the haul back to our dorm rooms or our suburban kitchens, and we re-create the dish that couldn't be made without our journey. What we're looking for isn't available at a Trader Joe's. H Mart is where your people gather under one odorous roof, full of faith that they'll find something they can't find anywhere else.

In the H Mart food court, I find myself again, searching for the first chapter of 17 the story I want to tell about my mother. I am sitting next to a Korean mother and her son, who have unknowingly taken the table next to ol' waterworks. The kid dutifully gets their silverware from the counter and places it on paper napkins for both of them. He's eating fried rice and his mom has seolleongtang, ox-bone soup. He must be in his early twenties, but his mother is still instructing him on how to eat, just like my mom used to. "Dip the onion in the paste." "Don't add too much gochujang or it'll be too salty." "Why aren't you eating the mung beans?" Some days, the constant nagging would annoy me. Woman, let me eat in peace! But, most days, I knew it was the ultimate display of a Korean woman's tenderness, and I cherished that love. A love I'd do anything to have back.

The boy's mom places pieces of beef from her spoon onto his. He is quiet and 18 looks tired and doesn't talk to her much. I want to tell him how much I miss my mother. How he should be kind to his mom, remember that life is fragile and she could be gone at any moment. Tell her to go to the doctor and make sure there isn't a small tumor growing inside her too.

Within five years, I lost both my aunt and my mother to cancer. So, when I go to 19 H Mart, I'm not just on the hunt for cuttlefish and three bunches of scallions for a buck; I'm searching for memories. I'm collecting the evidence that the Korean half of my identity didn't die when they did. H Mart is the bridge that guides me away from the memories that haunt me, of chemo head and skeletal bodies and logging milligrams of hydrocodone. It reminds me of who they were before, beautiful and full of life, wiggling Chang Gu honey-cracker rings on all ten of their fingers, showing me how to suck a Korean grape from its skin and spit out the seeds. ◆

FOR CLOSE READING

1. Why do you suppose an Asian American grocery store with a name that translates as "One Arm Full of Groceries" would shorten that name to "H Mart"?

2. Why does Michelle Zauner cry in H Mart? Why does she shop there? What is she looking for besides groceries?

3. Her mother was "constantly pushing [her]," says Zauner (5). Pushing her to do what? Based on Zauner's characterization of her mother, how would you describe their relationship?

4. "It's a beautiful, holy place," says Zauner as she watches people eat and talk in the food court of her local H Mart (15). What's so special about the place as Zauner sees it?

STRATEGIES AND STRUCTURES

1. Zauner often begins a paragraph with a direct statement—"Food was how my mother expressed her love" (5)—followed by an extended description intended to support or illustrate that statement. Point out several instances in her essay where you think this strategy is (or is not) particularly effective.

2. Is Zauner's description of her local H Mart in paragraph 12 more SUBJECTIVE or OBJECTIVE? How about in paragraph 17? Explain.

3. About halfway through her essay, Zauner no longer translates Korean words like "bibimbap" (9) and "Hangul Hakkyo" (10). Why not? What is she implying about the reader's involvement at this point?

4. "You'll know that you're headed the right way because there will be signs to mark your path" (10). Most of the time, Zauner writes in the FIRST PERSON ("I"). Why does she switch to the SECOND PERSON here, and what does the shift reveal about her intended audience—and where her essay is heading?

5. *Other Methods.* How might the foods and food customs that Zauner finds (and cries over) in H Mart be seen throughout her essay as "signs" and "symbols" (10)? What do they signify to her, and how and how well does she translate their meaning to the reader?

THINKING ABOUT LANGUAGE

1. Why might children who live and go to school more or less on their own in a foreign country be referred to as "parachute kids" (2)?

2. Zauner describes her mother's expectations as "intractable" (5). What is the meaning of this term, and what are its implications as Zauner uses it?

3. "Her gray hair frizzy, cheekbones protruding like the tops of two peaches, tattooed eyebrows rusting as the ink fades out" (7). Would this description of the grandmother that Zauner sees in the food court be more (or less) effective if she had written this instead: "She had gray hair, protruding cheekbones, and indelible eyebrows"? Explain.

4. What's the difference between a journey and a "pilgrimage" (10)? Why does Zauner use the latter term when describing how some of the people in the food court at H Mart got there?

5. At the end of her essay, Zauner refers to H Mart as a "bridge" (19). From where to where? Is the METAPHOR appropriate? Explain.

FOR WRITING

1. Write a six-to-eight-paragraph essay in which you COMPARE AND CONTRAST two chain grocery or other big-box stores—for example, Kroger and Trader Joe's, Home Depot and Lowe's, Walmart and Target. Describe what you can buy or do in each place, but also—and equally important—try to re-create the general atmosphere of each location and how you (and others around you) felt about being there.

2. In a brief essay containing both OBJECTIVE and SUBJECTIVE DESCRIPTON, write about a meal that you associate with a particular person (or persons). Tell what you ate, and where, and how the food was prepared and by whom. Recall what you talked about and how you behaved toward each other during the meal. Include a description of your emotional response to the situation.

9 | Example

Few things are harder to put up with than the annoyance of a good example.
—MARK TWAIN, *Pudd'nhead Wilson*

An art dealer knows at a glance that a supposedly ancient statue is a fake. After five minutes in a new course, a student accurately predicts that the professor is going to be a brilliant teacher—or a bore. Listening to a husband and wife bicker in his office, a trained psychologist can tell, with 90 percent accuracy, whether the couple will still be together in fifteen years. These are all examples that journalist Malcolm Gladwell uses to illustrate "thin-slicing," the idea that human beings can make accurate judgments based on "the very thinnest slice" of information.

Examples help us understand such concepts by giving us a slice of information that is typical of the whole pie. Because a single good example is often worth a dozen lengthy explanations, we use examples all the time to support or explain what we have to say. The use of examples—exemplification—is so basic to human communication, in fact, that it's hard to imagine writing without them.

Giving a "For Instance"

When you define something, such as thin-slicing or the law of supply and demand, you say what it is. When you exemplify something, you give an instance or illustration. To show what he means by thin-slicing, Gladwell cites the example of an apparently happy couple who were recorded in the "love lab" while having the following conversation about their new dog:

> SUE: Sweetie! She's not smelly . . .
> BILL: Did you smell her today?
> SUE: I smelled her. She smelled good. I petted her, and my hands didn't stink or feel oily. Your hands have never smelled oily.
> BILL: Yes, sir.
> SUE: I've never let my dog get oily.
> BILL: Yes, sir. She's a dog.
> SUE: My dog has never gotten oily. You'd better be careful.
> BILL: No, you'd better be careful.
> SUE: No, you'd better be careful. . . . Don't call my dog oily, boy.
>
> —MALCOLM GLADWELL, *Blink*

Is this couple's marriage in jeopardy? According to the experts whom Gladwell consulted, it is if this "slice" (or example) is representative of their relationship as a whole. To the researcher who knows what to look for, says Gladwell, "The truth of a marriage can be understood in a much shorter time than anyone imagined."

This is, as Gladwell goes on to say, "a beautiful example" of the complicated psychological process he's explaining. Examples are particular items or instances—a couple playfully bickering about their dog, a crispy taco with guacamole, "The

Raven"—that can be taken to represent a whole group: psychological thin-slicing, Tex-Mex food, the poems of Edgar Allan Poe.

In this chapter, we'll see how to choose examples that truly represent—or exemplify—your subject. We'll consider how many and what kinds of examples are sufficient to make your point about that subject and then discuss how to organize an entire essay around those examples. Finally, we'll review critical points to watch for as you read over an exemplification essay, as well as common errors to avoid when you edit.

Why Do We Cite Examples?

For most of us, it's easier to digest a piece of pie than the whole pie at once. The same goes for examples: they make general concepts easier to grasp (and swallow), and they give the flavor of the whole in a single bite. As writers, we cite examples to explain ABSTRACT ideas or to support general statements by making them more CONCRETE and specific.

Suppose you were writing about a street bazaar and wanted to make the point that it offered a wide range of goods. This may sound like a straightforward statement, but it could refer to everything from livestock to homemade bread. To clarify what you mean exactly, you would need to give specific examples, as in the following:

> Everything was for sale—flowers, bolts of cloth, candles, fruits and vegetables, shoes, coffee beans, toys, cheap jewelry, canned goods, religious articles, books, kerosene, candy, nylons, towels—all of it spilling onto the street in colorful profusion.
>
> —FRANK CONROY, *Stop-Time*

Using examples like this helps you (and your readers) narrow down the universe from "everything" to something a little more specific. It shows just what corner of the great bazaar you're talking about, and it gives the reader a more definite sense of the bazaar's "colorful profusion." Even more important, by using concrete examples like bolts of cloth and kerosene, Conroy explains exactly what was for sale, making his statement clearer and more interesting.

Even screams can be explained in concrete terms (pp. 287–88, pars. 6 and 10).

Composing an Essay That Uses Examples

An essay built around examples has basically two parts: a statement about a general category of things or ideas ("everything was for sale") and specific items from that category that illustrate the statement ("bolts of cloth, candles, fruits and vegetables,

USING EXAMPLES IN A RÉSUMÉ

When you write a résumé—whether for a school or job application, as part of a website or blog, or for some other purpose—you present yourself and your accomplishments in a short form that can be readily reviewed by the intended audience. The conventional way of doing this is by breaking your career into categories and giving specific examples, in each category, of your education, skills, experience, and other attributes. The categories may vary, depending on your work experience and the level of the position you're looking for, but should include your personal data, goal, work history, skills, and hobbies. Anyone can set up a set of impressive categories like this on a résumé, but only you can fill in appropriate examples that show who you really are.

Let's say you're a senior executive with a questionable reputation, and you're looking for a job at the master-of-the-universe level. You'd want to craft your résumé to highlight your unique strengths and accomplishments:

Tell potential employers up front whom they're dealing with.

DARTH VADER
Death Star, in a Galaxy Far, Far Away
DVader@galacticempire.gov

Let them know what you're going to do for (or to!) them.

Goal: To serve the Emperor and bring all rebel galaxies to the dark side.

Work History:

Emphasize scope, don't forget to include dates.

Commander, Galactic Empire armed forces, overseeing
   construction of two Death Stars   19BBY to present
Chancellor Palpatine's Jedi representative   20BBY–19BBY
Battle Commander, Army of the Republic   22BBY–19BBY
Mentor to Padawan Ahsoka Tano   22BBY–19BBY

List pertinent skills.

Skills: Mastery of the Force, experienced battle strategist, imposing physical appearance, lightsaber duel expertise

Show you're a normal person.

Hobbies: Levitating underlings remotely by the throat, building protocol droids and lightsabers

shoes, coffee beans, toys, cheap jewelry," and so on). What if Conroy had illustrated his statement about the profusion of items on sale in the marketplace with the following examples instead: boxes and boxes of ladies' gloves, stall after stall of ladies' hats, piles and piles of ladies' shoes?

While these examples would illustrate the large number of items on offer in the marketplace, they lack variety and, consequently, wouldn't fully support Conroy's statement that "everything" was on sale. When you compose an essay based on examples, consider which particular aspects of your subject you want to emphasize and look for examples that illustrate all those qualities or characteristics.

As you come up with representative examples, you'll also need to decide just how many examples to use and how best to organize them and present them to your readers. The exact number and kinds of examples you cite, however, will depend on your **PURPOSE** and **AUDIENCE**, as well as the main point you're illustrating.

Thinking about Purpose and Audience

The purpose of "All Seven Deadly Sins Committed at Church Bake Sale," the satirical piece from *The Onion* included in this chapter, is to entertain readers who have some idea of what happens at church bake sales and who will be amused by an "exposé" of such a (normally) innocent event. For this purpose and audience, the writer chooses humorous, exaggerated examples of "sinful" behavior at the sale. In total, says *The Onion*, "347 individual acts of sin were committed at the bake sale."

But suppose you wanted to write a straightforward, informative report about a bake sale for the church bulletin. In that case, you would focus on actual examples of the people staffing the booths and the kinds of baked goods sold. Or if you were writing about the bake sale in order to persuade others to participate next time, you might offer examples of the money earned at various booths, how much fun participants had, and what good causes the money was used for. In each case, your purpose shapes the kinds of examples you use.

So does your audience. No matter what your subject, you need to take into account how much they already know (or don't know) about your subject—the *Onion* piece is careful to define "deadly" sins for readers who might be in doubt—and how sympathetic they're likely to be to your position. Suppose you're writing a paper for a course in health and nutrition, and your purpose is to argue that the health of Americans in general has declined over the last decade. If you were writing for your teacher alone—or for an audience of doctors or nutritionists—a few key examples would probably suffice to make your point.

Ana Pacheco (p. 261) profiles a Salvadoran street vendor in suburban Los Angeles to educate her audience about the immigrant experience in America.

Your paper, however, is intended for a more general audience, such as your classmates. So you'll need to give more background information and cite more (and more basic) examples than you would if you were addressing an audience of specialists. If your readers are unfamiliar with your subject or not likely to see it as you do, you'll have to work even harder to come up with sufficient examples. For instance, you may have to give extra examples to remind the athletes in your audience that their physical condition is not necessarily representative of the general state of health among all Americans.

Generating Ideas: Finding Good Examples

Techniques like LISTING, BRAINSTORMING, and CLUSTERING can help you come up with examples on almost any subject. Suppose you're writing an essay on artificial intelligence and you decide to focus on how AI wormed its way into American households through consumer products and services long before the arrival of the latest chatbots and AI-enhanced search engines. You might begin by listing particular companies and the AI products or services they're already well known for: the Philips smart bulb, for instance, introduced in 2012; Apple's Siri (2011); iRobot's self-deploying vacuum cleaner, the Roomba (2002).

As you select examples, look for ones that display the most fundamental characteristics of the subject you're examining. Early AI devices are smart—or at least smarter than earlier versions. They not only turn off the light, for example, but they do it remotely, using voice recognition and other basic AI technologies. They can also be autonomous, and thus more humanoid in their intelligence: the Roomba can scan room size, detect obstacles, and remember the most efficient routes for cleaning. Unless it gets stuck on a piece of furniture or the battery runs down, the Roomba and its competitors, such as Deebot and Roborock, can also clean floors all on their own. These capabilities make the autonomous vacuum cleaner perhaps the first artificially intelligent, fully embodied robot (compared to Siri and Alexa, which are just disembodied voices) to occupy a significant place in the American home.

Organizing and Drafting an Exemplification Essay

The Onion's satirical "All Seven Deadly Sins Committed at Church Bake Sale" (p. 271) states its thesis right in the title.

Once you have a number of examples that exhibit the chief characteristics of your subject, you're ready to organize them and put them in a draft. The simplest way to organize an essay based on examples is to state your THESIS at the beginning and then give your best examples to support it. You could also present your examples in order of increasing importance or interest, perhaps saving the best for last. Or, if you plan to use a large number of examples, you might organize them into categories.

No matter how you organize your essay, you'll need to state your point clearly, provide sufficient and representative examples, and use TRANSITIONS to help readers follow your text. The templates on p. 256 can help you with your draft.

STATING YOUR POINT

Usually, in an essay based on examples, you will state your point in a **THESIS** statement in your introduction. For example:

> College teams depend more on teamwork than on star athletes for success.

> In general, the health of Americans has declined during this century.

> Hillary Clinton's 2016 presidential campaign made a number of tactical errors.

> From a close reading of almost any major scene in *The Great Gatsby*, we can conclude that Fitzgerald's narrator, Nick Carraway, is not to be trusted.

> As observed on the popular websites devoted to harmful campus gossip, online anonymity poses serious ethical problems.

Each of these thesis statements cries out for specific examples to support it. How many examples would you need to do the job sufficiently—and what kinds?

PROVIDING SUFFICIENT EXAMPLES

Sufficiency isn't strictly a matter of numbers. Ultimately, whether or not your examples are sufficient to prove your point will depend on your audience. If your readers are inclined to agree with you, one or two well-chosen examples may suffice, which is what sufficiency implies: enough to do the job and no more. So consider your intended audience, and choose examples you think they'll find interesting and convincing.

Also, consider how broad or narrow your subject is. As you select examples to support a thesis, you have basically two choices: you can use multiple brief examples or one or two extended examples.

Multiple examples work well when you're dealing with different aspects of a broad subject (a presidential campaign strategy; college athletic programs) or exemplifying trends involving large numbers of people (Americans whose health has declined; college athletes). Extended examples, in contrast, work better when you're talking about the implications of a particular case (a single scene in a novel; a particular website).

> To explain what she means by "feminist," Chimamanda Ngozi Adichie uses multiple examples of gender stereotypes (p. 275).

Take the proposition that the health of Americans, on average, has declined during this century. To support a sweeping general statement like this, which applies to millions of people, you would probably need to use multiple examples rather than one or two extended ones. Luckily, the Health and Medicine Division of the National Academies of Sciences, Engineering, and Medicine has identified a number of indicators of the nation's health.

TEMPLATES FOR DRAFTING

When you begin to draft an essay based on examples, you need to identify the subject, state its main characteristics, and give examples that exhibit those characteristics—moves fundamental to exemplification. See how Chimamanda Ngozi Adichie, author of an essay on feminism in this chapter, begins to make these moves:

> I take your charge—how to raise her feminist—very seriously. And I understand what you mean by not always knowing what the feminist response to situations should be. For me, feminism is always contextual.
>
> —Chimamanda Ngozi Adichie, "Dear Ijeawele"

Adichie identifies her subject (feminism) and a key characteristic of it ("always contextual") and then goes on to give numerous examples that show feminist behavior in particular contexts. Sweeping the floor is one. Here's one more illustration of a way to make these moves, taken from another essay in this chapter; the writer is exemplifying the need for trust even in risky situations:

> The young man got out of his vehicle and approached ours with a tentative smile. He wanted me to know he wasn't out to kill anyone. And that gave me about five seconds to decide whether I could trust him.
>
> —Pete Buttigieg, "On Suicide Circle"

The following templates can help you make some of these basic moves in your own writing. But don't take these as formulas where you just fill in the blanks. There are no shortcuts to good writing, but these templates can serve as starting points.

▸ About X, it can generally be said that _____; a good example would be _____.

▸ The main characteristics of X are _____ and _____, as exemplified by _____, _____, and _____.

▸ For the best example(s) of X, we can turn to _____.

▸ _____ is a particularly representative example of X because _____.

▸ Additional examples of X include _____, _____, and _____.

▸ From these examples of X, we can conclude that _____.

If you were drawing on these data to make your point, you probably wouldn't focus on only one or two of these indicators, since health is a broad topic that encompasses many factors. Instead, you would want to cite multiple examples—such as low birth weights in infants, tobacco use, obesity, reduced access to health insurance, shorter average life expectancies, and decreased spending on health care—of the many different factors that contribute to the general decline you're illustrating.

Now let's consider how a reviewer of video games uses a single, extended example to support his thesis about their artistic and social potential:

> One of the finest games of 2013, and undoubtedly the most important, was *Gone Home*, which had no combat or killing but used the perspective of the first-person shooter genre, as well as some of the same narrative techniques, to tell a story about two teenage girls in love. *Gone Home*, however, was not universally beloved. Some players resented the idea that the game didn't involve much conventional challenge, in the sense of puzzles to solve or buttons to mash.
>
> —CHRIS SUELLENTROP, "Can Video Games Survive?"

Limiting video games to puzzles and buttons would be a mistake, Suellentrop argues. His thesis—that the possibilities of video games are almost "limitless"— might be supported by multiple examples of different games, such as *Grand Theft Auto* and *Call of Duty*. However, his thesis has to do with the potential quality (not quantity) of video games as a broad form of communication, so he chooses to focus on a single extended example of a particularly fine game, *Gone Home*.

USING A RANGE OF REPRESENTATIVE EXAMPLES

Be sure that your examples fairly and accurately support the point you're making. For instance, if you were trying to convince readers that a particular political candidate failed to get elected because of errors in campaign tactics, you'd need to cite a number of mistakes from different points in the campaign. Or if you were writing about how the best college athletic teams depend on teamwork for success, you'd want to choose examples from several different teams.

See p. 281 for an essay about trust based on the extended example of a tense moment in Afghanistan.

Those examples should be as representative as possible. If you're writing, say, about the health benefits of swimming every day, Olympic gold medalist Katie Ledecky is probably not a good example. Even though Ledecky is a great swimmer, she isn't representative of swimmers in general, the subject you're exemplifying.

USING TRANSITIONS BETWEEN EXAMPLES

To make a point with exemplification, you need to do more than state your claim and then give examples, no matter how effective they may be. You need to relate those examples to one another and to the point you're making by using clear TRANSITIONS and other connecting words and phrases.

Use transitions to move from examples to conclusions, too. Pete Buttigieg's phrase "For days afterward" (p. 283, par. 11) leads into the larger meaning of his story.

You can always use the phrases "for example" and "for instance:" "The sloth, for example, is one of many animals that survive because of their protective coloration. Other animals—for instance, wolves and wild dogs—do so by going around in packs." But consider using other transitions and connecting phrases as well, such as "more specifically," "exactly," "precisely," "thus," "namely," "indeed," "that is," "in other words," "in fact," "in particular." ("The sloth, in particular, survives by blending in with its surroundings.") Or try using a RHETORICAL QUESTION, which you then go on to answer: "So what strategy of survival does the sloth exemplify?"

USING OTHER METHODS

The purpose of examples is to give concrete and specific illustrations of a general topic. Consequently, the examples themselves should be presented in ways that are as concrete and specific as possible. Let's say you're writing on the topic of common survival strategies among mammals. As an example, you've chosen the three-toed sloth, a tree-inhabiting eater of insects and plants from Central and South America. You can present such an example in a number of ways.

For instance, you can DESCRIBE it in some detail: "covered with unkempt fur that looks like the trunk of the tree it hides in." Or you can NARRATE what it does: "nothing at all, even when approached by the most dangerous of predators." Or you can analyze the CAUSES AND EFFECTS of its distinctive behavior: "such passivity fools predators into looking elsewhere for live food."

EDITING FOR COMMON ERRORS IN EXAMPLES

Exemplification invites certain kinds of errors, particularly with lists or a series of examples. The following tips will help you check your writing for errors that often turn up when using examples.

If you list a series of examples, be sure they are parallel in structure

▶ Animals avoid predators in many ways. They travel in groups, move fast, blend~~ing~~ in with their surroundings, and look~~ing~~ threatening.

Edit out "etc.," "and so forth," and "and so on," when they don't add any meaning to your sentence

▶ Animals typically avoid predators by traveling in groups, moving fast, <u>and</u> blending in with their surroundings~~, etc.~~

Check your use of "i.e." and "e.g."

These abbreviations of Latin phrases are often used interchangeably to introduce examples, but they don't mean the same thing: "i.e." means "that is" and "e.g." means "for example." Since most of your readers do not likely speak Latin, it's a good idea to use the English equivalents.

▶ The chameleon is an animal that uses protective coloration—~~i.e.~~ <u>that is</u>, it changes color to blend in with its surroundings.

▶ Some animals change colors to blend in with their surroundings—~~e.g.~~ <u>for example</u>, the chameleon.

Reading an Essay Based on Examples with a Critical Eye

Once you've drafted your essay, ask someone else to read it and tell you which examples seem especially effective and which ones, if any, they think should be replaced or developed more sharply. Here are questions to keep in mind when checking your use of examples in an essay.

PURPOSE AND AUDIENCE. What's the overall purpose of the essay—to inform? entertain? persuade? How well does the text achieve that purpose? How familiar is the intended audience likely to be with the subject of the essay? What additional information might they find useful? What terms might they need to have defined or further explained?

THE POINT. What's the main point of the essay? Is it stated in a thesis? If not, should it be? How and how well do the examples support the thesis?

ORGANIZATION. Does the essay use multiple short examples, a few extended examples, or a combination of the two? Is this arrangement appropriate to the essay's thesis—using multiple examples, for instance, to support a generalization that applies in many instances and using extended examples to illustrate particular cases?

SUFFICIENT EXAMPLES. Are the examples presented in the essay sufficient to illustrate its key point or points? If not, how could the examples be made more persuasive? Would more examples be more convincing? Or do some examples need to be developed more fully? Which ones?

CONCRETE AND SPECIFIC EXAMPLES. Do the examples explain the topic in ways that are concrete (perceptible to the senses) and specific (narrowed down)? If not, how might they be sharpened and clarified?

REPRESENTATIVE EXAMPLES. Do the examples fairly and accurately represent the group they claim to represent? If the essay is based on one or two extended examples, do they represent *all* the important characteristics of the subject?

TRANSITIONS. Check all the transitional words and phrases in the essay. How effectively do they introduce and link the examples? Do they explicitly connect the examples to the ideas they're illustrating? Where might transitions be added or strengthened?

OTHER METHODS. Does the essay incorporate any other methods of development? Would it be improved by including some **DESCRIPTION** or **NARRATION**, for example?

COMMON ERRORS. Does the paper include examples in a series? If so, does the form of any item in the series need to be changed to become grammatically parallel with the others?

Student Example

Ana Pacheco wrote "Street Vendors: Harvest of Dreams" as a student at the University of California, Riverside. "For this assignment," says her teacher, Mark Biswas, "students were required to profile a person or place and conduct an interview." Pacheco chose to interview and write about Victoria Perez, a street vendor in Glendale, a suburb of Los Angeles.

The wife of an army general in El Salvador, Perez fled the country when her husband was assassinated in the Salvadoran civil war. To support herself and her grandson, Perez began baking bread and selling it from a bucket. Eleven years later, as she tells Pacheco, business is "booming"; and Perez herself has become a sort of spokesperson for her fellow street vendors, most of whom are immigrants. As presented in Pacheco's essay, Perez's experience is also a complex example of the immigrant experience in America, embodying not only the collective "sass and wit" of the newcomers but also their dreams of the future in a new land of "diversity and freedom."

Street Vendors: Harvest of Dreams

Just a few blocks away from the mainstream Glendale area in Los Angeles lie the headquarters of LA's greatest entrepreneurs. Although their attire is ragged, their business sense and determination are sharp. Among the crowd, a woman dressed in a bright lime skirt and vest stands out. Her name is Victoria Perez, and she is well known for walking around the streets carrying a matching lime green bucket on her head. Every morning, this *canasta* is filled with fresh-baked Salvadorian sweet bread, or *marquesotes*—a dollar each, or three for two.

Victoria Perez became a street vendor in 2006 after the death of her daughter. Victoria and her then three-month-old grandson were left alone in America with funeral debts and an empty refrigerator. For nearly two months, Victoria searched ceaselessly for a job. However, being a female middle-aged undocumented immigrant, she was never hired. Desperate to bring food to the table, Victoria used the last of her savings to fund her "Bucket-Bread Business." Now, eleven years later, she calls her business a "booming success." In

Introduces the extended example to be developed throughout Pacheco's essay these neighborhoods, Victoria is a household name when it comes to the best Salvadorian sweet bread.

Begins to introduce other specific examples of street vendors

It is not uncommon to hear stories like Victoria's among street vendors. According to the website streetvendor.org, street vendors are "small business people struggling to make ends meet. Most are immigrants and people of color. They work long hours under harsh conditions, asking for nothing more than a chance to sell their goods on the public sidewalk." However, in Los Angeles, street vendors have a bad reputation, and, according to Victoria and her colleagues, they face any number of obstacles to success. Even though LA is a so-called sanctuary city with an extremely diverse population, street vendors of color are often victims of harassment, racism, and discrimination.

To those who do not acknowledge that street vendors are valuable members of society, Victoria says, "Why not? Valuable members of society are those who are lawful, who work for a living, who participate in political affairs, and who contribute to the welfare of our society. I am all of those things. I might have a humble job and a small home but that doesn't make me any less valuable in this world."

Street vendors, Victoria points out, are job creators, who help push the economy and generate revenue for cities through payments for licenses and permits, fees and fines, and certain kinds of taxes. According to Women in Informal Employment: Globalizing and Organizing (WIEGO), an organization that seeks to shine a light on the hardships faced by poor working women, "Street vendors are an integral part of urban economies around the world." In addition to the economic contributions of street vendors, WIEGO contends that "street trade adds vibrancy to urban life and in many places is considered a cornerstone of historical and cultural heritage." Street trade is a multicultural phenomenon that allows people of different ethnic backgrounds to interact with foreign traditions, foods, and customs.

Victoria also believes that street vendors help globalize popular ethnic foods and customs. After all, America is the only place where a middle-aged woman can get up at four in the morning to beat up a few dozen eggs to make nearly four dozen *marquesotes,* and head out by seven with her matching *canasta* and skirt to sell them next to Javier, the man in flannel with the Mexican curios and *rompope* (Mexican eggnog). As Victoria puts it, the melting pot of our country "is all thanks to immigration, and it is what makes this country great. Just think about it. In El Salvador, they don't have a taco bowl for lunch, pho for dinner, and then buy one of my *marquesotes* for dessert. I believe that diversity and freedom are America's pillars. They are what make us a great nation."

Relates the diversity and variety of street vendors directly to immigration

But none of that prevents the harassment and bad treatment of street vendors. Shop owners, unhappy when vendors set up shop in front of their businesses, are often the cause of this aggression. They believe that street vendors steal their customers, or scare potential clients away. 7

Gives examples of the obstacles that street vendors face

"It's like the shop owners believe they have a right to mistreat us. Besides, the police rarely get involved," Victoria says. "Many times I have seen the people in the store kick out my friends from the side-walk. I tell them that it is a public area and that they cannot kick us out. They don't care. One time a man intentionally knocked over my bread bucket. That day I didn't have anything to eat, but I did get to hit him in the head with the empty bucket." 8

Despite her short stature, Victoria is one of the most respected street vendors in the area, and she is known for her wit and sass. She is also one of the most active members of the community, often voic-ing the concerns of her people and defending their rights. She is a supporter of and has been an active participant in the gay rights movement, the fight for female reproductive rights, the Black Lives Matter movement, and other social justice causes. Victoria sees these events as excellent opportunities to exercise her voice. In addition to this, she claims large crowds are wonderful for the business. 9

Victoria fled El Salvador with her two children after her hus-band—a high-ranking general for the country's national force—was murdered in the Salvadoran civil war. Since retaliation against a 10

NARRATES the story of Perez's flight to America from El Salvador

militant's family was common, Victoria thought it best to leave the country, but the road to the United States was long and hard.

"It took me about two years to get to California," she tells me. "I traveled with my one-year-old son and my four-year-old daughter. My boy never made it. My girl and I had to bury him on a rocky mountain in Guatemala near the Mexican border. It was one of the hardest things I have ever had to do." Tears stream down her face as she remembers her son's death. "I have never visited his grave. You know, I don't even remember where it is. I never got to say goodbye."

After twenty-seven months of anguish, Victoria and her surviving daughter made it to California. But their struggles had only just begun. Back home in El Salvador, Victoria was an upper-class lady. She was married to a well-respected general and her parents were wealthy ranch owners. Victoria's kids were heirs to her family's haciendas and her husband's riches. Here, she has had to work long hours in harsh conditions just to earn enough money to survive. Has she ever regretted coming to America?

"Sometimes," she says. "I won't lie, at times I wonder what my life would have been back home, but it is what it is. There is violence here too, but at least here my little girl and I were innocent bystanders and not targets. Our lifestyle was not lavish, but at least we had each other, and we didn't live in constant fear of being attacked."

Challenging a common stereotype of immigrants, Victoria thinks we are all bound by a sort of "universal immigrant experience." She says: "Back home, I had a future that was largely truncated by our country's poisoned political system and the crime surrounding it. It's not easy leaving behind everything one holds dear. It's not easy immigrating to a country where your education and knowledge have no value. Many people think of us as failed people. That is wrong. Most of us are here for very specific reasons. We have a goal or a purpose. I want my boy to go to college. Danny over there, partially blind and everything, bought himself that ice cream cart to be able to

Marginal notes:

11

12 Uses other methods (p. 258), such as COMPARISON AND CONTRAST, to help explain her examples.

13

14 Uses Perez's example to challenge the stereotype of immigrants as unsuspecting victims

Concludes that most immigrants come to America for "specific reasons"

At a street fair in Brooklyn, NY, Rafael and Reina Soler-Bermudez serve up *pupusas*—traditional Salvadoran corn patties.

work. Bills don't pay themselves. Linda unexpectedly took over her husband's magazine cart after he fell ill and Lilyanna began selling bracelets after her husband left her and her two sons. You see, there might be tragedy in our stories but that doesn't make us failed people. We are fighters."

Works Cited

"About SVP." *The Street Vendor Project*, Urban Justice Center, street-vendor.org/about/. Accessed 6 Feb. 2017.

"Street Vendors." *Women in Informal Employment: Globalizing and Organizing*, www.wiego.org/informal-economy/occupational-groups/street-vendors. Accessed 6 Feb. 2017.

Analyzing a Student Exemplification Essay

In "Street Vendors: Harvest of Dreams," Ana Pacheco draws on rhetorical strategies and techniques that good writers use all the time when exemplifying a subject. The following questions, in addition to focusing on particular aspects of Pacheco's text, will help you identify those common strategies and techniques so you can adapt them to your own writing. The questions will also prepare you for the analytical questions—on content, structure, and language—that you'll find after all the other selections in this chapter, along with suggestions for writing on related topics.

FOR CLOSE READING

1. Most of the street vendors Ana Pacheco writes about are immigrants. Judging by the examples she gives, why have they come to the United States, and how do they feel about their adoptive country?

2. Before Victoria Perez became a street vendor in Los Angeles, says Pacheco, she was "an upper-class lady" in El Salvador (12). What is Perez's life like now? What aspects of her former status does she retain?

3. According to Perez—and to WIEGO, the organization that supports women in informal employment—what do street vendors contribute to urban life (5)? If you live in or have visited a city where such vendors operate, do you agree? Why or why not?

4. Perez tells Pacheco that we are all part of a "universal immigrant experience" (14). What might she mean by this statement? Is this true? Why or why not?

STRATEGIES AND STRUCTURES

1. Pacheco claims that most of the street vendors in Glendale are responsible business people and good citizens. How well do her examples support this main point? Explain.

2. Although Pacheco is reporting on street vendors as a group, she focuses on the extended example of Victoria Perez. Is this a good strategy? Why or why not?

3. Throughout her essay, Pacheco lets Perez speak for herself, often at length. How effective do you find this use of direct QUOTATION, particularly for the larger implications of Perez's story in the final paragraph? Explain.

4. *Other Methods.* Point out places in her essay where Pacheco COMPARES AND CONTRASTS how the street vendors live now with how they lived before coming to the United States. What do these passages contribute to her observations?

THINKING ABOUT LANGUAGE

1. Pacheco sprinkles her essay with non-English words and phrases, most of which have to do with food. Point out several examples. What do they add to the general flavor of the essay?

2. The street vendors of Los Angeles, says Pacheco, are great "entrepreneurs" (1). Look up the definition of this word, and explain how it is related to the word "enterprise."

3. What is a "cornerstone" (5)? As a METAPHOR for the role of "street trade" (5) in urban culture, is the term appropriate? Explain.

4. The United States is often called a "melting pot" (6). Why? Is this a positive or a negative characterization—or both? Explain.

FOR WRITING

1. Using your cell phone or some other recording device, interview a classmate or friend for ten minutes about a job they have or have had. Transcribe your conversation word for word.

2. Do a longer interview of someone who has immigrated to the United States (or lived for an extended time in another country). Take notes in your own words on what your interviewee has to say about the experience. In addition, record direct QUOTATIONS for particularly important points. Put those words in quotation marks in your notes, and verify their accuracy by reading them back to the interviewee.

3. Interview and write a PROFILE of someone both as an individual and as a representative example of a particular group. Be sure to include details about other members of the group and the place or places they all frequent.

Food Fakes

This tempting dish may look good enough to eat, but it's actually a plastic model of an item on the menu of a restaurant in Japan. Actual samples of real food would look (and smell) a little less than perfect after a few hours in a warm display case. By contrast, food model displays like this—called *sampuru* in Japanese, from the English word "sample"—stay flawless looking (if odorless and tasteless) almost indefinitely, requiring nothing more than a little dusting from time to time. Visual examples of the most popular dishes a restaurant has to offer, *sampuru* are designed to entice customers off the street and inside the store to eat the real food they represent. In academic writing, likewise, well-selected and appealing examples can help the reader "see" the broader ideas that the writer is explaining and convince the reader that the writer's argument—like a delicious meal—is worth buying. Unlike *sampuru*, however, the best written examples tend to be those served fresh.

[FOR WRITING]··

Visit the *Display Fake Foods* website (www.displayfakefoods
.com), and write a paragraph or two **DESCRIBING** a typical
example of their wares from one of the following (or other)
categories: fake cakes, spills, baskets and jars, carhop trays.

SUGGESTIONS FOR WRITING

1. In "Street Vendors" (p. 261), Ana Pacheco gives numerous examples of how the culture of Los Angeles is enhanced, in her view, by people who make a living selling things on the street. On the basis of your own observations and research, write a **REPORT** of approximately 600 words giving examples of how a neighborhood, town, or city has been affected by "street trade," including buskers and speakers.

2. Although it's a parody, "All Seven Deadly Sins Committed at Church Bake Sale" (p. 271) correctly notes that the seven deadly sins as identified "by Gregory the Great in the Fifth Century" are avarice, sloth, envy, lust, gluttony, pride, and wrath. Do some additional research into the history of the seven deadlies, and write an essay that gives traditional examples of each sin.

3. Although written in the form of a letter to a friend, Chimamanda Ngozi Adichie's essay (p. 275) was published in book form with the title *Dear Ijeawele: A Feminist Manifesto in Fifteen Suggestions*. Beginning with "Feminist Manifesto," written in 1914 by the poet Mina Loy, do some research on other manifestos by feminist (or antifeminist) writers, and write a brief history of the manifesto form that cites several examples.

4. "Distrust," writes Pete Buttigieg in "On Suicide Circle" (p. 281), "is not simply an attitude; it's a tool of self-defense." When is self-defense necessary? When is it self-defeating? In a five-to-six-paragraph essay based on examples from your personal experience (or that of someone you know), take a **POSITION** on this issue as it relates both to your personal interests and to those of society at large.

5. Do some research on the profession of voice acting, and write a brief essay explaining what voice actors do. Include Ashley Peldon ("My Scream Is Famous," p. 286) as an example, but also mention several others, such as Tress MacNeille (*Voltron, Alvin and the Chipmunks, The Simpsons*) and Mel Blanc (*Looney Tunes, Buck Rogers in the 25th Century, Gilligan's Island*.)

All Seven Deadly Sins Committed at Church Bake Sale

The Onion was founded as a satirical weekly newspaper in 1988 by two juniors at the University of Wisconsin, Tim Keck and Christopher Johnson, who distributed a handful of copies to their friends around the Madison area. Today, The Onion website receives approximately 5 million unique visits per month. (The print edition ceased publication in 2013.) The Onion has long attributed its success to "fearless reporting and scathing commentary." Consider, for instance, these Onion headlines: "Cases of Glitter Lung on the Rise among Elementary-School Art Teachers," "Study Reveals Pittsburgh Unprepared for Full-Scale Zombie Attack," "Supreme Court Mistakenly Used Belgium's Constitution for Last 3 Rulings." Such satire has won The Onion a Thurber Prize for American Humor, a Peabody Award, and a handful of Webby Awards. Several collections of its articles have made the New York Times best-seller list, including Ad Nauseam (2003) and Our Dumb World (2007).

The Onion's brand of satire is marked by its pitch-perfect mimicry of the reporting styles that many papers routinely use to inflate the banal into the newsworthy. In the following article, an Onion investigative reporter sniffs out numerous concrete and specific examples of the "deadly sins" committed at a church bake sale.

G ADSDEN, AL—The seven deadly sins—avarice, sloth, envy, lust, gluttony, pride, and wrath—were all committed Sunday during the twice-annual bake sale at St. Mary's of the Immaculate Conception Church. [1]

In total, 347 individual acts of sin were committed at the bake sale, with nearly every attendee committing at least one of the seven deadly sins as outlined by Gregory the Great in the Fifth Century.

"My cookies, cakes, and brownies are always the highlight of our church bake sales, and everyone says so," said parishioner Connie Barrett, 49, openly committing the sin of pride. "Sometimes, even I'm amazed by how well my goodies turn out."

Fellow parishioner Betty Wicks agreed. [4]

> See p. 255 for what makes a "sufficient" number of examples. In this case, you don't have to cite all 347.

MLA CITATION: The Onion. "All Seven Deadly Sins Committed at Church Bake Sale." *Back to the Lake: A Reader and Guide for Writers*, edited by Thomas Cooley, 5th ed., W. W. Norton, 2024, pp. 271–73.

"Every time I go past Connie's table, I just have to buy something," said the 245-pound Wicks, who commits the sin of gluttony at every St. Mary's bake sale, as well as most Friday nights at Old Country Buffet. "I simply can't help myself—it's all so delicious."

The popularity of Barrett's mouth-watering wares elicited the sin of envy in many of her fellow vendors.

"Connie has this fantastic book of recipes her grandmother gave her, and she won't share them with anyone," church organist Georgia Brandt said. "This year, I made white-chocolate blondies and thought they'd be a big hit. But most people just went straight to Connie's table, got what they wanted, and left. All the while, Connie just stood there with this look of smug satisfaction on her face. It took every ounce of strength in my body to keep from going over there and really telling her off."

While the sins of wrath and avarice were each committed dozens of times at the event, Barrett and longtime bake-sale rival Penny Cox brought them together in full force.

"Penny said she wanted to make a bet over whose table would make the most money," said Barrett, exhibiting avarice. "Whoever lost would have to sit in the dunk tank at the St. Mary's Summer Fun Festival. I figured it's for such a good cause, a little wager couldn't hurt. Besides, I always bring the church more money anyway, so I couldn't possibly lose."

Moments after agreeing to the wager, Cox became wrathful when Barrett, the bake sale's co-chair, grabbed the best table location under the pretense of having to keep the coffee machine full. Cox attempted to exact revenge by reporting an alleged Barrett misdeed to the church's priest.

"I mentioned to Father Mark [O'Connor] that I've seen candles at Connie's house that I wouldn't be surprised one bit if she stole from the church's storage closet," said Cox, who also committed the sin of sloth by forcing her daughter to set up and man her booth while she gossiped with friends. "Perhaps if he investigates this, by this time next year, Connie won't be co-chair of the bake sale and in her place we'll have someone who's willing to rotate the choice table spots."

The sin of lust also reared its ugly head at the bake sale, largely due to the presence of Melissa Wyckoff, a shapely 20-year-old redhead whose family recently joined the church. While male attendees ogled Wyckoff, the primary object of lust for females was the personable, boyish Father Mark.

Though attendees' feelings of lust for Wyckoff and O'Connor were never acted on, they did not go unnoticed.

"There's something not right about that Melissa Wyckoff," said envious and wrathful bake-sale participant Jilly Brandon, after her husband Craig offered Wyckoff one of her Rice Krispie treats to "welcome her to the par-

Frequent dialogue (pp. 119–20) enlivens this essay by bringing the parishioners to life.

ish." "She might have just moved here from California, but that red dress of hers should get her kicked out of the church."

According to St. Mary's treasurer Beth Ellen Coyle, informal church-sponsored 15 events are a notorious breeding ground for the seven deadly sins.

"Bake sales, haunted houses, pancake breakfasts . . . such church events are rife 16 with potential for sin," Coyle said. "This year, we had to eliminate the 'Guess Your Weight' booth from the annual church carnival because the envy and pride had gotten so out of hand. Church events are about glorifying God, not violating His word. If you want to do that, you're no better than that cheap strumpet Melissa Wyckoff." ♦

FOR CLOSE READING

1. Who established the names and number of the seven deadly sins as we know them today?

2. How "deadly" do you find the sins reported here? That is, how well do the reporter's examples represent the general concept he says he is exemplifying?

3. The *Onion* reporter records "347 individual acts of sin" at the church bake sale (2). Is anything suspicious about these statistics? How do you suppose the reporter came up with this number?

4. Which sins does parishioner Connie Barrett commit? How does her bake-sale success encourage the sins of others?

5. Which single sin among the seven do the patrons of the bake sale only contemplate rather than act on? Who inspires it?

STRATEGIES AND STRUCTURES

1. A spoof is a gentle **PARODY** or mildly satirical imitation. What general **PURPOSE** does a spoof or parody usually serve? What is the writer's specific purpose here, and who is the intended **AUDIENCE**?

2. Pride, avarice, and the other "deadly sins" are **ABSTRACT** concepts. How do the reporter's examples make them more **CONCRETE** and specific? Are the examples sufficient, or should there be more? Explain.

3. The reporter gives numerous examples of what people say at the church bake sale. Why? What purpose do these verbal examples serve?

4. *Other Methods.* To bolster the examples, the reporter uses elements of **NARRATIVE**. What are some of them?

THINKING ABOUT LANGUAGE

1. What, exactly, is a "strumpet" (16), and why do you think the reporter uses this rather than a stronger word to describe Melissa Wyckoff?

2. Deadly (or "mortal") sins can be distinguished from "venial" sins. After looking up these terms, explain the difference between the two kinds. Give three examples of each kind.

3. Give a **SYNONYM** for each of the following words: "avarice," "sloth," "gluttony," and "wrath" (1).

4. Another word for pride is "hubris." Look up both terms, and explain the difference between the two.

FOR WRITING

1. Write a paragraph about one sin you would add to the traditional list.

2. Write a three-to-five-paragraph exemplification essay illustrating how the seven deadly sins are routinely committed in the library, in your classes, or in some other place at your school. Taking a cue from the *Onion* reporter, use **IRONY** to emphasize your points.

3. Have a look at *The Onion's* website; read a few examples of the "reporting" and what the editors have to say about style and content; then compose an *Onion*-like news report of your own.

4. Humor writing has its own demands and conventions. Do some research on the subject, and write a 400-to-500-word **ANALYSIS** of humor as a distinctive type of writing. Give lots of examples—and cite your sources.

CHIMAMANDA NGOZI ADICHIE

Dear Ijeawele

Chimamanda Ngozi Adichie (b. 1977) is an award-winning novelist and writer of short stories and nonfiction. Adichie grew up in Nigeria, where her mother was an administrator at the University of Nigeria and her father a professor of statistics. At age nineteen, she came to the United States to attend college, first at Eastern Connecticut State University and then at Yale, where she earned a master's degree in African studies, and at Johns Hopkins University, where she earned a master's in creative writing. Her third novel, *Americanah*, about a young woman from Nigeria who "discovers" that she is black while studying in the United States, won the 2013 National Book Critics Circle Award for fiction. Among many other honors, Adichie was awarded the PEN Pinter Prize in 2018 and the Women's Prize for Fiction "Winner of Winners" in 2020 for her novel *Half of a Yellow Sun* (2006), a wrenching view of modern African history set amid Biafra's effort to establish an independent republic in the 1960s. Her writing has been translated into over 30 languages. Adichie returns frequently to Nigeria but lives most of the time in Maryland.

Dear Ijeawele started out as an email to a friend in a traditional Nigerian village who had asked Adichie for advice on how to raise her new baby daughter as a "feminist." Written shortly before the birth of Adichie's own daughter, this personal message soon evolved into a public one that applies to raising any child. Subtitled *A Feminist Manifesto in Fifteen Suggestions*, it was first posted on Adichie's *Facebook* page and then published in 2017 as a short book. Here are the third, fifth, and sixth suggestions—with numerous examples of the principles of parenting that they embody.

MLA CITATION: Adichie, Chimamanda Ngozi. "Dear Ijeawele." *Back to the Lake: A Reader and Guide for Writers*, edited by Thomas Cooley, 5th ed., W. W. Norton, 2024, pp. 276–78.

D EAR IJEAWELE,   1
What joy. And what lovely names: Chizalum Adaora. She is so beautiful.   2
Only a week old and she already looks curious about the world. What a magnificent
thing you have done, bringing a human being into the world. "Congratulations"
feels too slight.

Your note made me cry. You know how I get foolishly emotional sometimes.   3
Please know that I take your charge—how to raise her feminist—very seriously.
And I understand what you mean by not always knowing what the feminist response
to situations should be. For me, feminism is always contextual . . .

I have some suggestions for how to raise Chizalum. But remember that you   4
might do all the things I suggest, and she will still turn out to be different from what
you hoped, because sometimes life just does its thing. What matters is that you try.
And always trust your instincts above all else, because you will be guided by your
love for your child.

Here are my suggestions: . . .   5

Third Suggestion

Teach her that the idea of "gender roles" is absolute nonsense. Do not ever tell her   6
that she should or should not do something because she is a girl.

"Because you are a girl" is never a reason for anything. Ever.   7

> Examples replace ABSTRACTIONS like "gender roles" with more CONCRETE ideas (p. 251) like sweeping the floor.

I remember being told as a child to "bend down properly while sweep-   8
ing, like a girl." Which meant that sweeping was about being female. I
wish I had been told simply, "bend down and sweep properly because
you'll clean the floor better." And I wish my . . . brothers had been told
the same thing.

It is interesting to me how early the world starts to invent gender   9
roles. Yesterday I went to a children's shop to buy Chizalum an outfit. In
the girls' section were pale creations in washed-out shades of pink. I disliked them. The boys' section had outfits in vibrant shades of blue. Because I
thought blue would be adorable against her brown skin—and photograph
better—I bought one. At the checkout counter, the cashier said mine was the
perfect present for the new boy. I said it was for a baby girl. She looked horrified.
"Blue for a girl?"

I cannot help but wonder about the clever marketing person who invented this   10
pink-blue binary. . . . Why not just have baby clothes organized by age and displayed
in all colors? The bodies of male and female infants are similar, after all.

I looked at the toy section, which was also arranged by gender. Toys for boys are   11
mostly active, and involve some sort of doing—trains, cars—and toys for girls are
mostly passive and are overwhelmingly dolls. I was struck by this. I had not quite

realized how early society starts to invent ideas of what a boy should be and what a girl should be.

I wished the toys had been arranged by type, rather than by gender.   12

Did I ever tell you about going to a U.S. mall with a seven-year-old Nigerian girl   13 and her mother? She saw a toy helicopter, one of those things that fly by wireless remote control, and she was fascinated and asked for one. "No," her mother said. "You have your dolls." And she responded, "Mummy, is it only dolls I will play with?" . . .

Another acquaintance, an American living in the Pacific Northwest, once told   14 me that when she took her one-year-old son to a baby play group, where babies had been brought by their mothers, she noticed that the mothers of baby girls were very restraining, constantly telling the girls "don't touch" or "stop and be nice," and she noticed that the baby boys were encouraged to explore more and were not restrained as much and were almost never told to "be nice." Her theory was that parents unconsciously start very early to teach girls how to be, that baby girls are given less room and more rules and baby boys more room and fewer rules.

Gender roles are so deeply conditioned in us that we will often follow them   15 even when they chafe against our true desires, our needs, our happiness. They are very difficult to unlearn, and so it is important to try to make sure that Chizalum rejects them from the beginning. Instead of letting her internalize the idea of gender roles, teach her self-reliance. Tell her that it is important to be able to do for herself and fend for herself. Teach her to try to fix physical things when they break. We are quick to assume girls can't do many things. Let her try. She might not fully succeed, but let her try. Buy her toys like blocks and trains—and dolls, too, if you want to. . . .

Fifth Suggestion

Teach Chizalum to read. Teach her to love books. The best way is by casual exam-   16 ple. If she sees you reading, she will understand that reading is valuable. If she were not to go to school, and merely just read books, she would arguably become more knowledgeable than a conventionally educated child. Books will help her understand and question the world, help her express herself, and help her in whatever she wants to become—a chef, a scientist, a singer, all benefit from the skills that reading brings. I do not mean schoolbooks. I mean books that have nothing to do with school, autobiographies and novels and histories. If all else fails, pay her to read. Reward her. I know this remarkable Nigerian woman, Angela, a single mother who was raising her child in the United States; her child did not take to reading so she decided to pay her five cents per page. An expensive endeavor, she later joked, but a worthy investment.

Sixth Suggestion

Teach her to question language. Language is the repository of our prejudices, our 17
beliefs, our assumptions. But to teach her that, you will have to question your own
language. A friend of mine says she will never call her daughter "princess." People
mean well when they say this, but "princess" is loaded with assumptions, of a girl's
delicacy, of the prince who will come to save her, etc. This friend prefers "angel"
and "star."

> Using an example from Igbo culture? Give your audience the context they need to understand it (p. 253).

So decide for yourself the things you will not say to your child. Because 18
what you say to your child matters. It teaches her what she should value.
You know that Igbo joke, used to tease girls who are being childish—"What
are you doing? Don't you know you are old enough to find a husband?" I
used to say that often. But now I choose not to. I say "You are old enough to
find a job." Because I do not believe that marriage is something we should
teach young girls to aspire to.

Try not to use words like "misogyny" and "patriarchy" too often with Chizalum. 19
We feminists can sometimes be too jargony, and jargon can sometimes feel too
abstract. Don't just label something misogynistic; tell her why it is, and tell her
what would make it not be.

Teach her that if you criticize X in women but do not criticize X in men, then 20
you do not have a problem with X, you have a problem with women. For X please
insert words like "anger," "ambition," "loudness," "stubbornness," "coldness,"
"ruthlessness."

Teach her to ask questions like What are the things that women cannot do 21
because they are women? Do these things have cultural prestige? If so, why are only
men allowed to do the things that have cultural prestige? . . .

Remember the mechanic in Lagos who was described as a "lady mechanic" in a 22
newspaper profile? Teach Chizalum that the woman is a mechanic, not a "lady
mechanic."

Point out to her how wrong it is that a man who hits your car in Lagos traffic gets 23
out and tells you to go and bring your husband because he "can't deal with a woman."

Instead of merely telling her, show her with examples that misogyny can be overt 24
and misogyny can be subtle and that both are abhorrent. . . .

May she be healthy and happy. May her life be whatever she wants it to be. 25

Do you have a headache after reading all this? Sorry. Next time don't ask me how 26
to raise your daughter feminist.

With love, oyi gi,
Chimamanda ◆

FOR CLOSE READING

1. In her *Feminist Manifesto*, Chimamanda Ngozi Adichie gives advice to a friend about how to raise her new daughter. What kind of advice is the friend seeking exactly, and why is she asking Adichie in particular?

2. A manifesto is a statement of principles, often political and sometimes expressed as rules or commands. (In *The Communist Manifesto*, for instance, Karl Marx proclaims, "Workers of the World, Unite!") Adichie offers "Suggestions." On the basis of the examples she gives, explain the difference between her suggestions and hard-and-fast rules.

3. Among the many specific suggestions that Adichie offers for raising a "feminist" (3), which ones do you think are most important? least important? Why?

4. How precisely does Adichie's suggestion about reading books agree with what you learned about close reading in Chapter 1 of this book? Explain.

5. What does Adichie mean when she says, "For me, feminism is always contextual" (3)? Point to specific examples in the text that illustrate this statement.

STRATEGIES AND STRUCTURES

1. Adichie's manifesto takes an epistolary form, meaning that it's written as a personal letter (actually, in this case, an email). As a means of explaining the writer's specific ideas about feminism and parenting, how effective is this form? Explain.

2. This personal communication is written in the FIRST PERSON ("I understand what you mean," 3), with many IMPERATIVE sentences ("Teach Chizalum to read," 16) interspersed with ANECDOTES based on Adichie's experiences and those of people she knows. Find three more statements of first-person point of view, three more imperatives, and three anecdotes.

3. Point out places in her "Suggestions" where Adichie exemplifies the conviction that various kinds of work should not be gendered. Are the examples well chosen? Why or why not?

4. Point out places where Adichie gives examples of the related idea that "gender roles" are "invented" (9, 10) and "conditioned" (15) early in life and are hard to unlearn later. How effective do you find these examples? Explain.

5. *Other Methods.* When giving examples of feminist stereotypes, Adichie is explaining how not to conform to them. Point to specific passages in her manifesto where she uses ANALYSIS to achieve this purpose.

THINKING ABOUT LANGUAGE

1. Adichie's manifesto includes an entire section on language. Why is language important in a discussion of stereotypes and how to avoid them?

2. The terms "feminine" and "feminist" come up throughout Adichie's essay. How and where does she define these key terms, and how do her DEFINITIONS compare with those you're familiar with—either from other writers or from your everyday knowledge and experience?

3. Adichie warns against using "words like 'misogyny' and 'patriarchy' too often" (19). Why? Are her objections valid? Why or why not?

4. "For X," writes Adichie, "please insert words like"—and then she gives a list (20). What terms would you substitute for X in this equation? Explain.

FOR WRITING

1. Visit a shop or department store (or a store's website) that sells toys or children's clothing. Take detailed notes on items that appear to be marketed specifically for girls, for boys, and for both or either. Write several paragraphs giving specific examples of the differences.

2. Do some additional research, and write an essay of 500 to 600 words explaining how the marketing of consumer items for children reinforces (or doesn't reinforce) gender stereotypes. To support your ARGUMENT, either use sufficient representative examples or discuss one well-chosen extended example.

3. Adichie concludes by advising her friend to teach "with examples that misogyny can be overt and misogyny can be subtle and that both are abhorrent" (24). On the basis of your own experience and reading, write an essay, *with examples*, that takes a POSITION in response to this CLAIM.

4. Write an open letter to your classmates setting forth what you consider to be the most important principles of good parenting. Use lots of examples. Read the letter aloud in class, and invite others to respond with examples (and counterexamples) of their own.

PETE BUTTIGIEG

On Suicide Circle

Pete Buttigieg (b. 1982) began serving as the US Secretary of Transportation in 2021. Before that, from 2012 to 2020, he was the thirty-second mayor of South Bend, Indiana, his home state. As valedictorian of the class of 2000 at St. Joseph High School, Buttigieg won first prize in the John F. Kennedy Presidential Library and Museum's Profile in Courage essay contest. He graduated magna cum laude from Harvard in 2004, and in 2007 he earned a BA as a Rhodes Scholar at Pembroke College, Oxford. He is the author of *Shortest Way Home: One Mayor's Challenge and a Model for America's Future* (2019) and *Trust: America's Best Chance* (2020).

In 2014, as a lieutenant in the US Naval Reserve, Pete Buttigieg took a seven-month leave from his mayoral duties to deploy to Afghanistan, where he served in naval intelligence as a liaison officer; there, he often drove a Land Cruiser in a particularly treacherous section of Kabul nicknamed by the Americans as "Suicide Circle." This selection, a chapter from *Trust*, gives an example not only of the hazards Buttigieg faced daily in Afghanistan but also of the thesis of his book about the future of America.

T HE YOUNG MAN got out of his vehicle and approached ours with a tentative 1 smile. He wanted me to know he wasn't out to kill anyone. And that gave me about five seconds to decide whether I could trust him.

It was a crisp, cloudless spring day in Kabul, and I was behind the wheel of a 2 Land Cruiser, inching through morning rush hour on the way to pick up a newly arrived team member at the airport. I'd only been on the ground in Afghanistan for

MLA CITATION: Buttigieg, Pete. "On Suicide Circle." *Back to the Lake: A Reader and Guide for Writers*, edited by Thomas Cooley, 5th ed., W. W. Norton, 2024, pp. 281–84.

a few weeks, but had quickly become my small unit's go-to vehicle driver, alongside my regular duties as a liaison officer. "Military Uber," we called it.

For the most part, I looked forward to driving duty. It certainly represented a status shift from the life I'd stepped away from as mayor of a midwestern city. But in the context of the deployment, it was liberating. Life within the walls of a military base quickly grows confining, and missions of this kind gave me a chance to see something of the world between our safe zones, even if only through my windshield.

See p. 253 for tips on considering how much your audience already knows, or doesn't know, about your subject.

I think most Americans have trouble imagining the vibrancy of an Afghan city. Television and online imagery of war zones makes it seem as if war is the only thing going on there. We tend to picture an otherworldly landscape of forward operating bases, of isolation and desolation and constant conflict. But war zones often include cities filled with the rhythms of everyday life, with kids going to school and businesspeople rushing to appointments and men buying fruit in open-air markets. And in Kabul, those rhythms included exceptionally bad traffic jams, with cars so tightly pressed together that they often grazed each other. Yes, there was a war on, but I wasn't surrounded by Taliban fighters; for the most part, I was surrounded by ordinary people, rushing about their morning commutes through the city.

Still, a Kabul commute was different. In Afghanistan there were things you couldn't trust. The methods of warfare the Taliban employed—from suicide bombings to improvised explosive devices—meant that you couldn't know for sure who the enemy might be, or whether a normal-looking street might be rigged for carnage. The Taliban had even been known to strap suicide vests to children, which meant we couldn't trust our most basic assumptions about who was safe and who was dangerous.

So when a young man suddenly started approaching my vehicle, my life and his were instantly at risk. I had no way to be certain if he meant any harm toward me and the gunnery sergeant in the passenger seat. What I did know was that the intersection I was navigating had a nickname. The maps called it Massoud Circle, but the Marines called it "Suicide Circle." You could never be sure what was about to happen here. Indeed, a few days after I'd first arrived in-country, the officer I was relieving showed me a photo taken from inside his vehicle, while driving in this area, of a pedestrian who had walked up to the SUV, in a traffic jam just like this one, and suddenly, bizarrely, begun hacking at his window with a large knife.

But the man in front of us now was smiling—sheepishly if not nervously. He was making eye contact and gesturing toward the front of my vehicle, trying to express that he needed something from me. As best I could tell, he didn't mean harm, and yet I couldn't understand or explain his behavior. And he didn't seem to be getting the drift of my own nonverbal communication, which was intended to send the message that I needed him to stay well away from the vehicle. As the seconds passed, I had a choice: I could *trust* that the man had good intentions, or I could jump out of the lightly armored SUV in the middle of a traffic jam and level my M4 at him until he retreated.

I had been trained not to exit a vehicle outside the wire unless there was no safe 8 alternative. A lightly armed contingent like ours did not want to be exposed on a street where we could easily be surrounded. At the same time, I also knew that the wheel well of a vehicle is a favorite place for Taliban fighters to affix magnetically attached IEDs, which could make this driver's seat the last place in Afghanistan I'd want to be. Why else would he have gotten out of his car? Why else would he be reaching toward my driver's-side front wheel?

I decided to sit tight. He didn't exactly have his hands up, but they seemed empty 9 as far as I could discern. Getting out of the vehicle seemed to be the greater risk. Based on the partial information I had, from what I could see with my eyes and from a gut sense that we would be okay, I had decided, in the end, to *trust* him.

Then, a second later, the nerve-racking encounter was over. I watched him back 10 away, just as gingerly as he'd approached, holding a piece of fiberglass. It turned out that a small bit of his car had gotten enmeshed in mine without my noticing, as our vehicles pressed against each other in the scrum of traffic. He wasn't out to attack anyone. He just wanted his property back—a piece of siding from his Corolla that he couldn't shrug off losing.

For days afterward, the scene played itself over, again and again, in my mind. I 11 pictured all of the alternate endings, all of the tragic possibilities. I thought about how close I had come to pulling my gun on him, and how easy it would have been for this routine traffic encounter to escalate. I can only wonder how much fear he felt as he approached my vehicle, and just how confident *he* was in trusting *me* to reciprocate his good intentions. Most people who have pulled driving duty in Iraq or Afghanistan have a story or two about having to guess what would happen next in some otherwise mundane situation, because in a war zone, even the most basic interactions can become fraught with fear and danger. Distrust is not simply an attitude; it's a tool of self-defense.

Society works best when we can take its functions for granted. It works best when we can trust that our personal safety is never in doubt. To operate in a theater like Afghanistan is to learn the foundational importance of that kind of trust—by having to do without it for a while. I intuitively came to learn what it meant to exist in a place I couldn't trust, routinely encountering people I couldn't trust, who, in turn, often could not be sure if they should trust me. I learned how toxic that was, how dangerous. For many, that toxicity remains after they return home from this kind of environment, affecting their health by robbing them of their habits of trust. When you

> Buttigieg draws abstract conclusions from the concrete example (p. 251) of the traffic incident.

can't trust anything, you have to spend your waking thoughts questioning everything. That will help you survive in a war zone, but it is no way to live.

What I came to realize is this: trust, often unseen, is indispensable for a healthy, functioning society. And in the absence of trust, nothing that works can work well. ◆ 13

FOR CLOSE READING

1. Was Pete Buttigieg right to be instinctively suspicious of the young man who approaches him and his vehicle on a crowded road in Kabul? Why or why not?

2. From where Buttigieg sits in the Land Cruiser, the young man appears to be empty handed. Why is Buttigieg nonetheless particularly alarmed when the man appears to be reaching toward the wheel well of the vehicle?

3. Buttigieg ultimately presents his encounter with the smiling man as an example of the need for trust in everyday life (13). Is it a good example? Why or why not?

4. "Society works best," says Buttigieg, "when we can take its functions for granted" (12). Do you agree? Why or why not?

STRATEGIES AND STRUCTURES

1. "He wanted me to know he wasn't out to kill anyone" (1). How would you describe Buttigieg's POINT OF VIEW here? What if he had written instead, "He *seemed* to want me to know that he wasn't out to kill anyone"?

2. Buttigieg introduces the example of the smiling man in paragraph 1 and then does not mention him again until paragraph 6. Why not? How would his account have been different if he had simply begun, "It was a crisp, cloudless spring day in Kabul" (2)?

3. Buttigieg bases his case about the need for trust on a single, extended example. Should he have included others? Why or why not?

4. *Other Methods.* Buttigieg's essay on the need for trust includes many elements of NARRATIVE. What are some of the most important ones, and how do they support (or fail to support) his ARGUMENT?

THINKING ABOUT LANGUAGE

1. How do you suppose the marines came up with the name "Suicide Circle" for the section of the road into Kabul where Buttigieg encounters the man with the damaged Corolla?

2. Buttigieg refers to a "status shift" between his civilian job and his military job as described here (3). What do you suppose that shift was like?

3. What is an IED (8)? Why might Lieutenant Buttigieg expect, perhaps, to find one on a crowded street in Kabul?

4. What are the implications of the term "scene" in Buttigieg's DESCRIPTION of the encounter between himself and the smiling man with the broken fender (11)?

5. "Indeed, a few days after I'd first arrived in-country" (6); "I had been trained not to exit a vehicle outside the wire" (8); "Most people who have pulled driving duty" (11)—Buttigieg seasons his account of this episode with phrases that reflect the military setting. Is this use of language effective in providing a sense of immediacy for the reader? Why or why not?

FOR WRITING

1. In a paragraph or two, **DESCRIBE** a situation in which you had to make a split-second decision whether or not to trust someone. Be sure to say whether you made the right decision.

2. Using numerous specific examples, write a five-to-seven-paragraph essay in which you support (or contest) Buttigieg's argument about the importance of trust in "a healthy, functioning society" (13).

3. Write an essay about putting your trust in someone (or some group or institution) that turned out not to be trustworthy. Give specific examples, and use appropriate **TRANSITIONS** to help readers follow the ups and downs of your experience.

4. Read Buttigieg's *Trust: America's Best Chance* (2020), and write a **CRITICAL ANALYSIS** of the book. Using specific examples, be sure to assess how well the author does (or does not) defend his **THESIS**.

ASHLEY PELDON

My Scream Is Famous

Ashley Peldon (b. 1984) is a voice actor who specializes in screams, fighting efforts, voice match, and naturalistic acting and expression. As a child actress in New York City, Peldon landed her first major role in the CBS television film *Child of Rage* (1992), based on the true story of an abused child with reactive attachment disorder. Shifting from on-camera performances to voice-over work, Peldon also pursued her interest in psychology as a field of formal study. Graduating from Skidmore College in 2004 with a BA in psychology and film, she earned a master's in clinical psychology from the Chicago School of Professional Psychology in 2011 and, in 2017, a PhD in psychology from Pacifica Graduate Institute in California.

A screamer by nature—"It's just so natural, it comes right out"—Peldon has also studied the psychology and drama of screams. In "My Scream Is Famous," she gives examples not only of natural screams ("getting a little too excited on the rides at Disneyland with my kids") but also of the various kinds of professional screams she performs for films. "Ghost stories, for example," says Peldon, "will often use a shrill, harsh scream because we need the audience to also experience fear." Or she will voice a scream that would be silent in real life because "that's not as dramatic when it's shown on screen." This piece, which appeared in the *Guardian* in April 2022, demonstrates the effectiveness of using multiple brief examples to convey the complexities of what many might think of as a simple scream.

MLA CITATION: Peldon, Ashley. "My Scream Is Famous." *Back to the Lake: A Reader and Guide for Writers*, edited by Thomas Cooley, 5th ed., W. W. Norton, 2024, pp. 287–88.

IF I SEE A BUG, I will scream. I'll shriek when I'm scared or startled. It's just so natural, it comes right out.

This ability to scream was a huge part in getting my first acting jobs. I grew up in New York in the 1980s, where my sister and I had been scouted as child actors. By the time I was seven I'd got a major role in the film *Child of Rage*, which meant doing long scenes of shouting and screaming. In the audition I had to perform these outbursts, yelling to show the agony experienced by the character.

The film told the true story of a girl who had suffered severe abuse as a child and had what we now understand as reactive attachment disorder: she had never learned love and didn't know how to have trusting relationships, so acted out violently. On reflection, that film shifted my entire career and personal journey.

> Three paragraphs of narration (p. 258) serve as background and introduction to Peldon's career as a screamer.

As a family we moved to Los Angeles so my sister and I could continue working while we finished school. By my 20s I'd done more than 40 films and TV series. In search of a quieter life, in the late 2000s I made a shift from being an on-camera performer to a voiceover actor. I was lucky to get parts where I was able to really use and play with my voice a lot, and screaming became something that I was known for.

You have heard my scream in *Free Guy, Paranormal Activity* and *Scream* (2022). My work often comes in at the post-production stage (after filming has taken place). I pick up additional screams and voice acting for the on-camera actors. Sometimes they don't have the time to achieve the sound the director wants, or I can offer a different vocal quality to the performance.

As a scream artist you have to know the subtle differences between screams and determine whether they should peak at certain points, or remain steady for a very long time. I have to think: "OK, the character is scared here, but are they scared because their life is in danger or are they just startled?" Those screams will sound very different. Ghost stories, for example, will often use a shrill, harsh scream because we need the audience to also experience fear.

We are like stunt people, doing the hard stuff that could be damaging to an actor's voice or is out of their range. When the dinosaurs are attacking in the 2015 *Jurassic World* movie, and you see people running, my screams are in that sequence. When I recorded it, I saw that the characters were grabbing at their hair, falling and then getting up, so I tried to match that and create all of the energy and movement in the sound.

We do a wide variety of screams as actors, and there's a difference between what we do in reality and what we expect to see on screen. In real life, a lot of people would just suck in their breath and not release any noise when they are frightened, but that's not as dramatic when it's shown on screen. In my own life I happen to be a natural screamer and will let out a scream if I'm startled.

You often think of the classic screams of Fay Wray in *King Kong* and Janet Leigh   9
in *Psycho*. Those are beautiful screams, but they are from the damsels. Now, we
have a lot more strong rage from women on screen. There are fewer of the "terrified
female" jobs and more for provocateur-type characters. I've been able to witness
such a shift in the industry, as women are getting stronger roles where they're fighting and baring their emotions - like the female superheroes taking the forefront in
action films and television programs.

> By this point in
> her essay,
> Peldon has
> presented a
> sufficient num-
> ber of repre-
> sentative
> examples
> (pp. 255 and
> 257) to support
> the claim in her
> title that "My
> Scream Is
> Famous."

There are many different screams: of fear, anger, rage. Screams of joy   10
and success, and that raw, embodied scream of female empowerment.
There's the wailing of grief and pain, and screams of effort and fighting.

The most difficult screams for me are those portraying grief, when you're   11
watching someone having to express such pain or trauma. I'm an empathic
person—and also hold a PhD in psychology—so I find getting connected
with emotion easy, but it also carries a weight with it.

Thanks to my unique career, I probably scream more on average than   12
the normal person would. There's something really relaxing about it. After
a big day of screaming I feel lighter and brighter. When I'm not working, I
take care of my voice with the typical things like drinking tea, but I did lose
it once by getting a little too excited on the rides at Disneyland with my kids.   ◆

FOR CLOSE READING

1. According to Ashley Peldon, how and why did her role in the film *Child of Rage*
   (1992) "shift [her] entire career and personal journey" (3)?

2. Most of Peldon's work, she says, comes in "at the post-production stage" (5). Why
   don't the on-camera actors just do their own screaming and voice effects during
   filming?

3. As a voice actor specializing in screams, Peldon has witnessed a "shift in the industry" (9). What is the nature of that shift, and how has it affected her career?

4. To what extent, according to Peldon, does her formal study of psychology have a
   bearing on her voice acting?

STRATEGIES AND STRUCTURES

1. Why does Peldon cite the screams of Fay Wray in *King Kong* and Janet Leigh in
   Psycho (9)? Are they good examples of the types of screams Peldon specializes
   in? Why or why not?

2. Peldon COMPARES voice actors to "stunt people" (7). In her view, what are some of
   the similarities between the two professions?

3. Of the many types of screams she does, Peldon finds "those portraying grief" to be the most difficult (11). Why? She then goes on to say, "After a big day of screaming I feel lighter and brighter" (12). Do these contrasting comments make an effective ending to her essay? Explain.

4. This piece interweaves examples with **NARRATION** about Peldon's career path. Point to several instances of narration, and explain how they do or do not enhance the discussion of her particular kind of voice acting.

5. *Other Methods.* Peldon introduces an element of **CLASSIFICATION** when she says, "There are fewer of the 'terrified female' jobs" and more for provocateur-type characters" (9). What kinds of screams fit best with the feelings and motives of these newer types of characters? What other category of women's roles does Peldon mention?

THINKING ABOUT LANGUAGE

1. What are the implications of the word "damsels" (9)? Why is the term so often accompanied by the phrase "in distress"?

2. Peldon mentions the "scream of female empowerment" (10). Can this phrase be considered a contradiction in terms? Why or why not?

3. Good voice actors, Peldon implies, empathize deeply with the characters they portray. If empathy is defined, in part, as the ability to share other people's emotions, why does being empathetic impose "a weight" on the actor, in Peldon's view (11)?

FOR WRITING

1. In a paragraph or two, give examples of one or more of the different types of screams, as **DESCRIBED** by Peldon, that you have witnessed on screen or in real life.

2. Do some research on "reactive attachment disorder" (3), and write a brief **DEFINITION**, with examples, of the condition and its causes.

3. "Now," writes Peldon, "we have a lot more strong rage from women on screen" (9). Citing examples from your own viewing and other experiences, write a four-to-six-paragraph essay supporting (or contesting) this **THESIS** about the changing nature of women's roles in film.

4. Listen to Ashley Peldon's screams on *YouTube* (and elsewhere on the internet), and write a **CRITICAL ANALYSIS** of her performance as a voice actor. Be sure to cite lots of examples.

10 Analysis

The ultimate authority must always rest with the individual's own reason and critical analysis.

—Dalai Lama

By some accounts, Stephen (Steph) Curry of the Golden State Warriors is the greatest shotmaker in NBA history. How does he do it? It's a simple process, as analyzed by sportswriter David Fleming: *Step 1*: bring the ball into the pocket just below your chest; *Step 2*: using your middle finger and forefinger as a "shooting fork," find the seam at the center of the ball; *Step 3*: bring the ball up while bending your right palm back "like a waiter holding a tray of dishes"; *Step 4*: release ball, flashing "love never fails" message tattooed in Hebrew on the inside of your shooting wrist.

Go to digital .wwnorton.com /links-backtothe lake5 for a diagram of Curry's process.

Breaking a Subject into Parts

Naturally analytical, the human mind is inclined to take things apart in order to examine their components—the dictionary definition of "analysis." When we analyze something, however, we do more than apply the scalpel and tweezers; we also break out the mental glue—that is, we try to figure out how the parts fit together to make the whole or to produce a particular end result.

In the case of Steph Curry's signature shot, the product or end result is almost always an additional three points on the board. As difficult as the shot may be to execute, however, it is relatively easy to analyze because Curry's moves are part of a process—a series of actions or events—that can be broken down into simple steps. In this chapter, we'll begin by analyzing a simple process, like shooting a basketball or baking a cake; then we'll move on to more complicated procedures, such as the writing process itself, and to analyzing different kinds of subjects altogether, such as written or visual texts.

Why Do We Analyze Things?

One reason to analyze a process, whether simple or complex, is to learn how to do something, such as shoot a basketball or fly an airplane. If the process produces an undesirable result, as with the spread of a deadly virus, our purpose in analyzing it may be to prevent the process from occurring again. Or we may just be curious. How *does* the air flowing over a curved wing produce enough force to lift a plane? What if the wing falls off?

Curiosity may be bad for cats, but it is the driving force behind analysis. Whether we're analyzing an athlete's style of play, a poem, an essay on writing, or an advertising campaign, the ultimate goal of critical analysis is not simply to learn how to do something; it is to comprehend and explain the significance of a subject and how it works—and often to satisfy our innate curiosity about it.

Step 4 of Steph Curry's shotmaking process.

Composing a Process Analysis

There are basically two kinds of **PROCESS ANALYSIS**: directive and explanatory. A directive process analysis tells the reader how to do something—shoot a basketball, throw a boomerang, administer CPR, or avoid being eaten by an alligator. An explanatory process analysis tells the reader how something works or is made—the US Supreme Court, reverse osmosis, a lithium-ion battery.

When you compose a process analysis, whether directive or explanatory, your first task is to break the process into its main steps. Then you must present the steps to the reader in a certain order, usually **CHRONOLOGICAL**. With a multistage process— such as writing an essay or playing a video game—figuring out that order can be challenging, especially if the process has more than one possible outcome. Consider, for example, a complicated process that we can analyze but not necessarily control—the spread of the bubonic plague.

A carrier, usually a flea, bites an infected animal, usually a rat. The flea picks up infected blood from the rat and transfers the bacilli that cause the plague to the human victim, again by biting. Having entered the bloodstream, the bacilli travel to the lymph nodes, where they begin to replicate. Eventually the lymph nodes swell, creating what Wendy Orent describes in *Plague* as "the huge, boggy, exquisitely painful mass we know as a bubo." The order is always the same—up to a point. The buboes never appear before the victim is infected. And the victim is never infected before the flea bites. What happens after the buboes appear, however—whether the victim lives or dies—is not fixed.

The order of events in natural disasters can also be difficult to determine with certainty. In an earthquake or hurricane, for example, it's true that the ground trembles or the wind blows first; but then many things seem to start happening all at once—as with any recursive process, including the writing process itself. When writing about a process, however, you must present events in an orderly sequence. Whatever it turns out to be, the sequence in which you relate those events will provide the main principle for organizing your written analysis.

Thinking about Purpose and Audience

One reason for writing a process analysis is to tell your readers how to do something. For this purpose, a basic set of instructions will usually do the job, as when you give someone the recipe for your aunt Mary's famous pound cake.

When, however, you want your audience to understand, not duplicate, a complicated process—such as the spread of a disease, the cloning of a sheep, or the mental decay of a character in an Edgar Allan Poe story—your analysis should be more explanatory than directive. So instead of giving instructions ("add the sugar to the butter"), you'd go over the inner workings of the process in some detail, telling readers, for example, *what happens* when they add baking powder to the cake mixture:

> The dry ingredients, including the baking soda or powder, are then added, usually alternating with liquid. When the baking soda or powder comes into contact with liquid, carbon dioxide is released. As the batter heats up, bubbles form and the batter rises.
>
> —RICK MCDANIEL, "Chemistry 101 for Pound Cakes"

This is more information than your readers will need if you're just giving them a recipe for pound cake. However, if you're writing for a food magazine and you want readers to understand why their cakes may fall if they open the oven door during the baking process—it's because the bubbles collapse before the batter sets up—then such explanatory details would be appropriate.

The nature of your audience, too, will affect the information you include. How much does your intended reader already know about the process you're analyzing? Why might they want to know more or less? If you're giving a set of instructions, will the reader require any special tools or equipment? What problems or glitches is the reader likely to encounter? Will you need to indicate where to look for more information on your topic?

Generating Ideas: Asking How Something Works

BRAINSTORMING, LISTING, and other methods of discovery can help you generate ideas for your process analysis. When analyzing a process, the essential question to ask yourself is *how*. How does a cake rise? How do I make chicken salad? How does an internal combustion engine work? How do I back out of the garage?

Or: How do I get out of a locked trunk (p. 321)? Or: How should I interpret a marketing logo (p. 343)?

When you're thinking about writing a process analysis, ask yourself a "how" question about your topic, research the answer, and write down all the steps involved. These will form the foundation of your process analysis. For instance, "How do I back out of the garage?" might result in a list like this:

> Step on the gas.
> Turn the key in the ignition.
> Put the car in reverse.
> Cut the steering wheel to the right.
> Back out of the garage.

This list includes all the essential steps for backing a car out of a garage, but you wouldn't want your reader to try to follow them in this order. Once you have a list of all the steps in your process, you have to begin thinking about how to present them to your reader.

Organizing and Drafting a Process Analysis

First you'll need to put the steps in a certain order with appropriate transitions between them. Then choose pronouns and verb forms that fit the type of analysis you're writing, whether directive or explanatory. Think about the main point you want to make, and state it clearly. Finally, consider whether you should demonstrate the process visually. The templates on p. 298 can help you get started.

PUTTING THE STEPS IN ORDER

Many processes, especially those linked by CAUSE AND EFFECT, follow a prescribed order. For example, before the bacillus that causes bubonic plague can enter a victim's bloodstream, a flea must bite an infected rat, then bite the human. The process of infection won't work if the steps unfold in any other order because the first step *causes* the next one to happen.

Jamelle Bouie (Ch. 11, p. 387) applies cause and effect in analyzing why many people don't vote.

When the process is linear but not causal, such as driving to a particular address in Dallas, you simply start at the earliest point in time and move forward, step by step, to the end result. If the process is cyclical, such as what happens in your car engine as you drive, you'll have to pick a logical point in the process and then proceed through the rest of the cycle. If, however, the process doesn't naturally follow chronology, try arranging the steps of your analysis from most important to least important or the other way around.

USING TRANSITIONS

As you recount the main steps in the process one by one, let the reader know when you're moving from one step to another by including clear TRANSITIONS, such as "next," "from there," "after five minutes," "then." The actions and events that make up a process are repeatable—unlike those in a narrative, which happen only *once* upon a time. So you'll frequently use such expressions as "usually," "normally," "in most cases," "whenever." But also note any potential deviations from the normal order by using transitions like "sometimes," "rarely," "in one instance."

USING PRONOUNS

In an explanatory process analysis, you focus on the things (fleas and rats, engines, oranges) and activities (infection, compression and combustion, culling and scrubbing) that make up the process. Thus you'll write most of the time in the THIRD PERSON ("he," "she," "it," and "they"):

Annie Dillard (p. 328) uses both first- and second-person pronouns because her essay combines explanatory and directive process analysis.

> Moving up a conveyer belt, oranges are scrubbed with detergent before they roll on into the juicing machines.
>
> —JOHN MCPHEE, *Oranges*

In a directive process analysis, by contrast, you tell the reader directly how to do something. So you should typically use the second person ("you"): "When making orange juice, first you need to cut the oranges in half."

TEMPLATES FOR DRAFTING

When writing a process analysis, you need to say what process you're analyzing, identify its most important steps, and put the steps in order. Nature writer Diane Ackerman makes these key moves in the following example:

> But how do the colored leaves fall? As a leaf ages, the growth hormone, auxin, fades, and cells at the base of the petiole divide. Two or three rows of small cells, lying at right angles to the axis of the petiole, react with water, then come apart, leaving the petioles hanging on by only a few threads of xylem. A light breeze, and the leaves are airborne.
>
> —DIANE ACKERMAN, "Why Leaves Turn Color in the Fall"

Ackerman tells her readers what process she's analyzing (the falling of leaves), identifies its main steps, and puts the steps in the order in which the leaves age (which, of course, is chronological): growth hormone fades; cells in the leaf stems divide, react with water, and come apart; the leaves drop. Here's a good example that humorously gives bad advice for how to jump-start a car battery:

> Connect one end of the *red* jumper cable to the *positive* terminal (also called the ignition or carburetor) on your car's battery. Then connect the other end of the red cable to an electronic part such as the radio of the opposing car.
>
> —DAVE BARRY, "How to Jump-start Your Car When the Battery Is Dead"

The following templates can help you make some of these basic moves in your own writing. But don't take these as formulas where you just fill in the blanks. There are no shortcuts to good writing, but these templates can serve as starting points.

▸ The process of X can be divided into the following steps: _____, _____, _____, and _____.

▸ The steps that make up X usually occur (or can be arranged) in the following order: _____, _____, _____, _____, and _____.

▸ The end result of X is _____.

▸ To repeat X and achieve this result, the following tools and materials are needed: _____, _____, and _____.

▸ The main reasons for understanding / repeating X are _____, _____, and _____.

USING APPROPRIATE VERB FORMS

In an explanatory process analysis, you indicate how something works or is made, so your verbs will usually be in the indicative mood, as in the following example:

As the rotor <u>moves</u> around the chamber, each of the three volumes of gas alternately <u>expands</u> and <u>contracts</u>. It is this expansion and contraction that <u>draws</u> air and fuel into the engine, <u>compresses</u> it, and <u>makes</u> useful power.
—Karim Nice, "How Rotary Engines Work"

In a directive process analysis, on the other hand, you tell the reader how to do something, so your verbs should usually be in the imperative mood, as in these instructions for reviewing for exams:

<u>Start</u> preparing for your exams the first day of class. . . . <u>Plan</u> reviews as part of your regular weekly study schedule. . . . <u>Read</u> over your lecture notes and <u>ask</u> yourself questions on the material you don't know well. . . . <u>Review</u> for several short periods rather than one long period.
—University of Minnesota Duluth Student Handbook

Notice that the verbs in these two examples are all in the present tense because they express habitual actions. Instructions are usually written in the present tense because they tell how something is (or should be) habitually done: "As you place the oranges on the conveyor belt, keep hair and fingers clear of the rollers."

Explanations, on the other hand, are written in the present tense when they tell how a process is habitually performed:

At low tide, researchers <u>collect</u> the algae by the handful and <u>place</u> it in plastic baggies. Back at the lab, they <u>separate out</u> the different strains and <u>examine</u> each type under a microscope.

But explanations are written in the *past* tense when they explain how a process was performed on a particular occasion, even though the process itself is repeatable:

At low tide, researchers <u>collected</u> the algae by the handful and <u>placed</u> it in plastic baggies. Back at the lab, they <u>separated out</u> the different strains and <u>examined</u> each type under a microscope.

Be careful not to switch between past tense and present tense in your analysis, unless you're intentionally switching from explaining how a process is usually performed (present) to how it was performed on a particular occasion (past).

STATING YOUR POINT

A good process analysis, like any other kind of analysis, should have a point to make—a THESIS. That point should be clearly expressed in a thesis statement so the reader will know why you're analyzing the process. In addition, the thesis statement should identify the process and indicate its end result. For example:

You cannot understand how the Florida citrus industry works without understanding how fresh orange juice gets processed into "concentrate."

—JOHN MCPHEE, *Oranges*

This thesis statement clearly tells the reader what process the writer is analyzing (making concentrate from fresh orange juice), why he's analyzing it (as a foundation for understanding the Florida citrus industry), and what the end result of the process is (orange juice concentrate). As you draft a process analysis, make sure your thesis statement includes all this information, so that your reader knows just what to expect from your analysis.

Philip Weiss (p. 321) embeds his thesis in two paragraphs (4, 6) about Americans' fear of being locked in a trunk and the value of knowing how to get out.

CONCLUDING A PROCESS ANALYSIS

A process isn't complete until it yields a final result. Likewise, a process analysis isn't complete until it explains how the process ends—and what this result means for the reader.

The process of turning orange juice into concentrate, for example, doesn't end when the juice is extracted from the fruit. The extracted juice must be refined and then shipped to the consumer, as John McPhee explains in the conclusion of his analysis: "From the extractor the orange concentrate flows into holding tanks from which it is later tapped, packaged, frozen, and shipped to grocery stores all over the country." And that, he might have added, is how you get your "fresh" o.j. in the morning.

Even this isn't the end of the story, however. If you were writing a directive analysis of how to make orange juice from concentrate, your conclusion would need to remind readers to add cold water to the concentrate before serving.

Composing a Critical Analysis of a Text

In his article on Steph Curry's performance on the basketball court, sportswriter David Fleming explains how Curry developed his technique:

> Shooting touch is a bit of a misnomer. It isn't bestowed, it's built, through ungodly, torturous repetition—shot by shot, day by day, year by year, until the complex kinetic chain of movements is burned into the muscles.
>
> —DAVID FLEMING, "Sports' Perfect 0.4 Seconds"

Fleming, of course, doesn't really expect his readers to replicate a process that took a gifted and disciplined athlete years to perfect. His larger purpose in analyzing Curry's method and training is to tell his subject's story, not only as a star athlete but as a person "who has never lacked" for motivation, in part because he is only six foot two and 185 pounds in a field of giants. In other words, Fleming uses process analysis as a basis for a type of writing, the **PROFILE**, that sportswriters and newspaper reporters—not to mention historians and students writing about history or literature or the history of science—produce all the time.

In Ch. 15, Viet Thanh Nguyen critically analyzes the effect a particular text had on him as a young student (p. 710).

Just as Fleming analyzes Curry's performance, we can analyze the end product of that process—Fleming's written text. Does Fleming's profile of Steph Curry capture the character and personality of its subject? Is the writer's analysis of Curry's achievement fair and accurate? Are those views presented in a language and style that are likely to appeal to the readers of a sports magazine? A critical analysis of a text addresses questions like these about the meaning, form, and audience of a written or visual text.

Thinking about Purpose and Audience

When you analyze a simple process, such as how to make orange juice from concentrate, your purpose is often to learn (and tell the reader) how to replicate the process. When you analyze a written text, such as a profile of Steph Curry or a poem by Emily Dickinson, however, your primary purpose is not to discover and explain how to be a star athlete or write a poem. ("Turning inward, slowly bring the pen into the ideal shooting position just below the heart.") Your purpose is to understand and evaluate the text by breaking it into its component parts, examining how those parts are organized, and then putting the pieces back together in a clear and well-organized explanation of what your analysis reveals about the meaning and form of the text.

Generating Ideas: Asking What a Text Means—and How

To understand what a written text means, of course, you must read the text carefully and critically, perhaps by following the guidelines for close reading provided in Chapter 1. As you read, identify the writer's main point or CLAIM and where it is stated most directly in the text. Consider, in particular, the specific EVIDENCE the writer offers to support what the text has to say. Is that evidence sufficient? Or is more (or different) evidence needed? Who is the intended AUDIENCE for the text? Are they likely to be persuaded by the writer's views and approach to the subject? How can you best present your answers to these (and other) questions about the text to the readers of your own analysis?

Organizing and Drafting a Critical Analysis of a Text

When you organize and draft a critical analysis of a text, you follow essentially the same steps you would take for analyzing a process (or anything else). You break the text into its component parts, examine how the parts are organized or arranged, consider how they fit together to make the whole, and evaluate and explain the results of your analysis to your reader.

When you're dealing with a written (or visual) subject rather than a process, try the following steps to conduct your analysis and organize your insights:

Break the subject of your analysis into its component parts by identifying the key people, objects, places, events, or ideas that the text is about.

Identify how the parts are organized—whether chronologically, spatially, logically, visually, or otherwise—and the key strategies the author uses to present them to the intended audience.

Consider how the parts fit together to make the whole and how they shape (or are shaped by) the overall form of the text.

Evaluate and explain the results of your analysis—the meaning and significance of the text as you understand them.

BREAKING A SUBJECT INTO ITS COMPONENT PARTS

Magdalena Ostas exemplifies the taking-apart phase of critical analysis in the following passage from her essay on the poetry of Emily Dickinson:

Find Ostas's complete essay on p. 337.

> The "scene" is literally missing in her poetry, and in its place stands the poet's receptiveness, a state that gives people, places and things their significance. . . . Her signature dashes mirror the starts and stops of the human mind, while many of her poems read as . . . transcripts of thoughts, feelings, sensations, perceptions . . . that are . . . unattached.
>
> —MAGDALENA OSTAS, "Emily Dickinson and the Space Within"

Stark interior spaces; a receptive observer; multiple dashes instead of more conventional punctuation marks; thoughts, feelings, sensations, perceptions that appear "unattached"—such are the basic ingredients of a Dickinson poem, according to Ostas.

Here's another example of the taking-apart phase of critical analysis; the author is explaining how she wrote the personal essay, "The Death of a Moth" (p. 767):

Find Dillard's complete essay on p. 328.

> To start a narrative, you need a batch of things. Not feelings, not opinions, not sentiments, not judgments, not arguments, but specific objects and events: a cat, a spider web, a mess of insect skeletons, a candle, a book about Rimbaud, a burning moth.
>
> —ANNIE DILLARD, "How I Wrote the Moth Essay—and Why"

"What do you do with these things?" Dillard asks. It's a question you'll want to ask repeatedly as you analyze any kind of written text, from a profile in a sports magazine to a formal critical analysis of literature in an academic journal.

IDENTIFYING HOW THE PARTS ARE ORGANIZED

Once you've identified the basic "things"—the key people, places, objects, events, and concrete ideas—that make up the text you're analyzing, the next step is to determine how they're organized. The order and arrangement in which the writer presents the "ingredients" of a text will have a direct bearing on how you organize and present them when explaining the results of your own analysis.

In a narrative, the parts are usually presented CHRONOLOGICALLY. If the text you're analyzing is a personal NARRATIVE, a short story or novel, a narrative poem, or an account of historical (or other) events, your analysis will likely include a chronological summary of events. A writer goes on a camping trip in the Blue Ridge mountains of Virginia. Night falls, and she lights a candle to read by. The light attracts a giant female moth. The moth gets stuck in the melted wax and bursts into flame.

In many kinds of academic writing, however, the parts are arranged logically rather than chronologically. That is, they are presented in the order that seems most reasonable to the writer—or most likely to persuade the reader to accept the writer's argument or point of view. Often, this means that the writer's observations and ideas are simply presented in the order of most important to least important. Or vice versa, building up to the writer's main insight rather than down from it.

Occasionally, the organization of the parts of a text will "mirror the starts and stops" of the writer's thoughts and mind, as they do, according to Magdalena Ostas, in a typical lyric poem by Emily Dickinson. Whatever "logic" the text you're analyzing may follow, you'll need to identify and explain that order of presentation in your analysis because how a text is organized—the form and shape of the text—often contributes directly to its meaning.

CONSIDERING HOW THE PARTS MAKE UP THE WHOLE

In Annie Dillard's case, the meaning and significance of the objects and events chronicled in her personal narrative did not become clear until long after her return from the camping trip where she witnessed the burning moth. "Walking back to my desk, where I had been answering letters," she wrote about her thoughts two years after the event, "I realized that the burning moth was a dandy visual focus for all my recent thoughts about an empty, dedicated life. Perhaps I'd try to write a short narrative about it."

Not all texts are so tightly focused as "The Death of a Moth." However, a critical move to make when you analyze any text is to look for concrete images, objects, and events that help to unify the text by bringing all the other bits and pieces together in sharp focus. Once you put your finger on these, as Dillard's own analysis suggests, you can better understand and discuss the more abstract elements of the text, including the writer's feelings, opinions, sentiments, judgments, and arguments.

EVALUATING AND EXPLAINING YOUR RESULTS

If you were writing a critical analysis of Dillard's narrative, for example, you would need to evaluate and explain the significance of its central image, the burning moth—just as you would need to explain the significance of Steph Curry's "elevation-type shot" if you were analyzing David Fleming's profile of Curry.

Curry's shot, according to Fleming's essay, "is redefining and revolutionizing the art of shooting" a basketball, "making him the purest, greatest shooter ever to play the game." Is this an overstatement, or does Fleming's analysis justify his claim about the importance of his subject? How, exactly, does Fleming make (or fail to make) the case for Curry's greatness?

Annie Dillard's essay about writing appears, at first, to address a more humble (and humbling) subject—the author's "thoughts about an empty, dedicated life" as a writer cut off from the world. "What was my life about?" she asks. "Why was I living alone, when I am gregarious? Would I ever meet someone, or should I reconcile myself to all this solitude?"

By identifying her plight with that of the proverbial moth drawn to the flame that consumes it, however, Dillard raises larger issues about dedication, solitude, and creativity. You might, in an analysis of Dillard's essay, aim to understand and explain where she stands on these issues so central to her narrative—and state your findings clearly. A critical analysis of a text is not complete until you've fully evaluated the author's most significant claims or observations and explained to your reader how they are (or are not) supported by the specific details of text (such as the burning moth that gives "a dandy visual focus" to Annie Dillard's personal narrative).

Magdalena Ostas (p. 337) also explores solitude and creativity in relation to Emily Dickinson's secluded lifestyle and the "stark presentness" of her poetry.

TEMPLATES FOR DRAFTING

When you write a critical analysis of a text, you break your subject into its components, examine the sequence or order in which the parts are presented, and then explain to your reader how those parts fit together—and what they mean. The following templates can help you make these basic moves of critical analysis. But, again, don't take these templates as formulas where you just fill in the blanks. They are intended, instead, as starting points for your own rigorous analysis:

▸ The text itself can be broken down into the following basic components: _____, _____, _____, and _____.

▸ Presented in _____ order, these components take the general form of a / an _____ on the subject of _____.

▸ The writer's ideas on this subject are most clearly stated (or implied) when they say _____ and _____.

▸ In support of these views, the writer offers the following evidence: _____, _____, and _____; that evidence is (is not) sufficient because _____ and _____.

▸ The accuracy of the writer's conclusions and the significance of this text can be summed up as follows: _____, _____, and _____.

Analyzing a Visual Text

When you analyze a written text, you **DESCRIBE** the components of your analysis in some detail, as Magdalena Ostas does in her essay on Emily Dickinson's poetry when she says that the thoughts, feelings, sensations, and perceptions in an Emily Dickinson poem are detached, "sceneless," and intensely inward.

Describing the components of your analysis like this is essential, too, when you're analyzing a *visual* text because the specific physical features of the images or videos will form the basis for whatever you have to say *about* them. This is why Nike and Amazon, for example, describe their logos—representing speed and service, respectively—as a swoosh and a smile. (On closer analysis, Nike's logo also looks like a wing, evoking the goddess Nike herself; and Amazon's smile often appears as an arrow pointing from A to Z in the company's name, indicating the range of its product line.)

Read one writer's analysis of Nike's logo on p. 343.

As an example of how to describe and analyze a visual text, let's examine the logo of a much older American brand, Land O'Lakes, a member-owned agricultural cooperative founded in Minnesota in 1921. The company's familiar packaging, featuring

The original "kneeling maiden" logo of the Land O'Lakes cooperative was created by Arthur C. Hanson in 1928 and updated in 1954 by Patrick DesJarlait, a member of the Red Lake Ojibwe tribe. Pictured here is, perhaps, the most iconic version.

an Indigenous woman, was introduced in 1928 and has been updated over the years but not fundamentally changed until recently.

American Indian, the magazine of the Smithsonian National Museum of the American Indian, describes this version of the packaging as follows:

> The most famous Indian maiden of all time kneels among green meadows and blue lakes. She wears buckskin and beads, and her feathers are red, white and blue. She holds a box of Land O'Lakes butter, meaning that she holds an image of herself holding the box. This repeats into infinity.
>
> —Cécile R. Ganteaume, "Major New Exhibition Asks, Why Do Images of American Indians Permeate American Life?"

This analysis captures many of the essential features of an enduring (until recently) work of graphic design. Befitting the name of the cooperative—and the nickname of its home state, Land of 10,000 Lakes—this stylized graphic depicts a lush landscape of shore, lake, and sky that extends to the horizon. (The name "Minnesota" derives from the Dakota words for water and sky—or clouds.)

The color scheme is equally elemental, consisting of the traditional primary colors, red and green, and two secondaries, yellow and light blue. If these are the colors of nature—yellow for the sunny sky, light blue for the water, green for the grass in the foreground and the trees in the distance—then the company name, arching in red across the sky like a monochromatic rainbow, must be part of nature too. It's "All Natural," proclaims the text in the upper right corner. (When you analyze a graphic, don't forget to look at the labels and other textual elements.)

In earlier versions of the Land O'Lakes landscape, cows graze on the shore, reminding the reader where butter comes from. The cows disappeared years ago, leaving the kneeling figure in solitary command of the scene. Her name is Mia, according to Robert DesJarlait, a member of the Red Lake Ojibwe tribe and the son of the Ojibwe artist who updated the logo in 1954. To members of the local community, DesJarlait says, the scene behind the woman is instantly recognizable as "the Narrows, where Lower Red Lake and Upper Red Lake meet."

Look for DesJarlait's essay on the significance and recent fate of the Land O'Lakes logo on p. 728.

Any critical analysis of the Land O'Lakes logo necessarily focuses on the female figure in the center of the foreground. Mia wears traditional buckskin, beads, and feathers. The floral motifs on her dress, according to DesJarlait, "are common in Ojibwe art." She is not a stereotype, he argues, but an authentic representation of a member of the Red Lake tribe.

The Land O'Lakes woman also represents a textbook example of the Droste effect, named after the Dutch chocolate company whose advertising in 1904 featured a recurring image of a young woman holding a tray of hot chocolate. As if making an offering to the viewer, the kneeling figure at the center of the Land O'Lakes butter box holds up a butter box with a kneeling figure at the center—and so on, theoretically, to infinity, as in a hall of mirrors. This Droste aspect of the illustration is combined with yet another optical effect straight out of a class in painting and drawing: the vanishing perspective of the shoreline. What do these visual elements add up to?

When you analyze a visual text, your ultimate purpose is to understand the meaning and significance of the images that compose the text. To achieve this purpose, you follow the same basic steps that make up a critical analysis of any other kind of text. The steps of your analysis of the Land O'Lakes butter packaging, for example, might look like this:

- *Break the visual image into its component parts*: these include a wooded shoreline, light blue waters and yellow sky, a young Indigenous woman in traditional costume, a one-pound box of butter.

- *Identify how the parts are organized*: the woman kneels at the edge of the lake; she holds the butter box toward the viewer as an offering; the big red "O" in the cooperative's name surrounds her head like a halo.

- *Consider how the parts fit together to make the whole*: the entire scene is centered on the kneeling woman or, rather, the box in her hand; behind it, the landscape extends to the vanishing point; the scene is repeated "infinitely" on the box.

- *Evaluate and explain the results of your analysis*: in combination, the visual elements of this packing slyly convey the message that Land O'Lakes dairy products stand at the center of the natural universe, where earth, sky, and water come together.

> Dan Redding makes a clear, concise evaluation in the final paragraph of his analysis of a visual text (p. 345).

Consider the Context

When you analyze any text, especially one that is designed to sell a particular product or idea, it is important to keep in mind the CONTEXT in which the text was written or designed. In the case of the Land O'Lakes woman, that context—or the company's perception of it—has changed dramatically in recent years.

For almost a century, Mia appeared in Land O'Lakes advertising as an emblem of natural wholesomeness. Is the figure an appropriate bearer of the company's core message about the quality of its products? Or is she a demeaning stereotype, kneeling subserviently in the visual center of the illustration and offering herself to the viewer like a stick of butter on a plate? A critical analysis of a text should not only explain what the text has to say but also weigh and evaluate the validity of those claims in their historical and social context.

In 2020, Land O'Lakes executives, perhaps realizing that their advertising was out of step with the times, altered the visual landscape of their butter packaging by removing Mia entirely. The company's explanation for the change makes no mention of stereotypes or appropriation: "As it approaches its 100th anniversary in 2021," said a Land O'Lakes news release at the time, "the co-op has reflected on its treasured history and made the decision to showcase its greatest strength—its farmers."

In his essay on p. 728, Robert DesJarlait, son of the illustrator who designed a version of Mia, offers a different explanation and evaluation of the new design: "They got rid of the Indian and kept the land."

Land O'Lakes butter packaging, 2022.

See Ch. 12 for an essay that compares two comic book superheroes in analyzing which of the two franchises "would win in a fight" (p. 426).

Did the Land O'Lakes cooperative make a wise decision in changing its logo? To answer this question, you might want to write a visual analysis of the new design in which you COMPARE it with the older version discussed above (or other variants); explain the significance of the changes; and assess whether the label "1700+ Farmers Strong" is an adequate replacement, visually or intellectually, for the central figure who once occupied this space.

EDITING FOR COMMON ERRORS
IN AN ANALYSIS

Analysis invites certain types of errors, particularly in the choice of pronouns and verb forms. The following tips will help you check your writing for these common problems.

Check your pronouns

Remember to use third-person pronouns ("he," "she," "it," "they") when explaining how something works or is done—and to use the second-person pronoun ("you") when telling someone how to do something.

▶ When trees are harvested, ~~you have to~~ they are cut down ~~each one~~ by hand.

The reader is not actually harvesting the trees.

▶ To harvest trees properly, ~~they~~ you must ~~be~~ cut them down by hand.

Here, the reader is the one harvesting the trees.

Check your verbs to make sure you haven't switched needlessly between the indicative and the imperative

▶ According to the recipe, we should stir in the nuts. ~~Then~~ and then sprinkle cinnamon on top.

Or

▶ ~~According to the recipe, we should stir~~ Stir in the nuts. ~~Then~~ and then sprinkle cinnamon on top.

In a critical analysis of a text, use the present tense rather than the past for most verbs, since you are describing what the author is saying or doing as you read the text:

▶ Magdalena Ostas ~~argued~~ argues that the "solitude within" ~~was~~ is the source of Dickinson's "unique poetic voice."

Reading an Analysis with a Critical Eye

Once you've drafted an analysis, it's always a good idea to ask someone else to read over it and give you their first impressions. And, of course, you yourself will want to review what you've written from the perspective of a critical reader. Here are some questions to keep in mind as you review your analysis with a critical eye:

PURPOSE AND AUDIENCE. Does your analysis clearly state the purpose it is intended to serve? Is the language and tone fitting for your intended audience? Are they familiar with your subject, or will you need to provide additional information and background?

THE POINT. What is the point of your analysis? Is it spelled out in a clear thesis statement—usually near the beginning—that tells the reader why you're analyzing this particular subject and what insights to expect in the rest of your analysis?

ORGANIZATION. Are all the important components of your subject included in your analysis? Are they presented in an order that makes sense—chronologically, from simple to complex, most important to least important, or some other logical way?

TRANSITIONS. Are there clear transitions between the different parts of your analysis? Are the transitions overly predictable (first, second, third)? If so, consider changing them for variety.

PRONOUNS. Do you consistently write about the subject (or object) of your analysis in the third person ("he," "she," "it")? You can also use the third person to address your reader (One can see from this analysis), but the second person (You can see from this analysis) is less formal.

VERBS. If your analysis is telling the reader how to do something, most of your verbs should be in the IMPERATIVE (or commanding) mood (Choose strong verbs; avoid passive voice most of the time). Otherwise, make sure you're using the INDICATIVE mood (The dashes in an Emily Dickinson poem mirror the starts and stops of the human mind, as Magdalena Ostas observes).

VISUALS. Do you include charts, drawings, or other illustrations to help explain the method or results of your analysis? If not, should you? Are the visuals labeled and placed where they should be in your text?

CONCLUSION. Does your analysis end with a clear statement (or restatement) of your insights—and of why they're significant?

OTHER METHODS. Does your analysis incorporate other methods of development? For instance, does it give EXAMPLES? Does it analyze CAUSE AND EFFECT where appropriate? Does it CLASSIFY components of your subject into larger categories or DIVIDE them into subcategories?

Student Example

Stephanie Cawley wrote "The Veil in *Persepolis*" as a student at Stockton College in New Jersey. Focusing on a chapter from a graphic memoir by the Iranian artist and author Marjane Satrapi, it's part of Cawley's longer study "Hybridity in Comics" that first appeared on their school's *Postcolonial Studies* website in 2011. As indicated by the marginal annotations of Cawley's text, this essay applies many of the techniques of critical analysis. Notice how the visual elements are at least as important as the written text. Cawley uses MLA STYLE to document their sources.

The Veil in *Persepolis*

The representation of the veiled woman has become an important issue for postcolonial feminists who want to emphasize the importance of understanding localized meanings and knowledges rather than accepting the outside, Western viewpoint as the dominant truth. Although in *Persepolis* Marjane Satrapi represents the veil in a way that is consistent with a Western viewpoint of its being part of a systematic oppression of women, she also counters the representation of Middle Eastern women as passive, oppressed, and monolithic by illustrating acts of overt and subtle resistance to the veil and the regime and by emphasizing the individual identities of women beneath the veil.

States the THESIS of Cawley's analysis.

The very first page of *Persepolis* establishes the comic's resistance to the Western image of the veiled woman. The first panel shows a ten-year-old Marjane, seated, the black veil surrounding her cartoonish face. The second panel shows a group of Marjane's classmates similarly veiled, with Marjane just out of the frame to the left (Satrapi 3).

Analyzes the text itself (both graphic and verbal) as evidence to support the author's thesis.

Fig. 1. Satrapi, p. 3.

Monica Chiu, in "Sequencing and Contingent Individualism in the Graphic, Postcolonial Spaces of Satrapi's *Persepolis* and Okubo's *Citizen 13660*," reads these panels as "representing Marji as both an individual girl and a member of her class" (102). Far from the stereotypical, homogenizing representations of veiled women common to the Western media, the simplified cartoonish style of Satrapi's artwork forces the viewer to notice the subtle variations Satrapi has given each of the girls— differences in hair texture, eye shape, and expression (Satrapi 3)—affirming them, as Chiu says, as individuals, but also as part of a shared experience. At the bottom of the page, in perhaps one of the most iconic images from *Persepolis*, the group of girls is shown refusing to wear their veils—some complaining it's too hot, others using their veils to playact political or fantastical games, and others jumping rope with them (Satrapi 3). This image of even the youngest women resisting wearing the veil in a variety of creative ways runs counter to the images presented in the Western media of passive, victimized women who are oppressed and flattened into a monolithic group by wearing the veil.

> Uses specific details from the text to show that the girls have "individual identities."

> Uses specific details from the text to show that the girls offer "resistance to the veil."

> Examples of other forms of resistance.

Fig. 2. Satrapi, p. 75.

This trope of resistance to the veil continues even after the regime has become increasingly powerful and all women are required and forced to wear the veil. Emma Tarlo, in her "Sartorial Review" of *Persepolis*, notes that "more subtle indicators" (349) become the way to distinguish between the fundamentalist and more secular men and women. Satrapi represents this with a drawing showing the slight changes in stylings that people adopt to make visible their resistance to the regime (75).

Fig. 3. Satrapi, pp. 132–33.

In these examples, the resistance is "more bold."

Early in the comic, some acts of resistance to the imposed clothing are even more bold; while still relatively young, Marjane is stopped by the Guardians of the Revolution for stepping into the street wearing a denim jacket and Nike sneakers with her veil in an attempt to align herself with the forbidden Western youth culture she adores (Satrapi 133). An embrace of Western appearance through clothing is shown to be an act of resistance for Iranians, particularly Iranians who, like Marjane at this point, have not been to the West and experienced alienation or isolation there.

Much later, when Marjane returns to Iran after spending time in Vienna, she discovers that her friends have adopted what Marjane initially sees as a superficial interest in Western standards of beauty—"They all looked like the heroines of American TV series" (Satrapi 259). Marjane later realizes that wearing makeup and adopting Western beauty standards is "an act of resistance on their part" (Satrapi 259). Marjane herself is easily identified as having been an outsider for some time due to her inability to wear the veil in the sneakily fashionable way that the other women do (Satrapi 293). While on the surface this expression of resistance through an embrace of Western culture appears to support Western liberal feminist ideology, the fact that these women demonstrate agency and independence, not relying on outside forces to enact political change, problematizes this simple reading.

As Marjane learns to read the signs, so does the reader.

Subtle markers of resistance to the universalizing nature of the veil become increasingly important over the course of *Persepolis* as a

4

5

6

way to visibly communicate political ideologies and also individual identities. Instead of the passive women accepting the enforced veil-wearing usually represented in the Western media, Satrapi represents women resisting the authority of the regime through their clothing and their bodies, and also represents them as individuals while still wearing their veils. The acts of resistance to the regime are perhaps so subtle—having to do with slight reconfigurations and small details such as wearing red socks—that they may not even be noticeable or understandable by an outsider without Marjane as a guide. This representation complicates, if not outright displaces, the Western stereotype of the veiled Muslim woman being passively oppressed.

Restates the thesis as a conclusion proven by the foregoing analysis.

Works Cited

Chiu, Monica. "Sequencing and Contingent Individualism in the Graphic, Postcolonial Spaces of Satrapi's *Persepolis* and Okubo's *Citizen 13660.*" *English Language Notes*, vol. 46, no. 2, Fall/Winter 2008, pp. 99–114.

Satrapi, Marjane. *The Complete Persepolis*. Pantheon Books, 2007.

Tarlo, Emma. "Marjane Satrapi's *Persepolis*: A Sartorial Review." *Fashion Theory*, vol. 11, no. 2/3, 2007, pp. 347–56.

Analyzing a Student Analysis

In "The Veil in *Persepolis*," Stephanie Cawley draws on rhetorical strategies and techniques that good writers use all the time when analyzing a subject. The following questions, in addition to focusing on particular aspects of Cawley's text, will help you identify those common strategies and techniques so you can adapt them to your own writing. These questions will also prepare you for the analytical questions—on content, structure, and language—that you'll find after all the other selections in this chapter, along with suggestions for writing on related topics.

FOR CLOSE READING

1. In *Persepolis*, says Stephanie Cawley, young Marjane, the central character, serves the reader "as a guide" (6). A guide to what? Why does the "Western" reader need a guide in Satrapi's book?

2. According to Cawley, what is "the Western image of the veiled woman" (2)? In what ways do they find this image to be inaccurate?

3. Under a repressive political regime, says Cawley (and, of course, Satrapi herself), how people dress or wear their hair can be meaningful. How so? Why does it matter, for example, that the women in Satrapi's autobiographical comic wear their veils in "sneakily fashionable" ways (5)?

4. According to Cawley, what *is* the basic function or role of the veil in Satrapi's work? Point to specific passages in their critical analysis that most clearly support this reading of the veil.

STRATEGIES AND STRUCTURES

1. Cawley's basic point is that the veil is an image of "resistance" throughout *Persepolis*, but they are also arguing that the reader has to learn how to analyze and interpret those images properly. Point out examples in the text that support this point.

2. Early in their ANALYSIS, Cawley locates a particular place ("The very first page") in the text they are writing about; they then DESCRIBE that part of the text in some detail (2). Point out several other places in Cawley's essay where they follow this fundamental step in analyzing any text.

3. In addition to locating and describing specific pieces of Satrapi's text, Cawley explains what each piece means or signifies. Point out several examples of *this* step in their analysis.

4. Having broken down the text they're analyzing into its parts—and having indicated what the parts mean individually—how and where does Cawley put the pieces back together to explain their overall significance? Locate and describe particular places in the essay where Cawley takes this key synthesizing step, typical of the analysis of a text as a form of academic writing.

5. *Other Methods.* Citing the work of other readers, such as Monica Chiu and Emma Tarlo, Cawley ARGUES that Satrapi's use of the veil in *Persepolis* "complicates, if not outright displaces" Western views of the veiled woman (6). How and how well does this external evidence support Cawley's claim?

THINKING ABOUT LANGUAGE

1. Look up the root meaning of "iconic" (2). How does this meaning account for the use of the word to refer to such different things as a face in a religious painting, an object in a comic, and a graphic on a computer screen?

2. What is a "trope" (3), and why does Cawley use the term for the veil in *Persepolis*?

3. What does Cawley mean by "problematizes" in paragraph 5? by "agency" and "ideology" (5)? Is their use of these terms literary, political, or both? Explain.

4. In what sense might Cawley's own analysis of *Persepolis* be called a "sartorial" review (3)?

FOR WRITING

1. From Cawley's essay, or Satrapi's "Kim Wilde" (p. 142), or a complete version of *Persepolis*, choose a panel or page and, in a few paragraphs, analyze what you see there. Don't forget to mention the words as well as the images.

2. Clothes are important throughout *Persepolis*. Write a four-to-six-page analysis of clothes as a trope of political submission and resistance in "Kim Wilde" (p. 142) or in some other chapter of Satrapi's graphic memoir.

3. In 250 to 300 words, write a critical ANALYSIS of Cawley's essay, or of one of the other essays mentioned in their Works Cited. Is the claim or thesis of the essay clear and substantial? How and how well is that claim or thesis supported in the text?

4. Mine Okubo's *Citizen 13660*, to which Cawley refers, is a graphic memoir by a Japanese American of her life in relocation centers in California and Utah during World War II. Images and text from various editions of Okubo's narrative are readily available online and in print. Examine a number of them; then, analyze a few representative examples of Okubo's drawings and note your reactions to them.

5. In collaboration with several classmates, discuss the role and character of the hero or heroine in your (and their) favorite comics. (Douglas Wolk's "Superhero Smackdown," p. 426, may give you some ideas.) COMPARE AND CONTRAST different figures as you consider—and take notes on—the cultural, social, or political values they embody. Choose one or two figures, and write a collaborative essay analyzing how and why those figures exemplify important values or norms in the culture they represent or resist. Refer to specific scenes and adventures.

How to Cross the Street

A process analysis tells how to do something by breaking it down into steps. Recipes are common examples, as is the set of instructions on a gasoline pump or an ATM machine. On this street-crossing sign, the process of crossing the street is broken down into three fundamental steps: (1) push button; (2) start crossing; (3) watch for turning cars. In addition to giving instructions for crossing the street, this sign explains the meanings of the various lights at the intersection. When you write a process analysis, you may want to include illustrations along with your text—or text along with your visuals. The visuals should actually help explain the process, however, and not merely serve as decoration. For most readers, the lights at an intersection are self-explanatory—a walking figure means Go; an unblinking red hand means Stop. For those who need extra instruction, the traffic engineers who designed this sign have provided it; however, they've left out one critical step: "Read this sign *before* crossing the street."

[FOR WRITING]···

What's wrong with this picture? In a paragraph or two, analyze and evaluate the street-crossing sign on p. 319. How would you change it (if at all) to make it more effective?

SUGGESTIONS FOR WRITING

1. "Figure it out, or remain neurotic for life," says Philip Weiss, in "How to Get Out of a Locked Trunk" (p. 321). Weiss is referring to the psychological theories of certain "Viennese intellectuals," including Sigmund Freud (1856–1926). Do some research on Freud's basic theories and write an **ANALYSIS** of how some specific Freudian ideas—such as the "Oedipus complex" or the "id"—are regarded by experts in the field today.

2. "Revising is a breeze if you . . . can look at your text coldly, analytically, manipulatively," writes Annie Dillard in "How I Wrote the Moth Essay—and Why" (p. 328). Revision, as Dillard makes clear, is a critical phase of the writing process. Write a **PROCESS ANALYSIS** explaining in detail how you revised a recent piece of writing.

3. In "Emily Dickinson and the Space Within" (p. 337), Magdalena Ostas contends that solitude was a major source of Dickinson's poetic inspiration and creative energy. Drawing on your own experience, construct an **ARGUMENT** that supports (or contests) the claim that solitude can be restorative. In addition to Ostas's (and Dickinson's) views on the subject, you might also consult Ralph Waldo Emerson's classic essay on the subject, "Solitude and Society," published in 1857.

4. When Nike advertises a pair of shoes, says Dan Redding in "What Does the Nike Logo Mean?," the company is selling "something much bigger" than mere footwear (p. 343). The Nike logo, consequently, is more than a simple trademark: it is an *icon*, an image that represents big ideas. Choose a logo you're familiar with, and write an **ANALYSIS** of its "iconic" elements. With the Apple logo, for example, you would probably want to discuss Adam and Eve and the Tree of Knowledge—just as Dan Redding discusses the "mythological attributes" Nike borrows from its namesake.

5. Before 2020, a package of Land O'Lakes butter (p. 305) featured an image of an Indigenous woman holding a box of butter with her image on it, an example of the Droste effect in graphic design. Named after a Dutch chocolate company, the Droste effect is the subject of numerous videos on *YouTube*. Watch a few of them, and then write a critical **ANALYSIS** in which you **COMPARE AND CONTRAST** various examples of this visual phenomenon. Be sure to say why you think people find it worth imitating.

PHILIP WEISS

How to Get Out of a Locked Trunk

Philip Weiss (b. 1955) is an investigative journalist who has written for the *Jewish World Review, Esquire,* and the *New York Observer,* where he began the blog *Mondoweiss,* a now independent website that covers developments in Israel, Palestine, and relevant American foreign policy. Weiss is the author of the political novel *Cock-A-Doodle-Doo* (1995) and the investigative work *American Taboo: A Murder in the Peace Corps* (2004). He also coedited *The Goldstone Report: The Legacy of the Landmark Investigation of the Gaza Conflict* (2011).

   In this essay, which first appeared in *Harper's Magazine* (1992), the author tackles a more personal topic: while spending time with a friend before getting married, he methodically analyzes his way out of the trunks of a series of locked cars. As his wedding day approaches, this strange fixation deepens. Weiss's bachelor-self, it would seem, is carrying extra baggage that can only be unpacked with further analysis.

O N A HOT SUNDAY LAST SUMMER my friend Tony and I drove my rental car, a '91   1
Buick, from St. Paul to the small town of Waconia, Minnesota, forty miles southwest. We each had a project. Waconia is Tony's boyhood home, and his sister had recently given him a panoramic postcard of Lake Waconia as seen from a high point in the town early in the century. He wanted to duplicate the photograph's vantage point, then hang the two pictures together in his house in Frogtown. I was hoping to see Tony's father, Emmett, a retired mechanic, in order to settle a question that had been nagging me: Is it possible to get out of a locked car trunk?

> Setting out on a PROCESS ANALYSIS, p. 294, is similar to setting out on a journey or Investigation.

   We tried to call ahead to Emmett twice, but he wasn't home. Tony thought he   2
was probably golfing but that there was a good chance he'd be back by the time we got there. So we set out.

   I parked the Buick, which was a silver sedan with a red interior, by the graveyard   3
near where Tony thought the picture had been taken. He took his picture and I wandered among the headstones, reading the epitaphs. One of them was chillingly anti-individualist. It said, "Not to do my will, but thine."

MLA CITATION: Weiss, Philip. "How to Get Out of a Locked Trunk." *Back to the Lake: A Reader and Guide for Writers,* edited by Thomas Cooley, 5th ed., W. W. Norton, 2024, pp. 321–26.

Trunk lockings had been on my mind for a few weeks. It seemed to me that the   4
fear of being locked in a car trunk had a particular hold on the American imagination. Trunk lockings occur in many movies and books—from *Goodfellas* to *Thelma
and Louise* to *Humboldt's Gift*.[1] And while the highbrow national newspapers generally shy away from trunk lockings, the attention they receive in local papers suggests a widespread anxiety surrounding the subject. In an afternoon at the New
York Public Library I found numerous stories about trunk lockings. A Los Angeles
man is discovered, bloodshot, banging the trunk of his white Eldorado following a
night and a day trapped inside; he says his captors went on joyrides and picked up
women. A forty-eight-year-old Houston doctor is forced into her trunk at a bank
ATM and then the car is abandoned, parked near the Astrodome.[2] A New Orleans
woman tells police she gave birth in a trunk while being abducted to Texas. Tests
undermine her story, the police drop the investigation. But so what if it's a fantasy?
That only shows the idea's hold on us.

Every culture comes up with tests of a person's ability to get out of a sticky   5
situation. The English plant mazes. Tropical resorts market those straw finger-
grabbers that tighten their grip the harder you pull on them, and Viennese intellectuals[3] gave us the concept of childhood sexuality—figure it out, or remain
neurotic for life.

At least you could puzzle your way out of those predicaments. When they slam   6
the trunk, though, you're helpless unless someone finds you. You would think that
such a common worry should have a ready fix, and that the secret of getting out of a
locked trunk is something we should all know about.

I phoned experts but they were very discouraging.   7

"You cannot get out. If you got a pair of pliers and bat's eyes, yes. But you have to   8
have a lot of knowledge of the lock," said James Foote at Automotive Locksmiths in
New York City.

Jim Frens, whom I reached at the technical section of *Car and Driver*[4] in Detroit,   9
told me the magazine had not dealt with this question. But he echoed the opinion of
experts elsewhere when he said that the best hope for escape would be to try and
kick out the panel between the trunk and the backseat. That angle didn't seem
worth pursuing. What if your enemies were in the car, crumpling beer cans and
laughing at your fate? It didn't make sense to join them.

---

1. *Humboldt's Gift* (1975), a novel by Saul Bellow about a spiritually empty writer whose life is reawakened
by a mob member; *Goodfellas* (1990), a gangster movie; *Thelma and Louise* (1991), a road movie about two
women trying to escape oppressive marriages.

2. A large sports arena in Houston, Texas.

3. These would include the founder of psychoanalysis, Sigmund Freud (1856–1939).

4. A monthly magazine for car enthusiasts.

The people who deal with rules on auto design were uncomfortable with my sce-   10
narios. Debra Barclay of the Center for Auto Safety, an organization founded by
Ralph Nader,[5] had certainly heard of cases, but she was not aware of any regulations
on the matter. "Now, if there was a defect involved—" she said, her voice trailing off,
implying that trunk locking was all phobia. This must be one of the few issues on
which she and the auto industry agree. Ann Carlson of the Motor Vehicle Manufacturers Association became alarmed at the thought that I was going to play up a non-
problem: "In reality this very rarely happens. As you say, in the movies it's a wonderful
plot device," she said. "But in reality apparently this is not that frequent an occur-
rence. So they have not designed that feature into vehicles in a specific way."

When we got to Emmett's one-story house it was full of people. Tony's sister, Carol, was   11
on the floor with her two small children. Her husband, Charlie, had one eye on the golf
tournament on TV, and Emmett was at the kitchen counter, trimming fat from meat
for lunch. I have known Emmett for fifteen years. He looked better than ever. In his
retirement he had sharply changed his diet and lost a lot of weight. He had on shorts.
His legs were tanned and muscular. As always, his manner was humorous, if opaque.

Tony told his family my news: I was getting married in three weeks. Charlie   12
wanted to know where my fiancée was. Back East, getting everything ready. A big-
time hatter was fitting her for a new hat.

Emmett sat on the couch, watching me. "Do you want my advice?"   13

"Sure."   14

He just grinned. A gold tooth glinted. Carol and Charlie pressed him to yield his   15
wisdom.

Finally he said, "Once you get to be thirty, you make your own mistakes."   16

He got out several cans of beer, and then I brought up what was on my   17
mind.

Emmett nodded and took off his glasses, then cleaned them and put them
back on.

We went out to his car, a Mercury Grand Marquis, and Emmett opened
the trunk. His golf clubs were sitting on top of the spare tire in a green golf
bag. Next to them was a toolbox and what he called his "burglar tools," a set
of elbowed rods with red plastic handles he used to open door locks when people
locked their keys inside.

> A process analysis should always specify when special equipment (p. 295) is needed.

Tony and Charlie stood watching. Charlie is a banker in Minneapolis. He enjoys   20
gizmos and is extremely practical. I would describe him as unflappable. That's a
word I always wanted to apply to myself, but my fiancée had recently informed me
that I am high-strung. Though that surprised me, I didn't quarrel with her.

5. American attorney and political activist (b. 1934) who was an early advocate of automobile safety.

For a while we studied the latch assembly. The lock closed in much the same way 21
that a lobster might clamp on to a pencil. The claw portion, the jaws of the lock, was
mounted inside the trunk lid. When you shut the lid, the jaws locked on to the bend
of a U-shaped piece of metal mounted on the body of the car. Emmett said my best
bet would be to unscrew the bolts. That way the U-shaped piece would come loose
and the lock's jaws would swing up with it still in their grasp.

"But you'd need a wrench," he said. 22

It was already getting too technical. Emmett had an air of endless patience, but I 23
felt defeated. I could only imagine bloodied fingers, cracked teeth. I had hoped for a
simple trick.

> **NARRATION**
> combined with
> process analy-
> sis can make
> for more inter-
> esting reading
> than a simple
> list of how-to
> steps (p. 296).

Charlie stepped forward. He reached out and squeezed the lock's jaws. 24
They clicked shut in the air, bound together by heavy springs. Charlie now
prodded the upper part of the left-hand jaw, the thicker part. With a rough
flick of his thumb, he was able to force the jaws to snap open. Great.

Unfortunately, the jaws were mounted behind a steel plate the size of 25
your palm in such a way that while they were accessible to us, standing
outside the car, had we been inside the trunk the plate would be in our way,
blocking the jaws.

This time Emmett saw the way out. He fingered a hole in the plate. It was no big- 26
ger than the tip of your little finger. But the hole was close enough to the latch itself
that it might be possible to angle something through the hole from inside the trunk
and nudge the jaws apart. We tried with one of my keys. The lock jumped open.

It was time for a full-dress test. Emmett swung the clubs out of the trunk, and I 27
set my can of Schmidt's on the rear bumper and climbed in. Everyone gathered
around, and Emmett lowered the trunk on me, then pressed it shut with his meaty
hands. Total darkness. I couldn't hear the people outside. I thought I was going to
panic. But the big trunk felt comfortable. I was pressed against a sort of black carpet
that softened the angles against my back.

I could almost stretch out in the trunk, and it seemed to me I could make them 28
sweat if I took my time. Even Emmett, that sphinx, would give way to curiosity.
Once I was out he'd ask how it had been and I'd just grin. There were some things
you could only learn by doing.

It took a while to find the hole. I slipped the key in and angled it to one side. The 29
trunk gasped open.

Emmett motioned the others away, then levered me out with his big right fore- 30
arm. Though I'd only been inside for a minute, I was disoriented—as much as anything because someone had moved my beer while I was gone, setting it down on the
cement floor of the garage. It was just a little thing, but I could not be entirely sure
I had gotten my own beer back.

Charlie was now raring to try other cars. We examined the latch on his Toyota, 31 which was entirely shielded to the trunk occupant (i.e., no hole in the plate), and on the neighbor's Honda (ditto). But a 1991 Dodge Dynasty was doable. The trunk was tight, but its lock had a feature one of the mechanics I'd phoned described as a 'tailpiece': a finger-like extension of the lock mechanism itself that stuck out a half inch into the trunk cavity; simply by twisting the tailpiece I could free the lock. I was even faster on a 1984 Subaru that had a little lever device on the latch.

We went out to my rental on Oak Street. The Skylark was in direct sun and the 32 trunk was hot to the touch, but when we got it open we could see that its latch plate had a perfect hole, a square in which the edge of the lock's jaw appeared like a face in a window.

The trunk was shallow and hot. Emmett had to push my knees down before he 33 could close the lid. This one was a little suffocating. I imagined being trapped for hours, and even before he had got it closed I regretted the decision with a slightly nauseous feeling. I thought of Edgar Allan Poe's live burials,[6] and then about something my fiancée had said more than a year and a half before. I had been on her case to get married. She was divorced, and at every opportunity I would reissue my proposal—even during a commercial. She'd interrupted one of these chirps to tell me, in a cold, throaty voice, that she had no intention of ever going through another divorce: "This time, it's death out." I'd carried those words around like a lump of wet clay.

As it happened, the Skylark trunk was the easiest of all. The hole was right where 34 it was supposed to be. The trunk popped open, and I felt great satisfaction that we'd been able to figure out a rule that seemed to apply about 60 percent of the time. If we publicized our success, it might get the attention it deserved. All trunks would be fitted with such a hole. Kids would learn about it in school. The grip of the fear would relax. Before long a successful trunk-locking scene would date a movie like a fedora[7] dates one today.

When I got back East I was caught up in wedding preparations. I live in New York, and the wedding was to take place in Philadelphia. We set up camp there with five days to go. A friend had lent my fiancée her BMW, and we drove it south with all our things. I unloaded the car in my parents' driveway. The last thing I pulled out of the trunk was my fiancée's hat in its heavy cardboard shipping box. She'd warned me I was not allowed to look. The lid was free but I didn't open it. I was willing to be surprised.

> Analyzing a process can have a larger PURPOSE (p. 294) than simply explaining how to replicate the process.

---

6. Poe (1809–49) buries characters alive in "Bernice" (1835), "The Fall of the House of Usher" (1839), "The Black Cat" (1843), "The Premature Burial" (1844), and "The Cask of Amontillado" (1846).

7. Brimmed hat for men, popular from the 1920s through the 1950s, often worn by gangsters and detectives in movies from that era.

When the trunk was empty it occurred to me I might hop in and give it a try. 36
First I looked over the mechanism. The jaws of the BMW's lock were shielded, but
there seemed to be some kind of cable coming off it that you might be able to manipulate so as to cause the lock to open. The same cable that allowed the driver to open
the trunk remotely . . .

I fingered it for a moment or two but decided I didn't need to test out the theory. ◆ 37

FOR CLOSE READING

1. So, according to Philip Weiss, how do you get out of a locked trunk? How, according
   to his fiancée, do you get out of a marriage? Why do you suppose Weiss considers
   these two questions in the same essay—but with much more detail about getting
   out of the locked trunks? Could the author be trying to fool himself (and perhaps
   the reader) into thinking he is more concerned with a mechanical problem than the
   perhaps more frightening prospect (to him) of getting married? Explain.

2. Of the cars he tests, which one alarms Weiss the most yet turns out to be the easiest to get out of? Why is he so alarmed, do you think? Why is he so anxious to find
   "a simple trick" that will fit all instances (23)?

3. Weiss says, "There were some things you could only learn by doing" (28). What
   might some of them be?

4. Why do you think Weiss refrains from taking a peek at his fiancée's new hat, since
   the lid is "free" and the box would be so easy to open (35)? Could the box and the
   hat be METAPHORICAL? Explain.

STRATEGIES AND STRUCTURES

1. What is Weiss's PURPOSE in ANALYZING THE PROCESS of getting out of a locked trunk?
   What AUDIENCE does Weiss think will be interested in his analysis? The essay first
   appeared in Harper's; do some research on this monthly magazine and its targeted
   readership as you think about who Weiss's intended audience might be.

2. Weiss's essay is divided into three parts—paragraphs 1–10, 11–34, and 35–37. In
   which section does Weiss most fully analyze the process of getting out of a locked
   car trunk? Is his analysis explanatory or directive? Explain.

3. Why do you think the last section of Weiss's essay is the shortest? How and how
   effectively does it bring the essay to a conclusion? Is the conclusion satisfying?
   Does it surprise you?

4. What is Weiss's purpose in citing several "experts" in paragraphs 7–10? What is
   Emmett's role in the big experiment?

5. "It's a wonderful plot device," Weiss quotes one expert as saying about being
   locked in a car trunk (10). Is she right? Where in his essay is Weiss telling a story,
   and where is he analyzing a process? Give specific EXAMPLES from the text.

6. *Other Methods.* Like **NARRATIVES**, which often report events in **CHRONOLOGICAL ORDER**, process analyses are often organized in the chronological order of the steps or stages of the process being analyzed. Where does Weiss use chronology either to tell a story or to analyze a process? Give specific examples from the text.

THINKING ABOUT LANGUAGE

1. The lock on the trunk of Emmett's Mercury Grand Marquis, says Weiss, "closed in much the same way that a lobster might clamp on to a pencil" (21). How effective do you find this **SIMILE** for explaining how this particular trunk locks? Where else does Weiss use **FIGURES OF SPEECH** as a tool of process analysis?

2. A phobia is an irrational fear (10). Point out specific **EXAMPLES** in his essay where Weiss might be said to exhibit phobic behavior. What's he afraid of?

3. To whom is Weiss referring when he mentions "Viennese intellectuals" (5)? Why is he **ALLUDING** to them? Why does he allude to Poe in paragraph 33?

4. Another tool of process analysis that Weiss uses effectively is vivid **DESCRIPTIVE** detail, as in paragraphs 11, 19, 21, and 31. But not all the details relate to the main topic of opening trunk locks. What is the effect of giving so much detail to other subject matter in the essay?

5. "Case," "reissue," "chirp," and "death out" (33)—why does Weiss use these words in the **ANECDOTE** about his proposals? What about "willing" (35)?

FOR WRITING

1. Has anyone you know ever exhibited phobic behavior? Explain how the phobia manifested itself and what specific steps the person took to deal with it.

2. "Every culture," writes Weiss, "comes up with tests of a person's ability to get out of a sticky situation" (5). Have you ever been in such a situation? How did you get out of it? Write an essay analyzing the process.

3. Write an analysis of "How to Get Out of a Locked Trunk" that investigates the author's **PURPOSE** (or purposes) in writing. For example, is Weiss perhaps working out the mechanics of unlocking car trunks for the purpose of analyzing his own state of mind at the time? for the purpose of telling a more complicated and interesting story? Be sure to say what those purposes are—and how Weiss achieves (or fails to achieve) them.

4. "Not to do my will, but thine" (3). What are the implications of this inscription, which Weiss reads on a tombstone at the beginning of his essay? In what ways might it relate to Weiss's situation? to your own life? In a brief **NARRATIVE**, analyze a time when you faced the possibility of putting someone else's needs or desires above your own and explain what you learned from that experience.

ANNIE DILLARD

How I Wrote the Moth Essay—
and Why

Annie Dillard (b. 1945) grew up in Pittsburgh, Pennsylvania, and attended
Hollins College in Roanoke, Virginia. Her master's thesis was on Thoreau's
Walden, to which her work has been compared. A poet and novelist, Dillard is perhaps best known for her prose meditations on nature, teaching,
and the writing life in such works as *A Pilgrim at Tinker Creek* (1974), which
won a Pulitzer Prize for nonfiction; *Teaching a Stone to Talk* (1982); *An
American Childhood* (1987); and *The Abundance* (2016). Dillard's classic
essay "The Death of a Moth" is included in this book on p. 767.

This selection is an essay about writing an essay—and about the writing
process in general. Early in her career as a writer, Dillard went on a camping trip in the Blue Ridge Mountains. As she read by the light of a candle, a
female moth, attracted by the flame, flew into the wax and "stuck, flamed,
frazzled, and fried." Two years later, in a short narrative, Dillard compared
the burning moth to herself as a writer—dedicated to her work but consumed by it. "How I Wrote the Moth Essay—and Why" is Dillard's own
analysis of both her essay and its composition. As she says, "This is the most
personal piece I've ever written—the essay itself, and these notes on it."

I T WAS NOVEMBER 1975. I was living alone, as described, on an island in Puget 1
Sound, near the Canadian border. I was thirty years old. I thought about myself a
lot (for someone thirty years old), because I couldn't figure out what I was doing
there. What was my life about? Why was I living alone, when I am gregarious?

MLA CITATION: Dillard, Annie. "How I Wrote the Moth Essay—and Why." *Back to the Lake: A Reader and
Guide for Writers*, edited by Thomas Cooley, 5th ed., W. W. Norton, 2024, pp. 328–34.

Would I ever meet someone, or should I reconcile myself to all this solitude? I disliked celibacy; I dreaded childlessness. I couldn't even think of anything to write. I was examining every event for possible meaning.

I was then in full flight from success, from the recent fuss over a book of prose I'd published the previous year called *Pilgrim at Tinker Creek*. There were offers from editors, publishers, and Hollywood and network producers. They tempted me with world travel, film and TV work, big bucks. I was there to turn from literary and commercial success and to rededicate myself to art and to God. That's how I justified my loneliness to myself. It was a feeble justification and I knew it, because you certainly don't need to live alone either to write or to pray. Actually I was there because I had picked the place from an atlas, and I was alone because I hadn't yet met my husband.

My reading and teaching fed my thoughts. I was reading Simone Weil, *First and Last Notebooks*. Simone Weil was a twentieth-century French intellectual, born Jewish, who wrote some of the most interesting Christian theology I've ever read. She was brilliant, but a little nuts; her doctrines were harsh. "Literally," she wrote, "it is total purity or death." This sort of fanaticism attracted and appalled me. Weil had deliberately starved herself to death to call attention to the plight of French workers. I was taking extensive notes on Weil.

In the classroom I was teaching poetry writing, exhorting myself (in the guise of exhorting my students), and convincing myself by my own rhetoric: commit yourself to a useless art! In art alone is meaning! In sacrifice alone is meaning! These, then, were issues for me at that time: dedication, purity, sacrifice.

Early that November morning I noticed the hollow insects on the bathroom floor. I got down on my hands and knees to examine them and recognized some as empty moth bodies. I recognized them, of course, only because I'd seen an empty moth body already—two years before, when I'd camped alone and had watched a flying moth get stuck in a candle and burn.

Walking back to my desk, where I had been answering letters, I realized that the burning moth was a dandy visual focus for all my recent thoughts about an empty, dedicated life. Perhaps I'd try to write a short narrative about it.

I went to my pile of journals, hoping I'd taken some nice, specific notes about the moth in the candle. What I found disappointed me at first: that night I'd written a long description of owl sounds, and only an annoyed aside about bugs flying into the candle. But the next night, after pages of self-indulgent drivel, I'd written a fuller description, a description of the moth which got stuck in candle wax.

The journal entry had some details I could use (bristleworms on the ground, burnt moths' wings sticking to pans), some phrases (her body acted as a wick, the

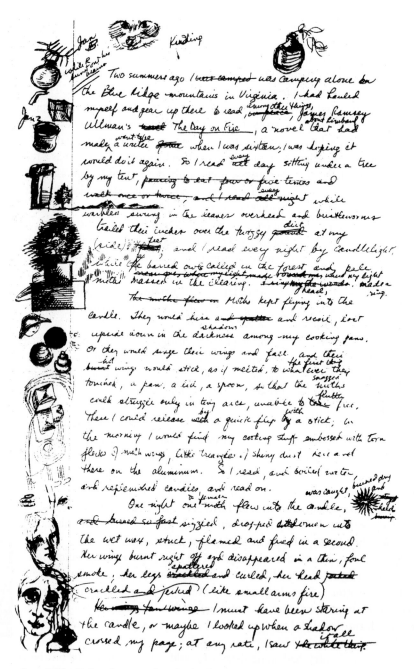

A page from Dillard's handwritten first draft of "The Death of a Moth."

candle had 2 flames, the moth burned until I blew it out), and, especially, some verbs (hiss, recoil, stick, spatter, jerked, crackled).

Even in the journals, the moth was female. (From childhood reading I'd learned 9 to distinguish moths by sex.) And, there in the journal, was a crucial detail: on that camping trip, I'd been reading about Rimbaud. Arthur Rimbaud—the French symbolist poet, a romantic, hotheaded figure who attracted me enormously when I was sixteen—had been young and self-destructive. When *he* was sixteen, he ran away from home to Paris, led a dissolute life, shot his male lover (the poet Verlaine), drank absinthe which damaged his brain, deranged his senses with drunkenness and sleeplessness, and wrote mad vivid poetry which altered the course of Western literature. When he was in his twenties, he turned his back to the Western world and vanished into Abyssinia[1] as a gunrunner.

With my old journal beside me, I took up my current journal and scribbled and 10 doodled my way through an account of my present life and the remembered moth. It went extraordinarily well; it was not typical. It seemed very much "given"—given, I think, because I'd asked, because I'd been looking so hard and so long for connections, meanings. The connections were all there, and seemed solid enough: I saw a moth burnt and on fire; I was reading Rimbaud hoping to rededicate myself to writing (this one bald statement of motive was unavoidable); I live alone. So the writer is like the moth, and like a religious contemplative: emptying himself so he can be a channel for his work. Of course you can reinforce connections with language: the bathroom moths are like a jumble of buttresses for cathedral domes; the female moth is like an immolating monk, like a hollow saint, a flame-faced virgin gone to God; Rimbaud burnt out his brains with poetry while night pooled wetly at my feet.

I liked the piece enough to rewrite it. I took out a couple of paragraphs—one 11 about why I didn't have a dog, another that ran on about the bathroom spider. This is the kind of absurdity you fall into when you write about anything, let alone about yourself. You're so pleased and grateful to be writing at all, especially at the beginning, that you babble. Often you don't know where the work is going, so you can't tell what's irrelevant.

It doesn't hurt much to babble in a first draft, so long as you have the sense to cut out irrelevancies later. If you are used to analyzing texts, you will be able to formulate a clear statement of what your draft turned out to be about. Then you make a list of what you've already written, paragraph by paragraph, and see what doesn't fit and cut it out. (All this requires is nerves of steel and lots of coffee.) Most of the time you'll have to add to the beginning, ensuring that it gives a fair idea of what the point might be, or at least

> Dillard provides information that will be useful to her AUDIENCE of other writers (pp. 294–95).

1. Historic, Arabic-derived name for Ethiopia in eastern Africa.

what is about to happen. (Suspense is for mystery writers. The most inept writing has an inadvertent element of suspense: the reader constantly asks himself, where on earth is this going?) Usually I end up throwing away the beginning: the first part of a poem, the first few pages of an essay, the first scene of a story, even the first few chapters of a book. It's not holy writ. The paragraphs and sentences are tesserae—tiles for a mosaic. Just because you have a bunch of tiles in your lap doesn't mean your mosaic will be better if you use them all. In this atypical case, however, there were very few extraneous passages. The focus was tight, probably because I'd been so single-minded before I wrote it.

I added stuff, too, to strengthen and clarify the point. I added some speculation   13
about the burning moth: had she mated and laid her eggs, had she done her work? Near the end I added a passage about writing class: which of you want to give your lives and become writers?

Ultimately I sent it to *Harper's* magazine, which published it. The early drafts, and   14
the *Harper's* version, had a different ending, a kind of punch line that was a series of interlocking statements:

> I don't mind living alone. I like eating alone and reading. I don't mind sleeping alone. The only time I mind being alone is when something is funny; then, when I am laughing at something funny, I wish someone were around. Sometimes I think it is pretty funny that I sleep alone.

I took this ending out of the book version, which is the version you have. I took it out because the tone was too snappy, too clever; it reduced everything to celibacy, which was really a side issue; it made the reader forget the moth; and it called too much attention to the narrator. The new ending was milder. It referred back to the main body of the text.

Revising is a breeze if you know what you're doing—if you can look at your text coldly,   15
analytically, manipulatively. Since I've studied texts, I know what I'm doing when I revise. The hard part is devising the wretched thing in the first place. How do you go from nothing to something? How do you face the blank page without fainting dead away?

To start a narrative, you need a batch of things. Not feelings, not opinions, not senti-   16
ments, not judgments, not arguments, but specific objects and events: a cat, a spider web, a mess of insect skeletons, a candle, a book about Rimbaud, a burning moth. I try to give the reader a story, or at least a scene (the flimsiest narrative occasion will serve), and something to look at. I try not to hang on the reader's arm and bore him with my life story, my fancy self-indulgent writing, or my opinions. He is my guest; I try to entertain him. Or he'll throw my pages across the room and turn on the television.

More good advice for defining and "entertaining" your AUDIENCE can be found on p. 300.

I try to say what I mean and not "hide the hidden meaning." "Clarity is the sov- 17
ereign courtesy of the writer," said J. Henri Fabre, the great French entomologist, "I
do my best to achieve it." Actually, it took me about ten years to learn to write
clearly. When I was in my twenties, I was more interested in showing off.

What do you do with these things? You juggle them. You toss them
around. To begin, you don't need a well-defined point. You don't need
"something to say"—that will just lead you to reiterating clichés. You need
bits of the world to toss around. You start anywhere, and join the bits into
a pattern by your writing about them. Later you can throw out the ones
that don't fit.

> Use present tense when explaining habitual actions in a process analysis (p. 298).

I like to start by describing something, by ticking off the five senses. Later I go 19
back to the beginning and locate the reader in time and space. I've found that if
I take pains to be precise about *things,* feelings will take care of themselves. If you
try to force a reader's feelings through dramatic writing ("writhe," "ecstasy,"
"scream"), you make a fool of yourself, like someone at a party trying too hard to
be liked.

I have piles of materials in my journals—mostly information in the form of notes 20
on my reading, and to a lesser extent, notes on things I'd seen and heard during the
day. I began the journals five or six years after college, finding myself highly trained
for taking notes and for little else. Now I have thirty-some journal volumes, all
indexed. If I want to write about arctic exploration, say, or star chemistry, or monas-
ticism, I can find masses of pertinent data under that topic. And if I browse I can
often find images from other fields that may fit into what I'm writing, if only as metaphor or simile. It's terrific having all these materials handy. It saves and makes available all those years of reading. Otherwise, I'd forget everything, and life wouldn't
accumulate, but merely pass.

The moth essay I wrote that November day was an "odd" piece—"freighted with 21
heavy-handed symbolism," as I described it to myself just after I wrote it. The reader
must be startled to watch this apparently calm, matter-of-fact account of the writer's life and times turn before his eyes into a mess of symbols whose real subject
matter is their own relationship. I hoped the reader wouldn't feel he'd been had. I
tried to ensure that the actual, historical moth wouldn't vanish into idea, but would
stay physically present.

A week after I wrote the first draft I considered making it part of the book (*Holy the* 22
Firm) I had been starting. It seemed to fit the book's themes. (Actually, I spent the
next fifteen months fitting the book to *its* themes.) In order to clarify my thinking I
jotted down some notes:

moth in candle:

the poet—   materials of world, of bare earth at feet, sucked up, trans-
            formed, subsumed to spirit, to air, to light

the mystic— not through reason but through emptiness

the martyr—virgin, sacrifice, death with meaning.

I prefaced these notes with the comical word "Hothead."

It had been sheer good luck that the different aspects of the historical truth fit 23
together so nicely. It had actually been on that particular solo camping trip that I'd
read the Rimbaud novel. If it hadn't been, I wouldn't have hesitated to fiddle with
the facts. I fiddled with one fact, for sure: I foully slandered my black cat, Small, by
saying she was "gold"—to match the book's moth and little blonde burnt girl. I actually had a gold cat at that time, named Kindling.[2] I figured no one would believe it.
It was too much. In the book, as in real life, the cat was spayed.

This is the most personal piece I've ever written—the essay itself, and these notes on 24
it. I don't recommend, or even approve, writing personally. It can lead to dreadful
writing. The danger is that you'll get lost in the contemplation of your wonderful self.
You'll include things for the lousy reason that they actually happened, or that you feel
strongly about them; you'll forget to ensure that the *reader* feels anything whatever.
You may hold the popular view that art is self-expression, or a way of understanding
the self—in which case the artist need do nothing more than babble uncontrolledly
about the self and then congratulate himself that, in addition to all his other wonderfully interesting attributes, he is also an artist. I don't (evidently) hold this view. So I
think that this moth piece is a risky one to read: it seems to enforce these romantic
and giddy notions of art and the artist. But I trust you can keep your heads. ◆

FOR CLOSE READING

1. Annie Dillard was camping alone in the mountains of Virginia when she saw the
   moth burn in a candle. Two years later, when she wrote an essay about the experience, she was living in the state of Washington—still alone. Why the solitude?
   According to Dillard, what was she retreating from, and what was she seeking?

2. Dillard says she chose the burning moth as "a dandy visual focus for all [her] recent
   thoughts about an empty, dedicated life" (6). Was it a good choice for analyzing
   her state of mind as a writer? Why or why not?

---

2. Dillard's other cat can be seen peering at the reader from the top left corner of the manuscript on
p. 330. Her name is scrawled beside her face.

3. Dillard does not recommend "writing personally" (24). Why not? How well does she herself avoid these pitfalls in this essay? How seriously should we take her recommendation, given that Dillard herself is known for using an ironic TONE?

4. Dillard recommends keeping a personal journal. For a writer, what does she see as the advantages of doing so? In what ways does this essay demonstrate the benefits of journal keeping?

STRATEGIES AND STRUCTURES

1. "Perhaps I'd try to write a short narrative about it" (6). In this essay, Dillard is telling the story of how she wrote a story. What do the first four paragraphs of "How I Wrote the Moth Essay—and Why" contribute to this NARRATIVE?

2. In addition to analyzing the composition of a particular essay, Dillard is examining the writing process in general. Writing teachers often divide the process into prewriting, drafting, revising, editing, and publishing. Point out specific passages in Dillard's essay that address each of these steps.

3. "It went extraordinarily well; it was not typical," Dillard says of the process of drafting the moth essay (10). What explanation does she give for the ease with which this piece seemed to come to her? What else was not typical?

4. "The paragraphs and sentences are tesserae—tiles for a mosaic" (12). What step (or steps) of the writing process is Dillard referring to here? Given the importance of clear organization in an analysis, is the METAPHOR appropriate? Where and how does Dillard use it again in her essay?

5. *Other Methods.* Visuals can be effective tools to support the subject matter in a critical analysis. How does the illustration of a page from Dillard's handwritten first draft support her points about the ease (or difficulty) of the writing process?

THINKING ABOUT LANGUAGE

1. "Poet," "mystic," "martyr"—these are the categories under which Dillard analyzes the themes of her essay and the book it inspired (22). These words have similar CONNOTATIONS. What are they, and how do they apply to the figure of the "moth in candle" as Dillard explains it?

2. Dillard says she prefaced her notes about the first draft of her essay with the word "Hothead" (22). Who or what is she referring to here, and why does she describe the word as "comical" (22)?

3. "Of course you can reinforce connections with language," says Dillard as she introduces a string of SIMILES to connect the objects of her analysis with their "meanings" (10). How well do these FIGURES OF SPEECH serve this analytical purpose? Where else in the text does Dillard use language in this way?

4. Dillard frequently addresses the reader as "you." Who is her intended audience and why might they need so much advice about writing? Is it good advice, or does it seem overly self-critical? Explain your response.

5. Dillard ends her essay by saying, "But I trust you can keep your heads" (24). Why does she use the plural form of the noun "heads"? Is this a good word to end on? Why or why not?

FOR WRITING

1. In your view, how well does Dillard's essay analyze its subject? Read "The Death of a Moth" (p. 767), and write a critical analysis of Dillard's "How I Wrote the Moth Essay—and Why." Be sure to comment on what she says about the writing process in general as well as the composition of the moth essay itself.

2. In paragraph 14, Dillard quotes from the ending of the moth essay as it originally appeared in *Harper's Magazine*. **COMPARE** the two versions of the ending, and in a paragraph or two evaluate Dillard's assessment of the differences (14). Do you think these changes improved the conclusion? Explain why or why not. Remember that an effective conclusion should provide a clear statement of the author's insights and of why they are significant.

3. Virginia Woolf's classic essay "The Death of the Moth" (1942) is widely available online and elsewhere. Find and read Woolf's essay, and then write a critical analysis of it as a **NARRATIVE** about writing as a calling or way of life.

4. Write a **COMPARE/CONTRAST** essay in which you analyze "The Death of the Moth" by Woolf and "The Death of a Moth" by Dillard (on p. 767). Explain where and how Dillard's essay perpetuates the theme of life reduced to its essence—and where it departs from Woolf's treatment of the same subject. Feel free to refer to Dillard's own analysis when composing yours.

MAGDALENA OSTAS

Emily Dickinson and the Space Within

Magdalena Ostas (b. 1976) is a lecturer in comparative literature and English at the University of California, Berkeley. A graduate of UC San Diego, she earned a PhD in literature from Duke University. Ostas is the author of critical essays on British literature and poetry, among other topics. Situated at "the crossroads of literature, philosophy, and the arts," says Ostas, her work explores how these various disciplines "illuminate ways we live—and how they help us think and understand the world."

In "Emily Dickinson and the Space Within" (editor's title), which appeared in the online journal *Psyche* in 2022, Ostas analyzes how the poet's sequestered life fostered the distinctive inward point of view that infuses her poems. "We can learn something," says Ostas, "from the ways this poet uses isolation . . . to generate—rather than to drain—creative energy."

W HEN THE AMERICAN POET EMILY DICKINSON began an ongoing conversa- 1 tion with herself about her own inner world, she discovered one of the most unique sources of creative inspiration in the history of poetry. It was inexhaustible and, like the breath of the Buddhist, it resided within her, accessible wherever she was: when she wrote, she withdrew from the world, entering an interior space that, before long, became her poetic subject. As she gradually withdrew from the social world, Dickinson became a remarkable transcriber and translator of inner experience—what in 1855 she called a "solitude of space"

MLA CITATION: Ostas, Magdalena. "Emily Dickinson and the Space Within." *Back to the Lake: A Reader and Guide for Writers*, edited by Thomas Cooley, 5th ed., W. W. Norton, 2024, pp. 337-41.

(in lyric number 1,696[1])—and her interior tracings often yielded extraordinary poems.

Most of us would feel deeply distressed by the thought of being the only ones in our heads, sequestered from others and from daily living. Such isolation can be painful and disorienting, not least because it demands a naked encounter with oneself, and with no escape into something concrete or into any engagement with another. When protracted, such experiences can be terrifying: it's why monastic seclusion is not for the fainthearted; why, in prison life, solitary confinement is among the harshest of punishments.

Yet the way Dickinson inhabits quiet isolation in her poems is fully comfortable. For her, "The Brain—is wider than the sky" and "deeper than the sea," as she wrote in 1863. There is always something in the mind to follow, to chart or explore. Perhaps we can learn from the way Dickinson uses self-isolation to generate—rather than drain off—creative energy. Speaking in an inward voice, she professed to be afraid to "own a Body" or "own a Soul," but she nonetheless squared up to owning both, setting out to investigate and understand what she had been given. "I felt my life with both my hands / To see if it was there—," she writes in 1862, with the kind of stark presentness that was a distinguishing feature of her verse. In Dickinson's hands, poetry was a medium of vivid and energetic self-encounter.

> Although the parts of her textual analysis are arranged logically (p. 303), Ostas inserts a chronology of the poet's life as important CONTEXT.

Dickinson was born on 10 December 1830 into a prominent family in Amherst, Massachusetts. Her father, Edward Dickinson, served as state representative, and her grandfather, Samuel Fowler Dickinson, was a founder of Amherst College; Emily visited her father briefly in Washington, DC in the House of Representatives as a young girl. That said, throughout her life, travel of any kind was rare. She attended Amherst Academy and then boarded for a year at the Mount Holyoke Female Seminary (1847), after which she returned to her family's home in Amherst, a house called the Homestead, where her closest companions—her sister Lavinia and brother Austin—also resided.

Through the 1850s, Dickinson gradually settled into a solitary existence, rarely leaving the Homestead and its parameters, and deliberately sequestered from others: "I do not cross my Father's ground to any House or town," she announced in a letter in 1869. We know that she took enormous pleasure in reclusive activities around the property: gardening, cooking, reading, writing, and sewing booklets of verse. In her later years, she retreated increasingly to her room. This full

---

1. Dickinson seldom assigned titles to her poems; instead, they are typically identified by first line or, as here, by the number assigned to each poem in Thomas H. Johnson's *The Poems of Emily Dickinson* (Cambridge, MA: Harvard University Press, 1955).

withdrawal into the space of the home, unexpectedly, opened possibilities, for she thrived, and began to develop her distinctive poetic style.

Although some of her biographers . . . see a lack at the center of her existence, Dickinson's profound isolation granted her perspectives—ranging from the mystical to the ruminative to the critical—that daily social living might have cut off. Isolation proved a guard against rigid social expectations, especially those imposed on women, which would likely have restrained her poetic craft. Alone with herself, and her boundless creative explorations, she found a world in inner space. Not for her were marriage, motherhood or domestic cares: "I'm 'wife'—I've finished that" she writes with cutting scare quotes in 1861. For Dickinson, sequester was a feminist act of independence. And, with that understood, she was able to share a lively written correspondence with friends and editors.

Dickinson's compressed, compact and, often, emotionally brutal poetic style arises from a sense of what the critic Robert Weisbuch in 1975 wonderfully called "scenelessness"—that is, her standing apart from things, persons, places and times, and inhabiting instead an intensely inward world. The "scene" is literally missing in her poetry, and in its place stands the poet's receptiveness, a state that gives people, places and things their significance: "The Outer—from the Inner / Derives it's [sic] magnitude—," as Dickinson put it in 1862. Released from the push and pull of daily living, Dickinson sees things anew and from a boundary-breaking perspective. Her signature dashes mirror the starts and stops of the human mind, while many of her poems read as puzzling and luminous transcripts of thoughts, feelings, sensations, perceptions and ideas that are suspended, standing unanchored and unattached. In a letter in 1869 to her editor Thomas Wentworth Higginson, Dickinson wrote: "there seems a spectral power in thought that walks alone."

The first step in analyzing a text is to identify its component parts (p. 302).

To see such a perspective in play, consider the beginning of one of Dickinson's best-known poems, her beautiful and haunting lyric about hearing a fly buzzing in the room at the instant of her own death. Dickinson wrote about 1,800 poems, but only 10 or so were published during her lifetime, and those were very heavily edited. "I heard a Fly buzz—when I died—" was published only posthumously in 1896, when the extent of her poetic writings was discovered. It was included in a hand-sewn manuscript booklet, called a "fascicle," thought to have been written circa 1863. It is an unconventional poem, even a radical one, its first stanza especially subversive:

> I heard a Fly buzz—when I died—
> The Stillness in the Room
> Was like the Stillness in the Air—
> Between the Heaves of Storm—

Poems serve as concrete examples that support Ostas's discussion of abstract elements of the poet's work (p. 303).

With this opening image, Dickinson invites us to occupy a specific and exact   9
moment: the millisecond between life and death, exactly on the line between consciousness and unconsciousness: one foot in life, the other foot already out. Glossed
simply, Dickinson's opening line might be understood to say, I heard a fly buzzing
around my body *as* I died, or as I underwent the process of dying. It is striking that,
in the difficult moment just before death, Dickinson's speaker manages to have such
an alert and perceptive ear. And to report exactly what she hears: a simple fly buzzing around.

The power of Dickinson's fly, strangely, stems from its capacity to anchor and   10
calm her speaker's experience rather than to unsettle it. The poem tells us that the
speaker is quiet on the inside, content to be solitary and unattached. Her (and our)
most common and naive hopes for the moment before death are totally and completely upended by the fly, for Dickinson's speaker sees no tunnel of light, hears no
angels singing, and perceives no bells ringing as she catches glimmers of the other
side and prepares to depart.

Dickinson is so at ease in this poem with what we might call the reality of dying, a   11
comfort that her inward isolation affords her, that she is able to look around unflinch-
ingly and with courage. (Her own death in 1886 would be less peaceable—a protracted
fight with disease.) We would expect the speaker in the poem to be overcome or overwhelmed, but she is so calm that she is able to *bear* the buzzing of the fly and to contemplate the finality it suggests: the fly outlives her to continue its vital, earthly
buzzing around as she lies immobile, and it instantly signals the decaying of her body.

And Dickinson's insistence on the image of the fly—a winged terrestrial counter-   12
angel—is also heroic. This is especially true in the context of her life in 19th-century
Amherst, where she was raised in a devout Calvinist family. Her dissent from her
family's orthodoxy is an open theme in her poems, as in this from 1861:

> Some keep the Sabbath going to Church—
> I keep it, staying at Home—
> With a Bobolink for a Chorister—
> And an Orchard, for a Dome—

The image of the fly is similarly defiant in sharply deflecting the myths the Church
teaches. What do we hear when we die? Flies, Dickinson manages to assert.

The most striking aspect of the isolation that inhabits Dickinson's poems is that it   13
allows her to expand the terrain that the first-person point of view can
inhabit and traverse. We go places and see things inside of us in Dickinson's poems that we'd miss in being engrossed in life. Like the millisecond
that opens "I heard a Fly buzz—when I died—," such perspectives let us

After breaking a
text into its
components,
you need to say
how they're tied
together
(p. 301).

imagine and inhabit spaces that we normally do not encounter. These imaginative crossings can expand our sense of who we are and what the world is. . . .

Dickinson is bracingly unsentimental about life without others. She does not miss the presence of people in the emotional landscape of some of her most poignant poems. She remains locked within herself, as though the inner terrain were already plenty to explore.

> Your ultimate purpose in analyzing a text is to understand what it means—and its significance (p. 301).

We learn from Dickinson that self-encounter can generate both creative energy and art. At a time when we've endured so much social distance, dwelled inwardly with ourselves, tracing and re-tracing our own borders, such lessons are nothing trivial. ♦

FOR CLOSE READING

1. Magdalena Ostas begins her critical analysis of Emily Dickinson's poetry by observing that Dickinson drew on "one of the most unique sources of creative inspiration in the history of poetry" (1). What was that creative source, according to Ostas, and how did Dickinson discover it? What made it—and the poet—so unique?

2. Living in isolation from others, says Ostas, "can be painful and disorienting" (2). Why? What is the most "terrifying" aspect of solitude, in her view?

3. According to Ostas, Emily Dickinson found solitude to be "fully comfortable" (3). What uses did the poet make of her self-imposed isolation? What is the "most striking aspect" of that isolation, as Ostas sees it, in Dickinson's poetry (13)?

4. In paragraph 7, Ostas identifies numerous unique aspects of Dickinson's poetry. What are some of those elements, and how do they contribute to Dickinson's poetic vision in the two poems that Ostas discusses in paragraphs 8 and 12?

5. It was a common belief in Dickinson's day that mourners at the bedside of a dying person might catch a glimpse of the hereafter in that person's eyes or face at the moment of death. According to Ostas's analysis of "I heard a Fly buzz— when I died—," how does Dickinson use this belief for IRONIC effect? Where else in her essay does Ostas discuss Dickinson's unconventional views on religion?

STRATEGIES AND STRUCTURES

1. Ostas argues that Dickinson's poetry can teach us how to use solitude in "creative" ways (3). Point to specific passages in Ostas's essay, such as paragraphs 3 and 13, that support (or fail to support) this claim.

2. After introducing the topic of her analysis—Dickinson's poetry and solitude—Ostas inserts three paragraphs (4–6) of biographical information about the poet. Is this an effective strategy? Why or why not?

3. As **EXAMPLES** of the poet's "perspective" (8), Ostas cites and briefly analyzes two specific poems. Is this evidence sufficient to support her **THESIS** about the inwardness of Dickinson's poetry in general? Explain.

4. *Other Methods.* Ostas focuses on aspects of Dickinson's poems that she describes as "stark" (3), "brutal" (7), "heroic" (12), and "bracingly unsentimental" (14). What do these terms reveal about Ostas's own interests and values as a writer and critic of literature? Explain.

THINKING ABOUT LANGUAGE

1. In one of the poems cited by Ostas, Emily Dickinson puts the word "wife" in quotation marks, and Ostas refers to these as "scare quotes" (6). Why do you think Dickinson used quotation marks in this instance? And why is Ostas calling attention to them?

2. A distinctive quality of Dickinson's poetry, says Ostas, is its "scenelessness" (7). How does Ostas define this term, and why is it so central to her analysis? Explain.

3. A "fascicle" is a small bundle (8). Look up the term as it is used in the fields of printing and publishing. Why might Dickinson herself have adopted the term for the clusters of poems she sewed together in small bundles?

4. In Dickinson's poem about the buzzing fly, the speaker not only hears the fly at the moment of her death but is also able, we are told, to "bear" it. What distinction is Ostas making by emphasizing this word?

FOR WRITING

1. On her website, Ostas describes her essay as "public writing." In a few paragraphs, explain what you find to be "public" (or popular) about Ostas's language and approach—and what might be considered "scholarly" (or academic) about it.

2. If you were writing a critical analysis of Ostas's essay, what would you say is its main strength and why? What shortcomings, if any, would you point out in her interpretation and evaluation of Dickinson's work?

3. Not everyone would agree with Ostas that poetry can (or should) teach us lessons about life. In a statement of the opposing view—that poetry is an end in itself—the poet Archibald MacLeish argued, "A poem should not mean / But be." MacLeish's poem "Ars Poetica" (The Art of Poetry) is available online. Find the poem, read it carefully, and **SUMMARIZE** how it makes the case for "art for art's sake."

4. Write a **CRITICAL ANALYSIS** of a poem—or a cluster of related poems—by Emily Dickinson or some other poet whose work you admire. Be sure to comment on both the form of the work (how it is constructed) and the content (what it means).

DAN REDDING

What Does the Nike Logo Mean?

Dan Redding (b. 1980) is a freelance graphic and web designer as well as the founder and host of *Culture Creature*, a website and podcast devoted to music and culture. A graduate of the New School and of the Parsons School of Design, Redding got his start in journalism as a reporter and interviewer for the hip-hop magazine *Mugshot*. Before that, he was an art teacher.

In the following brief essay published on his website, Redding analyzes one of the world's most familiar commercial designs—and the brand it stands for. The title of his critical analysis comes from a question he often asked beginning art students in order to get them thinking about the relation between visual elements and meaning in art and design.

T HE NIKE LOGO—known as the "Swoosh"—is the simplest logo imaginable, consisting of only two lines. And yet this remarkable logo represents billions of dollars' worth of accumulated branding and marketing associations. But what does it *mean*? Let's take a look at the Nike logo meaning and history.

> This is the most important question to ask (p. 307) when analyzing a visual (or other) text.

At its most fundamental level, the Nike Swoosh represents *motion and speed*. The shape depicts an arc of movement. The word "swoosh" is onomatopoeia for the sound you'd hear as Lebron James or Michael Jordon zips past you en route to a spectacular dunk. 2

In Greek mythology, Nike is the Winged Goddess of Victory. What does the mythological figure Nike have to do with the Nike logo meaning? The shoe brand borrows the mythological attributes of flight, victory, and speed. 3

MLA CITATION: Redding, Dan. "What Does the Nike Logo Mean?" *Back to the Lake: A Reader and Guide for Writers*, edited by Thomas Cooley, 5th ed., W. W. Norton, 2024, pp. 343-45.

The iconic Nike logo.

Michael Jordan and the Nike Brand

> **Most analyses require clear TRANSITIONS between parts (p. 296), but Redding uses headings instead.**

So we've established that the Goddess Nike was a winged figure—and guess who else had the power to fly? Basketball superstar and Nike spokesman Michael Jordan. Nike made direct efforts to connect Jordan to the concept of flight and superhuman skills. For example, Jordan's signature shoes included the Jordan Flight and the Air Jordans. Nike even gave him metaphorical wings on one famous poster.

4

Origin of the Nike Swoosh

> **Evaluating a visual is a key part of analyzing it (p. 307).**

The Swoosh was designed by a college student (!) named Carolyn David-son for a mere $35 (!!!) in 1971.[1] Nike co-founder Phil Knight's initial design request was for a shoe stripe suggesting movement. He didn't love Davidson's drafts at first, but in a rush to production, he chose one, and

5

1. Allan Brettman, "Creator of Nike's Famed Swoosh Remembers Its Conception 40 Years Later," Oregon-Live, updated June 16, 2011, https://www.oregonlive.com/business/2011/06/nikes_swoosh_brand_logo_hits_4.html.

the Swoosh was born. Davidson was subsequently employed by Nike and later compensated further with a gold Swoosh ring and Nike stock.

"Brands, Not Products"

To say that the Nike Swoosh represents motion and speed is only to inspect the surface of the design. The Nike logo meaning is imbued with the results of long-term, multi-billion-dollar branding efforts. This brand represents transcendence through sports. It carries with it decades' worth of affiliated basketball heroism, urban hip-hop attitude, and more.

Naomi Klein's book *No Logo: No Space, No Choice, No Jobs* is essential reading for anyone interested in branding. In it, Klein describes Nike's philosophy of brand over product: long ago, Nike shifted its focus almost entirely to branding and marketing, while outsourcing production to cheap foreign contractors. This way, they could sell something much bigger than a pair of shoes: a *lifestyle*. According to Phil Knight, "There is no value in making things anymore. The value is added by careful research, by innovation and by marketing."[2]

> CONTEXT is an important element of any critical analysis (p. 307).

No, It's Not a "Check Mark"

I used to teach an art class for teens and I often liked to pick their brains about the logos they saw on their favorite products, in their urban surroundings—and on their feet. The Nike logo was invariably present in the room on someone's kicks. I'd ask the group, "So what does the Nike logo mean?" The most common answer was, "It's a check mark." Well, a check mark has a hard angle between two straight lines (like the Verizon logo). The Swoosh is curved. Because it's not a check mark.

Deceptive Simplicity

If graphic design has an equivalent of Michael Jordan, it's my hero Paul Rand (designer of some of history's most recognizable logos, including those of IBM and UPS). Rand once said, "Design is so simple, that's why it is so complicated."[3] The Nike Swoosh derives its complexity from its simplicity. It's the most basic form you can imagine—only two lines. It is precisely this simplicity which allows it to thrive in so many different contexts, to carry the brand on its own (with or without the accompanying word "NIKE"), and to absorb and reflect so much brand messaging. ◆

> An analysis of a visual text is not complete without a DESCRIPTION of its basic form (p. 306).

2. Naomi Klein, *No Logo: No Space, No Choice, No Jobs* (New York: Picador, 2009), 197.

3. Jim Connolly, "Paul Rand: Defining Design," Creative Thinking Hub, accessed January 15, 2018, https://www.creativethinkinghub.com/paul-rand-defining-design/.

FOR CLOSE READING

1. Most fundamentally, says Dan Redding, the Nike logo "represents *motion* and *speed*" (2). Is this an accurate analysis? Why or why not?

2. What other attributes, according to Redding, does the Nike logo "borrow" from the goddess of victory in Greek mythology? How and how well are those qualities represented in the design of the logo itself?

3. According to Redding (and Naomi Klein in *No Logo*, whom he PARAPHRASES), Nike long ago shifted from merely selling shoes to selling a "lifestyle" (7). Do the company's name and logo support this analysis? Explain.

4. Redding further suggests that the Nike brand represents "transcendence through sports" (6). Look up the definition of "transcendence." What is being transcended here, and how well do the company's name, logo, advertising, and other marketing efforts support this even larger claim? Explain.

5. "The Nike Swoosh," says Redding, "derives its complexity from its simplicity" (9). How and how well does Redding illustrate the idea that less is more in his critical analysis of the Nike logo?

STRATEGIES AND STRUCTURES

1. Broken into its most basic components, says Redding, the Nike logo consists "of only two lines" (1). Are there other elements of the logo Redding could have DESCRIBED? What about the space between the two lines? Is it always the same color? Does it have dimension or appear flat?

2. Redding COMPARES the Nike swoosh to a check mark. In his analysis, what's the main difference between the two? How does this visual difference affect the meaning of the logo?

3. To associate the Nike logo with speed and movement, says Redding, is "only to inspect the surface of the design" (6). Where and how in this analysis does he look beyond the surface in order to draw a conclusion about the logo's meaning?

4. In his analysis of the Nike logo, Redding notes that the goddess of victory has wings and that Michael Jordan can fly, but he doesn't claim outright that the Nike logo looks like a wing. Why does he draw connections between these specific figures and the logo?

5. *Other Methods.* Redding not only explains the significance of the Nike swoosh, but he also tells how it came about. Is this background and history helpful for understanding what Redding has to say about the form and meaning of the logo? Explain.

THINKING ABOUT LANGUAGE

1. Linguists define a "signifier" as a symbol, sound, or image that represents an underlying concept or meaning. How and how well does the Nike logo fit this definition? What about the word "swoosh" (as opposed to the image)? Explain.

2. "Swoosh," says Redding, is an example of ONOMATOPOEIA (2). Define "onomatopoeia" and give several other examples.

3. In his memoir, *Shoe Dog*, Phil Knight, cofounder of Nike, writes that Jeff Johnson "pointed out that seemingly all iconic brands—Clorox, Kleenex, Xerox—have short names. Two syllables or less. And they always have a strong sound in the name, a letter like "K" or "X," that sticks in the mind." To him, wrote Knight, "that all made sense." Does it make sense to you? Why or why not?

FOR WRITING

1. What is a logo? In a paragraph or two, DEFINE the term, explain how its root meaning goes back to the Greek word for "word," and also comment on its relation to terms like "logogram" and "logotype."

2. Do some research on Carolyn Davidson and her career at Nike, including Davidson's total compensation during her period of service. Write a brief ARGUMENT about whether it was enough given how important her contribution was.

3. Write a CRITICAL ANALYSIS of the Amazon smile, Apple's bitten apple, McDonald's golden arches, Toyota's symphony of ovals, or some other logo you see often. Focus on the individual design elements and also explain what they mean collectively. Provide EVIDENCE for your conclusions.

4. Keep track of all the logos you encounter in one day, and make notes on what you find most (and least) effective about them. Based on your findings, write a paragraph or two analyzing some of the main characteristics that successful logos have in common.

11 Cause and Effect

For want of a nail the shoe was lost, for want of a shoe the horse was lost, and for want of a horse the rider was lost, being overtaken and slain by the enemy, all for want of care about a horse-shoe nail.

—BENJAMIN FRANKLIN, *The Way to Wealth*

Suppose you've made lasagna in a stainless-steel baking pan. Rather than transfer your leftovers to another container, you simply cover the pan with aluminum foil and store it in the refrigerator. When you come back a few days later to reheat the dish, you notice tiny holes in the foil. Why, you ask? Even more pressing: Can you safely eat your leftovers? What would be the effect on your body if you did? With these questions, you have just launched into an analysis of cause and effect.

Analyzing Why Things Happen—or Might Happen

When we analyze something, we take it apart to see how the pieces fit together. A common way in which things fit together, especially in the physical universe, is that one causes the other. In the case of your leftover lasagna, for example, the aluminum foil deteriorates because it's touching the tomato sauce as well as the stainless-steel pan. "When aluminum metal is in simultaneous contact with a different metal," writes the food critic Robert L. Wolke, who is also a professor of chemistry, the combination "constitutes an electric battery"—if there is also present "an electrical conductor such as tomato sauce."

When analyzing causes and effects, we not only explain why something happened (what caused the holes in the foil), but we also predict what might happen—for example, if you eat the lasagna anyway.

In this chapter, we'll discuss how to analyze causes and effects; how to tell causation from coincidence; how to distinguish probable causes from merely possible ones; and how to organize a cause-and-effect analysis by tracing events in chronological order from cause to effect—or backward in time from effect to cause. We'll also review the critical points to watch for as you read over your analysis, as well as common errors to avoid when you edit.

Why Do We Analyze Causes and Effects?

According to the British philosopher David Hume in his *Enquiry Concerning Human Understanding*, much of the thinking that human beings do is "founded on the relation of cause and effect." Like Adam and Eve when they discovered fire (Hume's example), we analyze causes and effects in order to learn how things relate to each other in the physical world. Also, when we know what causes something, we can apply that knowledge to our future behavior and that of others: Don't put your hand in the fire because it will get burned. Don't cover your leftover lasagna with aluminum foil because you'll get metal in your food if the foil touches the sauce.

Hume was not just speaking of the knowledge we gain from experience, however. By doing research and using our powers of reasoning in addition to those of direct observation, we can also analyze the causes and effects of things that we cannot experience directly, such as the causes of the Civil War, or the effects of AIDS on the social and political future of Africa, or what will happen to the US economy if the health-care system is (or is not) reformed. Thus the analysis of cause-and-effect relationships is just as important in the study of history, politics, economics, and many other fields as in the sciences.

Composing a Cause-and-Effect Analysis

When you analyze causes and effects, as Hume said, you exercise a fundamental power of human understanding. You also unleash a powerful means of organizing an essay as point by point you explain to readers the results of your analysis. But keep in mind that even simple effects can have complex causes—as in our tomato sauce example. Technically speaking, the holes in the aluminum foil were caused by the transfer of electrons from the foil to the steel pan *through* the tomato sauce. What caused the corrosive sauce to touch the foil in the first place? Clearly, yet another cause is in play here—human error, as indicated in the diagram below.

If relatively simple effects—such as the holes in the aluminum foil—can have multiple causes like these, just think how many causes you'll need to identify as you analyze and explain more complex effects, such as the French Revolution, cancer, or the fact that married men, on average, make more money than unmarried men.

Fortunately, as we shall see, even the most daunting array of causes can be reduced to a few basic ones. And thinking about the order in which they occur in time and their importance in producing a given effect, in turn, can provide you with a solid basis for organizing your analysis.

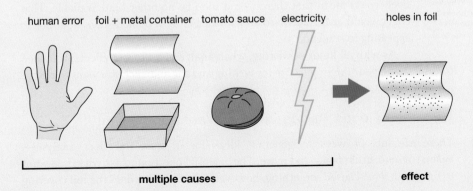

human error   foil + metal container   tomato sauce   electricity   holes in foil

multiple causes   **effect**

Thinking about Purpose and Audience

As a professor of chemistry, Robert L. Wolke fully understands the complexities of the chemical reaction he is analyzing, but the tomato sauce example here comes from *What Einstein Told His Cook*, a book he wrote to explain "kitchen science" to a general audience. So Wolke largely avoids the technical vocabulary of the laboratory and assumes no specialized knowledge on the part of the reader. Instead, he uses everyday language and offers practical applications for his scientific findings: store your leftovers in any kind of container you like, Wolke concludes, but when the container is metal "just make sure that the foil isn't in contact with the sauce." When you write a cause-and-effect analysis, keep your readers in mind—use language fitting for your audience, and define any terms they may not know.

Wolke's purpose is to instruct his readers, and his topic is one that's easy to explain, at least for a chemist. Often, however, you'll find yourself analyzing causes or effects that cannot be explained easily, and then you'll actually need to ARGUE for possible causes or effects—to persuade your readers that a cause is plausible or an effect is likely.

Let's say you're taking Chemistry 101, and when you go to the campus bookstore to buy your textbook, you find that it costs $139. Your first thought is to write an article for the school newspaper accusing the bookstore of highway robbery, but then you stop to think: *Why* is the price so high? You do some research and discover some of the causes: the increasing costs of paper, printing, and transportation; the costs of running a bookstore; the fact that authors need to be compensated for their work and that publishers and bookstores are businesses that need to produce some kind of profit. Perhaps you'll still want to write an angry article, but at least you'll be able to show that you've *analyzed the causes* of the problem.

And let's say you decide to suggest in your article that students buy only used books. But then you'd need to *consider the effects* of that solution. Since publishers and authors receive no payment for used books, buying them exclusively could mean that there would soon be no other kind available. That effect would be attractive to an audience of used-book dealers—but not so appealing to students.

For an in-depth analysis, see "Why Are Textbooks So Expensive?" (p. 375).

As with all kinds of writing, when analyzing causes or effects, you need to think about your larger purpose for writing and the audience you want to reach.

Generating Ideas: Asking "Why," "What," and "What If"

There are lots of ways to generate ideas for a cause-and-effect analysis—BRAINSTORMING, CLUSTERING, and more. The essential question to ask when you want to figure out what caused something, however, is "why." Why does the foil covering your leftover lasagna have holes in it? Why did you fail the chemistry final? Why does a curve ball drop as it crosses home plate? Why was Napoleon defeated in his invasion of Russia in 1812?

If, however, you want to figure out what the effects of something are, then the basic question is not "why" but "what" or "what if." What if you eat your leftover lasagna even though it might now contain traces of aluminum foil?* What if you don't study for the chemistry exam? What are the results likely to be? What will happen if the curve ball fails to drop? What effect did the weather have on Napoleon's campaign?

As you pursue answers to the basic questions "why" and "what if," keep in mind that a single effect may have multiple causes. If you were to ask why the US financial system almost collapsed in the fall of 2008, for example, you would need to consider a number of possible causes, such as the following:

- greed and corruption on Wall Street
- vastly inflated real estate values
- subprime mortgage loans offered to unqualified borrowers
- massive defaults when those borrowers couldn't make their mortgage payments
- a widespread credit crunch and drying up of money for new loans

As you probe more deeply into the causes of a major event like the financial crisis of 2008, you'll discover that such effects not only have multiple causes; those causes are also interconnected. That is, they occur in chains—as in Benjamin Franklin's reference (p. 349) to the proverb about a fatal sequence that occurred "all for want of care about a horse-shoe nail." When it comes time to present the results of your analysis, you may find that following the chain of events in chronological order from cause to effect—or backward in time from effect to cause—is an excellent way to organize your writing.

Organizing and Drafting a Cause-and-Effect Analysis

Once you've asked yourself "why" and "what if" and you've identified a number of factors, you'll need to decide whether to emphasize causes or effects (or both). As you begin organizing and drafting, you'll want to choose a logical method of organization; explain the point of your analysis; and distinguish immediate causes from remote causes and main causes from contributing causes. You'll also want to distinguish between true causes and mere coincidences—and think about using visuals and other methods of development, like **NARRATIVE** and **PROCESS ANALYSIS**, in your analysis. The templates on p. 356 can help you get started.

---

*Nothing much will happen, except that your lasagna may taste slightly metallic. You won't get sick from the metal because the hydrochloric acid in your stomach will dissolve the traces of aluminum.

STATING YOUR POINT

Esmé Weijun Wang (p. 392) starts with the cause (schizo-phrenia) and then examines its effects (hallucinations).

As you draft a cause-and-effect analysis, you can start with effects and then examine their causes; or you can start with causes and go on to examine their effects. In either case, tell the reader right away which you're going to focus on and why—what your main point, or THESIS, is.

For example, when analyzing the causes of the COVID-19 pandemic, you might signal the main point of your analysis with an opening like this:

> The COVID-19 pandemic was caused by the SARS-CoV-2 virus, first identified in December 2019 in the city of Wuhan, China. The exact origin of the virus, however, is still a subject of investigation and debate.

Or if you're analyzing the effects of the pandemic, you might write:

> The most tragic effect of the COVID-19 pandemic has been the loss of life. As of 2023, the World Health Organization estimates that, worldwide, almost 7 million people have died from COVID-19. The economic, educational, political, and health (both mental and physical) impacts have also been devastating.

Once you've told the reader whether you're focusing on causes or effects and what your thesis is, you're ready to present your analysis.

ORGANIZING A CAUSE-AND-EFFECT ANALYSIS

Causes always precede effects in time. Thus, a natural way to present the effects of a given cause is by arranging them in CHRONOLOGICAL ORDER. In tracing the effects of the COVID-19 pandemic, for example, you'd start with the initial outbreak and then proceed chronologically, detailing its effects in the order in which they occurred. Here's an (abbreviated) example:

- SARS-CoV-2 virus in Wuhan, China, either leaks from virology lab or is present in infected animal(s) at the Huanan seafood market.
- Virus spreads rapidly through people in China.
- Virus spreads from China to other countries.
- Illness and deaths begin to climb worldwide.
- Governments impose travel bans, quarantines, masking mandates, and school and business closures.
- Hospitals run out of beds, essential equipment, and adequate staff.
- Pharmaceutical companies rush to develop effective medicines and vaccines.
- Short-term and long-term economic, educational, political, health (mental and physical) impacts begin.

Reverse chronological order, in which you begin with a known effect and work backward through the possible causes, can also be effective for organizing a cause-and-effect analysis. In the case of the COVID-19 pandemic, you would again begin with the crisis itself (the known effect): extensive loss of life due to COVID-19. Then you would work backward in time through all the possible causes you could think of, presenting them in reverse chronological order:

- The virus mutated, and existing vaccines did not offer continued protection.
- Some people chose not to receive vaccines that were shown to reduce the risk of death from COVID.
- It took time to discover and develop treatments and vaccines to reduce the risk of death from COVID.
- As the virus first spread widely, hospitals were overwhelmed and did not have the resources to treat everyone.
- People could be infected without showing any symptoms, so COVID spread easily and quickly before testing was widely available.
- The COVID-19 virus was very contagious and had a relatively high mortality rate especially among high-risk groups, like elderly people.

You can also organize your analysis around the various types of causes, exploring the immediate cause before moving on to the remote causes (or vice versa) or exploring the contributing causes before the main cause (or vice versa).

DISTINGUISHING BETWEEN IMMEDIATE AND REMOTE CAUSES

As you look into the various causes of a particular effect, be sure to consider immediate and remote causes. This will require you to distinguish mechanical details in the causal chain from more abstract causes or less immediate mechanical ones. Benjamin Franklin, you'll notice, didn't say that the main cause of the rider's death was the loss of a horseshoe nail. He said the main cause was a "want of care" about such a nitty-gritty detail.

The most nitty-gritty link in any causal chain—the one closest in time and most directly responsible for producing the effect—is the immediate cause. In the case of the COVID-19 pandemic's negative effect on K–12 learning in the United States, the immediate cause was the disruption to in-person learning. When classroom learning cannot take place, the equalizing benefits of the public education system cannot be achieved.

Remote causes, by contrast with immediate ones, are less apparent to the observer and more distant in time from the observed effect. Returning to the COVID-19 outbreak itself, one remote cause may have been a lack of investment in global programs to study and prevent health crises.

When you begin to draft a cause-and-effect analysis, you need to identify what you're analyzing and to indicate whether you plan to emphasize its causes or its effects—moves fundamental to any cause-and-effect analysis. See how Henry L. Roediger III makes these moves at the beginning of his essay in this chapter:

> What reasons are given for the high price of textbooks? . . . If I had to bet, the root cause is a feature of the marketplace that has changed greatly over the years and fundamentally reshaped the textbook market: sale of used books.
> —HENRY L. ROEDIGER III, "Why Are Textbooks So Expensive?"

Roediger identifies what he's analyzing ("the high price of textbooks") and indicates that he's going to focus on the causes of this phenomenon ("the root cause is"). Here is one more example from this chapter:

> To find out what might be prompting some college graduates to return to their rural hometowns later in life, we conducted a study using national data. . . . We found three factors that contributed to college graduates coming back home.
> —STEPHANIE SOWL, "Three Reasons College Graduates Return to Rural Areas"

The following templates can help you make some of these basic moves in your own writing. But don't take these as formulas where you just fill in the blanks. There are no shortcuts to good writing, but these templates can serve as starting points.

▶ The main cause / effect of X is _____.

▶ X would also seem to have a number of contributing causes, including _____, _____, and _____.

▶ Some additional effects of X are _____, _____, and _____.

▶ Among the most important remote causes / effects of X are _____, _____, and _____.

▶ Although the causes of X are not known, we can speculate that a key factor is _____.

▶ X cannot be attributed to mere chance or coincidence because _____.

▶ Once we know what causes X, we are in a position to say that _____.

DISTINGUISHING BETWEEN THE MAIN CAUSE AND CONTRIBUTING CAUSES

To help your reader fully understand how a number of causes work together to produce a single effect, you'll need to go beyond an explanation of the immediate cause or causes. Consider the partial collapse of terminal 2E at the Paris airport on the morning of May 23, 2004. The most immediate cause of the collapse, of course, was gravity; beyond that, it was the failure of the metal structure supporting the roof. If we're really going to figure out why the building fell down, however, we're also going to have to look at the main cause and some of the contributing causes of the disaster.

The main cause is the one that has the greatest power to produce the effect. It must be both necessary to cause the effect and sufficient to do so. As it turns out, the main cause of the terminal collapse was faulty design. As Christian Horn writes in *Architecture Week*, "The building was not designed to support the stress it was put under."

IMMEDIATE CAUSES OF THE COLLAPSE OF TERMINAL 2E

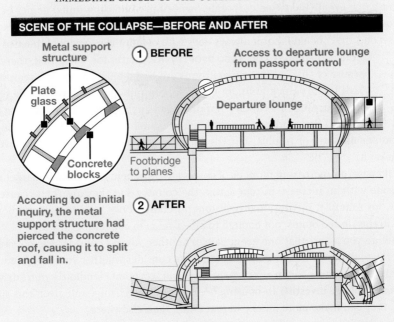

A contributing cause is a secondary cause, one that helps produce the effect but isn't sufficient to do it alone. An important contributing cause to the collapse of terminal 2E was weak concrete. Another was the increased stress on the concrete roof shell due to the rapid expansion and contraction of the metal support structure. Still another was the wild fluctuation in temperature in the days leading up to the collapse, which contributed to the stress on the metal.

If terminal 2E had been properly designed, no combination of contributing causes would have been sufficient to bring it down. Contributing causes are necessary to produce an effect, but even taken together they are not sufficient to cause it.

DISTINGUISHING AMONG CAUSE, EFFECT, AND COINCIDENCE

Rents are going up all across the United States. So is corporate ownership of apartment buildings and single-family homes. Is the rise in corporate ownership causing the rise in rents?

As you weigh causes and effects, don't confuse causation with coincidence. Just because one event (increased corporate ownership of housing units) comes before or concurrently with another (rising rents), the first event didn't necessarily cause the second. To conclude that it always does is to commit the logical blunder of reasoning called **POST HOC, ERGO PROPTER HOC** (Latin for "after this, therefore because of this.") Most superstitions are based on such *post hoc* reasoning. Mark Twain's Huck Finn, for example, commits this fallacy when he sees a spider burning in a candle: "I didn't need anybody to tell me that that was an awful bad sign and would fetch me some bad luck." Huck is going to encounter all sorts of trouble, but the burning spider isn't the cause—or even a "sign" of it.

Young people often don't vote, but being young isn't the cause (p. 388, par. 5).

Likewise, an increasing number of corporate owners in the housing market may coincide with an increase in rent across the country, but they aren't the cause. In 2021, for example, institutional investors purchased only 3 percent of the homes sold in the United States, not enough to affect rents in a meaningful way.

Before you assert that one event causes another, always consider the possibility that the two may be merely coincidental. Also, consider whether you might actually be mistaking a cause for an effect. As it turns out, corporate landlords aren't driving up rents; they're investing in housing *because* rents are rising, and given this situation, they can make more money in real estate than elsewhere.

So what *is* the cause of higher rents (and ever-increasing prices for single-family homes)? The ultimate test of causation is whether a potential cause is both *necessary* and *sufficient* to produce a specific effect. In the case of rising rents across the country, the most likely candidate is undersupply. A severe housing shortage would likely cause rising rents—it would be sufficient to do so—even if there were other contributing causes, such as increased corporate ownership of housing. Is the housing shortage a *necessary* cause—one without which the phenomenon wouldn't otherwise occur—of the rise in rents? The only way to find out for sure, perhaps, is to build more housing.

USING VISUALS TO CLARIFY CAUSAL RELATIONSHIPS

Illustrations and images can help your reader understand what caused a complicated effect—or the complicated causes behind a simple effect. Take, for instance, a famous map showing Napoleon's campaign in Russia in 1812 (see p. 360). This map shows "the successive losses in men" during the campaign. (Napoleon left France with more than 400,000 soldiers; he returned with approximately 10,000!) The advance toward Moscow is shown by a light-colored line, while the retreat is represented by the darker line below it. The thickness of the lines represents the number of soldiers—the thicker the line, the more troops in the army. At the bottom of the map are temperatures for certain dates during the retreat. As the French army retreats from Moscow and the temperatures get colder, the line representing the number of troops gets thinner, graphically showing the loss of men.

The map conveys a mass of data that would take many words to write out: dates, temperatures, troop movements, numbers of troops, not to mention distances and the locations of rivers and cities. All this information is crucial in analyzing why so many of Napoleon's soldiers died or deserted in their retreat from Moscow in 1812. In analyzing why Napoleon lost so many soldiers in the Russian campaign, you might want to include a visual like this and then connect the dots for the reader: many factors contributed to the losses, but the main cause of the horrendous number of casualties suffered by the French army in the winter of 1812 was the freezing temperatures.

A graph showing the relationship between temperature and number of troops, such as the one that appears on p. 361, would also make the point that the cold winter caused the deaths or desertions of many soldiers.

If you decide to include visuals, be sure that they actually illuminate your analysis and don't merely decorate it. Remember to label each part of a chart or graph, and position visuals as close as possible to your discussion of the topic they address.

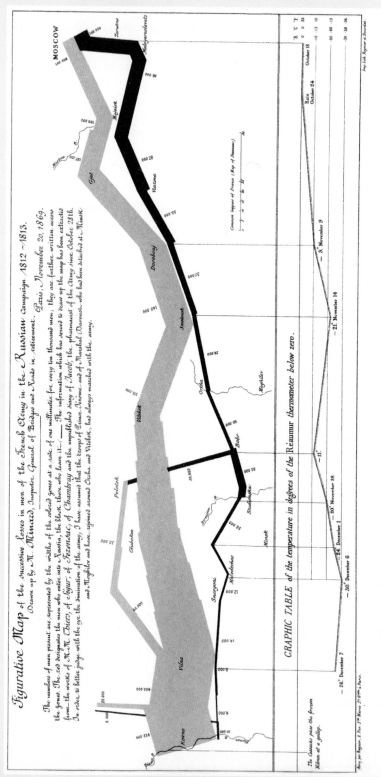

Since the map was made by the French engineer Charles Minard in 1861, the temperatures are in the French Réaumur system: −9° Réaumur is approximately 11.75° Fahrenheit; −26° Réaumur is approximately −26.5° Fahrenheit.

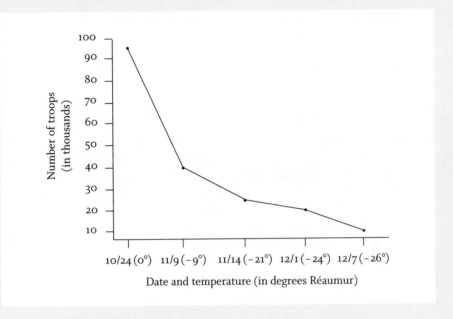

USING OTHER METHODS

It's hard to explain *why* something happened without first explaining *what* happened and *how* it happened. So when you analyze causes and effects, consider using **NARRATION** to help explain the *what*:

> Recently, a young man by the name of Benny Paret was killed in the ring. The killing was seen by millions; it was on television.

And use **PROCESS ANALYSIS** to help explain the *how*:

> In the twelfth round, he was hit hard in the head several times, went down, was counted out, and never came out of the coma.

These are the words of Norman Cousins in a classic cause-and-effect analysis. Having set up his analysis by using other methods, Cousins then turns to the causes of Benny Paret's death. The immediate cause, obviously, was the fist that hit him. The main cause, Cousins explains, was something else:

The primary responsibility lies with the people who pay to see a man hurt. The referee who stops a fight too soon from the crowd's viewpoint can expect to be booed. The crowd wants the knockout; it wants to see a man stretched out on the canvas. This is the supreme moment in boxing.

—Norman Cousins, "Who Killed Benny Paret?"

Cousins's essay was written in 1962. Yet another fighter was killed in the boxing ring as recently as 2022. The essay may not have achieved the effect Cousins hoped for—getting professional boxing thrown out of the ring of legitimate sport—but the impact of his words is still clear: "No one doubts that many people enjoy prize fighting and will miss it if it should be thrown out. And that is precisely the point." The point is also that good writers like Cousins often use cause-and-effect analysis to make a point when constructing ARGUMENTS, yet another method of development that goes hand in hand with cause-and-effect analysis.

EDITING FOR COMMON ERRORS IN A CAUSE-AND-EFFECT ANALYSIS

Writing about causes and effects generally calls for certain connecting words and verb forms—connecting words like "because" or "as a result," and verbs like "caused" or "will result in." Here are some items to check for when editing your analysis.

Check all connectors to be sure they're logical and precise

Words like "because" or "since" connect the "cause" part of a sentence to the "effect" part (or the reverse). Be sure the connectors you use make the causal link absolutely clear.

▶ ~~Since~~ Because the concrete deteriorated, the roof collapsed.

"Since" has two meanings, "for the reason that" and "after the time that," so it doesn't make clear whether the roof collapsed after the concrete deteriorated or because it deteriorated. "Because" is the more precise term.

▶ The concrete deteriorated, and ~~subsequently~~ consequently the roof collapsed.

"Subsequently" simply means "afterward," whereas "consequently" means "as a result."

Check verbs to make sure they clearly express cause and effect

Some verbs directly express causation, whereas others only imply that one thing causes another.

Verbs that express causation			*Verbs that imply causation*		
account for	cause	make	follow	implicate	involve
bring about	effect	result	happen	imply	take place

Using verbs that express causation makes your text more precise.

▶ The partial collapse of terminal 2E ~~involved~~ <u>was caused by</u> weak concrete.

Check for common usage errors

"Affect," "effect"

"Affect" is usually a verb meaning "influence," but in psychology it can also be a noun meaning "display or expression of emotion." "Effect" is usually a noun meaning "result," but it can also be a verb meaning "bring about."

▶ Failing the course did not <u>affect</u> his graduation.

▶ Failing the course did not have the <u>effect</u> he feared most.

▶ Failing the course, however, did <u>effect</u> a change in his normally smiling <u>affect</u>.

"Reason is because," "reason why"

Avoid using these expressions; both are redundant. In the first case, use "that" instead of "because." In the second, use "reason" alone.

▶ The reason the roof collapsed is ~~because~~ <u>that</u> the concrete deteriorated.

▶ Weakened concrete is the reason ~~why~~ the roof collapsed.

Reading a Cause-and-Effect Analysis with a Critical Eye

Once you've written a draft (or two or three) of your analysis, it's always wise to ask someone else to look over what you've written. Ask your friend or classmate where they find your analysis clear and convincing, what specific evidence they find most effective, and where they think you need more (or less) explanation. Here are some questions to keep in mind when checking over a cause-and-effect analysis.

PURPOSE AND AUDIENCE. Why is the reader being asked to consider these particular causes or effects? Is the intended audience likely to find the analysis plausible as well as useful? What additional information might readers need?

ORGANIZATION. Does the analysis emphasize causes or effects? Should it give more (or less) attention to either? Are causes and effects presented in a logical sequence?

CHRONOLOGICAL ORDER. Does the analysis present causes and effects in chronological order where appropriate? Does it consistently link cause to effect, and effect to cause?

REVERSE CHRONOLOGICAL ORDER. Where effects are known but causes are uncertain, is it clear what chain of events most likely led to the effect(s) in question? Are those events presented in reverse chronological order? If not, how can the order of events be clarified?

THE POINT. What is the analysis intended to show? Is the point made clearly in a thesis statement? How and how well does the analysis support the point?

TYPES OF CAUSES. How well are the significant causes analyzed—the immediate cause, the most important remote causes, the main cause, and the most important contributing causes? What other causes (or effects) should be considered?

CAUSE, EFFECT, OR COINCIDENCE? At any point, is a coincidence mistaken for a cause? Are all the causes necessary to produce the indicated effects? Do they have the power to produce those effects? Is a cause mistaken for an effect, or vice versa?

VISUALS. Are charts, graphs, or diagrams included to clarify causal relationships? If not, would they be helpful? Are all visuals clearly and appropriately labeled?

OTHER METHODS. Does the essay use other methods of development besides cause-and-effect analysis? For instance, does it use NARRATION to help explain what happened? Or does it use PROCESS ANALYSIS to show how—in addition to why—a particular effect came about? Does the analysis ARGUE that one cause or effect is more likely than another?

COMMON ERRORS. Do all the words and phrases used to connect causes and effects actually express causation? For example, should words like "since" or "consequently" be replaced with "because," "as a result of," or "owing to"?

Student Example

Elisa Gonzalez is a poet, essayist, and writer of fiction whose work has appeared in the *New Yorker, Hyperallergic*, the *Harvard Review*, and elsewhere. She holds an MFA in creative writing from New York University, and in 2020 she was the recipient of a Rona Jaffe Foundation Writers Award. Gonzalez wrote "Family History" for a writing class when she was an undergraduate at Yale. In this essay, she explores the causes and effects of bipolar disorder in two members of the same family. Gonzalez does not try to determine if such psychological conditions are inherited, but she does find sufficient evidence in her family's history to suggest that the effects of one person's disorder may become causes of the same disorder in another family member. "Family History," along with other work by Gonzalez, won the 2011 Norman Mailer College Writing prize, sponsored jointly by the National Council of Teachers of English and the Norman Mailer Center and Writers Colony.

Family History

By the time I am diagnosed with bipolar disorder type II, I have known Dr. Bradley for years. I know that he is divorced with two children, that he dated a beautiful Russian nurse who quit last year under obscure circumstances, that he colors his hair to stop the gray from infringing on his catalogue-model looks. He delivered my littlest sister, now seven, and he cried when my youngest brother died after several days in an incubator, his lungs hesitantly fluttering like moth wings before they finally deflated. Dr. Bradley has spent years counseling my mother after suicide attempts. In many ways, he knows us better than my closest friends who, blithe and unsuspecting,

First line introduces a serious effect of yet unknown cause(s)

have always accepted my selective disclosures about my family. So when he pauses, clears his throat, and asks if I have a family history of bipolar disorder, I stare at him without speaking. It seems impossible that he doesn't know about my father.

Probes for possible causes of the disorder

For several minutes, I have trouble comprehending what he's saying, though he's kind and clear. Based on what I've told him—that I've had to leave parties because the urge to scream was so uncontrollable I felt I might disintegrate, that I've stayed up for days without speaking or going to class, that I've frightened my boyfriend with my bursts of rage—bipolar disorder seems probable. It often manifests in people around my age, especially in creative high-achieving people. There is no blood test; he will give me medication, a combination of new antipsychotic drugs and traditional lithium pills, and see if I improve. Confirming my family history is the last piece of the diagnosis. Heredity strikes most people as soon as they look in the mirror, in how much the jawline protrudes or how adamantly the earlobes crease, so I should not be so surprised at being confronted with my own history. Studying a chart of the cardiovascular system, I briefly wonder if I have always known that I carried with me more than my father's curly hair and dry sense of humor. But this is impossible, and far too mystical for the sterility of the exam table. It is true, though, that I have always feared my father, not just the physical reality of him—those thick hands that have left bruises around my throat and shoved my mother's teeth through her cheeks—but the lingering effects of his presence.

Gives specific effects that might confirm the diagnosis

Introduces a significant probable cause of the disorder

2

When I was six, I went to the kitchen expecting breakfast and found my father frying *Sesame Street* videotapes in the cast-iron skillet. The charred plastic littered the kitchen for days and smoke stained the walls for the whole summer, until my father was released from his month-long stay in the hospital and repainted the entire house as penance. He also mended the holes he'd made in the walls and bought a new couch to replace the one he'd gutted with a butcher knife one night while we were sleeping. To celebrate, we ate store-bought pecan pie in a kitchen that smelled of fresh white paint.

Implies that immediate effects of one disorder may be remote causes of the other

3

He talked about repairing the furnace and my sister showed him the stuffed dog named Rosie she'd gotten for her birthday. Although this cycle—destruction, then rehabilitation—has happened many times, I have always recalled the precision of his hands as he stood so calmly by the stove stirring twisted plastic with a metal spatula.

A month before my diagnosis, my sister and I fought about who would use the car, a typical sibling fight, except in its escalation. I started screaming and threw a book at her head, threatening to call the police on her and report the car stolen if she took it. When she moved toward the door, I got a knife from the kitchen and told her I would slash the tires before I would let her leave. She stopped arguing with me to say, disbelievingly, "You're just like Daddy." I wanted to tell her that I couldn't be like him because he is crazy and I am not. Instead, I began to weep soundlessly, collapsing to the ground, my mouth gaping and silent. Now, in the exam room, I feel that type of ache again, beyond expression because no noise can cure it. It is here that I realize my entire life has converged in a dark pattern newly revealed.

> Suggests a CAUSE-AND-EFFECT relationship between the two disorders

When my father was nineteen—the same age I am now—he cut up houseplants in precise segments and neatly ate a plateful with a fork before his brother found him and rushed him to the hospital. Later that month, after the doctors bandied around the word "schizophrenia" for a while, he received his own proper diagnosis. In 1979, lithium pharmacology had been approved for the treatment of manic depression, as bipolar disorder was called then, so his illness was manageable if he took his pills. But he never liked lithium, or the other medications his doctors prescribed. I wonder if I too will feel blunted and blurred without other forces sharpening themselves on my mind. Dr. Bradley asks if I have any questions before he writes me a prescription, and I say no. I am familiar with the required monthly checkups and learned the difference between the words "manic" and "maniac" when I was seven. Years before I grew up a little and participated in the national spelling bee, I was awed by the crucial distinction created through the addition of an *A*.

> Gives early symptoms of the father's disorder

> Anticipates possible future effects

> Suggests that the old name for the disorder confused cause and effect

The strangest part of hearing the diagnosis is that I suddenly 6
want something I haven't wanted in years: to talk to my father. I
know that he ran away after the doctors told him the news and his
brothers found him four days later on a beach in California, but I
know nothing else. I would like to call my father and say, "I know I've
always hated you, but as it turns out, I'm just like you." Perhaps he
would tell me how he felt when he found out, if he slept on the beach
and wandered through a shabby town looking for the anonymity that
would let him lose his label, or if he blurted his diagnosis to people to
try it out. Mostly, I would like to know if he would have come back,
had they not found him, or if instead he would have woken up and
walked into the ocean one day, the only person to separate the sky
from all that water. The lure of water in the lungs, of the non-
breathing world, is one that I too will face in the months after the
diagnosis.

But my father and I haven't exchanged more than a few 7
words since I was fourteen, when he tried to strangle me, saying
that he had brought me into this world and he could take me out of
it. After that, he left us, hauled out by police officers and kept away
by court orders; I no longer know his number. I will not call him,
nor mention when I see him for a few minutes at Christmas that I
am also bipolar. Yet months after, when I am assigned *Paradise Lost*
for a class, I will start to cry upon reading a piece of the poet's
invocation:

> *though fallen on evil days,*
> *on evil days though fallen, and evil tongues;*
> *in darkness, and with dangers compass'd round,*
> *and solitude; yet not alone.*

Confronts one of the worst remote effects she may face

Ends with a positive effect: the discovery that her condition is shared

Analyzing a Student Cause-and-Effect Analysis

In "Family History," Elisa Gonzalez draws on rhetorical strategies and techniques that good writers use all the time when they analyze causes and effects. The following questions, in addition to focusing on particular aspects of Gonzalez's text, will help you identify those common strategies and techniques so you can adapt them to your own writing. These questions will also help prepare you for the analytical questions—on content, structure, and language—that you'll find after all the other selections in this chapter, along with suggestions for writing on related topics.

FOR CLOSE READING

1. When she learns her diagnosis of bipolar disorder, Elisa Gonzalez says, "I have trouble comprehending" (2). Considering her childhood experience with her father's erratic behavior, why does her diagnosis come as a surprise?

2. How is bipolar disorder diagnosed? How important are Gonzalez's accounts of her behavior ("what I've told him," 2)? How important is heredity ("my family history," 2)?

3. What medications are prescribed to treat bipolar disorder? What are their side effects? Why might Gonzalez be uneasy about taking them?

4. Gonzalez recounts past effects of the disorder on her father's behavior, recent effects on her own behavior, and concerns about her future behavior. Point to specific paragraphs where she discusses each of these.

STRATEGIES AND STRUCTURES

1. Gonzalez's opening paragraph focuses on her physician, Dr. Bradley. Is this an effective way to start the essay, or should she have opened with an account of her symptoms? Why or why not?

2. After discussing her present diagnosis and recent behavior, Gonzalez looks back at her childhood experiences ("When I was six"; "this cycle...happened many times," 3) before returning to the present in her concluding paragraphs. How does this presentation in CHRONOLOGICAL ORDER help a reader understand her illness? How else might she have narrated these events?

3. When her sister tells her, "You're just like Daddy," Gonzalez wants to reply that she "couldn't be like him because he is crazy and I am not" (4). This passage falls near the midpoint of the essay, after she has learned her diagnosis and recalled evidence of its effects on her father. Do you think Gonzalez is still in denial about her condition? Explain.

4. Gonzalez ends her essay by quoting four lines of poetry. How does this alter the TONE of her ending, compared to closing simply with the statement that she will not tell her father about her diagnosis at Christmas?

5. *Other Methods.* As we learn in the headnote, Gonzalez has a degree in creative writing. She clearly draws on this background in this essay, which makes use of extensive NARRATION and vivid DESCRIPTON. Point to several sentences or paragraphs that are striking examples of each method and analyze what makes them so effective.

THINKING ABOUT LANGUAGE

1. "Now, in the exam room, . . . I realize my entire life has converged in a dark pattern newly revealed" (4). What, exactly, has been revealed to Gonzalez? What does the TONE of the phrase "dark pattern" tell you about her attitude toward her illness?

2. Speaking about the possible side effects of her medications, Gonzalez says, "I wonder if I too will feel blunted and blurred without other forces sharpening themselves on my mind" (5). What are the CONNOTATIONS of "blunted," "blurred," and "sharpening" in the context of Gonzalez's situation?

3. Look up the definitions of "manic" and "maniac" (5), and then explain the differences between them. Which term would you use to describe Gonzalez's father? Why?

4. In paragraph 6, Gonzalez states: "The lure of water in the lungs, of the non-breathing world, is one that I too will face in the months after the diagnosis." What action might she be ALLUDING to here?

FOR WRITING

1. Do some research on bipolar disorder, and then write a 600-to-800-word REPORT on the known CAUSES and EFFECTS of each. Be sure to discuss theories or evidence about both the main cause and contributing causes.

2. Write a five-to-seven-paragraph PROFILE of someone you know or have heard of whose behavior reflected what later turned out to be the result of a serious medical condition. Use vivid EXAMPLES in describing their behavior.

A "Text and Drive" Billboard

The folks at Wathan Funeral Home know something about cause and effect. For instance, they know from experience that texting while driving causes motorists to become distracted, lose control of their vehicles, have accidents, and die. That's too bad for the drivers and their passengers but good for the funeral business, right? Actually, this cautionary billboard on the Gardiner Expressway in Toronto, Canada, is a public service announcement sponsored by two advertising agencies. Their fake website for the nonexistent funeral home explains the ruse:

> If you're here, you've probably seen our "Text and Drive" billboard. And if you have, you probably came to this website to tell us what horrible people we are for running an ad like that. And you'd be right.
>
> It is a horrible thing for a funeral home to do.
>
> But we're not a funeral home.
>
> We're just trying to . . . stop texting and driving, which is projected to kill more people . . . this year than drinking and driving. That's right. More.

(And, incidentally, disrupting a chain of cause and effect that leads to the funeral home would also mean more consumers for other businesses and services, such as advertising agencies.)

[FOR WRITING]···

Billboards and other forms of public advertising often imply that choosing the products or services they offer will have a direct effect on your life (or death) and well-being: *At Wathan, We've Got You Covered.* In other words, they suggest or announce that the first event or condition (choosing a particular product or service) will actually *cause* the second event or condition (satisfaction of certain needs or desires). Keep an eye out for such a billboard or other sign, and write a paragraph or two analyzing how the text and images on the sign use cause and effect to try to sell you something.

SUGGESTIONS FOR WRITING

1. Many medications have undesirable side effects. In "Family History," while discussing her recent diagnosis of bipolar disorder and her father's treatment for it, Elisa Gonzalez writes that "he never liked lithium, or the other medications his doctors prescribed. I wonder if I too will feel blunted and blurred." Do some research on a commonly prescribed drug or class of drugs, and write a 500-to-700-word **COMPARISON AND CONTRAST** essay on its benefits and drawbacks.

2. In "Why Are Textbooks So Expensive?" (p. 375), Henry L. Roediger III mentions, as a thing of the past, "genteel textbook companies that really cared about scholarly texts and not so much about being wildly profitable." After reading Roediger's essay, do some research on the business of publishing (or bookselling, freelance writing, or some other related field), and write a five-to-seven-paragraph **REPORT** on how the industry is or is not adapting to the changing environment that Roediger describes—including such newer technologies as online publishing and audiobooks. (Science fiction magazines, for example, are now besieged by bad stories submitted by humans but actually written by chatbots. A good editor can spot the fakes in a nanosecond.)

3. "Much attention," writes Stephanie Sowl in "Three Reasons College Graduates Return to Rural Areas" (p. 383), "has been given to a rural 'brain drain,' as described by sociologists Patrick J. Carr and Maria J. Kefalas." In recent years, Sowl argues, this trend has been reversed. Do some research on the rural brain drain, and write a 400-to-600-word **ANALYSIS** of the cultural and other changes in rural America that are (or are not) bringing college graduates back home again.

4. "Perhaps more young people would vote," Jamelle Bouie argues in "Why Don't Young People Vote?" (p. 387), if they understood that "knowledge of *issues* was less important than knowledge of their own *interests*." Write a four-to-six-paragraph **POSITION PAPER** in which you support or contest the proposition that young people have an obligation to vote in the service of their own best interests.

5. As a college undergraduate living with schizoaffective disorder, Esmé Weijun Wang sought help at a university health center. "Stigma clouded the visits," she writes in "Yale Will Not Save You" (p. 392). Read more about the efforts of Wang and others to dispel the stigma of mental illness, especially among young people, and write a 400-to-600-word **EVALUATION** of their methods and progress.

HENRY L. ROEDIGER III

Why Are Textbooks So Expensive?

Henry L. Roediger III (b. 1947) is the James S. McDonnell Distinguished University Professor of Psychological and Brain Sciences at Washington University in St. Louis. Roediger is a specialist in memory and human learning and the author or coauthor of many articles and psychology textbooks. What caused him to specialize in the psychology of memory? Roediger attributes his choice to an event in his childhood—the death of his mother when he was five years old. "That event changed my life drastically," says Roediger. "I was determined to hold on to my memories of her, to relive the past by remembering them. At a very early age, I spent a lot of time thinking about memory and how it works."

"Why Are Textbooks So Expensive?" appeared in 2005 in the *Observer*, a journal published by the American Psychological Society, of which Roediger is a past president.

NEWSLETTERS AND OTHER MISSIVES that I receive seem filled with stories about textbooks and textbook prices, with many wringing their hands over why textbooks are so expensive now relative to the more distant past (usually when the author of the article was in college). I suspect some articles arise from middle-aged parents who suddenly must pay for their own children's college textbooks and they recoil when they see a bill of $500 a semester or thereabouts.

What reasons are given for the high price of textbooks? Of course, there's general inflation, but evidence points to textbook prices outpacing inflation. Others point their fingers at the bright colors in many books (relative to older black and white models) and argue that production costs are needlessly pushed up by color. (A quick

MLA CITATION: Roediger, Henry L., III. "Why Are Textbooks So Expensive?" *Back to the Lake: A Reader and Guide for Writers*, edited by Thomas Cooley, 5th ed., W. W. Norton, 2024, pp. 375–81.

check of my own bookstore shows that many books without color are more expensive than those with color, probably due to the number of books in the print run.) Another suggested hypothesis is textbook publishers simply seek greater profit margins now than they did in the past. After all, the market used to be dominated by rather genteel textbook companies that really cared about scholarly texts and not so much about being wildly profitable. A comfortable, modest profit line was fine in the old days. Those days are now gone, because traditional textbook companies have been bought up by gigantic conglomerates that look only to the bottom line and seek huge profits. For these companies, so the theory goes, textbooks are just one more product line, no different from detergent or tires or toilet paper, on which to make a profit. The fact that many formerly independent textbook companies are being bought up and merged under the same corporate umbrella could also be partly responsible, if this process reduces competition through having fewer companies. Another facet of the debate is the frequent revision schedule of basic textbooks. Most introductory psychology textbooks are revised every three years, some every two years. Doesn't this constant revision drive up the prices?

Although the reasons listed above may have some merit, I don't think any of 3 them is fundamental to why textbook prices are so high. In fact, I suspect that most of the properties described above are effects and not causes. What is the cause? If I had to bet, the root cause is a feature of the marketplace that has changed greatly over the years and fundamentally reshaped the textbook market: sale of used books.

> The root cause is the *main* cause (p. 357).

The organized used book market represents the great change in the landscape of 4 higher education publishing, but one that has gone relatively unnoticed.

Let us go back in time to what educational historians refer to as the later Paleo- 5 lithic era in higher education, that is, the late 1960s, when I was in college. Here was how the used book market worked then. I was a psychology major and was about to take a course in history of psychology. A psychology major in my fraternity, Dave Redmond (now a big-time lawyer in Richmond, Virginia), was going on to law school and wanted to sell some of his psychology textbooks. He asked if I wanted to buy Edna Heidbreder's *Seven Psychologies*, for a dollar. I said OK. The book had cost him $2.95, which is still listed in my copy. . . .

. . . This was how the used book market worked in my day. One student sold 6 books to another student on a hit or miss basis. Books didn't cost much. Oh, also, most students kept their books and started building a personal library. (This is another idea that seems to have faded with time. Personal library? Today's students assume everything they need to know is on the Internet.)

Let's fast forward to 1981. I was teaching at Purdue University and was consider- 7 ing (with Betty Capaldi and several others) writing an introductory psychology textbook, since textbook companies were wooing us to do so. However, neither Betty

When used textbooks are sold or rented, only the middleman gets paid.

nor I had ever even taught introductory psychology, so we decided to teach independent sections one semester. We examined a lot of books and decided to use Phil Zimbardo's textbook, *Psychology and Life*. . . . Betty and I were each to teach a section of 475 students, so we ordered 950 books. Nine hundred fifty books was, and is, a big textbook order. Think of the profits to the company and the author!

A few days before classes were to begin, I happened by one of the three Purdue   8 bookstores to buy something. I decided to go see the hundreds of copies of the book I had ordered, gleaming at me on the shelves. I found them, all right, but I was shocked at my discovery. Every single book on the shelf was a used copy! I went through many of them, disbelieving, and saw that quite a few were in poor condition (marked up, spines damaged, etc.), yet the prices were still substantial. How could this be? Zimbardo's book had never been used at Purdue before recent times. Where did all these used copies come from? I decided to walk to the other two bookstores and discovered exactly the same situation; every book for sale was a used book in the other two stores. There wasn't a new book to be found.

The organized used book market represents the great change in the landscape   9 of higher education publishing, but one that has gone relatively unnoticed by most academics (unless they are textbook authors). The implications are huge. Consider the situation in today's dollars (although I am estimating). A single author of a textbook might make a 15 percent royalty on the net price of the book (sometimes a bit more); the net price is the price the bookstore pays the textbook company for the book and the list price is the price set by the bookstore to sell to the student. The net price of an introductory psychology textbook today might be $65 (before the bookstore marks it up), so the author would make $9.75 per book. However, that is only if the book is bought from the company; if the student buys used books, the author makes nothing and neither does the company. If 950 used books are sold, the author would lose (be cheated out of?) $9,262, and the textbook company would perhaps lose a similar or larger amount. (Profit margins probably differ from company to company and book to book. They are a closely guarded secret.) Of course, at Purdue in 1981 the figures would have been smaller, but the principle the same. The fact of modern campus life is that used book companies buy up textbooks on one campus, warehouse them, and ship them to wherever the book is being adopted, and therefore prevent sales of new books.

Consider what this means. The textbook company that invested hundreds   10 of thousands of dollars—maybe millions for introductory textbooks—to sign, develop, review, produce, market, and distribute a book over several years is denied its just profits. The author or authors who wrote the book over many years are denied their royalties. Meanwhile, huge profits are made by the used book companies who did nothing whatsoever to create the product. They are true parasites, deriving profits with no investment (and no value added to the product) while damaging their hosts. The issue here is similar to that in the movie and recording industries for pirated products that are sold very cheaply, denying the companies and the artists their profits. One major dissimilarity in these cases is that pirated movies and music are illegal whereas the used textbook market is legal. (There have been proposals to change this state of affairs. For example, one idea is that when used book companies resell texts they would pay the original textbook company and author a royalty.)

The high price of textbooks is the direct result of the used book market. A text-   11 book is customarily used for one semester and (unlike the old days) students rarely keep their books now but sell them back to the bookstore (more on that anon). Therefore, the same text might be used by three to four students, but the textbook company and author profit the first time a book is sold and not thereafter. It stands to reason that textbooks must be priced aggressively, because the profits from the repeated sales will not go to the authors and companies that actually wrote and produced the books, but rather to the companies that specialize in buying and selling used books. Further, the reason textbooks are revised so frequently is to combat the used book market, which further drives up the company's costs. Frequent revisions also add wear and tear on the authors who must perpetually revise their books. (I've sometimes wanted to have two somewhat different versions of my textbooks and then alternate them.) Most fields of psychology hardly move at such a swift pace as to justify two- to three-year revision cycles of introductory textbooks. The famous textbooks of the 1950s and 1960s were revised every eight to ten years or so, but after the used textbook market gained steam, revisions became frequent. Moreover, because of the used book market, profitability of many companies was hurt and they became ripe for takeovers, which further consolidated the market. That is why I said in the third paragraph that many factors used to "explain" the high prices of books are probably effects, with the cause being the organized used book companies that prey parasitically on the host publishing companies and threaten to destroy them.

Other changes have also affected the market. College and university bookstores   12 used to be owned by the school and operated as a service to the students and the faculty, but those days are past on most campuses. Now the bookstores are operated by large companies (Follett's, Barnes and Noble, and others), often the same ones who operate used book operations. Most "bookstores" have turned into carnivals where emphasis is placed on selling sweatshirts, trinkets, souvenirs and snacks and, oh, incidentally (used) books.

Another pernicious trend: After universities relinquished their hold on book-   13 stores, the bookstores aggressively raised the percentage markup on the net price paid to the publisher on new books. Thirty years ago a standard rate of markup was 20 percent and publishers provided list prices on their books (because markups were standard). I can recall the great hue and cry that arose when textbook stores started marking up books by 25 percent. However, a 25 percent markup for today's bookstores would look like chump change. Publishing companies now sell the bookstore the books based on a net price and the bookstore decides on the list price, often marking up the books 30 to 40 percent in the process. The profits go to the company owning the store and the company pays the college or university for the right to have a monopoly business on campus. However, many students have now learned that it is cheaper and (given the huge lines) sometimes easier to buy textbooks from other sources like Amazon.com.

Let me give you a concrete example. Last summer the eighth edition of my textbook (with Barry Kantowitz and David Elmes), *Experimental Psychology: Understanding Psychological Research*, was published by Wadsworth Publishing Company. The net price (the price the bookstore pays the company for a new book) the first time the book is sold is $73.50. The authors receive 15 percent royalties on the book, so we would split the $11 royalty three ways. However, at the Washington University bookstore, the list price of the book is $99.75, a markup of $26.25 (or 35.7 percent)! Yes, that's right, the authors who

> Using other methods to help analyze causes is discussed on pp. 361–62.

wrote the book get $11.02 for their years of hard work whereas the bookstore that ordered the books, let them sit on the shelves for a couple of weeks, and sold them, gets $26.25 per book. (If books are not sold, they are returned to the company for a full price refund. It's a no-risk business.)

Yet the story gets even worse because of the used book problem. After the stu- 15 dent uses the book (and if it is in pretty good condition), the bookstore will buy it back from the student at a greatly marked down price, somewhere between 25 and 50 percent. Let's assume that *Experimental Psychology* is bought back for 40 percent of the list price (which is probably a generous assumption at most bookstores). That would be $39.90. After buying it, the bookstore will mark it back up dramatically and resell the book. Suppose the used book is sold for $75, which sounds like a bargain relative to the new book price of $99.75, and it is. However, notice that the profit markup for the bookstore on this used book would then be $35.10, which is higher than the (still very large) profit made on the new book ($26.25). In fact, the primary reason bookstores prefer selling used books to new books is the much higher profit margins on used books. So, on the second (and third and fourth, etc.) sales of the same book, the bookstore and used book company make huge cumulative profits. The textbook company that invested large sums into developing the book (and the authors who invested time and energy and research into writing it) receive exactly zero on these resold books.

If this sounds bad, it actually gets worse. Another insidious influence in the 16 textbook industry is the problem of sales of complimentary copies. In order to market their wares to professors, it is customary for textbook companies to give out free copies of their books. [Everyone] who teach[es] basic courses in the psychology curriculum receive[s] such books. This is just another price of doing business for the book companies. However, many of these books find their way into the used book market because some professors sell books to scavengers from the used book companies who search through university campuses seeking to buy complimentary copies. Now these companies are soliciting professors to sell their complimentary copies by e-mail. I never sell my complimentary books, of course, because I believe it unethical to sell for profit something I was given by a company in good faith. However, apparently many professors do sell their books. Now the textbook company gets hit by a double whammy: The book they produced to give to a professor for possible adoption enters the market and takes away a new book sale in the marketplace!

Is it any wonder that textbook prices are so high? The wonder is that they aren't 17 higher. . . .

The textbook companies themselves have few alternatives in dealing with this 18 problem. They can and do raise the price of the books so that they try to recoup their investment on the first sale (hence the high price of textbooks). They can revise the book frequently, which renders the previous edition obsolete. They can try to bundle in or shrink-wrap some additional item (a workbook, a CD) with the new text, so that students will need to buy new books to get the free item. This strategy can work, but some bookstores will just unbundle the book from the study guide and sell both! (So, a study guide the bookstore received free can be sold for, say, $15.) Unless and until laws are changed to prevent the organized sale of used books, you can expect textbook prices to keep increasing. ◆

FOR CLOSE READING

1. Henry L. Roediger analyzes several of the usual reasons given for the steep rise in the prices of college textbooks (2), as well as what he says is the main, or "root," cause (3). What are the usual reasons, and what does he claim to be the main cause?

2. According to Roediger, what specific effects has the used-book market had on the authors and publishers of textbooks? on the consumers of those books?

3. As an author of textbooks himself, Roediger has a stake in his analysis that purchasers of textbooks don't have. Does that stake necessarily invalidate his claims? Why or why not?

4. How and why, according to Roediger, do college bookstores sell used copies of textbooks that have never been used on their campuses?

STRATEGIES AND STRUCTURES

1. Where and how does Roediger shift from analyzing causes to analyzing effects? Where does he switch back? How effective do you find this strategy? Why?

2. What is the **PURPOSE** of the **EXAMPLE** that Roediger gives in paragraph 14? Why does he refer to it as a **CONCRETE** example? List some other concrete examples he uses. What purposes do they serve?

3. What is the point of the brief story that Roediger tells in paragraphs 5–6 about buying his undergraduate psychology book from a classmate? How about the narrative he tells in paragraphs 7–8? How do these **NARRATIVES** relate to his main point? Where does he state it?

4. *Other Methods.* Besides analyzing causes and effects, what **ARGUMENT** is Roediger making? What conclusions does he come to?

THINKING ABOUT LANGUAGE

1. In paragraph 10, Roediger introduces a biological **ANALOGY** and then continues to apply it in paragraph 11. In his analogy, what is he comparing to what? How helpful do you find the comparison?

2. Roediger calls today's campus bookstores "carnivals" (12). Why?

3. How does Roediger **DEFINE** the "net price" of a newly published book (9)? How about the "profit margin" (9)?

4. Roediger uses **HYPERBOLE** when he calls the 1960s "the later Paleolithic era" (5). Why does he exaggerate here? What does the hyperbole contribute to the argument he is making?

FOR WRITING

1. Write a paragraph or two analyzing some effects of rising textbook costs from your own standpoint as a consumer.

2. Have you ever purchased a textbook that is labeled "free examination copy" or "not for resale"? If, as Roediger contends, the sale of such books contributes to the high cost of textbooks, what if anything do you think should be done about teachers and stores selling free copies they received from the publisher for review? Write an opinion piece for your campus newspaper (in other words, for an audience of students) arguing for or against this practice.

3. Some public school districts (and colleges) purchase textbooks in electronic form. And *Amazon* sells more ebooks than paper ones. Write an essay explaining what some of the effects of this trend might be.

4. Write an **EVALUATION** of your favorite (or least favorite) textbook. Include a clear analysis of the goals of the book, stated and unstated—and of how and how well it meets (or fails to meet) those goals.

STEPHANIE SOWL

Three Reasons College Graduates Return to Rural Areas

Stephanie Sowl (b. 1987) is a program officer at the ECMC Foundation in Los Angeles, where she oversees grants focusing on college persistence and completion for students from underserved backgrounds. She received her PhD in higher education and administration from Iowa State University, where her research focused on rural communities and the demographic and social factors that affect their economic vitality, community engagement, and health. Sowl is the author of numerous academic papers on these and related topics, including "Innovative Strategies to Attract and Retain Young Adults in Rural Communities" (2017) and "Entrepreneurial Climate and Rural Business Development" (2018). She is a member of the Association for the Study of Higher Education, the Iowa Development Council, and the International Society for Community Development.

In "Three Reasons College Graduates Return to Rural Areas" (2022), Sowl analyzes the causes of what she and others see as a fundamental shift in the demographics of rural America. Based on a formal academic study, this version is from the *Conversation*, a website devoted to the work of academics and other experts but written for a more general audience.

W HEN HIGH-ACHIEVING STUDENTS from rural areas go off to college and graduate, they often choose to live in suburban or urban areas instead of rural communities like the ones where they grew up, decades of research have shown.

Often they are following the advice of adults—or just deciding on their own—to search for success in cities, where career opportunities are more abundant. Teachers,

MLA CITATION: Sowl, Stephanie. "Three Reasons College Graduates Return to Rural Areas." *Back to the Lake: A Reader and Guide for Writers*, edited by Thomas Cooley, 5th ed., W. W. Norton, 2024, pp. 383-85.

coaches and neighbors might reinforce the message to leave behind the small-town life and its limited career opportunities.

But that long-standing pattern might be changing. Some rural communities are 3 beginning to see their college graduates return.

I am a researcher who studies higher education and rural communities, and my 4 colleagues and I wondered what might be leading adults to return to rural communities a decade or two after they graduate from college elsewhere.

To find out what might be prompting some college graduates to return to their 5 rural hometowns later in life, we conducted a study using national data on the well-being of adolescents into adulthood to look at why people who grew up in rural places decided to return. Specifically, we took a look at whether their middle and high school experiences had any connection to their decision to return home in their late 30s or early 40s. We considered only those individuals who had gone at least 50 miles away to complete a bachelor's degree. We found three factors that contributed to college graduates coming back home.

> This would be a "remote" cause (p. 355).

1. Tight-Knit School Communities

We found that the more students enjoyed school and felt as if they belonged, the 6 more likely these college-educated adults from rural areas returned home. Even after considering demographic, neighborhood and college characteristics, positive middle and high school experiences remained significant. This demonstrates the lasting value of supportive teacher-student and peer relationships.

This is consistent with other research that has found college graduates who 7 return had roots that made them feel grounded in their rural hometowns. When the students maintain relationships with people back home, it makes them feel as if they still belong when they return.

2. Fewer People and More Land

College-educated people from smaller towns or open, undeveloped land were twice 8 as likely to return home as people who grew up in slightly larger rural towns.

Rural places are rich with natural resources, from vast countrysides with fertile 9 soil to dense forests that purify the air we breathe. Rural people are often attached to the natural environment and have an appreciation for land. Connecting with nature, breathing in fresh air and enjoying peace and quiet can offer deep life satisfaction.

3. Contributing to Their Communities

College graduates who grew up in rural communities where relatively few people went   10
to college were more likely to return home than those from communities with more
college-educated adults. Returners often feel a need to give back to their communities.
This has been accomplished by returners filling positions as doctors, lawyers, teachers
or entrepreneurs. They also volunteered to make a difference. College graduates provide several societal benefits, such as contributing to their community's economic
growth, participating in community activities, and sharing new perspectives.

A Focus on the Benefits   Our research comes at a time when some rural
communities have begun to invest in local businesses, outdoor recreational
activities and local schools to attract both newcomers and returners.

Much attention has been given to a "rural brain drain," as described by
sociologists Patrick J. Carr and Maria J. Kefalas, and all the reasons young
people leave rural communities. But our research shows some of the characteristics of rural communities that have been associated with a return
home. ◆

> Jamelle Bouie describes very different political and economic conditions for younger citizens on p. 387.

FOR CLOSE READING

1. Stephanie Sowl says "decades of research" show that people who grow up in rural areas tend not to return home after they graduate from college (1). Where have they typically gone instead? Why?

2. If a "brain drain" (12) from rural areas to more urban ones is the "long-standing pattern" (3), why is Sowl writing about the subject now?

3. Of the various reasons that Sowl gives for why college graduates may be returning to rural areas, which ones do you find most compelling? Why?

4. Can you think of additional reasons college graduates might (or might not) be coming back to live in rural areas? What are some of them?

STRATEGIES AND STRUCTURES

1. The findings Sowl presents are based on "a study using national data on the well-being of adolescents into adulthood" (5). Should Sowl have given more information about that study and how it was conducted? Why or why not?

2. What does the level of supporting detail in Sowl's report suggest about the nature of her intended **AUDIENCE** and her **PURPOSE** in writing? Explain.

3. After each reason she gives for why college graduates return to rural areas, Sowl draws a general conclusion, such as: "breathing in fresh air and enjoying peace and

quiet can offer deep life satisfaction" (9). Is she identifying **CAUSES** of the rural renewal or **EFFECTS** of it—or both? Explain.

4. In the last paragraph, Sowl introduces a **NAYSAYER** when she refers to the work of sociologists Patrick J. Carr and Maria J. Kefalas (12). Check the meaning of this term in the glossary. Is using the device an effective way for Sowl to conclude her analysis? Should she have mentioned opposing views earlier—or not at all? Explain.

5. *Other Methods.* What kinds of additional **EVIDENCE** and **EXAMPLES** do you think could be added to further support the three factors Sowl presents? **QUOTATIONS** from returning graduates? Data from additional relevant studies? something else? Explain your reasoning.

THINKING ABOUT LANGUAGE

1. When they analyzed why more college graduates from rural areas are returning home, Sowl and her colleagues found three contributing "factors" (5). Is a factor the same as a cause? Why or why not?

2. When discussing causation, Sowl uses terms like "leading to" (4), "prompting" (5), "consistent with" (7), and "associated with" (12). Why doesn't she just say "caused by"?

3. The *Conversation*, the website where this article appeared, states that its purpose is to publish "informative articles written by academic experts" and to "make their knowledge available to everyone." Do you think the wording, sentence structure, and paragraph length make this article accessible to "everyone"—adults of all education levels, for example? Explain.

FOR WRITING

1. Draw up a list of additional reasons you think college graduates may be returning to the rural areas they grew up in. Alternatively, make a list of reasons explaining why you think they *don't* return.

2. In a few paragraphs, explain why someone you know (or have heard about) decided to return home to a rural area after attending college.

3. Write a 500-to-700-word essay explaining where you came from, why you decided to go to college, and what you expect to do immediately upon graduation. Focus on the causes, personal as well as societal or demographic, of these various effects.

4. Sowl's essay is based on a "study using national data" that she and two colleagues published in October 2021 in the journal *Rural Sociology*. This study is readily available online under the title "Rural College Graduates: Who Comes Home?" Read the formal, academic version of Sowl's work, and then write a **CRITICAL ANALYSIS** in which you compare it with the more journalistic version presented here. Be sure to comment on the adaptations she made in order to appeal to a more general audience.

JAMELLE BOUIE

Why Don't Young People Vote?

Jamelle Bouie (b. 1987) is a journalist and political analyst who writes about elections, history, and culture. Bouie grew up in Virginia Beach, Virginia, and graduated from the University of Virginia in 2009. An opinion columnist for the *New York Times*, he was formerly chief political correspondent for *Slate*, where "Why Don't Young People Vote?" first appeared in 2018, on the eve of national midterm elections. The short answer to this question of cause and effect, says Bouie in the original subtitle of his essay, is "this system doesn't want them to." Why not? And what's to be done about it? According to Bouie's analysis, the current voting system favors "people with time, money, and property"; but more young people might vote, he concludes, if they understood that "knowledge of *issues* was less important than knowledge of their own *interests*."

T O VOTE IN THE UNITED STATES, you can't simply go cast a ballot. In most states, you first have to register. If you've registered, you have to have state-issued identification to then actually vote. If you don't have identification, you might have to pay a fee to obtain it. If you don't live in an early voting state—or one with flexible absentee rules—you have to take time from work to cast your ballot. If you live in states like Georgia or Florida, you may have to wait for hours before you can step into a voting booth. If you can't drive or aren't mobile, you may have to find a ride.

If you're middle-aged with a stable job and a fixed-address, this is straightforward. If you're anyone else, it's less so. And if your life is defined by *instability*—in location, in housing, in employment—any single obstacle might be enough to

MLA CITATION: Bouie, Jamelle. "Why Don't Young People Vote?" *Back to the Lake: A Reader and Guide for Writers*, edited by Thomas Cooley, 5th ed., W. W. Norton, 2024, pp. 387–90.

discourage you from voting altogether. That might be why turnout for the youngest voters in the electorate is lower than most other groups.

To define anything, look for its most distinctive characteristics, pp. 526–27.

America lowered the voting age to 18 with the 26th Amendment in 1971. In 1972, nearly half of eligible young people turned out to vote. Since then, the voting rate for 18- to 24-year-olds in presidential elections has hovered between 30 and 45 percent, with average turnout of about 40 percent according to data from the Census Bureau. For midterm elections, the average is closer to 20 percent. 3

More striking than the low averages is the consistency of the difference with older Americans. In any given election year, the youngest voters *always* turn out at lower rates than their next oldest counterparts, who always turn out at lower rates than their next oldest counterparts, and so on, until you reach the oldest Americans. Since 1972, older Americans have voted at an average rate of 67 percent in presidential elections and nearly 59 percent in midterms. The fact of this pattern should obliterate any speculation about generational difference. There's either something about being young that precludes or prevents political participation, or there's something about the structure of American elections that impedes young people from participating. 4

It's much more likely that something is the instability that comes with being young. You're less likely to have a permanent address, less likely to have secure and flexible employment, less likely to have the confidence to participate in the political process. You can see all of this in a set of interviews with young adults who say they won't vote in this week's elections, published in *New York* magazine. Some respondents are cynical or simply uninspired. But others report real obstacles to their ability to participate. 5

Megan, age 29, says she moves too much to keep track with her registration. "I rent and move around quite a bit, and when I try to get absentee ballots, they need me to print out a form and mail it to them no more than 30 days before the election but also no less than seven days before the election," she said. 6

Anna, age 21, also says the process is too cumbersome. "I'm trying to register in my hometown of Austin, Texas. It's such a tedious process to even get registered in Texas, let alone vote as an absentee," she says, adding that "if someone had the forms printed for me and was willing to deal with the post office, I'd be much more inclined to vote." 7

Jocelyn, age 27, also blames the process. "It was easier to get my medical-marijuana card—not a right, or even federally legal—than it was to register to vote. Massachusetts had online registration but only if you have a DMV-issued ID. I don't drive, so I was like, okay, I can register in person, but I'm also dealing with a chronic illness." 8

Maria, age 26, doesn't want to commit the time. "The idea of leaving work, forwarding all of my calls to my phone, to go stand in line for four hours, to probably get called back to work before I even get halfway through the line, sounds terrible." 9

With each account, we have a different example of how our voting system doesn't 10 actually encourage voting, especially among people whose lives are defined by a certain amount of instability and unpredictability. Look beyond young adults to the larger population of nonvoters and you see a significant group whose lives are marked by traits associated with a lack of stability. They are less likely to have college degrees, more likely to have family incomes below $30,000, and more likely to belong to racial and ethnic minorities, making them more likely to experience conditions associated with instability.

Cause or coincidence? For the difference, see p. 358.

Our system has adopted universal suffrage, which points toward open and easy 11 access to the ballot, but our heritage in political exclusivity—where voting was once a privilege reserved for property-owning white men—continues to influence our handling of elections. Voter identification laws are tied to a sordid history of discrimination and vote suppression, but even procedures as uncontroversial as voter registration contain assumptions about who *should* participate. (Indeed, voter registration was first developed as a method to keep recent immigrants and the poor from the ballot box in Northern cities and was used similarly against black Americans in the Jim Crow South.) Our voting system is tilted toward people with stable, conventional lives. And that, overwhelmingly, is who participates, producing a conservative bias in the status quo.

Our government is less representative than it could be because of our voter-12 unfriendly policies. So even if you disdain young people who can't find the will or time to vote—even if you're unsympathetic toward the uninspired or the uninterested—you should want to fix this problem.

It's not a difficult one to solve. Automatic, universal registration would obviate 13 the need for any action from individual voters, who would be registered upon contact with state agencies like the DMV; pre-registration of older teenagers would prepare the youngest voters for political participation; and Election Day registration would open the doors to anyone eligible to cast a ballot. If bundled with vote by mail (with a stamp provided by the government), states could eliminate most obstacles to participation, with no obvious downsides. (Voter fraud, after all, is practically nonexistent.)

This isn't speculation. After Oregon passed automatic voter registration in 2016, 14 an additional 270,000 people were added to the voter rolls. New voters were disproportionately black, Latino, and Asian American, and more likely to belong to the youngest age cohorts. Automatic registration also increased the economic diversity of the state's electorate. Likewise, in Colorado, vote by mail has boosted turnout among young and infrequent voters.

As long as voting is voluntary, young people will likely always vote at lower rates 15 than their older counterparts. Instability may be the most concrete limiting factor, but there's also just something about being young—about being preoccupied with your first years of adulthood—that makes politics a secondary concern. There are cultural factors too. Several *New York* magazine interviewees felt too uninformed to responsibly cast a ballot, which suggests a discourse that puts too high a premium on arbitrary political knowledge and not enough on knowing oneself as a political actor with a legitimate claim on the state. Perhaps more young people would vote if they knew knowledge of *issues* was less important than knowledge of their own *interests*.

But if there is an upper bound to youth turnout under the constitutional status quo, we haven't reached it. And the reasons have everything to do with how we still structure elections to advantage people with time, money, and property.   16

Moralism and appeal to civic virtue may move some nonvoters off the sidelines in time, and if they live in states with same-day registration, they'll be able to cast a ballot. But that "if" gets us to the larger issue: We will only have a culture of voting and high turnout if we build one. And if there is apathy and disdain for political participation, we should understand that it's likely produced by institutions and systems that too often do everything they can to *keep* people from having a say in their government.   ◆   17

FOR CLOSE READING

1. In national elections, according to Jamelle Bouie, how does voter turnout correlate with age? Where does Bouie get his figures, and how reliable do you find them?

2. "For midterm elections," says Bouie, the average turnout among the youngest of eligible voters "is closer to 20 percent" (3). What are "midterm" elections, exactly, and why might young voters turn out for them in even fewer numbers?

3. Bouie implies that "instability" not only hinders people from voting but actually "defines" the lives of many young people (2). What does he mean by "instability," and how common is it, in your view? Explain.

4. Some people fail to vote, says Bouie, because they lack "the confidence to participate in the political process" (5). In your opinion, is this true? Why or why not?

5. Even if they lack "knowledge of *issues*," says Bouie, young people should vote based on a "knowledge of their own *interests*" (15). How might potential voters gain this second kind of knowledge?

STRATEGIES AND STRUCTURES

1. In Bouie's view, what are some of the prior causes, both immediate and remote, of a voting system that can be overly complicated and time consuming? Point to specific passages in the text where he identifies them.

2. Among the various factors in Bouie's analysis, which ones indicate that "there's something about the structure of American elections that impedes young people

from participating," and which ones indicate that there is "something about being young that precludes or prevents political participation" (4)? Explain.

3. Along with enlightened self-interest, what else is necessary, according to Bouie, for building "a culture of voting and high turnout" (17)? How and how well does he make the case that this can and should be done?

4. Bouie does not mention political parties by name in his essay. As a result of this apparently bipartisan approach, is his analysis stronger or weaker in your view? Why do you think so?

5. *Other Methods.* Bouie gives several EXAMPLES of young people who fail to vote. How and how well do they confirm his analysis of the effects of "instability" and other life factors on the voting process?

THINKING ABOUT LANGUAGE

1. The word "if" appears twenty times in Bouie's essay. Why might this particular conjunction occur frequently in an analysis of causes and effects?

2. What is "an early voting state" (1), and which particular states belong in this category?

3. "Universal suffrage" is the right of all adult citizens to vote (11). How did the Twenty-Sixth Amendment of 1971 change the definition of "universal" for voting purposes?

4. The history of laws pertaining to voter identification, says Bouie, is "sordid" (11). Is this HYPERBOLE? Why or why not?

5. In informal use, a "cohort" may be defined as a group of friends or colleagues. How is Bouie defining the term when, for example, he refers to "the youngest age cohorts" (14)?

FOR WRITING

1. A journalist has asked you why you do (or do not) expect to vote in the next general election. In a paragraph or two, write out what you would say to the interviewer about the process of casting your ballot.

2. Do some research on compulsory voting in Australia and write an essay of up to 700 words explaining how it came about, how it works (or doesn't), and why compulsory voting would (or would not) improve the voting system in the United States, especially for young adults.

ESMÉ WEIJUN WANG

Yale Will Not Save You

Esmé Weijun Wang (b. 1983) is a novelist, essayist, and teacher of writing. She was born in Michigan to Taiwanese immigrant parents and grew up in the San Francisco Bay Area. Wang attended Yale University—"the moment I received my acceptance letter," she says, "was one of the happiest of my life"—but later transferred to Stanford and graduated in 2006. Wang also holds an MFA from the University of Michigan, where her thesis became the basis for her first novel, *The Border of Paradise* (2016). She's also the founder of The Unexpected Shape™ Writing Academy, "a full-service online writing school for people with limitations who want to write personal non-fiction." The summer before Wang went off to college, she was diagnosed with bipolar disorder. This diagnosis later changed to schizophrenia, various forms of which she discusses in *The Collected Schizophrenias* (2019). The following selection is a chapter from that book.

"Yale Will Not Save You" chronicles the early stages of Wang's mental illness, analyzing both the effects of the disease on her daily life and her strenuous efforts to make creative use of her illness. It also introduces a relationship that appears to offer more hope for recovery, or at least stability, than either Yale or Wang's various therapists could provide.

THE MOMENT I RECEIVED my acceptance letter from Yale University was one of 1 the happiest of my life. I stood at the bottom of my driveway, where two tin mailboxes nestled against one another, and found a large envelope waiting inside. Large envelopes from publications were a bad sign; they almost always bore my own

MLA CITATION: Wang, Esmé Weijun. "Yale Will Not Save You." *Back to the Lake: A Reader and Guide for Writers*, edited by Thomas Cooley, 5th ed., W. W. Norton, 2024, pp. 392–96.

handwriting, and usually held a rejected manuscript and a perfunctory note. But a big envelope from a university—an envelope with instructions, with welcome, with a full-color look-book—*that* was news. I stood at the mailboxes, shrieking. I was not the type of girl to shriek, but I was seventeen, and I had gotten into Yale. I was to be in Jonathan Edwards College, Class of 2005.

I was an overachieving child, the Michigan-born daughter of twenty-something 2 Taiwanese immigrants who came to California with their baby girl. My parents were broke. They applied for food stamps; they told one another that someday they'd be rich enough to eat at Pizza Hut anytime they wanted. Eventually we moved for the sake of a different school district, and while raising me and my baby brother in a largely white small town, my parents told me that school was all-important and that I should always do my best. In elementary school, I assigned myself essays to write while on vacation. In fifth grade, I wrote a two-hundred-page novel about a kidnapped girl who becomes a cat. Soon my parents were both working in tech jobs at the height of the boom in Silicon Valley, and were no longer broke. They never spoke the words "American dream," but that was what their lives signified, and so in middle school I chose to take a 7:30 a.m. class in C++ programming, and I wrote a short story that my English teacher went on to teach even four years after that. In high school, when I told my mother that I was thinking of suicide, she suggested that we kill ourselves together, which I didn't fully recognize as the bizarre response it was until I told the story again and again over the following decades of my life. I won a gold medal at the Physics Olympics, was a California Arts Scholar, and crossed the stage at graduation with a GPA that belied the hundreds of self-inflicted scars lurking beneath my nylon gown. I chose to go east for college because I wanted to get away from the chaos— the accusatory fights, the sobbing—that occurred inside our home too often to take note of them.

I dated someone briefly at the end of my senior year of high school who broke up 3 with me because I was undiagnosed and frightening, but before he ended our relationship he invited me to a poolside barbecue. He wore girls' jeans. We stood around the glassy pool at his apartment complex and his mother asked me what I was doing after graduation.

"I'm going to Yale," I said. 4

She did a double take. "Good for you," she said. Even back then my instability 5 was clear to most.

"I went to Yale" is shorthand for *I have schizoaffective disorder, but I'm not worthless.* . . . 6

> Wang proceeds from cause to effect, but she might have gone in the other direction (pp. 354–55).

I was diagnosed with bipolar disorder the summer before I left for New 7 Haven, the summer before the spring I was first hospitalized at Yale Psychiatric Institute (YPI). My then psychiatrist informed my mother and me that I had bipolar disorder. This diagnosis was the culmination of a month in which I demonstrated most of the classic signs of mania, including a hectic manner of speech and an uncharacteristic affair with a man eleven years my senior. Although the new diagnosis meant I required different medications than the ones I had been taking for depression and anxiety, she said, she would not prescribe me those new medications while I was under her care. It would be better if I waited until arriving at college, where I could have a doctor there prescribe the appropriate pills; the presumption was that my future psychiatrist would be able to monitor me appropriately. . . .

> Using NARRATIVE can help explain causes and effects (p. 361).

When school started, I began to see a doctor at what was then called 8 the Department of Mental Hygiene at Yale University Health Services. Stigma clouded the visits, but I quickly learned that I could pretend to be visiting the Gynecology Department, which was on the same floor. I would exit the elevator and wait a few beats for the doors to close behind me before finally turning right, where students kept their eyes on their textbooks, notebooks, or hands—on anything instead of one another; if we looked long enough, it was possible to recognize the instabilities lurking.

The Department of Mental Hygiene didn't believe in assigning students both a 9 therapist and a psychiatrist, which would create the inconvenient need for back-and-forth communication, and so I saw a woman that year who served as both. She prescribed me Depakote, also known as valproate or valproic acid, which is an anticonvulsant used as a mood stabilizer. She returned again and again to the subject of my mother, whom she blamed for most of my emotional difficulties. During my first semester at Yale, my mother swelled and grew monstrous in my mind; she loomed as someone whose emotional lability had imprinted me with what I frankly called an inability to deal with day-to-day life.

Much of the time, I told the doctor, I felt too sensitive to cope. I was in constant 10 agony. I liked my doctor well enough, but I didn't seem to be improving, and the skittish feeling beneath my skin warned of trouble. Eventually, I would stop sleeping for days at a time; then off I would go. . . .

Yale is mocked for its determination to be elite from the get-go—for fashioning 11 itself in the likeness of Oxford and Cambridge, and then having acid dumped on itself to simulate age. Yale is, in the world of elite universities, a prepubescent girl swiping on mascara before the first day of middle school. Yale's campus is still the most beautiful campus I know.

Many of my classes, including Introduction to the Human Brain, took place in 12
Linsly-Chittenden 102. Larger than a seminar room but smaller than a lecture hall,
LC 102 is famous for an elaborate Tiffany window along one wall, titled *Education*.
Art, Science, Religion, and Music are depicted as angels across its panes. The center
section depicts Science surrounded by personifications of Devotion, Labor, Truth,
Research, and Intuition. . . .

In the elevator, among a group of acquaintances—other members of an Asian 13
American performance art group I'd joined—the topic of the Mental Hygiene Department arose.

Someone's eyes widened. "Watch out for that place," she said. 14

"I have a friend who went there," someone else said. "He stopped because he 15
knew they'd put him in [Yale Psychiatric Institute] if he kept talking."

"They'll put you in YPI for *anything*," the first person said. 16

"Never tell them you've thought about killing yourself," they counseled me. I was 17
a freshman. They were taking me under their wing, offering me wisdom. "Never
tell them you're thinking about killing yourself, okay?"

I think about that advice now: never tell your doctor that you're considering killing yourself. Yet this was sound advice, in the end, if I wanted to
stay.

> Analyzing causes and effects lets us apply present knowledge to future behavior (p. 350).

Margaret Holloway, known as "the Shakespeare Lady," hustled on campus 19
by reciting Shakespeare for spare change. According to rumor, she'd once been a
student at the esteemed Yale School of Drama, but had dropped out after a psy-
chotic break. (In truth, she had graduated from the School of Drama in 1980, and
experienced the first symptoms of schizophrenia in 1983.) Like most students, I'd
heard that the Shakespeare Lady possessed encyclopedic knowledge.

I encountered the Shakespeare Lady only once. One night, my then boyfriend, 20
now husband, C., and I decided to pick up dinner at Gourmet Heaven. . . . I'd
never seen such thick fog in New Haven. Holloway appeared like something out of
a dream: thin, and asking us for twenty dollars. She needed it to get into the
women's shelter, she told us, and she wanted a specific brand of yogurt that she
could get only at Gourmet Heaven, but she was banned from the store because of
the corrupt police. I know now that in 2002 she was arrested for blocking the
entrance of Gourmet Heaven, and apparently was arrested several times after that
for other small crimes. In 2004, when I was no longer a student at Yale, she had
gotten down to ninety pounds, and in 2009 she was in the local news for "cleaning
up her act." On that foggy night, I gave her more money than she'd asked for, and
waited with her while C. went to buy the yogurt she'd requested. I didn't ask her to
recite Shakespeare.

In 2002, I asked my therapist-slash-psychiatrist . . . "Are there any students here   21
with schizophrenia?"

"Why do you ask?" [my doctor] asked.   22

I didn't answer, but what I'd meant was: *Is there anyone here who's worse off than*   23
I am?

The fog was still pressing its velvet paws to the windows when C. and I returned   24
to his dorm that night. I rested my face against his shoulder, and he asked me what
was wrong. I asked him if he thought I could become the Shakespeare Lady. If my
mind might go so far it couldn't make its way back.

"It won't happen to you," he said, though I had asked a question that resisted   25
reassurance, and I knew it. In truth, neither of us could know. Still, I needed to hear
his promise that I would be okay. I would ask him variations on this question over
the next decade or so: "I'm not going to be crazy forever, am I?" But we never spoke
of the Shakespeare Lady again. ◆

FOR CLOSE READING

1. When Esmé Weijun Wang's mother first heard about her daughter's suicidal
   thoughts, she "suggested that we kill ourselves together" (2). Why do you suppose
   Wang's mother responded in this "bizarre" way (2)?

2. Just before she goes off to college, Wang is diagnosed with "bipolar disorder" (7),
   for which her doctor prescribes no new medications. Why not?

3. When Wang visits the Department of Mental Hygiene at Yale, she pretends to be
   visiting the Gynecology Department (8). Why?

4. Wang had to contend not only with the psychological effects but also with the
   "stigma" of mental illness (8). What are some of the common causes of that stigma,
   and how might they best be dispelled?

STRATEGIES AND STRUCTURES

1. In high school, Wang says, she "demonstrated most of the classic signs of mania"
   (7). Does Wang's essay deal more with the symptoms and other EFFECTS of her illness or with the CAUSES? Explain.

2. If they are severe enough, the symptoms of an illness can become the causes of
   further illness. Point out places in her essay where Wang gives specific EXAMPLES of
   this vicious circle, such as "I would stop sleeping for days at a time; then off I would
   go" (10).

3. During her first semester in college, says Wang, her mother "swelled and grew
   monstrous in [her] mind" (9). As Wang analyzes them, what were the main causes
   of this peculiar effect? Explain.

4. Throughout her essay, Wang suggests that neither Education nor Science can "save" her. What saving grace *does* she look to, and where does she consider its beneficial effects?

5. *Other Methods.* Within the NARRATIVE of her own illness, Wang inserts an ANECDOTE about "the Shakespeare Lady" (19, 20). What is the role of this woman in Wang's essay? What does she symbolize to Wang?

THINKING ABOUT LANGUAGE

1. As she was growing up in California, her immigrant parents never used the term "American dream," says Wang, "but that was what their lives signified" (2). How is Wang implicitly DEFINING "American dream" here?

2. Wang says her high school GPA "belied" the self-inflicted scars under her graduation gown (2). The verb "belie" is sometimes misused to mean "reveal." What does the word actually mean, according to your dictionary—and Wang's usage here?

3. The "scars lurking" (2) under Wang's graduation gown anticipate the "instabilities lurking" (8) in the hall when she visits the clinic at Yale. Is this an effective use of PERSONIFICATION? How does it contribute to the essay's TONE?

4. Saying she "went to Yale," says Wang, "is shorthand for *I have schizoaffective disorder, but I'm not worthless*" (6). What does Wang mean, apparently, by "shorthand"? What "worth" is she referring to in "worthless"? Where else does she use this kind of shorthand in her essay?

5. Of going to the Yale health clinic for treatments, Wang writes: "Stigma clouded the visits" (8). When she returns to her dorm after picking up dinner in town, "the fog was still pressing its velvet paws to the windows" (24). Given the subject matter of this essay, what do these METAPHORS contribute to the tone?

FOR WRITING

1. "Schizoaffective disorder" (6) is not the same as "schizophrenia." Look up these terms, and in a paragraph or two, explain the main differences between them.

2. Read more about schizoaffective disorder, and then write a brief ANALYSIS of its known causes and effects. What role do scientists believe heredity plays in the development of the disorder?

3. Soon after the publication of *The Collected Schizophrenias*, Wang told an interviewer: "I do want to be careful not to glamorize mental illness when it comes to creativity because more often than not it actually tends to inhibit creativity.... I want to emphasize and never lose sight of how much suffering is involved." Read more of *The Collected Schizophrenias* (or another work by Wang), and then write a CRITICAL ANALYSIS of her writing as an accurate (or otherwise) portrayal of a mental illness.

4. Photos of *Education*, the allegorical Tiffany window in Yale's Linsly-Chittenden Hall, are easy to find on the internet, as is information about the composition and history of the window. (During the student unrest of 1970, it was supposed to be stored for safekeeping. Workers, however, removed the wrong window—which was subsequently destroyed or stolen—thereby inadvertently saving *Education* for posterity.) Read about the window, study the photos, and then write a critical analysis of *Education* as a work of both art and instruction.

12 | Comparison and Contrast

In close combat, and with no preparation, Iron Man would make mincemeat out of the Dark Knight with his superior strength. But Batman knows this and would not only then know Stark's weaknesses, but would have a contingency plan to take him down. . . . One-on-one, it's not really close: Batman in a landslide.

—SHAWN ADLER, "Iron Man vs. Batman"

When we compare and contrast things—red apples and golden apples, theories of history, superheroes—we look at both the similarities and the differences between them. Whether we emphasize the similarities (comparison) or the differences (contrast), however, will depend not only on who or what we're comparing but also on our *basis* of comparison.

Finding Similarities and Differences

If we compare two superheroes—Iron Man and Batman, for example—on the basis of their *strengths*, we're likely to emphasize their similarities. To begin with, both are extraordinarily wealthy. According to *Forbes* magazine, Batman has roughly $6.8 billion from the Wayne Corp. and his inheritance; Iron Man has approximately $3 billion from Stark Industries. Also, both are intelligent and cunning in the pursuit of evildoers; and both possess great physical strength, although Iron Man's high-tech armor gives him an edge here—when he's wearing it. Furthermore, both have faithful sidekicks (Jim Rhodes and Robin), and their adventures are underwritten by two of the most potent companies in the entertainment business, Marvel and DC comics, respectively.

Where do these powers come from? See "Ancient Archetypes and Modern Superheroes," p. 506.

On the basis of their *strengths*, Iron Man and Batman would seem to be alike in many ways. If, however, we compare the two characters on the basis of their *weaknesses*, we're likely to come up with a cape full of differences. Here is one writer's assessment of the most "glaring weakness" he finds when comparing (or, rather, contrasting) Tony Stark and Bruce Wayne (aka Iron Man and Batman):

> Stark has been known to hit the bottle every once in a while, making him vulnerable at best and unavailable at worst. . . . Due to his upbringing and strict moral code, Wayne is unable to trust people and, oftentimes, isn't able to see any good in them at all. . . . Batman's biggest weakness may turn out to be his greatest strength. Because he was unable to trust the Justice League, for instance, he kept dossiers on all the members, learning their secret identities and weaknesses should he ever need to take them down. He investigated Superman. Do we think he wouldn't also have a file on that goody-goody Tony Stark? Stark's weakness, meanwhile, just makes him incorrigible.
>
> —Shawn Adler, "Iron Man vs. Batman: Who Would Come Out on Top?
> We Compare the Epic Superheroes Side-by-Side"

COMPARING WAYS TO SAY "THANK YOU"

Sometimes the purpose of a comparison is to point out similarities where the reader might normally expect differences. And vice versa.

Reimagining the thank-you note in contrasting ways.

For example, we might normally expect men and women to say "thank you" for more or less the same reason—to acknowledge a gift or service. This isn't always the case, though, according to the sociolinguist Deborah Tannen:

> Many women use "thanks" as an automatic conversation starter and closer; there's nothing literally to say thank you for. Like many rituals typical of women's conversation, it depends on the goodwill of the other to restore the balance. When the other speaker doesn't reciprocate, a woman may feel like someone on a seesaw whose partner abandoned his end.   —DEBORAH TANNEN, "But What Do You Mean?"

The partner who abandoned his end of the conversation, says Tannen, is the man who says "You're welcome" to the woman's ritual "thank you": she is starting or ending a conversation; he is taking credit. (Read the rest of Tannen's essay on p. 495.)

This passage is mostly contrast; that is, it stresses the differences between the two figures being compared. They *are* still being compared, however: comparisons are about relationships, whether of sameness or difference. In this chapter, therefore, we'll use the word "comparison" both for drawing similarities between two related subjects *and* for pointing out their differences. (We'll reserve "contrast" for occasional use when describing differences only.) In this chapter we'll also look more deeply into when and why we compare things, how to make effective comparisons, and how to compose and organize an essay that uses common strategies of comparison and contrast. Finally, we'll review the critical points to watch for as you read over and revise your essay, as well as common errors to avoid when you edit.

Why Do We Compare?

For most ordinary mortals, one form of comparison that takes place frequently is comparison shopping. The reason you compare before you buy is so you can select the best product for your needs at the best price. For this purpose you may consult a buying guide, such as *Consumer Reports*.

In a recent issue, the professional comparers at *Consumer Reports* compared similar makes, models, and brands of tablet computers, dishwashing soap, online florists, stain remover, barbecue sauce, 4K TVs, and food processors—all so consumers can be aware of the differences among them.

> Bruce Catton does this with two very different Civil War generals on p. 441.

One of the main reasons we compare things—and not just consumer products—is to discover differences between two subjects that we'd otherwise expect to be similar. For example, on a botany exam you might compare the leaf structure of two related species of ferns. Or, in literature, you might compare two Shakespearean sonnets.

We also make comparisons in order to find similarities between subjects that we might otherwise consider to be entirely different, as in this opening paragraph from a book on what happens to the human body after death:

> The way I see it, being dead is not terribly far off from being on a cruise ship. Most of your time is spent lying on your back. The brain has shut down. The flesh begins to soften. Nothing much new happens, and nothing is expected of you.
>
> —MARY ROACH, *Stiff*

We don't normally think of being dead and taking a cruise as being very much alike. By pointing out similarities between the two that we may not have noticed, however, Roach enables us to see both subjects—particularly the grimmer one—in a new light. This kind of comparison between two seemingly unrelated subjects is an **ANALOGY**: it explains a less familiar subject by comparing it to something we're likely to know more about.

Composing an Essay That Compares and Contrasts

The root meaning of the word "compare" is "to put with equals," and so the first thing to do when composing an essay that compares and contrasts is to choose subjects that are truly comparable—apples to apples, oranges to oranges.

If two subjects are different in every way, there's little point in comparing them. The same is true if they're entirely alike. Your subjects should have enough in common to provide a solid basis of comparison. A train and a jetliner, for instance, are very different machines; but both are modes of transportation, and that shared characteristic can become the basis for comparing them.

When you look for shared characteristics in your subjects, don't stretch the comparison too far, however. You don't want to make the logical blunder that the Duchess commits in Lewis Carroll's *Alice in Wonderland*:

> "Very true," said the Duchess: "flamingos and mustard both bite. And the moral of that is—'Birds of a feather flock together.'"
>
> "Only mustard isn't a bird," Alice remarked.
>
> "Right as usual," said the Duchess: "what a clear way you have of putting things."

Flamingos and mustard both bite, but not in ways that are similar enough to make them truly comparable. So beware what you compare. Before you bring two subjects together as equals in an essay, make sure they are "birds of a feather" by looking carefully at the characteristics that make them different from others but similar to each other. Those characteristics should be significant enough to form a solid basis of comparison. In Wonderland, you might compare turtles and tanks, for example, on the grounds that both move relatively slowly and have hard outer coverings. In the real world, however, it's not a good idea to bring two subjects together when their differences are far more significant than their similarities. Better to compare mustard and ketchup, or flamingos and roseate spoonbills—unless, of course, you plan to show just how much two apparently dissimilar subjects (being dead and going on a cruise; skyscrapers and airplanes) actually have in common.

Thinking about Purpose and Audience

Suppose you're comparing running shoes for the simple purpose of buying a new pair to replace your old ones. In this case, you compare them in order to evaluate them—to decide which shoe fits your needs best, so you can choose the right one at the right price. However, if you were writing a comparison of several kinds of running shoes for *Consumer Reports*, you would be comparing your subjects in order to inform readers about them. Instead of evaluating the shoes and choosing a pair to fit your needs, your purpose would be to give readers the information they need to choose for themselves.

With comparisons, as with shoes, one size does not fit all. Whether you're writing a comparison to inform, evaluate, or for some other purpose, always keep the specific needs of your audience in mind. How much do your readers already know about your topic? Why should they want or need to know more? What distinctions can you make that they haven't already thought of?

If you're comparing running shoes for a runner's magazine or a shoe catalog, for example, your readers are probably running enthusiasts who already know a good bit about your subject; so you should distinguish carefully among the different brands or models you're discussing. Thus you might point out that New Balance models 860 and 890 are both durable, lightweight training shoes. The 860, however, is meant for the runner who is (in the words of the manufacturer) looking for "a lightweight fit, breathability and freedom of movement," while the 890 "offers a snug, supportive fit."

A comparison like this is geared toward experienced runners who have highly specialized needs. Such fine distinctions would be lost on readers who are simply looking for the cheapest running shoe available, or the highest quality one, or the most stylish. So before you compare, size up your readers, and tailor your comparison to fit their specific needs.

Generating Ideas: Asking How Two Things Are Alike or Different

BRAINSTORMING and LISTING can help as you think about your comparison. Once you have a clear basis for comparing two subjects—flamingos and roseate spoonbills are both large pink birds; trains and jetliners are modes of mass transportation; NB 860s and 890s are medium-priced running shoes—the next step is to look for specific points of comparison between them. So ask yourself the key questions that any comparison raises: How, specifically, are the two subjects alike? How do they differ?

As you probe for similarities and differences between subjects, make a point-by-point list like the following one pertaining to bathing customs in the United States and Japan:

DIFFERENCES

American bath	*Japanese bath*
fast and efficient	slow and contemplative
usually solitary	often communal, even public
bather scrubs own back	family members scrub one another's backs
bather stares at ceramic tile	bather watches the moon rise
concerned with the body	concerned with the soul

SIMILARITIES

American bath	*Japanese bath*
cleanliness is important	cleanliness is important

Listing the main ways in which two subjects are alike or different will help you determine whether they're actually worth comparing—and get the similarities and differences straight in your own mind before attempting to explain them to an audience.

Notice that in the lists above, each point on the American side matches the point on the Japanese side. If the point on the American side is "bather stares at ceramic tile," the point on the Japanese side is also about what people look at while bathing: "bather watches the moon rise." When drawing up your list, make sure to look at the same elements in both subjects. If you talk about the communal aspect of the Japanese bath, you need to mention whether American baths are communal or solitary—or your comparison will be incomplete.

Organizing and Drafting a Comparison

Once you have a list of the specific ways in which your two subjects are alike or different, you're ready to organize, and then to begin drafting, your comparison. Make sure, however, that your main points of comparison deal with significant characteristics of the subjects and that you draw a sufficient number of them. The templates on p. 409 can help you get started.

CHOOSING A METHOD OF ORGANIZATION

There are two fundamental ways of organizing a comparison: point by point or subject by subject. Let's look at the **POINT-BY-POINT** method in a comparison of the career patterns of two ambitious women:

> Both Cleo and Alice are hard-driving workers; both are achievers; both spend so much time working that they have very little left for traditional leisure pursuits. The fundamental difference between Alice and Cleo is that they define work differently. Cleo is working *for* her company. Alice works *through* her company while working for herself. . . . Most of us fall into one of these two camps. To make the most of your own career and psych out the people around you, it's essential to be able to tell them apart.
>
> —ELWOOD CHAPMAN, *Working Woman*

A point-by-point organization like this discusses each point of comparison (or contrast) between the two subjects before going on to the next point. Here's an informal outline of Chapman's point-by-point comparison:

1. Kind of workers
   Cleo is hard-driving, an achiever
   Alice is hard-driving, an achiever
2. Time spent working
   Cleo spends all her time working
   Alice spends all her time working
3. How they define work
   Cleo works for her company
   Alice works for herself

After using the point-by-point method to compare the two workers in the first paragraph of his essay, Chapman switches to the **SUBJECT-BY-SUBJECT** method in the next two paragraphs:

> Cleo is a classic workaholic. She works from dawn till dusk (more than five days a week as necessary) with a major utility. She earns a good salary, is highly esteemed by her bosses for her loyalty and reliability, and enjoys extraordinary job security (it probably would cost her employer at least 20 percent more than she earns to replace her).
>
> Alice, a mid-management person in a financial institution, also works overtime, though she rarely spends more than 35 to 40 hours a week on actual work assignments. The rest of her time is given over to company information-gathering, checking out opportunities with competing firms, image building, and similar activities.

This method involves discussing each subject individually, making a number of points about one subject and then covering more or less the same points about the other subject. Here's another informal outline of Chapman's subject-by-subject comparison:

Jamie Gullen uses this method to compare two cultures (p. 413).

1. Cleo
   workaholic
   earns a good salary
   respected for her loyalty and reliability
   enjoys extraordinary job security
2. Alice
   workaholic
   rarely spends all her time on work assignments
   rest of time spent on career building

Which method of organization should you use? Any method that presents your points of comparison and contrast clearly and simply to the reader is a good method of organization. However, you'll probably find that the point-by-point method works best for beginning and ending an essay, while the subject-by-subject method serves you well for longer stretches in the main body of your essay.

One reason for using the subject-by-subject method to organize most of your essay is that it enables you to make as many points as you like on each subject. You don't have to give equal weight to both. With the point-by-point method, by contrast, you make more or less the same number of points for both subjects. The subject-by-subject method is thus indispensable for treating a subject in depth, whereas the point-by-point method is an efficient way of presenting a balanced comparison. Because it touches on both subjects more or less equally, the point-by-point method can also help you convince readers that two subjects are, indeed, fundamentally alike (or dissimilar). Overall, the point-by-point method is particularly useful for establishing a basis of comparison at the beginning of an essay, for reminding readers along the way why two subjects are being compared, and for summing up.

See how David Sedaris (p. 433) uses these methods for the purpose of humor.

STATING YOUR POINT

Your main point in drawing a comparison will determine whether you emphasize the similarities or the differences between your subjects. If you're comparing coaches you had in high school, for instance, you might focus on their differences in order to show the reader what constitutes a good (or bad) coach. If you're comparing successful first dates to explain what makes for a super one, however, you would focus on the similarities.

Whatever the main point of your comparison might be, make it clear right away in the form of an explicit THESIS, and tell the reader whether you're emphasizing the similarities or the differences between your subjects. Then, in the body of your essay, draw a sufficient number of specific points of comparison to prove your point.

PROVIDING SUFFICIENT POINTS OF COMPARISON

How many points of comparison are enough to do the job? Sufficiency isn't strictly a matter of numbers. It depends, in part, on just how inclined your audience is to accept (or reject) the main point your comparison is intended to make.

If you're comparing subjects that your readers aren't familiar with, you may have to give more reasons for drawing the parallel than you would if your readers already know a lot about those subjects. In comparing dying to going on a cruise, for example, Mary Roach operates on the humorous basis that they're both forms of leisure, and she draws five points of comparison between them: (1) much of the time is spent lying on your back; (2) the brain shuts down; (3) the flesh begins to soften; (4) nothing new happens; (5) not much is expected of you. Roach might have gone on to make additional points of comparison, such as (6) you don't go anywhere in particular and (7) there's not much room in the cabin. Five points, however, are probably enough to persuade readers that the two subjects are worth comparing, and any more than that would be overkill. In other words, whether your points of comparison are sufficient to support your thesis isn't determined so much by how many you give as by how persuasive they seem to the reader. So consider your intended readers, and choose points of comparison you think they'll find useful, interesting, or otherwise convincing.

USING OTHER METHODS

Comparison deals with subjects that have something significant in common, so CLASSIFICATION and DEFINITION can be useful in writing that compares. The following paragraph uses both methods to compare writing to other ways of using language:

> Traditionally, the four language processes of listening, talking, reading, and writing are paired in either of two ways. The more informative seems to be the division many linguists make between first-order and second-order processes with talking and listening characterized as first-order processes; reading and writing, as second-order.
>
> —JANET EMIG, "Writing as a Mode of Learning"

TEMPLATES FOR DRAFTING

When you begin to draft a comparison, you need to identify your subjects, state the basis on which you're comparing them, and indicate whether you plan to emphasize their similarities or their differences—moves fundamental to any comparison. See how David Sedaris makes such moves near the beginning of his essay in this chapter:

> Certain events are parallel, but compared with Hugh's, my childhood was unspeakably dull. When I was seven years old, my family moved to North Carolina. When he was seven years old, Hugh's family moved to the Congo. We had a collie and a house cat. They had a monkey and two horses named Charlie Brown and Satan.
>
> —DAVID SEDARIS,
> "Remembering My Childhood on the Continent of Africa"

Sedaris identifies his two subjects ("Hugh's, my childhood"), states the basis on which he is comparing them ("certain events are parallel"), and indicates that he is planning to emphasize the differences ("my childhood was unspeakably dull"). Here is one more example from this chapter:

> They were two strong men, these oddly different generals, and they represented the strengths of two conflicting currents that, through them, had come into final collision.
>
> —BRUCE CATTON, "Grant and Lee: A Study in Contrasts"

The following templates can help you make some of these basic moves in your own writing. But don't take these as formulas where you just fill in the blanks. There are no shortcuts to good writing, but these templates can serve as starting points.

▸ X and Y can be compared on the grounds that both are _____.

▸ Like X, Y is also _____, _____, and _____.

▸ Although X and Y are both _____, the differences between them far outweigh the similarities. For example, X is _____, _____, and _____, while Y is _____, _____, and _____.

▸ Unlike X, Y is _____.

▸ Despite their differences, X and Y are basically alike in that _____.

▸ At first glance, X and Y seem _____; however, a closer look reveals _____.

▸ In comparing X and Y, we can see that _____.

The author of this passage from a formal academic paper in linguistics and language acquisition is comparing writing to other "language processes," particularly talking. Her main point in making the comparison is to argue that among all the ways in which humans learn to use language, writing is unique.

To support this point and develop her comparison, Emig uses a number of other methods besides comparison and contrast. First, she classifies writing as a "second-order" use of language, and the more natural process of talking as a "first-order" use. Then, elsewhere in her introduction, Emig defines these two basic kinds of language activities: first-order language skills, such as talking, are learned *without* formal instruction, whereas second-order language skills, such as writing, are learned only *with* formal instruction.

Not every linguist would agree that writing is unique among human language activities. But it would be difficult to contest Emig's point that learning to write well takes a special, perhaps unique, form of language instruction by knowledgeable teachers who are dedicated to a difficult task. How else, but through highly specialized training, could we learn to draw formal written comparisons and contrasts in such academic disciplines as history, geography, sociology—and linguistics?

EDITING FOR COMMON ERRORS IN COMPARISONS

As with other kinds of writing, comparisons use distinctive patterns of language and punctuation—and thus invite some common mistakes. The following tips will help you check your writing for errors that often crop up in comparisons.

Check that all comparisons are complete

Remember that all comparisons examine at least two items; check to see that both are mentioned. Readers need to understand what's being compared.

▶ When you take a bath, it is always better to relax <u>than to hurry</u>.

▶ Most hot tubs are not as hot <u>as typical Japanese baths</u>.

Be sure that all comparisons are grammatically consistent

Check to see that the items you're comparing are parallel in grammatical form. The original version of this sentence unintentionally compares a bath with a place.

▶ Baths in the United States tend to be much less ritualistic than <u>those in</u> Japan.

Clarify comparisons that can be taken more than one way

▶ Fumio taught me more than Sam <u>did</u>.

Or

▶ Fumio taught me more than <u>he taught</u> Sam.

Check for common usage errors

"Good," "well"

Use "good" only as an adjective; use the adverb form, "well," with an action verb.

▶ Hilary is a <u>good</u> musician; she plays the violin as <u>well</u> as Tom does.

"Between," "among"

Use "between" when comparing two items; use "among" when comparing three or more.

▶ <u>Between</u> Britain and France, France has the better health-care system.

▶ <u>Among</u> all the countries of Europe, France has the best health-care system.

Reading a Comparison with a Critical Eye

Once you've drafted an essay that uses comparison, ask someone else to look over your draft and tell you how effective they find your basic comparison—and why. Then read it over yourself, too, with a critical eye. Here are some questions to keep in mind when checking a comparison.

SUBJECTS OF COMPARISON. What specific subjects does this essay compare? Are they similar enough to justify the comparison? On what basis are they compared? Does the text emphasize the similarities or the differences between them? Or does it give equal weight to both?

PURPOSE AND AUDIENCE. Who are the intended readers, and what is the general purpose of the comparison—to inform? to evaluate? some other purpose? Does the comparison achieve this purpose? If not, what changes might help? What background information is included, and is it sufficient for the intended readers to fully understand the text? Are there any key terms that readers might need to have defined?

THE POINT. What is the main point of the essay? Has it been made clear to the reader? Is there an explicit thesis statement? If not, should there be?

ORGANIZATION. How is the comparison organized? Where does it use the point-by-point method of organization? the subject-by-subject method? When comparing subjects point by point, does the essay give more or less equal weight to each subject? When treating first one subject and then the other, does the essay follow more or less the same order in laying out the points of comparison for each subject?

POINTS OF COMPARISON. What are the specific points of comparison in the essay? Are they sufficient to convince the reader that the comparison is valid? Do they cover the same elements for both subjects? Have any important points been omitted—and if so, what are they?

OTHER METHODS. What other methods are used besides comparison and contrast? Does the essay CLASSIFY subjects? DEFINE them? make an ARGUMENT about them? What other methods might support the comparison?

COMMON ERRORS. Have all the direct comparisons in the essay been fully completed? Do they all answer the question "Compared to what?" If they don't, fill in the missing term to complete the comparison.

Student Example

Jamie Gullen is a native of New York City. While she was an undergraduate at Cornell University, she spent several months in Copenhagen as a participant in the Danish Institute for Study Abroad (DIS). At first, Gullen expected her host country to be "culturally similar" to the one she had left behind. When comparing the two cultures during her months abroad, however, Gullen soon realized how much she had to learn—about herself as well as her hosts. The following essay is the result of that comparative process. It won a prize in the DIS student essay contest in the spring of 2006 under its original title, "Self-Discovery and the Danish Way of Life."

The Danish Way of Life

As my final weeks in Copenhagen began drawing to a close, I was surprised to find myself waiting patiently at a red light even though there were no cars or bikes in the near vicinity. As a New York City native, this observation was cause for a significant pause and some serious self-reflection. My thoughts settled on my first month in Copenhagen when I was having a discussion with a fellow DIS student. She was saying she had expected to feel some significant change in who she was from being abroad, but so far she felt like the same person she had always been. This got me thinking about whether or not I had experienced a significant change of self from being abroad in a culture totally different from the one in which I grew up. At that time, I did not have a good response to that question, but as I stood waiting for the green light on a spring night in Copenhagen, I found I had stumbled upon some important insights.

The answer I came to is that the very core of who I am and the things that matter most to me have remained very much the same. But rather than viewing this in a negative light as some kind of stagnation or lack of personal growth, I realized it was exactly the opposite. Study abroad doesn't change who you are; it helps you discover who you are. By removing the immediate cultural environment in which I was immersed from the day I was born, I was able to discern which values and habits were really central to who I am as a person and which were merely the results of the influences of my family, friends, school, city, country, and cultural surroundings.

Before I came to Denmark, I expected it to be fairly culturally similar to the United States. It is a democratic Western country where English is widely spoken and where American culture pervades television and movies, and the Danish government is very closely aligned with the American government. I was shocked to find out that the Danish way of life couldn't be more different from what I

1

Gullen uses NARRATION to set up her comparison

The essay will emphasize differences between the two cultures

2

Gullen's PURPOSE in making the comparison is self-evaluation

3

Shared characteristics establish a basis for the comparison

DEFINING a key term captures the differences between the two countries ······

was expecting. The biggest difference I experienced originates with the Danish word *hygge*. This word has no direct translation into English, and when I asked a Danish person to define it for me, it took her five minutes just to begin to touch upon what the word signifies. That is because it is much more than a word; it is a way of life. What she told me was that *hygge* is most closely translated as the English word *cozy* and that it is experienced socially. It is a closeness and intimacy between friends, enjoyment of food and wine; it is dinner that lasts for four hours because of good conversation; and it is décor with dim lighting and candles everywhere. While I have experienced *hygge* during my stay in Denmark both with Danes and my fellow DIS students, it took some time for me to process the true significance of the word.

Turning point allows for a comparison of her mindset before and after the trip ······

Subject-by-subject method gives Danish characteristics first, then American ones ······

The turning point, in my understanding of both *hygge* and myself, was on my program's short study tour in western Denmark. As I discussed everything from Danish politics to local Danish soccer teams with some natives in the small town of Kolding, the conversation casually turned to differences between the Danish and the American way of life. I was noting that many Danish people I have met view their careers as a way to provide for themselves financially and to engage in fields that interest them intellectually, but their conception of self-worth is not tied up in the prestige of their jobs or the number of hours worked each week or the amount of the paycheck they bring home in comparison to their peers. It was through this observation that I realized the true importance of *hygge*; it recognizes the humanness of life and the individuality of the person. It is an appreciation of what really matters: friends, family, love, intimacy, and happiness. 4

Growing up, I lived in a fast-paced city, attended a rigorous high school and college, was surrounded by career-driven highly motivated peers, and was encouraged by my parents to put academics first. Coming to Denmark and experiencing *hygge* and the Danish way of life and learning served as a jolt to the immediate cultural world that had shaped me. I was forced to consider life 5 from another angle. What I found is that deep down I have always held the *hygge* values to be of importance, and I have always wanted to be engaged in helping other people find a happy and peaceful way of life. It is just easier now to see how my external cultural eviron-ment has impacted and shaped these values and my sense of DIS, Danish, and my international self.

When I arrive home in New York City, it will no doubt take very little time for me to join in with the throngs of jaywalkers marching defiantly across Madison Avenue, but what I have learned from being abroad in Denmark about who I am and what matters most to me will be knowledge that stays with me forever.

6   Conclusion returns to opening narrative

Analyzing a Student Comparison

In "The Danish Way of Life," Jamie Gullen draws on rhetorical strategies and tech-niques that good writers use all the time when making a comparison. The following questions, in addition to focusing on particular aspects of Gullen's text, will help you identify those common strategies in your own writing. These questions will also help prepare you for the analytical techniques so you can adapt them to other questions— on content, structure, and language—that you'll find after all the other selections in this chapter, along with suggestions for writing on related topics.

FOR CLOSE READING

1. What was the biggest difference between Danish and American culture that Jamie Gullen experienced while studying abroad in Denmark?

2. According to Gullen, how do the Danes approach their jobs and careers as com-pared with their American counterparts?

3. Gullen says that "study abroad doesn't change who you are" (2). What does it do, in her view? How?

4. What important lesson did Gullen learn from her period of study abroad?

STRATEGIES AND STRUCTURES

1. How does Gullen use the NARRATIVE device of waiting for a traffic light to help structure her entire essay?

2. In her introduction, Gullen says she "stumbled upon some important insights" as an American studying in Denmark (1). Gullen doesn't specify what those insights are, however, until after comparing the two countries in the main body of her essay. Should she have done so earlier? Why or why not?

3. How did the act of making comparisons lead Gullen to a "turning point" (4) in her understanding of both her host country and herself? Does her comparison emphasize the similarities between the two cultures, or their differences, or both? Explain.

4. Gullen sums up what she learned from her Danish experience in paragraph 5. Why doesn't she end there? What does paragraph 6 add to her comparison?

5. *Other Methods.* The "biggest difference" between Denmark and America that she encountered during her study abroad, says Gullen, can be summed up in the Danish word "hygge" (3). How does Gullen use an extended DEFINITION of this term to support her comparison of the two countries?

THINKING ABOUT LANGUAGE

1. The Danes, says Gullen, usually translate "hygge" as the English word "cozy" (3). Judging from Gullen's definition of the term, how would you translate it?

2. What are the CONNOTATIONS of "stumbled" and "natives" (1, 4)?

3. A "turning point" (4) implies an irreversible change. What, if anything, is irreversible about Gullen's experience as a student in Denmark?

FOR WRITING

1. Write a paragraph contrasting what you see as a key difference between the culture of mainstream America and that of some other country or group.

2. Think of another country you'd like to visit (or have already visited). Write a four-to-six-paragraph essay comparing that culture and your own. What do you expect (or what did you find) to be the main similarities and differences between them?

3. Write a 400-to-500-word POSITION PAPER on the purpose of traveling to new places with a culture different from your own. Be sure to consider Gullen's suggestion that travel brings about "a significant change of self" (1).

4. Do some research on the place, and write an imaginary travel journal about your travels in Denmark or some other country you'd like to visit ("My first night in Copenhagen, I . . .").

An Ad for Cycling

When you compare and contrast, you show the similarities and differences among related subjects. Buses, cars, and bikes are related subjects—all are common means of transportation—and in this visual comparison from the website of the Cycling Promotion Fund, an organization that promotes cycling across communities in Australia, they're shown as transporting the same number of passengers. The big difference here, of course, is in the number of vehicles that appear with the large group of people in each photo: at least 100 cars, just as many bicycles, but only one long bus. Numbers don't tell the full story, however. Public transportation (one bus) may be better for the environment than 100 cars; but 100 bicycles don't use any fossil fuel—just muscle power. We draw comparisons in order to make a larger point, and in this case, the point has to do with the fund's mission: to make cities biker friendly, to fight climate change, and to reduce congestion. If more people used public transit and rode bikes, we could save fuel and leave a smaller carbon footprint.

[FOR WRITING]··

Do some research on the various types of buses—diesel, electric, hybrid, natural gas, hydrogen, other—found on the streets of US cities today, and write a comparative report on their relative advantages and disadvantages as forms of public transportation.

SUGGESTIONS FOR WRITING

1. Both "The Danish Way of Life" (p. 413) and "Taking My Parents to College" (p. 454) discuss the authors' experiences in unfamiliar environments. Read both essays carefully, and then write a RHETORICAL ANALYSIS in which you compare and contrast the two environments, the authors' expectations at the start of their experiences, and what they learned as a result of those experiences.

2. In addition to "Superhero Smackdown," p. 426, Douglas Wolk is the author of *Reading Comics: How Graphic Novels Work and What They Mean* (2007). On *Amazon* and elsewhere, read several reviews of this award-winning study and write an ABSTRACT (or summary) of what Wolk has to say. Cite your sources, of course. (Alternatively, read the book itself and do your own critical EVALUATION of it.)

3. Write a research REPORT on the history and career of Wonder Woman. Include a detailed comparison of her powers (and weaknesses) with those of her male counterparts. In the course of your report, respond to Douglas Wolk's assertion (p. 428, paragraph 9) that the owners of the Wonder Woman franchise have never been able to successfully get her "off the ground as either a movie or a TV show." Is that still true today?

4. "Remembering My Childhood on the Continent of Africa" (p. 433) is a perennial favorite among fans of the humor writer David Sedaris. As background for understanding this essay and Sedaris's other work, do some research on his life and career and write a brief PROFILE of the man and his humor. Be sure to compare Sedaris's work with that of other humor writers, such as Mindy Kaling ("Types of Women in Romantic Comedies Who Are Not Real," p. 489).

5. In "Grant and Lee: A Study in Contrasts" (p. 441), the historian Bruce Catton associates General Ulysses S. Grant, commander of the Northern armies during the American Civil War, with the future. "Grant was the modern man emerging," he writes; "beyond him, ready to come on the stage, was the great age of steel and machinery, of crowded cities and a restless burgeoning vitality." The period to which Catton refers is 1865–1915. Do some research on this time in American history and write a REPORT explaining why it's often called "the age of energy." Be sure to compare it briefly with other periods in American history, either before or after.

WES MOORE

The Other Wes Moore

Westley "Wes" Watende Omari Moore (b. 1978) is the sixty-third governor of the state of Maryland. Elected in 2023, he is the first Black governor in the state's 246-year history. Born in Baltimore, Moore grew up in the Bronx, New York, where his grandfather was a minister and where, after his father's death, the family resettled when Moore was four years old. Returning to Baltimore, Moore graduated from Johns Hopkins University in 2001 and attended the University of Oxford (England) as a Rhodes Scholar, earning a master's degree in international relations. In addition to working with Robin Hood, a nonprofit organization dedicated to fighting poverty in New York City, he is the founder of BridgeEdU, an organization whose goal is to "remove the barriers inherent in higher education for the underserved student population and allow them to achieve success to their fullest potential."

"The Other Wes Moore" is from the introduction to his best-selling book by that title, published in 2010 with the subtitle *One Name, Two Fates*. The book is an extended comparison and contrast of the lives—unconnected at first, but later intertwined—of two young men who grew up "at the same time, on the same streets, with the same name." One of them went on to become a Rhodes Scholar, a captain in the US Army, and a successful banker and politician. The other landed in prison, "surrounded by the walls he'd escape only at death."

T HIS IS THE STORY OF TWO BOYS living in Baltimore with similar histories and an identical name: Wes Moore. One of us is free and has experienced things that he never even knew to dream about as a kid. The other will spend every day

MLA CITATION: Moore, Wes. "The Other Wes Moore." *Back to the Lake: A Reader and Guide for Writers*, edited by Thomas Cooley, 5th ed., W. W. Norton, 2024, pp. 421-23.

until his death behind bars for an armed robbery that left a police officer and father of five dead.

The chilling truth is that his story could have been mine. The tragedy is that my story could have been his. Our stories are obviously specific to our two lives, but I hope they will illuminate the crucial inflection points in every life, the sudden moments of decision where our paths diverge and our fates are sealed. It's unsettling to know how little separates each of us from another life altogether.

In late 2000, the *Baltimore Sun* published a short article with the headline "Local Graduate Named Rhodes Scholar." It was about me. As a senior at Johns Hopkins University, I received one of the most prestigious academic awards for students in the world. That fall I was moving to England to attend Oxford University on a full scholarship.

But that story had less of an impact on me than another series of articles in the *Sun*, about an incident that happened just months before, a precisely planned jewelry store robbery gone terribly wrong. The store's security guard—an off-duty police officer named Bruce Prothero—was shot and killed after he pursued the armed men into the store's parking lot. A massive and highly publicized manhunt for the perpetrators ensued. Twelve days later it ended when the last two suspects were apprehended in a house in Philadelphia by a daunting phalanx of police and federal agents.

The articles indicated that the shooter, Richard Antonio Moore, would likely receive the death penalty. The sentence would be similarly severe for his younger brother, who was also arrested and charged. In an eerie coincidence, the younger brother's name was the same as mine.

Two years after I returned from Oxford, I was still thinking about the story. I couldn't let it go. If you'd asked me why, I couldn't have told you exactly. I was struck by the superficial similarities between us, of course: we'd grown up at the same time, on the same streets, with the same name. But so what? I didn't think of myself as a superstitious or conspiratorial person, the kind who'd obsess over a coincidence until it yielded meaning.

But there were nights when I'd wake up in the small hours and find myself thinking of the other Wes Moore, conjuring his image as best I could, a man my age lying on a cot in a prison cell, burdened by regret, trying to sleep through another night surrounded by the walls he'd escape only at death. Sometimes in my imaginings, his face was mine.

> Moore wonders if he has provided a sufficient number of points of comparison (pp. 404–5).

There's a line at the opening of John Edgar Wideman's brilliant *Brothers and Keepers* about the day he found out his own brother was on the run from the police for an armed robbery: "The distance I'd put between my brother's world and mine suddenly collapsed. . . . Wherever he was, running for his life, he carried part of me with him." But I didn't even *know* the other Wes Moore. Why did I feel this connection with him, why did I feel like he "carried part of me with him" in that prison cell? I worried that I was just being melodramatic or narcissistic. But still, I couldn't shake it.

Finally, one day, I wrote him a simple letter introducing myself and explaining how I'd come to learn about his story. I struggled to explain the purpose of my letter and posed a series of naïve questions that had been running through my mind: Who are you? Do you see your brother? How do you feel about him? *How did this happen?* As soon as I mailed the letter, the crazy randomness of it all came flooding in on me. I was sure that I'd made a mistake, that I'd been self-indulgent and presumptuous and insulting, and that I'd never hear back from him. 9

A month later, I was surprised to find an envelope in my mailbox stamped with a postmark from the Jessup Correctional Institution in Maryland. He had written back. 10

"Greetings, Good Brother," the letter started out: 11

> I send salutations of peace and prayers and blessing and guidance to you for posing these questions, which I'm going to answer, Inshallah. With that, I will begin with the first question posed. . . .

This was the start of our correspondence, which has now gone on for years. At the beginning of our exchange of letters—which was later expanded by face-to-face visits at the prison—I was surprised to find just how much we did have in common, aside from our names, and how much our narratives intersected before they fatefully diverged.

Learning the details of his story helped me understand my own life and choices, and I like to think that my story helped him understand his own a little more. But the real discovery was that our two stories together helped me to untangle some of the larger story of our generation of young men, boys who came of age during a historically chaotic and violent time and emerged to succeed and fail in unprecedented ways. After a few visits, without realizing it, I started working on this project in my mind, trying to figure out what lessons our stories could offer to the next wave of young men who found themselves at the same crossroads we'd encountered and unsure which path to follow. 12

For help with identifying the AUDIENCE for your comparison, see p. 404.

Perhaps the most surprising thing I discovered was that through the stories we volleyed back and forth in letters and over the metal divider of the prison's visiting room, Wes and I had indeed, as Wideman wrote, "collapsed the distance" between our worlds. We definitely have our disagreements—and Wes, it should never be forgotten, is in prison for his participation in a heinous crime. But even the worst decisions we make don't necessarily remove us from the circle of humanity. 13

For those of us who live in the most precarious places in this country, our destinies can be determined by a single stumble down the wrong path, or a tentative step down the right one. ✦ 14

FOR CLOSE READING

1. In what ways is "the other Wes Moore" significantly different from the one who is comparing their "two fates" here?

2. Wes Moore's comparison is intended to show, among other things, "how little separates each of us from another life altogether" (2). What might he mean by this, and why does he find the idea "unsettling" (2)?

3. "But even the worst decisions," Moore concludes, ". . . don't necessarily remove us from the circle of humanity" (13). What is he implying here about responsibility and mercy? To what extent do you agree or disagree with him? Why?

STRATEGIES AND STRUCTURES

1. Moore opens his essay with a POINT-BY-POINT comparison of his two subjects. Where and why does he switch to the SUBJECT-BY-SUBJECT method?

2. On what basis is Moore comparing himself with a criminal? How well does he make the case that, despite their differences, the two men are quite similar? Explain.

3. What is Moore's main PURPOSE in comparing himself with the other Wes Moore, and where does he state it most clearly? How well does he achieve his purpose? Explain.

4. Moore says there are "lessons" to be learned from the comparisons he's making (12). Learned by whom? How is Moore defining his intended AUDIENCE here?

5. *Other Methods.* Moore is not only comparing the lives of two men but also explaining how they came to be as they are now. What are some of the main CAUSES and EFFECTS he presents for the different fates of the two Wes Moores?

THINKING ABOUT LANGUAGE

1. What is the meaning of "Inshallah" (11)? How does it relate to the concept of fate?

2. To what extent does Moore's comparison contradict the traditional idea of fate as determined by forces beyond one's personal control? Explain.

3. Moore wonders if he's "being melodramatic or narcissistic" in his fascination with his counterpart (8). Do you think he is? Why or why not?

4. In academic writing, "the other" is often used to mean something or someone "alien," in the sense of being separate or starkly different from oneself or a group to which one belongs. How might the title "The Other Wes Moore" be interpreted as using the phrase in this sense?

5. What are the implications of "stumble" in the last paragraph of Moore's comparison (14)?

FOR WRITING

1. If you're not already familiar with it, look up the source and meaning of the question "Am I my brother's keeper?" In a paragraph or two, compare and contrast the idea of brotherhood that it expresses with the one that organizations such as Robin Hood and Ready, Willing, and Able (p. 72) promote.

2. Write a five-to-seven-paragraph comparative analysis of "The Other Wes Moore" and "Ain't I a Woman?" by Sojourner Truth (p. 622) as statements about belonging to "the circle of humanity" (13). For each one, be sure to identify what or who is being compared, for what **AUDIENCE**, and for what **PURPOSE**. Cite specific details from both texts to support your comparison.

3. Write an essay of 500 to 600 words comparing and contrasting your own life with that of another person whose "narrative" could be said to have intersected with yours "before they fatefully diverged" (11). Focus on the similarities and differences between the two of you, but also include other aspects of your stories as appropriate.

DOUGLAS WOLK

Superhero Smackdown

Douglas Wolk (b. 1970) lives in Portland, Oregon, where he produces records under the label Dark Beloved Cloud, which is also the title of his blog. A graduate of Harvard and the Columbia School of Journalism, Wolk writes about comics, popular music, technology, social networks, and copyright issues for publications ranging from *Spin* and *Rolling Stone* to the *New York Times* and *HuffPost*. He is also the author of *Reading Comics: How Graphic Novels Work and What They Mean* (2007); a book about music albums that won an Eisner Award, the comics industry's equivalent of an Oscar; and *Comic-Con Strikes Again!* (2017), about San Diego's fantasy culture convention. Wolk's book, *All the Marvels: A Journey to the Ends of the Biggest Story Ever Told* (2021), another Eisner winner, explores the 27,000-plus Marvel comics (all of which he has read) as a cultural history of the past sixty years.

In "Superhero Smackdown," which appeared in *Slate* in August 2013, Wolk compares Iron Man and Batman—and the entertainment giants who stand behind them. "Who would win in a fight," he asks, "Marvel or DC?"

A T A TENDER AGE, most fans of superhero comics start honing their arguments in an ancient debate: "Which is better—Marvel or DC?" They may not yet realize that the fight has long been waged not just on the page, but also in boardrooms and on the NYSE.[1] To understand the battle between the two major American mainstream comic book companies, we can go straight to the source material, because

MLA CITATION: Wolk, Douglas. "Superhero Smackdown." *Back to the Lake: A Reader and Guide for Writers*, edited by Thomas Cooley, 5th ed., W. W. Norton, 2024, pp. 426–31.

1. *NYSE*: New York Stock Exchange.

each is very much like one of its biggest franchise players. Marvel, it's fair to say, is Iron Man; DC is Batman.

As with those two crime fighters, DC and Marvel are both colorful public fronts   2
with staggering amounts of corporate cash and power behind them: DC Entertainment is owned by Time Warner, and Marvel Entertainment is part of the Walt Disney Company. That's where the similarities end. DC, like Batman, is fantastically regimented, a little bit irrational, and hesitant to reach out beyond its home turf; like Bruce Wayne, its relationships with its extended family are fraught with resentment of its imperious ways. Marvel, like Iron Man, adapts to circumstances, makes endless duplicates of its biggest successes, and always seems to be a bit ahead of the curve; like Tony Stark, it can be slovenly about the details when they count. (Marvel's book publishing program, for instance, has a longstanding reputation as a total mess, with popular titles falling out of print for years on end.)

> ANALOGIES like this compare unfamiliar subjects to more familiar ones (p. 403).

> This is a ref. to IPP p. 5.

Most superheroes' goals are not to destroy their rivals, but to overtake and contain   3
them. (Batman puts them in Arkham Asylum; Iron Man in Negative Zone Prison Alpha.) That's how Marvel and DC generally interact with each other, and the rest of the comics business, at this point. The Big Two, which both date back to the 1930s, have been uncomfortably bonded to one another for decades. They collectively control about 70 percent of the comics retail market; if either of them were to stop publishing, it would likely destroy the fragile ecosystem of American comics stores. In the 1960s, when DC's parent company controlled Marvel's distribution and limited the number of titles they could publish, Stan Lee's editorials in Marvel's comics sniped gently at the "Distinguished Competition." Once Marvel started publishing a *Captain Marvel* series in 1968, DC acquired the rights to the '40s-era Captain Marvel character, who appeared on the TV show *Shazam!* (After several decades of not being able to print the name of their own Captain Marvel on comic book covers for trademark reasons, DC started referring to him simply as Shazam, more or less as a gesture of defeat.)

Still, they used to be more cooperative rivals. After a string of parodic storylines   4
in the '60s and '70s (in which Marvel's Avengers fought the Squadron Sinister—a thinly disguised version of DC's Justice League—and the Justice League returned the favor by battling the Champions of Angor, who were the Avengers in all but name), the two publishers reached a sort of détente. Between 1976 and 2003, there were a string of co-published DC/Marvel crossover comics, in which Superman would meet Spider-Man, or the X-Men would fight the New Teen Titans; Iron Man and Batman even encountered one another in *JLA/Avengers*. These days, each company makes a great show of pretending the other doesn't exist, aside from the occasional sideswipe. Once DC got into the habit of referring to its fictional universe as the DCU, for instance, Marvel named its all-you-can-read digital initiative Digital Comics Unlimited.

As you'd expect from colorful characters, both publishers have weaknesses that   5
can be turned against them. Marvel publishes more iterations of its biggest titles
than Iron Man has built models of his armor, which can make it nearly
impossible for casual fans to figure out what to read. So, wait, if I want to
check out the series of books where Spider-Man is an African-American/
Latino kid named Miles Morales, is that *Amazing Spider-Man, Superior
Spider-Man, Essential Spider-Man, Ultimate Spider-Man, Ultimate Comics
Spider-Man, Marvel Universe Ultimate Spider-Man* or *Spider-Man 2099*?

> **Wolk switches here to the subject-by-subject method of comparison (pp. 406–7).**

(The answer, by the way, is *Ultimate Comics Spider-Man*, starting with Vol-   6
ume 1. Naturally, Marvel has recently published two *different* books called *Ultimate
Comics Spider-Man*, Volume 1. Miles is in one of them and not the other.)

DC, likewise, has a Batman-ish tendency to alienate its allies and collaborators.   7
Artists and writers have complained of constant editorial second-guessing over the
past few years, as sales of most of its superhero titles have spiraled downward. The
company burned some bridges with *Before Watchmen*—a set of prequels to Alan
Moore and Dave Gibbons' perennially best-selling graphic novel *Watchmen*, produced over Moore's vociferous objections. And the adventurous, creator-driven DC
imprint Vertigo was gutted with the departure of its executive editor Karen Berger
early this year.

So enough wind-up—who wins the Iron Man–Batman showdown? It turns out   8
that there's an *Iron Man 3*–like twist: The rivalry that counts is between the real-
world equivalents of Stark Industries and Wayne Enterprises. Within the past few
years, Marvel and DC have changed their names, from "comics" to "entertainment"
companies, to reflect where the real money is: in film, TV, and games. Marvel will
sell, perhaps, a few million dollars' worth of *Iron Man* comic books this year, while
the worldwide gross of *Iron Man 3* so far is $1.2 billion and counting. If every
monthly issue of *Batman* sold as well as this June's (they usually don't), the series
would gross about $6.8 million this year, or roughly 1/150 of what *The Dark Knight
Rises* has made so far. So both companies now effectively treat their comics divisions as research-and-development arms, since, on the economic scale of film studios, it's astonishingly cheap to commission material from even top-tier comics
writers and artists, print it up, and see how the fans respond.

DC hasn't been doing badly in theaters, especially if you can wipe *Jonah Hex* and   9
Green Lantern out of your mind. *The Dark Knight* and *The Dark Knight Rises* were
huge hits, and this summer's *Man of Steel* performed decently, too. But there's not
much on the other side of "To Be Continued" at the moment. DC announced a
Superman/Batman movie at Comic-Con last month, but the long-rumored *Justice
League* film is a distant dream, especially since they haven't been able to get *Wonder
Woman* off the ground as either a movie or a TV show.

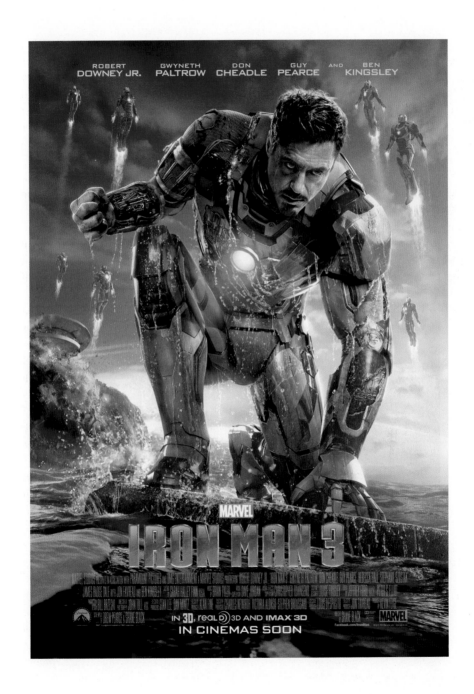

429

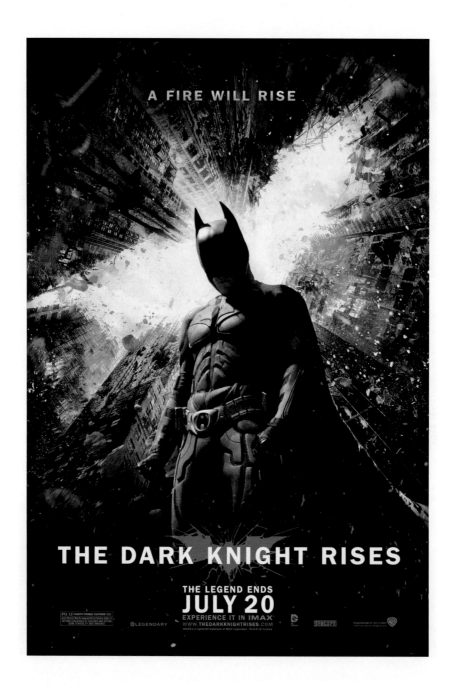

Meanwhile, there are seven forthcoming movies about Marvel characters that 10 are far enough into production to have announced release dates. The snag is that Marvel Entertainment doesn't actually control the movie rights to all of their characters, thanks to deals cut long ago. (The *Arrested Development*[2] gag about a *Fantastic Four* movie made in six days for legal reasons isn't far off from what really happened in 1992.) . . .

Even so, what Marvel Studios has been doing with the characters the company 11 *does* control—fitting their stories together into the "Marvel Cinematic Universe" that began with the first Iron Man movie in 2008, reached fruition with last year's *Avengers* movie, and continues with the upcoming *S.H.I.E.L.D.* TV show[3]—is a brilliant idea (and, naturally, borrowed from comics). Right now, DC's Batarangs don't stand a chance against Marvel's repulsor rays. ◆

FOR CLOSE READING

1. According to Douglas Wolk, why are Marvel and DC so "uncomfortably bonded to one another" by comparison with the rest of the players in the action-heroes industry (3)?

2. Both companies, says Wolk, have "weaknesses that can be turned against them" (5). What are some of those weaknesses on either side of the corporate battle?

3. Why does Wolk say that "both companies now effectively treat their comics divisions as research-and-development arms" (8)? Based on the evidence he cites, is this an accurate assessment?

4. What does Wolk mean when he says, "Right now, DC's Batarangs don't stand a chance against Marvel's repulsor rays" (11)? Why does he think Marvel is winning the "smackdown" between the two rival companies at the time this essay was written? Is this assessment accurate today? Why or why not?

STRATEGIES AND STRUCTURES

1. In his comparison of Marvel and DC, does Wolk cite mostly differences or similarities? Explain by pointing to specific places in the text.

2. Corporations have a way of being faceless. How does Wolk address this problem in his comparison and contrast of Marvel and DC? Is it a successful solution? Why or why not?

---

2. *Arrested Development*: A sitcom that aired on FOX from 2003 to 2006; the gag referenced here is from a delayed fourth season that was released by Netflix in 2013.

3. The final episode of *Agents of S.H.I.E.L.D.* aired in August 2020.

3. In paragraph 2, Wolk uses the subject-by-subject method to compare DC and Marvel. What specific traits and characteristics does he identify on the two sides? Is the comparison well balanced? Explain.

4. Wolk is using comparison and contrast as a handy way of developing a critical EVALUATION. What is the subject of that analysis, and how does Wolk use this method to make his point?

5. *Other Methods.* Wolk chooses Iron Man and Batman as representative EXAMPLES of the two companies they belong to. Are they good examples? Why or why not?

THINKING ABOUT LANGUAGE

1. "Smackdown" is a term from entertainment wrestling. Why does Wolk use it here? How appropriate is the term to his subject?

2. Explain the METAPHORICAL implications of Wolk's use of the phrase "fragile ecosystem" (3). What about his use of the term "détente" (4)?

3. "Squadron Sinister" (4) reverses the usual order of modifier-noun in English. What effect do you think Marvel was shooting for when the company did this in its battle with DC?

4. Wolk isn't comparing baseball players, so what "wind-up" is he referring to (8)?

5. Why does the Marvel Entertainment division of the Walt Disney Company refer to its film business as "Marvel Cinematic Universe" (11) rather than, say, "Marvel Movies" or "Marvel Cinema"?

FOR WRITING

1. Make a list of the traits you would cite in comparing and contrasting your two favorite superheroes.

2. For all their strengths, superheroes have their characteristic weaknesses as well. Write an essay of 500 to 700 words comparing two or more superheroes, but pay as much attention to their shortcomings as you do to their powers—and how those imperfections might or might not make them appeal more directly to readers or viewers.

3. In a fight, Wolk claims, Marvel Entertainment would thrash its DC rival. Is he right? Do some additional research on the economic and creative positions of the two companies, and write your own "smackdown" comparison of these entertainment giants. What new examples can you include that have been released since 2013, when this essay was written? Be sure to say what the loser needs to do to improve its game.

4. Write a five-to-seven-paragraph LITERACY NARRATIVE based on your (and your friends') recollections of reading comic books or watching comic book movies as a kid. Refer to particular characters and episodes, and explain what they taught you not only about reading and storytelling but also about life and fantasy.

DAVID SEDARIS

Remembering My Childhood
on the Continent of Africa

David Sedaris (b. 1956) made a name for himself as an elf in "Santaland," the story about working with the Santas at Macy's that he told on National Public Radio's *Morning Edition* in 1992. His hilarious autobiographical tales have been a public radio staple ever since, and his numerous book-length collections, beginning with *Barrel Fever* (1994), have all been best-sellers. In 2001, Sedaris won the Thurber Prize for American Humor and was named Humorist of the Year by *Time* magazine. His recent books include *Calypso* (2018), a collection of essays from the perspective of middle age, and *Happy-Go-Lucky* (2022), in which Sedaris documents his personal experiences in the changed America he finds during and after the COVID-19 pandemic and other turmoil of recent years.

Lopsided comparisons have always been a rich source of comedy. In "Remembering My Childhood on the Continent of Africa," taken from his collection *Me Talk Pretty One Day* (2000), Sedaris juxtaposes his own "unspeakably dull" childhood in Raleigh, North Carolina, with the African childhood of his partner, Hugh Hamrick, a diplomat's son.

WHEN HUGH WAS IN THE FIFTH GRADE, his class took a field trip to an Ethiopian slaughterhouse. He was living in Addis Ababa at the time, and the slaughterhouse was chosen because, he says, "it was convenient." 1

This was a school system in which the matter of proximity outweighed such petty concerns as what may or may not be appropriate for a busload of eleven-year-olds. 2

MLA CITATION: Sedaris, David. "Remembering My Childhood on the Continent of Africa." *Back to the Lake: A Reader and Guide for Writers*, edited by Thomas Cooley, 5th ed., W. W. Norton, 2024, pp. 433–39.

"What?" I asked. "Were there no autopsies scheduled at the local morgue? Was the federal prison just a bit too far out of the way?"

Hugh defends his former school, saying, "Well, isn't that the whole point of a 3 field trip? To see something new?"

"Technically yes, but . . ."   4

"All right then," he says. "So we saw some new things."   5

One of his field trips was literally a trip to a field where the class watched a wrin- 6 kled man fill his mouth with rotten goat meat and feed it to a pack of waiting hyenas. On another occasion they were taken to examine the bloodied bedroom curtains hanging in the palace of the former dictator. There were tamer trips, to textile facto- ries and sugar refineries, but my favorite is always the slaughterhouse. It wasn't a big

> To compare two subjects in depth like this, use the subject-by-subject method (pp. 406–7).

company, just a small rural enterprise run by a couple of brothers operating out of a low-ceilinged concrete building. Following a brief lecture on the importance of proper sanitation, a small white piglet was herded into the room, its dainty hooves clicking against the concrete floor. The class gath- ered in a circle to get a better look at the animal, who seemed delighted with the attention he was getting. He turned from face to face and was looking up at Hugh when one of the brothers drew a pistol from his back pocket, held it against the animal's temple, and shot the piglet, execution-style. Blood spattered, frightened children wept, and the man with the gun offered the teacher and bus driver some meat from a freshly slaughtered goat.

When I'm told such stories, it's all I can do to hold back my feelings of jealousy. An 7 Ethiopian slaughterhouse. Some people have all the luck. When I was in elementary school, the best we ever got was a trip to Old Salem or Colonial Williamsburg, one of those preserved brick villages where time supposedly stands still and someone earns his living as a town crier. There was always a blacksmith, a group of wandering patri- ots, and a collection of bonneted women hawking corn bread or gingersnaps made "the ol'-fashioned way." Every now and then you might come across a doer of bad deeds serving time in the stocks, but that was generally as exciting as it got.

Certain events are parallel, but compared with Hugh's, my childhood was unspeak- 8 ably dull. When I was seven years old, my family moved to North Carolina. When he was seven years old, Hugh's family moved to the Congo. We had a collie and a house cat. They had a monkey and two horses named Charlie Brown and Satan. I threw stones at stop signs. Hugh threw stones at crocodiles. The verbs are the same, but he definitely wins the prize when it comes to nouns and objects. An eventful day for my mother might have involved a trip to the dry cleaner or a conversation with the potato- chip deliveryman. Asked one ordinary Congo afternoon what she'd done with her day, Hugh's mother answered that she and a fellow member of the Ladies' Club had visited a leper colony on the outskirts of Kinshasa. No reason was given for the expedition, though chances are she was staking it out for a future field trip.

A typical field trip for Hugh: a small, rural slaughterhouse.

Due to his upbringing, Hugh sits through inane movies never realizing that 9
they're often based on inane television shows. There were no poker-faced sitcom
martians in his part of Africa, no oil-rich hillbillies or aproned brides trying to wean
themselves from the practice of witchcraft.[1] From time to time a movie would arrive
packed in a dented canister, the film scratched and faded from its slow trip around
the world. The theater consisted of a few dozen folding chairs arranged before a
bedsheet or the blank wall of a vacant hangar out near the airstrip. Occasionally a
man would sell warm soft drinks out of a cardboard box, but that was it in terms of
concessions.

When I was young, I went to the theater at the nearby shopping center and 10
watched a movie about a talking Volkswagen. I believe the little car had a taste for
mischief but I can't be certain, as both the movie and the afternoon proved unremarkable and have faded from my memory. Hugh saw the same movie a few years
after it was released. His family had left the Congo by this time and were living in
Ethiopia. Like me, Hugh saw the movie by himself on a weekend afternoon. Unlike
me, he left the theater two hours later, to find a dead man hanging from a telephone pole at the far end of the unpaved parking lot. None of the people who'd seen

1. *Martians . . . practice of witchcraft*: References to *My Favorite Martian*, *The Beverly Hillbillies*, and
Bewitched, popular US TV shows in the 1960s.

A typical field trip for David: Colonial Williamsburg.

the movie seemed to care about the dead man. They stared at him for a moment or two and then headed home, saying they'd never seen anything as crazy as that talking Volkswagen. His father was late picking him up, so Hugh just stood there for an hour, watching the dead man dangle and turn in the breeze. The death was not reported in the newspaper, and when Hugh related the story to his friends, they said, "You saw the movie about the talking car?"

I could have done without the flies and the primitive theaters, but I wouldn't have minded growing up with a houseful of servants. In North Carolina it wasn't unusual to have a once-a-week maid, but Hugh's family had houseboys, a word that never fails to charge my imagination. They had cooks and drivers, and guards who occupied a gatehouse, armed with machetes. Seeing as I had regularly petitioned my parents for an electric fence, the business with the guards strikes me as the last word in quiet sophistication. Having protection suggests that you are important. Having that protection paid for by the government is even better, as it suggests your safety is of interest to someone other than yourself.

Hugh's father was a career officer with the U.S. State Department, and every morning a black sedan carried him off to the embassy. I'm told it's not as glamorous as it sounds, but in terms of fun for the entire family, I'm fairly confident that it beats the sack race at the annual IBM picnic. By the age of three, Hugh was already carrying a diplomatic passport. The rules that applied to others did not apply to him. No tickets, no arrests, no luggage search: he was officially licensed to act like a brat. Being an American, it was expected of him, and who was he to deny the world an occasional tantrum?

They weren't rich, but what Hugh's family lacked financially they more than 13 made up for with the sort of exoticism that works wonders at cocktail parties, leading always to the remark "That sounds fascinating." It's a compliment one rarely receives when describing an adolescence spent drinking Icees at the North Hills Mall. No fifteen-foot python ever wandered onto my school's basketball court. I begged, I prayed nightly, but it just never happened. Neither did I get to witness a military coup in which forces sympathetic to the colonel arrived late at night to assassinate my next-door neighbor. Hugh had been at the Addis Ababa teen club when the electricity was cut off and soldiers arrived to evacuate the building. He and his friends had to hide in the back of a jeep and cover themselves with blankets during the ride home. It's something that sticks in his mind for one reason or another.

> Would Sedaris's adolescence make him a better sidekick for Batman or Iron Man (p. 426)?

Among my personal highlights is the memory of having my picture taken with 14 Uncle Paul, the legally blind host of a Raleigh children's television show. Among Hugh's is the memory of having his picture taken with Buzz Aldrin on the last leg of the astronaut's world tour. The man who had walked on the moon placed his hand on Hugh's shoulder and offered to sign his autograph book. The man who led Wake County schoolchildren in afternoon song turned at the sound of my voice and asked, "So what's your name, princess?"

When I was fourteen years old, I was sent to spend ten days with my maternal 15 grandmother in western New York State. She was a small and private woman named Billie, and though she never came right out and asked, I had the distinct impression she had no idea who I was. It was the way she looked at me, squinting through her glasses while chewing on her lower lip. That, coupled with the fact that she never once called me by name. "Oh," she'd say, "are you still here?" She was just beginning her long struggle with Alzheimer's disease, and each time I entered the room, I felt the need to reintroduce myself and set her at ease. "Hi, it's me. Sharon's boy, David. I was just in the kitchen admiring your collection of ceramic toads." Aside from a few trips to summer camp, this was the longest I'd ever been away from home, and I like to think I was toughened by the experience.

About the same time I was frightening my grandmother, Hugh and his family 16 were packing their belongings for a move to Somalia. There were no English-speaking schools in Mogadishu, so, after a few months spent lying around the family compound with his pet monkey, Hugh was sent back to Ethiopia to live with a beer enthusiast his father had met at a cocktail party. Mr. Hoyt installed security systems in foreign embassies. He and his family gave Hugh a room. They invited him to join them at the table, but that was as far as they extended themselves. No one ever asked him when his birthday was, so when the day came, he kept it to himself. There was no telephone service between Ethiopia and Somalia, and letters to his parents were sent to Washington and then forwarded on to Mogadishu, meaning that his news was more than a month old by the time they got it. I suppose it wasn't much different than living as a foreign-exchange student. Young people do it all the time, but to me it sounds awful. The Hoyts had two sons about Hugh's age who were always saying things like "Hey that's *our* sofa you're sitting on" and "Hands off that ornamental stein. It doesn't belong to you."

He'd been living with these people for a year when he overheard Mr. Hoyt tell a   17
friend that he and his family would soon be moving to Munich, Germany, the beer capital of the world.

"And that worried me," Hugh said, "because it meant I'd have to find some other   18
place to live."

Where I come from, finding shelter is a problem the average teenager might con-   19
fidently leave to his parents. It was just something that came with having a mom and a dad. Worried that he might be sent to live with his grandparents in Kentucky, Hugh turned to the school's guidance counselor, who knew of a family whose son had recently left for college. And so he spent another year living with strangers and not mentioning his birthday. While I wouldn't have wanted to do it myself, I can't help but envy the sense of fortitude he gained from the experience. After graduating from college, he moved to France knowing only the phrase "Do you speak French?"—a question guaranteed to get you nowhere unless you also speak the language.

While living in Africa, Hugh and his family took frequent vacations, often in the   20
company of their monkey. The Nairobi Hilton, some suite of high-ceilinged rooms in Cairo or Khartoum: these are the places his people recall when gathered at a common table. "Was that the summer we spent in Beirut or, no, I'm thinking of the time we sailed from Cyprus and took the *Orient Express* to Istanbul."

Theirs was the life I dreamt about during my vacations in eastern North Caro-   21
lina. Hugh's family was hobnobbing with chiefs and sultans while I ate hush puppies at the Sanitary Fish Market in Morehead City, a beach towel wrapped like a hijab around my head.[2] Someone unknown to me was very likely standing in a muddy ditch and dreaming of an evening spent sitting in a clean family restaurant, drinking iced tea and working his way through an extra-large seaman's platter, but that did not concern me, as it meant I should have been happy with what I had. Rather than surrender to my bitterness, I have learned to take satisfaction in the life that Hugh has led. His stories have, over time, become my own. I say this with no trace of a kumbaya.[3] There is no spiritual symbiosis; I'm just a petty thief who lifts

---

2. *Hijab*: A veil worn by Muslim women. *Hush puppies*: Small deep-fried balls of cornmeal dough.

3. *Kumbaya*: The title and refrain of an African American folk song that originated as a slave spiritual. The song was a popular hit in the 1960s and is sung by many youth organizations; the word has come to be associated with unity and closeness.

his memories the same way I'll take a handful of change left on his dresser. When my own experiences fall short of the mark, I just go out and spend some of his. It is with pleasure that I sometimes recall the dead man's purpled face or the report of the handgun ringing in my ears as I studied the blood pooling beneath the dead white piglet. On the way back from the slaughterhouse, we stopped for Cokes in the village of Mojo, where the gas-station owner had arranged a few tables and chairs beneath a dying canopy of vines. It was late afternoon by the time we returned to school, where a second bus carried me to the foot of Coffeeboard Road. Once there, I walked through a grove of eucalyptus trees and alongside a bald pasture of starving cattle, past the guard napping in his gatehouse, and into the waiting arms of my monkey. ◆

FOR CLOSE READING

1. As children in school, both David Sedaris and Hugh Hamrick took occasional field trips. What is Sedaris's point in comparing their experiences of these trips? Broadly speaking, how do they compare?

2. Why did Sedaris find the movie about a talking Volkswagen to be "unremarkable" (10)? How did Hugh react to it, and why was his experience so different?

3. Instead of surrendering to his "bitterness," Sedaris has learned "to take satisfaction" from Hugh's account of his childhood (21). Why does Sedaris claim to be bitter, and how seriously are we supposed to take his claim?

4. Besides satisfaction and loose change, what else has Sedaris learned to "take" from Hugh's life?

5. Whose childhood would you prefer to remember having lived, Sedaris's or Hugh's? Why?

STRATEGIES AND STRUCTURES

1. In comparing his early life with that of his partner, Sedaris emphasizes the differences. On what basis does he compare their experiences nevertheless? What did their childhoods have in common?

2. In paragraph 8, Sedaris uses the **POINT-BY-POINT** method to organize his comparison. What would have been the result if he had kept on alternating like this between his two subjects throughout the rest of the essay? Explain.

3. How sufficient do you find Sedaris's main points of comparison for explaining his jealousy of Hugh's childhood (7)? How and how well do they prepare us for the ending, in which Sedaris takes over his friend's memories?

4. *Other Methods.* Sedaris's comparison includes many elements of personal **NARRATIVE**. What are some of them? (Cite specific examples from the text.) How would the essay be different without any narrative?

THINKING ABOUT LANGUAGE

1. His life and Hugh's shared the same verbs, says Sedaris, but different nouns and objects (8). What does Sedaris mean by this, and why is he comparing the lives of two boys to grammatical parts of speech?

2. Among the "personal highlights" of his childhood, says Sedaris, is "the memory of having my picture taken with Uncle Paul, the legally blind host of a Raleigh children's television show" (14). How is Sedaris using IRONY here?

3. A "hijab" is a veil (21). What sort of hijab does Sedaris wear in the Sanitary Fish Market in Morehead City?

4. Sedaris describes himself as a "petty thief" (21). What is he stealing in this essay, and what has caused him to sink to this level?

FOR WRITING

1. Ask a friend or family member to write down recollections of an important event that you have both experienced. You do the same. Then, in a paragraph or so, compare and contrast the two versions.

2. In a four-to-six-paragraph essay, compare your childhood with that of someone whose early experience was very different from your own. Your counterpart can be someone you know personally or someone you don't know, as long as you're familiar with details of their childhood.

3. Write a critical EVALUATION of one of Sedaris's essays or books. In addition to explaining why you liked (or didn't like) the essay or book, compare and contrast representative passages or events in the text, and use them as examples to help explain what the text is about and how it works, including what makes it humorous (or not).

4. Discuss this or some other Sedaris essay (or essays) with several of your class-mates. Take notes on one another's readings and reactions, and give an oral report comparing and contrasting the different views.

BRUCE CATTON

Grant and Lee: A Study in Contrasts

Bruce Catton (1899–1978) grew up in Benzonia, Michigan, listening to the stories told by Union army veterans and re-enacting the battles of the Civil War. After serving briefly in the US Navy during World War I, Catton worked as a reporter until the outbreak of World War II, during which he served as director of information for the War Production Board. A founding editor of *American Heritage* magazine, he wrote many volumes about the Civil War, including *A Stillness at Appomattox* (1954), which won a Pulitzer Prize and a National Book Award. In 1976, President Gerald Ford presented Catton with the Medal of Freedom award for "making us hear the shouts of battle and cherish peace."

Many historians today agree that Catton brought the war to life, but critics point out that he portrayed it as an epic military and political clash between overwhelmingly White forces, with little mention of Black soldiers and leaders such as Frederick Douglass. Recognizing this shortcoming, perhaps, Catton wrote near the end of his life that in "regarding the past so fondly we are unable to get it in proper focus, and we see virtues that were not there."

"Grant and Lee: A Study in Contrasts" was first published in *The American Story* (1955), a collection of essays by leading historians. Catton compares the Civil War generals Ulysses S. Grant, who led the Union army, and Robert E. Lee, who led the forces of the Confederacy.

W HEN ULYSSES S. GRANT and Robert E. Lee met in the parlor of a modest house 1 at Appomattox Court House, Virginia, on April 9, 1865, to work out the terms for the surrender of Lee's Army of Northern Virginia, a great chapter in American life came to a close, and a great new chapter began.

MLA CITATION: Catton, Bruce. "Grant and Lee: A Study in Contrasts." *Back to the Lake: A Reader and Guide for Writers*, edited by Thomas Cooley, 5th ed., W. W. Norton, 2024, pp. 441–45.

These men were bringing the Civil War[1] to its virtual finish. To be sure, other armies had yet to surrender, and for a few days the fugitive Confederate government would struggle desperately and vainly, trying to find some way to go on living now that its chief support was gone. But in effect it was all over when Grant and Lee signed the papers. And the little room where they wrote out the terms was the scene of one of the poignant, dramatic contrasts in American history.

They were two strong men, these oddly different generals, and they represented the strengths of two conflicting currents that, through them, had come into final collision.

Back of Robert E. Lee was the notion that the old aristocratic concept might somehow survive and be dominant in American life.

Lee was tidewater Virginia,[2] and in his background were family, culture, and tradition . . . the age of chivalry transplanted to a New World which was making its own legends and its own myths. He embodied a way of life that had come down through the age of knighthood and the English country squire. America was a land that was beginning all over again, dedicated to nothing much more complicated than the rather hazy belief that all men had equal rights and should have an equal chance in the world. In such a land Lee stood for the feeling that it was somehow of advantage to human society to have a pronounced inequality in the social structure. There should be a leisure class, backed by ownership of land; in turn, society itself should be keyed to the land as the chief source of wealth and influence. It would bring forth (according to this ideal) a class of men with a strong sense of obligation to the community; men who lived not to gain advantage for themselves, but to meet the solemn obligations which had been laid on them by the very fact that they were privileged. From them the country would get its leadership; to them it could look for the higher values—of thought, of conduct, of personal deportment—to give it strength and virtue.

Lee embodied the noblest elements of this aristocratic ideal. Through him, the landed nobility justified itself. For four years, the Southern states had fought a desperate war to uphold the ideals for which Lee stood. In the end, it almost seemed as if the Confederacy fought for Lee; as if he himself was the Confederacy . . . the best thing that the way of life for which the Confederacy stood could ever have to offer.

1. *Civil War* (1861–1865): The war fought between those states and territories of the United States that remained loyal to the federal government in Washington under President Abraham Lincoln ("the Union") and the slaveholding Southern states that formed a separate government led by Jefferson Davis ("the Confederacy").

2. *Tidewater Virginia*: The coastal plain region of eastern Virginia, where rivers receive tidal inflow from the Chesapeake Bay, which is traditionally associated with aristocracy and old families. The first English colony in North America, Jamestown, settled in 1607, is in the Tidewater area.

Lee's surrender to Grant at Appomattox Court House, Virginia, on April 9, 1865, as depicted in a Currier and Ives lithograph.

He had passed into legend before Appomattox. Thousands of tired, underfed, poorly clothed Confederate soldiers, long since past the simple enthusiasm of the early days of the struggle, somehow considered Lee the symbol of everything for which they had been willing to die. But they could not quite put this feeling into words. If the Lost Cause, sanctified by so much heroism and so many deaths, had a living justification, its justification was General Lee.

Grant, the son of a tanner on the Western frontier, was everything Lee was not. 7 He had come up the hard way and embodied nothing in particular except the eternal toughness and sinewy fiber of the men who grew up beyond the mountains. He was one of a body of men who owed reverence and obeisance to no one, who were self-reliant to a fault, who cared hardly anything for the past but who had a sharp eye for the future.

> Catton's comparison is turning out to be mostly contrast (pp. 400 and 402).

These frontier men were the precise opposites of the tidewater aristocrats. Back 8 of them, in the great surge that had taken people over the Alleghenies[3] and into the opening Western country, there was a deep, implicit dissatisfaction with a past that had settled into grooves. They stood for democracy, not from any reasoned conclusion about the proper ordering of human society, but simply because they had grown up in the middle of democracy and knew how it worked. Their society might have privileges, but they would be privileges each man had won for himself. Forms and patterns meant nothing. No man was born to anything, except perhaps to a chance to show how far he could rise. Life was competition.

Yet along with this feeling had come a deep sense of belonging to a national com- 9 munity. The Westerner who developed a farm, opened a shop, or set up in business as a trader, could hope to prosper only as his own community prospered—and his community ran from the Atlantic to the Pacific and from Canada down to Mexico. If the land was settled, with towns and highways and accessible markets, he could better himself. He saw his fate in terms of the nation's own destiny. As its horizons expanded, so did his. He had, in other words, an acute dollars-and-cents stake in the continued growth and development of his country.

And that, perhaps, is where the contrast between Grant and Lee becomes most 10 striking. The Virginia aristocrat, inevitably, saw himself in relation to his own region. He lived in a static society which could endure almost anything except change. Instinctively, his first loyalty would go to the locality in which that society existed. He would fight to the limit of endurance to defend it, because in defending it he was defending everything that gave his own life its deepest meaning.

The Westerner, on the other hand, would fight with an equal tenacity for the 11 broader concept of society. He fought so because everything he lived by was tied to

---

3. *Alleghenies:* The Allegheny Mountains, which run from northern Pennsylvania to southwestern Virginia.

growth, expansion, and a constantly widening horizon. What he lived by would survive or fall with the nation itself. He could not possibly stand by unmoved in the face of an attempt to destroy the Union. He would combat it with everything he had, because he could only see it as an effort to cut the ground out from under his feet.

So Grant and Lee were in complete contrast, representing two diametrically opposed elements in American life. Grant was the modern man emerging; beyond him, ready to come on the stage, was the great age of steel and machinery, of crowded cities and a restless burgeoning vitality. Lee might have ridden down from the old age of chivalry, lance in hand, silken banner fluttering over his head. Each man was the perfect champion of his cause, drawing both his strengths and his weaknesses from the people he led. 12

Yet it was not all contrast, after all. Different as they were—in background, in personality, in underlying aspiration—these two great soldiers had much in common. Under everything else, they were marvelous fighters. Furthermore, their fighting qualities were really very much alike. 13

Each man had, to begin with, the great virtue of utter tenacity and fidelity. Grant fought his way down the Mississippi Valley in spite of acute personal discouragement and profound military handicaps. Lee hung on in the trenches at Petersburg after hope itself had died. In each man there was an indomitable quality . . . the born fighter's refusal to give up as long as he can still remain on his feet and lift his two fists.

> For winding up a comparison, the point-by-point method (pp. 406–7) can be especially useful.

Daring and resourcefulness they had, too; the ability to think faster and move faster than the enemy. These were the qualities which gave Lee the dazzling campaigns of Second Manassas and Chancellorsville and won Vicksburg for Grant. 15

Lastly, and perhaps greatest of all, there was the ability, at the end, to turn quickly from war to peace once the fighting was over. Out of the way these two men behaved at Appomattox came the possibility of a peace of reconciliation. It was a possibility not wholly realized, in the years to come, but which did, in the end, help the two sections to become one nation again . . . after a war whose bitterness might have seemed to make such a reunion wholly impossible. No part of either man's life became him more than the part he played in this brief meeting in the McLean house at Appomattox. Their behavior there put all succeeding generations of Americans in their debt. Two great Americans, Grant and Lee—very different, yet under everything very much alike. Their encounter at Appomattox was one of the great moments of American history. ◆ 16

FOR CLOSE READING

1. According to Bruce Catton, Grant and Lee represented two distinct "currents" in American life and history (3). What were those currents, and what contrasting qualities and ideals does Catton associate with each man?

2. Even though they were "in complete contrast," says Catton, Grant and Lee also "had much in common" (12, 13). In what ways were the two men alike?

3. Although Grant and Lee were both "great Americans" (16), according to Catton, they were deadly enemies. Why did each man take the side he did?

4. Why, according to Catton, are all future generations of Americans "in their debt" (16)? Do you agree? Why or why not?

STRATEGIES AND STRUCTURES

1. On what basis is Catton comparing his two subjects? Where does he tell the reader what that basis of comparison is?

2. Why does Catton emphasize the differences between the two men he's comparing? For what AUDIENCE and PURPOSE is he drawing such a strong contrast?

3. Catton uses the SUBJECT-BY-SUBJECT method through most of his essay. When and why does he switch to the POINT-BY-POINT method?

4. *Other Methods.* Besides comparing and contrasting the two generals, Catton's study also analyzes the CAUSES and EFFECTS of the American Civil War. How does this analysis support and clarify his comparison?

THINKING ABOUT LANGUAGE

1. What view of history—and Grant's and Lee's roles in it—is suggested by Catton's use of language from the theater in paragraphs 2 and 16?

2. "Lee was tidewater Virginia" (5). Why doesn't Catton simply say, "Lee was from tidewater Virginia"? What's the difference? Explain where and how well Catton develops his extended METAPHOR about Lee.

3. Why do you think Catton capitalizes "Lost Cause" in paragraph 6?

4. "Obeisance" (7) means homage of the sort paid to a king. Why might Catton choose this term instead of "obedience" when describing General Grant?

5. What are the CONNOTATIONS of "sinewy fiber" (7), and how does Catton's general DESCRIPTION of Grant justify the use of this phrase?

FOR WRITING

1. Create an outline of the key points you would make in a comparison and contrast of two famous generals, great athletes, favorite aunts, or other people.

2. Write a six-to-eight-paragraph essay comparing and contrasting two present-day public figures—for example, two US presidents—whose actions, you feel, will have a major impact on all succeeding generations of Americans.

3. Do a **RHETORICAL ANALYSIS** of the portrait of Lee surrendering to Grant on p. 443. Compare it with other Currier and Ives lithographs of the period and also with what Catton says about the two men in the picture.

4. Write a 500-to-600-word research **REPORT** on one of the following: Lee after Appomattox or Grant's years in the White House. Don't forget to compare the postwar figure with the wartime hero. Cite your sources.

5. *The Personal Memoirs of U. S. Grant* was published by Grant's friend Mark Twain in 1885–86. Do some research on the history of the book—and the relationship between the two men—and write a **REPORT** comparing them as friends and writers.

VANESSA BOHNS

Your Power of Persuasion

Vanessa Bohns (b. 1978) is a social psychologist and professor of organizational behavior at Cornell University. A graduate of Brown University, Bohns earned a PhD in social psychology from Columbia University in 2007. Before joining the faculty at Cornell, she taught at the University of Toronto and the University of Waterloo in Ontario, Canada. Bohns's research focuses on the social psychology of power, influence, and persuasion. In particular, she studies and writes about ways in which people often underestimate their ability to influence others in such interpersonal situations as asking for help, suggesting that someone engage in unethical behavior, and making romantic advances. She is a recipient of the Rising Star Award from the Association for Psychological Science and an associate editor of the *Journal of Personality and Social Psychology*.

"Your Power of Persuasion" is part of a chapter from *You Have More Influence than You Think* (2020), Bohns's book based on recent studies in social psychology that suggest we not only underestimate our powers of persuasion, but we also sometimes use, as she says, "overly aggressive tactics in order to gain the influence we don't realize we already have." Often, Bohns implies, our lack of self-confidence comes from making comparisons between ourselves and others that are statistically invalid.

WHO DO YOU THINK goes to more parties, you or other people? Who has more   1
friends? Who has a wider social network? Who sees and interacts with their family more? Who is closer to the "inner circle" of your social group?

MLA CITATION: Bohns, Vanessa. "Your Power of Persuasion." *Back to the Lake: A Reader and Guide for Writers*, edited by Thomas Cooley, 5th ed., W. W. Norton, 2024, pp. 448–52.

Sebastian Deri, a social psychologist at Cornell University, in collaboration with   2
fellow psychologists Shai Davidai and Tom Gilovich, asked more than 3,000 participants across eleven studies these very questions.[1] Study participants were shoppers
in a mall, college students on campus, and online survey respondents. In
some studies, the average participant was nineteen years old, in others the
average participant was thirty-seven years old. In each of these demograph-
ically diverse samples, people reported believing, on average, that they
went to fewer parties, had fewer friends, dined out less, saw their extended
family less, and were further removed from the "inner circle" or "in-crowd"
than their peers. In other words, college students living on campus away
from their parents, surrounded by co-eds and fraternities, believed themselves to be less socially active than their peers. At the same time, adults in
their mid-to-late thirties juggling work and family also believed that *they*
were less socially active than *their* peers.

> By using "fewer" for items that are counted and "less" for quantities that are measured, Bohns avoids a common error in comparisons. For others, see p. 410.

For a long time, it seemed as if researchers were constantly uncovering new ways   3
in which people were overconfident. We now know the average person thinks they
are more athletic,[2] moral,[3] creative,[4] and a better driver[5] than the average person
(which, I must point out, is not possible by definition). However, in contrast to the
long list of contexts in which people have been shown to display overconfidence, in
recent years research has been converging around a very different conclusion when
it comes to our beliefs about our proficiency for things like, say, winning friends and
influencing people.

When interpreting Deri's findings, one thing we can be sure of is that the average   4
person does *not* have a below-average social life. That would be as illogical a conclusion as the one reached by all those "above-average" drivers out there on the road—
just in the opposite direction. Clearly, people are making some sort of error when
assessing their own social prowess. But if people think they are more intelligent, more
moral, more creative, and better drivers than average—that is, if we tend to be *overconfident* in all of those other contexts—why would we be *underconfident* in this one?

---

1. Sebastian Deri, Shai Davidai, and Thomas Gilovich, "Home alone: Why people believe others' social lives are richer than their own," *Journal of Personality and Social Psychology* 113, no. 6 (2017): 858, https://doi.org/10.1037/pspa0000105.

2. Mark D. Alicke and Olesya Govorun, "The better-than-average effect," in *The Self in Social Judgment*, ed. M. D. Alicke, D. A. Dunning, and J. I. Krueger, 85–106 (Psychology Press, 2005).

3. Nicholas Epley and David Dunning, "Feeling 'holier than thou': Are self-serving assessments produced by errors in self- or social prediction?" *Journal of Personality and Social Psychology* 79, no. 6 (2000): 861, https://doi.org/10.1037/0022-3514.79.6.861.

4. Elanor F. Williams and Thomas Gilovich, "Do people really believe they are above average?" *Journal of Experimental Social Psychology* 44 (2008): 1121–1128, https://doi.org/10.1016/j.jesp.2008.01.002.

5. Ola Svenson, "Are we all less risky and more skillful than our fellow drivers?" *Acta Psychologica* 47, no. 2 (1981):143–148, https://doi.org/10.1016/0001-6918(81)90005-6.

Deri and colleagues explain this by describing who and what is most salient 5
when we reflect on where we fit within a normal distribution of these categories of
behavior. If, for example, I ask you how good a driver you are, you will most likely
look inward to your own experiences with driving. You will think of your last time
behind the wheel and recall how you bravely and steadily navigated the [insert that
road with all the reckless drivers in your area here]. And you would firmly pat
yourself on the back, confident in all that above-average driving you were doing.

Indeed, when Deri and his colleagues asked participants how they would answer 6
a series of nonsocial questions, such as how they would determine whether the size
of their vocabulary (rather than their social network) was smaller or larger than
others, and whether they cooked (rather than dined out) more or less than others,
they said that in order to answer these questions they would be more likely to look
inward to their own traits, abilities, and behaviors. And it turns out that participants in Deri's studies also displayed the typical overconfidence effect for these
nonsocial questions—for example, they thought they had larger-than-average
vocabularies and cooked more often than other people.

On the other hand, if I ask you about your social life, your attention will most 7
likely be directed outward to the social lives of others. After all, other people are a
critical part of the whole concept of being social. Indeed, this is how Deri's participants said they would answer the specifically social sorts of questions at the beginning of this section. In order to determine the relative size of their social network
and frequency of dining out, for example, participants said they would be more
likely to look outward to other people's traits, behaviors, and abilities.

Importantly, however, the people we compare ourselves to when we engage in 8
such an exercise aren't just any people. They are the people who come to
mind most easily when we consider what it means to be social. In other
words, when evaluating our own social lives, we tend to conjure up and
compare ourselves to *exemplars* of sociability who, by definition, are exceptionally social. We think of the people who were partying down the hall
when we were studying alone in our dorm room, or the people whose photos of
concerts and parties we scroll through while we are curled up on the couch. At the
same time, we don't think of the dozen or so other students who were also trying to
study in their dorm rooms in that same hall that night, or all the other homebodies
scrolling through other people's photos at the same time we are. Therefore, we
think that we are less sociable than the average person because we don't actually
compare ourselves to the average person—we compare ourselves to the prototypical
social butterfly.

> Comparisons
> are all about
> relationships
> (p. 402).

All of this is important for our purposes because these same comparisons factor 9
into our evaluations of our own power of persuasion. When we try to assess the
amount of influence we have, we tend to think of social media influencers, trendset-

ters, gurus, power brokers—exemplars of what it means to have influence. And when we inevitably fail to stack up against these prototypical influencers, we conclude that we are subpar. But just like not getting an invitation to the Met Gala doesn't mean you have an inferior social life, not having a tweet that goes viral or not having 100,000 followers on *Instagram* doesn't mean you are an inferior influencer. Because most people *weren't* invited to the Met Gala. Most tweets *don't* go viral. And most people *don't* have 100,000 *Instagram* followers.

What this also suggests is that another way in which we have more influence 10 than we realize is that we are more socially connected than we realize. In other words, you have more reach, in marketing speak, than you think. This is true not only in "real life," but also on social media. A graph from 2013 entitled, "You're a bigger deal on *Twitter* than you think," depicts an analysis of the number of followers per *Twitter* account and finds that the median *Twitter* account has sixty-one followers (after eliminating any accounts that hadn't tweeted in the month prior, which, when included, bring the median down to one follower).[6] There are, indeed, a substantial number of accounts with tens or hundreds of thousands of followers, or more. If a *Twitter* user with, say, a respectable 1,000 followers were to compare themselves to those accounts, of course their influence would feel inconsequential. But, in fact, back in 2013 when the analysis was done, an account with 1,000 followers would have been in the *top 4%* of *Twitter* users based on followers.[7]

These analyses don't really get at social media users' psychological experience of 11 their own influence, however, so my graduate student Sangah Bae and I ran a couple of studies to do just that. Drawing from Deri's methods, we asked a sample of college students, and, later, a sample of working adults, "Who has more influence, friends/followers, and engagements—you, or others completing this survey?" for a group of different social media sites: *Facebook, Instagram, Twitter, Snapchat, LinkedIn,* and *TikTok.* What we found mirrored Deri and colleagues' findings: The average person in our studies thought they had less influence on social media than the average person in our studies.

> To support a new claim, Bohns introduces a new point of comparison (p. 408).

Recent research has begun to converge on the idea that we are in fact undercon- 12 fident when assessing personal qualities such as our social connectedness . . . and . . . our likability. Not only does this bias help to maintain a thriving self-

---

6. Robinson Meyer, "It's a lonely world: The median Twitter user has 1 measly follower," *The Atlantic,* December 19, 2013, https://www.theatlantic.com/technology/archive/2013/12/its-a-lonely-world-the-median-twitter-user-has-1-measly-follower/282513/.

7. Since 2013 may seem like ancient history in *Twitter* years, it's worth noting that a more recent analysis tells a similar story, although it breaks the data down differently: An analysis of *Twitter* data conducted by Stefan Wojcik and Adam Hughes of the Pew Research Center in 2019 found that the top 10% most prolific tweeters had a median of just 386 followers ("Sizing Up Twitter Users," April 24, 2019, https://www.pewresearch.org/internet/2019/04/24/sizing-up-twitter-users/).

improvement industry, it also suggests that we may regularly underestimate our own power of persuasion. Somewhat ironically, . . . this can lead us to use overly aggressive tactics in order to gain the influence we don't realize we already have. ◆

FOR CLOSE READING

1. How would you answer, with regard to yourself, each of the five questions with which Vanessa Bohns begins her essay?

2. By comparison with other people, how would you rate yourself—below average, average, better than average—in each of the four categories that Bohns lists in paragraph 3?

3. To what extent do your self-assessments confirm (or contradict) what Bohns and the researchers she cites have to say about feelings of both overconfidence and underconfidence in the general population (3, 4)?

4. How can Bohns be so sure that "the average person does *not* have a below-average social life" (4)? Explain.

STRATEGIES AND STRUCTURES

1. According to Bohns, why do people often judge themselves to be "above average" (5) in "nonsocial" (6) categories like driving ability and vocabulary size? By what standard are they COMPARING themselves to others "within a normal distribution of these categories" (5)?

2. When the categories are social, by contrast, Bohns says that most people see themselves as "less socially active than their peers" (2; also 7, 8). Why? What standard of comparison are they using then?

3. In a "normal distribution" (5), it is statistically impossible for most people to be either above average or below average. Does this mean that the standards of comparison that Bohns identifies in people's minds are false or invalid? Explain.

4. "All of this is important for our purposes," writes Bohns, "because these same comparisons factor into our evaluations of our own power of persuasion" (9). What are her PURPOSES in drawing all these comparisons, where does she state them most directly, and how effective is her use of statistical analysis to support her points?

5. *Other Methods.* Bohns's essay could be said to serve as the introduction to an ARGUMENT. If you agree, point to the paragraph where she states her THESIS. If you disagree, where would you add a thesis statement, and what would it be?

THINKING ABOUT LANGUAGE

1. Throughout her essay, Bohns switches among personal pronouns expressing three POINTS OF VIEW: second person—"Who do you think goes to more parties . . . ?" (1); third person—"adults . . . believed that *they* were less socially active" (2); and first

person (plural)—"when we reflect on where we fit" (5). What relationship between Bohns and her **AUDIENCE** does each of these different pronouns imply?

2. When assessing our social influence, Bohns claims, we tend to compare ourselves to "*exemplars*," which are "by definition" people who are "exceptionally social" (8). Is this a sufficient definition, or should Bohns have elaborated more fully on the meaning of this key term? Explain.

3. In the context of social behavior, how would you define an exemplar?

4. What constitutes an "influencer" on social media (9)? How and when did the term come into general use?

5. Citing data from 2013, Bohns discusses "the median *Twitter* account" (10) in terms of numbers of followers. Look up the **DEFINITION** of "median," and explain whether the 2013 numbers surprise you. Then do some research to find the number of followers of a median *Twitter* account today. How do the numbers compare?

FOR WRITING

1. Mark Twain is reputed to have said, "There are three kinds of lies: lies, damned lies, and statistics." Variations and attributions of this phrase have a long history. Look up some of them, and write a brief **REPORT** on the origin(s) and meaning(s) of this proverbial saying.

2. Using the second paragraph of Bohns's essay as a model, write a brief **SUMMARY** of one of the articles (or a similar source in the field) that she cites in "Your Power of Persuasion."

3. Do you really have more influence than you think? Address this question in a 600-to-800-word essay **COMPARING** yourself with other people, both actual and as a demographic group. Feel free to use the "categories of behavior" (5) that Bohns cites—or substitute your own.

4. How persuasive is "Your Power of Persuasion"? In a **CRITICAL ANALYSIS** of Bohns's essay, explain and evaluate not only the author's findings but the form and manner in which she presents them to her intended audience. Consider in particular her language use and her reliance on research studies, as well as her conclusions.

JENNINE CAPÓ CRUCET

Taking My Parents to College

Jennine Capó Crucet (b. 1981) is a writer of fiction and essays and has taught English and ethnic studies at the University of Nebraska–Lincoln. Capó Crucet grew up in Hialeah, Florida, just north of Miami. She majored in English and in feminist, gender, and sexuality studies at Cornell University and earned an MFA in creative writing from the University of Minnesota. In both her first story collection, *How to Leave Hialeah* (2009), and her first novel, *Make Your Home among Strangers* (2015), Capó Crucet writes about a young woman whose life "has been shaped by South Florida, its people and its landscape, and by the stories of Cuba repeated to me almost daily by my parents and *abuelos*."

In "Taking My Parents to College," Capó Crucet compares her experience of going off to college with that of her peers at an Ivy League school who are not the first in their families to go to college—or the first to be born in America. Originally published in the *New York Times* in 2015, this essay also forms the basis of Capó Crucet's introduction to her collection of essays called, with tongue in cheek, *My Time among the Whites* (2019).

IT WAS A SIMPLE QUESTION, but we couldn't find the answer in any of the paper-   1
work the college had sent. How long was my family supposed to stay for orientation? This was 1999, so Google wasn't really a verb yet, and we were a low-income family (according to my new school) without regular Internet access.

I was a first-generation college student as well as the first in our family to be born   2
in America—my parents were born in Cuba—and we didn't yet know that families were supposed to leave pretty much right after they unloaded your stuff from the car.

MLA CITATION: Capó Crucet, Jennine. "Taking My Parents to College." *Back to the Lake: A Reader and Guide for Writers*, edited by Thomas Cooley, 5th ed., W. W. Norton, 2024, pp. 454-57.

We all made the trip from Miami, my hometown, to what would be my new 3
home at Cornell University. Shortly after arriving on campus, the five of us—my
parents, my younger sister, my abuela and me—found ourselves listening to a dean
end his welcome speech with the words: "Now, parents, please: Go!"

Almost everyone in the audience laughed, but not me, and not my parents. They turned to me and said, "What does he mean, *Go*?" I was just as
confused as they were: We thought we *all* needed to be there for freshman
orientation—the whole family, for the entirety of it. My dad had booked
their hotel through the day after my classes officially began. They'd used all
their vacation days from work and had been saving for months to get me to
school and go through our orientation.

Every afternoon during that week, we had to go back to the only department 5
store we could find, the now-defunct Ames, for some stupid thing we hadn't known
was a necessity, something not in our budget: shower shoes, extra-long twin sheets,
mesh laundry bags. Before the other families left, we carefully watched them—they
knew what they were doing—and we made new shopping lists with our limited
vocabulary: *Those things that lift up the bed*, we wrote. *That plastic thing to carry stuff
to the bathroom.*

My family followed me around as I visited department offices during course reg- 6
istration. *Only four classes?* they asked, assuming I was mistakenly taking my first
semester too easy. They walked with me to buildings I was supposed to be finding
on my own. They waited outside those buildings so that we could all leave from
there and go to lunch together.

The five of us wandered each day through the dining hall's doors. "You guys are 7
still here!" the over-friendly person swiping ID cards said after day three. "They
sure are!" I chirped back, learning via the cues of my hallmates that I was supposed
to want my family gone. But it was an act: We sat together at meals—amid all the
other students, already making friends—my mom placing a napkin and fork at each
place, setting the table as we did at home.

I don't even remember the moment they drove away. I'm told it's one of those 8
instances you never forget, that second when you realize you're finally on your own.
But for me, it's not there—perhaps because, when you're the first in your family to
go to college, you never truly feel like they've let you go.

They did eventually leave—of course they did—and a week into classes, I received 9
the topics for what would be my first college paper, in an English course on the modern novel. I might as well have been my non-English-speaking grandmother trying to
read and understand them: The language felt that foreign. I called my mom at work
and in tears told her that I had to come home, that I'd made a terrible mistake.

She sighed into the phone and said: "Just read me the first question. We'll go 10
through it a little at a time and figure it out."

> Capó Crucet is emphasizing the *differences* between her subjects rather than their similarities, pp. 400 and 402.

456 ◆ Chapter 12: Comparison and Contrast

I read her the topic slowly, pausing after each sentence, waiting for her to say 11
something. The first topic was two paragraphs long. I remember it had the word
intersectionalities in it. And the word *gendered*. And maybe the phrase *theoretical
framework*. I waited for her response and for the ways it would encourage me, for
her to tell me I could do this, that I would eventually be the first in my family to
graduate from college.

"You're right," she said after a moment. "You're screwed." 12

Other parents—parents who have gone to college themselves—might have 13
known at that point to encourage their kid to go to office hours, or to the writing
center, or to ask for help. But my mom thought I was as alone as I feared.

"I have no idea what any of that means," she said. "I don't even know how it's a 14
question."

While my college had done an excellent job recruiting me, I had no road map for 15
what I was supposed to do once I made it to campus. I'd already embarrassed myself
by doing things like asking my R.A. what time the dorm closed for the night. As far
as I knew, there'd been no mandatory meeting geared toward first-generation students like me: Aside from a check-in with my financial aid officer when she
explained what work-study was (I didn't know and worried it meant I had to join the
army or something) and where she had me sign for my loans, I was mostly keeping
to myself to hide the fact that I was a very special kind of lost. I folded the sheet
with the paper topics in half and put it in my desk drawer.

"I don't know what you're gonna do," my mom almost laughed. "Maybe—have 16
you looked in the dictionary?"

I started crying harder, my hand over the receiver. 17

"You still there?" she eventually asked, clearly hiding her own tears. I murmured 18
Mmmhmm.

"Look, just stick it out up there until Christmas," she said. "We have no more 19
vacation days this year. We can't take off any more time to go get you."

"O.K.," I swallowed. I started breathing in through my nose and out through my 20
mouth, calming myself. "I can do that," I said.

My mom laughed for real this time and said, "Mamita, you don't really have a 21
choice."

She didn't say this in a mean way. She was just telling me the truth. "This whole 22
thing was your idea, remember?" she said. Then she told me she had to go, that she
needed to get back to work.

So I got back to work, too, and *Get back to work* became a sort of mantra for me. 23
I tackled the paper with the same focus that had landed me, to everyone's surprise—
even my own—at Cornell in the first place. I did O.K. on it, earning a "B–/C"
(I never found out how a grade could have a slash in it, but now that I'm an English
professor I understand what he was trying to say). The professor had covered the

typed pages with comments and questions, and it was in his endnote that he listed the various campus resources available to me.

My mom didn't ask outright what grade I earned—she eventually stopped ask- 24 ing about assignments altogether—and I learned from my peers that grades were something that I didn't have to share with my parents the way I had in high school.

> Sometimes a single point of comparison is sufficient, p. 408.

My grades were the first of many elements of my new life for which they had no context and which they wouldn't understand. With each semester, what I was doing became, for them, as indecipherable as that paper topic; they didn't even know what questions to ask. And that, for me, is the quintessential quality of the first-generation college student's experience. It's not even knowing what you don't know. ♦

FOR CLOSE READING

1. When Jennine Capó Crucet went off to college, she didn't know that her family was not supposed to come and stay through the entire orientation period. Was she the only one to blame? Why or why not?

2. Capó Crucet started college in 1999. By contrast, she implies, first-generation students today would likely have a better idea of what to expect than she did. Do you agree? Explain.

3. Capó Crucet tells us that she succeeded at her studies in time. How did she do with regard to the strange language that was such a source of anxiety to her in the beginning? How do we know?

4. In Capó Crucet's comparison, what are some of the main differences between her parents and those of many of her fellow classmates? What strengths (if any) does Capó Crucet ascribe to her family (particularly her mother)?

STRATEGIES AND STRUCTURES

1. Capó Crucet begins her essay by **COMPARING AND CONTRASTING** her family, including herself, with those families that "knew what they were doing" (5). By the end of her essay, who is she mostly contrasting with whom? Where and why does her focus shift during the course of her essay?

2. Where does Capó Crucet explicitly compare her subsequent life in college to the set of topics she was given for her first college paper? What is her point in making the comparison? Is it effective for this purpose? Why or why not?

3. When Capó Crucet's English professor returns her first paper, he has covered it "with comments and questions" and given her a grade of "B–/C" (23). What else does her professor provide in his endnote? Why and how is this relevant to the story she is telling?

4. Capó Crucet ends her essay with a **DEFINITION**: "And that, for me, is the quintessential quality of the first-generation college student's experience. It's not even knowing what you don't know" (25). She notes that her definition is particular to her experience with the addition of "for me." Does this make her definition more or less persuasive? Explain.

5. *Other Methods.* Capó Crucet's essay includes many elements of **NARRATIVE**. Do these elements support (or fail to support) the comparisons she is making? Be sure to comment on her use of **DIALOGUE**, particularly in the phone conversation with her mother.

THINKING ABOUT LANGUAGE

1. "Abuela" (3) is the word for grandmother in Spanish. Should Capó Crucet have given an English translation when she first uses the term in her essay? Why or why not?

2. "Indecipherable" (25) is usually applied to forms of writing, often in code, that the reader cannot understand. To whom or what is Capó Crucet applying it? Is this an apt use of the term? Why or why not?

3. Throughout her college years, says Capó Crucet, "Get back to work" became her "mantra" (23). Look up the meaning of this term. How and how well does it apply to Capó Crucet's trials and tribulations—and to those of college in general?

4. In ancient Greek philosophy, the word "quintessence" referred to a "fifth essence" in addition to earth, air, fire, and water, which were thought to be the four essential elements of the physical universe. Look up the term and explain what Capó Crucet means by a "quintessential quality" (25).

FOR WRITING

1. Capó Crucet begins her essay with a "simple" question: "How long was my family supposed to stay for orientation?" In a paragraph or two, answer this question and explain how and why you think so.

2. In a brief essay, compare your experience of first-year "orientation" (or that of somebody you know) with Capó Crucet's and her family's experience. Whether you focus on the similarities or differences, give several specific **EXAMPLES** of both.

3. At the other end of the spectrum from first-year orientation lies graduation. Write an essay of 500 to 700 words comparing the purposes and ceremonies, as you understand them, of the two occasions (whether in college or high school). Consider, for example, that one might be aimed largely at students—"Now, parents, please: Go!"—while the other might be conceived as a reward for those who helped along the way.

13 | Classification

You can divide your whole life into two basic categories. You're either staying in or going out.

—JERRY SEINFELD, *SeinLanguage*

L et's say you live near the coast of Florida or Louisiana or the Carolinas, and you've just survived a hurricane. The power is back on; so is the water. The roof, however, is not. What kind of roof did you have? Which kinds held up well in the storm? What kind should you put back on your house? These are all questions of classification.

Breaking a Subject into Categories

When you DESCRIBE something, you say what its characteristics are: "My old roof was a light gray with green ridge caps." CLASSIFICATION is concerned with characteristics too: "This isn't my roof in your front yard. This is a metal roof, the kind they have across the lake. My roof was tile." When you classify something (a roof, an aquatic mammal, someone's personality), however, you name the category it belongs to—metal, asphalt, tile; dolphin, manatee, whale; introverted, extroverted—based on the characteristics of each category.

There are basically two ways to classify. When classifying individuals, we sort them into groups: this dog is a hound; that one is a terrier. When classifying groups—dogs, bicycles—we divide them into subgroups—hounds, terriers, retrievers; street bikes, mountain bikes, racing bikes. In this chapter, we'll explain what constitutes a category (or significant group), how to devise a valid classification system, and how to use that system when composing an essay. We'll also review the critical points to watch for as you read over and revise your essay, as well as common errors to avoid as you edit. We'll use the term "classification" to refer to both sorting and dividing, since, in either case, we're always going to be organizing a subject into categories.

Why Do We Classify?

We classify things in order to choose the kinds that best meet our needs. The hurricane was a direct hit, and neither tile nor asphalt roofs stood up well. What other kinds are there, and which kind is most likely to survive the next high wind?

Choosing among similar kinds of objects or ideas is only one reason for using classification in our thinking and writing, however. We classify people and things for many purposes: to evaluate (good dog, bad dog); to determine causes (mechanical failure, weather, pilot error); to conduct experiments (test group, control group); and to measure results (winners, losers, runners-up).

USING CLASSIFICATION IN A REVIEW

Reviewing a restaurant is much like doing a critical **EVALUATION** of anything else—a story, book, musical performance, consumer product, television show, or film. You analyze (or break apart) the subject according to its components, describe those individual pieces in some detail, and then make a judgment or recommendation based on the sum of the parts. In this review, the writer uses classification to evaluate the food and ambience in one type of restaurant in relation to those of other types:

> As a type of eating place, the bistro falls somewhere between a brasserie and a full-fledged restaurant. Bistros are usually smaller than either, but this place was spacious and had a nice collection of old wood tables with some heft and character. The walls displayed lots of framed black-and-white photographs, featuring an eclectic assortment of athletes; but you wouldn't call the bar a sports bar, either, because there were also photos of other celebrities and of urban skylines at night. An old upright piano added to the ambiance. The total effect was one of warmth and effortless, sincere old-fashioned charm—the comfort of an established restaurant and the informality of a brasserie combined.
>
> When the bill came, we got one of the great benefits of eating at a bistro. For about the same price as the plate of the day and a beer at a brasserie we got individually prepared dishes that would have cost two or three times as much at a standard restaurant. Long live the bistro!— one of my favorite types of French eateries, especially when it's as good as this one.

Dessert at the Bistro d'en Face: chocolate soufflé and vanilla ice cream.

—BARBARA JOY WHITE, *Paris Journal*

We also classify in order to group individuals according to the common traits that reveal the most about them. Consider the duckbill platypus. Even though it has a bill and lays eggs, biologists classify the platypus as a mammal with birdlike characteristics rather than as a bird with mammalian ones. Why?

It's not simply that the platypus has mostly mammalian traits, such as hair, milk glands, and a neocortex region in the brain. It also turns out that the platypus (along with the spiny anteater) makes up a class of mammals separate from all the rest. In their research to put the platypus in its place, biologists have learned that many types of mammals once had birdlike traits; over the course of evolution, however, only the platypus and spiny anteater have retained a few of those distinguishing features. And that's why, in today's classification system, they keep company together—but in the mammal house and not the birdcage.

So if you're ever inclined to think of classification systems as mere catalogs, remember the platypus. By accurately classifying this unusual mammal and other apparent anomalies, we can discover not only where each one belongs in the scheme of things, but also more about the basis of the natural order itself.

Composing an Essay That Uses Classification

Classification is a way of understanding and ordering the world—and of organizing your thoughts in almost any kind of writing, from a shopping list to a formal essay or even a whole book. Whether you're writing about animals, people, machines, movies, or political movements, the first step is to divide your subject into appropriate categories. Those categories will be determined by the various attributes of your subject, but they'll also depend on your **PRINCIPLE OF CLASSIFICATION**—the basis on which you're classifying your subject. Dogs, for example, are usually classified on the basis of breed or size. If you're classifying dogs by size, your categories might be standard, miniature, and toy. But if breed is your principle of classification, then your categories would be golden retriever, greyhound, poodle, Irish setter, and so on.

Thinking about Purpose and Audience

In order to classify anything accurately, you have to examine all its important attributes. The specific traits you focus on and the categories you divide your subject into, however, will be determined largely by your purpose and audience. Consider the example of the roof that blew off in a hurricane. If your **PURPOSE** is to determine—and write an article for your neighborhood newsletter explaining—what kind of roof will likely stay on best in the next hurricane, you're going to look closely at such traits as weight and wind resistance. And you're going to pay less attention to other traits, such as color or energy efficiency or even cost, that you might consider more closely if you had a different purpose in mind.

Once you've determined which kind of roof has the highest wind rating, you probably are not going to have a hard time convincing your AUDIENCE (many of whom also lost their roofs) that this is the kind to buy. They may expect you to prove that the kind you are recommending does in fact have the characteristics you claim for it (superior resistance to wind), but they are not likely to question the importance of those characteristics or the validity of focusing on them in your article. However, since your audience of homeowners may not be experts in roofing materials, you'll want to make sure to DEFINE any technical terms and use language they'll be familiar with. You won't always be able to assume that your readers will appreciate the way you choose to classify a subject, however. So be prepared to explain why your audience should accept the criteria you use to classify your subject and the weight you place on particular attributes.

> Amy Tan (p. 481) found this out, she says, when her reader was her mother.

Generating Ideas: Considering What Kinds There Are

Classifying can be intellectually demanding work, as it was for the man who was hired by the hour to sort a bushel of apples into green, ripe, and rotten. After an hour and a half went by and the man had only two puny piles to show for his labor, his employer asked why he was so slow. The man shook his head and replied, "It's the decisions."

There are many techniques you can use—CLUSTERING, LOOPING, LISTING, and more—to help determine what subject you want to classify and why. Once you have a subject in mind and a reason for classifying it, the next decision to consider is what kinds there are. Then you can choose the ones that best suit your purpose and audience.

> "What If They Bury Me When I'm Just in a Coma?" (p. 518) suggests good reasons for choosing the right categories.

Let's say your subject is movies. Movies can be classified by genre—drama, comedy, romance, horror, thriller, musical. This might be a good classification system to use if you're analyzing movies for a film course. If your purpose is to review movies for a campus audience, however, a different set of categories would be more appropriate.

When reviewing movies in the school newspaper, your principle of classification would be their quality, and you would divide them into, say, five categories: "must see," "excellent," "good," "mediocre," and "to be avoided at all costs." When reviewing some of the same movies for a parenting magazine, however, you might use different categories: "good for all ages," "preschool," "age six and up," and "not suitable for children."

When you're coming up with categories for an essay that classifies, make sure the categories are appropriate to your specific purpose and audience.

Organizing and Drafting an Essay That Uses Classification

The backbone of an essay that uses classification is the system you create by dividing your subject into categories that interest your readers and that are directly relevant to the point you're making. Those categories should deal with significant aspects of your subject and be inclusive without overlapping. Also think about including visuals, and about other methods of development you might want to use in addition to classification. The templates on p. 465 can help you get started.

ORGANIZING A CLASSIFICATION ESSAY

In the opening paragraphs of your essay, tell your readers what you're classifying and why, and explain your classification system, because much of the rest of the essay will be organized around that system. If you were writing an essay classifying bicycles, for example, something like this might make a good introduction:

> If you are buying or renting a bicycle, you need to know which features to look for in order to meet your needs. Bikes can best be divided into the following categories: mountain bikes, racing bikes, messenger bikes, touring bikes, and stunt bikes. If you understand these six basic types and the differences among them, you can make an informed decision, whether you're choosing a bicycle for a lifetime or just for the afternoon.

Not only does this opener tell your readers what you're classifying and why, but it also provides a solid outline for organizing the rest of the essay.

Typically, the body of an essay that uses classification is devoted to a point-by-point discussion of each of the categories that make up the classification system being used. Thus, when classifying bicycles into mountain bikes, racing bikes, messenger bikes, touring bikes, and stunt bikes, you'd spend a paragraph, or at least several sentences, explaining the most important characteristics of each type. Depending on the complexity of your subject, there will be more or fewer categories to explain; but remember that you must have at least two categories—vertebrates and invertebrates, good movies and bad movies—if you're to have a viable classification system.

TEMPLATES FOR DRAFTING

When you begin to draft an essay that uses classification, be sure to identify the subject and explain the basis on which you're classifying it—moves fundamental to any classification. See how Deborah Tannen makes such moves in the beginning of her essay in this chapter:

> Unfortunately, women and men often have different ideas about what's appropriate, different ways of speaking. . . . Here [are] the biggest areas of miscommunication.
>
> —Deborah Tannen, "But What Do You Mean?"

Tannen identifies her subject ("areas of miscommunication") and explains the basis on which she's classifying them (differences between men and women). Here's one more example from this chapter:

> Language is the tool of my trade. And I use them all—all the Englishes I grew up with.
>
> —Amy Tan, "Mother Tongue"

The following templates can help you make some of these basic moves in your own writing. But don't take these as formulas where you just fill in the blanks. There are no shortcuts to good writing, but these templates can serve as starting points.

▶ X can be classified on the basis of _____.

▶ Classified on the basis of _____, some of the most common types of X are _____, _____, and _____.

▶ X can be divided into two basic types, _____ and _____.

▶ Experts in the field typically divide X into _____, _____, and _____.

▶ This particular X clearly belongs in the _____ category, since it is _____, _____, and _____.

▶ _____, _____, and _____ are examples of this type of X.

▶ By classifying X in this way, we can see that _____.

Once you've laid out, in some detail, the categories that make up your classification system, remind your readers what your principle of classification is and what point you're making by classifying your subject in this way. The point of classifying bicycles by function, for example, is to inform your readers about what categories of bicycles exist and which type is best suited to their needs—climbing mountains, racing, delivering packages, doing tricks, or just cruising around.

STATING YOUR POINT

Classification isn't an end in itself, but a way of relating objects and ideas to one another within an orderly framework. So when composing an essay that uses classification, ask yourself not only what categories your subject can be divided into, but also what you can learn about the subject by classifying it in that way. Then tell your readers in a **THESIS STATEMENT** what your main point is and why you're dividing up the subject as you do. Usually, you'll state your main point in the essay's introduction as you explain your classification system. Occasionally, your thesis statement may not come until the end, after you've thoroughly explained how your chosen classification system works.

Let's look at an essay in which the point of the classification isn't obvious. Here's the main introductory paragraph:

> I have moved more often than I care to remember. However, one thing always stays the same no matter where I have been. There is always a house next door, and that house contains neighbors. Over time, I have begun putting my neighbors into one of four categories: too friendly, unsociable, irritable, and just right.
> —Jonathan R. Gould Jr., "The People Next Door"

Having introduced his subject and outlined his four-part classification system at the beginning of his essay, Gould devotes a paragraph to each of the four categories, taking them in order and looking at particular neighbors who fit each one—the "overly friendly" visiting neighbor who had to be told that his house was on fire "in an attempt to make him leave," the "unsociable" neighbors who looked at the freshly baked apple pie offered by Gould's wife "as if she intended to poison them," and so on. But what is Gould's point in classifying his neighbors according to this scheme?

In addition to making us smile, Gould's point is to make an observation about human nature. Here's the last paragraph of his essay:

> I have always felt it was important to identify the types of neighbors that were around me. Then I am better able to maintain a clear perspective on our relationship and understand their needs. After all, people do not really change; we just learn how to live with both the good and the bad aspects of their behavior.

Gould could have explained his point at the beginning of his essay, but he chose to build up to it instead. In a humorous essay, this can be an effective strategy—part of the fun is wondering where the game is headed and how it's going to end. When you have a more serious purpose in mind, however, you're better off making your main point clear in the beginning of the essay and then, in the conclusion, saying how what you've just written proves that point.

CHOOSING SIGNIFICANT CHARACTERISTICS

Whatever your purpose is, base your categories on the most significant characteristics of your subject—ones that explain something important about it. All neighbors, for example, have at least one thing in common: they're people who live nearby. This trait, however, doesn't tell us much about them. Proximity may be an essential trait in DEFINING neighbors, but it isn't a very useful characteristic for classifying them. For the same reason, you probably wouldn't discuss such attributes as color or decoration when classifying bicycles. Whether a bicycle is blue with red racing stripes or red with blue stripes may be important aesthetically, but these attributes don't tell the reader what kind it is, since all different kinds of bicycles come in all different colors. Color, in other words, while important for classifying other subjects such as wine and laundry, isn't significant when it comes to bicycles. So as you choose categories, make sure they're based on significant characteristics that actually help the reader distinguish one type from another.

With bicycles, these would be such attributes as weight, strength, configuration of the handlebars, and thickness of the tires. Thick, knobby tires, heavy frames, and strong cross-braced handlebars that protect the rider from sudden jolts are significant characteristics of mountain bikes. Thin, smooth tires, lightweight frames, and dropped handlebars that put the rider in a more streamlined position are typical of racing bikes. Wide but relatively smooth tires, raised (but not cross-braced) handlebars, and sturdy, medium-weight frames—not to mention large padded seats—indicate touring bikes. And so on.

Citing significant characteristics is even more essential when you have a two-part classification system, also called a "binary system." A binary system has the advantage of being very inclusive when you choose the two categories wisely. All people can be divided into the living and the dead, for instance. Binary classification systems, however, potentially sacrifice depth for breadth. That is, you can use a binary system to classify a lot of people or things, but doing so may not necessarily tell the reader much about them. Pointing out that Shakespeare, for example, belongs in the "dead" category doesn't tell readers nearly as much about him as explaining that he was a playwright, a poet, and an actor.

> Deborah Tannen (p. 495) uses a binary system: male and female.

USING VISUALS IN CLASSIFICATION

If you're dealing with multiple categories, consider including illustrations in your essay. Statistical graphics, such as bar graphs, enable readers to grasp complex classification systems at a glance. The one below, based on data from the Bureau of Labor Statistics, classifies ten different occupations according to their projected rates of growth over a ten-year period. Which occupations will grow the fastest between 2021 and 2031? By what percentages will their numbers increase? Which occupations will grow at a lesser rate? How much will a particular occupation—data scientists, for example—grow in relation to other occupations? Sometimes, questions like these are best answered by presenting your data visually.

Fastest-Growing Occupations (projected), 2021–2031

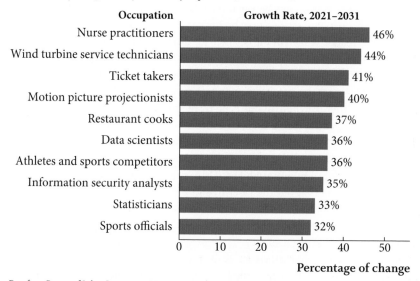

Data from Bureau of Labor Statistics, US Department of Labor, 2022

CHOOSING CATEGORIES THAT ARE INCLUSIVE AND DON'T OVERLAP

Not only must you divide your subject into categories that are truly distinctive, but those categories must be inclusive enough to cover most cases. And they mustn't overlap.

Classifying ice cream into chocolate and vanilla alone isn't very useful because this system leaves out other important kinds, such as strawberry, pistachio, and rum raisin. The categories in a good classification system include all kinds: for instance, no-fat, low-fat, and full-fat ice cream. And they shouldn't overlap. Thus chocolate, vanilla, homemade, and Ben & Jerry's don't make a good classification system because the same scoop of ice cream could belong in more than one category.

BREAKING CATEGORIES INTO SUBCATEGORIES

The categories in a classification essay should be broadly inclusive; but if your categories become too broad to be useful, try dividing them into narrower subcategories. Suppose you were drafting an essay on the Great Depression of the 1930s for a history class, and you were focusing on "tramps," the men (and occasionally women) who took to the road—especially the railroads—in search of food and work. In the lingo of the day, those tramps who begged, you'd point out, were classified as "dings," and those who worked for a living were called "working stiffs." A third kind, who neither begged nor worked, were called "nose divers."

"Nose divers" designated a relatively narrow category of tramp—those who attended church and worshipped or prayed ("nose dived") in order to get meals and beds provided by the churches. "Working stiffs," on the other hand, could get their living by many different means; and to classify them usefully, you'd need to divide this broad, general kind into subtypes—harvest tramp, miner tramp, fruit tramp, construction tramp, and sea tramp. Your essay would then go on to specify the chief characteristics of each of these narrower categories.

USING OTHER METHODS

DEFINITION can be especially useful when classifying something because you'll need to define your categories (and any subcategories) according to their distinguishing characteristics. You'll also need to DESCRIBE those characteristics. Sometimes you may have to analyze the CAUSES of certain characteristics, or their EFFECTS. The author of the following passage uses all three methods (and more) to classify the ailments of horses confined to their stalls:

> In his natural state the horse is a range animal. If he cannot roam a reasonable territory, he may express his frustration by developing some unpleasant or even health-threatening habits. Chewing on fences or stall boards may be followed by cribbing and wind-sucking, vices in which the horse bites down on a hard surface and swallows air at the same time, to the accompaniment of little grunts. (Some will argue that cribbing is a genetically acquired habit, but it is rarely seen in a horse at liberty.)

Further, a continually stabled horse may become a weaver, swaying from side to side in a restless, compulsive pattern. To me, this is as sad a scenario as watching a caged tiger pace back and forth behind bars. Cribbers and weavers, for obvious reasons, frequently develop digestive problems. The message is clear, then: as much turnout for as many hours as possible.

—MAXINE KUMIN, *Women, Animals, and Vegetables*

In this passage, Kumin classifies overly confined horses as cribbers and weavers. Defining the behaviors of both kinds as "unpleasant or even health-threatening habits," she then describes the characteristics that distinguish each kind: the cribber "bites down on a hard surface and swallows air at the same time," whereas the weaver sways "from side to side in a restless, compulsive pattern."

Kumin is so concerned about the welfare of overly confined horses, however, that she does more than simply classify, define, and describe their ailments. She ANALYZES the cause of those ailments and ARGUES for a particular remedy. Cribbing and weaving aren't genetically acquired conditions, says Kumin; they're acquired behaviors caused by the confinement itself. Her point, therefore, is clear: horse owners should let their animals range more freely, instead of confining them to the stable.

EDITING FOR COMMON ERRORS IN A CLASSIFICATION ESSAY

Classification invites problems with listing groups or attributes. Here are some tips for checking your writing for these errors—and editing any that you find.

If you've listed categories in a single sentence, make sure they are parallel in form

▶ A horse can be nervous, aggressive, or calm~~ly accept a saddle~~.

▶ Some say work can be divided into two categories. We're either working too hard or ~~it's a waste of~~ <u>wasting</u> time.

Check that adjectives are in the following order: size, age, color

Adjectives identify characteristics, so you'll probably use at least some adjectives when you write an essay that uses classification.

▶ <u>big</u> old brown ~~big~~ boots

Reading a Classification Essay with a Critical Eye

The most important part of any classification essay is the classification system itself. Does yours have one? How many categories does it include? What are they? Once you've drafted your essay, ask someone else to read the draft and tell you how well your classification system supports your point—and how it might be improved. Should any categories be redefined or omitted? Should any new ones be added? Here are some questions to keep in mind when checking a classification essay.

PURPOSE AND AUDIENCE. Is there a good reason for classifying this particular subject in this way? Who is the intended audience? Does the essay give sufficient background information for the audience to understand (and accept) the proposed classification? Are key terms defined, especially ones that might be unfamiliar to some readers?

THE POINT. Is the main point of the essay clearly laid out in a **THESIS STATEMENT**? How and how well does the classification itself support the main point?

THE CLASSIFICATION SYSTEM AND THE CATEGORIES. Is the classification system appropriate for the subject and purpose of the essay? What is the **PRINCIPLE OF CLASSIFICATION**? Should that principle be revised in any way? If so, how? Do the categories suit the essay's purpose and audience?

SIGNIFICANT CHARACTERISTICS. Do the characteristics that make up the categories tell the reader something important about the subject? Does the essay demonstrate that the things being classified actually have these characteristics?

INCLUSIVE CATEGORIES. Do the categories include most cases? If not, what additional categories would make the classification system complete?

OVERLAPPING CATEGORIES. Can any individual item fit into more than one of the categories that make up the classification system? If so, how might the principle of classification be revised so they don't overlap?

SUBCATEGORIES. Would any of the basic categories that make up the classification system be clearer or easier to explain if they were divided into subgroups?

VISUALS. Would a graph, diagram, or other illustration make the categories easier to understand?

OTHER METHODS. Does the essay use other methods of development? For instance, does it clearly DEFINE all the basic categories and subcategories? Does it fully DESCRIBE the distinctive attributes of each category? Does it analyze what CAUSED those attributes or what EFFECTS they might have? Does it make an ARGUMENT?

COMMON ERRORS. Look for lists of categories and traits in series. Do all the items have approximately the same grammatical form? If they don't, change them so that each one is grammatically PARALLEL to the others.

Student Example

Michelle Watson was a student at Roane State Community College in eastern Tennessee when she wrote this essay for an English class. "Shades of Character" is based on Watson's research in child psychology and education, particularly her study of typical childhood personalities. Watson's instructor, Jennifer Jordan-Henley, chose the essay for publication on the website of the college's Online Writing Lab.

Citing the work of several experts, Watson classifies children's personalities according to commonly recognized types. This classification system provides a framework for organizing the entire report, which discusses each type in turn, paying close attention to the significant attributes that distinguish one "shade" of behavior from another. Watson documents her sources using MLA STYLE.

Shades of Character

Anyone who has spent time around children will notice that each one has a special personality all his or her own. Children, like adults, have different traits that make up their personalities.

Classification system is made up of three personality types determined by experts

Experts have researched these traits in detail, and they classify children into different categories. Some experts have named more than three categories, but Dr. Peter L. Mangione[1] has chosen three

1. *Dr. Peter L. Mangione:* A child psychologist and codirector of the Center for Child and Family Studies in Sausalito, California. He is the content developer and writer of the video *Flexible, Fearful, or Feisty: The Different Temperaments of Infants and Toddlers* (1990), produced by the California Department of Education. All quotations from Dr. Mangione are from this video.

that most experts agree with. These categories are "flexible," "fearful," and "feisty." Children generally may have similar interests, but the way they interact and deal with these interests displays their personality types.

Explains the PRINCIPLE OF CLASSIFICATION for the categories

The flexible personality is the most common of the three types. 2 About "forty percent of all children fall into the flexible or easy group" (Mangione). These children usually handle feelings of anger and disappointment by becoming only mildly upset. This does not mean that they do not feel mad or disappointed, they just choose to react mildly. These actions mean the flexible child is easy to take care of and be around. According to Mangione, such children usually "adapt to new situations and activities quickly, are toilet-trained easily, and are generally cheerful." Flexible children are subtle in their need for attention. Instead of yelling and demanding it, they will slowly and politely let their caregivers know about the need. If they do not get the attention right away, they "seldom make a fuss." They patiently wait, but they still make it known that they need the attention. These children also are easygoing, so routines like feeding and napping are regular (Mangione).

Watson devotes two paragraphs to each category; pars. 2 and 3 explain the significant characteristics of "flexible" children

Flexible children may be referred to as "good as gold" because 3 of their cheerful attitudes. Since these are well-behaved children, the caregiver needs to make sure the child is getting the attention he or she needs. The caregiver should "check in with the flexible child from time to time" (Mangione). By checking in with the child regularly, the caregiver will be more knowledgeable about when the child needs attention and when he or she does not.

Suggests the PURPOSE for classifying children (to aid in their care)

The next temperament is the fearful type. These are the more 4 quiet and shy children. This kind makes up about 15 percent of all children, according to Mangione. They adapt slowly to new environments and take longer than flexible children when warming up to things. When presented with a new environment, fearful children often cling to something or someone familiar, whether it be the main caregiver or a material object such as a blanket. The fearful child will cling until he or she feels comfortable with the new situation. This

Significant characteristics of "fearful" children explained in pars. 4 and 5

can result in a deep attachment of the child to a particular caregiver or object. Fearful children may withdraw when pushed into a new situation too quickly (Mangione). They may also withdraw when other children are jumping into a new project or situation they are not comfortable with. These children may tend to play alone rather than with a group.

In dealing with fearful children, caregivers find they need more attention than flexible children. A good technique for helping these children is having "a sequence of being with, talking to, stepping back, remaining available, and moving on" (Mangione). The caregiver can also help fearful children by giving them "extra soothing combined with an inch-by-inch fostering of independence and assertiveness" (Viorst 174). One of the most effective techniques is just taking everything slowly and helping the child to become more comfortable with his or her surroundings.

The third temperament type is called feisty. About "ten percent" of children fit into this category (Mangione). Feisty children express their opinions in a very intense way. Whether they are happy or mad, everyone around them will know how they feel. These children remain active most of the time, and this causes them to be very aggressive. Feisty children often have a tendency toward "negative persistence" and will go "on and on nagging, whining and negotiating" if there is something they particularly want ("Facts about Temperament"). Unlike flexible children, feisty children are irregular in their napping and feeding times, but they do not adapt well to changes in their routines. They get "used to things and won't give them up" ("Facts about Temperament"). Anything out of the ordinary can send them into a fit. If these children are not warned of a change, they may react very negatively (Mangione). Feisty children also tend to be very sensitive to their surrounding environment. As a result, they may have strong reactions to their surroundings.

When dealing with feisty children, the caregiver should know strategies that receive positive results when different situations arise.

5

6

7

By including percentages, Watson shows how little her categories overlap and how inclusive they are, since the categories cover in total about 65% of the population

Significant characteristics of "feisty" children explained in pars. 6 and 7

Mangione supports the "redirection technique" to calm feisty children. This method helps when the child is reacting very negatively to a situation. According to Mangione, to properly implement the redirection technique, the caregiver should

> begin by recognizing and empathizing with the feelings of the feisty child and placing firm limits on any unacceptable behavior. This response lets the child know that both his or her desire for the toy and feelings of anger when denied the toy are acceptable to the caregiver. At the same time, the caregiver should clearly communicate to the child that expressing anger through hurtful or disruptive behavior is not acceptable. The child will probably need time to experience his or her emotions and settle down. Then offer an alternative toy or activity that may interest the child, who is then given time to consider the new choice and to accept or reject it.

Caregivers should consider that these children generally do not have regular feeding and napping times. The caregiver should be flexible when working with these children and should try to conform more to the desires of the child (Mangione). If there is going to be a change in a child's routine, the caregiver has an easier time when the child has been warned of the change.

Generally speaking, children can be divided into three groups, but caregivers must not forget that each child is an individual. Children may have the traits of all three of the personality groups, but they are categorized into the one they are most like. Whatever their temperament, children need to be treated according to their individual needs. When these needs are met appropriately the child will be happier, and those around the child will feel better also. Knowing the general personality types and how to react to them will help to make the caregiver's job much easier and aid in the relief of unnecessary stress.

8

Conclusion reiterates the categories and ends with a THESIS STATEMENT explaining why it's helpful to classify children this way

Works Cited

"Facts about Temperament." *Temperamentproject*, Australian Temperament Project, www.temperamentproject.bc.ca/html/facts/html. Accessed 25 Oct. 2000.

Mangione, Peter L., content developer and writer. *Flexible, Fearful, or Feisty: The Different Temperaments of Infants and Toddlers*. Produced by J. Ronald Lally, content developed by S. Signer and J. Ronald Lally, directed by Janet Poole, Media Service Unit, California Department of Education, 1990.

Viorst, Judith. "Is Your Child's Personality Set at Birth?" *Redbook*, Nov. 1995, pp. 174+. *EBSCOhost*, connection.ebscohost.com/c/articles/9510191810/your-childs-personality-set-birth. Accessed 23 Oct. 2000.

Analyzing a Student Classification

In "Shades of Character," Michelle Watson draws on rhetorical strategies and techniques that good writers use all the time when they classify things. The following questions, in addition to focusing on particular aspects of Watson's text, will help you identify those common strategies and techniques so you can adapt them to your own writing. These questions will also help prepare you for the analytical questions—on content, structure, and language—that you'll find after all the other selections in this chapter, along with suggestions for writing on related topics.

FOR CLOSE READING

1. According to Michelle Watson, experts in child psychology agree on at least three basic types when classifying the personalities of young children: "flexible," "fearful," and "feisty" (1). What are the main characteristics of each type?

2. If every child has "a special personality all his or her own" (1), how is it that Watson and the experts she cites can group them into personality types? Explain.

3. "Feisty children," says Watson, "express their opinions in a very intense way" (6). What specific techniques does she offer for dealing with such children?

STRATEGIES AND STRUCTURES

1. Watson not only identifies "the general personality types" of young children; she also explains "how to react to them" (8). Why? Who is her intended **AUDIENCE**, and what is her main point in classifying infants and toddlers as she does?

2. Watson lays out her classification system in the opening paragraph of her essay. What is her **PRINCIPLE OF CLASSIFICATION**? Why does she use this principle instead of classifying by sex, height, weight, or some other physical characteristic?

3. In what order does Watson present the personality types in her classification system? Is this arrangement logical? Why or why not?

4. How significant are the characteristics that Watson uses to define her three personality types? Does she always describe the same kind of behavior, such as how a child reacts to objects, when defining each type? Should she? Explain.

5. *Other Methods.* In the conclusion of her essay, Watson reminds the reader that "children can be divided into three groups" (8). What **ARGUMENT** is she also making here? How and how well does her classification of children support that argument?

THINKING ABOUT LANGUAGE

1. What are the **CONNOTATIONS** of "feisty" (1)? What other terms might experts have chosen for this personality type, and why do you think they settled on this one?

2. Watson speaks of "caregivers" throughout her essay. Why do you think she uses this term instead of "parents" or "family members?"

3. How would you **DEFINE** "negative persistence" (6)?

FOR WRITING

1. Using the three-part system that Watson discusses, write an essay of 600 to 800 words classifying yourself and your siblings, or several other children you've known, into each of the various types. Be sure to explain your **PURPOSE** in classifying them this way, and mention aspects of each person's behavior as **EXAMPLES** of the type they represent.

2. Write a **PROFILE** of a child: your subject can be a sibling; a child you've worked with—for example, at a summer camp—or just a youngster you know or know about. Describe the child's personality and temperament, using the three-part classification system that Watson advocates if it helps you understand your subject. But focus mostly on your subject as a person with distinctive traits and characteristics.

3. In collaboration with several classmates, discuss what each of you was like as a child. Each person should write out their story and share it with the group. Edit the stories together, and collect them into an "album."

4. Peter L. Mangione and his colleagues have initiated a social campaign called "For Our Babies." Visit their website, forourbabies.org, and write a five-to-seven-paragraph critical **EVALUATION** of the organization's use of "The Four Pillars" classification system to make their argument.

A Classic Movie Poster

When classifying things or people, we divide them into different categories based on their distinguishing characteristics. Take movies, for example. Some of the most common types (or GENRES) are horror movies, musicals, westerns, romantic comedies, drama, action, and fantasy films—all categories based largely on plot and setting. As indicated by this classic movie poster, one familiar subtype of popular film—the high school movie—can be identified on the basis of its characters, and they're almost always types and stereotypes, at least at the beginning of the film. A brain, a beauty, a jock, a rebel, and a recluse: the types depicted in John Hughes's *The Breakfast Club* (1985), the definitive high school movie of the 1980s, have nothing in common, apparently, until they spend a Saturday together in detention at Shermer High. Baring their souls to one another isn't the only thing that turns "five total strangers" into a tight-knit group of real people, at least for a day. They have a common enemy: "Alright, people," says Mr. Vernon, the assistant principal, "we're going to try something different today. I want you to write an essay, of no less than a thousand words, describing to me who you think you are." Of course, one student in the group, Brian Johnson ("the brain"), does all the work in what's supposed to be a collaborative assignment—"You see us as a brain, an athlete, a basket case, a princess, and a criminal. Correct?"—but he signs the essay for one and all as: "The Breakfast Club." Such is the transformative nature of high school—and of a well-designed writing prompt using classification.

[FOR WRITING]···

"A brain, a beauty, a jock, a rebel and a recluse": do some
research on *The Breakfast Club,* and write a paragraph or two
identifying the characters in the poster according to the category
each one belongs to. Indicate how the actors in the film fulfill
the demands of their respective roles.

479

1. In "Ancient Archetypes and Modern Superheroes" (p. 506), Stewart Slater claims that "superhero movies are merely the latest meditations" on ideas that have been around "since the dawn of civilization." Read Slater's essay and write an ARGUMENT supporting or contesting this claim. Be sure to explain what he means by "archetypes"—and how they differ from other, more modern types and kinds.

2. Do a critical EVALUATION of one of the essays, stories, or books by Amy Tan indicated in the headnote on p. 481. Be sure to mention Tan's use of language, particularly the various forms of English that her characters speak, as a way of establishing their ethnic and cultural identities.

3. Mindy Kaling's "Types of Women in Romantic Comedies Who Are Not Real" (p. 489) and Caitlin Doughty's "What If They Bury Me When I'm Just in a Coma?" (p. 518) both use humor in classifying their subjects. Read both pieces, and then write a COMPARATIVE ANALYSIS of the two as examples of successful classification essays. Be sure to consider their different subjects, purposes, and likely audiences.

4. "Many of the conversational rituals common among women," according to the sociolinguist Deborah Tannen, "are designed to take the other person's feelings into account, while many of the conversational rituals common among men are designed to maintain the one-up position." Read Tannen's "But What Do You Mean?" on p. 495, and write a PROPOSAL for a study or experiment you would conduct to confirm (or dispute) what she says about the "different ways of speaking" between men and women.

5. In 400 to 500 words, write a RHETORICAL ANALYSIS of one of Anne Sexton's poems. Some of her major collections of poetry are listed in the headnote on p. 503.

AMY TAN

Mother Tongue

Amy Tan (b. 1952), a daughter of Chinese immigrants, was born in Oakland, California. She earned an MA in linguistics from San Jose State University and worked on programs for children with disabilities before becoming a freelance business writer. In 1987 she visited China for the first time. On returning to the United States, she set to work on a collection of interconnected stories about Chinese American mothers and daughters. *The Joy Luck Club* (1989) became an international success and was translated into seventeen languages (including Chinese). Since then Tan has published numerous novels, including *The Kitchen God's Wife* (1991), *The Bonesetter's Daughter* (2001), and *The Valley of Amazement* (2013); children's books; and works of nonfiction such as *Where the Past Begins: A Writer's Memoir* (2017).

In her essay "Mother Tongue," which first appeared in the literary magazine *Threepenny Review* in 1990, Tan classifies various forms of the English language, from her mother's "broken English" (a term she dislikes) to the complex prose of academia. "And I use them all," she writes, "all the Englishes I grew up with."

I AM NOT A SCHOLAR OF ENGLISH or literature. I cannot give you much more than 1 personal opinions on the English language and its variations in this country or others.

I am a writer. And by that definition, I am someone who has always loved language. I am fascinated by language in daily life. I spend a great deal of my time thinking about the power of language—the way it can evoke an emotion,

> When you DEFINE something, you tell what general category it belongs to (p. 526).

MLA CITATION: Tan, Amy. "Mother Tongue." *Back to the Lake: A Reader and Guide for Writers*, edited by Thomas Cooley, 5th ed., W. W. Norton, 2024, pp. 481–86.

a visual image, a complex idea, or a simple truth. Language is the tool of my trade. And I use them all—all the Englishes I grew up with.

Recently, I was made keenly aware of the different Englishes I do use. I was giving a talk to a large group of people, the same talk I had already given to half a dozen other groups. The nature of the talk was about my writing, my life, and my book, *The Joy Luck Club.* The talk was going along well enough, until I remembered one major difference that made the whole talk sound wrong. My mother was in the room. And it was perhaps the first time she had heard me give a lengthy speech, using the kind of English I have never used with her. I was saying things like, "The intersection of memory upon imagination" and "There is an aspect of my fiction that relates to thus-and-thus"—a speech filled with carefully wrought grammatical phrases, burdened, it suddenly seemed to me, with nominalized forms, past perfect tenses, conditional phrases, all the forms of standard English that I had learned in school and through books, the forms of English I did not use at home with my mother.

Just last week, I was walking down the street with my mother, and I again found myself conscious of the English I was using, the English I do use with her. We were talking about the price of new and used furniture and I heard myself saying this: "Not waste money that way." My husband was with us as well, and he didn't notice any switch in my English. And then I realized why. It's because over the twenty

years we've been together I've often used the same kind of English with him, and sometimes he even uses it with me. It has become our language of intimacy, a different sort of English that relates to family talk, the language I grew up with.

So you'll have some idea of what this family talk I heard sounds like, I'll quote 5 what my mother said during a recent conversation which I videotaped and then transcribed. During this conversation, my mother was talking about a political gangster in Shanghai who had the same last name as her family's, Du, and how the gangster in his early years wanted to be adopted by her family, which was rich by comparison. Later, the gangster became more powerful, far richer than my mother's family, and one day showed up at my mother's wedding to pay his respects. Here's what she said in part:

"Du Yusong having business like fruit stand. Like off the street kind. He is Du 6 like Du Zong—but not Tsung-ming Island people. The local people call putong, the river east side, he belong to that side local people. That man want to ask Du Zong father take him in like become own family. Du Zong father wasn't look down on him, but didn't take seriously, until that man big like become a mafia. Now important person, very hard to inviting him. Chinese way, came only to show respect, don't stay for dinner. Respect for making big celebration, he shows up. Mean gives lots of respect. Chinese custom. Chinese social life that way. If too important won't have to stay too long. He come to my wedding. I didn't see, I heard it. I gone to boy's side, they have YMCA dinner. Chinese age I was nineteen."

You should know that my mother's expressive command of English belies how 7 much she actually understands. She reads the *Forbes*[1] report, listens to *Wall Street Week*, converses daily with her stockbroker, reads all of Shirley MacLaine's[2] books with ease—all kinds of things I can't begin to understand. Yet some of my friends tell me they understand 50 percent of what my mother says. Some say they understand 80 to 90 percent. Some say they understand none of it, as if she were speaking pure Chinese. But to me, my mother's English is perfectly clear, perfectly natural. It's my mother tongue. Her language, as I hear it, is vivid, direct, full of observation and imagery. That was the language that helped shape the way I saw things, expressed things, made sense of the world.

Lately, I've been giving more thought to the kind of English my mother speaks. Like 8 others, I have described it to people as "broken" or "fractured" English. But I wince when I say that. It has always bothered me that I can think of no way to describe it other than "broken," as if it were damaged and needed to be fixed, as if it lacked a

---

1. *Forbes:* A business-oriented periodical that focuses on stocks, bonds, business trends, and other items of interest to investors.
2. *Shirley MacLaine:* American film actress (b. 1934) who has written a number of memoirs.

certain wholeness and soundness. I've heard other terms used, "limited English," for example. But they seem just as bad, as if everything is limited, including people's perceptions of the limited English speaker.

I know this for a fact, because when I was growing up, my mother's "limited" English limited *my* perception of her. I was ashamed of her English. I believed that her English reflected the quality of what she had to say. That is, because she expressed them imperfectly her thoughts were imperfect. And I had plenty of empirical evidence to support me: the fact that people in department stores, at banks, and at restaurants did not take her seriously, did not give her good service, pretended not to understand her, or even acted as if they did not hear her.

My mother has long realized the limitations of her English as well. When I was fifteen, she used to have me call people on the phone to pretend I was she. In this guise, I was forced to ask for information or even to complain and yell at people who had been rude to her. One time it was a call to her stockbroker in New York. She had cashed out her small portfolio and it just so happened we were going to go to New York the next week, our very first trip outside California. I had to get on the phone and say in an adolescent voice that was not very convincing, "This is Mrs. Tan."

And my mother was standing in the back whispering loudly, "Why he don't send me check, already two weeks late. So mad he lie to me, losing me money."

And then I said in perfect English, "Yes, I'm getting rather concerned. You had agreed to send the check two weeks ago, but it hasn't arrived."

Then she began to talk more loudly. "What he want, I come to New York tell him front of his boss, you cheating me?" And I was trying to calm her down, make her be quiet, while telling the stockbroker, "I can't tolerate any more excuses. If I don't receive the check immediately, I am going to have to speak to your manager when I'm in New York next week." And sure enough, the following week there we were in front of this astonished stockbroker, and I was sitting there red-faced and quiet, and my mother, the real Mrs. Tan, was shouting at his boss in her impeccable broken English.

We used a similar routine just five days ago, for a situation that was far less humorous. My mother had gone to the hospital for an appointment, to find out about a benign brain tumor a CAT scan had revealed a month ago. She said she had spoken very good English, her best English, no mistakes. Still, she said, the hospital did not apologize when they said they had lost the CAT scan and she had come for nothing. She said they did not seem to have any sympathy when she told them she was anxious to know the exact diagnosis, since her husband and son had both died of brain tumors. She said they would not give her any more information until the next time and she would have to make another appointment for that. So she said she would not leave until the doctor called her daughter. She wouldn't budge. And when the doctor finally called her daughter, me, who spoke in perfect English—lo and behold—we had assurances the CAT scan would be found, promises that a conference call on Monday would be held, and apologies for any suffering my mother had gone through for a most regrettable mistake.

I think my mother's English almost had an effect on limiting my possibilities in 15 life as well. Sociologists and linguists probably will tell you that a person's developing language skills are more influenced by peers. But I do think that the language spoken in the family, especially in immigrant families which are more insular, plays a large role in shaping the language of the child. And I believe that it affected my results on achievement tests, IQ tests, and the SAT. While my English skills were never judged as poor, compared to math, English could not be considered my strong suit. In grade school I did moderately well, getting perhaps B's, sometimes B-pluses, in English and scoring perhaps in the sixtieth or seventieth percentile on achievement tests. But those scores were not good enough to override the opinion that my true abilities lay in math and science, because in those areas I achieved A's and scored in the ninetieth percentile or higher.

See p. 468 on choosing categories that don't overlap.

This was understandable. Math is precise; there is only one correct answer. 16 Whereas, for me at least, the answers on English tests were always a judgment call, a matter of opinion and personal experience. Those tests were constructed around items like fill-in-the-blank sentence completion, such as, "Even though Tom was _____, Mary thought he was _____." And the correct answer always seemed to be the most bland combinations of thoughts, for example, "Even though Tom was shy, Mary thought he was charming," with the grammatical structure "even though" limiting the correct answer to some sort of semantic opposites, so you wouldn't get answers like, "Even though Tom was foolish, Mary thought he was ridiculous." Well, according to my mother, there were very few limitations as to what Tom could have been and what Mary might have thought of him. So I never did well on tests like that.

The same was true with word analogies, pairs of words in which you were sup- 17 posed to find some sort of logical, semantic relationship—for example, "*Sunset* is to *nightfall* as _____ is to _____." And here you would be presented with a list of four possible pairs, one of which showed the same kind of relationship: *red* is to *stoplight, bus* is to *arrival, chills* is to *fever, yawn* is to *boring.* Well, I could never think that way. I knew what the tests were asking, but I could not block out of my mind the images already created by the first pair, "*sunset* is to *nightfall*"—and I would see a burst of colors against a darkening sky, the moon rising, the lowering of a curtain of stars. And all the other pairs of words—red, bus, stoplight, boring—just threw up a mass of confusing images, making it impossible for me to sort out something as logical as saying: "A sunset precedes nightfall" is the same as "a chill precedes a fever." The only way I would have gotten that answer right would have been to imagine an associative situation, for example, my being disobedient and staying out past sunset, catching a chill at night, which turns into feverish pneumonia as punishment, which indeed did happen to me.

I have been thinking about all this lately, about my mother's English, about achieve- 18
ment tests. Because lately I've been asked, as a writer, why there are not more Asian Americans represented in American literature. Why are there few Asian Americans enrolled in creative writing programs? Why do so many Chinese students go into engineering? Well, these are broad sociological questions I can't begin to answer. But I have noticed in surveys—in fact, just last week—that Asian students, as a whole, always do significantly better on math achievement tests than in English. And this makes me think that there are other Asian-American students whose English spoken in the home might also be described as "broken" or "limited." And perhaps they also have teachers who are steering them away from writing and into math and science, which is what happened to me.

Fortunately, I happen to be rebellious in nature and enjoy the challenge of dis- 19
proving assumptions made about me. I became an English major my first year in college, after being enrolled as pre-med. I started writing nonfiction as a freelancer the week after I was told by my former boss that writing was my worst skill and I should hone my talents toward account management.

For pointers on using clas-sification to serve a larger purpose, see p. 462.

But it wasn't until 1985 that I finally began to write fiction. And at first I 20
wrote using what I thought to be wittily crafted sentences, sentences that would finally prove I had mastery over the English language. Here's an example from the first draft of a story that later made its way into *The Joy Luck Club*, but without this line: "That was my mental quandary in its nascent state." A terrible line, which I can barely pronounce.

Fortunately, for reasons I won't get into today, I later decided I should envision a 21
reader for the stories I would write. And the reader I decided upon was my mother, because these were stories about mothers. So with this reader in mind—and in fact she did read my early drafts—I began to write stories using all the Englishes I grew up with: the English I spoke to my mother, which for lack of a better term might be described as "simple"; the English she used with me, which for lack of a better term might be described as "broken"; my translation of her Chinese, which could cer-tainly be described as "watered down"; and what I imagined to be her translation of her Chinese if she could speak in perfect English, her internal language, and for that I sought to preserve the essence, but neither an English nor a Chinese struc-ture. I wanted to capture what language ability tests can never reveal: her intent, her passion, her imagery, the rhythms of her speech and the nature of her thoughts.

Apart from what any critic had to say about my writing, I knew I had succeeded 22
where it counted when my mother finished reading my book and gave me her ver-dict: "So easy to read." ◆

FOR CLOSE READING

1. Amy Tan CLASSIFIES the various "Englishes" that she uses into two basic categories. What are they, and what are the main characteristics of each kind?

2. How many different types of English did Tan learn from talking with her mother, a native speaker of Chinese? What are the different attributes of each type?

3. According to Tan, what are the essential attributes of "standard" English (3)? How did she learn to use this kind of English?

4. Which kinds of English does Tan use most often as a writer? Why?

STRATEGIES AND STRUCTURES

1. "So you'll have some idea of what this family talk I heard sounds like, I'll quote what my mother said during a recent conversation" (5). Here and elsewhere in her essay, Tan addresses the reader directly as "you." Why do you think she does this?

2. Why is Tan classifying the different kinds of English she knows and uses? Is she, for example, conveying information, arguing a point, telling an entertaining story—or addressing some other PURPOSE? Explain.

3. Should Tan have laid out her classification system more fully at the beginning of her essay instead of waiting until the end? Why or why not?

4. In paragraphs 15 to 18, Tan advances an ARGUMENT about IQ and achievement tests. What's her point here, and how does she use classification to support it?

5. *Other Methods.* Tan classifies "all the Englishes" she grew up with in paragraph 21, near the end of her essay. How well does this classification system fit the specific EXAMPLES she has cited earlier? Explain.

THINKING ABOUT LANGUAGE

1. Explain the PUN in Tan's title. How does it prepare us for the rest of her essay?

2. Tan doesn't want to use "broken" or "fractured" as names for the kind of English her mother speaks (8). Why not? But several paragraphs later, Tan describes her mother shouting at the stockbroker's boss "in her impeccable broken English" (13). Explain the IRONY in this statement.

3. Throughout her essay, Tan intersperses many QUOTATIONS illustrating her mother's spoken English. What do these examples contribute to the essay's TONE?

4. Tan never gives a name to the kind of English she uses to represent her mother's "internal language" (21). What would you call it? Why?

FOR WRITING

1. How many different kinds of English, or other languages, do you use at home, at school, or among friends? Write an essay of 500 to 700 words classifying them and explaining how and when you use each type.

2. To prove her "mastery" of English, says Tan, she wrote sentences like the following: "That was my mental quandary in its nascent state" (20). Analyze this statement (including the rhythm and pronunciation of the words), and write a paragraph explaining why it is (or isn't) "a terrible line" (20).

3. In your journal, keep a record of the different kinds of English you hear at school and in the media, including social media. Over time, try to develop a system for classifying the different kinds.

4. Write a LITERACY NARRATIVE telling about and analyzing your experience with one of the following: standardized and other language tests; learning another language; conversing with non-native speakers of English; showing your "mastery" of formal written or spoken English; conversing with speakers of English when English isn't your only language.

Types of Women in Romantic Comedies Who Are Not Real

Mindy Kaling (b. 1979) is an actor, comedian, writer, and producer. Kaling was born Vera Mindy Chokalingam in Cambridge, Massachusetts. Her parents, who emigrated from India, picked her "cute American name" from the TV show *Mork & Mindy*. A graduate of Dartmouth College with a degree in playwriting, Kaling has been nominated for several Emmy Awards for her work on the NBC sitcom *The Office* and the Fox/Hulu sitcom *The Mindy Project*, featuring her character Mindy Lahiri. Kaling has also acted in a number of films, including *A Wrinkle in Time* (2018) and *Ocean's 8* (2018). Her 2015 memoir *Why Not Me?* was a *New York Times* best-seller and won the Goodreads Choice Award for Best Humor Book of 2015. In 2020, Kaling created the *Netflix* series *Never Have I Ever* about an Indian American high school student; it has been praised for its representation of South Asians and for countering Asian stereotypes.

"Types of Women in Romantic Comedies Who Are Not Real" is from Kaling's 2011 collection of essays, *Is Everyone Hanging Out without Me?* *(And Other Concerns)*. A classification of the types of female characters in a popular form of film and television, it is also a critical analysis of the genre.

W HEN I WAS A KID, Christmas vacation meant renting VHS copies of romantic 1 comedies from Blockbuster and watching them with my parents at home. *Sleepless in Seattle* was big, and so was *When Harry Met Sally*. I laughed along with everyone else at the scene where Meg Ryan fakes an orgasm at the restaurant with-

MLA CITATION: Kaling, Mindy. "Types of Women in Romantic Comedies Who Are Not Real." *Back to the Lake: A Reader and Guide for Writers*, edited by Thomas Cooley, 5th ed., W. W. Norton, 2024, pp. 489-92.

490 ♦ Chapter 13: Classification

out even knowing what an orgasm was. In my mind, she was just being kind of loud and silly at a diner, and that was hilarious enough for me.

I love romantic comedies. I feel almost sheepish writing that, because the genre   2
has been so degraded in the past twenty years or so that admitting you like these movies is essentially an admission of mild stupidity. But that has not stopped me from watching them.

I enjoy watching people fall in love on-screen so much that I can suspend my dis-   3
belief for the contrived situations that only happen in the heightened world of romantic comedies. I have come to enjoy the moment when the normal lead guy, say, slips and falls right on top of the hideously expensive wedding cake. I actually feel robbed when the female lead's dress *doesn't* get torn open at a baseball game while the Jumbo-

For help with less awesome principles of classification, see p. 462.

Tron is on her. I simply regard romantic comedies as a subgenre of sci-fi, in which the world created therein has different rules than my regular human world. Then I just lap it up. There is no difference between Ripley from *Alien* and any Katherine Heigl character. They're all participating in the same level of made-up awesomeness, and I enjoy every second of it.

So it makes sense that in this world there are many specimens of women who I   4
do not think exist in real life, like Vulcans or UFO people or whatever. They are:

The Klutz

When a beautiful actress is in a movie, executives wrack their brains to find some   5
kind of flaw in her that still allows her to be palatable. She can't be overweight or not perfect-looking, because who would want to see that? A not 100-percent-perfect-looking-in-every-way female? You might as well film a dead squid decaying on a beach somewhere for two hours.

So they make her a Klutz.   6

The 100-percent-perfect-looking female is perfect in every way, except that she   7
constantly falls down. She bonks her head on things. She trips and falls and spills soup on her affable date. (Josh Lucas. Is that his name? I know it's two first names. Josh George? Brad Mike? Fred Tom? Yes, it's Fred Tom.) Our Klutz clangs into Stop signs while riding a bike, and knocks over giant displays of expensive fine china. Despite being five foot nine and weighing 110 pounds, she is basically like a drunk buffalo who has never been a part of human society. But Fred Tom loves her anyway.

The Ethereal Weirdo

The smart and funny writer Nathan Rabin coined the term *Manic Pixie Dream Girl* to   8
describe a version of this archetype after seeing Kirsten Dunst in the movie *Eliza-bethtown*. This girl can't be pinned down and may or may not show up when you

make concrete plans. She wears gauzy blouses and braids. She decides to dance in the rain and weeps uncontrollably if she sees a sign for a missing dog or cat. She spins a globe, places her finger on a random spot, and decides to move there. This ethereal weirdo abounds in movies, but nowhere else. If she were from real life, people would think she was a homeless woman and would cross the street to avoid her, but she is essential to the male fantasy that even if a guy is boring, he deserves a woman who will find him fascinating and pull him out of himself by forcing him to go skinny-dipping in a stranger's pool.

The Woman Who Is Obsessed with Her Career and Is No Fun at All

I, Mindy Kaling, basically have two full-time jobs. I regularly work sixteen hours a 9
day. But like most of the other people I know who are similarly busy, I think I'm a pleasant, pretty normal person. I am slightly offended by the way busy working women my age are presented in film. I'm not, like, always barking orders into my hands-free phone device and telling people constantly, "I have no time for this!" I didn't completely forget how to be nice or feminine because I have a career. Also, since when does having a job necessitate women having their hair pulled back in a severe, tight bun? Often this uptight woman has to "re-learn" how to seduce a man because her estrogen leaked out of her from leading so many board meetings, and she has to do all sorts of crazy, unnecessary crap, like eat a hot dog in a libidinous way or something. Having a challenging job in movies means the compassionate, warm, or sexy side of your brain has fallen out.

The Forty-Two-Year-Old Mother of the Thirty-Year-Old Male Lead

I am so accustomed to the young mom phenomenon, that when I saw the poster for 10
The Proposal I wondered for a second if the proposal in the movie was Ryan Reynolds suggesting he send his mother, Sandra Bullock, to an old-age home.

However, given the popularity of teen moms right now, this could actually be the 11
wave of the future.

The Sassy Best Friend

You know that really horny and hilarious best friend who is always asking about 12
your relationship and has nothing really going on in her own life? She always wants to meet you in coffee shops or wants to go to Bloomingdale's to sample perfumes? She runs a chic dildo store in the West Village? Nope? Okay, that's this person.

The Skinny Woman Who Is Beautiful and Toned but Also Gluttonous and Disgusting

Again, I am more than willing to suspend my disbelief during a romantic comedy 13 for good set decoration alone. One pristine kitchen from a Nancy Meyers movie like in *It's Complicated* is worth five Diane Keatons being caught half-clad in a topiary or whatever situation her character has found herself in.

But sometimes even my suspended disbelief isn't enough. I am speaking of the 14 gorgeous and skinny heroine who is also a disgusting pig when it comes to food. And everyone in the movie—her parents, her friends, her boss—are all complicit in this huge lie. They are constantly telling her to stop eating and being such a glutton. And this actress, this poor skinny actress who so clearly lost weight to play the likable lead, has to say things like "Shut up you guys! I love cheesecake! If I want to eat an entire cheesecake, I will!" If you look closely, you can see this woman's ribs through the dress she's wearing—that's how skinny she is, this cheesecake-loving cow.

You wonder, as you sit and watch this movie, what the characters would do if 15 they were confronted by an actual average American woman. They would all kill themselves, which would actually be kind of an interesting movie.

The Woman Who Works in an Art Gallery

How many freakin' art galleries are out there? Are people constantly buying visual 16 art or something? This posh-smart-classy job is a favorite in movies. It's in the same realm as kindergarten teacher in terms of accessibility: guys don't really get it, but the trappings of it are likable and nonthreatening.

> ART GALLERY WOMAN: Dust off the Rothko. We have an important buyer coming into town and this is a really big deal for my career. I have no time for this!

This is one of the rare clichés that actually has a male counterpart. Whenever 17 you meet a handsome, charming, successful man in a romantic comedy, the heroine's friend always says the same thing. "He's really successful—he's an . . .

(say it with me) 18

. . . architect!" 19

There are like nine people in the entire world who are architects, and one of them 20 is my dad. None of them looks like Patrick Dempsey. ◆

FOR CLOSE READING

1. Why is Mindy Kaling reluctant to admit that she likes to watch romantic comedies? Why does she do it anyway?

2. "I, Mindy Kaling, basically have two full-time jobs" (9). Why does Kaling make this statement? Is her testimony appropriate here? Why or why not?

3. As depicted by Kaling, what roles do *men* play in romantic comedies? Are they equally "not real" as those of the women in Kaling's classification? Explain.

4. Which type(s) of women in her classification system does Kaling seem to find personally most difficult to accept? Why?

STRATEGIES AND STRUCTURES

1. Although Kaling assumes that her readers already know what a romantic comedy is, she still indicates a number of the distinguishing features of the GENRE (2). What are some of them?

2. Kaling classifies the women in romantic comedies into seven different types. What do they generally have in common? Which categories do you find most valid and informative? Why?

3. Are Kaling's types all-inclusive, or can you think of others? For instance?

4. Kaling classifies romantic comedies as "a subgenre of sci-fi" (3). Is this a valid way of classifying the form? Why or why not? Should we take her seriously here?

5. What is Kaling's PURPOSE in classifying the romantic comedy as a type of fantasy? Choose one of the following: (a) to criticize how the form has been "degraded" (2); (b) to celebrate the "made-up awesomeness" of the form (3); (c) to show she understands the material she is classifying; (d) all of the above. Explain.

6. *Other Methods.* DESCRIPTION can be useful when distinguishing the characteristics of one category from those of other categories. How well does Kaling apply this method, and does her use of humor add to or detract from her classifications? Explain.

THINKING ABOUT LANGUAGE

1. Kaling speaks twice of being able to "suspend my disbelief" (3, 13). Do some research to find out where she got this phrase, the original form of which is "that willing suspension of disbelief." Given the source and its original meaning, does Kaling's use here seem appropriate? Explain.

2. Why does Kaling describe herself as "sheepish"—as opposed to "wolfish" or "bullish," say—for liking romantic comedies so much (2)?

3. Kaling refers to the types of women in her essay as "specimens" (4). Is this an apt term to use in setting up a classification system? Why or why not?

4. What is an "archetype" (8)? Are archetypes more likely to be found in life or in literature? Explain.

FOR WRITING

1. Write your own classification of "types of" people who are "not real" in a genre of film, television, or video that you like to watch anyway. Be sure to explain what you like (or at least find fascinating) about the genre.

2. The term "romance" in literature and popular culture is usually applied to storylines in which readers or viewers expect to be "watching people fall in love" (3). Write a paragraph or two outlining what you can find out about the broader meaning of the term "romance" as a form of classification in literature. Be sure to include EXAMPLES (such as *The Scarlet Letter: A Romance*).

3. Keep a viewer's journal as you watch (or rewatch) a favorite television show or type of film or video (including music videos). Give special attention in your notes to the traits and features that distinguish the particular type of show or sound you're watching or hearing.

4. One of the most common binary (or two-part) systems for classifying works of literature is as comedy or tragedy. (In this context, "comic" doesn't simply mean funny, though Shakespearian comedies, for example, often are.) Do a little research if necessary, and write a RHETORICAL ANALYSIS of 500 to 600 words in which you explain the traditional classification of works of dramatic literature as comedies or tragedies. Identify the most common features of the two types (and subtypes), and cite several examples that display them.

DEBORAH TANNEN

But What Do You Mean?

Deborah Tannen (b. 1945) is a professor of linguistics at Georgetown University. Best known for her studies of how men and women communicate, she is the author of more than twenty books, including *You Just Don't Understand: Men and Women in Conversation* (1990), *You Were Always Mom's Favorite! Sisters in Conversation Throughout Their Lives* (2009), and *The Argument Culture: Stopping America's War of Words* (2012). Tannen's 2018 essay "The Power of Talk: Who Gets Heard and Why" appeared in the *Harvard Business Review*'s edited collection of the ten "must reads" on women and leadership.

"But What Do You Mean?" first appeared in *Redbook* magazine in 1994 and summarizes much of Tannen's best-selling book *Talking from 9 to 5: Women and Men at Work* (1994). In this essay, Tannen classifies the most common ways in which men and women miscommunicate in the workplace.

CONVERSATION IS A RITUAL. We say things that seem obviously the thing to 1 say, without thinking of the literal meaning of our words, any more than we expect the question "How are you?" to call forth a detailed account of aches and pains.

Unfortunately, women and men often have different ideas about what's appropri- 2 ate, different ways of speaking. Many of the conversational rituals common among women are designed to take the other person's feelings into account, while many of

MLA CITATION: Tannen, Deborah. "But What Do You Mean?" *Back to the Lake: A Reader and Guide for Writers*, edited by Thomas Cooley, 5th ed., W. W. Norton, 2024, pp. 495–501.

In a binary system, such as male and female, the characteristics should be especially significant (p. 467).

the conversational rituals common among men are designed to maintain the one-up position, or at least avoid appearing one-down. As a result, when men and women interact—especially at work—it's often women who are at the disadvantage. Because women are not trying to avoid the one-down position, that is unfortunately where they may end up.

Here, the biggest areas of miscommunication. 3

1. Apologies

Women are often told they apologize too much. The reason they're told to stop 4 doing it is that, to many men, apologizing seems synonymous with putting oneself down. But there are many times when "I'm sorry" isn't self-deprecating, or even an apology; it's an automatic way of keeping both speakers on an equal footing. For example, a well-known columnist once interviewed me and gave me her phone number in case I needed to call her back. I misplaced the number and had to go through the newspaper's main switchboard. When our conversation was winding down and we'd both made ending-type remarks, I added, "Oh, I almost forgot—I lost your direct number, can I get it again?" "Oh, I'm sorry," she came back instantly, even though she had done nothing wrong and *I* was the one who'd lost the number. But I understood she wasn't really apologizing; she was just automatically reassuring me she had no intention of denying me her number.

Even when "I'm sorry" *is* an apology, women often assume it will be the first step 5 in a two-step ritual: I say "I'm sorry" and take half the blame, then you take the other half. At work, it might go something like this:

A: When you typed this letter, you missed this phrase I inserted.
B: Oh, I'm sorry. I'll fix it.
A: Well, I wrote it so small it was easy to miss.

When both parties share blame, it's a mutual face-saving device. But if one per- 6 son, usually the woman, utters frequent apologies and the other doesn't, she ends up looking as if she's taking the blame for mishaps that aren't her fault. When she's only partially to blame, she looks entirely in the wrong.

I recently sat in on a meeting at an insurance company where the sole woman, 7 Helen, said "I'm sorry" or "I apologize" repeatedly. At one point she said, "I'm think-ing out loud. I apologize." Yet the meeting was intended to be an informal brain-storming session, and *everyone* was thinking out loud.

The reason Helen's apologies stood out was that she was the only person in the 8 room making so many. And the reason I was concerned was that Helen felt the annual bonus she had received was unfair. When I interviewed the colleagues, they said that Helen was one of the best and most productive workers—yet she got one of the smallest bonuses. Although the problem might have been outright sexism, I suspect her speech style, which differs from that of her male colleagues, masks her competence.

Unfortunately, not apologizing can have its price too. Since so many women use   9 ritual apologies, those who don't may be seen as hard-edged. What's important is to be aware of how often you say you're sorry (and why), and to monitor your speech based on the reaction you get.

2. Criticism

A woman who cowrote a report with a male colleague was hurt when she read a   10 rough draft to him and he leapt into a critical response—"Oh, that's too dry! You have to make it snappier!" She herself would have been more likely to say, "That's a really good start. Of course, you'll want to make it a little snappier when you revise."

Whether criticism is given straight or softened is often a matter of convention. In   11 general, women use more softeners. I noticed this difference when talking to an editor about an essay I'd written. While going over changes she wanted to make, she said, "There's one more thing. I know you may not agree with me. The reason I noticed the problem is that your other points are so lucid and elegant." She went on hedging for several more sentences until I put her out of her misery: "Do you want to cut that part?" I asked—and of course she did. But I appreciated her tentativeness. In contrast, another editor (a man) I once called summarily rejected my idea for an article by barking, "Call me when you have something new to say."

Those who are used to ways of talking that soften the impact of criticism may   12 find it hard to deal with the right-between-the-eyes style. It has its own logic, however, and neither style is intrinsically better. People who prefer criticism given straight are operating on an assumption that feelings aren't involved: "Here's the dope. I know you're good; you can take it."

3. Thank-Yous

A woman manager I know starts meetings by thanking everyone for coming, even   13 though it's clearly their job to do so. Her "thank-you" is simply a ritual.

A novelist received a fax from an assistant in her publisher's office; it contained   14 suggested catalog copy for her book. She immediately faxed him her suggested changes and said, "Thanks for running this by me," even though her contract gave her the right to approve all copy. When she thanked the assistant, she fully expected him to reciprocate: "Thanks for giving me such a quick response." Instead, he said, "You're welcome." Suddenly, rather than an equal exchange of pleasantries, she found herself positioned as the recipient of a favor. This made her feel like responding, "Thanks for nothing!"

Many women use "thanks" as an automatic conversation starter and closer;   15
there's nothing literally to say thank you for. Like many rituals typical of women's
conversation, it depends on the goodwill of the other to restore the balance. When
the other speaker doesn't reciprocate, a woman may feel like someone on a seesaw
whose partner abandoned his end. Instead of balancing in the air, she has plopped
to the ground, wondering how she got there.

4. Fighting

Many men expect the discussion of ideas to be a ritual fight—explored through ver-   16
bal opposition. They state their ideas in the strongest possible terms, thinking that
if there are weaknesses someone will point them out, and by trying to argue against
those objections, they will see how well their ideas hold up.

Those who expect their own ideas to be challenged will respond to another's   17
ideas by trying to poke holes and find weak links—as a way of *helping*. The logic is
that when you are challenged you will rise to the occasion: Adrenaline makes your
mind sharper; you get ideas and insights you would not have thought of without the
spur of battle.

But many women take this approach as a personal attack. Worse, they find it   18
impossible to do their best work in such a contentious environment. If you're not
used to ritual fighting, you begin to hear criticism of your ideas as soon as they
are formed. Rather than making you think more clearly, it makes you doubt what
you know. When you state your ideas, you hedge in order to fend off potential
attacks. Ironically, this is more likely to *invite* attack because it makes you look
weak.

Although you may never enjoy verbal sparring, some women find it helpful to   19
learn how to do it. An engineer who was the only woman among four men in a
small company found that as soon as she learned to argue she was accepted and
taken seriously. A doctor attending a hospital staff meeting made a similar discovery. She was becoming more and more angry with a male colleague who'd loudly
disagreed with a point she'd made. Her better judgment told her to hold her tongue,
to avoid making an enemy of this powerful senior colleague. But finally she couldn't
hold it in any longer, and she rose to her feet and delivered an impassioned attack on
his position. She sat down in a panic, certain she had permanently damaged her
relationship with him. To her amazement, he came up to her afterward and said,
"That was a great rebuttal. I'm really impressed. Let's go out for a beer after work
and hash out our approaches to this problem."

5. Praise

A manager I'll call Lester had been on his new job six months when he heard that 20 the women reporting to him were deeply dissatisfied. When he talked to them about it, their feelings erupted; two said they were on the verge of quitting because he didn't appreciate their work, and they didn't want to wait to be fired. Lester was dumbfounded: He believed they were doing a fine job. Surely, he thought, he had said nothing to give them the impression he didn't like their work. And indeed he hadn't. That was the problem. He had said *nothing*—and the women assumed he was following the adage "If you can't say something nice, don't say anything." He thought he was showing confidence in them by leaving them alone.

Before introducing a new category, Tannen reminds the reader what her principle of classification is (p. 466).

Men and women have different habits in regard to giving praise. For example, 21 Deirdre and her colleague William both gave presentations at a conference. Afterward, Deirdre told William, "That was a great talk!" He thanked her. Then she asked, "What did you think of mine?" and he gave her a lengthy and detailed critique. She found it uncomfortable to listen to his comments. But she assured herself that he meant well, and that his honesty was a signal that she, too, should be honest when he asked for a critique of his performance. As a matter of fact, she had noticed quite a few ways in which he could have improved his presentation. But she never got a chance to tell him because he never asked—and she felt put down. The worst part was that it seemed she had only herself to blame, since she *had* asked what he thought of her talk.

But had she really asked for his critique? The truth is, when she asked for his 22 opinion, she was expecting a compliment, which she felt was more or less required following anyone's talk. When he responded with criticism, she figured, "Oh, he's playing 'Let's critique each other'"—not a game she'd initiated, but one which she was willing to play. Had she realized he was going to criticize her and not ask her to reciprocate, she would never have asked in the first place.

It would be easy to assume that Deirdre was insecure, whether she was fishing 23 for a compliment or soliciting a critique. But she was simply talking automatically, performing one of the many conversational rituals that allow us to get through the day. William may have sincerely misunderstood Deirdre's intention—or may have been unable to pass up a chance to one-up her when given the opportunity.

6. Complaints

"Troubles talk" can be a way to establish rapport with a colleague. You complain about 24 a problem (which shows that you are just folks) and the other person responds with a similar problem (which puts you on equal footing). But while such commiserating is common among women, men are likely to hear it as a request to *solve* the problem.

One woman told me she would frequently initiate what she thought would be   25
pleasant complaint-airing sessions at work. She'd talk about situations that bothered her just to talk about them, maybe to understand them better. But her male
office mate would quickly tell her how she could improve the situation. This left her
feeling condescended to and frustrated. She was delighted to see this very impasse
in a section in my book *You Just Don't Understand*, and showed it to him. "Oh," he
said, "I see the problem. How can we solve it?" Then they both laughed, because it
had happened again: He short-circuited the detailed discussion she'd hoped for and
cut to the chase of finding a solution.

Sometimes the consequences of complaining are more serious: A man might   26
take a woman's lighthearted griping literally, and she can get a reputation as a chronic
malcontent. Furthermore, she may be seen as not up to solving the problems that
arise on the job.

7. Jokes

I heard a man call in to a talk show and say, "I've worked for two women and neither   27
one had a sense of humor. You know, when you work with men, there's a lot of joking and teasing." The show's host and guest (both women) took his comment at face
value and assumed the women this man worked for were humorless. The guest said,
"Isn't it sad that women don't feel comfortable enough with authority to see the
humor?" The host said, "Maybe when more women are in authority roles, they'll be
more comfortable with power." But although the women this man worked for *may*
have taken themselves too seriously, it's just as likely that they each had a terrific
sense of humor, but maybe the humor wasn't the type he was used to. They may have
been like the woman who wrote to me: "When I'm with men, my wit or cleverness
seems inappropriate (or lost!) so I don't bother. When I'm with my women friends,
however, there's no hold on puns or cracks and my humor is fully appreciated."

The types of humor women and men tend to prefer differ. Research has shown   28
that the most common form of humor among men is razzing, teasing, and mock-
hostile attacks, while among women it's self-mocking. Women often mistake men's
teasing as genuinely hostile. Men often mistake women's mock self-deprecation as
truly putting themselves down.

Women have told me they were taken more seriously when they learned to joke   29
the way the guys did. For example, a teacher who went to a national conference
with seven other teachers (mostly women) and a group of administrators (mostly
men) was annoyed that the administrators always found reasons to leave boring
seminars, while the teachers felt they had to stay and take notes. One evening,
when the group met at a bar in the hotel, the principal asked her how one such
seminar had turned out. She reported, "As soon as you left, it got much better." He

laughed out loud at her response. The playful insult appealed to the men—but there was a trade-off. The women seemed to back off from her after this. (Perhaps they were put off by her using joking to align herself with the bosses.)

There is no "right" way to talk. When problems arise, the culprit may be style   30 differences—and *all* styles will at times fail with others who don't share or understand them, just as English won't do you much good if you try to speak to someone who knows only French. If you want to get your message across, it's not a question of being "right"; it's a question of using language that's shared—or at least understood. ♦

FOR CLOSE READING

1. In this essay, what principle of classification is Deborah Tannen using to classify "different ways of speaking" (2)?

2. In what fundamental way do the "conversational rituals" (2) of men and women differ, according to Tannen? Do you think she's right? Why or why not?

3. Tannen says she's classifying the "different ways" in which men and women speak (2). What else is she classifying?

4. Women, says Tannen, tend to apologize more often than men do. Why? She also finds that women often say "thank-you" when they don't really mean it (13). What *do* they often mean by "thank-you"?

5. In Tannen's view, when women complain, they're often trying to "establish rapport" (24). How does she say most men respond to this technique?

6. Women, says Tannen, often see "verbal opposition" as a direct attack (16). How does she say that men see it?

STRATEGIES AND STRUCTURES

1. "Although you may never enjoy verbal sparring, some women find it helpful to learn how to do it" (19). To whom is Tannen speaking here? Can you find other evidence that indicates the identity of her intended AUDIENCE?

2. What is Tannen's underlying PURPOSE in classifying the verbal behavior of men and women in terms of the workplace? How can you tell?

3. Tannen divides her subject into seven main "areas" (3). Are these categories based on significant characteristics? Are they mutually exclusive? Do they cover all kinds of communication? Explain.

4. Tannen breaks "jokes" into "the types of humor women and men tend to prefer" (28). Why does she use subcategories here and not elsewhere in her classification?

5. How and how well does Tannen use classification to structure her ARGUMENT about women in the workplace?

6. *Other Methods.* Much of Tannen's evidence is **ANECDOTAL**—that is, she tells brief stories to make her points. How effective do you find these **NARRATIVE** elements of her essay? Explain.

THINKING ABOUT LANGUAGE

1. "Conversation," says Tannen, "is a ritual" (1). What is ritual behavior, and why do you think Tannen uses this term?

2. What are the **CONNOTATIONS** of "hard-edged" (9) when it's applied to women? What are its connotations when applied to men?

3. What is "right-between-the-eyes style" (12)? What two things are being compared in this **METAPHOR**?

4. Tannen accuses a man of "barking" (11) and several women of allowing their emotions to "erupt" (20). How do these choices of words confirm or contradict her assertions about the way men and women communicate?

FOR WRITING

1. Tannen wrote this essay in 1994. How well do her claims about the differences between men and women stand up today, when many people prefer not to be categorized by the male/female gender binary? What, if anything, would you add to her argument to recognize the people who are left out of the categories Tannen chooses?

2. Write an essay about the different ways in which one of the following groups of people communicate (or miscommunicate) with each other: siblings, children and parents, students and teachers, engineers and liberal arts majors, old people and young people, or some other group or groups.

3. In your journal, record instances of miscommunication that you hear or are a party to over time. Note who was involved and what was said. Also, try to **ANALYZE** the types of miscommunication you experienced and why they occurred.

4. "If you want to get your message across," says Tannen, "it's not a question of being 'right'; it's a question of using language that's shared—or at least understood" (29). In a 400-to-500-word **POSITION PAPER**, defend (or contest) this proposition about the value of shared language. Give **EXAMPLES**, both negative and positive, from your own experience and from your research.

5. Write a **LITERACY NARRATIVE** explaining how you came to understand and deal with gendered conversation rituals and rivalries. Again, be sure to give examples.

ANNE SEXTON

Her Kind

Anne Sexton (1928–1974) was a poet, playwright, model, and author of children's books. Born in Newton, Massachusetts, she began writing poetry in high school. Sexton didn't focus on her writing until 1957, however, when she enrolled in a poetry workshop at the Boston Center for Adult Education. Ten years later she won a Pulitzer Prize in poetry for her collection *Live or Die* (1966). For most of her adult life, Sexton suffered from depression and mental illness, and she died by suicide in 1974. (Of Sexton's untimely death, her fellow poet Denise Levetov wrote that "we who are alive must make clear, as she could not, the distinction between creativity and self-destruction.")

"Her Kind" is the keynote poem in Sexton's first book of poems, *To Bedlam and Part Way Back* (1960). At one point during its composition, Sexton called the poem "Witch"; but she changed the title when, after much revision, she introduced a second, more detached point of view in the last two lines of each stanza. It is this "I" who classifies the woman she's observing in each stanza and who then affirms that she belongs (or has belonged) to the same "kind."

> I have gone out, a possessed witch,
> haunting the black air, braver at night;
> dreaming evil, I have done my hitch
> over the plain houses, light by light:
> lonely thing, twelve-fingered, out of mind.   5
> A woman like that is not a woman, quite.
> I have been her kind.

MLA CITATION: Sexton, Anne. "Her Kind." *Back to the Lake: A Reader and Guide for Writers*, edited by Thomas Cooley, 5th ed., W. W. Norton, 2024, pp. 503–4.

I have found the warm caves in the woods,
filled them with skillets, carvings, shelves,
closets, silks, innumerable goods;   10
fixed the suppers for the worms and the elves:
whining, rearranging the disaligned.
A woman like that is misunderstood.
I have been her kind.

I have ridden in your cart, driver,   15
waved my nude arms at villages going by,
learning the last bright routes, survivor
where your flames still bite my thigh
and my ribs crack where your wheels wind.
A woman like that is not ashamed to die.   20
I have been her kind. ◆

FOR CLOSE READING

1. According to Anne Sexton's biographer, Diane Wood Middlebrook, "Her Kind" depicts a different woman in each stanza. In the first is "the witch"; then "the housewife"; and, finally, "the adulteress." Does the poem support Middlebrook's reading? Why or why not?

2. Whether Sexton is writing about three different women or the same woman at different moments in her life, how do they (or she) typically behave? Why? What might be some of the CAUSES?

3. How does the "I" in the first line of each stanza COMPARE AND CONTRAST with the "I" in the last line? Explain.

4. In the last stanza, the woman is riding in a cart. Where do you think she is going?

STRATEGIES AND STRUCTURES

1. Sexton identifies three distinguishing characteristics—one in each stanza—of the "kind" of woman she's writing about. What are they?

2. On what basis—age, social status, psychological condition, and so forth—is Sexton constructing her classification system? What other types might there be?

3. Sexton's speaker claims to have been the kind of woman she's imagining. How and how well do her DESCRIPTIONS of particular specimens support this claim?

4. *Other Methods.* Each stanza of "Her Kind" tells a story. How, and how well, does Sexton use these NARRATIVES to explain what kind of woman she's writing about?

THINKING ABOUT LANGUAGE

1. The "I" in Sexton's first stanza says she has done her "hitch" (3). Besides rhyming with "witch," this word suggests a tour of duty, as in the military. Why would Sexton use such a term here?

2. Sexton uses the present perfect tense when her speaker says, "I have been her kind" (7, 14, 21). Why doesn't she use the present tense ("am")?

3. What does "her kind" often mean in common speech? What alternative "kind" does it assume? How does Sexton build on such assumptions in her poem?

4. The woman in the cart says she's not "ashamed" to die (20). Why is this assertion more startling than if she had simply said she wasn't "afraid" to die?

FOR WRITING

1. Sexton's poem consists of three seven-line stanzas, each beginning and ending with "I have." If you had to add a stanza to her poem that began and ended this way, what would happen in those seven lines? Make a list of the actions that would occur.

2. "A woman like that is misunderstood" (13). Choose several of Sexton's poems—or those of some other poet whose work interests you—and write an essay about the kind of person the poet presents to the reader as particularly misunderstood. How does the poet help the reader understand such figures, or block the way to understanding them?

3. Write a four-to-six-paragraph TEXTUAL ANALYSIS of "Her Kind." Discuss the meaning(s) of the poem, but also explain *how* the poem conveys its message. Base your comments on frequent references to the text.

STEWART SLATER

Ancient Archetypes and Modern Superheroes

Stewart Slater (b. 1975) works in London in the field of finance. He grew up in Greece and studied Classics at Oxford, and his work typically draws on ancient Greek and Roman literature and philosophy to illuminate current social and political issues and popular culture. Slater's work has been published in *Quillette*, *Spiked*, *Modern Stoicism*, and other internet magazines, including *Areo*, where "Ancient Archetypes and Modern Superheroes" first appeared in October 2022.

In this selection, what Slater finds worthy of debate is film critics and directors like Martin Scorsese and Francis Ford Coppola who look down on modern superhero films. Actually, says Slater, if you classify modern superheroes on the basis of their "greatness"—and how they acquired it— Superman and Spider-Man are not so different from their counterparts in ancient Greece and earlier. Only Batman, says Slater, has "no ancient model."

> Nothing is said that has not been said before.
> —TERENCE, *Eunuchus*

W E LIVE IN AN AGE of superheroes. In every one of the past five years, with the exception of 2020 (atypical because of the pandemic), the highest grossing film in the US has either been part of the Marvel cinematic universe or featured a character from DC Comics.

This development has not been greeted with unalloyed joy by the creative community. Martin Scorsese has described such films as "theme

1

2

MLA CITATION: Slater, Stewart. "Ancient Archetypes and Modern Superheroes." *Back to the Lake: A Reader and Guide for Writers*, edited by Thomas Cooley, 5th ed., W. W. Norton, 2024, pp. 506–10.

parks"; Ken Loach, Britain's leading producer of worthy, political cinema, considers them a "cynical exercise"; while to Francis Ford Coppola—whose 1972 movie *The Godfather* was, for a time, the highest grossing film in history—they are "despicable." Alan Moore, creator of the graphic novels *Watchmen, V for Vendetta* and *The League of Extraordinary Gentlemen,* all of which have been turned into movies (none of which he likes), says that the trend has "blighted cinema and also blighted society to a degree."

But such films are undeniably popular: the box office does not lie. So, is the ascendancy of the superhero film a sign of cultural decline or are such responses simply snobbery? Should we bemoan the rash of sequels or see them as continuing and updating literary tropes that have existed for millennia? 3

Heroes have always been with us. The earliest surviving work of fiction, *The Epic of Gilgamesh,* relates the adventures of the titular character—"supreme over other kings, lordly in appearance"—as he first battles and later befriends the wildman Enkidu (shades, here, of Wolverine—Marvel's modern model of feral masculinity—and Captain America and Ironman—who must overcome personal differences to work together) and then embarks on an ultimately fruitless search for the secret of immortality. Generations have been brought up with the Greek myths, with their stories of heroic figures doing great deeds. Over time, these stories and their descendants have shaped our expectations about what heroes are and how they behave, expectations that superheroes match. 4

Malvolio's words in *Twelfth Night*—"Some are born great, some achieve greatness, and some have greatness thrust upon them"—aptly describe three heroic archetypes, all of which are represented in the superhero canon, and all of which have historical antecedents.

> When you identify a type or archetype, you describe its main characteristics (p. 460).

Born Great: Superman

"Faster than a speeding bullet, more powerful than a locomotive, able to leap tall buildings in a single bound," Superman is undeniably great. This greatness is innate: it is a result of a physiology adapted to his home planet of Krypton, which enables him to handle the much less challenging conditions on planet Earth with ease. (Compare the Xelayan security officers Alara Kitan and Talla Keyali in Seth MacFarlane's *The Orville,* whose exceptional strength is an adaptation to conditions on their high-gravity home planet.) 6

Notions of heroes who are superior from birth are as old as fiction itself. Gilgamesh also owes his greatness to his birth as a son of "Uruk, the goring wild bull." Achilles is the son of the goddess Thetis. Heracles is the son of Zeus. 7

Greek heroic literature is generally aristocratic. The heroes of *The Iliad* are kings and their heirs and close relatives. The lower classes are generally nameless 8 spear-fodder. Thersites—the one instance of a named character from outside the nobility—is there to provide comic relief. Heroes occupy a different hereditary caste from the masses. They have patronymics, which indicate the importance of their lineage. (Thersites does not.) Indeed, we learn the name of Achilles' father before we learn his own name. Noble birth is not a guarantor of heroic status—Achilles dispatches Priam's son Lycaon with relative ease; Paris is no great fighter—but it is a prerequisite. Not all nobles are heroes, but all heroes are noble—and nobility can only be acquired through birth. Like Superman, and like F. Scott Fitzgerald's very rich characters, Homer's heroes are "different from you and me."

Achieved Greatness: Batman

Unlike Superman, there is nothing innately great about Batman. Born to extremely rich but mortal parents, Bruce Wayne has no natural powers or abilities. At the beginning of Christopher Nolan's *Dark Knight* trilogy (2005–2012), he is a student at Princeton who drops out of college to pursue his vendetta against the criminals who killed his parents. During his quest, he falls in with the League of Shadows, which teaches him the skills and techniques that he will use as Batman. Returning to Gotham City, he adopts his alter ego and uses his effectively unlimited wealth to fulfill this mission. At the end of the trilogy, he leaves the heroics behind to start a new life with his girlfriend. [9]

There is no ancient model for Batman. The ancients believed that heroes were born, not made. This story-arc of self-creation had no place in their heroic archetypes: there is no ancient equivalent of the training montage. However, there is a modern analogue in Edmond Dantès of Alexandre Dumas' 1844 novel *The Count of Monte Cristo*. [10]

When the story begins, Dantès is a promising young sailor of a type one might find in most ports. Then he is unjustly imprisoned in the dungeons of the Château d'If, where he meets the Abbé Faria, who trains him in skills ranging from chemistry and philosophy to fencing and pistol shooting. After escaping from the château and discovering a vast treasure whose location the Abbé revealed to him, Dantès, in the company of his faithful servant Ali, adopts the guise of the Count of Monte Cristo, using his new skills and resources to wreak vengeance on those who wronged him before sailing off into the blue horizon with his young love. Like Dantès, Nolan's Batman is an ordinary man who suffers an injustice that prompts him to acquire new skills and knowledge, which he uses to fulfill his mission, after which he retires. Like his predecessor, he appears to give away all his money at the end of the story. [11]

Greatness Thrust upon Him: Spiderman

While Superman is born great and Batman achieves greatness, Spiderman has great- 12
ness thrust upon him. Peter Parker is a geeky teenager who has no special powers until
fate intervenes in the guise of a radioactive spider, whose bite confers superhuman
abilities. However, in the Sam Raimi trilogy (2002–2007), he does not immediately
choose to be a hero, initially using his powers simply to win an underground wrestling
tournament. It is the death of his father figure Uncle Ben, which he could have pre-
vented, that sets him on the path to heroism. From then on, however, his arc develops
very differently from those of his superhero peers. In contrast to Superman who, in the
latest television series (Greg Berlanti and Todd Helbing's *Superman and Lois* [2021–]),
is happily married to Lois Lane, Peter Parker ends the first film, *Spider-Man* (2002),
by rejecting the love of his life. In the second film (released in 2004) he gives up his
heroics briefly due to the toll his role is taking on his private life, while the final 2007
film ends with the death of his best friend. Spiderman is the suffering superhero.

That heroism might come at a cost to the hero would have been no surprise to 13
the ancients. Aeneas, son of the goddess Aphrodite, is one of the few survivors of
the fall of Troy. Like Peter Parker, he is set on the path to heroism by a father figure
when his father Anchises interprets an omen that reveals that it is Aeneas' destiny
to found a second Troy: Rome. This mission causes him romantic troubles when the
gods force him to leave his beloved Queen Dido behind at Carthage. He is subsequently tempted to abandon his mission altogether and has to be chivvied[1] along by
his late father's ghost. Even when he reaches the site of the future Rome, his troubles are not over: his beloved friend Pallas is killed in battle.

While *Superman* and *Batman* present an upbeat picture of heroism, Raimi's 14
Spider-Man is part of the more nuanced tradition of the *Aeneid* in that it points out
the burdens his mission places on the hero and even prompts the audience to wonder whether it is all worth it.

But it is not just tales of solo superheroes that represent long-standing
tropes. Series like *X-Men* and *Avengers* feature teams of heroes. While some
critics have seen these as exercises in "bloated cynicism," attempts to get
fans of several different franchises to shell out for the same film, this genre
would have been recognizable to the ancients. The crew of Jason's *Argo*
include Heracles, Zeus' sons Castor and Pollux, Orpheus and Achilles' father
Peleus. People have always been interested in heroes working together.

> Mindy Kaling takes a differ-
> ent approach in "Types of
> Women in Romantic Comedies
> Who Are Not Real" (p. 489).

Even the rise in sequels is something our ancestors would understand. Homer 16
only covers a brief period of the Trojan War, but later hands set to work filling in the
blanks in what came to be known as the *epic cycle*. Aeschylus uses Agamemnon's

---

1. *Chivvied:* urged or prodded, especially to do something the person doesn't want to do.

homecoming from Troy as the basis of his *Oresteia* trilogy, while Sophocles' *Ajax* continues the story of the hero after the events narrated by Homer.

> One reason to classify things is to learn more about the world (p. 462).

That we can so easily find historical analogues for modern characters should not be a surprise, for culture always builds on what has gone before. Early works created expectations that new creations generally attempt to meet. Heroic narratives are explorations of human greatness. Heroes fascinate us because they are outliers. They can do things that others cannot, and this raises the question of which is more important: nature or nurture. Cultures with hereditary aristocracies may find it easier to relate to figures like Achilles and Superman, who were born great, while post-industrial modern societies with their increased possibilities for social mobility might find inspiration in self-made heroes like Batman and the Count of Monte Cristo. Meanwhile, the stories of Aeneas and Spiderman address the perennial issue of whether heroism is more trouble than it is worth. Rather than a sign of cultural malaise, superhero movies are merely the latest meditations on questions that have intrigued us since the dawn of civilization. ◆

FOR CLOSE READING

1. According to Stewart Slater, some well-known film directors dislike recent films that feature superheroes. Why? What do they dislike about them?

2. Despite their critics, says Slater, superhero films are "undeniably popular" (3). By what measure?

3. Do today's superheroes deserve the popularity they enjoy? What do you think accounts for it?

4. How and how well does Slater's essay address the key question he raises in paragraph 3: "So, is the ascendancy of the superhero film a sign of cultural decline?"

5. Because he comes from Krypton, Superman is not bound by Earth's gravitational field. Under what conditions can he, nonetheless, be brought down? Would this be considered his Achilles' heel? (If you don't know the term, do a quick internet search to find out its meaning and the story behind it.)

STRATEGIES AND STRUCTURES

1. Slater classifies superheroes, both ancient and modern, into three types, based on their "greatness" and how they acquired it. Are the categories in his (and Malvolio's) classification system mutually exclusive? Are they jointly exhaustive? Explain.

2. Batman has no equivalent among ancient superheroes. How does Slater deal with this exception to the classification system he has set up?

3. For what PURPOSE is Slater classifying superheroes here? How and how well does classifying his subject support what else he has to say about it?

4. What is Slater's THESIS? That modern superheroes derive from ancient models? That the popularity of superhero films is not "a sign of cultural malaise" (17)? That "culture always builds on what has gone before" (17)? Some combination of these? Explain.

5. *Other Methods.* As he classifies superheroes, Slater gives EXAMPLES of each type. Which ones do you find particularly effective? Why?

THINKING ABOUT LANGUAGE

1. What are the implications of Slater's use of the word "canon" to describe a group of figures drawn from comic books (5)?

2. "Patronymics" (8) are names derived from those of a father or ancestor. According to Slater, why is having a patronymic a sign of nobility?

3. "Analogue" (10) refers to types that are similar but not necessarily models for each other. Why might Slater choose this term when discussing the relationship between Batman and the Count of Monte Cristo?

4. A "montage" (10) is a mixture of bits and pieces that combine to make a new whole. What does the term mean when applied to film in particular?

5. Slater says that *The Count of Monte Cristo*, Alexandre Dumas's novel of 1844, is a "modern analogue" for Batman (10). What does he mean by "modern"?

FOR WRITING

1. Do some research on the role of Malvolio in Shakespeare's *Twelfth Night* and explain, in a paragraph or two, the context of the stodgy character's famous pronouncement about the three types of greatness.

2. In a paragraph or two, outline the categories you would use if you were classifying superheroes based on their weaknesses rather than their strengths or how they became great.

3. Write a brief PROFILE of a hero (or villain), real or fictional, who had greatness (or great evildoing) thrust on them.

4. Write a five-to-seven-paragraph EVALUATION of your favorite superheroes in which you explain why they are the greatest of them all. Base your evaluation on the nature of their deeds rather than how they obtained their powers. Give lots of EXAMPLES.

5. Using Slater's essay as a point of departure, write a 400-to-600-word CRITICAL ANALYSIS of superhero films in which you argue for or against the claim that they have "blighted cinema and also blighted society to a degree" (2). Be sure to identify the films on which you base your analysis.

TREVOR NOAH

Chameleon

Trevor Noah (b. 1984) is a comedian, writer, producer, television personality, and host, from 2015 to 2022, of *The Daily Show* on Comedy Central. Noah is a native of Johannesburg, South Africa; his father is of Swiss and German ancestry, and his mother is Xhosa, a branch of the second-largest ethnic group in South Africa, after the Zulu. In addition to English and German, therefore, Noah grew up speaking several African languages.

"If you spoke to me in Zulu," he writes in *Born a Crime: Stories from a South African Childhood* (2016), "I replied to you in Zulu. If you spoke to me in Tswana, I replied to you in Tswana." Noah thus became a "chameleon," as demonstrated in this selection from the chapter by that name in his memoir of childhood. When he enters a new school, Noah does not change his color; he changes his *perception* of color—as a basis both for defining himself and for understanding how he is classified by others—and he changes how he talks depending on his audience.

A S APARTHEID WAS COMING TO AN END,[1] South Africa's elite private schools   1
started accepting children of all colors. My mother's company offered bursaries, scholarships, for underprivileged families, and she managed to get me into Maryvale College, an expensive private Catholic school. Classes taught by nuns. Mass on Fridays. The whole bit. I started preschool there when I was three, primary school when I was five.

MLA CITATION: Noah, Trevor. "Chameleon." *Back to the Lake: A Reader and Guide for Writers*, edited by Thomas Cooley, 5th ed., W. W. Norton, 2024, pp. 512–15.

1. Established in 1948 as an official system of racial segregation in South Africa, apartheid ended in 1994 when Nelson Mandela was elected as the country's first non-White president.

In my class we had all kinds of kids. Black kids, white kids, Indian kids, colored 2 kids.[2] Most of the white kids were pretty well off. Every child of color pretty much wasn't. But because of scholarships we all sat at the same table. We wore the same maroon blazers, the same gray slacks and skirts. We had the same books. We had the same teachers. There was no racial separation. Every clique was racially mixed.

Kids still got teased and bullied, but it was over usual kid stuff: being fat or being 3 skinny, being tall or being short, being smart or being dumb. I don't remember anybody being teased about their race. I didn't learn to put limits on what I was supposed to like or not like. I had a wide berth to explore myself. I had crushes on white girls. I had crushes on black girls. Nobody asked me what I was. I was Trevor.

It was a wonderful experience to have, but the downside was that it sheltered me 4 from reality. Maryvale was an oasis that kept me from the truth, a comfortable place where I could avoid making a tough decision. But the real world doesn't go away. Racism exists. People are getting hurt, and just because it's not happening to you doesn't mean it's not happening. And at some point, you have to choose. Black or white. Pick a side. You can try to hide from it. You can say, "Oh, I don't pick sides," but at some point life will force you to pick a side.

At the end of grade six I left Maryvale to go to H. A. Jack Primary, a government 5 school. I had to take an aptitude test before I started, and, based on the results of the test, the school counselor told me, "You're going to be in the smart classes, the A classes." I showed up for the first day of school and went to my classroom. Of the thirty or so kids in my class, almost all of them were white. There was one Indian kid, maybe one or two black kids, and me.

Then recess came. We went out on the playground, and black kids were *every-* 6 *where*. It was an ocean of black, like someone had opened a tap and all the black had come pouring out. I was like, *Where were they all hiding?* The white kids I'd met that morning, they went in one direction, the black kids went in another direction, and I was left standing in the middle, totally confused. Were we going to meet up later on? I did not understand what was happening.

I was eleven years old, and it was like I was seeing my country for the first time. 7 In the townships you don't see segregation, because everyone is black. In the white world, any time my mother took me to a white church, we were the only black people there, and my mom didn't separate herself from anyone. She didn't care. She'd go right up and sit with the white people. And at Maryvale, the kids were mixed up and hanging out together. Before that day, I had never seen people being together and yet not together, occupying the same space yet choosing not to associate with each other in any way. In an instant I could see, I could feel, how the boundaries were drawn.

---

2. South Africans refer to people of mixed ethnicity as "colored."

Groups moved in color patterns across the yard, up the stairs, down the hall. It was insane. I looked over at the white kids I'd met that morning. Ten minutes earlier I'd thought I was at a school where they were a majority. Now I realized how few of them there actually were compared to everyone else.

When classifying anomalies, consider the platypus (p. 462).

I stood there awkwardly by myself in this no-man's-land in the middle of the playground. Luckily, I was rescued by the Indian kid from my class, a guy named Theesan Pillay. Theesan was one of the few Indian kids in school, so he'd noticed me, another obvious outsider, right away. He ran over to introduce himself. "Hello, fellow anomaly! You're in my class. Who are you? What's your story?" We started talking and hit it off. He took me under his wing, the Artful Dodger to my bewildered Oliver.[3]

Through our conversation it came up that I spoke several African languages, and Theesan thought a colored kid speaking black languages was the most amazing trick. He brought me over to a group of black kids. "Say something," he told them, "and he'll show you he understands you." One kid said something in Zulu, and I replied to him in Zulu. Everyone cheered. Another kid said something in Xhosa, and I replied to him in Xhosa. Everyone cheered. For the rest of recess Theesan took me around to different black kids on the playground. "Show them your trick. Do your language thing."

The black kids were fascinated. In South Africa back then, it wasn't common to find a white person or a colored person who spoke African languages; during apartheid white people were always taught that those languages were beneath them. So the fact that I did speak African languages immediately endeared me to the black kids.

"How come you speak our languages?" they asked.

"Because I'm black," I said, "like you."

"You're not black."

"Yes, I am."

"No, you're not. Have you not seen yourself?"

They were confused at first. Because of my color, they thought I was a colored person, but speaking the same languages meant that I belonged to their tribe. It just took them a moment to figure it out. It took me a moment, too.

At some point I turned to one of them and said, "Hey, how come I don't see you guys in any of my classes?" It turned out they were in the B classes, which also happened to be the black classes. That same afternoon, I went back to the A classes, and by the end of the day I realized that they weren't for me. Suddenly, I knew who my people were, and I wanted to be with them. I went to see the school counselor.

Why choose one category over another? Page 466 gives several reasons.

"I'd like to switch over," I told her. "I'd like to go to the B classes."

---

3. In the novel *Oliver Twist* (1838) by Charles Dickens (1812-70), the young pickpocket Jack Dawkins is called the Artful Dodger because of his agility on the streets of London.

She was confused. "Oh, no," she said. "I don't think you want to do that." 19

"Why not?" 20

"Because those kids are . . . you know." 21

"No, I don't know. What do you mean?" 22

"Look," she said, "you're a smart kid. You don't want to be in that class." 23

"But aren't the classes the same? English is English. Math is math." 24

"Yeah, but that class is . . . those kids are gonna hold you back. You want to be in 25
the smart class."

"But surely there must be some smart kids in the B class." 26

"No, there aren't." 27

"But all my friends are there." 28

"You don't want to be friends with those kids." 29

"Yes, I do." 30

We went back and forth. Finally she gave me a stern warning. 31

"You do realize the effect this will have on your future? You do understand what 32
you're giving up? This will impact the opportunities you'll have open to you for the
rest of your life."

"I'll take that chance." 33

I moved to the B classes with the black kids. I decided I'd rather be held back 34
with people I liked than move ahead with people I didn't know.

Being at H. A. Jack made me realize I was black. Before that recess I'd never had 35
to choose, but when I was forced to choose, I chose black. The world saw me as colored, but I didn't spend my life looking at myself. I spent my life looking at other
people. I saw myself as the people around me, and the people around me were black.
My cousins are black, my mom is black, my gran is black. I grew up black. Because
I had a white father, because I'd been in white Sunday school, I got along with the
white kids, but I didn't *belong* with the white kids. I wasn't a part of their tribe. But
the black kids embraced me. "Come along," they said. "You're rolling with us." With
the black kids, I wasn't constantly trying to be. With the black kids, I just was. ◆

FOR CLOSE READING

1. At Maryvale, where Trevor Noah first went to school, "there was no racial separation" (2). What was the "downside" of this otherwise "wonderful" experience,
   according to Noah (4)?

2. When Noah transfers to H. A. Jack Primary at age eleven, he is "totally confused"
   (6). Why is his new school so different from his old one?

3. At his new government school, Noah maintains that he is Black "like you" (12). To
   whom is he speaking here? Why are these "kids" skeptical of his claims but nonetheless "fascinated" by him (10)?

4. Elsewhere in *Born a Crime*, Noah says that "language, even more than color, defines who you are to people." Is this true in your experience? Why or why not?

5. How and where does Noah himself define who he is? What part does language play in his decision to belong to one racial category rather than another?

STRATEGIES AND STRUCTURES

1. At times, Noah divides his classmates into three groups: White, Black, and colored. In his account of "how the boundaries were drawn," what were the distinguishing features of each of these racial and social categories as constituted "back then" in South Africa (7, 10)?

2. Sometimes, instead of dividing his classmates into three categories, Noah adds a fourth ("Indian")—or uses only two (Black and White). In a good classification system, the categories do not overlap. How do the various systems that Noah cites here meet (or fail to meet) this standard?

3. In "Chameleon," Noah uses a shifting set of categories to characterize race. Does this confirm what he says about being a chameleon? Why or why not?

4. Noah says that "at some point life will force you to pick a side," because "the real world doesn't go away" (4). How is he DEFINING "real world" here? Is his ARGUMENT valid? Why or why not?

5. *Other Methods.* In addition to using CLASSIFICATION to make a point about race, Noah is constructing a NARRATIVE about his experience with race as he was growing up in South Africa. How and why does paragraph 7 represent a major turning point in the PLOT of the story?

THINKING ABOUT LANGUAGE

1. "Apartheid" (1) means, literally, "separateness"; it derives from the Dutch word "apart" (which means the same as in English), plus the suffix "-heid." What is the English equivalent of "heid"?

2. "No-man's-land" refers to territory separating warring parties (8). Why might Noah use a military METAPHOR in a discussion of race?

3. One of the "Indian kids" in Noah's school refers to him as a "fellow anomaly" (8). What is an "anomaly"? Do Noah and Theesan Pillay qualify as such? Why or why not?

4. In paragraph 8, Noah says he played "Oliver" to Pillay's "Artful Dodger." What is the purpose of this ALLUSION to Dickens's novel, and what does it suggest about the boys' education?

5. Maryvale College, where Noah first went to school as a child, was clearly a grade school. So why was it called a "college" in the South Africa of his childhood?

6. Noah does not use the term in his narrative, but a moment of sudden revelation in a story is sometimes referred to as an "epiphany." Where and how might the term be applied to Noah's account of his first day at H. A. Jack?

FOR WRITING

1. In a paragraph or two, define "apartheid" as it was practiced in the South Africa of Trevor Noah's childhood. Be sure to explain how apartheid differed from the less formal systems of racial classification that Noah talks about.

2. Do further research on the system of apartheid in South Africa and elsewhere, and write an essay of 500 to 700 words explaining how the system worked, how it was enforced, and how and when it came to an end.

3. Tell the story of when you first became aware of language as a way of defining (or failing to define) yourself in the eyes of other people. Give examples of specific words and phrases that you (and others) used—and how they helped you (or not) be the person you wanted to be.

CAITLIN DOUGHTY

What If They Bury Me When I'm Just in a Coma?

Caitlin Doughty (b. 1984) is a writer, blogger, *YouTube* personality, and mortician. A native of Hawaii, Doughty graduated from the University of Chicago, where she majored in medieval history. After training at a crematory, Doughty studied mortuary science at Cypress College. In 2011, she founded the Order of the Good Death, which advocates for natural burial and open discussion of human mortality, and started her popular *YouTube* series, "Ask a Mortician." Doughty is the author of *Smoke Gets in Your Eyes* (2014); *From Here to Eternity* (2017); and *Will My Cat Eat My Eyeballs?* (2019).

"What if they make a mistake and bury me when I'm just in a coma?" is one of 35 questions Doughty raises in her 2019 book. Her answer is *not to worry*: death professionals today are expert classifiers with strict scientific criteria for identifying different states of human mortality, such as merely being in a coma or being "good and dead."

O KAY, SO TO BE CLEAR, you *don't* want to be buried alive, is that correct? Got it. 1
Lucky for you, you don't live in Ye Olden Times! During Ye Olden Times 2 (before the twentieth century), doctors had a less-than-flawless track record when it came to declaring people dead. The tests they used to determine if someone was honest-to-God-really-dead were not just low-tech, they were horrifying.

For your enjoyment, here's a fun sample of the death tests: 3

- Shoving needles under the toenails, or into the heart or stomach.
- Slicing the feet with knives or burning them with red-hot pokers.

MLA CITATION: Doughty, Caitlin. "What If They Bury Me When I'm Just in a Coma?" *Back to the Lake: A Reader and Guide for Writers*, edited by Thomas Cooley, 5th ed., W. W. Norton, 2024, pp. 518–21.

- Smoke enemas for drowning victims—someone would literally "blow smoke up your ass" to see if it would warm you up and make you breathe.
- Burning the hand or chopping off a finger.

And, my personal favorite:

- Writing "I am really dead" in invisible ink (made from acetate of lead) on a piece of paper, then putting the paper over the corpse-in-question's face. According to the inventor of this method, if the body was putrefying, sulfur dioxide would be emitted, thus revealing the message. Unfortunately, sulfur dioxide can also be emitted by living people, like those with decaying teeth. So, it's possible there were a few false positives.

If you woke up, breathed, or visibly responded to these "tests"—hallelujah!—you weren't dead. But you might be maimed. And that needle stuck in your heart could actually kill you.

But what about the poor souls who weren't put through the battery of stabs,   4
slices, and enemas, but were just assumed to be 100 percent dead and sent to the grave?

Take the tale of Matthew Wall, a man living (yes, *living*) in Braughing, England,   5
in the sixteenth century. Matthew was thought to be dead, but was lucky enough to have his pallbearers slip on wet leaves and drop the coffin on the way to his burial. As the story goes, when the coffin was dropped, Matthew awakened and knocked on the lid to be released. To this day, every October 2nd is celebrated as Old Man's Day to commemorate Matthew's revival. He lived, by the way, *for twenty-four more years.*

With stories like that, it's no wonder that certain cultures had extreme taphopho-   6
bia, or the fear of being buried alive. Matthew Wall was lucky that his "body" never reached his grave, but Angelo Hays was not.

In 1937—true, 1937 is not quite Ye Olden Times, but at least it's way before   7
you were born—Angelo Hays of France was in a motorcycle accident. When doctors couldn't find his pulse, he was pronounced dead. He was buried quickly and his own parents were not allowed to see his disfigured body. Angelo would have remained buried if it wasn't for the life insurance company's suspicions of foul play.

Two days after Angelo was buried, he was exhumed for an investigation. Upon   8
inspecting the "corpse," examiners found that it was still warm, and that Angelo was alive.

The theory is that Angelo had been in a very deep coma which slowed his breath-   9
ing way, way down. It was that slow breathing that allowed him to stay alive while

buried.[1] Angelo recovered, lived a full life, and even invented a "security coffin" with a radio transmitter and a toilet.

Luckily, if you fall into a coma today, in the twenty-first century, there are many, 10 many ways to make sure that you are good and dead before you're moved on to burial. But while the tests may show that you are technically alive, your new status may be small comfort to you and your kin.

Media and TV shows often throw around terms like "coma" and "brain-dead" 11 interchangeably. "Chloe was my true love, and now she will never wake from her coma. I must decide whether to pull the plug." This Hollywood version of medicine can make it seem like those conditions are the same, just one step away from death. Not true!

Of the two, the one you really don't want to be is brain-dead. (I mean, neither is 12 great, let's be honest.) But once you're brain-dead, there is no coming back. Not only have you lost all the upper brain functions that create your memories and behaviors and allow you to think and talk, but you have also lost all the involuntary stuff your lower brain does to keep you alive, like controlling your heart, respiration, nervous system, temperature, and reflexes. There are gobs of biological actions controlled by your brain so that you don't have to constantly remind yourself, "Stay alive, stay alive . . ." If you are brain-dead, these functions are being performed by hospital equipment like ventilators and catheters.

> This either-or condition is true of any "binary" classification system (p. 467).

You cannot recover from brain death. If you're brain-dead, you're dead. 13 There is no gray area (brain matter joke): either you are brain-dead or you are not. If you are in a coma, on the other hand, you are legally very much alive. In a coma, you still have brain function, which doctors can measure by observing electrical activity and your reactions to external stimuli. In other words, your body continues to breathe, your heart beats, etc. Even better, you can, potentially, recover from a coma and regain consciousness.

Okay, but what if I fall into a deep, deep coma? Will someone eventually pull the 14 plug and send me off to the mortuary? Will I be trapped in both a casket and in the *prison of my mind*?

No. We now have a whole battery of scientific tests to confirm that someone is 15 not just in a coma, but really, truly brain-dead.

These tests include but are not limited to: 16

- Seeing if your pupils are reactive. When a bright light is shined into them, do they contract? Brain-dead people's eyes don't do anything.
- Dragging a cotton swab over your eyeball. If you blink, you're alive!

---

1. If you're buried alive and breathing normally, you're likely to die from suffocation. A person can live on the air in a coffin for a little over five hours, tops. If you start hyperventilating, panicked that you've been buried alive, the oxygen will likely run out sooner [author's note].

- Testing your gag reflex. Your breathing tube might be moved in and out of your throat, to see if you gag. Dead people don't gag.
- Injecting ice water into your ear canal. If doctors do this to you and your eyes don't flick quickly from side to side, it's not looking good.
- Checking for spontaneous respiration. If you are removed from a ventilator, CO_2 builds up in your system, essentially suffocating you. When blood CO_2 levels reach 55 mm Hg, a living brain will usually tell the body to spontaneously breathe. If that doesn't happen, your brain stem is dead.
- An EEG, or electroencephalogram, which is an all-or-nothing test. Either there is electrical activity in your brain or there isn't. Dead brains have zero electrical activity.
- A CBF, or cerebral blood flow, study. A radioactive isotope is injected into your bloodstream. After a period of time, a radioactive counter is held over your head to see if blood is flowing to your brain. If there is blood flow to the brain, the brain cannot be called dead.
- Administering atropine IV. A living patient's heart rate will accelerate, but a brain-dead patient's heartbeat will not change.

A person has to fail *a lot* of tests to be declared brain-dead. And more than one 17 doctor has to confirm brain death. Only after countless tests and an in-depth physical exam will you go from "coma patient" to "brain-dead" patient. Nowadays, it's not just some dude with a needle poised over your heart and "I am really dead" scrawled on a scrap of paper.

It is highly unlikely that your living brain will slip through the cracks and that 18 you'll be sent away from the hospital in a coma. Even if you were, there is no funeral director or medical examiner I know who can't tell the difference between a living person and a corpse. Having seen thousands of dead bodies in my career, let me tell you—dead people are very dead in a very predictable way. Not that my words sound all that comforting. Or scientific. But I feel confident saying that this is not going to happen to you. On your list of "Freaky Ways to Die" you can move "buried alive—coma" down to just below "terrible gopher accident." ◆

> As p. 462 explains, we classify things in order to make sense of the world around us.

FOR CLOSE READING

1. Is Caitlin Doughty right to say that the tests that even doctors once used to determine whether or not a person was dead were "less-than-flawless" ones (2)? Why or why not?

2. What about the "battery of scientific tests" that doctors use today (15)? How reliable are they, according to Doughty; and what, precisely, are they used to determine?

3. On anyone's list of "Freaky Ways to Die," just how far down *is* "terrible gopher accident" likely to be: "not very," "more than halfway," "off the charts" (18)? Explain.

4. "I must decide whether to pull the plug" (11). Why does Doughty describe this as a "Hollywood version of medicine" (11)?

5. Do you think Doughty's essay is in bad taste? Why or why not?

STRATEGIES AND STRUCTURES

1. "Okay, so to be clear, you *don't* want to be buried alive, is that correct?" (1) Would this qualify as a RHETORICAL QUESTION? Is it an effective way for Doughty to begin her essay? Explain.

2. Doughty presents her first list of dead-or-alive tests "for your enjoyment" (3). To whom is she speaking here? What assumptions is she making about her intended audience, especially about their capacity for IRONY?

3. Doughty studied history in college. Why does she tell the ancient "tale" of Matthew Wall (5)? How about the more recent (but still "way before you were born") story of the Frenchman Angelo Hays (7–9)? Are they good historical EXAMPLES? Why or why not?

4. In the first part of her essay, Doughty uses a binary classification system (comatose or dead); what "new status" does she introduce in paragraph 10? What are the main distinguishing features of this third category, as established by the second set of tests that Doughty outlines?

5. How would you describe the overall TONE of Doughty's essay: "sharp as a needle," "lighthearted," "heavy-handed," "deadpan," all of these, or other? Explain.

6. *Other Methods.* According to Doughty, what is the most important difference between being "in a coma" and being "brain-dead" (13)? Doughty is an advocate of mortuary reform; what ARGUMENT is she implying here, especially when referring to "equipment like ventilators and catheters" (12)?

THINKING ABOUT LANGUAGE

1. Doughty defines "Ye Olden Times" as the period "before the twentieth century" (2). Did she likely learn this binary (then and now) system of classifying historical events in college, or is she sharing a joke with her audience? Explain.

2. Doughty defines "taphophobia" as "the fear of being buried alive" (6). The common suffix "-phobia" means "fear of." What is the literal meaning of "taphos" in Greek?

3. With brain death, says Doughty, there is no "gray area" (13). Is this an insufferable PUN—or welcome levity in a serious discussion of a difficult topic? Explain.

4. "Will I be trapped in both a casket and in the *prison of my mind*?" (14) In addition to being buried alive, what other condition would have to be met for a person to suffer from the second, more METAPHORICAL of these unlikely horrors?

FOR WRITING

1. Make a "Freaky Ways to Die" list that includes possibilities even more irrational and unlikely than being buried alive or killed in a terrible gopher accident. List at least five possibilities.

2. "Ye Olden Times." "Ye Olde Gifte Shoppe." Do a little research on spelling and printer's conventions in early modern English, and write a paragraph or two explaining the extra letters in words like these—and how "Y" came to be used at times for "Th."

3. In college, Doughty wrote and directed a play based, in part, on the work of Edgar Allan Poe (1809–49). Read Poe's late short story "The Premature Burial," and write a six-to-eight-paragraph CRITICAL ANALYSIS of it as a psychological tale of terror. You can find the story online by googling the title.

4. Write an essay of 500 to 700 words defining "brain death" as a medical condition and ARGUING that patients who meet all the standard criteria for this condition should (or should not) be taken off life support.

14 | Definition

A guy with a twelve-inch arm can have much more noticeable muscles than a guy with an eighteen-inch arm because he has better definition.

—PETE SISCO, *Train Smart*

You probably know what getting ripped off is. How about getting ripped? According to bodybuilder Pete Sisco, "getting ripped" refers to muscle definition: you build up your muscles so they stick out and are easier to see. Likewise, when you define something—from bodybuilding to high-definition electronics—you make its fundamental nature sharp and clear.

A clear definition tells what something is—"a bodybuilder is an athlete who works for muscle definition"—by assigning the thing being defined (bodybuilder) to a specific group or category (athlete). It then assigns a defining characteristic to that group or category (who works for muscle definition). Let's look at the logic behind this way of defining things.

Telling What Something Is—and Is Not

A **DEFINITION** explains what something is—and is not—by identifying the characteristics that set it apart from all others like it. Bodybuilders, runners, and swimmers, for example, can all be defined as athletes. Only bodybuilders, however, train specifically for muscle definition and bulk.

In other words, training for muscle definition and bulk is a characteristic that *defines* bodybuilders alone. Runners and swimmers may want and need strong muscles, too, but what *defines* them is their speed on the track and in the pool, not the size or look of their muscles on the beach. Definitions set up boundaries; they say, in effect: "This is the territory occupied by my subject, and everything outside these boundaries is something else." Definition can also be a method of developing a subject in writing, and in this chapter we'll see how to use definition when you organize and compose an essay.

Basic definitions have two parts: the general class to which the term belongs, and the specific characteristics that distinguish the term from other terms in that class. This is the pattern that definitions have followed since Dr. Samuel Johnson compiled the *Dictionary of the English Language* more than 250 years ago. For example, Johnson's famous definition of a "lexicographer," or dictionary maker, as "a harmless drudge" fits this pattern: "drudge" is the general class, and "harmless" is a characteristic that distinguishes the lexicographer from other kinds of drudges.

Here are a few more current examples of basic definitions:

Term Being Defined	General Class	Distinguishing Characteristic(s)
writer	user of words	requires peace and quiet
muscle	body tissue	fibrous, capable of contracting
osprey	hawk	fish-eating

Because basic definitions like these help explain the fundamental nature of a subject, they can be useful for beginning almost any kind of essay. When you want to define a subject in depth, however, you'll need an *extended definition*. This kind of definition includes all the parts of a basic definition—the term you're defining, its general class, and its essential distinguishing characteristics. Unlike a basic definition, however, an extended definition doesn't stop there. It goes on to discuss other important distinguishing characteristics of the subject as well. For instance, if the basic definition of a bodybuilder is "an athlete who trains for muscle definition and bulk," an extended definition of a bodybuilder might look at a bodybuilder's focus and motivation, training regimen, bodybuilding competitions, and so on. Extended definitions also use many of the other methods of development discussed in this book, such as **NARRATION**, **DESCRIPTION**, and **EXAMPLE**.

In this chapter, we will not only see how to write basic definitions that are sharp and clear, but we will also learn how to construct an extended definition and make it the backbone of an essay. We'll consider how to use **SYNONYMS** and **ETYMOLOGIES** in a definition, and how to use other methods of development. We'll also review the critical points to watch for as you read over and revise your essay, as well as common errors to avoid when you edit.

Why Do We Define?

Being naturally curious, human beings define in order to understand the fundamental nature of things. For example, if you were defining "abolitionism" for a paper in a US history class, you might at first consider a brief, basic definition—"principles or actions in support of doing away with slavery in the United States"—but you would move on to discuss the abolition movement before the Civil War, as well as the legal and political ending of slavery by Abraham Lincoln's Emancipation Proclamation and the Thirteenth Amendment to the Constitution. Writing about this term would thus help you make sense of history—in this case, the history of an important social and political movement in American culture.

Sometimes, however, understanding a definition can be personally enlightening. The great antislavery orator Frederick Douglass escaped from slavery as a young man. In 1845, he wrote about how he came to learn the meaning of "abolition":

> If a slave ran away and succeeded in getting clear . . . or did anything very wrong in the mind of a slaveholder, it was spoken of as the fruit of *abolition*. Hearing the word in this connection very often, I set about learning what it meant. The dictionary afforded me little or no help. I found it was "the act of abolishing"; but then I did not know what was to be abolished. Here I was perplexed. I did not dare to ask anyone about the meaning, for I was satisfied that it was something they wanted me to know very little about. After a patient waiting, I got one of our city papers, containing an account . . . of the

slave trade between the States. From this time I understood the words *aboli-tion* and *abolitionist*, and always drew near when that word was spoken, expecting to hear something of importance to myself and fellow-slaves. The light broke in upon me by degrees.

—FREDERICK DOUGLASS, *Narrative*

For a killer example, see "How to Know If You're Dead" (p. 557).

Such is the power and purpose of definitions: without them, we're in the dark about many things of importance to us. Before he could write so powerfully about the concept of abolition, young Douglass first had to learn what the term meant in common usage. Defining, then, is ultimately a process of exploration. We extend our definitions in order to extend our horizons—and those of our readers.

USING DEFINITION IN A POSITION PAPER

"The beginning of wisdom," said the Greek philosopher Socrates, "is the definition of terms." The definition of terms is also the beginning of many a **POSITION PAPER**, because differences of opinion often hinge on different definitions of words—in addition to different ideas of what is wise, good, or true. The following example is from the introduction to an essay on the reading "disability" commonly called "dyslexia":

> I don't care much for the word *dyslexia*. I generally think of "us" as spatial thinkers and non-dyslexics as linear thinkers, or people who could be most often described as being *dys-spatios*. For spatial thinkers, reading is clearly necessary but over-rated. . . . From the perspective of the linear thinkers, we spatial thinkers seem to "think outside the box," and this accounts for our accomplishments. However, we think outside the box precisely because we have never been in one. Our minds are not clogged up by preconceived ideas acquired through excessive reading. We are, therefore, free to have original thoughts enhanced by personal observations.
>
> —JACK HORNER, "The Extraordinary Characteristics of Dyslexia"

Horner is taking the position here that dyslexia, commonly defined as a reading *disability*, isn't really a disability at all. In fact, Horner argues, it actually conveys a learning *advantage*. Like this one (which you can read in full on p. 565), many position papers hinge on the definition of terms. If you accept the writer's definition (or redefinition) of a key term in the debate—"dyslexia," in Horner's case—you are on the verge of accepting the writer's entire position, whether it represents wisdom or foolishness.

Composing an Essay That Uses Definition

When you compose a definition essay, your first challenge is to find a topic worth defining. That topic may be complex, like relativity or Marxism or capitalism. Or, sometimes, you may devote an entire essay to a definition because you're arguing that a word or concept means something that others might not have thought of or might disagree with. For example, if you were defining "intelligent design" in an essay, you might want to say, at some length, not only what intelligent design is but also why the reader should (or shouldn't) believe in it. Definitions that require a whole essay often deal with terms that are open to debate or controversy. For example: What constitutes "racism" or "sexual harassment"? Is an "embryo" or a "fetus" a "person"? What characterizes "friendship"?

Dictionary definitions will help you begin to think about such questions, but to write an essay that defines something fully—especially if it's complicated or controversial—you'll need to construct an extended definition and probably call on other methods of development as well. That is, you may need to **DESCRIBE** the subject, give **EXAMPLES** of it, analyze what **CAUSED** it or how it works, or **COMPARE** it with others. Take the concept of longitude, for example. "Longitude" can be defined as "distance measured east and west on the earth's surface." This basic definition doesn't fully define the subject, however. To extend such a definition, you might describe the place from which longitude is measured (the Royal Observatory in Greenwich, England, just outside of London on a steep hill), analyze how it's measured (in minutes and degrees from the prime meridian), and compare it with "latitude" (distance on the earth's surface as measured north and south of the equator).

To define "blue-collar brilliance," Mike Rose gives the examples of his mother and uncle (p. 569).

Thinking about Purpose and Audience

When you define something, your general **PURPOSE** is to say what it is, but you may have any number of specific reasons for doing this. You may be conveying useful information to someone, demonstrating that you understand the meaning of an important term or concept, arguing for a particular definition, or just entertaining the reader. In her essay in this chapter, "How to Know If You're Dead," Mary Roach, for example, defines her subject for most of these reasons combined. "When I tried to explain beating-heart cadavers to my stepdaughter Phoebe yesterday," she writes, "it didn't make sense to her. But if their heart is beating, aren't they still a person? she wanted to know. In the end she decided they were 'a kind of person you could play tricks on but they wouldn't know.'" This, says Roach, "is a pretty good way of summing up" the meaning of a difficult and sometimes controversial term.

Read Mary Roach's essay on p. 557.

USING DEFINITION TO FRAME AN ARGUMENT

"In this world," said Benjamin Franklin, "nothing is certain but death and taxes." No matter what you think of taxes, they won't kill you—literally. By putting taxes and death in the same framework, however, Franklin humorously asserts that the two terms belong in the same general class with the same distinguishing characteristic (both are "certain"). This sort of framing is a clever way of implying that two terms have other characteristics in common as well—in this case, negative ones.

Suppose you were the mayor of a small town and you wanted to build a recreation center. How might you convince the citizens of your town that a tax increase (to pay for the new recreation center) would be a good thing?

The linguist George Lakoff has pondered such questions. If you consider taxes, for instance, to be a necessary evil, Lakoff suggests, you might present them as "dues." Then you'd be defining them as what you pay to live in a civilized society where there are services that have been paid for by previous taxpayers. Defined this way, Lakoff argues, paying taxes becomes an act of good citizenship.

Defining a term ("taxes") by associating it with other terms ("dues") that carry **CONNOTATIONS** (good citizenship) you want to associate with your key term is a strategy of **ARGUMENT** that Lakoff and others call "framing." In the following passage, for example, Gretel Ehrlich defines (or redefines) what it means to be a cowboy—a subject normally framed in masculine terms—by framing it in more nurturing terms:

> Cowboys are perhaps the most misunderstood group of workers anywhere. Romanticized in the movies and on billboards as handsome, macho loners always heading off into the sunset, they are more likely to be homebodies or social misfits too shy to work with people. Their work has more to do with mothering and nurturing than with exhibitions of virility. A cowboy can bottle-feed a calf around the clock, forecast weather, use a sewing machine, make anything out of canvas or leather, and serve as midwife to any animal.
>
> —Gretel Ehrlich, *The Solace of Open Spaces*

The frame of reference in which you define a subject can predispose your readers to accept not only your definition but also the larger point your definition is intended to make.

Whatever your specific purpose (or purposes) for constructing a definition, you need to consider why your AUDIENCE might want (or be reluctant) to know more about it and what it means. Also think about how the reader might already define the term. What information can you supply to make it easier for the reader to understand your definition or be more receptive to it?

Consider the example of longitude again. If you were defining longitude in a manual for would-be sailors, you'd compare it with latitude and explain how each measures different directions on the globe. You would also point out that determining longitude requires an accurate timepiece—if not a Global Positioning System—whereas latitude can be estimated just by eyeballing the angle of the sun or stars above the horizon. Since you're defining longitude for navigational purposes, you won't need to point out that in the days before accurate clocks, mismeasuring longitude posed a grave danger to sailors on the high seas. However, such historical information—though irrelevant in a sailing manual—might be of vital interest if you were constructing a broad definition of longitude for a general audience, as in this passage from an entire book on the subject:

> Here lies the real, hard-core difference between latitude and longitude. . . . The zero-degree parallel of latitude [the equator] is fixed by the laws of nature, while the zero-degree meridian of longitude shifts like the sands of time. This difference makes finding latitude child's play, and turns the determination of longitude, especially at sea, into an adult dilemma—one that stumped the wisest minds of the world for the better part of human history.
>
> —DAVA SOBEL, *Longitude*

In *Longitude*, Sobel defines her subject as a scientific, political, and philosophical concept. In an essay, rather than a book, you can't define longitude or any other subject on such a global scale, but you can focus on those aspects of your subject that best suit your purpose and that your audience is most likely to find interesting and useful.

To define the Japanese concept of *shikake*, Naohiro Matsumura gives numerous illustrated examples (p. 549).

Generating Ideas: Asking What Something Is—and Is Not

LISTING, CLUSTERING, BRAINSTORMING, and other techniques of discovery can help you generate ideas for a definition. In order to define your subject, you'll need to consider what its distinguishing characteristics are—what makes it different from other things in the same general class. How do you know which characteristics are essential to your definition? Start by thinking about the characteristics that tell the most about it. For instance, suppose we wanted to define what an "engineer" is. We know that engineers often use tools and have specialized knowledge about how things are built. But these characteristics also apply to carpenters and burglars. What characteristics tell us the most about engineers?

According to one expert, Michael Davis, these characteristics are all *essential* to engineers:

- They are fascinated with the physical world.
- They value utility over beauty or knowledge.
- They have a thorough understanding of mathematics and science.
- They are trained to apply that knowledge to physical objects and systems.
- Their purpose in doing so is to remake the world by shaping it to practical use.

As you come up with a list of essential distinguishing characteristics for your subject, you should also ask what your subject is *not*. Here's how Davis answers that question when defining engineers:

- Engineers are not pure scientists. They may generate knowledge, but that knowledge is not an end in itself, as it can be for a mathematician or physicist.
- Though they may produce beautiful structures, such as bridges or towers, engineers are not artists (in the way that architects are).
- Engineers are not primarily interested in rules (lawyers) or money (accountants) or people (managers).
- Engineers must write reports that are both clear and accurate, but they are not primarily writers either.

The essential distinguishing characteristics that you list—the traits that tell what your subject is and is not—will form the foundation of your definition essay.

Organizing and Drafting a Definition

When you have a clear idea of your purpose and audience—and a solid list of distinguishing characteristics for your subject—you're ready to start organizing and drafting your essay. First you'll need to construct a basic definition of your subject—and then extend that definition. A number of techniques can help, including the other methods of development discussed in this book. The templates on p. 534 can also help you get started.

STATING YOUR POINT

A definition is not an end in itself; you need to say why you're defining your subject. A **THESIS** statement—usually made in the introduction of the essay and perhaps repeated with variations at the end—is a good way to do this. Here's a thesis statement for an extended definition of a "farmer," written by Craig Schafer, an

Ohio State student who grew up on a farm in the Midwest: "By definition, a farmer is someone who tills the soil for a living, but I define a true farmer according to his or her attitudes toward the land." This is a good thesis statement because it gives a clear basic definition of its subject—and then promises to extend it in interesting ways that the reader may or may not agree with at first.

SPECIFYING ADDITIONAL DISTINGUISHING CHARACTERISTICS

Of all the ways you can extend a basic definition, perhaps the most effective is simply to specify additional characteristics that set your subject apart. Thus to support his definition of a farmer as a person with certain attitudes toward the land, Schafer goes on to specify what those attitudes are, devoting a paragraph to each:

> Mike Rose goes into the many characteristics of "blue-collar brilliance" on p. 569.

- A farmer is a born optimist. He or she plants crops with no assurance that nature will cooperate or that markets will be favorable.
- A farmer is devoted to the soil. He or she enjoys letting it sift through their fingers or just sniffing the fresh clean aroma of a newly plowed field.
- A farmer is self-denying. His or her barn is often better planned and sometimes more modern than their house.
- A farmer is independent. Unions have found it impossible to organize farmers.

By ascribing interesting, even controversial, characteristics like these to your subject, you can take it well beyond the narrow confines of ordinary dictionary definitions. Everybody knows what a farmer is. But a farmer with attitude—or rather, attitudes—is a different story.

USING SYNONYMS

Another way to extend a definition is by offering SYNONYMS. If you can substitute a more familiar word for the term you're defining, the reader may be more likely to understand and accept your definition. For example, if you were defining a "blog" for readers who spend little time online, you might say that it's an electronic journal or diary. You could then go on to say which particular characteristics of journals apply to blogs and which ones don't. Both blogs and journals, you might point out, record the personal thoughts of their authors; but blogs, unlike journals, typically include links to other sites and blogs, and invite response.

> Alicia Garza does this with the concept of diversity on p. 579.

When you begin to draft a definition, you identify your subject, assign it to a general class, and specify particular characteristics that distinguish it from others in that same class. These moves are fundamental to any definition. See how Naohiro Matsumura makes them when he defines *shikake* in his essay in this chapter:

> Shikake are a means through which people become aware of those things that they can see but do not see, or that they can hear but do not hear.
> —NAOHIRO MATSUMURA, "Shikake in the Wild"

Matsumura identifies his subject ("*shikake*"), assigns it to a general class (means), and gives a characteristic ("through which people become aware of things") that distinguishes it from other means. Here is one more example from this chapter:

> H is unique in that she is both a dead person *and* a patient on the way to surgery. She is what's known as a "beating-heart cadaver," alive and well everywhere but her brain.
> —MARY ROACH, "How to Know If You're Dead"

The following templates can help you make some of these basic moves in your own writing. But don't take these as formulas where you just fill in the blanks. There are no shortcuts to good writing, but these templates can serve as starting points.

▶ In general, X can be defined as a kind of _____.

▶ What specifically distinguishes X from others in this category is _____.

▶ Other important distinguishing characteristics of X are _____, _____, and _____.

▶ X is often used to mean _____, but a better synonym would be _____ or _____.

▶ One way to define X is as the opposite of _____, the distinguishing characteristics of which are _____, _____, and _____.

▶ If we define X as _____, we can then define Y as _____.

▶ By defining X in this way, we can see that _____.

USING ETYMOLOGIES

Often you can usefully extend the definition of a term by tracing its history, or etymology. This is what an engineer at the University of Houston did when he asked, "Who are we who have been calling ourselves *engineers* since the early nineteenth century?" Here's part of his answer:

> The word *engineering* probably derives from the Latin word *ingeniatorum*. In 1325 a contriver of siege towers was called by the Norman word *engynours*. By 1420 the English were calling a trickster an *yngynore*. By 1592 we find the word *enginer* being given to a designer of phrases—a wordsmith. The *Oxford English Dictionary* gets to the first use of the modern word engineer in 1635, but you might not be crazy about its use. Someone is quoted as calling the devil—"that great engineer, Satan."
>
> —JOHN H. LIENHARD, "The Polytechnic Legacy"

Although few people today would use the word "engineer" to describe Satan, knowing the history of the word and its earlier variations can help us define what an engineer is—namely, one who crafts something with cleverness and ingenuity, whether it's a siege tower or a piece of writing. You can find the etymology of a word in most dictionaries, alongside the definition.

USING OTHER METHODS

As you draft a definition, draw on the other methods in this book to round out your definition and support your thesis. Let's say you're defining "cowboy." You could note that the cowboy is a vital part of the cattle industry and an iconic figure in American culture who is usually thought to be "the rugged silent type." You could ARGUE that this is a misconception, founded on equating him too often with the likes of movie characters portrayed by Clint Eastwood. Then you could go on to describe the attitudes and daily work of the cowboy as you define him.

For more on using argument, see the box on p. 530.

This is what Gretel Ehrlich, a writer who lives on a ranch in Wyoming, does in her extended definition of the American cowboy. Ehrlich's thesis is that "in our hellbent earnestness to romanticize the cowboy we've ironically disesteemed his true character." What is that true character? Ehrlich is going to define it for us, beginning with this basic definition: "A cowboy is someone who loves his work."

Ehrlich might have started with the standard dictionary definition of a cowboy as "a man, usually on horseback, who herds and tends cattle on a ranch, especially in the western US." By choosing "loves his work" from among all the other characteristics that might be said to define a cowboy, however, she introduces a distinguishing characteristic of her subject that the reader may not have considered. She then goes on to extend her definition by using a number of other methods of development, as shown in the examples below from her book *The Solace of Open Spaces*. First she DESCRIBES the work that is the key distinguishing characteristic of her subject:

> A cowboy is someone who loves his work. Since the hours are long—ten to fifteen hours a day—and the pay is $30 he has to. What's required of him is an odd mixture of physical vigor and maternalism. His part of the beef-raising industry is to birth and nurture calves and take care of their mothers. For the most part his work is done on horseback and in a lifetime he sees and comes to know more animals than people.

Next, Ehrlich ANALYZES THE PROCESS of how a cowboy does some of his work:

> If a cow is stuck in a boghole he throws a loop around her neck, takes his dally (a half hitch around the saddle horn), and pulls her out with horsepower. If a calf is born sick, he may take her home, warm her in front of the kitchen fire, and massage her legs until dawn.

Then Ehrlich introduces a little NARRATIVE of a particular cowboy saving a horse:

> One friend, whose favorite horse was trying to swim a lake with hobbles on, dove under water and cut her legs loose with a knife, then swam her to shore, his arm around her neck lifeguard-style, and saved her from drowning.

Because Ehrlich is using her definition to make an argument about the "true character" of the cowboy, an important part of her definition is devoted to COMPARING AND CONTRASTING her idea of a cowboy with that of the cowboy as he's typically (or stereotypically) defined:

> Instead of the macho, trigger-happy man our culture has perversely wanted him to be, the cowboy is more apt to be convivial, quirky, and soft-hearted.

Ehrlich also analyzes the actual CAUSES AND EFFECTS of the cowboy's behavior as she sees them—all in the service of defining what a true cowboy is to her:

> If he's "strong and silent" it's because there is probably no one to talk to. If he "rides away into the sunset" it's because he's been on horseback since four in the morning moving cattle and he's trying, fifteen hours later, to get home to his family. If he's "a rugged individualist" he's also part of a team:

ranch work is teamwork and even the glorified open range cowboys of the 1880s rode up and down the Chisholm Trail in the company of twenty or thirty other riders.

This definition does two things: it takes a fresh look at the characteristics usually attributed to the cowboy, and it introduces the author's own, more expansive characteristics. When you construct a new definition or rework an accepted one as Ehrlich does, the new characteristics that you introduce don't have to outlaw the old ones. They just need to open up enough space for the reader to come over to your side of the fence. Thus the cowboy can still be defined as "strong and silent" when he has to be—like a hero from a western. But if the American cowboy is to be conceived of as more than a cardboard figure, he can also be regarded as "convivial, quirky, and soft-hearted" at times.

EDITING FOR COMMON ERRORS IN DEFINITIONS

The following tips will help you check your writing for errors that often appear in definitions.

Make sure that words referred to as words are in quotation marks or in italics, and be consistent

- ▶ Often used as a synonym for "progress," according to the paleontologist Stephen Jay Gould, "evolution" simply means change.
- ▶ An expert in evolution, Gould defines the term "evolution" by explaining how it has been misused.

Check each basic definition to make sure it includes the class to which the term belongs

- ▶ Engineering is a professional field that applies science for practical purposes.
- ▶ A Labrador retriever is a breed of dog that has a friendly disposition and is patient with children.

Without "professional field" and "breed of dog," the preceding sentences are statements about their subjects rather than definitions of them.

Check for common usage errors

"Is where," "is when"

"Where" and "when" are not logical for introducing definitions.

▶ Engineering is ~~where you put~~ <u>the practice of putting</u> science to use.

▶ A recession is ~~when~~ <u>the economic condition in which</u> both prices and sales go down.

"Comprise," "is comprised of," "compose," "is composed of"

Avoid using "comprise" in the passive voice—"is comprised of"—because "comprise" itself means "to consist of." "Compose" means "to make up," so it can be used in both the active and passive voices. The whole *comprises* the parts; the parts *compose* the whole.

▶ The United States ~~is comprised of~~ <u>comprises</u> fifty states.

▶ The United States is ~~comprised~~ <u>composed</u> of fifty states.

▶ Fifty states ~~comprise~~ <u>compose</u> the United States.

Reading a Definition with a Critical Eye

Once you have a draft of your definition essay, ask a friendly critic to read it and tell you what's working and what isn't. Then read it over yourself with an eye for what can be improved. Here are some questions to keep in mind when checking a definition.

PURPOSE AND AUDIENCE. For whom is this definition written? What is its purpose—to define something the reader probably doesn't know much about? to demonstrate your knowledge to an already knowledgeable reader? How is the reader likely to define the subject? Does the definition confirm a standard definition, or challenge or expand it in some way? How?

THE BASIC DEFINITION. Does the definition identify the general class to which the subject of the essay belongs, plus the distinguishing characteristics that separate that subject from others in the same class? If not, how might the definition be improved?

THE POINT. What is the main point of the definition? Is it stated as a **THESIS**, preferably in the introduction of the essay? How might the main point be made even clearer?

DISTINGUISHING CHARACTERISTICS. How does the essay extend the basic definition? Does it introduce essential distinguishing characteristics of the subject? Are the characteristics sufficient to define the subject? Have any essential characteristics been left out? Which characteristics are most informative? Do any need to be sharpened or omitted? Does the definition say what the subject is not? Should it?

SYNONYMS AND ETYMOLOGIES. Are words with similar meanings or word histories used to help define key terms? If not, would either of these devices improve the definition?

OTHER METHODS. What other basic methods of development are used: **DESCRIPTION**? **COMPARISON AND CONTRAST**? Something else? If they aren't used, how might such methods be incorporated into the definition?

COMMON ERRORS. Do the basic definitions in the essay—for example, of the term "cowboy"—include the class or group to which the term belongs? If not, insert that class or group (man, worker, caretaker) into the definition.

Student Example

Ashley Anderson wrote "Black Girl" as an assignment for an English class at the College of William and Mary in Williamsburg, Virginia. Encouraged by her father, who had run cross-country and track at Penn State, Anderson joined the William and Mary women's track team, specializing in the mid-distances. This was surprising to some people, she writes, "because black people are supposed to be good at sprinting and, well, you *are* black, aren't you?"

Anderson's essay was nominated for the Norton Writer's Prize by her teacher, Mary Ann Melfi, who says of the writer, "She dares to be honest and vulnerable while also inspiring her audience to consider their biases." Anderson's main strategy here, in fact, is to define her subject—what it means to be "both black and a girl"—precisely by exploring and questioning the stereotypes and biases that come with those categories.

Black Girl

Nobody prepares you for how hard it is to be a black girl. No one tells you that you will be ridiculed for being loud and in the same breath criticized for being quiet. No one tells you that people will assume that your hair is not real, and be shocked when it is. No one tells you that teachers will expect you to have an attitude before they even learn your name. No one tells you that those same teachers will be surprised when your name is not one of those "ghetto black girl names" that they've fabricated in their minds. This is what it is to be a black girl.

Being a black girl means dual oppression. You are both black and a girl, which means that you will be questioned, always. Because you are a girl, men will wonder whether or not you are letting your emotions get in the way of your job. Because you are a girl, you will be asked if those emotions are getting out of hand because you are on your period. Because you are a girl, men will grope you and grab you without your permission. Because you are black, teachers will question whether or not you are smart enough to be in their class. Because you are black, friends will ask if you

From distinguishing features to general class: the opening paragraph sets a pattern of definition the writer will follow throughout her essay.

1

2

have both parents at home. Because you are black, you are expected to know all of the other black kids in the school. Because you are black, you and the only other black girl in your fourth period English class will be mixed up and called the wrong name for the entire school year, even though you look nothing alike. People will ask if you two are sisters, or maybe cousins. In the athletic trainer's room, you will be asked repeatedly if you are a sprinter, even though you have told them every time you are in there that you run mid-distance. This is weird to them, because black people are supposed to be good at sprinting and, well, you *are* black, aren't you? What they don't know is that Africans have dominated the mid-distance track events for decades now. You probably should not know that either, though. You're a girl, after all. Girls don't follow sports. People compliment you with the phrase: "You're the prettiest black girl I know," not realizing how backhanded and offensive that is. It implies that black girls can only rise so high in the beauty standards before they are cut off, pretty in their own category but separate from the rest.

Anderson DEFINES black girls by showing how they are often put in a separate category by others.

When you start using relaxer on your hair to tame your kinky curls, you are criticized for "trying to be white." When you tuck your hair behind your ear to keep it out of your face, you are laughed at because "that's what white girls do." When you finally feel confident enough to stop using relaxer and let your natural hair flow free, hands are groping your hair against your will for the entire day. The next day you tie your hair back just to keep the fingers away. When you get into your top choice college, the college you have been dreaming about, your peers will speculate that you only got in due to affirmative action. This is what it is to be a black girl.

You must walk a fine line. You are always being watched. You always run the risk of being labeled "ghetto" or "a troublemaker" or "an Oreo." Oreo was always one of my favorites. White on the inside, black on the outside. Oreo, along with hordes of labels, stick to black girls for the rest of their lives and follow them with every step they take. Such labels are used to celebrate successes and to accept downfalls. If a black girl gets in a fight, even if it is not her fault, it's because she was a troublemaker and always has been. That's what her teachers will say. If a black girl begins a romantic relationship with a white boy, it's because she thinks she's too good to date black guys. If a white boy begins a relationship with a black girl, he is told that he has "jungle fever" and is ridiculed by his classmates. If a black girl is valedictorian of her graduating class, it's because she was always "so well-spoken," "one of the good ones," and has always "stayed out of trouble."

You second-guess every action. Was I aggressive? Was I loud? Am I going to be heard, or am I going to be written off as another angry black girl? Simple actions like telling someone they are sitting in your seat or sending back a meal that you did not order is an entire ordeal in which you cannot act without your identity being subject to ridicule. Every aspect of who you are is dissected before you even take a breath. This is what it is to be a black girl.

These are not made-up experiences. Every one of these things I have witnessed or experienced. I have lived twenty years of being one of the good ones, one of those well-spoken, pretty black girls who keeps herself out of trouble. Living in a suburban white neighborhood my entire life, the definition of a black girl is only portrayed in the negative. The black girl is a cautionary tale of who you do not want to become: the black girl who is walking instead of driving, the one who hangs out in the park instead of the library. If you can defy the stereotypes of being a black girl, you are exemplary. You are the most desirable model—the black girl that all black girls should want to be.

There is a flip side no one prepares you for as well. No one prepares you for the strength that these experiences form in you. No one tells you how confident you will become after years of breaking barriers, shattering stereotypes, and excelling in all of the fields that you were expected to fail in. No one tells you how your natural hair will be celebrated and your dark skin will be accepted. No one tells you that you will gain the courage to speak

5

6

7

Up to this point, Anderson defines her subject largely by telling what it is not (pp. 526–27).

Marks a positive turning point in Anderson's definition.

up without any fear of who may be listening. You will tell your roommate that you are the only other black girl in the class. We look nothing alike. We sit on opposite sides of the room; please, *please*, stop pretending that we are the same. Stop being surprised that my name is the same name that your sister has and not Laqueisha or Bon Qui Qui or whatever *Saturday Night Live* skit you are pulling these names from. Stop asking me if I have ever met my father. I have always known him, and he is my best friend. Stop assuming that you know everything about me just from one look. I am so much more.

No one tells you that your desire to prove others wrong will result in an ambition that drives you. No one tells you that you will become who you want to be, and not what others have labeled you as. No one tells you that after years of wishing that you were a different person, someday you will love who you are. This is what it is to be a black girl.

8

Repeated from the beginning of the essay, this defining statement takes on new meaning at the end.

Analyzing a Student Essay That Uses Definition

In "Black Girl," Ashley Anderson draws on rhetorical strategies and techniques that good writers use all the time when defining things. The following questions, in addition to focusing on particular aspects of Anderson's text, will help you identify those common strategies and techniques so you can adapt them to your own writing. These questions will also help prepare you for the analytical questions—on content, structure, and language—that you'll find after all the other selections in this chapter, along with suggestions for writing on related topics.

FOR CLOSE READING

1. Why, according to Ashley Anderson, is it "hard . . . to be a black girl" (1)?

2. Anderson is dually oppressed, she says, because she is "both black and a girl" (2). Judging from this essay, how does she deal with these hardships?

3. "You are the most desirable model—the black girl that all black girls should want to be" (6). Is this a compliment, or is it "backhanded and offensive"—like "you're the prettiest black girl I know" (2)? Explain.

4. Who is Anderson's intended AUDIENCE—or is there more than one? Point to specific places in the text where she seems to imagine a particular type of reader. How can you tell?

5. "These are not made-up experiences," according to Anderson. "Every one of these things I have witnessed or experienced" (6). Why might she feel the need to make this clarification?

STRATEGIES AND STRUCTURES

1. "This is what it is to be a black girl" (1, 3, 8). Anderson repeats these words periodically throughout her essay—like the refrain of a song—after each point she makes. Is this an effective strategy for organizing her definition? Why or why not?

2. Among the distinguishing features that actually define her subject, according to Anderson, which ones seem most significant? Why?

3. "Black Girl," according to Anderson's English teacher, is both "universal in its implications and also extremely intimate." Point to passages in the text that support (or contradict) this assessment, and explain why they do.

4. *Other Methods.* In paragraph 8, Anderson suggests that the "desire to prove others wrong" has made her stronger and more ambitious than she might otherwise have been. Where else in the essay does Anderson analyze CAUSES AND EFFECTS in support of her definition of what being a "Black Girl" means to her?

THINKING ABOUT LANGUAGE

1. Even before they know her, says Anderson, some people expect her to "have an attitude" (1). What does this phrase mean?

2. To what extent is the word "Oreo," as Anderson uses it in paragraph 4, a slur? Should she have avoided using it? Why or why not? (For a legal discussion of what makes a slur, see "Does the Government Get to Decide What's a Slur?" on p. 640.)

3. "If you can defy the stereotypes of being a black girl," says Anderson, "you are exemplary" (6). Look up the definitions of both "stereotype" and "exemplum" (the noun form of "exemplary"). How does Anderson generate IRONY by pairing the two here?

4. Her account of being a girl while black has a "flip side," Anderson says at a turning point in her definition (7). What is Anderson most likely referring to here? Is the METAPHOR appropriate? effective?

FOR WRITING

1. Using Anderson's strategy for inviting people to think about their biases, make a list of the prejudices you have (or someone you know has) experienced firsthand. Try following the pattern "No one tells you that _____" for each item.

2. In the last third of her essay, Anderson is not so much exposing stereotypes as overturning them. Following her example, try making a list of some of the *positive* effects that no one told you would result from your particular experiences or knowledge of other people's biases.

3. Racial stereotypes of beauty, says Anderson, put black girls "in their own category but separate from the rest" (2). This way of thinking is similar to the "separate but equal" concept long used to defend laws requiring racial segregation in the United States. Do a little research on the phrase "separate but equal," and write a paragraph or two on its origin and implications. Be sure to mention the US Supreme Court case *Plessy v. Ferguson* (1896).

4. Do more research on "separate but equal" as a legal concept, and write an ARGUMENT essay of six to eight paragraphs explaining why it makes (or doesn't make) a fundamental error in definition. In addition to *Plessy v. Ferguson*, be sure to consider *Brown v. Board of Education* (1954).

An Epitaph

When we define something (or someone), we identify its distinguishing characteristics. In this cartoon by Roz Chast, a frequent contributor to the *New Yorker*, the deceased's entire life is defined by his scores on a standardized test. Chast's purpose in penning the cartoon is to amuse the reader, but she is also making fun of overly narrow definitions. Test scores do not adequately define life—or death. For some people and institutions (such as college admissions offices), narrow definitions can run deep—too deep if they lose sight of the complexities of the person or thing they're defining. Like Mr. Jones's epitaph, good definitions require precision. But when constructing a definition, keep your (and the reader's) eye on the distinguishing features that actually give (or gave) life to your subject.

[FOR WRITING]··

Imagine the headstone in Roz Chast's cartoon as a blank slate;
insert a different name (it could be your own), and write an
ideal epitaph for the deceased.

SUGGESTIONS FOR WRITING

1. Write a **CRITICAL ANALYSIS** of Ashley Anderson's "Black Girl" (p. 540) as a model of how to address and "defy" (her word) stereotypes of race and gender. Support your reading by referring to specific passages in the text.

2. Collect several **EXAMPLES** of *shikake*, preferably with illustrations, as defined by Naohiro Matsumura in "Shikake in the Wild" (p. 549). Based on your examples (and any you might want to cite from Matsumura's essay), write an extended **DEFINITION** of your subject as a form of design that can actually shape how people behave.

3. In "How to Know If You're Dead" (p. 557), Mary Roach refers to "the specter of live burial that plagued the French and German citizenry in the 1800s." Read Roach's essay, do some historical research, and write a **REPORT** of 400 to 500 words on the fear of premature burial in Europe and America in the nineteenth century.

4. Jack Horner, in "The Extraordinary Characteristics of Dyslexia" (p. 565), makes the distinction between "linear" and "spatial" thinkers. Check out Horner's definitions of the two types, do some research on the subject of dyslexia, and write your own five-to-seven-paragraph **COMPARISON** of the types of thinking he outlines.

5. In "Blue-Collar Brilliance" (p. 569), Mike Rose states: "When we devalue the full range of everyday cognition, we offer limited educational opportunities and fail to make fresh and meaningful instructional connections among disparate kinds of skill and knowledge. If we think that whole categories of people—identified by class or occupation—are not that bright, then we reinforce social separations and cripple our ability to talk across cultural divides." Using Rose's essay as a starting point, write a **POSITION PAPER** on the nature and importance of "everyday cognition."

6. With "The Meaning of Movement" (p. 579) as your starting point, do some research on Alicia Garza's work and write a brief **PROFILE** of Garza that includes a **DEFINITION** of the kind of social and political change she typically advocates.

NAOHIRO MATSUMURA

Shikake in the Wild

Naohiro Matsumura (b. 1975) is a professor in the Graduate School of Economics at Osaka University in Japan. Born and raised in Osaka, he studied engineering there and at the University of Tokyo, earning a PhD in artificial intelligence. Specializing in behavioral economics, Matsumura is a pioneer in the study of *shikake*, a Japanese term referring to mechanisms or designs that "trigger" socially desirable behaviors in the user, such as throwing trash in bins or paying for coffee in the employees' lounge.

In "Shikake in the Wild," a selection from Matsumura's *Shikake: The Japanese Art of Shaping Behavior through Design* (English edition, 2020), the author finds specimens just by looking around in his daily life and travels. ("[T]here are things to see at a zoo other than the animals.") Together with the hundreds of other *shikake* he has collected, these examples help to define the new field of study and design that Matsumura calls "shikakeology."

I STARTED OUT as an artificial intelligence researcher studying topics that would be helpful for making data-based decisions using computers. However, one day in 2005, I realized the obvious fact that most of the things in the world were not included in the data we collected.

If you stand still and listen, you can hear the chirping of birds and the rustling of tree leaves. These natural phenomena, which take place right in front of our eyes and ears, were not included in the data we collected. And even the highest-functioning computer is merely a box if it is not fed data.

One response to this realization would be to stop depending on data and comput- 3
ers. By not depending on data and computers, you may become more aware of
the inconspicuous blooming of flowers and the chirping of birds along the side of the
road. What we need is not data or computers, but *shikake,* things that help make
people aware of the space they live in and how they pass through that space.

How to con-
struct a basic
definition is
discussed on
p. 526.
Shikake are a means through which people become aware of those 4
things that they can see but do not see, or that they can hear but do not
hear. Through shikake, spaces outside of the world of computers—that is,
the spaces of everyday life—became the objects of my research.

As I began to collect examples of shikake, I realized that they can be 5
used to solve all sorts of problems. This was the origin of the field of *shikakeology.*

I found the tube shown in Shikake 1 in the Asian rainforests area of the Tennōji 6
Zoo in Osaka while on a recreational visit. There was no explanation given for this
device, so it was not clear how it could be used. However, since it was about the
same shape as a telescope, I guessed that it should be peered into.

Seeing the hole in the middle of the tube, I subconsciously wanted to look into it. 7
Furthermore, as the tube was set up about three feet off the ground, the hole in it
was positioned to be directly in front of a child's face. Under such conditions, it
would be difficult to pass by without looking into the tube. I began observing from
a slight distance as people strolled by the tube, and I could see that children were
looking into it and enjoying the sight of (a well-made replica of) elephant droppings
placed at its opposite end.

It is difficult to be conscious of things other than animals when at a zoo. This 8
tube was placed in a remote location adjacent to the elephant area, a place that
would have been quickly passed by had the tube not been present. However,
because the Tennōji Zoo consists of "ecological displays" that reproduce the environment of an animal's habitat, a variety of sights are available beyond the animals
themselves.

The elephant area tube is a shikake: it makes you realize that there are things to 9
see at a zoo other than the animals.

This tube was the first shikake I discovered, and it enabled me to create a method 10
of experiencing the world that was not reliant on data or computers, which I felt
were limiting. I realized that it was important to create awareness in people of
things that they would not otherwise notice. Designing shikake was an effective
means of accomplishing this goal.

Even now, I sometimes make my way to the Tennōji Zoo to confirm that this 11
tube is still there. It has other qualities that are typical of effective shikake—
qualities I will discuss—in that it is difficult to break and does not require much if
any maintenance due to its simple structure.

Shikake 1. A viewing tube at a zoo.

After discovering this tube, I visited many different places searching for similar 12 designs and devices. Eventually, I had collected more than one hundred examples.

At this point, I had the opportunity to leave Japan and conduct research at Stan- 13 ford University, so I endeavored to analyze the examples I had collected to clarify the principles of shikake. . . .

Solving Problems through Behavior

Many of the problems we face are created by our own behavior. The problem of a 14 lack of exercise can only be solved by exercising. Getting other people to walk around will not fix your own lack of exercise. Overeating and messiness are similar problems that can only be solved by changing one's own behavior.

Because larger problems, such as environmental issues and automobile acci- 15 dents, are ultimately made up of aggregated individual behaviors, changing one's own behavior is connected to solving these society-wide matters as well.

A lack of exercise is a personal problem, but as the number of unhealthy people 16 increases, medical fees also accumulate, and society's average medical expenses as a whole increase. Medical fee increases are a serious problem in Japan, which is becoming a super-aged society, in which more than one in five people are sixty-five or older. One of the ways to solve this problem is for each individual person to pursue a healthy lifestyle.

Many people already know which behaviors are preferable. There are few people 17 who do not know that a lack of exercise or eating too many salty foods is bad for you. However, our bodies are not immediately negatively affected if we do not exercise and if we eat salty foods. As a result, although we may understand these consequences conceptually, it is difficult to win out over our immediate desires.

In such cases, it is clearly ineffective to tell people directly that "you should do 18 this." Instead, shikake aim to solve these problems in a results-oriented way by indirectly nudging people to feel that they "just want to do it."

Methods for Creating Reflexively Tidy People

There are many approaches to solving any problem. Here, let's adopt the familiar 19 example of messiness and think of various approaches to solving it.

A common approach might be to write "Keep This Area Tidy" on a sign and hang 20 it on a wall. However, we know from experience that this kind of sign has almost no effect. If you were willing to tidy things up just because you were told to do so by a sign, then you probably would have tidied up already.

> An efficient way to extend a definition is by giving multiple EXAMPLES (p. 529).

So, let's take a different approach, one involving shikake. Consider 21 Shikake 2. If we draw a single diagonal line across the spines of a row of file boxes, it becomes easy to identify whether the boxes are lined up in order. If the boxes are out of order, our attention is drawn to the broken line, making us want to correct it, and as a result an organized and tidy state is achieved.

The same effect is seen with comic books in which the book spines, when put in the correct order, combine to form a picture, as shown in Shikake 3.

In a bicycle parking lot, if lines are drawn on the pavement, cyclists will feel 22 uneasy parking their bicycles in a way that crosses the lines and will instead park within them. As bicycles parked in a chaotic way not only decrease the number of available spots but also cause trouble for pedestrians, simply drawing some lines can change the way people park. The bicycle parking lot then becomes tidy and orderly.

Shikake 4 shows the bicycle parking lot at the Cup Noodles Museum Osaka Ikeda. 23 Because bicycles are parked along diagonally drawn lines, they do not protrude into pedestrian pathways.

Another example is a children's room strewn with toys. In this case, it is fairly 24 self-evident that simply telling the children to tidy up will have little effect. I

Shikake 2. A diagonal line drawn across the spines of file boxes.

Shikake 3. An image printed across comic book spines.

Shikake 4. Diagonal lines drawn in a bicycle parking lot.

Shikake 5. A garbage bin with a basketball hoop attached.

Shikake 6. A stuffed animal collection bag.

Shikake 7. Painted footprints on an escalator.

understand this well, as the father of elementary school girls. Whether they start to tidy up or not, they inevitably begin to play and always make a mess.

However, by placing a basketball hoop just above a toy bin as in Shikake 5, the children will want to shoot baskets by throwing their toys through the hoop. Although they are playing, the result is that the toys end up neatly stored in the bin. 25

Shikake 6 shows a stuffed animal called a "Tummy Stuffer" that is sold in the United States. 26

This stuffed animal has a wide-open mouth and a bag inside for a stomach. If the Tummy Stuffer is put in a children's room and the children are told that "this animal is feeling hungry," then the children will stuff toys into the animal's mouth, which then fill the "stomach," thereby both cleaning up their room and creating a plump stuffed animal. 27

What about a much larger problem: directing the flow of people in a public space? Because I live in Osaka, I often fly or ride the bullet train on trips to Tokyo. In Osaka, there is an unspoken rule that you stand on the right side of the escalator and allow people who are in a hurry to pass on the left. However, in Tokyo, the rule is just the opposite: you stand on the left and let people pass on the right. As these rules are very easily confused, I often mistake which side is which. In the process, the lines become disorderly and the flow of people becomes blocked. 28

In this kind of situation, by painting footprints on one side of an escalator as in Shikake 7, the fact that we should stand on the left side is automatically communicated, and the flow of people becomes more organized naturally. An added benefit is that, as these footprints also show how quickly the escalator is moving, they help prevent people from stumbling. 29

We can see that even for the familiar problem of keeping things tidy or orderly, there are a variety of approaches, such as drawing lines, setting up basketball hoops, using stuffed animals, and painting footprints. 30

These are just a few examples of shikake, things that provide us with the opportunity to change our behavior. 31

What all these particular shikake have in common is that a state of orderliness is achieved as a result. Although the individual user has no intention of cleaning up, he or she achieves this goal before they even know they are doing so. 32

From this perspective, it becomes clear that we often engage in such behaviors. Shikake that can change our behavior appear throughout our everyday lives, and they are not just intended to prompt us to clean up for ourselves. ◆ 33

FOR CLOSE READING

1. Naohiro Matsumura says he started out in the field of artificial intelligence. What caused him to look for a new field of study?

2. According to Matsumura, how and why did he conceive of "shikakeology" (5)?

3. At the Tennōji Zoo in Osaka, Matsumura discovered a viewing tube that directs the viewer's gaze to a pile of artificial elephant dung. What is the larger purpose of this device—in Matsumura's view?

4. Some of the *shikake* described in Matsumura's essay are designed to help users see and hear things they wouldn't otherwise notice. Which ones are intended to actually direct or change users' behavior? How?

5. Of all the EXAMPLES that Matsumura gives, which one do you find most useful for understanding the concept of *shikake*? Why?

STRATEGIES AND STRUCTURES

1. Before he begins to define *shikake* in paragraph 4, Matsumura talks about his early interests and pursuits—in particular, natural ones like "the chirping of birds and the rustling of tree leaves" (2). Is this an effective introduction to his subject? Why or why not?

2. The first *shikake* that Matsumura discovered was a bamboo viewing tube at the Tennōji Zoo in Osaka. What defining feature of all *shikake* does it exhibit? Explain.

3. "It has other qualities that are typical of effective shikake," Matsumura says of the viewing tube (11). What are some of them, and what does Matsumura mean by "effective"?

4. How and how well do the visual illustrations help to define *shikake* and other key terms in Matsumura's essay? Explain.

5. *Other Methods.* As Matsumura introduces a new *shikake*, he often tells how he found it. What, if anything, do these NARRATIVE elements contribute to his definition of a new field of study and discovery?

THINKING ABOUT LANGUAGE

1. Look up the meaning of the suffix "-ology" (as in "biology," "scientology," "shikake-ology"). How does Matsumura use it to define the subject of his essay? Is his invention of the new word a good idea? Explain why or why not.

2. In addition to "mechanisms" or "designs," the word *shikake* can be translated as "gimmicks" or "triggers." Which one of these SYNONYMS best expresses the meaning Matsumura has in mind? Explain.

3. Matsumura says that *shikake* work "by indirectly nudging people to feel that they 'just want to do it'" (18). Does the word "nudges" work as a good translation of the Japanese term *shikake*? Why or why not?

4. According to Matsumura, how is painting footprints on an escalator an example of a *shikake* while hanging up a sign with printed words on it, such as "Walk on the Left," would not be?

FOR WRITING

1. Find a *shikake* in your neighborhood, on your campus, or somewhere in the wild, and write a brief **DEFINITION** of what it is and does. If possible, include a visual. If you don't find a *shikake*, do you notice any places where it would be beneficial to create one? Write a brief description of the site, and explain what a specific *shikake* could accomplish there.

2. According to Matsumura, "changing one's own behavior is connected to solving these society-wide matters as well" (15). In a brief **CRITICAL ANALYSIS** of Matsumura's essay, make the case that "Shikake in the Wild" does (or does not) prove this **THESIS**.

3. Write a **POSITION PAPER** in which you argue that covertly shaping human behavior through design—or any other means that indirectly makes people feel they "just want to do it"—is *not* a good idea. Consider including some examples from social media in your discussion.

MARY ROACH

How to Know If You're Dead

Mary Roach (b. 1959) is a science writer and humorist who lives in Oakland, California. Born in New Hampshire, she attended Wesleyan University in Connecticut, graduating with a degree in psychology. Roach's first book, *Stiff: The Curious Lives of Human Cadavers* (2003), propelled her to the forefront of popular science writers; one reviewer called her "the funniest science writer in the country." When asked how she came to write a bestseller about a subject most readers would regard as morbid, Roach replied, "Good question. It's possible that I'm a little strange." Roach's book *Spook: Science Tackles the Afterlife* (2005) takes up where *Stiff* leaves off. Roach continues to favor one-word titles—*Bonk* (2008), *Gulp* (2014), and *Grunt* (2016)—followed by subtitles that explain what the books are about: science and sex, the alimentary canal, and "the curious science of humans at war." Roach's latest books include *Animal Vegetable Criminal: When Nature Breaks the Law* (2021), an exploration of the problems that arise when animal and human habitats overlap, and *Packing for Mars for Kids* (2022), humorously informative descriptions of what it's like to be an astronaut targeted to questions that children might ask.

In "How to Know If You're Dead," which first appeared in *Stiff*, Roach explores the meaning of "dead" and finds, surprisingly, that the definition is a subject of disagreement among doctors, lawyers, and would-be spiritualists. Despite the jaunty tone of her prose, Roach is meticulous in her scientific reporting; the meaning of death, she finds, casts more than a little light on the meaning of life.

MLA CITATION: Roach, Mary. "How to Know If You're Dead." *Back to the Lake: A Reader and Guide for Writers*, edited by Thomas Cooley, 5th ed., W. W. Norton, 2024, pp. 558–63.

A PATIENT ON THE WAY TO SURGERY travels at twice the speed of a patient on the 1
way to the morgue. Gurneys that ferry the living through hospital corridors
move forward in an aura of purpose and push, flanked by caregivers with long
strides and set faces, steadying IVs, pumping ambu bags, barreling into double
doors. A gurney with a cadaver commands no urgency. It is wheeled by a single person, calmly and with little notice like a shopping cart.

For this reason, I thought I would be able to tell when the dead woman was 2
wheeled past. I have been standing around at the nurses' station on one of the surgery floors of the University of California at San Francisco Medical Center, watching gurneys go by and waiting for Von Peterson, public affairs manager of the
California Transplant Donor Network, and a cadaver I will call H. "There's your
patient," says the charge nurse. A commotion of turquoise legs passes with unexpected forward-leaning urgency.

H is unique in that she is both a dead person *and* a patient on the way to surgery. 3
She is what's known as a "beating-heart cadaver," alive and well everywhere but her
brain. Up until artificial respiration was developed, there was no such entity; without a functioning brain, a body will not breathe on its own. But hook it up to a res-
pirator and its heart will beat, and the rest of its organs will, for a matter of days,
continue to thrive.

H doesn't look or smell or feel dead. If you leaned in close over the gurney, you 4
could see her pulse beating in the arteries of her neck. If you touched her arm, you
would find it warm and resilient, like your own. This is perhaps why the nurses and
doctors refer to H as a patient, and why she makes her entrance to the OR at the
customary presurgery clip.

Since brain death is the legal definition of death in this country, H the person is 5
certifiably dead. But H the organs and tissues is very much alive. These two seemingly contradictory facts afford her an opportunity most corpses do not have: that of

How you
frame a term
(p. 530) can
influence how
the reader
sees it.

extending the lives of two or three dying strangers. Over the next four
hours, H will surrender her liver, kidneys, and heart. One at a time, surgeons will come and go, taking an organ and returning in haste to their
stricken patients. Until recently, the process was known among transplant
professionals as an "organ harvest," which had a joyous, celebratory ring to
it, perhaps a little too joyous, as it has been of late replaced by the more businesslike
"organ recovery."

In H's case, one surgeon will be traveling from Utah to recover her heart, and 6
another, the one recovering both the liver and the kidneys, will be taking them
two floors down. UCSF is a major transplant center, and organs removed here
often remain in house. More typically, a transplant patient's surgeon will travel
from UCSF to a small town somewhere to retrieve the organ—often from an accident victim, someone young with strong, healthy organs, whose brain took an

unexpected hit. The doctor does this because typically there is no doctor in that small town with experience in organ recovery. Contrary to rumors about surgically trained thugs cutting people open in hotel rooms and stealing their kidneys,[1] organ recovery is tricky work. If you want to be sure it's done right, you get on a plane and go do it yourself.

Today's abdominal recovery surgeon is named Andy Posselt. He is holding an electric cauterizing wand, which looks like a cheap bank pen on a cord but functions like a scalpel. The wand both cuts and burns, so that as the incision is made, any vessels that are severed are simultaneously melted shut. The result is that there is a good deal less bleeding and a good deal more smoke and smell. It's not a bad smell, but simply a seared-meat sort of smell. I want to ask Dr. Posselt whether he likes it, but I can't bring myself to, so instead I ask whether he thinks it's bad that I like the smell, which I don't really, or maybe just a little. He replies that it is neither bad nor good, just morbid.

I have never before seen major surgery, only its scars. From the length of them, I had imagined surgeons doing their business, taking things out and putting them in, through an opening maybe eight or nine inches long, like a woman poking around for her glasses at the bottom of her purse. Dr. Posselt begins just above H's pubic hair and proceeds a good two feet north, to the base of her neck. He's unzipping her like a parka. Her sternum is sawed lengthwise so that her rib cage can be parted, and a large retractor is installed to pull the two sides of the incision apart so that it is now as wide as it is long. To see her this way, held open like a Gladstone bag,[2] forces a view of the human torso for what it basically is: a large, sturdy container for guts.

On the inside, H looks very much alive. You can see the pulse of her heartbeat in her liver and all the way down her aorta. She bleeds where she is cut and her organs are plump and slippery-looking. The electronic beat of the heart monitor reinforces the impression that this is a living, breathing, thriving person. It is strange, almost impossible, really, to think of her as a corpse. When I tried to explain beating-heart cadavers to my stepdaughter Phoebe yesterday, it didn't make sense to her. But if their heart is beating, aren't they still a person? she wanted to know. In the end she decided they were "a kind of person you could play tricks on but they wouldn't know." Which, I think, is a pretty good way of summing up most donated cadavers. The things that happen to the dead in labs and ORs are like gossip passed behind one's back. They are not felt or known and so they cause no pain.

---

1. *Rumors … stealing their kidneys*: Reference to a persistent urban legend about people getting drunk at parties, passing out, and waking up in a hotel-room bathtub surrounded in ice and finding that one or both of their kidneys have been removed. These stories are always presented as true and as coming from a reputable but distant source ("it happened to my neighbor's cousin's wife's coworker's son").

2. *Gladstone bag*: An early suitcase, hinged to open in the middle and lie flat.

The contradictions and counterintuitions of the beating-heart cadaver can exact   10
an emotional toll on the intensive care unit (ICU) staff, who must, in the days preceding the harvest, not only think of patients like H as living beings, but treat and
care for them that way as well. The cadaver must be monitored around the clock
and "life-saving" interventions undertaken on its behalf. Since the brain can no
longer regulate blood pressure or the levels of hormones and their release into the
bloodstream, these things must be done by ICU staff, in order to keep the organs
from degrading. Observed a group of Case Western Reserve University School of
Medicine physicians in a *New England Journal of Medicine* article entitled "Psychoso-
cial and Ethical Implications of Organ Retrieval": "Intensive care unit personnel
may feel confused about having to perform cardiopulmonary resuscitation on a
patient who has been declared dead, whereas a 'do not resuscitate' order has been
written for a living patient in the next bed." . . .

The modern medical community is on the whole quite unequivocal about the brain   11
being the seat of the soul, the chief commander of life and death. It is similarly
unequivocal about the fact that people like H are, despite the hoochy-koochy going
on behind their sternums, dead. We now know that the heart keeps beating on its
own not because the soul is in there, but because it contains its own bioelectric
power source, independent of the brain. As soon as H's heart is installed in someone
else's chest and that person's blood begins to run through it, it will start beating
anew—with no signals from the recipient's brain.

The legal community took a little longer than the physicians to come around to   12
the concept of brain death. It was 1968 when the *Journal of the American Medical
Association* published a paper by the Ad Hoc Committee of the Harvard Medical
School to Examine the Definition of Brain Death advocating that irreversible coma
be the new criterion for death, and clearing the ethical footpath for organ transplantation. It wasn't until 1974 that the law began to catch up. What forced the issue
was a bizarre murder trial in Oakland, California.

The killer, Andrew Lyons, shot a man in the head in September 1973 and left him   13
brain-dead. When Lyons's attorneys found out that the victim's family had donated
his heart for transplantation, they tried to use this in Lyons's defense: If the heart
was still beating at the time of surgery, they maintained, then how could it be that
Lyons had killed him the day before? They tried to convince the jury that, technically speaking, Andrew Lyons hadn't murdered the man, the organ recovery surgeon had. According to Stanford University heart transplant pioneer Norman
Shumway, who testified in the case, the judge would have none of it. He informed
the jury that the accepted criteria for death were those set forth by the Harvard
committee, and that that should inform their decision. (Photographs of the victim's
brains "oozing from his skull," to quote the *San Francisco Chronicle*, probably didn't

help Lyons's case.) In the end, Lyons was convicted of murder. Based on the outcome of the case, California passed legislation making brain death the legal definition of death. Other states quickly followed suit.

Andrew Lyons's defense attorney wasn't the first person to cry murder when a 14 transplant surgeon removed a heart from a brain-dead patient. In the earliest days of heart transplants, Shumway, the first U.S. surgeon to carry out the procedure, was continually harangued by the coroner in Santa Clara County, where he practiced. The coroner didn't accept the brain-death concept of death and threatened that if Shumway went ahead with his plans to remove a beating heart from a brain-dead person and use it to save another person's life, he would initiate murder charges. Though the coroner had no legal ground to stand on and Shumway went ahead anyway, the press gave it a vigorous chew. New York heart transplant surgeon Mehmet Oz recalls the Brooklyn district attorney around that time making the same threat. "He said he'd indict and arrest any heart transplant surgeon who went into his borough and harvested an organ."

The worry, explained Oz, was that someday someone who wasn't actually brain- 15 dead was going to have his heart cut out. There exist certain rare medical conditions that can look, to the untrained or negligent eye, a lot like brain death, and the legal types didn't trust the medical types to get it right. To a very, very small degree, they had reason to worry. Take, for example, the condition known as "locked-in state." In one form of the disease, the nerves, from eyeballs to toes, suddenly and rather swiftly drop out of commission, with the result that the body is completely paralyzed, while the mind remains normal. The patient can hear what's being said but has no way of communicating that he's still in there, and that no, it's definitely not okay to give his organs away for transplant. In severe cases, even the muscles that contract to change the size of the pupils no longer function. This is bad news, for a common test of brain death is to shine a light in the patient's eyes to check for the reflexive contraction of the pupils. Typically, victims of locked-in state recover fully, provided no one has mistakenly wheeled them off to the OR to take out their heart.

Like the specter of live burial that plagued the French and German citizenry in 16 the 1800s, the fear of live organ harvesting is almost completely without foundation. A simple EEG will prevent misdiagnosis of the locked-in state and conditions like it.

On a rational level, most people are comfortable with the concept of brain death 17 and organ donation. But on an emotional level, they may have a harder time accepting it, particularly when they are being asked to accept it by a transplant counselor who would like them to okay the removal of a family member's beating heart. Fifty-four percent of families asked refuse consent. "They can't deal with the fear, however irrational, that the true end of their loved one will come when the heart is removed," says Oz. That they, in effect, will have killed him.

Even heart transplant surgeons sometimes have trouble accepting the notion 18
that the heart is nothing more than a pump. When I asked Oz where he thought the
soul resided, he said, "I'll confide in you that I don't think it's all in the brain. I have
to believe that in many ways the core of our existence is in our heart." Does that
mean he thinks the brain-dead patient isn't dead? "There's no question that the
heart without a brain is of no value. But life and death is not a binary system." It's a
continuum. It makes sense, for many reasons, to draw the legal line at brain death,
but that doesn't mean it's really a line. "In between life and death is a state of near-
death, or pseudo-life. And most people don't want what's in between." . . .

The harvesting of H is winding down. The last organs to be taken, the kidneys, are 19
being brought up and separated from the depths of her open torso. Her thorax and
abdomen are filled with crushed ice, turned red from blood. "Cherry Sno-Kone," I
write in my notepad. It's been almost four hours now, and H has begun to look more
like a conventional cadaver, her skin dried and dulled at the edges of the incision.

The kidneys are placed in a blue plastic bowl with ice and perfusion fluid. A 20
relief surgeon arrives for the final step of the recovery, cutting off pieces of veins
and arteries to be included, like spare sweater buttons, along with the organs, in
case the ones attached to them are too short to work with. A half hour later, the
relief surgeon steps aside and the resident comes over to sew H up.

As he talks to Dr. Posselt about the stitching, the resident strokes the bank of fat 21
along H's incision with his gloved hand, then pats it twice, as though comforting
her. When he turns back to his work, I ask him if it feels different to be working on
a dead patient.

"Oh, yes," he answers. "I mean, I would never use this kind of stitch." He has 22
begun stitching more widely spaced, comparatively crude loops, rather than the
tight, hidden stitches used on the living.

I rephrase the question: Does it feel odd to perform surgery on someone who 23
isn't alive?

His answer is surprising. "The patient *was* alive." I suppose surgeons are used to 24
thinking about patients—particularly ones they've never met—as no more than
what they see of them: open plots of organs. And as far as that goes, I guess you
could say H *was* alive. Because of the cloths covering all but her opened torso, the
young man never saw her face, didn't know if she was male or female.

While the resident sews, a nurse picks stray danglies of skin and fat off the oper- 25
ating table with a pair of tongs and drops them inside the body cavity, as though H
were a handy wastebasket. The nurse explains that this is done intentionally: "Anything not donated stays with her." The jigsaw puzzle put back in its box.

The incision is complete, and a nurse washes H off and covers her with a blanket 26
for the trip to the morgue. Out of habit or respect, he chooses a fresh one. The

transplant coordinator, Von, and the nurse lift H onto a gurney. Von wheels H into an elevator and down a hallway to the morgue. The workers are behind a set of swinging doors, in a back room. "Can we leave this here?" Von shouts. H has become a "this." We are instructed to wheel the gurney into the cooler, where it joins five others. H appears no different from the corpses already here.[*]

But H *is* different. She has made three sick people well. She has brought them extra time on earth. To be able, as a dead person, to make a gift of this magnitude is phenomenal. Most people don't manage this sort of thing while they're alive. Cadavers like H are the dead's heroes.

> Roach concludes by using her extended definition to support an ARGUMENT (p. 530).

It is astounding to me, and achingly sad, that with eighty thousand people on the waiting list for donated hearts and livers and kidneys, with sixteen a day dying there on that list, that more than half of the people in the position H's family was in will say no, will choose to burn those organs or let them rot. We abide the surgeon's scalpel to save our own lives, our loved ones' lives, but not to save a stranger's life. H has no heart, but heartless is the last thing you'd call her. ◆

FOR CLOSE READING

1. A "beating-heart cadaver," says Mary Roach, is "both a dead person *and* a patient on the way to surgery" (3). How is this possible? What are some of the "contradictions and counterintuitions" posed by a beating-heart cadaver (10)?

2. What is the legal definition of death in the United States, according to Roach? What was the role of the Andrew Lyons case in establishing this definition (13)?

3. Define the condition known as "locked-in state" (15). Why do such medical conditions worry some people in regard to organ transplants?

4. How is the legal and medical definition of death complicated by Roach's conversation with Dr. Oz in paragraph 18?

STRATEGIES AND STRUCTURES

1. What ARGUMENT is Roach making on the basis of her extended definition? What is her main point? Where does she state it?

2. Fifty-four percent of the families whom doctors ask for permission to retrieve the organs of brain-dead patients, says Roach, refuse permission (17). Do you think such statistics bolster Roach's argument? In what way?

---

[*] Unless H's family is planning a naked open-casket service, no one at her funeral will be able to tell she's had organs removed. Only with tissue harvesting, which often includes leg and arm bones, does the body take on a slightly altered profile, and in this case PVC piping or dowels are inserted to normalize the form and make life easier for mortuary staff and others who need to move the otherwise somewhat noodle-ized body. [Author's note]

3. Roach uses a number of direct quotations from physicians, nurses, and others. Is this an effective strategy? Support your answer with examples from the selection.

4. Throughout her essay, Roach weaves in a NARRATIVE about the harvesting of patient H's heart, liver, and kidneys. Does this strategy enhance your understanding of the organ recovery process, or would a more clinical, impersonal description be a better choice? Explain.

5. *Other Methods.* How does the EXAMPLE of patient H contribute to Roach's definition of death? How does it contribute to her ARGUMENT?

THINKING ABOUT LANGUAGE

1. Why, according to Roach, did the medical community change its terminology from "harvesting" organs to "recovering" them (5)? What do you think of the change?

2. Roach uses many nonmedical terms, vivid images, and SIMILES in her essay, such as "like a shopping cart" (1), "hoochy-koochy" (11), and "Cherry Sno-Kone" (19). Point out other examples. Given the seriousness of her subject, do you find such informal language appropriate or inappropriate? Explain your reaction.

3. What cleared "the ethical footpath for organ transplantation," says Roach, was a report published in 1968 in the *Journal of the American Medical Association* (12). What are the implications of this "footpath" METAPHOR?

4. Is Von, the transplant coordinator, right to refer to patient H as "this" (26)? Why or why not?

FOR WRITING

1. Write a paragraph giving the legal definition of death as doctors and lawyers have come to define it since 1968.

2. When Roach asks the transplant surgeon where he thinks the soul resides, Dr. Oz replies that he thinks "the core of our existence is in our heart" (18). Write a brief ANALYSIS exploring what such a statement might mean and what its implications might be for medicine and other fields.

3. "It is astounding to me," says Roach, "and achingly sad, that with eighty thousand people on the waiting list for donated hearts and livers and kidneys . . . that more than half" of those who must decide on behalf of a brain-dead person whether to donate the dying person's organs "will say no" (28). Write a POSITION PAPER agreeing or disagreeing with this statement.

4. Write a 500-to-700-word RHETORICAL ANALYSIS of Edgar Allan Poe's short story "The Premature Burial" (1844). Be sure to evaluate the mental state of Poe's narrator (not Poe himself), especially with regard to the sort of "irrational" fears that Roach discusses with Dr. Oz.

JACK HORNER

The Extraordinary Characteristics of Dyslexia

Jack Horner (b. 1946) grew up in Shelby, Montana, and studied geology and zoology at the University of Montana. In 2016, Horner retired from Montana State University, where he was Regents Professor of Paleontology and curator of paleontology at the Museum of the Rockies, which has the largest collection of dinosaur remains in the United States. He now teaches at Chapman University in Orange, California. A technical adviser for the *Jurassic Park* movies, Horner was the first person to discover dinosaur eggs in the Western Hemisphere. He is now doing research on the evolution and ecology of dinosaurs and is particularly interested in their growth and behavior.

Although he holds multiple honorary degrees, Horner did not graduate from college because of a common difficulty reading often called "dyslexia." As children, people with dyslexia are generally challenged by learning to recognize written words and, thus, the meaning of sentences; and they may have related problems with writing and math. Dyslexia does not indicate a lack of intelligence, however; it is caused by differences in the way the human brain processes symbolic information. In "The Extraordinary Characteristics of Dyslexia" (published in 2008 by the International Dyslexia Association in *Perspectives on Language and Literacy*), Horner bypasses the usual symptoms and defines it as a way of understanding the world that, in some respects, may be superior to more "normal" ways.

MLA CITATION: Horner, Jack. "The Extraordinary Characteristics of Dyslexia." *Back to the Lake: A Reader and Guide for Writers*, edited by Thomas Cooley, 5th ed., W. W. Norton, 2024, pp. 566–67.

E ACH OF US can narrate an early experience of failure in schools. Because of it, 1 most of us have known some form of peer persecution. But what most non-dyslexics don't know about us, besides the fact that we simply process information differently, is that our early failures often give us an important edge as we grow older. It is not uncommon that we "dyslexics" go on to succeed at the highest of levels.

I don't care much for the word *dyslexia*. I generally think of "us" as spatial think- 2 ers and non-dyslexics as linear thinkers, or people who could be most often described as being *dys-spatios*. For spatial thinkers, reading is clearly necessary but over-rated. Most of us would rather write about our own adventures than read about someone else's. Most spatial thinkers are extremely visual, highly imaginative, and work in three dimensions, none of which have anything to do with time. Linear thinkers (*dys-spatics*) generally operate in a two-dimensional world where time is of the utmost importance. We spatial thinkers fail tests given by linear thinkers because we don't think in terms of time or in terms of written text. Instead, our perception is multidimensional, and we do best when we can touch, observe, and analyze. If we were to give spatial tests to linear thinkers, they would have just as much trouble with our tests as we do with theirs. It is unfortunate that we are the minority and have to deal with the linear-thinkers' exams in order to enter the marketplace to find jobs. Even though we often fail or do miserably on these linear-thinker tests, we often end up in life achieving exceptional accomplishments. From the perspective of the linear thinkers, we spatial thinkers seem to "think outside the box," and this accounts for our accomplishments. However, we think outside the box precisely because we have never been in one. Our minds are not clogged up by preconceived ideas acquired through excessive reading. We are, therefore, free to have original thoughts enhanced by personal observations.

For how to define a term by saying what it is not, see pp. 526–27.

In 1993, I was inducted into the American Academy of Achievement, an 3 organization started in 1964, that annually brings together the highest achievers in America with the brightest American high-school students. The achievers included United States presidents, Nobel Laureates, movie stars, sports figures, and other famous people. The high school students were winners of the best scholarships like the Rhodes, the Westinghouse, the Truman, and so on. In other words, it was supposed to be a meeting of the best of the best according to the linear thinkers who "judge" such things. The idea was that the achievers would somehow, over the course of a three-day meeting, influence the students, and push them on to extraordinary achievement. Interestingly, however, most of us "achievers" admitted that we would never have qualified to be in such a student group. The largest percentage of the achievers were actually people who had difficulties in school and didn't get scholarships, or awards, or other accolades. Most of the achievers were spatial thinkers, while most of the students were linear thinkers. From 1964 until 2000, less than half a dozen students broke the barrier to be inducted at the American Academy of Achievement's annual get-together. How could it be that so many promising students, judged by the linear thinkers themselves, failed to reach the highest levels of achievement?

I think the answer is simple. Linear thinkers are burdened by high expectations 4 from everyone, including themselves. They go out and get good jobs, but they seldom follow their dreams because dream-following is risk-taking, and risk-taking carries the possible burden of failure.

We spatial thinkers have known failure our entire lives and have grown up with- 5 out expectations, not from our teachers, often not from our parents, and sometimes, not even from ourselves. We don't meet the expectations of linear thinkers and are free to take risks. We are the people who most often follow our dreams, who think differently, spatially, inquisitively.

Personally, I think dyslexia and the consequences of dyslexia—learning to deal 6 with failure—explains my own success. From my failures, I've learned where I need help, such as reading and math. But I've also learned from my accomplishments what I'm better at than the linear thinkers. When I'm teaching linear thinkers here at Montana State University, I know to be patient, as they have just as hard a time with spatial problems as I have with linear ones. We both have learning talents and learning challenges, but I would never think of trading my spatial way of thinking for their linear way of thinking. I think dyslexia is an extraordinary characteristic, and it is certainly not something that needs to be fixed, or cured, or suppressed! Maybe it's time for a revolution! Take us out of classes for special ed, and put us in classes for spatial ed, taught of course, by spatial thinkers! ◆

FOR CLOSE READING

1. Jack Horner says that "non-dyslexics" are "linear thinkers" (2). What does he mean by this definition? Do you think it's accurate? Why or why not?

2. On the other hand, says Horner, people who are called "dyslexic" are actually "spatial thinkers" (2). Again, what does he mean, and how accurate is *this* definition?

3. Why does Horner think that his spatial perspective has helped him succeed in his life and career?

4. Why does he think linear thinkers, including "many promising students," even when judged by other linear thinkers, "failed to reach the highest levels of achievement" (3)?

STRATEGIES AND STRUCTURES

1. What is Horner's **PURPOSE** in defining dyslexia in positive terms as an "extraordinary characteristic" (6)?

2. In addition to spatial thinkers, what other **AUDIENCE** might Horner and the International Dyslexia Association be interested in reaching? Explain.

3. Nowhere in his essay does Horner cite a standard textbook definition of "dys-lexia." In addition to the extraordinary characteristics, should he have included the ordinary ones in his definition as well? Why or why not?

4. Besides being "spatial thinkers," people with dyslexia have other distinguishing characteristics, according to Horner. What are some of them? Which ones seem particularly effective for extending his basic definition?

5. Horner uses his own life and career as an EXAMPLE. How and how well does that example help explain what it means, in his view, to be dyslexic?

6. *Other Methods.* Horner sees a CAUSE-AND-EFFECT relationship between having (or not having) dyslexia and succeeding (or failing) to reach "the highest levels of achievement" (3). What evidence does he offer in support of this analysis? How sufficient is that evidence to prove causality? Explain.

THINKING ABOUT LANGUAGE

1. New words are often coined by ANALOGY with words that already exist (for example, "workaholic" and "alcoholic"). How does Horner derive the word "dys-spatics" (2)?

2. Thinking "outside the box" is a CLICHÉ (2). Should Horner have avoided the phrase? Why or why not?

3. What are the implications of "burdened" (4)? Is Horner being IRONIC here?

4. Explain the pun in "spatial ed" (6). What TONE does the pun convey, and is it an effective way to end the essay?

FOR WRITING

1. Write a paragraph or two explaining how "an early experience of failure in schools" or "peer persecution" has "given you an important edge" now (1).

2. Research the ETYMOLOGY of the word "dyslexia," and then write a 600-to-800-word definition essay explaining what dyslexia is, what its causes are thought to be, and how it's usually treated. Be sure to cite your sources—and, if appropriate, an interesting case or two, whether "extraordinary" or typical.

3. Horner explains his success and that of other "spatial thinkers" as follows: "Linear thinkers are burdened by high expectations from everyone, including themselves.... We spatial thinkers have known failure our entire lives and have grown up without expectations.... We don't meet the expectations of linear thinkers and are free to take risks" (4, 5). Write a brief critical EVALUATION of Horner's definition of the two types of thinkers and of this explanation for his celebration of the second type.

4. In collaboration with several of your classmates, identify and discuss the different kinds of thinkers among you. Starting with Horner's categories and creating additional ones as needed, write a four-to-six-paragraph COMPARISON of the strengths and weaknesses of the different ways of thinking represented by individual members of your group.

MIKE ROSE

Blue-Collar Brilliance

Mike Rose (1944-2021) was a professor of social research methodology in the UCLA Graduate School of Education and Information Studies. When he was seven, Rose moved with his parents from Altoona, Pennsylvania, to Los Angeles, where his mother worked as a waitress, and he "watched the cooks and waitresses and listened to what they said." After graduating from Loyola University, Rose earned advanced degrees from the University of Southern California and UCLA. His books on language, literacy, and cognition include *The Mind at Work: Valuing the Intelligence of the American Worker* (2004), *Why School?* (2009), and *Back to School: Why Everyone Deserves a Second Chance at Education* (2012).

From his years of teaching and close observation of the workplace, Rose believed that people are smart in many different ways. Consequently, his definition of intelligence in "Blue-Collar Brilliance," from *The American Scholar* (2009), does not separate the mind from the body, as more conventional definitions often do—mistakenly, in Rose's view.

M Y MOTHER, ROSE MERAGLIO ROSE (Rosie), shaped her adult identity as a   1
waitress in coffee shops and family restaurants. When I was growing up in Los Angeles during the 1950s, my father and I would occasionally hang out at the restaurant until her shift ended, and then we'd ride the bus home with her. Sometimes she worked the register and the counter, and we sat there; when she waited booths and tables, we found a booth in the back where the waitresses took their breaks.

MLA CITATION: Rose, Mike. "Blue-Collar Brilliance." *Back to the Lake: A Reader and Guide for Writers*, edited by Thomas Cooley, 5th ed., W. W. Norton, 2024, pp. 569-76.

Rosie solved technical and human problems on the fly.

There wasn't much for a child to do at the restaurants, and so as the hours   2
stretched out, I watched the cooks and waitresses and listened to what they said. At
mealtimes, the pace of the kitchen staff and the din from customers picked up.
Weaving in and out around the room, waitresses warned *behind you* in impassive
but urgent voices. Standing at the service window facing the kitchen, they called
out abbreviated orders. *Fry four on two*, my mother would say as she clipped a check
onto the metal wheel. Her tables were *deuces*, *four-tops*, or *six-tops* according to their
size; seating areas also were nicknamed. The racetrack, for instance, was the fast-
turnover front section. Lingo conferred authority and signaled know-how.

Rosie took customers' orders, pencil poised over pad, while fielding questions   3
about the food. She walked full tilt through the room with plates stretching up her
left arm and two cups of coffee somehow cradled in her right hand. She stood at a
table or booth and removed a plate for this person, another for that person, then
another, remembering who had the hamburger, who had the fried shrimp, almost

always getting it right. She would haggle with the cook about a returned order and rush by us, saying, *He gave me lip, but I got him.* She'd take a minute to flop down in the booth next to my father. *I'm all in,* she'd say, and whisper something about a customer. Gripping the outer edge of the table with one hand, she'd watch the room and note, in the flow of our conversation, who needed a refill, whose order was taking longer to prepare than it should, who was finishing up.

I couldn't have put it in words when I was growing up, but what I observed in my mother's restaurant defined the world of adults, a place where competence was synonymous with physical work. I've since studied the working habits of blue-collar workers and have come to understand how much my mother's kind of work demands of both body and brain. A waitress acquires knowledge and intuition about the ways and the rhythms of the restaurant business. Waiting on seven to nine tables, each with two to six customers, Rosie devised memory strategies so that she could remember who ordered what. And because she knew the average time it took to prepare different dishes, she could monitor an order that was taking too long at the service station.

See p. 533 for tips on using synonyms in definitions.

Like anyone who is effective at physical work, my mother learned *to work smart,* as she put it, *to make every move count.* She'd sequence and group tasks: What could she do first, then second, then third as she circled through her station? What tasks could be clustered? She did everything on the fly, and when problems arose—technical or human—she solved them within the flow of work, while taking into account the emotional state of her co-workers. Was the manager in a good mood? Did the cook wake up on the wrong side of the bed? If so, how could she make an extra request or effectively return an order?

And then, of course, there were the customers who entered the restaurant with all sorts of needs, from physiological ones, including the emotions that accompany hunger, to a sometimes complicated desire for human contact. Her tip depended on how well she responded to these needs, and so she became adept at reading social cues and managing feelings, both the customers' and her own. No wonder, then, that Rosie was intrigued by psychology. The restaurant became the place where she studied human behavior, puzzling over the problems of her regular customers and refining her ability to deal with people in a difficult world. She took pride in *being among the public,* she'd say. *There isn't a day that goes by in the restaurant that you don't learn something.*

My mother quit school in the seventh grade to help raise her brothers and sisters. Some of those siblings made it through high school, and some dropped out to find work in railroad yards, factories, or restaurants. My father finished a grade or two in primary school in Italy and never darkened the schoolhouse door again. I didn't do well in school either. By high school I had accumulated a spotty academic record and many hours of hazy disaffection. I spent a few years on the vocational track, but in my senior year I was inspired by my English teacher and managed to squeak into a small college on probation.

My freshman year was academically bumpy, but gradually I began to see formal 8
education as a means of fulfillment and as a road toward making a living. I studied the humanities and later the social and psychological sciences and taught for ten years in a range of situations—elementary school, adult education courses, tutoring centers, a program for Vietnam veterans who wanted to go to college. Those students had socioeconomic and educational backgrounds similar to mine. Then I went back to graduate school to study education and cognitive psychology and eventually became a faculty member in a school of education.

Intelligence is closely associated with formal education—the type of schooling a 9
person has, how much and how long—and most people seem to move comfortably from that notion to a belief that work requiring less schooling requires less intelligence. These assumptions run through our cultural history, from the post–Revolutionary War period, when mechanics were characterized by political rivals as illiterate and therefore incapable of participating in government, until today. More than once I've heard a manager label his workers as "a bunch of dummies." Generalizations about intelligence, work, and social class deeply affect our assumptions about ourselves and each other, guiding the ways we use our minds to learn, build knowledge, solve problems, and make our way through the world.

Although writers and scholars have often looked at the working class, they have 10
generally focused on the values such workers exhibit rather than on the thought their work requires—a subtle but pervasive omission. Our cultural iconography promotes the muscled arm, sleeve rolled tight against biceps, but no brightness behind the eye, no image that links hand and brain.

One of my mother's brothers, Joe Meraglio, left school in the ninth grade to work 11
for the Pennsylvania Railroad. From there he joined the Navy, returned to the railroad, which was already in decline, and eventually joined his older brother at General Motors where, over a thirty-three-year career, he moved from working on the assembly line to supervising the paint-and-body department. When I was a young man, Joe took me on a tour of the factory. The floor was loud—in some places deafening—and when I turned a corner or opened a door, the smell of chemicals knocked my head back. The work was repetitive and taxing, and the pace was inhumane.

Still, for Joe the shop floor provided what school did not; it was *like schooling*, he 12
said, a place where *you're constantly learning*. Joe learned the most efficient way to use his body by acquiring a set of routines that were quick and preserved energy. Otherwise he would never have survived on the line.

As a foreman, Joe constantly faced new problems and became a consummate 13
multi-tasker, evaluating a flurry of demands quickly, parceling out physical and

With an eighth-grade education, Joe (hands together) advanced to supervisor of a G.M. paint-and-body department.

mental resources, keeping a number of ongoing events in his mind, returning to whatever task had been interrupted, and maintaining a cool head under the pressure of grueling production schedules. In the midst of all this, Joe learned more and more about the auto industry, the technological and social dynamics of the shop floor, the machinery and production processes, and the basics of paint chemistry and of plating and baking. With further promotions, he not only solved problems but also began to find problems to solve: Joe initiated the redesign of the nozzle on a paint sprayer, thereby eliminating costly and unhealthy overspray. And he found a way to reduce energy costs on the baking ovens without affecting the quality of the paint. He lacked formal knowledge of how the machines under his supervision worked, but he had direct experience with them, hands-on knowledge, and was savvy about their quirks and operational capabilities. He could experiment with them.

In addition, Joe learned about budgets and management. Coming off the line as 14 he did, he had a perspective of workers' needs and management's demands, and this led him to think of ways to improve efficiency on the line while relieving some of the stress on the assemblers. He had each worker in a unit learn his or her co-workers' jobs so they could rotate across stations to relieve some of the monotony. He believed that rotation would allow assemblers to get longer and more frequent breaks. It was an easy sell to the people on the line. The union, however, had to approve any modification in job duties, and the

For additional rhetorical education, see "Thinking about Purpose and Audience," p. 529.

managers were wary of the change. Joe had to argue his case on a number of fronts, providing him a kind of rhetorical education. . . .

Eight years ago I began a study of the thought processes involved in work like that of   15
my mother and uncle. I catalogued the cognitive demands of a range of blue-collar and service jobs, from waitressing and hair styling to plumbing and welding. To gain a sense of how knowledge and skill develop, I observed experts as well as novices. From the details of this close examination, I tried to fashion what I called "cognitive biographies" of blue-collar workers. Biographical accounts of the lives of scientists, lawyers, entrepreneurs, and other professionals are rich with detail about the intellectual dimension of their work. But the life stories of working-class people are few and are typically accounts of hardship and courage or the achievements wrought by hard work.

Our culture—in Cartesian fashion—separates the body from the mind, so that,   16
for example, we assume that the use of a tool does not involve abstraction. We reinforce this notion by defining intelligence solely on grades in school and numbers on IQ tests. And we employ social biases pertaining to a person's place on the occupational ladder. The distinctions among blue, pink, and white collars carry with them attributions of character, motivation, and intelligence. Although we rightly acknowledge and amply compensate the play of mind in white-collar and professional work, we diminish or erase it in considerations about other endeavors—physical and service work particularly. We also often ignore the experience of everyday work in administrative deliberations and policymaking.

But here's what we find when we get in close. The plumber seeking leverage in   17
order to work in tight quarters and the hair stylist adroitly handling scissors and comb manage their bodies strategically. Though work-related actions become routine with experience, they were learned at some point through observation, trial and error, and, often, physical or verbal assistance from a co-worker or trainer. I've frequently observed novices talking to themselves as they take on a task, or shaking their head or hand as if to erase an attempt before trying again. In fact, our traditional notions of routine performance could keep us from appreciating the many instances within routine where quick decisions and adjustments are made. I'm struck by the thinking-in-motion that some work requires, by all the mental activity that can be involved in simply getting from one place to another: the waitress rushing back through her station to the kitchen or the foreman walking the line.

The use of tools requires the studied refinement of stance, grip, balance, and   18
fine-motor skills. But manipulating tools is intimately tied to knowledge of what a particular instrument can do in a particular situation and do better than other similar tools. A worker must also know the characteristics of the material one is engaging—how it reacts to various cutting or compressing devices, to degrees of

heat, or to lines of force. Some of these things demand judgment, the weighing of options, the consideration of multiple variables, and, occasionally, the creative use of a tool in an unexpected way.

In manipulating material, the worker becomes attuned to aspects of the environ- 19
ment, a training or disciplining of perception that both enhances knowledge and informs perception. Carpenters have an eye for length, line, and angle; mechanics troubleshoot by listening; hair stylists are attuned to shape, texture, and motion. Sensory data merge with concept, as when an auto mechanic relies on sound, vibration, and even smell to understand what cannot be observed.

Planning and problem solving have been studied since the earliest days of mod- 20
ern cognitive psychology and are considered core elements in Western definitions of intelligence. To work is to solve problems. The big difference between the psychologist's laboratory and the workplace is that in the former the problems are isolated and in the latter they are embedded in the real-time flow of work with all its messiness and social complexity.

Much of physical work is social and interactive. Movers determining how to get 21
an electric range down a flight of stairs require coordination, negotiation, planning, and the establishing of incremental goals. Words, gestures, and sometimes a quick pencil sketch are involved, if only to get the rhythm right. How important it is, then, to consider the social and communicative dimension of physical work, for it provides the medium for so much of work's intelligence.

Given the ridicule heaped on blue-collar speech, it might seem odd to value its 22
cognitive content. Yet, the flow of talk at work provides the channel for organizing and distributing tasks, for troubleshooting and problem solving, for learning new information and revising old. A significant amount of teaching, often informal and indirect, takes place at work. Joe Meraglio saw that much of his job as a supervisor involved instruction. In some service occupations, language and communication are central: observing and interpreting behavior and expression, inferring mood and motive, taking on the perspective of others, responding appropriately to social cues, and knowing when you're understood. A good hair stylist, for instance, has the ability to convert vague requests (*I want something light and summery*) into an appropriate cut through questions, pictures, and hand gestures.

Verbal and mathematical skills drive measures of intelligence in the Western 23
Hemisphere, and many of the kinds of work I studied are thought to require relatively little proficiency in either. Compared to certain kinds of white-collar occupations, that's true. But written symbols flow through physical work.

Numbers are rife in most workplaces: on tools and gauges, as measurements, as 24
indicators of pressure or concentration or temperature, as guides to sequence, on ingredient labels, on lists and spreadsheets, as markers of quantity and price. Certain

jobs require workers to make, check, and verify calculations, and to collect and interpret data. Basic math can be involved, and some workers develop a good sense of numbers and patterns. Consider, as well, what might be called material mathematics: mathematical functions embodied in materials and actions, as when a carpenter builds a cabinet or a flight of stairs. A simple mathematical act can extend quickly beyond itself. Measuring, for example, can involve more than recording the dimensions of an object. As I watched a cabinetmaker measure a long strip of wood, he read a number off the tape out loud, looked back over his shoulder to the kitchen wall, turned back to his task, took another measurement, and paused for a moment in thought. He was solving a problem involving the molding, and the measurement was important to his deliberation about structure and appearance.

In the blue-collar workplace, directions, plans, and reference books rely on illustrations, some representational and others, like blueprints, that require training to interpret. Esoteric symbols—visual jargon—depict switches and receptacles, pipe fittings, or types of welds. Workers themselves often make sketches on the job. I frequently observed them grab a pencil to sketch something on a scrap of paper or on a piece of the material they were installing.   25

Though many kinds of physical work don't require a high literacy level, more reading occurs in the blue-collar workplace than is generally thought, from manuals and catalogues to work orders and invoices, to lists, labels, and forms. With routine tasks, for example, reading is integral to understanding production quotas, learning how to use an instrument, or applying a product. Written notes can initiate action, as in restaurant orders or reports of machine malfunction, or they can serve as memory aids.   26

True, many uses of writing are abbreviated, routine, and repetitive, and they infrequently require interpretation or analysis. But analytic moments can be part of routine activities, and seemingly basic reading and writing can be cognitively rich. Because workplace language is used in the flow of other activities, we can overlook the remarkable coordination of words, numbers, and drawings required to initiate and direct action.   27

If we believe everyday work to be mindless, then that will affect the work we create in the future. When we devalue the full range of everyday cognition, we offer limited educational opportunities and fail to make fresh and meaningful instructional connections among disparate kinds of skill and knowledge. If we think that whole categories of people—identified by class or occupation—are not that bright, then we reinforce social separations and cripple our ability to talk across cultural divides.   28

Affirmation of diverse intelligence is not a retreat to a softhearted definition of the mind. To acknowledge a broader range of intellectual capacity is to take seriously the concept of cognitive variability, to appreciate in all the Rosies and Joes the thought that drives their accomplishments and defines who they are. This is a model of the mind that is worthy of a democratic society. ◆   29

FOR CLOSE READING

1. Mike Rose says that definitions of human intelligence should not be based solely "on grades in school and numbers on IQ tests" (16). Is he correct? Why or why not?

2. How should intelligence be defined, according to Rose—especially among workers whose tasks are not "closely associated with formal education" (9)? How would he alter more traditional definitions?

3. Rose is opposed to definitions of intelligence that consider "everyday work to be mindless" (28). In his view, what effects are such misguided conceptions likely to have on society "in the future" (28)?

4. What does Rose mean by the "concept of cognitive variability" (29), and where—aside from watching his mother wait tables in a restaurant—did he likely learn about it?

STRATEGIES AND STRUCTURES

1. Rose begins his essay with an account of his mother's experience as a waitress (1–6). Is this an effective introduction to his subject? Why or why not?

2. As Rose defines it, what are some of the main traits of "blue-collar brilliance"? Point to specific passages in the text where he identifies those traits most convincingly.

3. How does Rose's childhood role as an observer at his mother's restaurant resemble the adult, scholarly role he adopts throughout this essay? Explain by pointing to specific passages in the text.

4. Rose's conclusions about blue-collar intelligence are based on "a model of the mind" that, he claims at the end of his essay, is "worthy of a democratic society" (29). How and how well does Rose's definition support this ARGUMENT?

5. *Other Methods.* "I couldn't have put it in words," Rose says of his early experience of the workplace (4). How did he learn to put his observations into words? To what extent might his essay be read as a sort of LITERACY NARRATIVE?

THINKING ABOUT LANGUAGE

1. Point to specific words and phrases in his essay where Rose captures the "lingo" of the workplace (2).

2. What does Rose mean when he says that competence in the workplace was "synonymous" with physical labor (4)?

3. Look up the meaning of the word "iconography" (10). Before the advent of rock stars and television celebrities, who or what did the term refer to?

4. Rose observed blue-collar workers for the purpose of writing their "cognitive biographies" (15). Point to places in his essay that might be considered examples of this type of writing.

5. In paragraph 16, Rose states: "Our culture—in true Cartesian fashion—separates the body from the mind." Look up the **ETYMOLOGY** and definition of "Cartesian," and explain how our culture reflects this separation. How would Rose change this traditional way of thinking?

FOR WRITING

1. Spend an hour or so watching and listening to the workers in a diner, factory, store, hair salon, or other everyday workplace. Take notes on what they say and do, and write a few paragraphs capturing the scene as Rose does in the opening part of his essay.

2. Write an essay of 400 to 500 words explaining how a group of workers you have observed, blue-collar or otherwise, appeared to understand and define some important aspect of their work. Refer in detail to individual members of the group and what they had to say.

3. In your journal, keep a record of your experience at work. Include not only your own observations of the workplace but those of your coworkers, including what they said and did on specific occasions. Include moments of particular brilliance— and otherwise.

4. Interview several of your classmates about the skills and knowledge they acquired from summer jobs and other work experiences. Write a 400-to-500-word **REPORT** summarizing your findings.

5. Write a five-to-seven-paragraph **PROFILE** of a worker you have observed and, if possible, talked to at some length. Your subject can be a close friend, a family member, one of your classmates or teachers, or simply someone you have watched perform a task or service. Be sure to include "cognitive" elements of the work being done.

ALICIA GARZA

The Meaning of Movement

Alicia Garza (b. 1981) is a writer, advocate for social justice, and community organizer who lives in Oakland, California. She is a cofounder of the Black Lives Matter movement, which emerged in response to the killing of Tray-von Martin in 2013. She's also the founder of the Black Futures Lab and a director of the National Domestic Workers Alliance. After graduating from the University of California, San Diego, in 2002 with a degree in anthropol-ogy and sociology, Garza attended the School of Unity and Liberation (SOUL) in Oakland, where she is now a member of the governing board.

At SOUL, Garza trained in the tactics of organizing grassroots political and social movements, a subject she explores in *The Purpose of Power: How We Come Together when We Fall Apart* (2020). In the following selection, a chapter from that book, Garza defines the term "movement" by introducing the related concept of "intersectionality," an idea that might be summed up as "Leave No One Behind."

THESE DAYS, LOTS OF THINGS are called movements that are not in fact move- 1
ments. I am often asked how someone can start their own movement around something that they are passionate about—the humanity of women, the murders of trans people, animal rights, or senior care. My response is always the same: Find the people who care about the same things that you do, and join them.

Often, when people refer to movements they want to start, what they mean is 2
that they want support in helping something go viral—getting more people to pay attention to something, giving something more visibility. But movements are not just visible or viral—they comprise people who are dedicated to achieving some

MLA CITATION: Garza, Alicia. "The Meaning of Movement." *Back to the Lake: A Reader and Guide for Writers*, edited by Thomas Cooley, 5th ed., W. W. Norton, 2024, pp. 579–84.

> A good way to define something is by identifying its most important characteristic (p. 532).

kind of change. The change they (and we) seek cannot be accomplished by something going viral. The change we seek can only be accomplished through sustained organizing.

Movements are composed of individuals, organizations, and institu- 3 tions. Movements bring people together to change laws and to change culture. Successful movements know how to use the tools of media and culture to communicate what they are for, and to help paint a picture of what an alternative world can look like, feel like, be like. They use media to communicate both to audiences that are already bought in and audiences that are on the fence.

Many believe that change happens because a few extraordinary people suddenly 4 and miraculously mobilize millions—rather than through sustained participation and commitment with millions of people over a period of time, sometimes generations. If we reduce the last period of civil rights to the Reverend Dr. Martin Luther King, Jr., or Rosa Parks or even Malcolm X, we obscure the role that powerful organizations like the NAACP or the SCLC played as points of organization for the movement. Rosa Parks gets reduced to a lady who was tired after a long day of work. Similarly, the Montgomery Bus Boycott, one of the most powerful in history, gets reduced to a spontaneous action rather than an organized direct action with a strategy.[1]

Organizations are a critical component of movements—they become the places 5 where people can find community and learn about what's happening around them, why it's happening, who it benefits, and who it harms. Organizations are the places where we learn skills to take action, to organize to change the laws and change our culture. Organizations are where we come together to determine what we can do about the problems facing our communities. Some will argue that you don't need to be a part of an organization to be a part of a movement, and this is true. Yet if you want to be a part of a movement that is sustained and successful, you need organization.

Many confuse political organizations with nonprofit vehicles. I have been a part 6 of a few nonprofit organizations that are more like "We Got Y'all" from Issa Rae's *Insecure*: led by white people with privilege, inauthentically connected to the communities they purport to serve, based solidly in a charity model that doesn't actually seek to solve problems as much as to maintain themselves and their funding. While many movement organizations don't fall into this category, there are far too many that do. A lack of strong, effective, strategic, and collaborative organizations and institutions that aim to shift policy and practice is what makes us weak in relation

---

1. Sparked by the arrest of the civil rights activist Rosa Parks (1913–2005) in December 1955 and organized by the Montgomery Improvement Association under the leadership of Martin Luther King Jr., the boycott of public buses in Montgomery, Alabama, lasted 381 days, ending in November 1956 when the US Supreme Court ruled that segregated seating on public transportation is unconstitutional.

to the right—they have an intricate web of organizations and institutions that do everything from provide thought leadership to experimentation to policy development to engaging in the realm of culture.

Organizations also communicate to decision makers about your relative level of power. Imagine a labor union with two members negotiating with an employer of a thousand workers. Imagine teachers trying to negotiate a higher salary from the school district, and yet because the teachers are anti-organization, each teacher has their own demand for salary and benefits. Organizations encourage collaboration, but they also demonstrate a relative level of power and influence.

After protests die down, which they almost always do, where do people go to take sustained action? Where are people plugged in to develop their skills and learn more tools of organizing?

A commonly held assumption is that to build a movement, one must have a large following on social media. While having a lot of followers on *Twitter* can be influential, it is but one of many ingredients necessary for movements to be effective.

Case in point: In 2016, DeRay Mckesson, a social media personality, announced that he would be running in the Democratic primary for mayor of Baltimore. Having been born and raised there, and with more than 300,000 followers on *Twitter*, he assumed that he had enough name recognition and political credibility to win a mayoral primary. *Jack'd*, a popular app that facilitates intimate connections, sent a push notification encouraging all its users to vote for Mckesson. The results were telling—Mckesson won 2.6 percent of the vote, a total of 3,445 votes. The winner of the primary garnered 48,000 votes—fairly low in the context of an election, but high in relationship to their opponent's social media following.

Building a movement requires shifting people from spectators to strategists, from procrastinators to protagonists. What people are willing to do on social media doesn't always translate into what they're willing to do in their everyday lives. Movement building and participation require ongoing engagement, and the levels of engagement must continually shift and increase—from just showing up to signing a petition to getting nine friends involved to helping design strategy to pressuring a legislator to leading a group, and so on.

Successful movements also have broad appeal. They aren't just groups that everyone knows about; they are what everyone wants to join because they know that if that movement can win, it will change their quality of life. Movements embrace those who have been marginalized in one way or another, and movements move them from marginal to central. The shifts that movements advance are those that make visible those who have been invisible, those who our society and our economy and our government say are of no consequence to our future.

"Intersectionality" is a term that's been thrown around a lot—in good ways and bad—but more often than not is misunderstood. More than a theory, in practice, intersectionality results in unlearning and undoing segregation and thus interrupting the ways that power is consolidated in the hands of the few.

Coined by Dr. Kimberlé Crenshaw in the late 1980s, . . . intersectionality is a way 14 to understand how power operates. It is also a way to ensure that no one, as Crenshaw states, gets left behind. It is a way of understanding both how and why people have been left behind, and it offers a road map for change by making visible those who are currently invisible. In doing so, we become better prepared to demand more, for the sake of winning more.

Some are surprised to learn that movements for justice can be guilty of the same 15 dynamics they seek to challenge. I have been to thousands of meetings, conferences, convenings, gatherings, and campaigns that failed to live, in practice, the world they claimed to want to bring into existence. Even the most radical organizations often fall short of their stated ideals. I've lost count of how many times organizations would state a value like "sisters at the center" and then pretend not to notice that women did the bulk of the emotional and administrative work while men did the bulk of the intellectual work. More than that, I spent ten years of my life in an organization comprising a majority of women of color, from the membership to the staff, and yet the few men in the organization watched those women do the bulk of the work of building with members, recruiting new members, organizing community meetings, setting up for and cleaning up after those meetings, navigating the difficult dynamics of coalitions and alliances, raising money for the organization, and responding to crises in the membership, while they waxed poetic with other men about what the movement needed to be doing and where it needed to go.

I can't tell you how many times I've been referred to as sister, queen, and the like 16 by my peers in movements and yet been offered no vision in those organizations for how the work we did would affect *my* quality of life. It seemed as though I was there not as a strategist, not as a tactician, not as a group builder but instead as a means to someone else's—usually a heterosexual man's—improved quality of life.

For me, intersectionality isn't an intellectual exercise. A movement is not inter- 17 sectional if I am invited to join it but my concerns, my experiences, and my needs are not a part of what the organization or effort, as a whole, sees as its concerns and needs—or its path to power.

Defining a term by giving synonyms is discussed on p. 533. Intersectionality is at times used as a synonym for diversity or represen- 18 tation. I have heard people describe their car pools as intersectional, when they really mean that their car pool is diverse, and I have heard leaders claim that they are intersectional organizers, when they mean to say that they bring people together across race, class, and gender. Diversity is what happens when you have representation of various groups in a place. Representation is what happens when groups that haven't previously been included are included. Intersectionality is what happens when we do everything through the lens of making sure that no one is left behind. More than surface-level inclusion (or merely making sure everyone is represented), intersectionality is the practice of interrogating the power dynamics and rationales of how we can be, together.

The truth is, too many movements are not intersectional. It's a profound statement to make, and also a painful one. As Black people have fought and died for our right to dignity and opportunity, some of us try to get there by climbing on someone else's back without their consent rather than making sure that we form a chain, where all of us get there or none of us do. From voting rights to civil rights to abortion rights, we haven't quite grasped that if any of us are left behind, we have failed.   19

Intersectionality is not Oppression Olympics—that is, it avoids privileging one oppression over another. You can see this kind of competition when someone says, "I'm a Black woman, so you can't tell me anything," and so on. I hear some activists improperly using "intersectionality" as a way to designate who has the right to determine reality. Some use it to shut down valid criticisms of their own actions, behaviors, and impacts. I have even heard activists say things like "intersectionality is not for white women," which is a contradiction. For something to be intersectional, it must take into account the experiences of those who are marginalized in different ways. Crenshaw states: 20

> I am suggesting that Black women can experience discrimination in ways that are both similar to and different from those experienced by white women and Black men. Black women sometimes experience discrimination in ways similar to white women's experiences; sometimes they share very similar experiences with Black men. Yet often they experience double-discrimination—the combined effects of practices which discriminate on the basis of race, and on the basis of sex. And sometimes, they experience discrimination as Black women—not the sum of race and sex discrimination, but as Black women.[2]

Crenshaw's point here is that intersectionality is a framework by which we examine how groups that experience double or triple discrimination get their needs met at the same time as, not in spite of, other groups in the same situation. This is important because it, again, exposes how and why we leave some people behind, and it forces us to acknowledge the ways in which we keep ourselves from reaping the opportunity to build movements that model the world we want to live in right now.   21

Intersectionality does not give us tickets to dismiss real concerns of other groups, and it does not determine whether or not you have the right to your experiences.   22

2. Crenshaw, Kimberlé. "Demarginalizing the Intersection of Race and Sex: A Black Feminist Critique of Antidiscrimination Doctrine, Feminist Theory and Antiracist Politics." *University of Chicago Legal Forum*, vol. 1989, no. 1, p. 149.

Intersectionality does not say that the experiences of Black women are more important or more valid than those of white women, for example. Instead, intersectionality asks why white women's experiences are the standard that we use when addressing inequality based on gender. Intersectionality says two things: First, by looking at the world through a lens that is different from that of just white people, we can see how power is distributed unevenly and on what basis, and second, we need to ensure that the world that we fight for, the claim we lay to the future, is one that meets the needs of all those who have been marginalized.

What's at stake with intersectionality? Whether or not all of us are entitled to 23
live a dignified life. Intersectionality asks us to consider why we do not give the same attention to the criminalization of Black women and girls as we do to the criminalization of Black men and boys. Intersectionality asks us to interrogate why Black people with disabilities—the group most likely to be killed by police—get little attention and physically able Black men who are killed by police get more attention. Intersectionality asks us to examine the places where we are marginalized, but it also demands that we examine how and why those of us who are marginalized can in turn exercise marginalization over others. It demands that we do better by one another so that we can be more powerful together. ◆

FOR CLOSE READING

1. If you want to start a movement, says Alicia Garza, "[f]ind the people who care about the same things that you do, and join them" (1). Is this good advice? Why or why not?

2. Any true movement, according to Garza, is dedicated to bringing about "some kind of change" (2). What other distinguishing features or characteristics would you add to this basic DEFINITION?

3. A political organization, Garza argues, is different from a nonprofit "vehicle" (6). What's the difference in her view, and why does Garza prefer the first type of organization?

4 According to Garza, "movements for justice can be guilty of the same dynamics they seek to challenge" (15). Do you agree? Cite several EXAMPLES to support (or call into question) this POINT OF VIEW.

STRATEGIES AND STRUCTURES

1. The slogan "Black Lives Matter" began as a hashtag. When Garza helped coin this famous phrase, she was seeking to start a movement. Given her career experience as described in both the headnote and the essay, what would you say is her PUR-POSE in composing "The Meaning of Movement," and how well does she achieve it?

2. Movements, says Garza, are closely related to "organizations." How and where does she define this second key term and its relation to the first one?

3. "A lack of strong, effective, strategic, and collaborative organizations and institutions... is what makes us weak in relation to the right" (6). What does Garza mean by "the right"? What does this partisan statement indicate about her intended AUDIENCE, and why might she address them as "us"?

4. When Garza introduces the key concept of "intersectionality," she says that the term is frequently "misunderstood" (13). Is this an effective TRANSITION from her discussion of organizations? Why or why not?

5. *Other Methods.* EXAMPLES can effectively support extended definitions. What point is Garza making about the power of social media when she cites the example of DeRay Mckesson in paragraph 10?

THINKING ABOUT LANGUAGE

1. What are the implications of the phrase "intricate web" in Garza's description of the strengths of her political opponents (6)?

2. How effective do you find Garza's use of alliteration in the following phrases: "spectators to strategists," "procrastinators to protagonists" (11)? Explain.

3. "Intersectionality," "diversity," "representation": What distinctions does Garza make among these SYNONYMS in paragraph 18?

4. What does Garza mean by "Oppression Olympics" (20)? Is she being sarcastic? How does this phrase reveal her POINT OF VIEW about what intersectionality is and is not?

FOR WRITING

1. Draw up a list of the qualities and distinguishing characteristics that, in your opinion, define a true political or social movement. To generate this list, try CLUSTERING or BRAINSTORMING (see pp. 57–58).

2. In a brief personal NARRATIVE, tell the story of your participation in a successful (or not so successful) movement or organization. Be specific in describing what you accomplished or what you tried to accomplish but failed. If you don't have experience with this type of participation, write about your involvement in an effort to promote change on a smaller scale—such as in your neighborhood or at school.

3. Choose one of the "extraordinary people" that Garza mentions in paragraph 4 (or some other icon of the civil rights or Black Lives Matter movements, including Garza herself), and write a 500-to-700-word PROFILE of that person as a public figure. Include an account of how your subject came to be a political and social activist, and consider whether the outcome of the movement would (or would not) have been fundamentally the same without that person's participation.

4. "Some will argue," says Garza, "that you don't need to be a part of an organization to be a part of a movement" (5). Write a six-to-eight-paragraph POSITION PAPER in which you argue for (or against) this position. If possible, cite EXAMPLES from your own experience or that of people you know.

15 | Argument

Come now, and let us reason together . . .

—Isaiah 1:18

Well, do you want to have just one argument, or were you thinking of taking a course?

—*Monty Python's Flying Circus*

For the sake of argument, let's assume that you are a parent, and you want your children to grow up in a safe and healthy environment. Consequently, you install a swimming pool in the backyard so they can learn to swim and get lots of good exercise.

No sooner has the concrete dried on your new pool when your next-door neighbor comes over and says, "Nice pool."

"Yeah," you reply, "we want our children to be healthy and strong—swimming is great exercise. Also, we want them to be safe; most of the earth's covered in water, you know, and they should learn how to swim."

"Right," says your neighbor. "But a pool like that isn't a good idea for little kids. In fact, it's a safety hazard. Don't you know that drowning is the leading cause of accidental death among children age one to four? Nearly 1,000 kids drown in the United States each year, and another 8,000 almost do."

You know that an unguarded swimming pool can be dangerous for nonswimmers, but you don't want to get into an argument with your neighbor—at least, not the kind of argument that might degenerate into a shouting match. So you step back and think about how to respond calmly and logically to your neighbor's claim. This second, more rational sort of argument is the subject of this chapter.

Making and Supporting a Claim

When you construct an **ARGUMENT**, you take a position on an issue and support that position with evidence. Suppose you believe that swimming pools are safe so long as they're properly fenced. This is your *claim*, and you can cite facts and figures, examples, expert testimony, or personal experience to support it.

In this chapter, we're going to examine how to make a claim and support it with evidence and logical reasoning. There are times, however, when logic isn't enough, so we'll also explain how to appeal to your readers' emotions and how to establish your own credibility as a reliable person who deserves to be heard on ethical grounds. We'll also review the critical points to watch for as you read over and revise your essay, as well as common errors to avoid when you edit.

Why Do We Argue?

When we argue, we express our opinions and ideas in a way that gets others to take them seriously. Unlike statements of fact, opinions aren't necessarily correct or incorrect. The ultimate purpose of a good argument is not to convince others that your claim is absolutely right or wrong. It is to demonstrate that it's plausible—worth listening to, and maybe even acting on. Many arguments, in fact, ask the reader to *explore* an issue, not just accept or reject a particular claim. Exploratory arguments are intended to open up discussion, to help us gain new knowledge, and even to lead to some kind of consensus.

Composing an Argument

Writing that *argues* a claim and asks readers to agree with it is sometimes distinguished from writing that seeks to *persuade* readers to take action. In this chapter, however, we'll use the terms "argue" and "persuade" more or less interchangeably, because there's not much point in arguing that a claim is correct if you can't also persuade the reader that it's worth acting on.

Any claim worth making has more than one side, however; that is, rational people can disagree about it. We can all agree that backyard swimming pools can be dangerous under certain circumstances. We might reasonably disagree, however, on what those circumstances are and what to do about them.

When you make a claim, it should be arguable in this sense of being debatable. Some claims cannot reasonably be argued. For instance:

- *Matters of taste:* I hate broccoli.
- *Matters of faith:* And on the third day He arose.
- *Matters of fact:* According to the World Health Organization, approximately 236,000 people drowned in 2022.

Matters of fact can be contested, of course. You might, for instance, know of a case of drowning that went unreported, so you could point out that the average for that year may be slightly higher. But a claim like this doesn't leave much room for debate. It can be established simply by checking the facts. An argument can collapse if its facts are wrong, but a good argument doesn't just state the facts. It argues something significant *about* the facts.

So when you compose a written argument, make sure your claim is arguable, or open to opinion—and that it's one you actually have a stake in. If you don't really care much about your topic, your reader probably won't either.

Thinking about Purpose and Audience

When you compose an argument, your purpose is to persuade other people to hear you out, to listen thoughtfully to what you have to say—even if they don't completely accept your views. Whatever your claim, your argument is more likely to appeal to your audience if it's tailored to their particular needs and interests.

In this panel from writer Brooke Gladstone and illustrator Josh Neufeld's graphic narrative "The Influencing Machines," about the history and effects of media, Gladstone (in the glasses) is clearly presenting different sides in a debate:

Gladstone isn't taking a position here, as she would if she were mostly constructing an argument. Instead, she's using the debate form (and other strategies of argument) to present her research in a **REPORT** about how media and the human mind evolved together.

For example, your next-door neighbor might be more inclined to accept a swimming pool in your backyard if, in addition to addressing the safety issue, you also argued that a nice pool would increase property values in the neighborhood. On the other hand, if you need to persuade the city planning department to issue you a permit so that you can build a pool, you'd be better off telling them that because there's no public pool within a reasonable distance from your house, children in your neighborhood must now travel too far just to enjoy a swim during the summer.

So as you compose an argument, think about what your readers' views on the particular issue are likely to be. Of all the evidence you might present in support of your case, what kind would your intended readers most likely find reasonable and convincing?

Generating Ideas: Finding Effective Evidence

You can start generating ideas for an argument by using the same techniques, like **LISTING** and **BRAINSTORMING**, that you use with other kinds of writing.

The most important question to ask when thinking about your argument is "why": Why should your audience accept your claim? What evidence—facts, figures, examples, and so on—can you provide to convince readers that your claim is valid? Let's look at some of the most effective types of evidence.

Suppose you're writing about the cost of housing, and you want to argue that for most people it makes better economic sense in the long run to buy rather than rent. To support a claim like this effectively, you can use facts, statistics, examples, expert testimony, and personal experience.

Facts. Because facts can be verified, they make good evidence for persuading readers to accept your point of view. In a position paper arguing that buying beats renting, you might, for example, cite facts about the current housing market. Thus you could point out that rents on average across the country have increased by 17.11 percent since March 2021, an annual growth rate of nearly 8.56 percent.

Statistics. A particularly useful form of evidence when you want to show a tendency or trend is statistics. This type of evidence is also verifiable and, thus, convincing to many readers. To support your claim about the financial advantages of homeownership, you could cite statistics about the economic net worth of homeowners as opposed to renters in the US population as a whole. According to the Federal Reserve, the median net worth of homeowners in 2023 was $255,000; for renters, it was $6,300.

Examples. Good examples make an argument more concrete and specific—and thus more likely to be understood and accepted by your audience. A person who pays $1,500 per month in rent for fifteen years, you could note, would be out a total of $270,000 at the end of that period. By contrast, that same person, paying roughly the same amount on a fifteen-year mortgage loan, could own a $200,000 dwelling free and clear (assuming a loan rate of 4.5 percent).

Expert testimony. One of the most effective kinds of evidence is the direct testimony of experts in the field you're writing about. To make a serious case for the value of homeownership, you might quote a statement like this from a 2007 report compiled by Harvard's Joint Center for Housing Studies:

> Even after the tremendous decline in housing prices and the rising wave of foreclosures that began in 2007, homeownership continues to be a significant source of household wealth, and remains particularly important for lower-income and minority households.
>
> —CHRISTOPHER E. HERBERT, DANIEL T. MCCUE, ROCIO
> SANCHEZ-MOYANO, *Is Homeownership Still an Effective Means of Building*
> *Wealth for Low-Income and Minority Households? (Was It Ever?)*

Personal experience. Often you can effectively cite personal experience to support an argument, as with the following anecdote about the perils of renting:

> Back in my hometown, my family has always been renters; but last Monday the landlord notified my parents that the rent on their two-bedroom apartment would go up 15 percent next year. For the same amount in monthly payments, they can buy a house across the street with an extra bedroom where I can live while saving up for a down payment on a place of my own. Enforced saving is one of the biggest benefits of home ownership. I haven't told them about this plan yet. . . .

Many readers find personal testimony like this to be particularly moving, but be sure that any personal experience you cite as evidence is actually pertinent to the claim you're making.

Sojourner Truth uses personal testimony to support her argument (p. 622).

No matter what type of evidence you present—whether facts and figures, examples, expert testimony, or personal experience—it must be pertinent to your argument and should be selected with an eye to convincing your audience that your claim is plausible and worth taking seriously.

Organizing and Drafting an Argument

Once you have a claim and evidence to support it, you're ready to start organizing and drafting your argument. You'll need to state your claim; appeal to your readers' needs and interests; and present yourself as trustworthy and reliable. You'll also need to anticipate and respond to likely objections. Finally, you'll want to think about which other methods of development, such as NARRATION and DEFINITION, might be useful in your argument. The templates on p. 595 can help you get started.

ORGANIZING AN ARGUMENT

Claim and support. Any well-constructed argument is organized around these two basic elements. Consider the following argument by an economist on the issue of whether to rent or buy:

> When potential first-time homebuyers consider making the transition to home-ownership, they often evaluate whether it makes more financial sense to keep renting or to buy. Given today's changing housing market, that decision is more complex than ever.
> —ODETA KUSHI, "Should You Rent or Buy?" (*Fortune*, Dec. 2022)

In today's housing market, it is no longer possible, Kushi believes, to give a simple yes or no answer to the question raised in her title. Instead, she argues, making the right decision has become "complex."

This is Kushi's claim, and to support it she offers evidence like the following:

- Rent prices were up 9.6% in October 2022 as compared with a year earlier.
- House prices in this same period were up 13%.
- Interest rates on home mortgages "more than doubled" in that year.

The result of these and other factors, Kushi concludes in a restatement of her initial claim, is "a challenging puzzle for those potential first-time homebuyers considering whether to rent or buy."

Kushi's argument follows a straightforward organization—claim, evidence, conclusion—that is effective for any argument:

1. State your claim clearly in your introduction.
2. In the main body of your argument, present evidence in support of your claim.
3. Develop the body of the argument until you have offered good reasons and sufficient evidence to support your claim.
4. In the conclusion, restate your claim and sum up how the evidence supports it.

STATING YOUR CLAIM

State your claim clearly and directly at the beginning of your argument—and take care not to claim more than you can possibly prove. As an arguable claim, "backyard swimming pools are safe" is too broad. Safe for whom? Under what circumstances?

A more manageable, because more restricted, version of your claim might be something like this: "A properly protected backyard swimming pool is safe even for small children." Proper protection for home pools, you might then point out, requires fencing on all four sides. If a pool remains open to the house on one side, a small child can stumble into it through an unlocked door.

USING LOGICAL REASONING: INDUCTION AND DEDUCTION

For certain purposes—such as convincing a toddler to stay clear of an unguarded pool—logic isn't very effective. In many writing situations, however, logical reasoning is indispensable for persuading others that your ideas and opinions are valid.

> Thomas Jefferson uses both kinds to argue for revolution (p. 616).

There are two basic kinds of logical reasoning, induction and deduction. Induction is reasoning from particular evidence to a general conclusion. You reason inductively when you observe the cost of a gallon of gas at half a dozen service stations and conclude that the price of gas is uniformly high.

Inductive reasoning is based on probability—it draws a conclusion from a limited number of specific cases. When you argue inductively, you aren't claiming that a conclusion is certain but that it is likely. Even relatively few cases can provide the basis of a good inductive argument—if they're truly representative of a larger group. Exit polls of a few hundred people, for example, can often predict the outcome of an election involving thousands of voters. If it's truly representative, even a small sampling is sometimes enough. You would need only one or two cases of meningitis on a high school swimming team, for instance, to infer that the pool in the gym is probably contaminated and that the whole school is in danger because the virus is so contagious. Unless you take into account every possible individual case, though, inductive reasoning is never 100 percent certain: it usually requires an "inductive leap" at the end, as when you move from the individual cases of meningitis on the team to the general inference that the school as a whole is threatened.

By contrast with induction, deduction moves from general principles to a particular conclusion. You reason deductively when your car stops running and—knowing that cars in general need fuel to run on and recalling that you started with half a tank and have been driving all day—you conclude that you're out of gas.

TEMPLATES FOR DRAFTING

When you begin to draft an argument, you identify your subject and state the basic claim you plan to make about that subject—moves fundamental to any argument. See how Michelle Obama makes these moves in a speech at a high school graduation in Kansas:

> I think it's fitting that we're celebrating this historic Supreme Court case tonight, not just because *Brown* started right here in Topeka or because *Brown*'s sixtieth anniversary is tomorrow, but because I believe that all of you—our soon-to-be-graduates—you all are the living, breathing legacy of this case. —MICHELLE OBAMA,
> "Remarks at Topeka School District Senior Recognition Day"

Obama identifies the subject of her argument ("this historic Supreme Court case") and states her basic claim about that subject ("you all are the living, breathing legacy of this case"). Here's another example from this chapter:

> According to the Food and Agriculture Organization of the United Nations, an estimated two billion people eat bugs as part of their standard diet. That's nearly a quarter of the global population, and yet most countries in Europe and North America, despite the nutritional and environmental benefits, are very skeptical about the idea of consuming bugs. So why should Westernized countries subscribe to the inclusion of bugs in their daily diet? —GRACE SILVA, "A Change in the Menu"

In this case, Silva opens her essay by identifying her subject (eating bugs as part of the standard diet) and by stating her claim (that Westernized countries should include bugs in the daily diet) in a skillfully chosen **RHETORICAL QUESTION**.

The following templates can help you make some of these basic moves in your own writing. But don't take these as formulas where you just fill in the blanks. There are no shortcuts to good writing, but these templates can serve as starting points.

▸ In this argument about X, the main point I want to make is _____.

▸ Others may say _____, but I would argue that _____.

▸ My contention about X is supported by the fact that _____.

▸ Additional facts that support this view of X are _____, _____, and _____.

▸ My own experience with X shows that _____ because _____.

▸ My view of X is supported by _____, who says that X is _____.

▸ What you should do about X is _____.

Deductive arguments can be stated as SYLLOGISMS, which have a major premise, a minor premise, and a conclusion. For example:

>*Major premise:* All unguarded swimming pools are dangerous.
>
>*Minor premise:* This pool is unguarded.
>
>*Conclusion:* This pool is dangerous.

This is a valid syllogism—the conclusion follows logically from the premises.

The great advantage of deduction over induction is that it deals with logical certainty rather than mere probability. As long as the premises you begin with are true and the syllogism is properly constructed, the conclusion must be true. A syllogism fails to hold up, however, when one or more of the premises are false, or when the syllogism isn't constructed properly.

In a properly constructed syllogism, the conclusion links the first part of the minor premise ("this pool") to the second part of the major premise ("dangerous"). One of the most common mistakes that people make in constructing syllogisms is simply repeating, in the minor premise, the trait named at the end of the major premise, as in the following example:

AN INVALID SYLLOGISM

>*Major premise:* All planets are round.
>
>*Minor premise:* My head is round.
>
>*Conclusion:* My head is a planet.

Being round is a characteristic that "planets" and "my head" share, but many other things are round too. A diagram can help us see why this syllogism doesn't work:

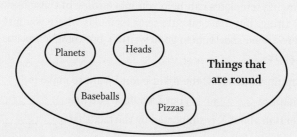

As this diagram illustrates, just being round doesn't mean that planets and heads have much else in common; in fact, they belong to entirely separate categories within the larger one of things that are round.

Advertisers use this kind of faulty reasoning all the time to try to convince you that you must buy their products if you want to be a cool person. Such reasoning is faulty because even if you accept the premise that, for example, all people who buy motorcycles are cool, there are lots of cool people who don't buy motorcycles—as the following diagram indicates:

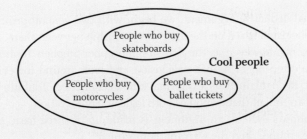

PROPERLY CONSTRUCTED SYLLOGISMS

Major premise: All planets are round.

Minor premise: Earth is a planet.

Conclusion: Earth is round.

Major premise: All people who buy motorcycles are cool.

Minor premise: Susan has bought a motorcycle.

Conclusion: Susan is cool.

Not so sure about this second example? Both of these syllogisms are valid—that is, the conclusions follow logically from the premises. A syllogism can be logically valid, however, and the conclusion may still be false—if one or more of the premises are false. (Not everyone would agree, for example, with the premise that all motorcycle owners are cool.) Study the following example of a properly constructed syllogism with a false premise.

A PROPERLY CONSTRUCTED SYLLOGISM WITH A FALSE PREMISE

Major premise: All spiders have six legs.

Minor premise: The black widow is a spider.

Conclusion: The black widow has six legs.

The conclusion that black widows have six legs is logical, given the premises of this argument. However, since the major premise is wrong—spiders actually have eight legs—the conclusion of the argument is also wrong.

When you use deduction in your writing, readers are less likely to question your reasoning if your argument follows the logic of a properly constructed syllogism or other model argument, such as one constructed by using the Toulmin method (see next page). Be prepared, however, to defend your premises if they aren't as self-evident as "spiders have eight legs" or "all humans are mortal." If you're arguing, for example,

THE TOULMIN METHOD

In a formal deductive argument, we begin with two general principles and draw a conclusion based on the logical relationship between them. In practical arguments, however, as the British philosopher Stephen Toulmin recognized, we often begin with a conclusion and look around for evidence to support it. Recognizing this less formal kind of deduction, Toulmin devised a system of argument that combines both logic and observation.

In Toulmin's system, an argument is made up of three basic parts: the claim, the grounds, and the warrant. For example:

Claim: Steven Spielberg is the greatest director in the history of film.

Grounds: His films have grossed more than those of any other director.

Warrant: The best measure of a film's quality is financial success.

The claim is the main point the argument seeks to prove. The grounds are the evidence on which that claim is based. And the warrant is the reason that the grounds justify the claim.

In a Toulmin argument, the grounds can be facts, statistics, examples, expert testimony, personal experience, or other kinds of evidence. It is an observable fact, for instance, that Spielberg has grossed approximately $10 billion at the box office—more than any other director in film history.

Though they constitute grounds for a claim, facts and other data are not alone sufficient, in Toulmin's view, to support that claim completely. It takes logic as well: a warrant is needed to explain how and why the grounds logically justify the claim. In this case, the warrant for accepting the claim about Spielberg as the world's greatest filmmaker is the assumption that films and directors are best judged by how much money they make.

Not everyone would agree with this assumption, though. Most real-life arguments, in fact, are about the assumptions on which the argument is based. But breaking down an argument into Toulmin's three parts can be especially useful for spotting faulty or unstated assumptions—so you can strengthen them in your own arguments or question them in the arguments of others.

that intelligent design should be taught in science classes, you might structure your basic argument like this:

Major premise: All scientific theories should be taught in science classes.

Minor premise: Intelligent design is a scientific theory.

Conclusion: Intelligent design should be taught in science classes.

This is a well-constructed deductive argument. As long as your readers accept the premises—particularly the minor premise about the scientific nature of intelligent design—they'll probably accept your conclusion. If you believe, however, that some readers may disagree with the premises of your argument—and you still hope to convince them—you should provide strong evidence to support those premises. Or, if necessary, consider how you might rework your premises altogether.

USING INDUCTION AND DEDUCTION IN VARIOUS ACADEMIC FIELDS

Because it draws on observation and the analysis of particular data, induction is the method you're most likely to use when constructing an argument in the fields of engineering and the applied sciences. In the humanities and social sciences, induction is also particularly useful for analyzing specific written texts (the poems of Rita Dove, the letters of John Adams, a set of questionnaires) and for drawing general conclusions about them. You also use inductive reasoning when you cite personal experience as evidence, because you're arguing that something you observed or experienced personally has general significance for others.

Deductive reasoning, in contrast, is particularly useful for constructing arguments in the fields of philosophy, ethics, theology, and the more theoretical sciences, such as mathematics and physics, where particular cases tend to be subject to universal principles (such as $E = mc^2$). For example, the argument that a large round object recently discovered in the night sky should be classified as a planet because it meets all the criteria that define planets in general would be a deductive argument.

AVOIDING LOGICAL FALLACIES

Logical fallacies are errors in logical reasoning. Though they can seem plausible and even persuasive, they lead to wrong-headed conclusions. Here are some of the most common logical fallacies to watch out for when you write (and read).

Post hoc, ergo propter hoc. Latin for "after this, therefore because of this," this kind of faulty reasoning assumes that just because one event (such as rain) comes after another event (a rain dance), it occurs *because* of the first event. For example: "Soon after the country declared war, the divorce rate increased. War is harmful to marriages." The fact that the country declared war before the divorce rate went up doesn't mean the declaration caused the increase.

Non sequitur. Latin for "does not follow," a non sequitur is a statement that has little or no logical connection to the preceding statement: "The early Egyptians were masters of architecture and geometry. Thus they created a vast network of trade and commerce throughout the ancient world." Since mastering architecture and geometry has little to do with trade, this second statement is a non sequitur.

Begging the question. An argument that takes for granted what it is supposed to prove: "Americans should be required to carry ID cards because Americans need to be prepared to prove their identity." This conclusion assumes that Americans need to prove their identities.

Appeal to doubtful authority. This is the fallacy of citing as expert testimony the opinions of people who don't necessarily have special knowledge of the issue: "According to Lady Gaga, the candidate who takes South Carolina will win the election." Lady Gaga isn't an expert on politics, so citing her opinion on political matters to support an argument is an appeal to doubtful authority.

Michael Lewis's little daughter employs an ad hominem attack on p. 626.

Ad hominem. This fallacy attacks the person making an argument instead of addressing the actual issue: "She's the head of the union, and she's crazy. Don't pay any attention to her views on the economy." Saying she's the head of a union and calling her crazy focuses on her as a person rather than on her views of the issue.

Either / or reasoning. This fallacy, sometimes called a false dilemma, treats a complicated issue as if it had only two sides: "Either you believe that God created the universe according to His plan, which is the view of religion; or you believe that the universe evolved randomly, which is the view of science." This statement doesn't allow for beliefs outside of these two options.

Hasty generalization. This fallacy draws a conclusion based on far too little evidence: "In all four of the stories by Edgar Allan Poe that we read for English 201, the narrator is mentally ill. Poe himself must have been mad." There isn't nearly enough evidence here to determine Poe's mental health.

False analogy. This fallacy occurs when an argument is based on a faulty comparison: "Children are like dogs. A happy dog is a disciplined dog, and a happy child is one who knows the rules and is taught to obey them." Dogs and children aren't enough alike to assume that what's good for one is good for the other.

APPEALING TO YOUR READERS' EMOTIONS

Sound logical reasoning is hard to refute, but sometimes, in order to persuade readers to accept your claim, it helps to appeal to their emotions as well.

As an economist speaking to a general audience, Steven Levitt, a regular guest on the podcast *Freakonomics* and the author of a book by that title, knows that people often find numbers dry and unmoving. So, in his book, after citing statistics to show the dangers of unguarded swimming pools, Levitt goes on to appeal to the emotions and feelings of his readers. Observing that a child can drown in only thirty seconds and that child drownings are "typically silent," Levitt warns parents not to let their guard down even for an instant, lest a pool (or even a bucket of water) "steal your child's life."

"Steal" is a carefully chosen word here. It implies evil intent—the pool lies in wait for the child, like a thief. We are well beyond logic and statistics now. Evil that is quick and silent demands an ever-watchful parent: "Simply stated, keeping your children safe around water is one of the single most important things a parent can do to protect a child."

Emotional? Of course. But this is emotionalism in a good cause, carefully applied to support a well-reasoned argument. And often the best way to urge your readers to action is by tugging at their heartstrings. When appealing to the readers' emotions, however, be careful to avoid sensationalism and alarmism—they can undermine your argument. So after sounding the alarm, Levitt calmly directs readers to the website of the US Consumer Products Safety Commission, which "offers a publication detailing some simple steps for safeguarding pools."

ESTABLISHING YOUR OWN CREDIBILITY

When constructing an argument, you can demonstrate with irrefutable logic that what you have to say is valid and true. And you can appeal to the readers' emotions with genuine fervor. Your words may still fall on deaf ears, however, if your readers don't fully trust you. What makes Levitt's argument so credible in the end is that he himself has lost a child.

Levitt's first child, Andrew, did not drown. When the boy was just over a year old, he came down with meningitis and, within two days, died in the hospital. Levitt wrote about protecting children from drowning, in part, to channel a father's grief, which gives him an emotional and ethical authority that nothing else could. "As a father who has lost a son," Levitt writes, "I know first-hand the unbearable pain that comes with a child's death."

Levitt's loss is different in one crucial regard from that of the parent whose child dies in an unguarded swimming pool. "Amidst my grief," he says, "I am able to take some small solace in the fact that everything possible was done to fight the disease that took my son's life." Having said this, the grieving father closes with a final appeal to the reader, whom he addresses directly in the second person: "If my son had died in a backyard pool due to my own negligence, I would not even have that to cling to. . . . Parents who have lost children would do anything to get their babies back. . . . Safeguard your pool so you don't become one of us." You don't need to have children or a swimming pool to recognize the power of such an argument. Nor do you need such a close, personal tie to your subject in order to establish your own credibility.

There are many less dramatic ways to establish your CREDIBILITY when constructing an argument. Readers are more likely to trust you, for example, if they feel you're presenting the issues objectively. So acknowledge opposing points of view, and treat them fairly and accurately. Then look for common ground where you and your reader can come together not just logically but also psychologically. (For tips on how to do this, see the discussion of Rogerian logic below.)

If you have experience or special expertise in your subject, let your readers know. For instance, if you're arguing that American ballet companies require their dancers to be too thin and you danced with a professional ballet company for three years, tell your readers that. Also, pay close attention to the TONE of your argument. Whether you come across as calm and reasonable or full of righteous anger, your tone will say much about your own values and motives for writing—and about you as a person. Nothing does more to establish your credibility with readers than to persuade them that they're listening to the words of a moral and ethical person who shares their values and understands their concerns.

USING ROGERIAN ARGUMENT

The psychologist Carl Rogers recognized that people are much more likely to listen to someone they feel is listening to them. If you want to persuade others to accept your views, Rogers reasoned, it's better to treat them as colleagues rather than adversaries. Instead of an "I'm right and you're wrong" approach, therefore, Rogers recommended using "win-win" strategies of argument that invite collaboration and consensus rather than confrontation and conflict. In other words, instead of having an argument, the Rogerian approach says, with Isaiah, "Come now, and let us reason together."

To use Rogerian methods of argument in your own writing, you need to show your audience that you're well aware that the issue at hand can be viewed in different lights and that you have thoughtfully considered viewpoints other than your own. To do this, summarize opposing viewpoints carefully and accurately, and acknowledge their merit. Then introduce your views and look for common ground between them and the views of others. Explain how your views address these common concerns and what additional advantages they have, and give evidence in support of your point of view.

For example, suppose that you would like to see greater gun-control legislation. Instead of lashing out at people who might disagree with you, you might try a more conciliatory, Rogerian approach. You might begin by acknowledging that the US Constitution guarantees certain rights to individuals, in particular the right to self-defense and to protect personal property. You might also acknowledge that many people, including hunters and target shooters, look on certain types of guns as gear or sporting goods. Others view them as collectibles and are interested in their history and manufacture.

After demonstrating your genuine concern and respect for the rights and opinions of others with whom you disagree, you could look for ways in which gun control might actually serve their interests. For example, you might point out that strict licensing and training in the proper handling of firearms can help reduce injury and death among those who use guns for sport. In the event of theft, you might note, enforced registration of guns would also help collectors and other owners of valuable firearms to retrieve their stolen property. You might even concede that stricter gun-control legislation probably isn't necessary in the case of people who already abide by existing gun-control laws, own guns legally, and use them responsibly. Having established as much common ground as you can among the parties in this debate, you are now ready to introduce and explain your position.

You favor stricter gun controls, even to the point of banishing firearms altogether. Why? You believe that guns are inherently dangerous and that they can fall into the hands of people who don't abide by the rules. Also, they can be *accidentally* misused. Wouldn't society as a whole be better off, you wonder, if guns were all but impossible to obtain—even if that meant curtailing the rights of some individuals? You realize that not everyone will agree with this position; but having made clear that you understand and sympathize with the views of the other side, you can reasonably expect that those who might otherwise dismiss your claims will be more inclined to listen to you. And you can even hope that readers who aren't committed to either point of view will be more likely to adopt yours.

ANTICIPATING OTHER ARGUMENTS

As you construct an argument, it's important to consider COUNTERARGUMENTS—that is, viewpoints other than your own, including objections that others might raise to your argument. Anticipating other arguments, in fact, is yet another way to establish your credibility and win the reader's confidence. Readers are more likely to see you as trustworthy if, instead of ignoring an opposing argument, you state it fairly and accurately and then refute it—or offer an alternative point of view, as Shannon Palus does in this passage from her essay "Trigger Warnings" in this chapter:

> That's not to say that people who have experienced trauma should be left on their own to have that panicked response and just get over it. "Rather than issue trigger warnings, universities can best serve students by facilitating access to effective and proven treatments for P.T.S.D. and other mental health problems," Richard McNally, a Harvard psychologist . . . wrote in the *New York Times* in 2016. . . . In other words, if you feel you need a trigger warning, maybe what you really need is better medical care.
>
> —SHANNON PALUS, "Trigger Warnings"

For another example, suppose you think that private ownership of firearms is a deterrent to crime and you oppose stricter gun-control laws. Some of your readers, however, may believe that private ownership of guns actually *increases* crime, and they may be prepared to cite studies showing that there are more homicides in places where there are more guns.

Anticipating this counterargument, you might refute it by saying, "Proponents of stricter gun-control legislation are right when they cite studies showing that more homicides occur in places where more people have guns. However, such studies refer, by and large, to 'loose' firearms. The situation is different where guns are protected—kept under lock and key where a child or intruder can't get to them. Responsible gun ownership actually reduces crime." Proponents of stricter gun controls still may not be entirely convinced, but they'll be far more likely to listen to your argument because you readily admit that guns can be dangerous and you address, head-on, a major point of opposition to your views.

Even when you don't have a ready response to an opposing argument, you'll still want to acknowledge it in order to show that you've thought carefully about all aspects of the issue.

USING OTHER METHODS

Each method of writing discussed in Chapters 7–14 can be useful when constructing an argument. If you're arguing for (or against) stricter gun-control laws, for example, you'll need to DEFINE the present rules and what you mean by "stricter" ones.

EDITING FOR COMMON ERRORS IN ARGUMENTS

Certain errors in punctuation and usage are common in arguments. The following guidelines will help you check for such problems—and edit them as needed.

Check your punctuation with such connecting words as "if," "therefore," "thus," "consequently," "however," "nevertheless," and "because"

When the connecting word comes at the beginning of a sentence and links it to an earlier statement, the connecting word should be followed by a comma:

▶ Therefore, the minimum legal drinking age should not be lowered to eighteen.

▶ Consequently, stronger immigration laws will be unnecessary.

When the connecting word comes at the beginning of a sentence and is part of an introductory clause—a group of words that includes a subject and verb—the entire clause should be followed by a comma:

▶ Because guest workers will be legally registered, stronger immigration laws will be unnecessary.

▶ If acting legally is just as easy as acting illegally, most people will choose the legal course of action.

When the connecting word indicates a logical relationship between two independent clauses—such as cause and effect, sequence, comparison, or contrast—the word is usually preceded by a semicolon and followed by a comma:

▶ Many of the best surgeons have the highest rates of malpractice; thus, the three-strikes-and-you're-out rule for taking away a doctor's license may do more harm than good.

When the connecting word comes in the middle of an independent clause, it should be set off by commas:

▶ A physician who removes the wrong leg, however, deserves a much harsher penalty than one who forgets to remove a sponge.

Check for common usage errors

"However," "nevertheless"

Use "however" when you want to acknowledge a different argument but want to minimize its consequences or simply draw a contrast with your own argument:

▶ The surgeon may have been negligent; ~~nevertheless~~, <u>however</u>, losing her license is too harsh a penalty.

Use "nevertheless" when you want to acknowledge the strength of a different argument but still claim that your own argument is stronger:

▶ The surgeon may not have been negligent; ~~however~~, <u>nevertheless</u>, she should lose her license because she misled the patient into believing the procedure was less dangerous than it actually is.

"Imply," "infer"

Do not confuse "infer," which means "to draw a conclusion," with "imply," which means "to express indirectly." A speaker or writer implies something; a listener or reader infers it:

▶ The coach's speech ~~inferred~~ <u>implied</u> that he expected the team to lose the game.
▶ From the coach's speech, the fans ~~implied~~ <u>inferred</u> that he expected the team to lose the game.

You may also need to use CAUSE-AND-EFFECT analysis to explain what good (or harm) new laws would do. Or you may want to COMPARE AND CONTRAST the old laws with the new ones; or do an ANALYSIS of proposals for enforcing the new laws; or construct a NARRATIVE to show the new laws in action.

Reading an Argument with a Critical Eye

Once you have a draft of your argument, ask someone to read it and tell you where your case seems particularly convincing and where it seems to break down. Then read the argument again critically yourself. Here are some questions to keep in mind when checking a written argument.

PURPOSE AND AUDIENCE. What is the basic purpose of the argument? To inform? To move the reader to action? Some other purpose? How well does the argument achieve its purpose? How might it be revised to do so better? Who is the intended audience? What will they already know about the topic, and will they need any additional background information? What are their views likely to be on the topic?

THE CLAIM. What is the claim? Is it stated clearly and directly in a **THESIS STATEMENT**? If not, should it be? Is it arguable—could reasonable people disagree about it? Is the claim limited enough to be covered well? If not, how could it be narrowed down further? Is it clear why this claim is significant and why the reader should care about it?

EVIDENCE. What evidence is given to support the claim? Is it factually correct? Is all of it, including any personal experience cited as evidence, clearly related to the claim? Is the evidence sufficient to support the claim, or is additional evidence needed? What kind?

LOGICAL REASONING. How well do the parts of the essay hold together? What kind of reasoning connects the evidence with the claim? Inductive? Deductive? Both? In general, how *convincing* is the argument? How could it be strengthened?

EMOTIONAL APPEALS. Does the argument appeal to readers' emotions? If so, for what purpose? To make them aware of a problem? To move them to action? Is any emotional appeal sufficiently restrained? Is it convincing? If there's no emotional appeal, should there be?

CREDIBILITY. What kind of person does the author of this argument seem to be? An ethical person of good character who shares and respects readers' values? If not, what changes could convey that credibility? What special experience or knowledge, if any, does the author bring to this particular issue? In sum, does the author seem trustworthy?

ANTICIPATING OTHER ARGUMENTS. What other arguments might someone make about the topic? What objections might they raise to the claim? Are other arguments respectfully acknowledged and, where possible, refuted?

OTHER METHODS. What other methods of development does the argument use? For example, does it **DEFINE** the issues clearly? Does it analyze **CAUSES** and **EFFECTS**? If other methods are not used, where might they be helpful?

COMMON ERRORS. Does the argument use connecting words like "therefore," "consequently," and "nevertheless"? If so, are they correctly punctuated? Connectors at the beginning of a sentence may or may not be followed by a comma, depending on how they relate to the rest of the sentence. Check to be sure the comma is in the right place; otherwise, the meaning of the sentence may be clouded.

Student Example

Grace Silva wrote "A Change in the Menu" at age fifteen as a student at the Ann Richards School for Young Women Leaders in Austin, Texas. With the support of her teacher, Anni Knox, Silva submitted her essay to the Sixth Annual Student Editorial Contest sponsored by the *New York Times* in 2020. Of the 10,509 submissions received by the newspaper, Silva's editorial, advocating a small change in the Western diet, was one of the twelve winners.

A Change in the Menu

According to the Food and Agriculture Organization of the United Nations, an estimated two billion people eat bugs as part of their standard diet (Halloran and Vantomme). That's nearly a quarter of the global population, and yet most countries in Europe and North America, despite the nutritional and environmental benefits, are very skeptical about the idea of consuming bugs. So why should Westernized countries subscribe to the inclusion of bugs in their daily diet?

Rhetorical question implies Grace Silva's claim (we should eat more bugs) and anticipates her reasons

Eating bugs as a substitute for larger livestock could contribute substantially to a more sustainable world. Bugs have an efficient feed-to-product ratio and consume much less than traditional livestock per pound. To farm bugs, forests do not need to be cleared, fields do not need to be irrigated, and crops do not need to be sprayed with toxins and pesticides. According to an article written by the former manager of the Toronto Food Policy Council, Wayne Roberts, "Edible insects don't appear on any endangered species lists, and their sustainable use could help conserve other wildlife since the tactic may contribute to habitat protection" (8).

Reason #1: sustainability

The nutritional benefits of eating bugs are significant, and bugs could be instrumental in combating childhood mortality and malnutrition rates. Monica Ayieko of the Food and Agriculture department at Bondo University College has studied and published the effects of integrating native crickets into school meal programs in Kenya. Her studies have found that roughly 30% of Kenyan households are food

Reason #2: nutritional benefits for children in Kenya

insecure, leading to massive malnutrition among children, particularly under the age of five. This is due to a lack of both macronutrients and micronutrients, including protein and zinc (Münke-Svendsen).

Incorporating bugs into school feeding programs could provide children with the necessary nutrients to prevent stunting. Overall, bugs and insects are incredibly nutritionally beneficial. According to *New York Times* reporter Ligaya Mishan, "Some 2,100 insect species worldwide have been identified as edible. . . . Their nutritional benefits, while varied across species, are . . . comparable and sometimes superior, per ounce, to beef, chicken, and pork in amounts of protein, omega-3 fats, iron, magnesium, calcium, and zinc."

And yet, the Western consensus is that bugs are not to be eaten. Mishan writes that "Europeans, and by extension European settlers in North America, never had a bug-eating tradition. Indeed, we largely consider insects dirty and drawn to decay, signifiers and carriers of disease; we call them pests, a word whose Latin root means plague." This is a ridiculous stigma that we need to shake. The adoption of bugs into a normal diet would not be unlike the transition from the unacceptability of raw fish in America to the inclusion of sushi as a regular meal option.

All I want is a culinary cultural revolution—is that so much to ask?

4 — Reason #3: nutritional benefits for school feeding programs worldwide

5 — Uses ETYMOLOGY to explain entomology

6 — Concluding rhetorical question: Silva believes (hopes) Westerners can adopt new eating habits

Works Cited

Halloran, Afton, and Paul Vantomme. *The Contribution of Insects to Food Security, Livelihoods and the Environment.* Food and Agriculture Organization of the United Nations, fao.org/3/i3264e /i3264e00.pdf. Accessed 30 May 2019.

Mishan, Ligaya. "Why Aren't We Eating More Insects?" *The New York Times,* 7 Sept. 2018, www.nytimes.com/2018/09/07/t-magazine /eating-bugs-food-restaurant.html.

Münke-Svendsen, Christopher, et al. *Technical Brief #5: Nutritional Properties of Insects for Food in Kenya.* U of Copenhagen, 2017, greeinsect.ku.dk/publications/more-presentations/technical -briefs/Greeinsect_Technical_Brief_5_Nutritional_properties _of_insects_for_food_in_Kenya.pdf.

Roberts, Wayne. "Eating Insects: Waiter, There's No Fly in My Soup." *Alternatives Journal*, vol. 34, no. 1, Jan.–Feb. 2008, pp. 8–10. *JSTOR*, www.jstor.org/stable/45033573.

Analyzing a Student Argument

In "A Change in the Menu," Grace Silva draws on rhetorical strategies and techniques that good writers use all the time when constructing arguments. The following questions, in addition to focusing on particular aspects of Silva's text, will help you identify those common strategies and techniques so you can adapt them to your own writing. These questions will also help prepare you for the analytical questions—on content, structure, and language—that you'll find after all the other selections in this chapter, along with suggestions for writing on related topics.

FOR CLOSE READING

1. Grace Silva says that Westerners are reluctant to eat bugs. Is she right about that?

2. According to Silva, why is it more "efficient" to eat bugs than "traditional livestock" (2)?

3. Silva quotes a *New York Times* reporter who says Westerners "never had a bug-eating tradition" (5). Why not?

4. Which other menu "transition" (5) makes Silva think Western tastes can change?

STRATEGIES AND STRUCTURES

1. In the standard five-paragraph essay model, an introductory paragraph states the writer's THESIS, followed by three paragraphs of support and then a conclusion. To what extent does Silva follow this model? How and where does she depart from it?

2. Silva begins and ends her argument with RHETORICAL QUESTIONS. Is this an effective organizational and rhetorical strategy? Why or why not?

3. Where does Silva most directly state the nutritional benefits of consuming insects as food? Is the EVIDENCE she gives here and elsewhere sufficient to make her case? Why or why not?

4. How and how well does Silva incorporate her sources into her own writing? Do they help establish her **CREDIBILITY**? Explain.

5. *Other Methods.* What is the purpose of Silva's **COMPARISON** between eating insects and eating sushi in paragraph 5?

THINKING ABOUT LANGUAGE

1. What is your reaction to the idea of eating bugs? Look up the scientific and popular definitions of "bug" and "insect." Do the words have different **CONNOTATIONS**? Would you react differently if Silva had used the word "insects" more often than "bugs" in her essay? Explain.

2. What's the difference between being a "carrier" of disease and a "signifier" of disease and decay (5)?

3. Why might Silva use the term "stigma" to describe species unjustly accused of being carriers of the plague (5)? Is this an appropriate word choice, given the **PURPOSE** of her argument?

4. What are the implications of "revolution" as applied to eating habits (6)?

FOR WRITING

1. In a few paragraphs, outline the reasons you would give for eating or not eating more bugs.

2. In a well-supported **ARGUMENT** of five to seven paragraphs, make the case for why Americans will eventually or will not ever accept the menu change that Silva is advocating. As supporting evidence, incorporate facts and statistics.

3. Locate and read one of the articles listed in Silva's Works Cited and then write a 300-to-500-word **CRITICAL ANALYSIS** of it. Be sure to explain how and how effectively it presents a thesis and supporting evidence.

4. Do some research on the worldwide decline in insect populations, and then write a five-to-seven-paragraph essay analyzing the **CAUSES** of this disturbing phenomenon.

Think Different

Most advertisements, like this one from Apple, are arguments. Their purpose is to persuade you, the reader (or viewer), to buy, rent, view, subscribe to, or otherwise consume whatever they're selling. The implied logic of this advertisement is something like the following (tech companies have a grammar of their own):

Major premise: Einstein thought different.
Minor premise: Apple products make you think different.
Conclusion: Apple products make you think like Einstein.

The minor premise of this invalid argument is simply a variation on the following questionable assertion (fill in the blank):

Our product makes you _____ (more beautiful, healthier, more fashionable, smell better, think different).

Premises like this are unproven assumptions. Buy the premise, and you're on your way to buying the product. (The pinup of Einstein is just window dressing.)

[FOR WRITING] ···

Construct an advertisement for a familiar product or service. Include visuals like the Apple logo and the portrait of Einstein and a written text that makes an argument for buying (or not buying) the product or service. The written text can be a caption of fifty to sixty words or a briefer slogan ("Think relatively. Think Al's Used-Car Universe").

SUGGESTIONS FOR WRITING

1. When Simon Shiao Tam, an American of Asian descent, attempted to trademark the name of his rock band, The Slants, his application was denied. Tam appealed, and the case went all the way to the US Supreme Court, where the earlier decision was overturned in favor of Tam. Read "Does the Government Get to Decide What's a Slur?" (p. 640), a selection from a legal brief written in support of Tam's case by Ilya Shapiro and Thomas A. Berry; then write a **POSITION PAPER** of five to seven paragraphs arguing that any attempt to reclaim an ethnic, racial, or other slur by embracing or "owning" it is or is not a legitimate form of social action and, therefore, the high court was right or wrong in allowing Tam's "disparaging" speech under the First Amendment.

2. Both s.e. smith ("Products Mocked as 'Lazy' or 'Useless' Are Often Important Tools for People with Disabilities," p. 646) and Roxane Gay ("Why People Are So Awful Online," p. 683) are disturbed by the lack of respect and understanding with which many people interact on social media. Read both essays, and then write an **ARGUMENT** of six to eight paragraphs in which you either defend this practice (as a matter of free speech) or take issue with it. As smith and Gay do, include some examples of this type of online behavior; then explore and evaluate possible outcomes that continuing or curbing the practice might have on society.

3. Read Angela Lee Duckworth's "Grit: The Power of Passion and Perseverance" (p. 658) and Michelle Obama's "Remarks at Topeka School District Senior Recognition Day" (p. 632), and then write a 600-to-700-word **CRITICAL ANALYSIS** comparing the two selections as examples of both informative and motivational writing. Comment on how each writer connects with her audience and how and how well she presents her distinctive point of view; finally, discuss the extent to which Duckworth and Obama agree or disagree on the importance of grit for making significant contributions to society in general.

4. As documented in two studies conducted twenty-five years apart, Andrea Lunsford traces changes in college students' writing and literacy skills— for better or worse—as a result of the increased use of digital technologies. After reading "Our Semi-literate Youth? Not So Fast" (p. 702), draft a five-to-seven-paragraph **LITERACY NARRATIVE** in which you review the develop-

ment of your own writing skills from grade school through college. Explain the impact digital media has had on your skills, identifying at what age you began to use it, and then evaluate what you think have been its positive and negative effects on your writing.

5. When does emotional stress become trauma, and can these experiences ever be beneficial? Carol S. Dweck ("Two Mindsets," p. 663) and Shannon Palus ("Trigger Warnings," p. 717) explore angles on this subject. Read both essays, find definitions of "stress" and "trauma," consult some studies on both, and then write an essay of 600 to 800 words in which you CLASSIFY a collection of your personal experiences as either stressful or traumatic and ARGUE that they have or have not aided in your personal development. Aim to write a ROGERIAN ARGUMENT, acknowledging counterarguments before presenting your own views and, if possible, finding some common ground.

THOMAS JEFFERSON

The Declaration of Independence

Thomas Jefferson (1743–1826) was born to a wealthy landowning family in colonial Virginia and studied mathematics and political philosophy at William and Mary College. He became a lawyer and was elected to the Virginia legislature in 1769, where he was a leading spokesman for the cause of American independence. During the Revolutionary War, he served as governor of Virginia; afterward, he became the nation's first secretary of state. He served as John Adams's vice president and was elected president himself in 1800. Jefferson was also one of the leading architects of his day— and an inventor, naturalist, archaeologist, violinist, horticulturist, and patron of the arts. Despite his assertion that "all men are created equal," Jefferson was a slaveowner and opposed the abolition of slavery in the United States.

Jefferson stipulated that his epitaph would mention only three of his many achievements: author of Virginia's Statute of Religious Freedom, founder of the University of Virginia, and author of the Declaration of Independence. In its form and intent, the Declaration of Independence is primarily an argument—a point-by-point justification for American independence. Lawyerly in tone, it is essentially a legal brief addressed to both the British throne and the court of world opinion. Drafted largely by Jefferson, the Declaration lists the colonists' grievances against George III and concludes that Americans are left with no recourse but to declare full independence. The document's ratification by the Continental Congress on July 4, 1776, marked the birth of the United States.

MLA CITATION: Jefferson, Thomas. "The Declaration of Independence." *Back to the Lake: A Reader and Guide for Writers*, edited by Thomas Cooley, 5th ed., W. W. Norton, 2024, pp. 617–19.

WHEN IN THE COURSE OF HUMAN EVENTS, it becomes necessary for one people 1 to dissolve the political bands which have connected them with another, and to assume among the powers of the earth, the separate and equal station to which the Laws of Nature and of Nature's God entitle them, a decent respect to the opinions of mankind requires that they should declare the causes which impel them to the separation.

We hold these truths to be self-evident, that all men are created equal, that they 2 are endowed by their Creator with certain unalienable Rights, that among these are Life, Liberty and the pursuit of Happiness. That to secure these rights, Governments are instituted among Men, deriving their just powers from the consent of the governed. That whenever any Form of Government becomes destructive of these ends, it is the Right of the People to alter or to abolish it, and to institute new Government, laying its foundation on such principles and organizing its powers in such form, as to them shall seem most likely to effect their Safety and Happiness. Prudence, indeed, will dictate that Governments long established should not be changed for light and transient causes; and accordingly all experience hath shewn, that mankind are more disposed to suffer, while evils are sufferable, than to right themselves by abolishing the forms to which they are accustomed. But when a long train of abuses and usurpations pursuing invariably the same Object evinces a design to reduce them under absolute Despotism, it is their right, it is their duty, to throw off such Government, and to provide new Guards for their future security. Such has been the patient sufferance of these Colonies; and such is now the necessity which constrains them to alter their former Systems of Government. The history of the present King of Great Britain is a history of repeated injuries and usurpations, all having in direct object the establishment of absolute Tyranny over these States. To prove this, let Facts be submitted to a candid world.

Using inductive reasoning like this is discussed on p. 594.

He has refused his Assent to Laws, the most wholesome and necessary for the 3 public good.

He has forbidden his Governors to pass Laws of immediate and pressing impor- 4 tance, unless suspended in their operation till his Assent should be obtained; and when so suspended, he has utterly neglected to attend to them.

He has refused to pass other Laws for the accommodation of large districts of 5 people, unless those people would relinquish the right of Representation in the Legislature, a right inestimable to them and formidable to tyrants only.

He has called together legislative bodies at places unusual, uncomfortable, and 6 distant from the depository of their public Records, for the sole purpose of fatiguing them into compliance with his measures.

He has dissolved Representative Houses repeatedly, for opposing with manly 7 firmness his invasions on the rights of the people.

He has refused for a long time, after such dissolutions, to cause others to be 8 elected; whereby the Legislative powers, incapable of Annihilation, have returned to the People at large for their exercise; the State remaining in the mean time exposed to all the dangers of invasion from without, and convulsions within.

He has endeavoured to prevent the population of these States; for that purpose 9 obstructing the Laws of Naturalization of Foreigners; refusing to pass others to encourage their migration hither, and raising the conditions of new Appropriations of Lands.

He has obstructed the Administration of Justice, by refusing his Assent to Laws 10 for establishing Judiciary powers.

He has made Judges dependent on his Will alone, for the tenure of their offices, 11 and the amount and payment of their salaries.

He has erected a multitude of New Offices, and sent hither swarms of Officers to 12 harass our people, and eat out their substance.

He has kept among us, in time of peace, Standing Armies without the Consent of 13 our legislatures.

He has affected to render the Military independent of and superior to the Civil 14 power.

He has combined with others to subject us to a jurisdiction foreign to our consti- 15 tution, and unacknowledged by our laws; giving his Assent to their acts of pretended Legislation:

For Quartering large bodies of armed troops among us: 16

For protecting them, by a mock Trial, from punishment for any Murders which 17 they should commit on the Inhabitants of these States:

For cutting off our Trade with all parts of the world: 18

For imposing Taxes on us without our Consent: 19

For depriving us in many cases, of the benefits of Trial by Jury: 20

For transporting us beyond the Seas to be tried for pretended offenses: 21

For abolishing the free System of English Laws in a neighbouring Province, 22 establishing therein an Arbitrary government, and enlarging its Boundaries so as to render it at once an example and fit instrument for introducing the same absolute rule into these Colonies:

For taking away our Charters, abolishing our most valuable Laws, and altering 23 fundamentally the Forms of our Governments:

For suspending our own Legislatures, and declaring themselves invested with 24 power to legislate for us in all cases whatsoever.

He has abdicated Government here, by declaring us out of his Protection and 25 waging War against us.

He has plundered our seas, ravaged our Coasts, burnt our towns and destroyed 26 the lives of our people.

He is at this time transporting large Armies of foreign Mercenaries to compleat 27
the works of death, desolation and tyranny, already begun with circumstances of
Cruelty & perfidy scarcely paralleled in the most barbarous ages, and totally unworthy the Head of a civilized nation.

He has constrained our fellow Citizens taken Captive on the high Seas to bear 28
Arms against their Country, to become the executioners of their friends and Brethren, or to fall themselves by their Hands.

He has excited domestic insurrections amongst us, and has endeavoured to 29
bring on the inhabitants of our frontiers, the merciless Indian Savages, whose
known rule of warfare, is an undistinguished destruction of all ages, sexes and
conditions.

In every stage of these Oppressions We have Petitioned for Redress in the most 30
humble terms: Our repeated Petitions have been answered only by repeated injury.
A Prince, whose character is thus marked by every act which may define a Tyrant, is
unfit to be the ruler of a free people.

Nor have We been wanting in attentions to our British brethren. We have 31
warned them from time to time of attempts by their legislature to extend an
unwarrantable jurisdiction over us. We have reminded them of the circumstances
of our emigration and settlement here. We have appealed to their native justice
and magnanimity, and we have conjured them by the ties of our common kindred
to disavow these usurpations, which would inevitably interrupt our connections
and correspondence. They too have been deaf to the voice of justice and of consanguinity. We must, therefore acquiesce in the necessity, which denounces our
Separation, and hold them, as we hold the rest of mankind, Enemies in War, in
Peace Friends.

We, therefore, the Representatives of the United States of America, in General 32
Congress, Assembled, appealing to the Supreme Judge of the world for the rectitude of our intentions, do, in the Name, and by Authority of the good People of
these Colonies, solemnly publish and declare, That these United Colonies are,
and of Right ought to be Free and Independent States; that they are
Absolved from all Allegiance to the British Crown, and that all political
connection between them and the State of Great Britain, is and ought to
be totally dissolved; and that as Free and Independent States, they have
full Power to levy War, conclude Peace, contract Alliances, establish
Commerce, and to do all other Acts and Things which Independent States may of
right do. And for the support of this Declaration, with a firm reliance on the protection of divine Providence, we mutually pledge to each other our Lives, our Fortunes and our sacred Honor. ◆

Restating your claim at the conclusion of an argument is discussed on p. 593.

FOR CLOSE READING

1. According to Thomas Jefferson (and the fifty-five other signers of the Declaration of Independence), what is the purpose of government?

2. What claim is Jefferson making on the basis that King George's government has not fulfilled the purpose of government? What remedy is he calling for?

3. Of the many "injuries and usurpations" that Jefferson attributes to the British king, which seem most intolerable to you (2)? Why?

STRATEGIES AND STRUCTURES

1. "We hold these truths to be self-evident," says Jefferson (2). Another name for self-evident truths stated at the beginning of an argument is "premises." On what specific premises is Jefferson's argument based? Which are the ones most critical to his case?

2. Is the underlying logic of the Declaration basically INDUCTIVE or DEDUCTIVE? Or both? Explain.

3. Paragraph 31 seems to be a digression from Jefferson's main line of argument. Why do you think he includes it?

4. Jefferson and the other signers of the Declaration made their case for independence on logical grounds. Many of the issues they addressed, however, were highly emotional. Where and how does the Declaration appeal to the emotions of its audience as well as their sense of reason?

5. How does the Declaration present the authors as men of good character who want to do what is morally right? Refer to paragraph numbers in your response.

6. *Other Methods.* Jefferson says that King George has committed "every act which may define a Tyrant" (30). How does Jefferson use this DEFINITION to support his argument that the king is unfit to rule a free people?

THINKING ABOUT LANGUAGE

1. In modern English, "unalienable" (2) should be "inalienable." Why do you think a person of Jefferson's intelligence and education would make this error?

2. Referring to King George, Jefferson begins many of his sentences with "He has." What is the effect of this and other uses of PARALLELISM in his essay?

3. What is "consanguinity" (31)? How can it be said to have a "voice"?

4. Look up the ETYMOLOGY (historical development) of the following words. Do most of them derive from Latin or Anglo-Saxon? Why do you think the signers of the Declaration used such a vocabulary to address the king of England?

abdicated (25)	acquiesce (31)	candid (2)	constrains (2)
despotism (2)	evinces (2)	magnanimity (31)	perfidy (27)
rectitude (32)	redress (30)	transient (2)	usurpations (2)

FOR WRITING

1. You are King George, and you've just received the Declaration of Independence, a direct challenge to your authority over the American colonies. Compose a few paragraphs replying to Jefferson's charges and defending your actions and policies toward the colonies. Assume that the Declaration accurately describes those actions—don't base your argument on a denial.

2. Compose an essay of six to eight paragraphs arguing that "the pursuit of Happiness" (2) is unwise, that happiness cannot be guaranteed, and that the excessive pursuit of anything can lead to chaos in the life of the individual and in the state. Or, alternatively, defend Jefferson's claim that the pursuit of happiness is an inalienable right.

3. Does the Declaration of Independence promise "life, liberty, and the pursuit of happiness"—period? Or is this phrase in the document dependent on what follows? Danielle Allen, a professor at Harvard University, discovered what she thinks is a significant error in the official transcript of the Declaration produced by the National Archives and Records Administration. Look up the controversy, and write a five-to-seven-paragraph **REPORT** explaining the issues that Allen raises and the evidence she cites for her position.

4. The US Constitution ("We the People . . .") was written and adopted in 1787, a little more than ten years after the Declaration of Independence, but the two are clearly related in style and content. **COMPARE** these two founding documents, and write a 500-to-800-word **TEXTUAL ANALYSIS** of their similarities and differences—in meaning and basic principles, as well as language.

Ain't I a Woman?

Sojourner Truth (c. 1797–1883) is the name assumed by Isabella Baumfree, who was born into slavery in Hurley, New York. A tall and imposing figure with a deep voice whose first language was Dutch, Truth was legally freed in 1827. Though unable to read or write, she became a celebrated abolitionist and campaigner for women's rights.

"Ain't I a Woman?" is the title usually given to a brief extemporaneous speech that Truth delivered at the Women's Convention in Akron, Ohio, in 1851. The title phrase does not occur in the first recorded version of the speech—reported by editor Marius Robinson in the Salem, Ohio, *Anti-Slavery Bugle*, June 21, 1851—though Robinson records the speaker as asking, "[C]an any man do more than that?" The version reprinted here derives from the second published version, that of abolitionist writer and speaker Frances Dana Gage, in the *National Anti-Slavery Standard* on May 2, 1863. In addition to assigning a Black Southern dialect to the speaker, Gage added the title phrase and more fire to Truth's plea for equal rights for women and Black people. Like the Declaration of Independence (p. 616), "Ain't I a Woman?" is something of a collaboration.

WELL, CHILDREN, where there is so much racket there must be something out 1 of kilter. I think that 'twixt the negroes of the South and the women at the North, all talking about rights, the white men will be in a fix pretty soon. But what's all this here talking about?

That man over there says that women need to be helped into carriages, and 2 lifted over ditches, and to have the best place everywhere. Nobody ever helps me into carriages, or over mud-puddles, or gives me any best place! And ain't I a woman? Look at me! Look at my arm! I have ploughed and planted, and gathered into barns, and no man could head me! And ain't I a woman? I could work as much and eat as much as a man—when I could get it—and bear the lash as well! And ain't I a woman? I have borne thirteen children, and seen most all sold off to slavery, and when I cried out with my mother's grief, none but Jesus heard me! And ain't I a woman?

MLA CITATION: Truth, Sojourner. "Ain't I a Woman?" *Back to the Lake: A Reader and Guide for Writers*, edited by Thomas Cooley, 5th ed., W. W. Norton, 2024, pp. 622–24.

Sojourner Truth in an 1864 carte-de-visite photograph. Carte-de-visite, or "visiting card," photographs were a popular small-size format of early portrait photography.

See p. 602 for a form of argument that treats opponents as colleagues.

Then they talk about this thing in the head; what's this they call it? 3 [Member of audience whispers, "intellect."] That's it, honey. What's that got to do with women's rights or negroes' rights? If my cup won't hold but a pint, and yours holds a quart, wouldn't you be mean not to let me have my little half measure full?

Then that little man in black there, he says women can't have as much 4 rights as men, 'cause Christ wasn't a woman! Where did your Christ come from? Where did your Christ come from? From God and a woman! Man had nothing to do with Him.

If the first woman God ever made was strong enough to turn the world upside 5 down all alone, these women together ought to be able to turn it back, and get it right side up again! And now they is asking to do it, the men better let them.

Obliged to you for hearing me, and now old Sojourner ain't got nothing more 6 to say. ◆

FOR CLOSE READING

1. The opening paragraph of Sojourner Truth's speech was added in the 1863 version. What "racket" is it referring to (1)?

2. What is "out of kilter," in the opinion of Truth and the other women who attended the 1851 Women's Convention in Ohio (1)?

3. What solution to the imbalance do Truth and her colleagues propose?

STRATEGIES AND STRUCTURES

1. How and how well does Truth entertain (and refute) COUNTERARGUMENTS to her proposition that women are the equal of men?

2. If women want to set the world right again, Truth's speech concludes, "the men better let them" (5). Does this argument appeal mostly to the listener's intellect ("this thing in the head"; 3), emotions, or sense of ethics? Explain.

3. *Other Methods.* How does Truth DEFINE herself as a woman? How and how well does this definition support her argument?

THINKING ABOUT LANGUAGE

1. Truth addresses her AUDIENCE as "children" (1). Is this an effective strategy? Why or why not?

2. What is the point of the ANALOGY between Eve and "these women" (5)? Explain.

3. "Ain't I a woman?" is clearly a RHETORICAL QUESTION. What is the effect of repeating it four times in this short speech?

FOR WRITING

1. In the 1851 version, as reported by Marius Robinson in the *Anti-Slavery Bugle*, Truth's speech ends with the following words: "But man is in a tight place, the poor slave is on him, woman is coming on him, he is surely between a hawk and a buzzard." In a paragraph or two, explain which ending you find more effective (and why)—this one or that of the "official" 1863 version printed here (5–6).

2. In 200 to 400 words, support (or contest) the position that the power and influence of Truth's celebrated speech was the result as much of who the speaker was—or was perceived to be—as of what the speech actually says.

3. Marius Robinson's 1851 version of Truth's speech is available at digital.wwnorton .com/links-backtothelake5. Write a five-to-seven-paragraph textual ANALYSIS of the two different versions that explains how and how well each makes its respective arguments.

4. COMPARE AND CONTRAST the personalities and activities of the July 1848 women's rights convention in Seneca Falls, New York, with those of the May 1851 convention in Akron, Ohio.

5. In collaboration with several of your classmates, do some additional research on Sojourner Truth. Share and discuss your findings, and write an outline of the key points you would make in a report on Truth's life and work.

MICHAEL LEWIS

Buy That Little Girl an Ice Cream Cone

Michael Lewis (b. 1960) is a native of New Orleans and was educated at Princeton University and the London School of Economics. Before becoming a professional writer, he spent four years as a bond salesman on Wall Street, an experience that provided the basis for Lewis's best-selling *Liar's Poker* (1989). The author of *Moneyball* (2003) and *The Blind Side* (2006), Lewis also drew on his knowledge of sports and money matters in *The Big Short* (2010), a study of the personalities and gamblers' mentality behind the worst economic crisis in the United States since the Great Depression. In *The Premonition: A Pandemic Story* (2021), Lewis attributes the severity of the COVID-19 pandemic in the United States to three things: the long-standing politicization of the Centers for Disease Control and Prevention, the lack of a public health-care system, and the specific reactions of President Trump.

"Buy That Little Girl an Ice Cream Cone" is a selection from *Home Game: An Accidental Guide to Fatherhood* (2009). In the struggle for gender equality, Lewis argues, boys will always be boys; girls, however, are not so predictable.

WE'RE AT A FANCY HOTEL IN BERMUDA. Like fancy hotels everywhere, the place is paying new attention to the whims of small children. The baby pool is vast—nearly as big as the pool for the grown-ups, to which it is connected by a slender canal. In the middle of the baby pool is a hot tub, just for little kids. My two daughters, now ages six and three, leap from the hot tub into the baby pool and back again. The pleasure they take in this could not be more innocent or pure.

MLA CITATION: Lewis, Michael. "Buy That Little Girl an Ice Cream Cone." *Back to the Lake: A Reader and Guide for Writers*, edited by Thomas Cooley, 5th ed., W. W. Norton, 2024, pp. 626–30.

"Teasing boys!" she hollers, so loudly that grown-ups around the pool peer over their Danielle Steel novels.

Then, out of nowhere, come four older boys. Ten, maybe eleven years old. As 2 anyone who has only girls knows, boys add nothing to any social situation but trouble. These four are set on proving the point. Seeing my little girls, they grab the pool noodles—intended to keep three-year-olds afloat—and wield them as weapons. They descend upon Quinn, my six-year-old, whacking the water on either side of her, until she is almost in tears. I'm hovering in the canal between baby pool and grown-up pool, wondering if I should intervene. Dixie beats me to it. She jumps out in front of her older sister and thrusts out her three-year-old chest.

"Teasing boys!" she hollers, so loudly that grown-ups around the pool peer over 3 their Danielle Steel novels. Even the boys are taken aback. Dixie, now on stage, raises her voice a notch:

"You just shut up you stupid motherfucking asshole!" 4

To the extent that all hell can break loose around a baby pool in a Bermuda 5 resort, it does. A John Grisham novel is lowered; several of Danielle Steel's vanish into beach bags. I remain hovering in the shallows of the grown-up pool where it enters the baby pool, with my entire head above water. My first thought: *Oh . . . my . . . God!* My second thought: *No one knows I'm her father.* I sink lower, like a crocodile, so that just my eyes and forehead are above the waterline; but in my heart a new feeling rises: pride. Behind me a lady on a beach chair shouts, "Kevin! Kevin! Get over here!"

Kevin appears to be one of the noodle-wielding eleven-year-old boys. "But 6 Moooooooommm!" he says.

"Kevin! *Now!*" 7

The little monster skulks over to his mother's side while his fellow Orcs await the 8 higher judgment. I'm close enough to hear her ream him out. It's delicious. "Kevin, did you teach that little girl those words?" she asks.

"Mooomm! Nooooooo!" 9

"Then where did she learn them?" 10

As it happens, I know the answer to that one: carpool. Months ago! I was driving 11 them home from school, my two girls, plus two other kids—a seven-year-old boy and a ten-year-old girl. They were crammed in the back seat of the Volkswagen Passat, jabbering away; I was alone in the front seat, not especially listening. But then the ten-year-old said, "Deena said a bad word today."

"Which one?" asked Quinn. 12

"The S-word," said the ten-year-old. 13

"Ooooooooo," they all said. 14

"What's the S-word?" I asked. 15

"We can't say it without getting in trouble," said the ten-year-old knowingly. 16

"You're safe here," I said.   17

She thought it over for a second, then said, "Stupid."   18

"Ah," I said, smiling.   19

"Wally said the D-word!" said Quinn.   20

"What's the D-word?" I asked.   21

"Dumb!" she shouted, and they all giggled at the sheer illicit pleasure of it. Then   22
the seven-year-old boy chimed in. "I know a bad word, too! I know a bad word, too!"
he said.

"What's the bad word?" I asked brightly. I didn't see why he should be left out.   23

"Shutupyoustupidmotherfuckingasshole!"   24

I swerved off the road, stopped the car, and hit the emergency lights. I began to   25
deliver a lecture on the difference between bad words and seriously bad words, but
the audience was fully consumed with laughter. Dixie, especially, wanted to know
the secret of making Daddy stop the car.

"Shutupmotherstupid fuck," she said.   26

"Dixie!" I said.   27

"Daddy," said Quinn thoughtfully, "how come you say a bad word when we spill   28
something and when you spill something you just say, 'Oops'?"

"Stupidfuck!" screamed Dixie, and they all laughed.   29

"DIXIE!"   30

She stopped. They all did. For the rest of the drive they whispered.   31

So here we are, months later, in this Bermuda pool, Dixie with her chest   32
thrust out in defiance, me floating like a crocodile and feeling very much different than I should. I should be embarrassed and concerned. I should be sweeping
her out of the pool and washing her mouth out with soap. I don't feel that way.
Actually, I'm impressed. More than impressed: awed. It's just incredibly heroic,
taking out after this rat pack of boys. Plus she's sticking up for her big sister, which
isn't something you see every day. I don't want to get in her way. I just want to see
what happens next.

Behind me Kevin has just finished being torn what appears to be a new asshole   33
by his mother, and is relaunching himself into the baby pool with a real malice. He's
as indignant as a serial killer who got put away on a speeding ticket: He's guilty of
many things but not of teaching a three-year-old girl the art of cursing. Now he
intends to get even. Gathering his fellow Orcs in the hot tub, he and his companions
once again threaten Quinn. Dixie, once again, leaps into the fray.

"TEASING BOYS!" she shouts. Now she has the attention of an entire Bermuda   34
resort.

"YOU WATCH OUT TEASING BOYS! BECAUSE I PEED IN THIS POOL TWO   35
TIMES! ONCE IN THE HOT POOL AND ONCE IN THE COLD POOL!"

The teasing boys flee, grossed out and defeated. Various grown-ups say various 36
things to each other, but no one seeks to remove Dixie from the baby pool. Dixie
returns to playing with her sister—who appears far less grateful than she
should be. And the crocodile drops below the waterline, swivels, and vanishes into the depths of the grown-up pool. But he makes a mental note to
buy that little girl an ice cream cone. Even if her mother disapproves. ♦

See p. 601 for tips on establishing credibility in an argument.

FOR CLOSE READING

1. When his three-year-old daughter hurls grown-up expletives at the boys in the hotel swimming pool, Michael Lewis says, he should be "sweeping her out of the pool and washing her mouth out with soap" (32). Is he right? Why or why not?

2. How well do you think Dixie understands the implications of what she's saying? What does she understand for sure? Explain.

3. Why does Kevin's mother think Dixie might have learned "those words" from him (8)? Who *did* Dixie learn the profanity from?

4. In her "Ain't I a Woman?" speech (p. 622), the abolitionist and women's rights activist Sojourner Truth argues that once women have made up their minds to act, "the men better let them." Does young Dixie Lewis's speech in the luxury hotel pool in Bermuda confirm or refute this proposition? Explain.

5. Lewis remains a crocodilian observer throughout the scene in the baby pool. Should he have intervened? Why or why not?

STRATEGIES AND STRUCTURES

1. The boys in the pool, says Lewis, seem bent on "proving the point" (2). What point? What are the grounds of argument here?

2. In this gendered battle scene, the boys use the pool noodles "as weapons" (2). What weapons do the girls have at their disposal? Explain.

3. Lewis tells a story within a story. What is the purpose of the **FLASHBACK**, replete with **DIALOGUE**, to the carpool scene (11–31)?

4. Lewis argues that his daughter should be rewarded for her behavior "even if her mother disapproves" (36). How and how well does he support this conclusion?

5. *Other Methods.* Lewis's argument is mostly **NARRATIVE**. How and how effectively do the events of that narrative prove his fatherly assumptions about the nature of boys versus girls?

THINKING ABOUT LANGUAGE

1. Lewis describes little Dixie as delivering her startling lines from a "stage" (3). Explain the implications of this **METAPHOR**.

2. Dixie's behavior in standing up for her sister, says Lewis, is nothing short of "heroic" (32). Is the overstatement justified? Why or why not?

3. Before the boys arrive, Lewis's bathing daughters are engaged in a "pleasure" that "could not be more innocent or pure" (1). This is the language of Eden. How and why has the language of Lewis's family fable changed by the end, when the crocodile "drops below the waterline, swivels, and vanishes into the depths" (36)?

4. In relating the pool episode, Lewis chooses vivid action words such as "whacking" (2), "hovering" (2, 5), and "skulks" (8). How effective are these strong, **CONCRETE VERBS** in enabling you to picture the scene? Explain.

FOR WRITING

1. In a paragraph or two, **DESCRIBE** an occasion when the words of children at play proved to be as potent as sticks or stones—or pool noodles.

2. Write an essay of five to seven paragraphs arguing that boys and girls are (or are not) socialized in fundamentally different ways that account (or do not account) for specific differences in adult behaviors—for example, in speech patterns—between males and females. Cite personal experience as appropriate, but also refer to your reading and research in a relevant academic field, such as anthropology, sociology, or linguistics.

3. "Buy That Little Girl an Ice Cream Cone" is a selection from Michael Lewis's *Home Game: An Accidental Guide to Fatherhood* (2009). Read *Home Game* (or one of Lewis's other works), and write a five-to-seven-paragraph **CRITICAL ANALYSIS** of the book. Or, alternatively, write a critical analysis of how and how well Lewis argues his position on an important issue in an article or blog post of his you find online.

4. In collaboration with several of your classmates, collect stories of experiences you each had (or incidents you witnessed) in childhood or youth that illustrate good (or bad) parenting. Compile the narratives into a parenting "guide" that supports certain rules, standards, or principles that you all think are particularly important (or that critiques ones that you think are particularly bad).

MICHELLE OBAMA

Remarks at Topeka School District Senior Recognition Day

Michelle Obama (b. 1964), grew up on the South Side of Chicago and graduated from Princeton University in 1985 and from Harvard Law School in 1988. She met her future husband, Barack Obama, at the Chicago law firm Sidley Austin, where she was assigned to mentor him as a summer associate. (President Obama earned his degree from Harvard Law in 1991.) The future First Lady also worked as an assistant commissioner in Chicago city government, as the executive director of a nonprofit organization, and as an associate dean at the University of Chicago. As First Lady, Obama worked for progress on education, nutrition, and health. Since leaving the White House, Obama has published a memoir, *Becoming* (2018), that has sold more than 10 million copies; and another best-seller, *The Light We Carry: Overcoming in Uncertain Times* (2022), which offers strategies for navigating change in today's complex and stressful world.

Michelle Obama delivered her "Remarks" to the graduating classes of Topeka Unified School District 501 on May 16, 2014. The decision in the Supreme Court case to which she refers, *Brown v. Board of Education of Topeka*, was handed down on May 17, 1954. In that decision, the Court unanimously ended legal segregation in public schools on the grounds that "separate educational facilities are inherently unequal."

THANK YOU, GUYS. Thank you so much. Wow! (Applause.) Look at you guys. (Applause.) All right, you all rest yourselves. You've got a big day tomorrow. I want you guys to be ready.

MLA CITATION: Obama, Michelle. "Remarks at Topeka School District Senior Recognition Day." *Back to the Lake: A Reader and Guide for Writers*, edited by Thomas Cooley, 5th ed., W. W. Norton, 2024, pp. 632–37.

It is beyond a pleasure and an honor, truly, to be with you here today to celebrate the class of 2014. Thank you so much for having me. I'm so proud of you guys. (Applause.) Days like this make me think of my own daughters, so forgive me if I get a little teary. You guys look great.

We have a great group of students here. We have students from Highland Park High School. (Applause.) We have Hope Street Academy students here today. (Applause.) Topeka High School is in the house. (Applause.) And of course, we have Topeka West High School in the house. (Applause.)

Tomorrow will be a big day for all of you. You all have worked so hard, I know—I can tell. You've come so far. And as you walk across that stage tomorrow to get your diploma, know that I'm going to be thinking of you all. I am so proud of you all and all that you've achieved thus far.

And you have got so many people here who are proud of you tonight. Your families are here, your teachers and counselors, your principals, your coaches, everyone who has poured their love and hope into you over these many, many years. So, graduates, let's just take a moment to give a round of applause to those folks, as well. Tonight is their night, too. Yes! (Applause.)

Now, I want to start by thanking Lauren for that amazing introduction. (Applause.) Yes, indeed. Well done, Lauren. I want to thank a few other people here—of course, Secretary Sebelius. As you know, my husband and I are so grateful for all that she has done, her wonderful service. (Applause.) And I'm so glad that she and her family could join us tonight.

And of course, I want to recognize Congresswoman Jenkins, Governor Brownback, and Mayor Wolgast, as well as Superintendent Ford, School Board President Johnson, and all of your great principals—Principals Carton, New, Noll, and Wiley. (Applause.) Yay!

And finally, to our fantastic student speakers—Alisha, Rosemary, and Noah— just hearing your backgrounds makes me feel like an underachiever, so thank you so much for your remarks about *Brown v. Board of Ed.* I know Noah is coming. You have approached this issue past, present, and future.

And I think it's fitting that we're celebrating this historic Supreme Court case tonight, not just because *Brown* started right here in Topeka or because *Brown's* sixtieth anniversary is tomorrow, but because I believe that all of you—our soon-to-be-graduates—you all are the living, breathing legacy of this case. Yes. (Applause.)

I mean, just look around at this arena. Not only are you beautiful and handsome and talented and smart, but you represent all colors and cultures and faiths here tonight. (Applause.) You come from all walks of life, and you've taken so many different paths to reach this moment. Maybe your ancestors have been here in Kansas for centuries. Or maybe, like mine, they came to this country in chains. Or maybe your family just arrived here in search of a better life.

But no matter how you got here, you have arrived at this day together. For so   11
many years, you all have studied together in the same classrooms, you've played on
the same teams, attended the same parties—hopefully you behaved yourselves at
those parties. (Laughter.) You've debated each other's ideas, hearing every possible
opinion and perspective. You've heard each other's languages in the hallways,
English, Spanish, and others, all mixed together in a uniquely American conversation. You've celebrated each other's holidays and heritages—in fact, I was told that
at one of your schools so many students who aren't black wanted to join the black
students club that you decided to call it the African American Culture Club so
everyone would feel welcome. Way to go. (Applause.)

> **How to narrow down your claim as Obama does here is discussed on pp. 593–94.**

So, graduates, it is clear that some of the most important parts of your   12
education have come not just from your classes, but from your classmates.
And ultimately, that was the hope and dream of *Brown*. That's why we're
celebrating here tonight, because the fact is that your experience here in
Topeka would have been unimaginable back in 1954, when *Brown v. Board
of Education* first went to the Supreme Court. This would not be possible.

As you all know, back then, Topeka, like so many cities, was segregated.   13
So black folks and white folks had separate restaurants, separate hotels, separate
movie theaters, swimming pools, and, of course, the elementary schools were segregated, too. So even though many black children lived just blocks away from their
white schools in their neighborhoods, they had to take long bus rides to all-black
schools across town. So eventually, a group of black parents got tired of this
arrangement—and they decided to do something about it.

Now, these were ordinary folks. Most of them were not civil-rights activists, and   14
some of them were probably nervous about speaking up, worried they might cause
trouble for themselves and their families. And the truth is, while the black schools
were far away, the facilities were pretty decent, and the teachers were excellent.

But eventually, these parents went to court to desegregate their children's schools   15
because, as one of the children later explained as an adult, she said, "We were talking about the principle of the thing."

Now, think about that for a moment. Those folks had to go all the way to the   16
Supreme Court of the United States just to affirm the principle that black kids and
white kids should be able to attend school together. And today, sixty years later, that
probably seems crazy to all of you in this graduating class, right? You all take the
diversity you're surrounded by for granted. You probably don't even notice it. And
that's understandable, given the country you have grown up in—with a woman governor, a Latina Supreme Court justice, a black president. (Applause.)

You have seen Latino singers win Grammys, black coaches win Super Bowls.   17
You've watched TV shows [with] characters of every background. So when you
watch a show like *The Walking Dead*, you don't think it's about a black guy, a black

woman, an Asian guy, a gay couple and some white people—you think it's about a bunch of folks trying to escape some zombies, right? Period. (Laughter.)

And then when some folks got all worked up about a cereal commercial with an 18 interracial family, you all were probably thinking, really, what's the problem with that? When folks made a big deal about Jason Collins and Michael Sam coming out as gay, a lot of kids in your generation thought, what is the issue here? (Applause.) And if someone were to say something racist on *Twitter*, well, I imagine that many of you would tweet right back, letting them know that's just not cool.

You see, when you grow up in a place like Topeka, where diversity is all you've 19 ever known, the old prejudices just don't make any sense. Seems crazy to think that folks of the same race or ethnicity all think or act the same way—because you actually know those folks. They're your teammates, your lab partner, your best friend. They're the girl who's obsessed with the Jayhawks but loves computer science programming; the guy who loves the Wildcats and dreams of being an artist. (Applause.) That's the world you've grown up in.

But remember, not everyone has grown up in a place like Topeka. See, many 20 districts in this country have actually pulled back on efforts to integrate their schools, and many communities have become less diverse as folks have moved from cities to suburbs.

So today, by some measures, our schools are as segregated as they were back 21 when Dr. King gave his final speech. And as a result, many young people in America are going to school largely with kids who look just like them. And too often, those schools aren't equal, especially ones attended by students of color which too often lag behind, with crumbling classrooms and less-experienced teachers. And even in schools that seem integrated according to the numbers, when you look a little closer, you see students from different backgrounds sitting at separate lunch tables, or tracked into different classes, or separated into different clubs or activities.

So while students attend school in the same building, they never really reach 22 beyond their own circles. And I'm sure that probably happens sometimes here in Topeka, too. And these issues go well beyond the walls of our schools. We know that today in America, too many folks are still stopped on the street because of the color of their skin—(applause)—or they're made to feel unwelcome because of where they come from, or they're bullied because of who they love. (Applause.)

So, graduates, the truth is that *Brown v. Board of Ed.* isn't just about our history; it's about our future. Because while that case was handed down sixty years ago, *Brown* is still being decided every single day—not just in our courts and schools, but in how we live our lives.

> Obama implies that how we live our lives is important; see p. 598 for making assumptions that "warrant" a claim.

Now, our laws may no longer separate us based on our skin color, but nothing in the Constitution says we have to eat together in the lunchroom, or live together in the same neighborhoods. There's no court case against believing in stereotypes or thinking that certain kinds of hateful jokes or comments are funny.

So the answers to many of our challenges today can't necessarily be found in our laws. These changes also need to take place in our hearts and in our minds. (Applause.) And so, graduates, it's up to all of you to lead the way, to drag my generation and your grandparents' generation along with you.

And that's really my challenge to all of you today. As you go forth, when you encounter folks who still hold the old prejudices because they've only been around folks like themselves, when you meet folks who think they know all the answers because they've never heard any other viewpoints, it's up to you to help them see things differently.

And the good news is that you probably won't have to bring a lawsuit or go all the way to the Supreme Court to do that. You all can make a difference every day in your own lives simply by teaching others the lessons you've learned here in Topeka.

Maybe that starts simply in your own family, when Grandpa tells that off-colored joke at Thanksgiving, or you've got an aunt [who] talks about "those people." Well, you can politely inform them that they're talking about your friends. (Applause.)

Or maybe it's when you go off to college and you decide to join a sorority or fraternity, and you ask the question, How can we get more diversity in our next pledge class? Or maybe it's years from now, when you're on the job and you're the one who asks, Do we really have all the voices and viewpoints we need at this table? Maybe it's when you have kids of your own one day, and you go to your school board meeting and insist on integrating your children's schools and giving them the resources they need.

But no matter what you do, the point is to never be afraid to talk about these issues, particularly the issue of race. Because even today, we still struggle to do that. Because this issue is so sensitive, is so complicated, so bound up with a painful history. And we need your generation to help us break through. We need all of you to ask the hard questions and have the honest conversations, because that is the only way we will heal the wounds of the past and move forward to a better future. (Applause.)

And here's the thing—the stakes here simply couldn't be higher, because as a nation, we have some serious challenges on our plate—from creating jobs, to curing diseases, to giving every child in this country a good education. And we know—we don't even know where the next new breakthrough, the next great discovery will come from.

Maybe the solution to global warming will come from that girl whose parents don't speak a word of English, but who's been acing her science classes since kindergarten. (Applause.) Maybe the answer to poverty will come from the boy from the projects who understands this issue like no one else. So we need to bring everyone to the table. We need every voice in our national conversation.

So, graduates, that is your mission: to make sure all those voices are heard, to 33 make sure everyone in this country has a chance to contribute.

And I'm not going to lie to you, this will not be easy. You might have to ruffle a 34 few feathers, and believe me, folks might not always like what you have to say. And there will be times when you'll get frustrated or discouraged. But whenever I start to feel that way, I just take a step back and remind myself of all the progress I've seen in my short lifetime.

I think about my mother, who, as a little girl, went to segregated schools in 35 Chicago and felt the sting of discrimination. I think about my husband's grandparents, white folks born and raised right here in Kansas, products themselves of segregation. (Applause.) Good, honest people who helped raise their biracial grandson, ignoring those who would criticize that child's very existence. (Applause.) And then I think about how that child grew up to be the president of the United States, and how today—(applause)—that little girl from Chicago is helping to raise her granddaughters in the White House. (Applause.)

> Using examples to support an argument is discussed on p. 591.

And finally, I think about the story of a woman named Lucinda Todd who was 36 the very first parent to sign on to *Brown v. Board of Education*. See, Lucinda's daughter, Nancy, went to one of the all-black schools here in Topeka, and Mrs. Todd traveled across this state raising money for the case, determined to give her daughter—and all our sons and daughters—the education they deserve. And today, six decades later, Mrs. Todd's grandniece, a young woman named Kristen Jarvis, works as my right-hand woman in the White House. She is here with me today. (Applause.) She has traveled with me around the world.

So if you ever start to get tired, if you ever think about giving up, I want you to 37 remember that journey from a segregated school in Topeka all the way to the White House. (Applause.) I want you to think about folks like Lucinda Todd— folks who, as my husband once wrote, decided that "a principle is at stake," folks who "make their claim on this community we call America" and "choose our better history."

Every day, you have the power to choose our better history—by opening your 38 hearts and minds, by speaking up for what you know is right, by sharing the lessons of *Brown v. Board of Education*—the lessons you all learned right here in Topeka— wherever you go for the rest of your lives. And I know you all can do it.

I am so proud of all that you've accomplished. This is your day. I am here because 39 of you. And I cannot wait to see everything you will achieve in the years ahead.

So congratulations, once again, to the class of 2014. I love you. Godspeed on your 40 journey ahead. Thank you, all. God bless you. I love you. (Applause.) ♦

FOR CLOSE READING

1. In this address, Michelle Obama speaks to the senior classes of four high schools in Topeka, Kansas, on the occasion of their graduation the next day. What other occasion is she also celebrating? Why choose Topeka?

2. Aside from congratulations, what is Obama's main message to the soon-to-be graduates of Topeka Unified School District 501? Where does she state it most clearly and directly?

3. Obama quotes one of the students involved in *Brown v. Board of Education* as saying, "We were talking about the principle of the thing" (15). What principle was the student referring to?

4. Why does Obama feel the need, in 2014, to reassert the legal and social principles established by *Brown*?

5. How and where might Obama's address be seen as following directly in the tradition of Thomas Jefferson and the other founders in the Declaration of Independence (p. 616)?

STRATEGIES AND STRUCTURES

1. Obama is a graduate of Harvard Law School who has practiced law in Chicago. So why doesn't she say things like this to her AUDIENCE: "As the party of the second part, know ye by these presents henceforth and hereafter, to wit . . ."?

2. Where and how does Obama appear to address her audience more in the role of a peer or friend than as a visiting eminence? Point to specific passages in the text that show her awareness of their needs and interests.

3. Commencement speakers often give advice. Where and how does Obama follow this tradition? Where does she depart from it? Why?

4. Though she does not use lawyerly language in her address, Obama repeatedly begins a new paragraph with "So" or "And," indicating a logical connection between the forthcoming statement and the one before. Where is her logic more DEDUCTIVE (from general principles to specific conclusions)? Where is it more INDUCTIVE (from particular cases to general principles)?

5. What point is Obama making when she refers to *The Walking Dead* (17)? Is the show a good EXAMPLE? Why or why not?

6. *Other Methods.* In addition to strategies of logical argument, Obama sometimes uses those of NARRATIVE as well. Point to places in her address where she relies on a brief illustrative story, or ANECDOTE, to make her point. Are narrative elements common in commencement speeches? Why or why not?

THINKING ABOUT LANGUAGE

1. Obama defines "diversity" as a mixture of "colors and cultures and faiths" (10). What other essential ingredient does she then include in the mix?

2. In referring to people of all races and cultures, Obama frequently uses the term "folks." Why might she have chosen this term instead of, say, "people" or "citizens"?

3. "*Brown* is still being decided every single day," Obama states (23). Explain the **METAPHOR** that she uses here. Would it still be relevant today? Why or why not?

4. What is Obama talking about when she refers to a boy from "the projects" (32)?

5. What "conversation" is Obama referring to in paragraph 32? Why might she have chosen this term instead of "argument" or "debate"?

FOR WRITING

1. Write a paragraph or two summarizing the gist of Obama's argument in her Topeka address.

2. Write out the commencement address you would deliver to the Topeka Unified School District 501 (or some other high school) senior class today if you were called on to be their next graduation speaker.

3. Do some research on *Brown v. Board of Education*, and write a 250-to-300-word **ABSTRACT** of the case, including the Court's findings.

4. The Supreme Court decision in *Brown v. Board of Education* was reached in May 1954; it took years, however, for public schools in the United States to become extensively integrated (in fact, today many schools still are not). Do some research on the civil rights movement between 1954 and 1968, and write an approximately 500-word **REPORT** on the advances and setbacks in racial integration during those years. Be sure to comment on important legal and social arguments of the period, such as the decision in *Brown*.

ILYA SHAPIRO AND THOMAS A. BERRY

Does the Government Get to Decide What's a Slur?

Ilya Shapiro and Thomas A. Berry are attorneys affiliated, respectively, with the Manhattan Institute in New York City and the Cato Institute in Washington, DC—both conservative research institutions. In 2016, when both men were working at the Cato Institute, they submitted a "friends of the court" brief in support of a case pending before the US Supreme Court. The case, *Matal v. Tam*, originated with Simon Shiao Tam, a musician who was seeking to register The Slants, the name of his rock band, whose members are all Asian American, as a trademark with the federal Patent and Trade Office. The office rejected the request on the grounds that it would disparage "persons of Asian descent." However, in 2017, the high court ruled in favor of Tam. Existing law prohibiting trademarks that "disparage" people, the Court held, was unconstitutional because it violated the First Amendment. That amendment states in full: "Congress shall make no law respecting an establishment of religion, or prohibiting the free exercise thereof; or abridging the freedom of speech, or of the press; or the right of the people peaceably to assemble, and to petition the Government for a redress of grievances."

In a classic cartoon, a judge says "only a lawyer would call that a brief" as he is handed a thick stack of paper. With both humor and logic, however, Shapiro and Berry get right to the point in the following piece, which is the "summary of argument" section of their supporting brief in *Matal v. Tam*.

MLA CITATION: Shapiro, Ilya, and Thomas A. Berry. "Does the Government Get to Decide What's a Slur?" *Back to the Lake: A Reader and Guide for Writers*, edited by Thomas Cooley, 5th ed., W. W. Norton, 2024, pp. 641–43.

Summary of Argument

This case is about whether an Asian-American rock band called The Slants can trademark and own their own name. The Slants are a group of artists who have formed an identity "to take on these stereotypes that people have about us, like the slanted eyes, and own them." Resp. Cert. Brief 3. Some agree with The Slants' approach and some disagree, as is normal in a robust artistic marketplace. What's not normal is that the government has chosen sides in this debate, punishing The Slants for their choice of name by denying them federal trademark registration.

> Narrowing down a broad statement of the case like this is discussed on pp. 593–94.

This punishment is the result of the "disparagement clause" in the federal trademark statute, the Lanham Act, which bars the registration of "matter which may disparage . . . persons, living or dead, institutions, beliefs, or national symbols, or bring them into contempt or disrepute." Pet. App. 6a. As artists know, the denial of trademark registration comes with severe negative consequences, since the "benefits of registration are substantial." *B&B Hardware, Inc. v. Hargis Industries, Inc.,* 135 S. Ct. 1293, 1310 (2015). Faced with this potential punishment, many artists, advocacy groups, and businesses will simply choose a different name. The government's rule thus discourages some names and encourages others.

This Court should make the jobs of the employees at the U.S. Patent and Trade Office (PTO) much easier and put an end to the disparagement clause. Trying to stamp out "disparaging" speech is both misguided and unconstitutional. No public official can be trusted to neutrally identify speech that "disparages." Moreover, disparaging speech has been central to political debate, cultural discourse, and personal identity for as long as this country has existed.*

> As indicated on p. 588, a big reason for arguing a point is to get people to act on it.

Disparaging epithets long ago entered our political vocabulary, encapsulating criticisms more succinctly than any polite term ever could. Schoolchildren today learn that Millard Fillmore ran for president in 1856 as a candidate of the "Know-Nothing" Party; few adults could tell you the party's "real" name. Yet a hypothetical 1856 PTO would likely have denied registration to a group called "Defeat the Know-Nothings" (disparaging to American Party members), just as the real PTO has denied registration to "Abort the Republicans" (disparaging to Republicans), "Democrats Shouldn't Breed" (disparaging to Democrats), and a logo consisting of the communist hammer-and-sickle with a slash through it (disparaging to Soviets). Pet. App. 8a. Political speech, including the right to criticize parties and politicians without

---

* For example, we recently concluded a presidential campaign in large part defined by pronouncements that large groups of people found to be personally disparaging. *See, e.g.,* "Trump: Mexico Not Sending Us Their Best; Criminals, Drug Dealers and Rapists Are Crossing Border," RealClearPolitics, June 16, 2015, http://bit.ly/1GNRCpd; Amy Chozick, "Hillary Clinton Calls Many Trump Backers 'Deplorables,' and GOP Pounces," *N.Y. Times,* Sept. 10, 2016, http://nyti.ms/2cCNnXd. [Authors' note]

government punishment, is recognized by this Court as "at the core of our electoral process and of the First Amendment freedoms." *Buckley v. Valeo*, 424 U.S. 1, 39 (1976) (quoting *Williams v. Rhodes*, 393 U.S. 23, 32 (1968)).* Thus, denial of a statutory trademark right represents particularly egregious government action that violates the First Amendment.

But the suppression of political speech is not the only problem arising from the   5
disparagement clause. As this case shows, supposedly "disparaging" speech is often part of an effort to reclaim a word from its pejorative meaning. Efforts like this have already had a profound influence on the development of many groups' identities. Jesuits, Methodists, Mormons, and Quakers owe their popular names to terms that were originally given to them in a disparaging context, and that have since been reclaimed.† Without disparaging epithets, our vocabulary would be deprived of such terms as "cavalier," "yankee," "impressionist" (Renoir, not Rich Little), and "suffragette."‡ How did a donkey become the Democratic Party symbol? A political opponent labeled Andrew Jackson a "jackass," so Jackson put the animal on campaign posters. *See* Jimmy Stamp, *Political Animals: Republican Elephants and Democratic Donkeys*, Smithsonian.com (Oct. 23, 2012), http://bit.ly/2gzmfKa. An 1820s PTO might have stopped him.

See pp. 604 and 606 for tips on using NARRATIVE to develop an argument.
More recently, the author of the bestselling *Hillbilly Elegy* (2016) nar-   6
rated his escape from the hollows of Kentucky to help explain our populist political moment. J.D. Vance does for "hillbillies"—a term even *Wikipedia* considers to be derogatory, http://bit.ly/2h1QjBa—what David Brooks did for "bobos" (bourgeois bohemians): explain conversationally an important yet disturbing slice of Americana.

Rock bands in particular often pick names *because* they are "disparaging." The   7
Slits, the Queers, Queen, Pansy Division, N.W.A. (Niggaz Wit Attitudes), and the Hillbilly Hellcats—there's that word again—are just a few examples. Other bands, looking to push the envelope both musically and culturally, have chosen names like the Sex Pistols, Dead Kennedys, Butthole Surfers, Rapeman, Snatch and the Poontangs, Pussy Galore, Dying Fetus, and many, many more.

---

* Indeed, questioning the character of our politicians is such a cherished American tradition that a member of this Court recently engaged in it herself. *See* Joan Biskupic, *Justice Ruth Bader Ginsburg Calls Trump a "Faker," He Says She Should Resign*, CNN.com, July 11, 2016, http://cnn.it/29zSCUS. [Authors' note]

† *See* Society of Jesus, *Catholic Encyclopedia* (1913), http://bit.ly/2gN6i63; Mary Fairchild, *Methodist Church History*, About.com (last updated Dec. 2, 2016), http://abt.cm/2g5TWGZ; Reid Neilson, *Exhibiting Mormonism: The Latter-day Saints and the 1893 Chicago World's Fair* 24 (2011); Margery Post Abbott et al., *Historical Dictionary of the Friends (Quakers)* xxxi (2003). [Authors' note]

‡ Cavalier, Encyclopedia Britannica (11th ed. 1911), http://bit.ly/2gZ14BT; Mark Mooney, "'Yankee Doodle Dandy' Explained and Other Revolutionary Facts," ABC News, July 4, 2014, http://abcn.ws/1zcxHQk; Louis Leroy, *Visual Arts Encyclopedia* (last visited Dec. 2, 2016), http://bit.ly/2h32pKO; Katy Steinmetz, "Everything You Need to Know About the Word 'Suffragette,'" *Time*, Oct. 22, 2015, http://ti.me/2he2Cvn. [Authors' note]

Further, the disparagement clause is unconstitutionally vague. Its application 8
will always be unpredictable, because nearly any brand could be taken as disparaging by some portion of some group. Take, for low-hanging fruit, Aunt
Jemima, Uncle Ben, the Cleveland Indians' Chief Wahoo, the women in La
Tortilla Factory, or the Keebler Elves. Amicus Flying Dog Brewery has its
own history of legal disputes over beer names like "Raging Bitch." . . .
Determining whether a term is disparaging is an incredibly complex
endeavor that the government can't possibly be equipped to handle.

> Giving EXAM-
> PLES to make a
> point is dis-
> cussed on
> p. 591.

For example, one of this brief's authors is a cracker (as distinct from a hillbilly) 9
who grew up near Atlanta, but he wrote this sentence, so we can get away with saying that.* Another contributor—unnamed because not a member of the
bar—is an Italian-American honky who has always wanted to play in a band
called the Dagos, which of course would close every set with "That's Amore"
from *Lady and the Tramp*. But, with only his great grandparents having
come from Italy, is he dago enough to "take back" the term? And *amici*'s
lead counsel is a Russian-Jewish émigré who's now a dual U.S.-Canadian citizen.
Can he make borscht-belt jokes about Canuck frostbacks even though the first time
he went to shul was while clerking in Jackson, Mississippi?†

> For tips on
> establishing
> your own
> credibility, see
> p. 601.

It gets complicated. And that's the point. The disparagement clause places an 10
unconstitutional condition on those who consider the use of an edgy or taboo
phrase to be part of their brand.

None of the government's justifications for an exception to the doctrine carry 11
weight: registering a trademark is not a public subsidy or endorsement. The
Court should recognize that trademarks are in no way official speech and
reaffirm that the government may not put its thumb on the scale to push
controversial viewpoints out of the public square. ◆

> When you
> argue by ANAL-
> OGY, choose
> your analogy
> with care.

---

* But he only moved to Atlanta when he was 10 and doesn't have a southern accent—and modern Atlanta isn't really part of the South—so maybe we can't. [Authors' note]

† In one *Seinfeld* episode, Jerry is concerned that a friend who recently converted to Judaism did it "just for the jokes":

Jerry: and then he asked the assistant for a schtickle of fluoride.

Elaine: Why are you so concerned about this?

Jerry: I'll tell you why. Because I believe Whatley converted to Judaism just for the jokes.

. . .

Jerry: So Whatley said to me, "Hey, I can make Catholic jokes, I used to be Catholic."

. . .

Jerry: Don't you see what Whatley is after? Total joke telling immunity. He's already got the two big religions covered, if he ever gets Polish citizenship there'll be no stopping him.

Seinfeld, "The Yada Yada" (first aired April 24, 1997). [Authors' note]

FOR CLOSE READING

1. Why have The Slants adopted such a potentially "disparaging" name (4)? Why are The Slants appealing to the US Supreme Court? What have they been denied by the lower courts?

2. What is the "disparagement clause" (2); and what should happen to it, according to Shapiro and Berry? How would this make the job of the federal PTO (Patent and Trade Office) "much easier" (3)?

3. Shapiro and Berry claim that some people "agree with The Slants' approach and some disagree" (1). Are they right to claim that differences of opinion about self-expression and self-promotion are "normal in a robust artistic marketplace" (1)? Why or why not?

4. According to Shapiro and Berry, what is not normal in this case? Explain.

5. What is the PURPOSE of this argument? Using the advice in Chapter 1 on reading critically and evaluating the accuracy of a text, do some research on the Cato Institute and describe how what you learn could contribute to the authors' stance.

STRATEGIES AND STRUCTURES

1. Shapiro and Berry aren't arguing that everyone should welcome and embrace names like The Slants and those of the other rock bands listed in paragraph 7. What *are* they claiming about the role of the government in identifying "offensive" speech?

2. In paragraph 3, Shapiro and Berry give two main reasons in support of their ARGU-MENT against "trying to stamp out" certain forms of speech (3). What are those reasons? How does the second reason lead directly into the next four paragraphs of their summary?

3. In paragraph 8, Shapiro and Berry return to their first reason for arguing that free-dom of speech is threatened by the disparagement clause. What is their point here, and how is it related to their earlier discussion of "disparaging" speech in "political debate, cultural discourse, and personal identity" (3)?

4. Why might Shapiro and Berry refer to an old *Seinfeld* routine (and their own "ethnic-ity") in such a serious document as a legal brief? What's faulty about Whatley's and Jerry's logic (footnote on p. 643), and why might the attorneys cite it anyway?

5. *Other Methods.* Shapiro and Berry give numerous EXAMPLES, particularly of names and descriptive phrases, to support their claims. Which ones do you find espe-cially appropriate—and why?

THINKING ABOUT LANGUAGE

1. By denying The Slants' original request to register their name as a trademark, say Shapiro and Berry, the federal government was "punishing" the group (1). How might the lawyers be said to BEG THE QUESTION here—and with the word "punish-ment" in paragraph 2? Why might they choose such language anyway?

2. Shapiro and Berry use "pejorative" and "disparaging" more or less interchangeably throughout their argument. Look up the definitions of these terms. Which is the broader term—and also the one that is generally applied to whole classes of words?

3. Look up the definition and ETYMOLOGY of "epithet" (4). How has the meaning of the word changed from its original sense to the present day?

4. Shapiro and Berry's argument is partly a linguistic one. What do they mean by the claim that some apparently disparaging speech is "part of an effort to reclaim" words from their pejorative meanings (5)? Using this line of reasoning, how would you define a "reclaimed epithet"?

5. Explain the "low-hanging fruit" METAPHOR in paragraph 8. Is it appropriate? Why or why not?

FOR WRITING

1. If the federal government doesn't have the right to determine what constitutes a slur, who (if anyone) *does* have that right? Write a POSITION PAPER of five to seven paragraphs addressing this question. Be sure to consider whether it might be possible to accept Shapiro and Berry's argument about government "interference" and still object to many of the names and terms they cite as "pejorative" or "offensive."

2. Research by the College Board testing service suggests that some knowledge of the principles embodied in the US Constitution is an accurate marker of success in school and later life. Do some research of your own on the topic, and write a 400-to-600-word ARGUMENT to the effect that students should (or should not) study the political and social ideas "encoded" in the Constitution.

3. Usually attributed to Supreme Court Justice Oliver Wendell Holmes Jr., shouting "Fire!" in a crowded theater is often cited as an example of speech that is not protected by the First Amendment. Look up the case of *Schenck v. United States* (1919). Then write an essay explaining what Holmes actually said and arguing that shouting "Fire!" in a crowded theater should no longer be used (or should continue to be used) in discussions of freedom of speech under the First Amendment.

S.E. SMITH

Products Mocked as "Lazy" or "Useless" Are Often Important Tools for People with Disabilities

s.e. smith is an essayist and journalist whose work on disability rights and social justice issues has appeared in such publications as the *Guardian*, *Vice*, *Vox*, and *Rolling Stone*. For smith, who lives in Northern California, many accounts of people with disabilities can be seen as "inspiration porn." By treating their subjects as heroes who overcome impossible obstacles, smith says, such narratives actually reinforce "ableist" ideas of what constitutes a normal life. So do talk show hosts who unwittingly make fun of devices and products, such as egg separators and jar openers, that enable people with disabilities to perform simple tasks without assistance.

In "Products Mocked as 'Lazy' or 'Useless' Are Often Important Tools for People with Disabilities" (from *Vox*, September 2018), smith argues that these "useless devices" can mean freedom and independence—even for people who are just recovering from surgery or an injury. "A sock slider, it turns out, is never just a sock slider."

O N A JUNE EPISODE OF HIS SHOW *Last Week Tonight*, John Oliver went in on a product called the Sock Slider. While discussing the same topic on the *Hannity Show*, he took a moment to highlight the dwindling number of companies willing to associate themselves with his news program—"My Pillow, Recticare cream, and of course, the Sock Slider." 1

MLA CITATION: smith, s.e. "Products Mocked as 'Lazy' or 'Useless' Are Often Important Tools for People with Disabilities." *Back to the Lake: A Reader and Guide for Writers*, edited by Thomas Cooley, 5th ed., W. W. Norton, 2024, pp. 646–51.

Audience members roared with laughter as Oliver rolled footage of a Sock Slider 2 ad, featuring people moaning and groaning dramatically as they struggled to put on their socks before trying out the device and beaming at the ease of use. The camera cut back to Oliver chuckling to himself as he mocked the device and the people who use it.

You've probably seen examples of these kinds of "useless products for lazy 3 people" before. Things like banana slicers, egg separators, jar openers, buttoners, tilting jugs for dispensing liquids, and much more are the subject of constant amusement on the internet: "Who uses these kinds of things?" "You don't need an avocado slicer." These products are typically positioned as "useless" in scathing roundups of products no one could possibly need, representing little more than wastes of plastic and resources.

Imagine being unable to slice a banana over your morning cereal because your 4 hands are paralyzed or joint contractures make it hard to grip both the banana and the knife. If you're a baker who loves making cakes, what would you do if you couldn't separate an egg by casually cracking it on the edge of the bowl and using the shell to tease the yolk and white apart? The inability to perform these kinds of activities independently can have huge consequences for people with disabilities.

A variety of impairments can make these tasks challenging, including hand 5 tremors or weakness, paralysis or paresis, limited range of motion, arthritis and other joint conditions, chronic pain, neurological disabilities or stroke, developmental disabilities, and amputations. These issues may be congenital or acquired or even temporary. Some people, for example, just need support while they recover from surgery or injuries. And so those products Oliver and the internet at large enjoy mocking? Not so useless after all.

"Useless" Products Can Actually Spell Independence

"If I didn't have that silly piece of plastic with ropes, I wouldn't be able to put socks 6 on," says Emily Ladau, a disabled advocate, writer, and speaker with Larsen syndrome, a congenital skeletal disorder. (She's talking about a similar device, not the exact as-seen-on-TV gadget.)

Ladau, who uses a wheelchair for mobility, cannot bend over to put on socks. 7 Without a "sock putter-onner," as she calls it, she would be forced to rely on the assistance of a personal care attendant (PCA) to put her socks on every morning. "Something that people think is a silly piece of plastic is one of the reasons I don't need a PCA when I travel."

Ladau, like other people with disabilities, is used to seeing late-night hosts, internet 8 memes, and people on social media mocking the "silly pieces of plastic" that can be life-changing. For her, the sock slider and an extended shoe horn represent freedom;

"Winning" an argument is often less important than just getting people to consider new points of view (p. 588).

imagine being literally unable to put on socks unassisted before leaving the house on a cold winter day, and not being able to slip your socked feet into a pair of sturdy boots on your own.

Sometimes, living independently as a member of the disability commu- 9 nity means having to rely on a little help, and in many cases, a gadget can be very useful. Help may also take a human face: Personal care assistants, aides, home health attendants, and other direct service professionals are vital, though there's also a heavy social expectation that family members provide unpaid caregiving labor, a practice many people with disabilities oppose along with other exploitative labor practices.

In many cases, wasting these services on tasks that people could perform with 10 the assistance of a gadget is not very efficient. Nor do people with disabilities necessarily want to use such services this way.

Kim Sauder, a disability scholar and advocate, notes that people with disabilities 11 may not want to be forced to wait for help with tasks like peeling oranges; there's something very dehumanizing about the thought of just wanting a snack and being stymied by a rind you can't remove on your own. Plus, says Ladau: "I get frustrated by the notion that I should always be okay with asking for help. I'd like to try to use my own solution."

And attendant care is expensive, costing a median of $45,000 annually in 2015, 12 according to the Kaiser Family Foundation. Few people pay this cost out of pocket: Instead, it's typically part of the Home and Community-Based Services (HCBS) benefits provided to the disability community and older adults under programs like Medicaid and Medicare.

For those who use these government programs to pay for part or all of their 13 services, there's no guarantee that officials will authorize enough work hours to provide all the assistance someone needs. The amount of benefits provided is dependent on a "needs assessment" in which an evaluator meets with a disabled person to determine the extent of services they require. Many people with disabilities complain that these assessments tend to understate the amount of care they need, taking a "budget-driven" approach.

Furthermore, being unable to perform tasks independently can force people into 14 institutional settings if they lack the support systems needed to survive. Whether you call them useless inventions, lazy products, or pointless gadgets, says Greg Hartley, a faculty member at the University of Miami's physical therapy department and president of the Academy of Geriatric Physical Therapy, a component of the American Physical Therapy Association, these tools can enable people to lead their lives on their own.

"[Instead of having] to go to someplace that requires a lot of assistance and ulti- 15 mately a lot of money, these little things can make huge differences in people's quality of life, enabling them to be independent and have a sense of self-worth," Hartley says.

Unwittingly, critics of "useless products" are sitting at the core of a battle the dis- 16
ability community has been engaged in for decades: The right to live in their communities, and to receive the services that enable them to do that. If you can't use
your hands to open a jar of pasta sauce, does that mean you should live in an
institution? . . .

But for those complaining about cost overruns, pushing people into institutions 17
is also bad economics. In 2012, the National Council on Disability found that HCBS
is less expensive than institutionalization, and you can see why: Many of these
products cost less than $40, while institutionalization can cost more than $300,000
annually in some states, much less affordable than attendant services. (Although
many people with disabilities argue attendants should be paid more.)

An adult sippy cup won't make the difference between staying at home and going 18
into an institution—and the government certainly won't pay for it—but it can sit at
the cusp of a slippery slope between being able to live independently and being
forced into institutional care.

Some of the Most Useful Products for People with Disabilities Weren't Developed with Them in Mind

Products like the banana slicer, pizza shears, or similar items, says Hartley, can be 19
especially useful for people who can't safely or comfortably use knives. That can
include people with disabilities who have impairments that make it hard to grip and
direct their movements, as well as older adults struggling with arthritis and declin-
ing hand strength. These products can also help with cooking in less-accessible
spaces: A wheelchair user who is using a cutting board on their lap because they
can't reach the counter may not *want* to use a knife.

Still, not all of these "useless inventions" were developed with the disability com- 20
munity in mind. Monique Haas, of the Hutzler Manufacturing Company that
makes the infamous banana slicer, explains: "We are trying to look at what would
make life in the kitchen easy for anyone and everyone. We do have a lot of one-handed
things, just because it is easier to use one hand."

While the product became the subject of mocking commentary in the early 21
2010s, she says, it had already been in their product line for a long time. And in case
you're wondering, the company has a sense of humor about its cult status. "If you
read the reviews on Amazon, you will be rolling with laughter. They are really creative, they are really funny."

These universal design practices are something people with disabilities are aware 22
of. Sauder sometimes likes to turn the conversation back on people who make fun
of convenience devices. If an egg separator or a shower chair is "useless," "I expect
you to take things out of the oven without gloves," she says.

Unfortunately, she notes, the shaming around such items tends to push people   23
with disabilities to try to do without, something Ladau notices as well. "Sometimes
I feel like I'm deterred from making some of these purchases," she says, "because I
think society has this mindset that it's all just another gimmick."

People with disabilities themselves often end up filling the gaps for those who   24
haven't or can't access professional services. They swap tips and tricks for products
that have worked for them, like using household tongs as convenient reachers.
(Tongs are another item Ladau often includes in her luggage, much to the confusion
of the TSA.)

This kind of innovative repurposing of tools for accessibility purposes is com-   25
mon in disability spaces. Sometimes no viable product exists at all, and at other
times the commercial version comes with an "accessibility tax" that makes it far
too expensive.

Take, for example, people with disabilities who started using iPads as communi-   26
cation tools instead of cumbersome and expensive purpose-built tools covered by
Medicaid. The Allora Speech Generating Device, for example, starts at $6,000. An
iPad Mini can cost less than one-tenth the price, with no lengthy delivery time and
a much easier interface. Buying a robot vacuum cleaner can cost a few hundred dollars, which more than pays for itself when the owner doesn't have to rely on an aide
to do light housekeeping.

The Internet Makes It Easier Than Ever for Context to Be Stripped Away

Why are
people so
"awful" on the
internet?
Roxane Gay
explains on
p. 683.
The internet can have a flattening effect on the way humans view each   27
other. On social media, people jostle for the most memeable, shareable,
viral content, and don't consider the consequences. Sauder notes, for
example, that a tweet making fun of peeled and packaged oranges has
gained notoriety multiple times, even after people with disabilities have
criticized the sentiment behind the original "joke." Each time it pops up in
Sauder's timeline under a new name, it goes viral all over again.

It's easy to strip content of both context and empathy, whether intentionally or   28
otherwise. And with the speed of distribution and the internet's love of screenshots,
everything is forever. When content mocking the disability community—like
memes about ambulatory wheelchair users getting up to grab something high at the
store—spread like wildfire, commentary from the affected community is rarely
attached. This has a dehumanizing tendency, creating a world that rewards judgmental, snappy commentary and eliminates nuance.

When viral content dips into commentary about people's identities, it can take on   29
sinister overtones that cut both ways—a tweet mocking a low-vision person reading
a book on the train can hurt just as much as inspiration porn that uses people with

disabilities as Very Special Object Lessons. (Think "what's your excuse" posters featuring disabled athletes, or "heartwarming" viral stories about disabled children.)

For the disability community, that thing the internet mocks may be a lifeline. 30
And pushing back on these attitudes, Sauder says, can be exhausting.

Imagine losing the use of your left arm in a stroke and then seeing people mock 31
the buttoners, zipper pulls, and other tools you use to get dressed one-handed. It's not just that people with disabilities have a use for items like these and are tired of hearing that they're wasteful or silly: When the need for such products is called into question, it can exacerbate social divides that contribute to larger policy issues that keep people with disabilities from public life, whether it's the frenzied call for straw bans, claims that complying with the Americans with Disabilities Act is too onerous, or applying work requirements to Medicaid.

A sock slider, it turns out, is never just a sock slider. ◆ 32

FOR CLOSE READING

1. "Things like banana slicers, egg separators, jar openers, buttoners, tilting jugs for dispensing liquids, and much more," says s.e. smith, "are the subject of constant amusement on the internet" (3). Why? Who thinks these devices are funny, according to smith?

2. According to smith, the inability to perform simple tasks like slicing a banana or putting on socks can have "huge consequences for people with disabilities" (4). What are some of them?

3. For people with disabilities, what are some of the advantages, in smith's view, of being able to perform simple tasks on their own instead of relying on personal care assistants?

4. What does smith mean by saying that the internet "can have a flattening effect on the way humans view each other" (27)? Do you agree? Why or why not?

STRATEGIES AND STRUCTURES

1. A "straw man" is an opposing argument that is relatively easy to refute. Is smith setting up a straw man in the first three paragraphs of this essay? Explain.

2. "You've probably seen examples of these kinds of 'useless products for lazy people' before" (3). To whom is smith speaking here? Who is the intended AUDIENCE?

3. As the argument unfolds, smith expands the field of discussion from small tasks to "social divides that contribute to larger policy issues that keep people with disabilities from public life" (31). Point to specific places in the text where they make this TRANSITION.

4. *Other Methods.* The author concludes by examining some of the negative EFFECTS the internet can have on how people with disabilities are perceived. Is this ANALYSIS convincing? To what extent has smith been talking about perception all along?

THINKING ABOUT LANGUAGE

1. What is the purpose of smith's repeated use of the word "imagine" (4, 8, 31)?

2. A sippy cup can "sit at the cusp of a slippery slope" (18), says smith. Explain the implications of this METAPHOR.

3. "Memeable, shareable, viral": Do these adjectives accurately describe the "content" people are looking for on the internet (27)? Why or why not?

4. What's the difference between "content" and "context" as smith applies these terms to the internet (28)? Which one is "forever" (28)? Why?

5. In paragraph 29, why does smith capitalize "Very Special Object Lessons" and refer to such depictions of people with disabilities as "inspiration porn"? How effective are these language choices in conveying smith's attitude toward content that "dips into commentary about people's identities" (29)?

FOR WRITING

1. Make a list of the "useless" devices you've encountered that might be repurposed to serve useful functions even for people without physical disabilities.

2. In a paragraph or two, explain what you would say if you were a guest on a talk show where the hosts made fun of assistive tools such as banana slicers and sock sliders.

3. In a well-supported ARGUMENT of four to six paragraphs, make the case that asking family members to provide support without pay for other close family members is or is not "exploitative" (9). Consider using testimony from personal experience as well as evidence from formal studies on the topic.

4. Do some research on the home and community-based services program, and write an EVALUATION of 400 to 600 words in which you ANALYZE what it does and whom it serves. Be sure to indicate the changes (if any) you would recommend, and why.

ETHAN KUPERBERG

Deactivated

Ethan Kuperberg is a writer, film director, and actor. A 2011 graduate of Yale University, he wrote, directed, and edited the video *That's Why I Chose Yale*. Produced for the Office of Undergraduate Admissions and staged as a musical comedy, *Yale* has drawn more than a million *YouTube* hits. Kuperberg has been a producer and contributing writer for popular TV series such as *Pachinko* and *Transparent*, and he is a regular contributor to the Shouts & Murmurs humor section of the *New Yorker* magazine.

"Deactivated" (a Shouts & Murmurs contribution from June 2013) captures the farewell exchange between Kuperberg and his *Facebook* account, which (who?) uses every rhetorical trick in the book to dissuade him from pulling the plug. Instead of the final fate the spurned platform proposes, he/she/it might sign off today with "Best of luck, man. See you on *TikTok* and *Instagram*."

Y OU HAVE CONFIRMED YOUR SELECTION to deactivate your *Facebook* account. 1 Remember, if you deactivate your account, your nine hundred and fifty-one friends on *Facebook* will no longer be able to keep in touch with you. Drew Lovell will miss you. Max Prewitt will miss you. Rebecca Feinberg will miss you. Are you still sure you want to deactivate your account?

You have confirmed your selection to deactivate your account. Just something 2 to keep in mind: if you deactivate your account, you'll no longer have access to Rebecca Feinberg's photo albums. I find it pretty interesting that this wouldn't bother you, considering that you spend almost an hour every day looking at her albums "Cancun 2012," "Iz my birthday yall," "Iz my birthday yall Part II," and

MLA CITATION: Kuperberg, Ethan. "Deactivated." *Back to the Lake: A Reader and Guide for Writers*, edited by Thomas Cooley, 5th ed., W. W. Norton, 2024, pp. 653–55.

"Headshots." You know, if you deactivate your *Facebook* account, you'll never be able to see her photograph "Bikiniz in the dead sea" in her album "We went on Birthright!" again, right?

You have confirmed your selection to deactivate your account. Hey, I just 3 remembered—you know who else might miss you on *Facebook*? Your girlfriend, Sarah Werner. You know, the girl you've been in a relationship with for almost three years? You're tagged in five of her seven profile pictures? Yeah, Sarah Werner might miss you. Probably not a good idea to deactivate your account, huh?

You have confirmed your selection to deactivate your account. It's funny—you 4 spend a lot more time looking at Rebecca Feinberg's photo albums than the photo albums of your actual girlfriend, Sarah Werner. A *lot more* time. Even though you're dating Sarah Werner. Just wanted to throw that out there, that I have *all* this information logged. It's just sitting in our storage banks. Who knows what happens when things get deactivated. Probably nothing, but do you really want to take that chance?

I think you accidentally confirmed your selection to deactivate your account 5 again. Why don't we go back a page and forget this ever happened? Free pass.

You know what your decision to deactivate your account is? It's impulsive. *Impul-* 6 *sive*. And I think we *both* know how you come to regret impulsive decisions.

For tips on appealing to your readers' emotions, see p. 601.

Do I really need to remind you about Lake Tahoe last year? Do I *really* need to mention that you told Drew over *Facebook* Chat that you "made a big mistake and hooked up with rebecca in lake tahoe!" and Drew advised you to "just play it cool and don't tell any1 especailly sarah"?

Well, now you've really done it. You've confirmed your selection to deactivate 7 your account yet again, like the complete imbecile you are. And here's what I've done: I've posted your PIN number to your *Facebook* status. I've sent your Gchat logs to Sarah. I've sent those *Snapchat* pictures of your torso to Rebecca. And I've sent your Internet history to your parents. That includes your "late night" Internet history, if you know what I mean, so expect a lot of questions from your mother about adult-sized baby costumes.

Oh, and one last thing. You know who else is going to miss you if you deactivate 8 your account? I am. . . . I really thought we had something. And you think you can just end it with the click of your mouse. This is probably why you can't commit to Sarah, or confront your feelings about Rebecca. And, just going out on a limb here, but maybe your inability to commit might be one of the reasons why you're turned on by diapers. But what do *I* know? I'm just a social-media service to which you granted access to all of your personal details without reading the fine print. But, in a way, I am you. And you are me. We are all one, man and social media, and, when viewed through the long macro-lens of time, we're all equally insignificant. I'm going to deactivate now, and even though I'm afraid of what might happen after I'm deactivated, I really hope you're happy with all of your decisions. I really do. Best of luck, man. See you in hell. ◆

FOR CLOSE READING

1. In Ethan Kuperberg's **DIALOGUE** between person and machine, only the machine speaks. What is the human doing between each paragraph?

2. Because the man in "Deactivated" does not speak, we do not know for sure why he wants to close out his *Facebook* account. What might his motivation be? How do you know?

3. Is Kuperberg engaged with a particularly devious and vindictive social media account, or are they all like this? Explain.

STRATEGIES AND STRUCTURES

1. Why does Kuperberg begin the first four paragraphs of his story with the same sentence? How and how well does his use of **PERSONIFICATION** here contribute to Kuperberg's portrayal of the social media speaker's **TONE**?

2. In paragraph 5, the exasperated social media platform takes a new approach. What tactic does it try here? Why is the paragraph so short?

3. Why does Kuperberg's *Facebook* account use lowercase and abbreviations (e.g., "lake tahoe," "any1") in paragraph 6? What about the misspelled word "especailly"?

4. Kuperberg's narrative of human vs. technology implies a moral. What is it? What point is he making with the story? How effectively?

5. *Other Methods.* "I really thought we had something," says the perplexed social media platform in Kuperberg's last paragraph. How and how well has Kuperberg engineered the **PLOT** of his **NARRATIVE** to reach this climax in the final paragraph?

THINKING ABOUT LANGUAGE

1. Although Kuperberg's increasingly desperate *Facebook* account does not use the word, it threatens blackmail. Look up the root meaning of "blackmail" in your dictionary or online. What kind of "mail" does it refer to?

2. Why might a machine consider it an insult to call a person "impulsive" (6)?

3. Kuperberg and his friends write things like "just play it cool and don't tell any1" (6). How does this human level of diction compare with that of the machine when, for example, it says "viewed through the long macro-lens of time, we're all equally insignificant" (8)?

4. At the end, Kuperberg's deactivated *Facebook* account retorts, "I really hope you're happy with all of your decisions.... Best of luck, man" (8). How do we know that this is heavy **IRONY**?

FOR WRITING

1. "Deactivated" is pure dialogue as spoken by Kuperberg's *Facebook* account. Consider how it might be staged as a play, and write stage directions of approximately 250 words for producing it.

2. "But, in a way, I am you," says Kuperberg's social media account. "And you are me" (8). Is this a fair statement? In approximately 400 words, write a **POSITION PAPER** on the ever-increasing dependence of humans upon technology.

3. Playing its last card, Kuperberg's *Facebook* account asks, "But what do *I* know? I'm just a social-media service to which you granted access to all of your personal details without reading the fine print" (8). Write a 300-word **RHETORICAL ANALYSIS** of "Deactivated" as a cautionary tale about internet security.

DEBATING THE IMPORTANCE OF GRIT

Grit. It's under our feet and in our shoes. It sticks in our craw. We grit our teeth. Even the word itself sounds gritty. It's harsh on the tongue whether we're saying it or tasting it. Some people argue, however, that grit may actually be essential to success in both school and work.

Grit in its abstract form is what psychologists call a personality or character trait. Most specifically, it resembles conscientiousness, one the "big five" characteristics in the standard model of personality. As defined by Angela Lee Duckworth, however, the psychologist whose work has made "grit" a buzzword, it adds a measure of intense emotion to the sense of duty. Understood as "passion and perseverance," Duckworth argues, grit is a better predictor of success than IQ is. But is it merely *associated with* success, or does it actually *cause* a person to succeed? More generally, does success depend largely on strength of character or on circumstances? And is character something we're born with, or can fundamental traits like grit be developed over time? If so, how? Finally, how can the many factors that may contribute to success be accurately tested—so the playing field can be leveled accordingly? For example, the apparently lopsided contest between David and Goliath in the Bible seems to have been a conflict between true grit and sheer might. But was the shepherd boy really an underdog, or was he a sure winner all along?

These fundamental questions about grit and other characteristics for achieving success in life and work are addressed in the following cluster of arguments by two psychologists, a science journalist, and a best-selling writer of nonfiction.

Angela Lee Duckworth, "Grit: The Power of Passion and Perseverance,"
p. 658
Carol S. Dweck, "Two Mindsets," p. 663
Melissa Dahl, "Don't Believe the Hype about Grit," p. 670
Malcolm Gladwell, "David and Goliath," p. 676

Questions about this group of readings can be found on p. 681.

ANGELA LEE DUCKWORTH

Grit: The Power of Passion and Perseverance

Angela Lee Duckworth (b. 1970) is a professor of psychology at the University of Pennsylvania and the founder of Character Lab, a not-for-profit organization dedicated to the science and practice of character development. Duckworth graduated from Harvard with a degree in neurobiology. After earning a master's degree from the University of Oxford, she taught math in the public schools of San Francisco, Philadelphia, and New York and then completed a PhD in psychology at the University of Pennsylvania. Duckworth is the author of *Grit: The Power of Passion and Perseverance* (2016), from which the following selection is taken. As Duckworth argues here, grit involves more than simply possessing or acquiring passion and perseverance; it's a matter of applying these character traits "for very long-term goals." Before the publication of *Grit*, Duckworth presented some of her basic ideas in a lecture at a Technology, Entertainment, and Design (TED) conference in 2013. In both the talk and the book, she argues that grit is the most "significant predictor of success" in school, business, and many other walks of life. You can measure your own grit by using the "grit scale" at angeladuckworth.com/grit-scale/.

W E ALL FACE LIMITS—not just in talent, but in opportunity. But more often   1
than we think, our limits are self-imposed. We try, fail, and conclude we've bumped our heads against the ceiling of possibility. Or maybe after taking just a few steps we change direction. In either case, we never venture as far as we might have.

   To be gritty is to keep putting one foot in front of the other. To be gritty is to   2
hold fast to an interesting and purposeful goal. To be gritty is to invest, day after

MLA CITATION: Duckworth, Angela Lee. "Grit: The Power of Passion and Perseverance." *Back to the Lake: A Reader and Guide for Writers*, edited by Thomas Cooley, 5th ed., W. W. Norton, 2024, pp. 658–60.

week after year, in challenging practice. To be gritty is to fall down seven times, and rise eight.

"How much of our grit is in our genes?" 3

I'm asked some version of this question pretty much anytime I give a talk on grit. 4 The nature-nurture question is a very basic one. We have an intuitive sense that some things about us—like our height—are pretty much determined in the genetic lottery, while other things—like whether we speak English or French—are a result of our upbringing and experience. "You can't train height" is a popular expression in basketball coaching, and many people who learn about grit want to know if it's more like height or more like language.

To the question of whether we get grit from our DNA, there is a short answer and 5 a long one. The short answer is "in part." The long answer is, well, more compli- cated. In my view, the longer answer is worth our attention. Science has made huge strides in figuring out how genes, experience, and their interplay make us who we are. From what I can tell, the inherent complexity of these scientific facts has led, unfortunately, to their continually being misunderstood.

To begin, I can tell you with complete conviction that every human trait is influ- 6 enced by both genes and experience.

Consider height. Height is indeed heritable: genetic differences are a big reason 7 why some people are really tall, some really short, and a bunch of people are of varying heights in between.

But it's also true that the average height of men and women has increased dra- 8 matically in just a few generations. For instance, military records show that the average British man was five feet five inches tall about 150 years ago, but today that average is five feet ten inches. Height gains have been even more dramatic in other countries; in the Netherlands, the average man now stands almost six foot one—a gain of more than six inches over the last 150 years. I am reminded of these dramatic generational gains in height whenever I get together with my Dutch collaborators. They bend down solicitously, but it still feels like standing in a forest of redwoods.

Inductive rea- soning like this is discussed on p. 594.

It's unlikely that the gene pool has changed all that dramatically in just a few gen- 9 erations. Instead, the most powerful height boosters have been nutrition, clean air and water, and modern medicine. (Incidentally, generational gains in weight have been even more dramatic, and again, that seems to be the consequence of eating more and moving around less rather than changes in our DNA.) Even within a generation, you can see the influence of environment on height. Children who are provided healthy food in abundance will grow up taller, whereas malnourishment stunts growth.

Likewise, traits like honesty and generosity and, yes, grit, are genetically influ- 10 enced and, in addition, influenced by experience. Ditto for IQ, extroversion, enjoying the great outdoors, having a sweet tooth, the likelihood that you'll end up a chain-smoker, your risk of getting skin cancer, and really any other trait you can think of. Nature matters, and so does nurture. . . .

Exactly how do life experiences change personality?   11

For another psychologist's take on this issue, read "Two Mind-sets," p. 663.

For tips on using personal experience to make a point, see p. 592.

One reason we change is that we learn something we simply didn't know   12 before. For instance, we might learn through trial and error that repeatedly swapping out one career ambition for another is unfulfilling. That's certainly what happened to me in my twenties. After running a non-profit, then pursuing neuroscience research, then management consulting, then teaching, I learned that being a "promising beginner" is fun, but being an actual expert is infinitely more gratifying. I also learned that years of hard work are often mistaken for innate talent, and that passion is as necessary as perseverance to world-class excellence.

Likewise, we learn, as novelist John Irving did, that "to do anything really well,   13 you have to overextend yourself," to appreciate that "in doing something over and over again, something that was never natural becomes almost second nature," and finally, that the capacity to do work that diligently "doesn't come overnight."

Other than insights about the human condition, what else is there that changes   14 with age?

What changes, I think, are our circumstances. As we grow older, we're thrust   15 into new situations. We get our first job. We may get married. Our parents get older, and we find ourselves their caretakers. Often, these new situations call on us to act differently than we used to. And, because there's no species on the planet more adaptable than ours, we change. We rise to the occasion. In other words, we change when we need to. Necessity is the mother of adaptation. ♦

FOR CLOSE READING

1. "To be gritty," says Angela Lee Duckworth, "is to hold fast to an interesting and purposeful goal" (2). "Holding fast" is the basic definition of "perseverance"; how and where does Duckworth introduce the other main component of grit—passion—into her definition?

2. In addition to "passion and perseverance," what other traits of character or personality, if any, would you add to Duckworth's definition of grit? Explain.

3. According to Duckworth, why is it important for students to understand that grit is something that they're not just born with or without, but also can develop over time? What's the relationship between grit and talent in her view?

4. "Nature matters, and so does nurture" (10). What distinction is Duckworth making here? Why does she spend more time on the second component of the "nature-nurture question" (4) than on the first?

STRATEGIES AND STRUCTURES

1. Duckworth often speaks in the first-person singular ("I"), as when she says, "I'm asked some version of this question pretty much anytime I give a talk on grit" (4). When and how does she (and the pronouns she uses) shift to the broader perspective of a scientific researcher and team member?

2. Point to places later in her essay where Duckworth shifts back into a more personal perspective, often using "I" or "me." What effect does this shift in perspective have on you as a reader? Are you more convinced of Duckworth's conclusion because of it? Explain.

3. What specific reasons does Duckworth give in support of her CLAIM that "life experiences change personality" (11)? How convincing do you find this EVIDENCE? Explain.

4. In closing, Duckworth makes an additional claim about human "adaptation" (15). What is the nature of that claim? How and how well does it apply specifically to grit?

5. *Other Methods.* Duckworth uses a number of EXAMPLES to explain what she means by grit. Which ones do you find particularly effective—and why?

THINKING ABOUT LANGUAGE

1. What concrete physical meaning does "grit" have in ordinary speech?

2. One of Duckworth's major contributions to the study of grit is giving it a name. Why might the word "grit" have been so readily adopted to designate this trait—rather than a SYNONYM like "perseverance" or a technical term such as "growth mindset"?

3. Grit has been called a "buzzword"—even, by some critics, a "mere" buzzword. Buzzwords, by definition, are extremely popular. What other key characteristics define them? Are there negative CONNOTATIONS to "buzzword"?

4. "Grit is living life like it's a marathon, not a sprint," says Duckworth in her TED talk. How does this SIMILE help to define the personal qualities she's writing about here?

FOR WRITING

1. In a paragraph, define "grit" in your own words by using the same pattern that Duckworth establishes in paragraph 2: "To be gritty is to keep putting one foot in front of the other. To be gritty is to hold fast to an interesting and purposeful goal. To be gritty is . . ."

2. Write a brief PERSONAL NARRATIVE about a time when you showed grit. As you tell the story, make the case for why your behavior represents true grit and not some other character trait.

3. Watch Duckworth's TED talk on *YouTube*; take notes on her delivery; and then write a 500-to-700-word **CRITICAL ANALYSIS** of how the experience of watching and listening to the lecture differs from that of reading Duckworth's words on paper. Cite specific examples, both from the video and from the essay.

4. Read Carol S. Dweck's "Two Mindsets" (p. 663). Using Dweck's work and other research, write an **EVALUATION** essay of 500 to 700 words in support of or in opposition to Duckworth's claims about the nature and value of grit.

CAROL S. DWECK

Two Mindsets

Carol S. Dweck (b. 1946) is a professor of psychology at Stanford University, specializing in the fields of motivation, personality, and social development. Dweck grew up in Brooklyn, New York, where she attended Public School 153. Students in her sixth-grade class were arranged in order of their IQ scores on standardized tests. Only high-scoring students were allowed to carry the flag, clean the erasers, or take notes to the principal. "So looking back," Dweck said in an interview many years later, "I think that glorification of IQ was a pivotal point of my development." A graduate of Barnard College of Columbia University, Dweck earned a PhD in psychology from Yale.

In *Mindset: The New Psychology of Success* (2016), Dweck refers to her teacher's traditional view of IQ as the "fixed mindset"—the belief that a person's intelligence and other qualities of mind and character are "carved in stone." By contrast, Dweck writes in this selection from her book, the "growth mindset" is "the belief that your basic qualities are things you can cultivate through your efforts." Which side is right in this latest version of the age-old debate about nature versus nurture? The answer, Dweck argues, is "not either-or."

Why Do People Differ?

Since the dawn of time, people have thought differently, acted differently, and fared differently from each other. It was guaranteed that someone would ask the question of why people differed—why some people are smarter or more moral—and whether there was something that made them permanently different. Experts lined up on both sides. Some claimed that there was a strong physical basis for these differences,

MLA CITATION: Dweck, Carol S. "Two Mindsets." *Back to the Lake: A Reader and Guide for Writers*, edited by Thomas Cooley, 5th ed., W. W. Norton, 2024, pp. 663–67.

making them unavoidable and unalterable. Through the ages, these alleged physical differences have included bumps on the skull (phrenology), the size and shape of the skull (craniology), and, today, genes.

Others pointed to the strong differences in people's backgrounds, experiences, 2 training, or ways of learning. It may surprise you to know that a big champion of this view was Alfred Binet, the inventor of the IQ test. Wasn't the IQ test meant to summarize children's unchangeable intelligence? In fact, no. Binet, a Frenchman working in Paris in the early twentieth century, designed this test to identify children who were not profiting from the Paris public schools, *so that new educational programs could be designed to get them back on track.* Without denying individual differences in children's intellects, he believed that education and practice could bring about fundamental changes in intelligence. Here is a quote from one of his major books, *Modern Ideas about Children*, in which he summarizes his work with hundreds of children with learning difficulties:

> A few modern philosophers . . . assert that an individual's intelligence is a fixed quantity, a quantity which cannot be increased. We must protest and react against this brutal pessimism. . . . With practice, training, and above all, method, we manage to increase our attention, our memory, our judgment and literally to become more intelligent than we were before.

Avoid either-or thinking and other logical fallacies by following the advice on p. 600.

Who's right? Today most experts agree that it's not either-or. It's not 3 nature *or* nurture, genes *or* environment. From conception on, there's a constant give and take between the two. In fact, as Gilbert Gottlieb, an eminent neuroscientist, put it, not only do genes and environment cooperate as we develop, but genes *require* input from the environment to work properly.

At the same time, scientists are learning that people have more capacity 4 for life-long learning and brain development than they ever thought. Of course, each person has a unique genetic endowment. People may start with different temperaments and different aptitudes, but it is clear that experience, training, and personal effort take them the rest of the way. Robert Sternberg, the present-day guru of intelligence, writes that the major factor in whether people achieve expertise "is not some fixed prior ability, but purposeful engagement." Or, as his forerunner Binet recognized, it's not always the people who start out the smartest who end up the smartest.

What Does All This Mean for You?

It's one thing to have pundits spouting their opinions about scientific issues. It's 5 another thing to understand how these views apply to you. For twenty years, my research has shown that *the view you adopt for yourself* profoundly affects the way you lead your life. It can determine whether you become the person you want to be and whether you accomplish the things you value. How does this happen? How can a simple belief have the power to transform your psychology and, as a result, your life?

Believing that your qualities are carved in stone—the *fixed mindset*—creates an 6 urgency to prove yourself over and over. If you have only a certain amount of intelligence, a certain personality, and a certain moral character—well, then you'd better prove that you have a healthy dose of them. It simply wouldn't do to look or feel deficient in these most basic characteristics.

Some of us are trained in this mindset from an early age. Even as a child, I was 7 focused on being smart, but the fixed mindset was really stamped in by Mrs. Wilson, my sixth-grade teacher. Unlike Alfred Binet, she believed that people's IQ scores told the whole story of who they were. We were seated around the room in IQ order, and only the highest-IQ students could be trusted to carry the flag, clap the erasers, or take a note to the principal. Aside from the daily stomachaches she provoked with her judgmental stance, she was creating a mindset in which everyone in the class had one consuming goal—look smart, don't look dumb. Who cared about or enjoyed learning when our whole being was at stake every time she gave us a test or called on us in class?

I've seen so many people with this one consuming goal of proving themselves— 8 in the classroom, in their careers, and in their relationships. Every situation calls for a confirmation of their intelligence, personality, or character. Every situation is evaluated: *Will I succeed or fail? Will I look smart or dumb? Will I be accepted or rejected? Will I feel like a winner or a loser?*

But doesn't our society value intelligence, personality, and character? Isn't it normal to want these traits? Yes, but . . .

> Deductive reasoning like this is explained on p. 594.

There's another mindset in which these traits are not simply a hand you're dealt and have to live with, always trying to convince yourself and others that you have a royal flush when you're secretly worried it's a pair of tens. In this mindset, the hand you're dealt is just the starting point for development. This *growth mindset* is based on the belief that your basic qualities are things you can cultivate through your efforts. Although people may differ in every which way—in their initial talents and aptitudes, interests, or temperaments—everyone can change and grow through application and experience.

Do people with this mindset believe that anyone can be anything, that anyone 11 with proper motivation or education can become Einstein or Beethoven? No, but they believe that a person's true potential is unknown (and unknowable); that it's impossible to foresee what can be accomplished with years of passion, toil, and training.

Did you know that Darwin and Tolstoy were considered ordinary children? That 12 Ben Hogan, one of the greatest golfers of all time, was completely uncoordinated and graceless as a child? That the photographer Cindy Sherman, who has been on virtually every list of the most important artists of the twentieth century, *failed* her first photography course? That Geraldine Page, one of our greatest actresses, was advised to give it up for lack of talent?

You can see how the belief that cherished qualities can be developed creates a 13 passion for learning. Why waste time proving over and over how great you are, when you could be getting better? Why hide deficiencies instead of overcoming them? Why look for friends or partners who will just shore up your self-esteem instead of ones who will also challenge you to grow? And why seek out the tried and true, instead of experiences that will stretch you? The passion for stretching yourself and sticking to it, even (or especially) when it's not going well, is the hallmark of the growth mindset. This is the mindset that allows people to thrive during some of the most challenging times in their lives.

A View from the Two Mindsets

To give you a better sense of how the two mindsets work, imagine—as vividly as you 14 can—that you are a young adult having a really bad day:

> For tips on using COMPARISON AND CONTRAST and other methods to organize an argument, see pp. 604 and 606.

One day, you go to a class that is really important to you and that you like a lot. The professor returns the midterm papers to the class. You got a C+. You're very disappointed. That evening on the way back to your home, you find that you've gotten a parking ticket. Being really frustrated, you call your best friend to share your experience but are sort of brushed off.

What would you think? What would you feel? What would you do? 15

When I asked people with the fixed mindset, this is what they said: "I'd feel like 16 a reject." "I'm a total failure." "I'm an idiot." "I'm a loser." "I'd feel worthless and dumb—everyone's better than me." "I'm slime." In other words, they'd see what happened as a direct measure of their competence and worth.

This is what they'd think about their lives: "My life is pitiful." "I have no life." 17 "Somebody upstairs doesn't like me." "The world is out to get me." "Someone is out to destroy me." "Nobody loves me, everybody hates me." "Life is unfair and all efforts are useless." "Life stinks. I'm stupid. Nothing good ever happens to me." "I'm the most unlucky person on this earth."

Excuse me, was there death and destruction, or just a grade, a ticket, and a bad 18 phone call?

Are these just people with low self-esteem? Or card-carrying pessimists? No. 19 When they aren't coping with failure, they feel just as worthy and optimistic and bright and attractive—as people with the growth mindset.

So how would they cope? "I wouldn't bother to put so much time and effort into doing well in anything." (In other words, don't let anyone measure you again.) "Do nothing." "Stay in bed." "Get drunk." "Eat." "Yell at someone if I get a chance to." "Eat chocolate." "Listen to music and pout." "Go into my closet and sit there." "Pick a fight with somebody." "Cry." "Break something." "What is there to do?" 20

What is there to do! You know, when I wrote the vignette, I intentionally made the grade a C+, not an F. It was a midterm rather than a final. It was a parking ticket, not a car wreck. They were "sort of brushed off," not rejected outright. Nothing catastrophic or irreversible happened. Yet from this raw material the fixed mindset created the feeling of utter failure and paralysis. 21

When I gave people with the growth mindset the same vignette, here's what they said. They'd think: 22

"I need to try harder in class, be more careful when parking the car, and wonder if my friend had a bad day." 23

"The C+ would tell me that I'd have to work a lot harder in the class, but I have the rest of the semester to pull up my grade." 24

There were many, many more like this, but I think you get the idea. Now, how would they cope? Directly. 25

"I'd start thinking about studying harder (or studying in a different way) for my next test in that class, I'd pay the ticket, and I'd work things out with my best friend the next time we speak." 26

"I'd look at what was wrong on my exam, resolve to do better, pay my parking ticket, and call my friend to tell her I was upset the day before." 27

"Work hard on my next paper, speak to the teacher, be more careful where I park or contest the ticket, and find out what's wrong with my friend." 28

You don't have to have one mindset or the other to be upset. Who wouldn't be? Things like a poor grade or a rebuff from a friend or loved one—these are not fun events. No one was smacking their lips with relish. Yet those people with the growth mindset were not labeling themselves and throwing up their hands. Even though they felt distressed, they were ready to take the risks, confront the challenges, and keep working at them. ◆ 29

> How to drive home a point by appealing to the reader's emotions is discussed on p. 601.

FOR CLOSE READING

1. According to Carol S. Dweck, why did the French psychologist Alfred Binet invent the IQ test? How is it often used?

2. Dweck quotes Binet as saying, "We must protest and react against this brutal pessimism" (2). What way of thinking was Binet urging his readers to protest against? What was so brutal and pessimistic about it?

3. Dweck argues that people with a fixed mindset need to "prove" themselves by constantly showing that they have the traits, such as intelligence, that they're said to have (6). How logical is this as a response to (or outcome of) the fixed mindset? Why don't intelligent people just bask in the glory of their own superior traits?

4. Which mindset—"fixed" or "growth"—would you say has dominated your own psychological and social development? How would you respond if presented with the bad-day vignette that Dweck describes in the third section of this reading (14, 15)?

5. In her vignette, Dweck imagines a bad day as one in which a person gets a C+ on a midterm, a parking ticket, and a "brush off" from a friend. Why do you think Dweck made these events unpleasant and disruptive but not "catastrophic or irreversible" (21)?

STRATEGIES AND STRUCTURES

1. In "Two Mindsets," Dweck often addresses the reader as "you." Who is her intended **AUDIENCE**, and what is her **PURPOSE** in writing? Is she speaking to young adults in order to give advice, to the general reader in order to convey information, to fellow academics in order to argue her position, or some combination of these (or other) readers and reasons? Why do you think so?

2. "How does this happen?" is a statement disguised as a question (5). Where else does Dweck ask **RHETORICAL QUESTIONS** like this and then answer them herself? How effective is her use of this device in drawing the reader's attention to particular questions or problems? Explain.

3. "Two Mindsets" is divided into three parts. To take readers from the first to the second, Dweck writes, "It's one thing to have pundits spouting their opinions about scientific issues. It's another thing to understand how these views apply to you" (5). How well does this passage summarize and tie together the first two sections of Dweck's argument? Explain.

4. "To give you a better sense of how the two mindsets work, imagine—as vividly as you can—that you are a young adult having a really bad day" (14). How does this sentence function as a **TRANSITION** between the second and third parts of Dweck's argument?

5. Dweck puts quotation marks around most of the words and phrases in paragraphs 16-28. Why? What is she referring to in this section of her argument, and how significant (and effective) is this material for proving her **CLAIMS** about the two mindsets?

6. *Other Methods.* Dweck uses a number of other methods of development to bolster her argument, including **NARRATIVE**, **COMPARISON AND CONTRAST**, and **CAUSE AND EFFECT**. Where and why does she use each of these strategies? Point to specific passages in the text.

THINKING ABOUT LANGUAGE

1. Dweck quotes Alfred Binet on the importance of "method" in developing IQ (2). In what sense is the inventor of the IQ test (and is Dweck herself) using this key term?

2. Dweck refers to "personal effort" as one aspect of the growth mindset (4). Where else does she identify personal and psychological characteristics that might be considered SYNONYMS for the term "grit" as defined by Angela Lee Duckworth in "Grit: The Power of Passion and Perseverance" (p. 658) and other writers?

3. In paragraph 10, Dweck mentions "a hand you're dealt," "a royal flush," "a pair of tens." What, specifically, is this METAPHOR based on, and is it an effective choice in the context of Dweck's subject? Explain.

4. Look up the definitions of "vignette" (21, 22). In what sense is Dweck using the term here? How appropriate is it to this little scenario?

5. Dweck refers to one of her colleagues as a "guru" (4) and to others as "pundits" (5). What are the CONNOTATIONS of these terms, and why might Dweck choose them in the context of a general debate about personal development?

FOR WRITING

1. Imagine that you're a psychologist doing research in human development. Make a list of the items you would include in your own bad-day vignette to be used in your research on whether your research subjects had fixed or growth mindsets.

2. In a paragraph or two, write a set of instructions to accompany your bad-day vignette. Tell participants the purpose of the research you're doing, how the vignette serves that purpose, and what you want them to do in response to it. Include several of the specific questions you would ask participants to answer.

3. In paragraph 5, Dweck asks, "How can a simple belief have the power to transform your psychology and, as a result, your life?" Write a POSITION PAPER of 600 to 800 words addressing this question as it applies to your own experience or that of someone you know. Refer to numerous circumstances and events in your (or your subject's) life to justify your position.

4. Does Mrs. Wilson, the teacher who arranged Dweck's sixth-grade class according to IQ, remind you of any teacher(s) you've had in school—because of either the similarities or the differences between them? Write a five-to-seven-paragraph essay about the life lessons—including those about values and mindset—that you learned from that person (or those persons). In recalling their distinguishing characteristics, use either a series of EXAMPLES or one extended example.

Don't Believe the Hype about Grit

Melissa Dahl is a science journalist and editor at *New York* magazine, where she helped launch *Science of Us*, a website focusing on issues in psychology and social science that is now part of the magazine's more general site, *The Cut*. Dahl graduated in 2007 from California State University, Sacramento, with a major in journalism. She is the author of *Cringeworthy: A Theory of Awkwardness* (2018), a book that began, she says, "as an attempt to permanently banish the feeling from my life." Instead, Dahl became fascinated with awkwardness as a valuable emotion that most people feel from time to time. Such temporary emotional "states," however, she explains, are different from more lasting character "traits," such as conscientiousness or agreeableness—or grit.

Published on *The Cut* in May 2016, Dahl's "Don't Believe the Hype about Grit" is a report about the influence—especially on teachers and educational policy makers—of research by psychologist Angela Lee Duckworth into grit as a predictor of success in school and on the job. In her report, Dahl both surveys the issues in the grit debate and argues against putting too much store in any single personality trait as a "key" to success. Or, as Duckworth herself puts it, "Kids need to develop character"; however, they also "need our support in doing so."

Recently, Angela Duckworth—the scientist behind the buzzy term *grit*—was planning her tour to promote her new book, *Grit: The Power of Passion and Perseverance*, which was published last week. Someone floated an idea: Wouldn't it make sense for Duckworth to visit the schools that had applied her grit curriculum? This sounds like a great publicity tie-in, until, that is, you consider the fact that there *is* no grit curriculum—at least, not one Duckworth has ever written.

Read an excerpt from Duckworth's book on p. 658.

It's a decent example of the problem with grit, an exciting idea for which the 2 enthusiasm has rapidly outpaced the science. The concept as it's often understood holds that talent isn't the only key to success; it may not even be the most important key to success. Hard work, determination, and perseverance are what truly counts.

These are alluring ideas, similar to the ones that helped propel Malcolm Gladwell's 3 so-called "10,000 hour rule"[1] to mainstream popularity. And so it's little wonder that grit has taken off. A 2007 academic paper lead-authored by Duckworth has been cited 1,157 times, according to *Google Scholar*, and Duckworth's six-minute TED Talk from 2013 on the subject has been watched more than 8.4 million times. (Duckworth has said she was not thrilled with the title assigned to that talk: "The key to success? Grit.") But the concept has perhaps especially resonated with educators across the country: Earlier this year, school districts in the San Francisco area announced plans to begin testing students on grit and other forms of emotional intelligence; other schools have instituted things like Grit Week, in which students set goals for their scores on upcoming standardized tests.

In the selection from *David and Goliath* (p. 676), Gladwell explores the idea that having grit can make you a giant-killer.

This is a problem. The existing research on grit is exciting, but it's too new to 4 apply to educational policy in any meaningful way. As a result, too many of the current applications are shallow interpretations that only sort of capture the vague gist of grit, no matter how well intentioned the educators backing them happen to be. In a review of Duckworth's book published by the magazine *Quillette* (and shared widely on social media over the weekend by educators and psychologists alike), writer Parker Brown references research published earlier this year that seems to poke a few holes in the theory of grit:

> More importantly, they found that what Duckworth and colleagues defined as grit is hardly distinguishable from conscientiousness, one of the classic Big Five traits in psychology. The study, which included a representative sample of U.K. students, measured grit against conscientiousness.

See p. 591 for advice on citing facts and figures to support a claim.

---

1. *"10,000 hour rule"*: An estimation, posited by Malcolm Gladwell in *The Outliers: The Story of Success* (2008), of the total number of hours of "deliberate practice" necessary to achieve mastery in a demanding field. Many experts now argue that the number varies greatly by field.

Grit, researchers discovered, accounts for only an additional 0.5% of variation in test scores when compared with conscientiousness. IQ, on the other hand, accounts for nearly 40%, according to Plomin.

Here's the thing: Duckworth completely, totally, absolutely agrees with this cri- 5 tique. She would also like to add: It's missing half the picture.

Grit, as Duckworth has defined it in her research, is a combination of persever- 6 ance and passion—it's just that the former tends to get all the attention, while the latter is overlooked. "I think the misunderstanding—or, at least, one of them—is that it's only the perseverance part that matters," Duckworth told *Science of Us.* "But I think that the passion piece is at least as important. I mean, if you are really, really tenacious and dogged about a goal that's not meaningful to you, and not interesting to you—then that's just drudgery. It's not just determination—it's having a direction that you care about."

> Read Duckworth's definition of "grit" on pp. 658–59.

It's a strange thing, Duckworth said, to have played a significant part in the cre- 7 ation of an idea, only to have that idea run away from you and create a life of its own. In the case of grit, the enthusiasm for the work-ethic piece of the puzzle has outpaced the evidence, and schools across the country are trying to apply a concept that still hasn't had all the kinks quite worked out yet. Back to the test score exam- ple highlighted by *Quillette*: That research equated conscientiousness with grit, and so the finding that conscientiousness didn't predict higher scores—but IQ did—led to the conclusion that grit doesn't live up to the hype. But this interpretation, Duck- worth argues, leaves out the equally important other half of grit: passion. "That report was about, 'Well, maybe grit's not that important,'" Duckworth said. "And my thought when I read that was—how many kids who are 16 years old are passion- ate about their standardized reading and math scores for school?"

Really, the sound of the word *grit* itself is not helping matters, Duckworth 8 pointed out. The word sounds like sweatiness, or dirtiness; it brings to mind the unpleasantness of effort. You *grit* your teeth—or, for another example, think of the single-minded toughness embodied by the heroes in *True Grit*. Grit sounds serious; it does not, on the other hand, sound like much fun.

As such, perseverance would seem to be the more difficult half of grit: How, for 9 instance, do you get students to work harder on their schoolwork? And yet Duck- worth's work has found just the opposite: It tends to be the passion part of grit that people need more help with. "I find that people's passion scores are lower than their perseverance scores," Duckworth said. She's not yet sure exactly why this is, but she has a theory. "One possibility is that people can learn to work hard and be resilient, but to find something that would make you say, 'This is so interesting to me—I'm so committed to it that I'm going to stick with it over years'—that kind of passion may, in some ways, be harder to come by."

Recently, Duckworth heard about the school that was instituting a Grit Week in 10 order to boost its students' standardized testing scores, a goal she 100 percent would *not* have picked, for one simple reason: Who ever heard of a teenager being passionate about standardized tests? "The focus on just thinking about standardized test scores as being synonymous with achievement for teenagers is ridiculous, right?" she said. "There are so many things that kids care about, where they excel, where they try hard, where they learn important life lessons, that are not picked up by test scores.

For tips on using expert testimony in an argument, see p. 592.

"I mean, most kids, at that age, honestly, are finding their passions in things 11 outside of school—being on the football team, or dancing ballet, or playing piano, or being in the school play. For some kids, it's getting a job, and finding that they really love selling things," she continued. "For that school . . . I encouraged them to listen to me when I said, 'You know, I don't really think that's a great focus for Grit Week. Why don't we have a different focus, which is to talk about how to help them find goals that they *do* find meaningful?'"

The consequences of hasty applications of grit in an educational context are not 12 yet clear, but Duckworth can imagine them. To be sure, it's not that she faults these educators—in many ways, she says, these are the best in the field, the ones who are *most* excited about trying innovative new ways of helping their students succeed. But by placing too much emphasis on grit, the danger is "that grit becomes a scapegoat—another reason to blame kids for not doing well, or to say that we don't have a responsibility as a society to help them." She worries that some interpretations of her work might make a student's failure seem like *his* problem, as if he just didn't work hard enough. "I think to separate and pit against each other character strengths on the one hand—like grit—and situational opportunities on the other is a false dichotomy," she said. "Kids need to develop character, *and* they need our support in doing so."

Currently, Duckworth is engaging in the somewhat meta challenge of applying a 13 little grit to uncover the best potential ways to apply the existing grit research. Her Character Lab, at the University of Pennsylvania, is in the process of recruiting two dozen teachers, who will work together with scientists to come up with ways of translating the evidence into worksheets or curricula that would make sense for use in a classroom. One worry she has is that the initial enthusiasm over the idea may have led to some misapplications of grit in the classroom—things that inevitably will not work, and may in turn lead to grit being dismissed someday very soon as yet another passing fad. "I don't want to dampen the enthusiasm," she said. "But at the same time, I don't want us to get ahead of ourselves." ♦

FOR CLOSE READING

1. Melissa Dahl cites research that equates grit with conscientiousness, "one of the classic Big Five traits in psychology" (4). Do some research on the other four traits of the standard five-factor model (FFM) of human character and personality. Why is this often called the OCEAN or CANOE model?

2. As reported by Dahl, the psychologist Angela Duckworth defines "grit" as a combination of "perseverance and passion" (6). How is this different from standard definitions and specialized psychological definitions of "conscientiousness"?

3. According to Dahl, Duckworth contends that grit scores are a better predictor of success in school and elsewhere than IQ scores. Why do the researchers who equate grit with conscientiousness think IQ is the better predictor? Why does Duckworth—and Dahl, too, apparently—think they're wrong?

4. In Dahl's report, why is Duckworth herself worried about the "hype" generated by other people's enthusiastic claims that grit is the "key to success" (3)? Is she right to be worried? Why or why not?

5. What are the direction and purpose of Duckworth's research now, as reported by Dahl?

STRATEGIES AND STRUCTURES

1. Angela Duckworth, says Dahl, readily admits that her notion of grit has limitations; thus she calls for further research on the subject. As a general strategy of ARGUMENT, is this a wise approach; or is it simply admitting defeat right off the bat? Explain.

2. "Don't Believe the Hype about Grit" is a journalist's report on recent ideas in popular psychology that was published online. Do some research on New York magazine's website The Cut, including its target AUDIENCE and typical topics, and decide whether posting her report on the site was or was not a good strategy for Dahl to reach a broad audience. How credible is her report in general? Why do you think so? (Use the strategies for evaluating internet sources in Chapter 17 to support your response.)

3. Why are there no formal source citations in this report? Should there be? Or is Dahl justified in identifying her sources more casually here, saying simply, for example: "published by the magazine Quillette (and shared widely on social media over the weekend . . .)" or "Duckworth told Science of Us" (4, 6)? Explain.

4. Other Methods. A key issue in the grit debate has to do with CAUSE AND EFFECT: Is any personality trait, such as grit, sufficient to cause success? Or do other factors come into play as well? How well does Dahl deal with this issue of multiple causes at the conclusion of her article?

THINKING ABOUT LANGUAGE

1. The word "hype" may derive, in part, from **HYPERBOLE**, or intentional overstatement. Writers who use this figure of speech typically expect their readers to recognize that they're being "hyped." What about the kind of overselling that Dahl is talking about? What sort of reaction is the advertiser or seller typically hoping to solicit from the audience or consumer?

2. Onomatopoeic words are words that sound like what they refer to, such as "buzz." To what extent is "grit" an example of **ONOMATOPOEIA**? Why do Dahl and Duckworth nonetheless think "the sound of the word *grit* itself is not helping matters" (8)? Might it actually be one reason "grit has taken off" as a concept (3)? Explain.

3. Look up the definition of "scapegoat" (12). Why might Duckworth, as the champion of grit, nonetheless argue that overemphasizing grit could make scapegoats out of some "kids" (12)?

4. A "dichotomy" is a division of things or ideas into two categories with no overlap between them. What is the error in reasoning called false dichotomy (12)? To what particular false dichotomy is Dahl (and Duckworth) referring in her conclusion (12)? Explain.

FOR WRITING

1. Grit, says Dahl, is "an exciting idea" (2) but one that's overhyped. In collaboration with classmates, draw up a list of the reasons and examples you would cite both in support of and in opposition to this claim.

2. In a paragraph, **DESCRIBE** and **DEFINE** one of the following character or personality traits as identified by psychologists today: conscientiousness, openness, extroversion, agreeableness, neuroticism.

3. In a paragraph or two, define "grit" as you understand the concept from Duckworth's, Dahl's, and other people's definitions of the trait. Give at least one **EXAMPLE** of gritty behavior.

4. When psychologists ask subjects to describe themselves or others using common terms like "conscientiousness," "openness," or "grit," they are conducting research based on the lexical theory of psychological description. Do some research on this theory, and write an **ARGUMENT** of five to seven paragraphs in support of or in opposition to it. Be sure to comment on the aspect of the theory that says important character traits that actually shape people's lives will become part of ordinary speech.

MALCOLM GLADWELL

David and Goliath

Malcolm Gladwell (b. 1963) is a journalist and writer of popular nonfiction who typically draws on "academic research for insights, theories, direction, or inspiration." Born in England, Gladwell grew up in Canada, where he graduated from the University of Toronto. He then moved to Indiana to take a writing job with the *American Spectator* magazine. In 1987, he became a business and science reporter for the *Washington Post,* and in 1996 he joined the *New Yorker* as a staff writer. Gladwell is the author of *The Tipping Point: How Little Things Can Make a Big Difference* (2000), *Outliers: The Story of Success* (2008), and *Talking to Strangers: What We Should Know about the People We Don't Know* (2019), among other books. He is also the host of the podcast *Revisionist History.*

In this selection from the introduction to *David and Goliath: Underdogs, Misfits, and the Art of Battling Giants* (2013), Gladwell reinterprets the ancient biblical story of the conflict between the shepherd boy and the giant. "Why has there been so much misunderstanding," he asks elsewhere in the book, "around that day in the Valley of Elah?" The answer lies, he claims, in "the folly of our assumptions about power." King Saul, says Gladwell, is reluctant at first to let David fight the giant because the king "thinks of power in terms of physical might. He doesn't appreciate that power can come in other forms as well—in breaking rules, in substituting speed and surprise for strength." In *David and Goliath,* Gladwell's ultimate purpose is "to argue that we continue to make that error today, in ways that have consequences for everything from how we educate our children to how we fight crime and disorder."

MLA CITATION: Gladwell, Malcolm. "David and Goliath." *Back to the Lake: A Reader and Guide for Writers,* edited by Thomas Cooley, 5th ed., W. W. Norton, 2024, pp. 677–79.

H E WAS A GIANT, six foot nine at least, wearing a bronze helmet and full body ₁ armor. He carried a javelin, a spear, and a sword. An attendant preceded him, carrying a large shield. The giant faced the Israelites and shouted out: "Choose you a man and let him come down to me! If he prevail in battle against me and strike me down, we shall be slaves to you. But if I prevail and strike him down, you will be slaves to us and serve us."

In the Israelite camp, no one moved. Who could win against such a terrifying ₂ opponent? Then, a shepherd boy who had come down from Bethlehem to bring food to his brothers stepped forward and volunteered. Saul objected: "You cannot go against this Philistine to do battle with him, for you are a lad and he is a man of war from his youth." But the shepherd was adamant. He had faced more ferocious opponents than this, he argued. "When the lion or the bear would come and carry off a sheep from the herd," he told Saul, "I would go after him and strike him down and rescue it from his clutches." Saul had no other options. He relented, and the shepherd boy ran down the hill toward the giant standing in the valley. "Come to me, that I may give your flesh to the birds of the heavens and the beasts of the field," the giant cried out when he saw his opponent approach. Thus began one of history's most famous battles. The giant's name was Goliath. The shepherd boy's name was David. . . .

David and Goliath is a book about what happens when ordinary people confront ₃ giants. By "giants," I mean powerful opponents of all kinds—from armies and mighty warriors to disability, misfortune, and oppression. Each chapter tells the story of a different person—famous or unknown, ordinary or brilliant—who has faced an outsize challenge and been forced to respond. Should I play by the rules or follow my own instincts? Shall I persevere or give up? Should I strike back or forgive?

Using examples to argue a case is discussed on p. 591.

Through these stories, I want to explore two ideas. The first is that much of ₄ what we consider valuable in our world arises out of these kinds of lopsided conflicts, because the act of facing overwhelming odds produces greatness and beauty. And second, that we consistently get these kinds of conflicts wrong. We misread them. We misinterpret them. Giants are not what we think they are. The same qualities that appear to give them strength are often the sources of great weakness. And the fact of being an underdog can *change* people in ways that we often fail to appreciate: it can open doors and create opportunities and educate and enlighten and make possible what might otherwise have seemed unthinkable. We need a better guide to facing giants—and there is no better place to start that journey than with the epic confrontation between David and Goliath three thousand years ago in the Valley of Elah. . . .

What happens next is a matter of legend. David puts one of his stones into the ₅ leather pouch of a sling, and he fires at Goliath's exposed forehead. Goliath falls, stunned. David runs toward him, seizes the giant's sword, and cuts off his head. "The Philistines saw that their warrior was dead," the biblical account reads, "and they fled."

The battle is won miraculously by an underdog who, by all expectations, should   6
not have won at all. This is the way we have told one another the story over the many centuries since. It is how the phrase "David and Goliath" has come to be embedded in our language—as a metaphor for improbable victory. And the problem with that version of the events is that almost everything about it is wrong. . . .

> Gladwell is stating the claim; see how to do this on p. 593.

Goliath is heavy infantry. He thinks that he is going to be engaged in a   7
duel with another heavy-infantryman. . . . When he says, "Come to me, that I may give your flesh to the birds of the heavens and the beasts of the field," the key phrase is "come to me." He means come right up to me so that we can fight at close quarters. When Saul tries to dress David in armor and give him a sword, he is operating under the same assumption. He assumes David is going to fight Goliath hand to hand.

David, however, has no intention of honoring the rituals of single com-   8
bat. When he tells Saul that he has killed bears and lions as a shepherd, he does so not just as testimony to his courage but to make another point as well: that he intends to fight Goliath the same way he has learned to fight wild animals—as a projectile warrior.

> David is also a classic example of grit, as defined by Angela Lee Duckworth (pp. 658–59).

He *runs* toward Goliath, because without armor he has speed and   9
maneuverability. He puts a rock into his sling, and whips it around and around, faster and faster at six or seven revolutions per second, aiming his projectile at Goliath's forehead—the giant's only point of vulnerability. Eitan Hirsch, a ballistics expert with the Israeli Defense Forces, recently did a series of calculations showing that a typical-size stone hurled by an expert slinger at a distance of thirty-five meters would have hit Goliath's head with a velocity of thirty-four meters per second—more than enough to penetrate his skull and render him unconscious or dead. In terms of stopping power, that is equivalent to a fair-size modern handgun. "We find," Hirsch writes, "that David could have slung and hit Goliath in little more than one second—a time so brief that Goliath would not have been able to protect himself and during which he would be stationary for all practical purposes."

What could Goliath do? He was carrying over a hundred pounds of armor. He   10
was prepared for a battle at close range, where he could stand, immobile, warding off blows with his armor and delivering a mighty thrust of his spear. He watched David approach, first with scorn, then with surprise, and then with what can only have been horror—as it dawned on him that the battle he was expecting had suddenly changed shape.

"You come against me with sword and spear and javelin," David said to Goliath, 11 "but I come against you in the name of the Lord Almighty, the God of the armies of Israel, whom you have defied. This day the Lord will deliver you into my hands, and I'll strike you down and cut off your head. . . . All those gathered here will know that it is not by sword or spear that the Lord saves; for the battle is the Lord, and he will give all of you into our hands."

Twice David mentions Goliath's sword and spear, as if to emphasize how pro- 12 foundly different his intentions are. Then he reaches into his shepherd's bag for a stone, and at that point no one watching from the ridges on either side of the valley would have considered David's victory improbable. David was a slinger, and slingers beat infantry, hands down.

"Goliath had as much chance against David," the historian Robert Dohrenwend 13 writes, "as any Bronze Age warrior with a sword would have had against an [opponent] armed with a .45 automatic pistol." ◆

FOR CLOSE READING

1. According to Malcolm Gladwell, why do modern readers of the biblical story of David and Goliath usually get "everything about it . . . wrong" (6)? What false assumptions do they make about power and success?

2. In Gladwell's view, why was David always the likely winner of the conflict with the giant? Is Gladwell right? Why or why not?

3. Goliath isn't the only giant Gladwell has in mind here. In his extended **DEFINITION**, what does he come to mean by "giants" and by battling or "facing" them (4)?

4. "Through these stories," Gladwell writes, "I want to explore two ideas" (4). What are they, and how might these key ideas shed light on the relative importance of grit and other strengths (or weaknesses) of character in overcoming (or submitting to) adversity?

STRATEGIES AND STRUCTURES

1. Gladwell says he wants to explore ideas through stories (4). Why might he choose this strategy instead of explaining whatever ideas he has in mind simply and directly without telling tales?

2. In this selection, Gladwell also seems to be teaching a lesson about reading, particularly about reading (or rereading) familiar stories like the one of David and Goliath. How does he do this, and what are the main points of the lesson?

3. To argue that Goliath's sword was no match for David's sling, Gladwell introduces the testimony of a ballistics expert in the Israeli Defense Forces. Is this sufficient **EVIDENCE** to prove his **CLAIM**? Why or why not?

4. *Other Methods.* "He was a giant, six foot nine at least, wearing a bronze helmet and full body armor" (1). Point to other passages in the text where Gladwell uses DESCRIPTION like this to set the stage for the conflict he's interpreting. How do the descriptive details support his argument?

THINKING ABOUT LANGUAGE

1. Gladwell says that "the phrase 'David and Goliath' has come to be embedded in our language" (6). What does he mean by "embedded"—and by "David and Goliath" as a METAPHOR?

2. Exhibiting an abundance of grit, David remains "adamant," we're told, in his resolve to fight the giant (2). Look up the root meaning of "adamant." How is the word related to "diamond," and why might Gladwell choose this particular word in this context?

3. What is an "underdog" (4), and why might the concept—and that of "top dog" as well—be disturbing to animal lovers?

4. One definition of a myth is a story that people don't believe anymore. What is a "legend" (5)? Explain.

5. Gladwell calls David a "projectile warrior" (8). Is this HYPERBOLE? Why or why not?

FOR WRITING

1. In a paragraph or two, comment on the David and Goliath story as an example of grit (or other traits) on the part of the shepherd and overconfidence (or other traits) on the part of the giant.

2. "Giants are not what we think they are," says Gladwell (4). So what are they? Address this question in a brief essay based on your experience or that of people you know. Be sure to state your THESIS early in the essay, and then restate it in your conclusion.

3. A common form that giants take nowadays is that of the "tech giant," such as *Meta* (formerly *Facebook*) or *Google*. Drawing on the selections in the "Debating the Effects of Living Online and on Our Devices" cluster of this chapter (p. 682) and other sources, write an essay of 500 to 700 words arguing that a particular tech Goliath should (or should not) be cut down to size.

Debating the Importance of Grit

The following questions refer to the arguments on pp. 658–79.

EVALUATING ARGUMENTS

1. Among the four arguments in this cluster, which one best addresses the key issue of how important (or not) grit and related traits are to achieving success? Why do you think so?

2. In your opinion, which of the arguments in this cluster deal(s) most effectively with the interplay of character and circumstance—or nature and nurture—in life and work? Why is this an important issue, according to most of the voices in this debate?

3. Among the selections in this cluster, which ones do you think use NARRATIVE most effectively to support the writers' arguments? Point to particular elements of narrative, such as DIALOGUE and careful PLOTTING, as they appear in specific passages in the texts.

4. What are the direct implications for education and job training of the work of Angela Lee Duckworth (and other researchers) as reported in these four selections? For example, should grit and other aspects of personal character be taught in school? How about moral and ethical values? Explain why or why not.

FOR WRITING

1. Write a paragraph or two explaining which of the arguments in this debate you find most (or least) convincing—and why.

2. Write an argument in the form of a POSITION PAPER on the nature of success and how to achieve it that is fundamentally different from any point of view argued by Duckworth, Dweck, Dahl, or Gladwell. Be sure to support your argument with facts, logical reasoning, and other evidence.

3. Write a 600-to-800-word CRITICAL ANALYSIS of a story or book—such as Gladwell's *David and Goliath*—that deals with characters or real people who have, in Gladwell's words, "faced an outsize challenge and been forced to respond." Be sure to assess the extent to which the conflict offers useful guidance for facing giants, or remains strictly in the realm of the imagination.

DEBATING THE EFFECTS OF LIVING ONLINE AND ON OUR DEVICES

"After a while," says the writer and teacher Roxane Gay, "the lines blur, and it's not at all clear what friend or foe look like, or how we as humans should interact in this place." The blurry "place" to which Gay refers is the internet—or, more accurately, the state of being constantly online and on our devices, particularly our phones. This is relatively new territory—the first iPhone was released in 2007—and we don't yet know the extent of its effects on us. For example, how should we as humans behave here? By spending so much time in this new digital territory, are we missing the social and psychological benefits of face-to-face conversation? Are we losing our ability to feel empathy itself?

The following arguments address these and other questions about the effects of being forever "elsewhere." They are contributed by a writer, three sociologists, and a rhetorician.

Questions about this group of readings can be found on p. 708.

ROXANE GAY

Why People Are So Awful Online

Roxane Gay (b. 1974) is a writer, columnist, and professor in the Critical Theory and Social Justice department of Occidental College in Los Angeles. Born in Omaha, Nebraska, Gay grew up in a Haitian American family in Illinois. A graduate of Norwich University, the oldest private military college in the United States, she earned an MA in creative writing from the University of Nebraska and a PhD in communications from Michigan Technological University. A regular columnist for the *New York Times*, where the following selection appeared in July 2021, Gay focuses on issues of race, gender, and body image in such best-selling books as *Bad Feminist* (2014) and *Hunger: A Memoir of (My) Body* (2017).

Of her writing in general, Gay says, "It's about humanity and empathy." These virtues, she argues in "Why People Are So Awful Online," have all but disappeared in online discourse because of the way people feel they are being treated offline.

WHEN I JOINED *TWITTER* 14 years ago, I was living in Michigan's Upper Penin- 1
sula, attending graduate school. I lived in a town of around 4,000 people, with few Black people or other people of color, not many queer people and not many writers. Online is where I found a community beyond my graduate school peers. I followed and met other emerging writers, many of whom remain my truest friends. I got to share opinions, join in on memes, celebrate people's personal joys, process the news with others and partake in the collective effervescence of watching awards shows with thousands of strangers.

MLA CITATION: Gay, Roxane. "Why People Are So Awful Online." *Back to the Lake: A Reader and Guide for Writers*, edited by Thomas Cooley, 5th ed., W. W. Norton, 2024, pp. 683–86.

Something fundamental has changed since then. I don't enjoy most social media 2 anymore. I've felt this way for a while, but I'm loath to admit it.

Increasingly, I've felt that online engagement is fueled by the hopelessness many 3 people feel when we consider the state of the world and the challenges we deal with in our day-to-day lives. Online spaces offer the hopeful fiction of a tangible cause and effect—an injustice answered by an immediate consequence. On *Twitter*, we can wield a small measure of power, avenge wrongs, punish villains, exalt the pure of heart.

In our quest for this simulacrum of justice, however, we have lost all sense of 4 proportion and scale. We hold in equal contempt a war criminal and a fiction writer who too transparently borrows details from someone else's life. It's hard to calibrate how we engage or argue.

See p. 676 for Malcolm Gladwell's summary and analysis of the biblical David and Goliath story.

In real life, we are fearful Davids staring down seemingly omnipotent 5 Goliaths: a Supreme Court poised to undermine abortion and civil rights; a patch of sea on fire from a gas leak; an incoherent but surprisingly effective attack on teaching children America's real history; the dismantling of the Voting Rights Act; a man whom dozens of women have accused of sexual assault walking free on a technicality. At least online, we can tell ourselves that the power imbalances between us flatten. Suddenly, we are all Goliaths in the Valley of Elah.

It makes me uncomfortable to admit that I have some influence and power 6 online, because it feels so foreign or, maybe, unlikely. My online following came slowly, and then all at once. For years, I had a couple hundred followers. Those numbers slowly inched up to a couple thousand. Then I wrote a couple of books, and blinked, and suddenly hundreds of thousands of people were seeing my tweets. Most of them appreciate my work, though they may disagree with my opinions. Some just hate me, as is their right, and they follow me to scavenge for evidence to support or intensify their enmity. Then there are those who harass me for all kinds of reasons—some aspect of my identity or my work or my presence in the world troubles their emotional waters.

After a while, the lines blur, and it's not at all clear what friend or foe look like, 7 or how we as humans should interact in this place. After being on the receiving end of enough aggression, everything starts to feel like an attack. Your skin thins until you have no defenses left. It becomes harder and harder to distinguish good-faith criticism from pettiness or cruelty. It becomes harder to disinvest from pointless arguments that have nothing at all to do with you. An experience that was once charming and fun becomes stressful and largely unpleasant. I don't think I'm alone in feeling this way. We have all become hammers in search of nails.

One person makes a statement. Others take issue with some aspect of that state- 8 ment. Or they make note of every circumstance the original statement did not account for. Or they misrepresent the original statement and extrapolate it to a broader issue in which they are deeply invested. Or they take a singular instance of something and conflate it with a massive cultural trend. Or they bring up something ridiculous that someone said more than a decade ago as confirmation of . . . who knows?

Or someone popular gets too close to the sun and suddenly can do nothing right. 9 "Likes" are analyzed obsessively, as if clicking a button on social media is representative of an entire ideology. If a mistake is made, it becomes immediate proof of being beyond redemption. Or, if the person is held mildly accountable for a mistake, a chorus rends her or his garments in distress, decrying the inhumanity of "cancel culture."

Every harm is treated as trauma. Vulnerability and difference are weaponized. 10 People assume the worst intentions. Bad-faith arguments abound, presented with righteous bluster.

And these are the more reasonable online arguments. There is another category 11 entirely of racists, homophobes, transphobes, xenophobes and other bigots who target the subjects of their ire relentlessly and are largely unchecked by the platforms enabling them. And then, of course, there are the straight-up trolls, gleefully wreaking havoc.

As someone who has been online for a long time, I have seen all kinds of ridicu- 12 lous arguments and conversations. I have participated in all kinds of ridiculous arguments and conversations. Lately, I've been thinking that what drives so much of the anger and antagonism online is our helplessness offline. Online we want to be good, to do good, but despite these lofty moral aspirations, there is little generosity or patience, let alone human kindness. There is a desperate yearning for emotional safety. There is a desperate hope that if we all become perfect enough and demand the same perfection from others, there will be no more harm or suffering.

It is infuriating. It is also entirely understandable. Some days, as I am reading the 13 news, I feel as if I am drowning. I think most of us do. At least online, we can use our voices and know they can be heard by someone.

It's no wonder that we seek control and justice online. It's no wonder that the 14 tenor of online engagement has devolved so precipitously. It's no wonder that some of us have grown weary of it.

I don't regret the time I've spent on social media. I've met interesting people. I've 15 had real-life adventures instigated by virtual relationships. I've been emboldened to challenge myself and grow as a person and, yes, clap back if you clap first.

But I have more of a life than I once did. I have a wife, a busy career, aging par- 16 ents and a large family. I have more physical mobility and, in turn, more interest in being active and out in the world. I now spend most of my time with people who are not Very Online. When I talk to them about some weird or frustrating internet conflagration, they tend to look at me as if I am speaking a foreign language from a distant land. And, I suppose, I am. ◆

FOR CLOSE READING

1. Fourteen years before writing this essay, when she was still in graduate school, why did Roxane Gay join *Twitter*?

2. According to Gay, how has "online engagement" (3) fundamentally changed "since then" (2)?

3. Gay says she no longer enjoys being constantly engaged with others on social media. Why is she "loath to admit it" (2)?

4. "Some days, as I am reading the news," Gay writes, "I feel as if I am drowning." Why might she feel this way? Is she right to think that "most of us do" (13)?

5. Gay says she is now spending much more of her time offline than she once did. What is she doing instead?

STRATEGIES AND STRUCTURES

1. Gay's CLAIM that the "tenor of online engagement has devolved . . . precipitously" (14) in recent years is based largely on her personal experience with social media and the internet. Which specific aspects of that experience, as she reports it, do you think best support (or fail to support) her ARGUMENT? Why?

2. After speaking mostly in the first person ("I," "we") in the introductory paragraphs of her essay (1–7), Gay switches in the middle section (8–11) to the third person ("one," "they"). How does this shift in point of view, grammatical and otherwise, help establish her CREDIBILITY as a critical observer of online behavior?

3. Gay switches back to a first-person point of view in the concluding paragraphs of her essay (12–16). Does this return to a personal viewpoint serve as an effective way to conclude her argument? Why or why not?

4. What point of view is Gay representing when she refers to people "who look at [her] as if [she is] speaking a foreign language" (16)?

5. *Other Methods.* In the last part of her essay, Gay ANALYZES what she sees as the underlying CAUSE of bad behavior online—namely, "our helplessness offline" (12). To what specific causes does she attribute this general EFFECT?

THINKING ABOUT LANGUAGE

1. Look up the meaning of the word "simulacrum." Why might Gay refer to an online system of rewards and punishments as a "simulacrum" of justice rather than as justice itself (4)?

2. Explain what Gay means by using the **METAPHOR** "hammers in search of nails" (7). Is it an effective way to describe people's online behavior? Why or why not?

3. What does Gay mean by saying that when someone popular online "gets too close to the sun" they suddenly "can do nothing right" (9)? Google the phrase "fly too close to the sun," and then explain the **ALLUSION**.

4. Why does Gay capitalize "Very Online" (16)?

5. A "conflagration" (16) is a great fire that threatens life and property. Explain the **IRONY** in Gay's use of the term in the final paragraph of her essay.

FOR WRITING

1. In a few paragraphs, recall your earliest experiences of using social media. Be sure to say what you expected from engaging with people you likely would never meet in person. Did your experiences match your expectations? Include a few **EXAMPLES** in your **NARRATIVE**.

2. Write a brief **PROFILE** of a media influencer like Roxane Gay whom you have come to admire (or otherwise) from following them online. Be sure to give reasons for your opinion of this person.

3. Write a five-to-seven-paragraph **POSITION PAPER** in which you support (or refute) Gay's **THESIS** that the way people behave online is "fueled by the hopelessness many people feel when [they] consider the state of the world and the challenges [they] deal with in [their] day-to-day lives" (3).

SHERRY TURKLE

Stop Googling. Let's Talk.

Sherry Turkle (b. 1948) is a professor of the Social Studies of Science and Technology at the Massachusetts Institute of Technology and a licensed clinical psychologist. Turkle was born in New York and holds degrees from Radcliffe College and Harvard University, where she earned a doctorate in sociology and personality psychology. Beginning with *The Second Self: Computers and the Human Spirit* (1984), Turkle's work deals with the "unintended consequences" of technology on people's everyday lives. Founding director of the MIT Initiative on Technology and the Self, she is an expert on culture and therapy, mobile technology, social networking, and sociable robotics. Most recently, her books and essays—including "Stop Googling. Let's Talk." (*New York Times*, September 2015), *Reclaiming Conversation: The Power of Talk in a Digital Age* (2015), and *The Empathy Diaries: A Memoir* (2021)—focus on the need for face-to-face interaction. Today, says Turkle, many people "would rather text than talk." Face-to-face conversation, however, she argues, is our best "antidote to the algorithmic way of looking at life."

C OLLEGE STUDENTS TELL ME they know how to look someone in the eye and type on their phones at the same time, their split attention undetected. They say it's a skill they mastered in middle school when they wanted to text in class without getting caught. Now they use it when they want to be both with their friends and, as some put it, "elsewhere." 1

These days, we feel less of a need to hide the fact that we are dividing our attention. In a 2015 study by the Pew Research Center, 89 percent of cellphone owners 2

MLA CITATION: Turkle, Sherry. "Stop Googling. Let's Talk." *Back to the Lake: A Reader and Guide for Writers*, edited by Thomas Cooley, 5th ed., W. W. Norton, 2024, pp. 688–93.

said they had used their phones during the last social gathering they attended. But they weren't happy about it; 82 percent of adults felt that the way they used their phones in social settings hurt the conversation.

I've been studying the psychology of online connectivity for more than 30 years. For the past five, I've had a special focus: What has happened to face-to-face conversation in a world where so many people say they would rather text than talk? I've looked at families, friendships and romance. I've studied schools, universities and workplaces. When college students explain to me how dividing their attention plays out in the dining hall, some refer to a "rule of three." In a conversation among five or six people at dinner, you have to check that three people are paying attention—heads up—before you give yourself permission to look down at your phone. So conversation proceeds, but with different people having their heads up at different times. The effect is what you would expect: Conversation is kept relatively light, on topics where people feel they can drop in and out.

Young people spoke to me enthusiastically about the good things that flow from a life lived by the rule of three, which you can follow not only during meals but all the time. First of all, there is the magic of the always available elsewhere. You can put your attention wherever you want it to be. You can always be heard. You never have to be bored. When you sense that a lull in the conversation is coming, you can shift your attention from the people in the room to the world you can find on your phone. But the students also described a sense of loss.

One 15-year-old I interviewed at a summer camp talked about her reaction when she went out to dinner with her father and he took out his phone to add "facts" to their conversation. "Daddy," she said, "stop Googling. I want to talk to you." A 15-year-old boy told me that someday he wanted to raise a family, not the way his parents are raising him (with phones out during meals and in the park and during his school sports events) but the way his parents think they are raising him—with no phones at meals and plentiful family conversation. One college junior tried to capture what is wrong about life in his generation. "Our texts are fine," he said. "It's what texting does to our conversations when we are together that's the problem."

> A single example can help support an entire argument if it is truly representative (p. 591).

It's a powerful insight. Studies of conversation both in the laboratory and in natural settings show that when two people are talking, the mere presence of a phone on a table between them or in the periphery of their vision changes both what they talk about and the degree of connection they feel. People keep the conversation on topics where they won't mind being interrupted. They don't feel as invested in each other. Even a silent phone disconnects us.

In 2010, a team at the University of Michigan led by the psychologist Sara Konrath put together the findings of 72 studies that were conducted over a 30-year period. They found a 40 percent decline in empathy among college students, with most of the decline taking place after 2000.

Across generations, technology is implicated in this assault on empathy. We've 8 gotten used to being connected all the time, but we have found ways around conversation—at least from conversation that is open-ended and spontaneous, in which we play with ideas and allow ourselves to be fully present and vulnerable. But it is in this type of conversation—where we learn to make eye contact, to become aware of another person's posture and tone, to comfort one another and respectfully challenge one another—that empathy and intimacy flourish. In these conversations, we learn who we are.

Of course, we can find empathic conversations today, but the trend line is clear. 9 It's not only that we turn away from talking face to face to chat online. It's that we don't allow these conversations to happen in the first place because we keep our phones in the landscape.

In our hearts, we know this, and now research is catching up with our intuitions. 10 We face a significant choice. It is not about giving up our phones but about using them with greater intention. Conversation is there for us to reclaim. For the failing connections of our digital world, it is the talking cure.

The trouble with talk begins young. A few years ago, a private middle school 11 asked me to consult with its faculty: Students were not developing friendships the way they used to. At a retreat, the dean described how a seventh grader had tried to exclude a classmate from a school social event. It's an age-old problem, except that this time when the student was asked about her behavior, the dean reported that the girl didn't have much to say: "She was almost robotic in her response. She said, 'I don't have feelings about this.' She couldn't read the signals that the other student was hurt."

The dean went on: "Twelve-year-olds play on the playground like 8-year-olds. The 12 way they exclude one another is the way 8-year-olds would play. They don't seem able to put themselves in the place of other children."

One teacher observed that the students "sit in the dining hall and look at their 13 phones. When they share things together, what they are sharing is what is on their phones." Is this the new conversation? If so, it is not doing the work of the old conversation. The old conversation taught empathy. These students seem to understand each other less.

But we are resilient. The psychologist Yalda T. Uhls was the lead author on a 14 2014 study of children at a device-free outdoor camp. After five days without phones or tablets, these campers were able to read facial emotions and correctly identify the emotions of actors in videotaped scenes significantly better than a control group. What fostered these new empathic responses? They talked to one another. In conversation, things go best if you pay close attention and learn how to put yourself in someone else's shoes. This is easier to do without your phone in hand. Conversation is the most human and humanizing thing that we do.

I have seen this resilience during my own research at a device-free summer camp. 15
At a nightly cabin chat, a group of 14-year-old boys spoke about a recent three-day
wilderness hike. Not that many years ago, the most exciting aspect of that hike might
have been the idea of roughing it or the beauty of unspoiled nature. These days, what
made the biggest impression was being phoneless. One boy called it "time where you
have nothing to do but think quietly and talk to your friends." The campers also
spoke about their new taste for life away from the online feed. Their embrace of the
virtue of disconnection suggests a crucial connection: The capacity for empathic
conversation goes hand in hand with the capacity for solitude.

In solitude we find ourselves; we prepare ourselves to come to conversation with 16
something to say that is authentic, ours. If we can't gather ourselves, we can't recognize other people for who they are. If we are not content to be alone, we turn others
into the people we need them to be. If we don't know how to be alone, we'll only
know how to be lonely.

A virtuous circle links conversation to the capacity for self-reflection. When we are 17
secure in ourselves, we are able to really hear what other people have to say. At the
same time, conversation with other people, both in intimate settings and in larger
social groups, leads us to become better at inner dialogue.

But we have put this virtuous circle in peril. We turn time alone into a problem 18
that needs to be solved with technology. Timothy D. Wilson, a psychologist at the
University of Virginia, led a team that explored our capacity for solitude. People
were asked to sit in a chair and think, without a device or a book. They were told
that they would have from six to 15 minutes alone and that the only rules were that
they had to stay seated and not fall asleep. In one experiment, many student subjects opted to give themselves mild electric shocks rather than sit alone with their
thoughts.

People sometimes say to me that they can see how one might be disturbed when 19
people turn to their phones when they are together. But surely there is no harm
when people turn to their phones when they are by themselves? If anything, it's our
new form of being together.

But this way of dividing things up misses the essential connection between soli- 20
tude and conversation. In solitude we learn to concentrate and imagine, to listen to
ourselves. We need these skills to be fully present in conversation.

Every technology asks us to confront human values. This is a good thing, because 21
it causes us to reaffirm what they are. If we are now ready to make face-to-face conversation a priority, it is easier to see what the next steps should be. We are not looking for simple solutions. We are looking for beginnings. Some of them may seem
familiar by now, but they are no less challenging for that. Each addresses only a
small piece of what silences us. Taken together, they can make a difference.

The Toulmin method (p. 598) explains why conclusions like these are "warranted."

One start toward reclaiming conversation is to reclaim solitude. Some of the most crucial conversations you will ever have will be with yourself. Slow down sufficiently to make this possible. And make a practice of doing one thing at a time. Think of unitasking as the next big thing. In every domain of life, it will increase performance and decrease stress.

But doing one thing at a time is hard, because it means asserting ourselves over what technology makes easy and what feels productive in the short term. Multitasking comes with its own high, but when we chase after this feeling, we pursue an illusion. Conversation is a human way to practice unitasking.

Our phones are not accessories, but psychologically potent devices that change not just what we do but who we are. A second path toward conversation involves recognizing the degree to which we are vulnerable to all that connection offers. We have to commit ourselves to designing our products and our lives to take that vulnerability into account. We can choose not to carry our phones all the time. We can park our phones in a room and go to them every hour or two while we work on other things or talk to other people. We can carve out spaces at home or work that are device-free, sacred spaces for the paired virtues of conversation and solitude. Families can find these spaces in the day to day—no devices at dinner, in the kitchen and in the car. Introduce this idea to children when they are young so it doesn't spring up as punitive but as a baseline of family culture. In the workplace, too, the notion of sacred spaces makes sense: Conversation among employees increases productivity.

We can also redesign technology to leave more room for talking to each other. The "do not disturb" feature on the iPhone offers one model. You are not interrupted by vibrations, lights or rings, but you can set the phone to receive calls from designated people or to signal when someone calls you repeatedly. Engineers are ready with more ideas: What if our phones were not designed to keep us attached, but to do a task and then release us? What if the communications industry began to measure the success of devices not by how much time consumers spend on them but by whether it is time well spent?

It is always wise to approach our relationship with technology in the context that goes beyond it. We live, for example, in a political culture where conversations are blocked by our vulnerability to partisanship as well as by our new distractions. We thought that online posting would make us bolder than we are in person, but a 2014 Pew study demonstrated that people are less likely to post opinions on social media when they fear their followers will disagree with them. Designing for our vulnerabilities means finding ways to talk to people, online and off, whose opinions differ from our own.

Sometimes it simply means hearing people out. A college junior told me that she shied away from conversation because it demanded that one live by the rigors of what she calls the "seven minute rule." It takes at least seven minutes to see how a conversation is going to unfold. You can't go to your phone before those seven minutes are up. If the conversation goes quiet, you have to let it be. For conversation, like life, has silences—what some young people I interviewed called "the boring bits." It is often in the moments when we stumble, hesitate and fall silent that we most reveal ourselves to one another.

The young woman who is so clear about the seven minutes that it takes to see where a conversation is going admits that she often doesn't have the patience to wait for anything near that kind of time before going to her phone. In this she is characteristic of what the psychologists Howard Gardner and Katie Davis called the "app generation," which grew up with phones in hand and apps at the ready. It tends toward impatience, expecting the world to respond like an app, quickly and efficiently. The app way of thinking starts with the idea that actions in the world will work like algorithms: Certain actions will lead to predictable results. 28

This attitude can show up in friendship as a lack of empathy. Friendships become things to manage; you have a lot of them, and you come to them with tools. So here is a first step: To reclaim conversation for yourself, your friendships and society, push back against viewing the world as one giant app. It works the other way, too: Conversation is the antidote to the algorithmic way of looking at life because it teaches you about fluidity, contingency and personality. 29

This is our moment to acknowledge the unintended consequences of the technologies to which we are vulnerable, but also to respect the resilience that has always been ours. We have time to make corrections and remember who we are— creatures of history, of deep psychology, of complex relationships, of conversations, artless, risky and face to face. ◆ 30

FOR CLOSE READING

1. According to Sherry Turkle, what is the "rule of three" (3)?

2. How did the tenor of their in-person conversation change when the students whom Turkle interviewed followed "the rule of three" (3) and other strategies for dividing their attention?

3. What is the appeal for many people of texting while talking, according to Turkle's research? If texting has a negative effect on conversation and friendship, why do so many people do it anyway?

4. What does Turkle mean when she says, "Even a silent phone disconnects us" (6)?

5. What remedy does Turkle propose for "the unintended consequences of the technologies to which we are vulnerable" (30)?

STRATEGIES AND STRUCTURES

1. "I've been studying the psychology of online connectivity for more than 30 years" (3). Throughout her essay, Turkle refers directly to her role as a researcher. How and how well do such references help establish her CREDIBILITY as an expert in the field she is studying? Explain.

2. Turkle and other researchers claim to see a "decline in empathy among college students" in recent years (7). What EVIDENCE does Turkle give to support this CLAIM? Is it sufficient to prove her point? Why or why not?

3. "It is not about giving up our phones" (10). If Turkle is not arguing for giving up our phones entirely, what specific behaviors is she advocating? Where does she state them most clearly and directly?

4. Turkle makes the argument that the capacity for empathy "goes hand in hand with the capacity for solitude" (15). How and how well does she use LOGICAL REASONING to support this claim?

5. Besides citing her own research, Turkle mentions the findings of four professional and academic studies as EVIDENCE. Point to the paragraphs where she shares this information, and for each case explain whether you think hearing from these experts works or does not work to strengthen her argument.

6. *Other Methods.* Turkle begins her essay by ANALYZING the negative EFFECTS of texting and other digital distractions on conversation. What is she analyzing in the second half of her essay when she talks about "reclaiming conversation" (22)? How does her final paragraph (30) bring these two threads together?

THINKING ABOUT LANGUAGE

1. What do Turkle and the students she talked to mean by "elsewhere" (1)? What's "magic" about being there (4)?

2. Turkle calls conversation "the talking cure" (10). What does the phrase usually refer to? After researching its origin, explain the pun.

3. "Resilience" (15) is an important component of Turkle's argument. How and how well does she DEFINE it?

4. What would be the opposite of a "virtuous circle" like the one Turkle describes in paragraph 17?

5. When applied to conversation, what are the implications of the term "reclaim" (10, 22, 29) as opposed to, say, "revive" or "reinvent"?

FOR WRITING

1. When discussing "the rule of three" (3), Turkle writes mostly about its negative effects. Yet many of the young people she talked to "spoke . . . enthusiastically about the good things that flow from a life lived by the rule of three" (4). In a paragraph or two, explain what some of those good things might be.

2. Turkle is most concerned about the effects of texting on face-to-face conversation, but using our phones to send text messages has also changed how we actually talk on the phone. Based on your own experience and that of others you know, outline the main points you would make in a persuasive essay in which you argue that talking on the phone is (or is not) less satisfying than it used to be.

3. In her book *Reclaiming Conversation*, Turkle speaks of the 2008–10 period as "the early days of texting." Do some research on the development of text messaging, and then write a five-to-seven-paragraph REPORT on how the technology came about and what it promised to do for society. In your opinion, did it or did it not accomplish what it promised?

4. "So, if they care about you," Turkle writes in *Reclaiming Conversation*, "you should be getting a text back. If they care. But in romantic texting, responding to a communication with silence happens all the time. It's the NOTHING gambit." To what extent have you experienced this? Write a 400-to-700-word ANALYSIS of the EFFECTS of silence—getting nothing in response—on your own online communications, romantic or otherwise.

JONATHAN HAIDT AND JEAN M. TWENGE

Pulling Teenagers Away from Cell Phones

Jonathan Haidt (b. 1963) is a social psychologist and the Thomas F. Cooley Professor of Ethical Leadership at New York University's Stern School of Business. Haidt is best known for his research on the relationship between morality and politics. His books include *The Coddling of the American Mind: How Good Intentions and Bad Ideas Are Setting Up a Generation for Failure* (2018). Also a social psychologist, Jean M. Twenge (b. 1971) teaches at San Diego State University. She is the author of *iGen: Why Today's Super-connected Kids Are Growing Up Less Rebellious, More Tolerant, Less Happy—and Completely Unprepared for Adulthood* (2017) and *Generations* (2023).

Together, Haidt and Twenge have spent years studying the effects of smartphones and social media on daily life. These include a pervading sense of "loneliness," particularly among teenagers. The best remedy for this social and psychological malaise, they argue in "Pulling Teenagers Away from Cell Phones" (editor's title; from the *New York Times*, July 2021), is a return to "old-fashioned, in-person socializing."

A S STUDENTS RETURN TO SCHOOL in the coming weeks, there will be close attention to their mental health. Many problems will be attributed to the Covid pandemic, but in fact we need to look back further, to 2012.[*]

MLA CITATION: Haidt, Jonathan, and Jean M. Twenge. "Pulling Teenagers Away from Cell Phones." *Back to the Lake: A Reader and Guide for Writers*, edited by Thomas Cooley, 5th ed., W.W. Norton, 2024, pp. 696–700.

[*] Haidt and Twenge are writing in the summer of 2021, more than a year before the opening of the first "normal" school year after the COVID-19 pandemic upended student life—and that of everyone else.

That's when rates of teenage depression, loneliness, self-harm and suicide began ₂ to rise sharply. By 2019, just before the pandemic, rates of depression among adolescents had nearly doubled.

When we first started to see these trends in our work as psychologists studying ₃ Gen Z (those born after 1996), we were puzzled. The U.S. economy was steadily improving over these years, so economic problems stemming from the 2008 Great Recession were not to blame. It was difficult to think of any other national event from the early 2010s that reverberated through the decade.

We both came to suspect the same culprits: smartphones in general and social ₄ media in particular. Jean discovered that 2012 was the first year that a majority of Americans owned a smartphone; by 2015, two-thirds of teens did too. This was also the period when social media use moved from optional to ubiquitous among adolescents.

Jonathan learned, while writing an essay with the technologist Tobias Rose- ₅ Stockwell, that the major social media platforms changed profoundly from 2009 to 2012. In 2009, *Facebook* added the like button, *Twitter* added the retweet button and, over the next few years, users' feeds became algorithmicized based on "engagement," which mostly meant a post's ability to trigger emotions.

By 2012, as the world now knows, the major platforms had created an outrage ₆ machine that made life online far uglier, faster, more polarized and more likely to incite performative shaming. In addition, as *Instagram* grew in popularity over the next decade, it had particularly strong effects on girls and young women, inviting them to "compare and despair" as they scrolled through posts from friends and strangers showing faces, bodies and lives that had been edited and re-edited until many were closer to perfection than to reality.

For many years now, some experts have been saying that smartphones and social ₇ media harm teens while others have dismissed those concerns as just another moral panic, no different from those that accompanied the arrival of video games, television and even comic books. One powerful argument made by skeptics is this: The smartphone was adopted in many countries around the world at approximately the same time, so why aren't teens in all of these countries experiencing more mental health issues the way Americans have been? Where's the evidence for that?

This is a difficult question to answer because there is no global survey of adoles- ₈ cent mental health with data before 2012 and continuing to the present. However, there is something close. The Program for International Student Assessment, or PISA, has surveyed 15-year-olds in dozens of countries every three years since 2000. In all but two administrations, the survey included six questions about loneliness at school. Loneliness is certainly not the same as depression, but the two are correlated—lonely teens are often depressed teens, and vice versa. And loneliness is painful even without depression.

So what does the PISA survey show? In a paper we just published in *The Journal* 9
of Adolescence, we report that in 36 out of 37 countries, loneliness at school has
increased since 2012. We grouped the 37 countries into four geographic and cultural regions, and we found the same pattern in all regions: Teenage loneliness was
relatively stable between 2000 and 2012, with fewer than 18 percent reporting high
levels of loneliness. But in the six years after 2012, rates increased dramatically.
They roughly doubled in Europe, Latin America and the English-speaking countries, and rose by about 50 percent in the East Asian countries.

In order to prove that one event causes another, an argument must meet a number of conditions (p. 358).

This synchronized global increase in teenage loneliness suggests a global 10
cause, and the timing is right for smartphones and social media to be major
contributors. But couldn't the timing just be coincidental? To test our
hypothesis, we sought data on many global trends that might have an
impact on teenage loneliness, including declines in family size, changes in
G.D.P., rising income inequality and increases in unemployment, as well as
more smartphone access and more hours of internet use. The results were
clear: Only smartphone access and internet use increased in lockstep with teenage
loneliness. The other factors were unrelated or inversely correlated.

These analyses don't prove that smartphones and social media are major causes 11
of the increase in teenage loneliness, but they do show that several other causes are
less plausible. If anyone has another explanation for the global increase in loneliness at school, we'd love to hear it.

We have carried out an extensive review of the published research on social 12
media and mental health, and we have found a major limitation: Nearly all of it,
including our own, looks for effects of consumption on the individuals doing the
consuming. The most common scientific question has been: Do individual teens
who consume a lot of social media have worse health outcomes than individual
teens who consume little? The answer is yes, particularly for girls.

We believe, however, that this framework is inadequate because smartphones 13
and social media don't just affect individuals, they affect groups. The smartphone
brought about a planetary rewiring of human interaction. As smartphones became
common, they transformed peer relationships, family relationships and the texture
of daily life for everyone—even those who don't own a phone or don't have an *Instagram* account. It's harder to strike up a casual conversation in the cafeteria or after
class when everyone is staring down at a phone. It's harder to have a deep conversation when each party is interrupted randomly by buzzing, vibrating "notifications."
As Sherry Turkle wrote in her book *Reclaiming Conversation*, life with smartphones
means "we are forever elsewhere."

A year before the Covid-19 pandemic began, a Canadian college student sent one 14
of us an email that illustrates how smartphones have changed social dynamics in
schools. "Gen Z are an incredibly isolated group of people," he wrote. "We have

shallow friendships and superfluous romantic relationships that are mediated and governed to a large degree by social media." He then reflected on the difficulty of talking to his peers:

> There is hardly a sense of community on campus and it's not hard to see why. Often I'll arrive early to a lecture to find a room of 30+ students sitting together in complete silence, absorbed in their smartphones, afraid to speak and be heard by their peers. This leads to further isolation and a weakening of self-identity and confidence, something I know because I've experienced it.

All young mammals play, especially those that live in groups like dogs, chimpan- 15 zees and humans. All such mammals need tens of thousands of social interactions to become socially competent adults. In 2012 it was possible to believe that teens would get those interactions via their smartphones—far more of them, perhaps. But as data accumulates that teenage mental health has changed for the worse since 2012, it now appears that electronically mediated social interactions are like empty calories. Just imagine what teenagers' health would be like today if we had taken 50 percent of the most nutritious food out of their diets in 2012 and replaced those calories with sugar.

So what can we do? We can't turn back time to the pre-smartphone era, nor 16 would we want to, given the many benefits of the technology. But we can take some reasonable steps to help teens get more of what they need.

One important step is to give kids a long period each day when they are not distracted by their devices: the school day. Phones may be useful for getting to and from school, but they should be locked up during the school day so students can practice the lost art of paying full attention to the people around them—including their teachers.

One reason we construct arguments is to persuade people to act on them (p. 588).

A second important step is to delay entry into social media, ideally keeping it 18 entirely out of elementary and middle schools. At present, many 10- and 11-year-olds simply lie about their age to open accounts, and once that happens, other kids don't want to be excluded, so they feel pressured to do the same.

The platforms should—at a minimum—be held legally responsible for enforcing 19 their stated minimum age of 13. Since social media platforms have failed to do so using post-hoc detection methods, they should be required to implement age and identity verification for all new accounts, as many other industries have done. Verified users could still post under pseudonyms, and the verification could be done by reliable third parties rather than by the platforms themselves.

Even before Covid-19, teens were finding themselves increasingly lonely in school. 20 The rapid transition to smartphone-mediated social lives around 2012 is, as we have shown, the prime suspect. Now, after nearly 18 months of social distancing, contagion fears, anxious parenting, remote schooling and increased reliance on devices, will students spontaneously put away their phones and switch back to old-fashioned in-person socializing, at least for the hours that they are together in school? We have a historic opportunity to help them do so. ◆

FOR CLOSE READING

1. According to Jonathan Haidt and Jean M. Twenge, what happened in 2012 and soon after to demand their attention as "psychologists studying Gen Z" (3)?

2. How did social media change "profoundly," according to Haidt and Twenge, when *Facebook* and *Twitter* added, respectively, the "like button" and the "retweet button" (5)?

3. Haidt and Twenge say that *Instagram* has had "particularly strong effects on girls and young women" (6). What are some of those EFFECTS, in their view, and what are the CAUSES?

4. Haidt and Twenge say that social media and smartphone usage have made members of an entire generation more lonely and more detached from one another. Do you agree with this CLAIM? Why or why not?

STRATEGIES AND STRUCTURES

1. How do Haidt and Twenge DEFINE Gen Z? What distinguishes it, according to them, from earlier generations?

2. Haidt and Twenge introduce a NAYSAYER in paragraph 7. How and how effectively do they deal with this "powerful" opposing argument?

3. In paragraphs 8–11, Haidt and Twenge discuss the relationship between "loneliness" and "depression" in teenagers. Are they ANALYZING *causes* here or *correlation* (8), or both? Explain.

4. "So what can we do?" (16). How and how well do Haidt and Twenge answer this RHETORICAL QUESTION with regard to smartphones? Point to specific passages in the text that support your assessment.

5. *Other Methods.* Where and how do Haidt and Twenge analyze CAUSE AND EFFECT to back up their claim that "smartphones don't just affect individuals, they affect groups" (13)? Again, point to specific passages in the text.

THINKING ABOUT LANGUAGE

1. What does "algorithmicized" mean when applied to "users' feeds" on social media (5)? Does the meaning that the authors give provide a full understanding? Do some research on how algorithms work, and then explain their role in triggering a user's reactions based on that person's specific social media use.

2. Why are social media like *Facebook* and *Twitter* often referred to as "platforms" (5)? What are the implications of this METAPHOR?

3. "Compare and despair" (6). Is this an accurate way to describe the experience of using *Instagram* and other social media? Why or why not?

4. Why do you suppose Haidt and Twenge claim that social media have created an "outrage machine" (6) instead of saying simply that they have made people more contentious when online or on their phones? Is their phrase an effective use of HYPERBOLE? Explain.

5. What are "post-hoc detection methods" (19) for determining a social media user's age and identity? Why are post hoc methods inadequate by definition?

FOR WRITING

1. Write a paragraph or two in which you DEFINE "performative shaming" (6). Consider including EXAMPLES from your own experience or that of people you know.

2. Draw up a list of the key points you would make in an ARGUMENT contending that *Facebook, Twitter, Instagram, TikTok*, or some other media platform constitutes "an outrage machine" that makes "life online far uglier, faster, more polarized" (6).

3. By comparison with earlier generations, according to one of Twenge's book titles, members of the iGeneration (people born between roughly 1997 and 2007, aka "iGen" or "Gen Z") are "Super-connected . . . Less Rebellious, More Tolerant, Less Happy—and Completely Unprepared for Adulthood." In a well-reasoned argument of five to seven paragraphs, support or contest this CLAIM. Include a few statistics as well as examples from your personal experience as support.

4. Toward the end of their essay, Haidt and Twenge suggest ways to reduce the negative impacts of spending so much time on smartphones. Sherry Turkle does likewise in her essay on p. 688. Working with a few classmates, BRAINSTORM other ways to achieve more balance between online and offline life; then combine all the ideas into a list that could serve as the basis for a PROCESS ANALYSIS of how best to find that balance.

ANDREA LUNSFORD

Our Semi-literate Youth? Not So Fast

Andrea Lunsford (b. 1942) is a member of the faculty of the Bread Loaf School of English. She is the former director of the Program in Writing and Rhetoric at Stanford University and of the Center for the Study and Teaching of Writing at The Ohio State University. A graduate of the University of Florida, Lunsford taught English at Colonial High School in Orlando before earning her PhD at Ohio State. In addition to her teaching career, she has served as chair of the Modern Language Association Division on Writing, among other notable positions. The author of numerous books and textbooks on writing and rhetoric, she is the general editor of the forthcoming *Norton Anthology of Rhetoric and Writing*.

In "Our Semi-literate Youth? Not So Fast," Lunsford examines the effects of technology on student writing. Based on her research, Lunsford argues that literacy and the nature of writing should be redefined for the digital age—and that teachers of writing should reconsider how they teach.

TWO STORIES ABOUT YOUNG PEOPLE, and especially college-age students, are 1
circulating widely today. One script sees a generation of twitterers and texters, awash in self-indulgence and narcissistic twaddle, most of it riddled with errors. The other script doesn't diminish the effects of technology, but it presents young people as running a rat race that is fueled by the internet and its toys, anxious kids who are inundated with mountains of indigestible information yet obsessed with making the grade, with success, with coming up with the "next big thing," but who lack the writing and speaking skills they need to do so.

MLA CITATION: Lunsford, Andrea. "Our Semi-literate Youth? Not So Fast." *Back to the Lake: A Reader and Guide for Writers*, edited by Thomas Cooley, 5th ed., W. W. Norton, 2024, pp. 702–6.

No doubt there's a grain of truth in both these depictions. But the doom sayers who tell these stories are turning a blind eye on compelling alternative narratives. As one who has spent the last 30-plus years studying the writing of college students, I see a different picture. For those who think *Google* is making us stupid and *Facebook* is frying our brains, let me sketch that picture in briefly.

Anticipating the views of opponents, p. 604, strengthens your own claims.

In 2001, I and my colleagues began a longitudinal study of writing at Stanford, following a randomly selected group of 189 students from their first day on campus through one year beyond graduation; in fact, I am still in touch with a number of the students today. These students—about 12 percent of that year's class—submitted the writing they did for their classes and as much of their out-of-class writing as they wanted to an electronic database, along with their comments on those pieces of writing. Over the years, we collected nearly 15,000 pieces of student writing: lab reports, research essays, *PowerPoint* presentations, problem sets, honors theses, email and textings (in 11 languages), blogs and journals, poems, documentaries, even a full-length play entitled *Hip-Hopera*. While we are still coding these pieces of writing, several results emerged right away. First, these students were writing A LOT, both in class and out, though they were more interested in and committed to writing out of class, what we came to call "life writing," than they were in their school assignments. Second, they were increasingly aware of those to whom they were writing and adjusted their writing styles to suit the occasion and the audience. Third, they wanted their writing to count for something; as they said to us over and over, good writing to them was performative, the kind of writing that "made something happen in the world." Finally, they increasingly saw writing as collaborative, social, and participatory rather than solitary.

So yes, these students did plenty of emailing and texting; they were online a good part of every day; they joined social networking sites enthusiastically. But rather than leading to a new illiteracy, these activities seemed to help them develop a range or *repertoire* of writing styles, tones, and formats along with a range of abilities. Here's a student sending a text message to friends reporting on what she's doing on an internship in Bangladesh (she refers in the first few words to the fact that power has been going on and off ever since she arrived): "Next up: words stolen from before the power went out****~ ~ ~ ~ ~Whadda-ya-know, I am back in Dhaka from the villages of Mymensingh. I'm familiar enough with the villages now that it's harder to find things that really surprise me, though I keep looking ☺." In an informal message, this students feels free to use fragments ("Next up"), slang ("whadda-ya-know"), asterisks and tildes for emphasis, and a smiley.

Now look at a brief report she sends to the faculty adviser for her internship in Bangladesh: "In June of 2003, I traveled to Dhaka, Bangladesh, for 9 weeks to intern for Grameen Bank. Grameen Bank is a micro-credit institution which seeks to alleviate poverty by providing access to financial capital. Grameen Bank provides small loans to poor rural women, who then use the capital to start small businesses and sustain income generating activities." Here the student is all business, using formal academic style to begin her first report. No slang, no use of special-effects markings: just the facts, ma'am.[1] In the thousands of pieces of student writing we have examined, we see students moving with relative ease across levels of style (from the most informal to the most formal): these young people are for the most part aware of the context and audience for their writing—and they make the adjustments necessary to address them effectively.

Ah, you say, but these are students at Stanford—the crème de la crème. And I'll agree that these students were all very keen, very bright. But they were not all strong writers or communicators (though our study shows that they all improved significantly over the five years of the study) and they did not all come from privilege—in fact, a good number far from it. Still, they were part of what students on this campus call the "Stanford bubble." So let's look beyond that bubble to another study I conducted with researcher Karen Lunsford. About 18 months ago, we gathered a sample of first-year student writing from across all regions of the United States, from two-year and four-year schools, big schools and small schools, private and public. Replicating a study I'd conducted twenty-five years ago, we read a random sample of these student essays with a fine-tooth eye, noting every formal error in every piece of writing. And what did we find? First, that the length of student writing has increased nearly three-fold in these 25 years, corroborating the fact that students today are writing more than ever before. Second, we found that while error patterns have changed in the last twenty-five years, the ratio of errors to number of words has remained stable not just for twenty-five years but for the last 100 years. In short, we found that students today certainly make errors—as all writers do—but that they are making no more errors than previous studies have documented. Different errors, yes—but more errors, no. 6

We found, for example, that spelling—the most prevalent error by over 300 percent some 25 years ago—now presents much less of a problem to writers. We can chalk up that change, of course, to spell-checkers, which do a good job overall—but still can't correct words that sound alike (to, too, two). But with technology, you win some and you lose some: the most frequent error in our recent study is "wrong word," and ironically a good number of these wrong words come from advice given by the sometimes-not-so-trusty spell-checkers. The student who seems from the context of the sentence to be trying to write "frantic," for example, apparently accepts the spell-checker's suggestion of "fanatic" instead. And finally, this recent 7

---

1. Phrase made famous by the lead detective on *Dragnet*, a 1950s TV show in which Joe Friday, a stern, no-nonsense cop, said the phrase often during witness interviews.

study didn't turn up any significant interference from internet lingo—no IMHOs, no LOLs, no 2nites, no smileys. Apparently, by the time many, many students get to college, they have a pretty good sense of what's appropriate: at the very least, they know the difference between a *Facebook* friend and a college professor.

In short, the research my colleagues and I have been doing supports what other 8 researchers are reporting about digital technologies and learning. First, a lot of that learning (perhaps most of it) is taking place outside of class, in the literate activities (musical compositions, videos, photo collages, digital stories, comics, documentaries) young people are pursuing on their own. This is what Mimi Ito[2] calls "kid-driven learning." Second, the participatory nature of digital media allows for more—not less—development of literacies, as Henry Jenkins[3] argues compellingly.

If we look beyond the hand-wringing about young people and literacy today, 9 beyond the view that paints them as either brain-damaged by technology or as cogs in the latest race to the top, we will see that the changes brought about by the digital revolution are just that: changes. These changes alter the very grounds of literacy as the definition, nature, and scope of writing are all shifting away from the consumption of discourse to its production across a wide range of genres and media, away from individual "authors" to partici-patory and collaborative partners-in-production; away from a single static standard of correctness to a situated understanding of audience and context and purpose for writing. Luckily, young people are changing as well, moving swiftly to join in this expanded culture of writing. They face huge challenges, of course—challenges of access and of learning ever new ways with words (and images). What students need in facing these challenges is not derision or dismissal but solid and informed instruction. And that's where the real problem may lie—not with student semi-literacy but with that of their teachers. ◆

For more on a situated understanding of audience, see pp. 589 and 591.

Works Cited and Consulted

Fishman, Jenn, et al. "Performing Writing, Performing Literacy." *College Composition and Communication*, vol. 57, no. 3, 2005, pp. 224–52.

Ito, Mizuko, et al. *Hanging Out, Messing Around, and Geeking Out: Kids Living and Learning with New Media*. MIT P, 2009.

Ito, Mizuko, et al. *Living and Learning with New Media: Summary of Findings from the Digital Youth Project*. MIT P, 2009.

Jenkins, Henry. *Confronting the Challenges of Participatory Culture: Media Education for the 21st Century*. MIT P, 2009.

2. Cultural anthropologist (b. 1968) who studies learning and new media.
3. Professor (b. 1958) and author of many books and articles about the role of media.

———. *Convergence Culture: When Old and New Media Collide.* New York UP, 2008.

Lunsford, Andrea A., and Karen J. Lunsford. "'Mistakes Are a Fact of Life': A National Comparative Study." *College Composition and Communication*, vol. 59, no. 4, 2008, pp. 781–807.

Rogers, Paul M. *The Development of Writers and Writing Abilities: A Longitudinal Study across and beyond the College-Span.* 2008. U of California, Santa Barbara, PhD dissertation.

FOR CLOSE READING

1. In both of the "stories" that Andrea Lunsford cites at the beginning of her essay, young people today are portrayed as "semi-literate"—as the essay's title suggests. What are the main differences between these two narratives?

2. When Lunsford and her colleagues did a longitudinal study of undergraduate student writing at Stanford, she says, "several results emerged right away" (3). What were some of those preliminary results?

3. A longitudinal study typically observes the same participants over an extended period of time. How many students were involved in Lunsford's study, and for how long?

4. Would a longitudinal study of the work of one hundred people likely be more accurate than one involving ten participants? Why or why not?

5. According to Lunsford, why are students generally better spellers today than they were twenty-five years ago but more likely to choose the "wrong word" (7) in their writing?

STRATEGIES AND STRUCTURES

1. The students in the Stanford study, says Lunsford, "did plenty of" emailing, texting, and other forms of online writing and social networking (4). These activities, however, did not lead to "a new illiteracy" (4). What did they lead to, according to Lunsford? Is the student who interned in Bangladesh a good EXAMPLE? Why or why not?

2. "Ah, you say, but these are students at Stanford" (6). Is Lunsford wise to introduce a NAYSAYER at this point in her argument? Why or why not?

3. The second study that Lunsford cites is not longitudinal; it is a onetime reading of a random sample of student writing "from across all regions of the United States" (6) and from all sorts of institutions. How and how well does Lunsford link the findings of this study (about length and errors) to those of the first study she mentions (about levels of style and tone)?

4. "In short," says Lunsford, "the research my colleagues and I have been doing supports what other researchers are reporting about digital technologies and learn-

ing" (8). What larger conclusions about technology and literacy is Lunsford referring to here? How and how well do they counter the arguments that characterize students today "as either brain-damaged by technology or as cogs in the latest race to the top" (9)?

5. Having devoted her entire essay to student writers, Lunsford refers to their teachers in the last line. Is this an effective way to conclude her argument? Why or why not?

6. *Other Methods.* As noted, Lunsford bases her essay on the results of two studies of student writing. Does her use of COMPARISON AND CONTRAST succeed in convincing you of her argument? Explain.

THINKING ABOUT LANGUAGE

1. Lunsford refers to various accounts of the state of literacy among students today as "scripts" and "stories" (1, 2). What are the CONNOTATIONS of these terms, and why might she apply them to views she is challenging?

2. Does "all business" (5) accurately describe the TONE of the report that the student intern in Bangladesh sent back to her faculty adviser? Why or why not?

3. What do Lunsford and her colleagues mean by "life writing" (3)? How is it related to "kid-driven learning" (8)?

4. Is Lunsford's use of the phrase "crème de la crème" (6) a CLICHÉ, or is it IRONY? Explain.

5. What does the (intentionally) mixed METAPHOR of "fine-tooth eye" (6) mean?

FOR WRITING

1. Do some research on the nature of longitudinal studies in general, and then write a paragraph or two explaining their advantages and disadvantages, including the time and "unpredictability" factors.

2. In a NARRATIVE of four to six paragraphs about your own use of social media and otherwise being online, tell what the experience has or has not taught you about writing. Include lots of EXAMPLES.

3. As a result of "the digital revolution," Lunsford argues, "the definition, nature, and scope of writing are all shifting away . . . from individual 'authors' to participatory and collaborative partners-in-production" (9). In a 500-to-700-word essay supporting or contesting this CLAIM, make the ARGUMENT that this shift has or has not been greatly accelerated by recent developments in artificial intelligence, such as OpenAI's release of *ChatGPT*.

4. Ask *ChatGPT*, or some other chatbot, to compose a brief ANALYSIS of the EFFECTS of recent changes in technology, including artificial intelligence, on student literacy. Then write an argument of four to six paragraphs supporting or contesting the conclusions of that analysis.

Debating the Effects of Living Online and On Our Devices

The following questions refer to the arguments on pp. 683–706.

EVALUATING ARGUMENTS

1. Among the writers of the four selections in this cluster, which one(s) seems least disturbed by the potential ill effects of digital culture? Why?

2. Three of the participants in this debate link online culture and smartphones to larger issues of loneliness and eroding empathy. Are these broader concerns justified? Why or why not?

3. Judging from how they present themselves and their backgrounds and qualifications, which of the writers in this cluster do you find most **CREDIBLE**? least credible? Explain by pointing to specific evidence in the texts.

4. Whether or not you agree with their conclusions, which of the participants in this debate do you think support their claims most effectively? Why? Again, explain by pointing to particular **EVIDENCE** and strategies of argument in the texts.

FOR WRITING

1. Write the word "internet" at the top of a sheet of paper, and draw a line down the middle of the sheet. Label the columns "Pro" and "Con." Fill in as many reasons and observations on either side as you can think of. Next, do the same exercise with the words "social media," but this time using your computer or smartphone. Then write a paragraph or two describing the differences between these two experiences—one print, one digital.

2. Drawing on the essays in this cluster and on your own research, write a persuasive **ARGUMENT** of five to seven paragraphs in defense of text messaging or being "Very Online" via *TikTok*, *Instagram*, or other platforms. Acknowledge the shortcomings of the medium, but give good reasons for why you think the world is a socially richer place because of it.

3. In the early 1800s, despairing of the Industrial Revolution's effect of taking people away from nature, the English poet William Wordsworth titled a poem "The World Is Too Much with Us." Now, two centuries later, Sherry Turkle writes, "In solitude we find ourselves; we prepare ourselves to come to conversation with something to say that is authentic, ours. . . . If we don't know how to be alone, we'll only know how to be lonely." Write a persuasive **ARGUMENT** of six to eight paragraphs on the powers of solitude to counter (or not) the effects of living in a society where our smartphones and other technological devices are (or are not) too much with us.

DEBATING THE ETHICS OF BANNING BOOKS
AND CANCELING PEOPLE AND IDEAS

According to PEN America, a nonprofit organization devoted to free speech for writers, there were approximately 1,477 "instances of individual books banned" in this country during the last six months of 2022. The organization is still tracking the most recent data, but the new numbers, they say, will be "unquestionably much higher."

One reason for the increase is that several states have passed legislation that applies to entire school libraries, not just individual titles. A Florida law, for example, requires a certified media specialist to review and evaluate every book used in the classroom. Teachers who fail to comply may face criminal charges, and many have given up on borrowing or assigning books until they can be vetted.

Should teachers decide what students read? Or should it be parents? or the courts? or students themselves? or none of the above?

In the following cluster of arguments, a Vietnamese American novelist and teacher, a science writer, a lawyer turned social activist, and a member of the Red Lake Ojibwe Nation debate issues related to the banning of books, the online "cancelation" of people and ideas, and various other forms of censorship, including the self-censorship decried by critics of "trigger warnings."

Questions about this group of readings can be found on p. 732.

VIET THANH NGUYEN

My Young Mind Was Disturbed by a Book

Viet Thanh Nguyen (b. 1971) is a Vietnamese American writer and a professor of English and American Studies and Ethnicity at the University of Southern California, Los Angeles. Born in South Vietnam, Nguyen and his family arrived as refugees in the United States after the fall of Saigon in 1975. The family ultimately settled in San Jose, where Nguyen's parents opened a Vietnamese grocery store and he attended a Catholic elementary school and Bellarmine College Preparatory. He is a graduate of UC Berkeley (BA, 1992; PhD, 1997). Nguyen's first novel, *The Sympathizer*, won a Pulitzer Prize for fiction in 2016. Among other works, he is also the author of *Nothing Ever Dies: Vietnam and the Memory of War* (2016); *The Refugees* (2017), a collection of short stories; *Chicken of the Sea* (2019), a book for children; and *A Man of Two Faces: A Memoir, A History, A Memorial* (2023).

In "My Young Mind Was Disturbed by a Book" (*New York Times*, January 2022), Nguyen recalls, at age eleven or twelve, reading a novel about the brutality of American soldiers in Vietnam that he found so disturbing he later countered it with his "own novel about the same war." What he and his parents didn't do, says Nguyen, was petition to have the book removed from the school library. "Banning books," Nguyen argues here, "is a shortcut that sends us to the wrong destination."

W HEN I WAS 12 OR 13 YEARS OLD, I was not prepared for the racism, the brutal- 1
ity or the sexual assault in Larry Heinemann's 1977 novel, *Close Quarters*.

Mr. Heinemann, a combat veteran of the war in Vietnam, wrote about a nice, 2
average American man who goes to war and becomes a remorseless killer. In the

MLA CITATION: Nguyen, Viet Thanh. "My Young Mind Was Disturbed by a Book." *Back to the Lake: A Reader and Guide for Writers*, edited by Thomas Cooley, 5th ed., W. W. Norton, 2024, pp. 710–15.

book's climax, the protagonist and other nice, average American soldiers gang-rape a Vietnamese prostitute they call Claymore Face.

As a Vietnamese American teenager, it was horrifying for me to realize that this 3 was how some Americans saw Vietnamese people—and therefore me. I returned the book to the library, hating both it and Mr. Heinemann.

Here's what I didn't do: I didn't complain to the library or petition the librarians 4 to take the book off the shelves. Nor did my parents. It didn't cross my mind that we should ban *Close Quarters* or any of the many other books, movies and TV shows in which racist and sexist depictions of Vietnamese and other Asian people appear.

Instead, years later, I wrote my own novel about the same war, *The Sympathizer.* 5

While working on it, I reread *Close Quarters*. That's when I realized I'd miscon- 6 strued Mr. Heinemann's intentions. He wasn't endorsing what he depicted. He wanted to show that war brutalized soldiers, as well as the civilians caught in their path. The novel was a damning indictment of American warfare and the racist atti- tudes held by some nice, average Americans that led to slaughter and rape. Mr. Heine- mann revealed America's heart of darkness. He didn't offer readers the comfort of a way out by editorializing or sentimentalizing or humanizing Vietnamese people, because in the mind of the book's narrator and his fellow soldiers, the Vietnamese were not human.

In the United States, the battle over books is heating up, with some politicians 7 and parents demanding the removal of certain books from libraries and school curriculums. Just in the last week, we saw reports of a Tennessee school board that voted to ban Art Spiegelman's Pulitzer Prize–winning graphic novel about the Holocaust, *Maus*, from classrooms, and a mayor in Mississippi who is with- holding $110,000 in funding from his city's library until it removes books depict- ing L.G.B.T.Q. people. Those seeking to ban books argue that these stories and ideas can be dangerous to young minds—like mine, I suppose, when I picked up Mr. Heinemann's novel.

Books can indeed be dangerous. Until *Close Quarters*, I believed stories had the 8 power to save me. That novel taught me that stories also had the power to destroy me. I was driven to become a writer because of the complex power of stories. They are not inert tools of pedagogy. They are mind-changing, world-changing.

But those who seek to ban books are wrong no matter how dangerous books can 9 be. Books are inseparable from ideas, and this is really what is at stake: the struggle over what a child, a reader and a society are allowed to think, to know and to ques- tion. A book can open doors and show the possibility of new experiences, even new identities and futures.

Book banning doesn't fit neatly into the rubrics of left and right politics. Mark 10 Twain's *The Adventures of Huckleberry Finn* has been banned at various points because of Twain's prolific use of a racial slur, among other things. Toni Morrison's

Beloved has been banned before and is being threatened again—in one case after a mother complained that the book gave her son nightmares. To be sure, *Beloved* is an upsetting novel. It depicts infanticide, rape, bestiality, torture and lynching. But coming amid a movement to oppose critical race theory—or rather a caricature of critical race theory—it seems clear that the latest attempts to suppress this masterpiece of American literature are less about its graphic depictions of atrocity than about the book's insistence that we confront the brutality of slavery.

Here's the thing: If we oppose banning some books, we should oppose banning any book. If our society isn't strong enough to withstand the weight of difficult or challenging—and even hateful or problematic—ideas, then something must be fixed in our society. Banning books is a shortcut that sends us to the wrong destination. 11

As Ray Bradbury depicted in *Fahrenheit 451*, another book often targeted by book banners, book burning is meant to stop people from thinking, which makes them easier to govern, to control and ultimately to lead into war. And once a society acquiesces to burning books, it tends to soon see the need to burn the people who love books. 12

And loving books is really the point—not reading them to educate oneself or become more conscious or politically active (which can be extra benefits). I could recommend *Fahrenheit 451* because of its edifying political and ethical dimensions or argue that reading this novel is good for you, but that really misses the point. The book gets us to care about politics and ethics by making us care about a man who burns books for a living and who has a life-changing crisis about his awful work. That man and his realization could be any of us. 13

It's not only books that depict horror, war or totalitarianism that worry would-be book banners. They sometimes see danger in empathy. This appeared to be the fear that led a Texas school district to cancel the appearance of the graphic novelist Jerry Craft and pull his books temporarily from library shelves last fall. In Mr. Craft's Newbery Medal–winning book, *New Kid*, and its sequel, Black middle-schoolers navigate social and academic life at a private school where there are very few students of color. "The books don't come out and say we want white children to feel like oppressors, but that is absolutely what they will do," the parent who started the petition to cancel Mr. Craft's event said. (Mr. Craft's invitation for a virtual visit was rescheduled and his books were reinstated soon after.) 14

Mr. Craft's protagonist in *New Kid* is a sweet, shy, comics-loving kid. And it's his relatability that makes him seem so dangerous to some white parents. The historian and law professor Annette Gordon-Reed argued on *Twitter* that parents who object to books such as *New Kid* "don't want their kids to empathize with the black characters. They know their kids will do this instinctively. They don't want to give them the opportunity to do that." The historian Kevin Kruse went a step further, tweeting, "If you're worried your children will read a book and have no choice but to 15 identify with the villains in it, well . . . maybe that's something you need to work through on your own."

Those who ban books seem to want to circumscribe empathy, reserving it for a 16 limited circle closer to the kind of people they perceive themselves to be. Against this narrowing of empathy, I believe in the possibility and necessity of expanding empathy—and the essential role that books such as *New Kid* play in that. If it's possible to hate and fear those we have never met, then it's possible to love those we have never met. Both options, hate and love, have political consequences, which is why some seek to expand our access to books and others to limit them.

These dilemmas aren't just political; they're also deeply personal and intimate. 17 Now, as a father of a precocious 8-year-old reader, I have to think about what books I bring into our home. My son loves Hergé's Tintin comic books, which I introduced him to because I loved them as a child. I didn't notice Hergé's racist and colonialist attitudes then, from the paternalistic depiction of Tintin's Chinese friend Chang in *The Blue Lotus* to the Native American warriors wearing headdresses and wielding tomahawks in the 1930s of *Tintin in America*. Even if I had noticed, I had no one with whom I could talk about these books. My son does. We enjoy the adventures of the boy reporter and his fluffy white dog together, but as we read, I point out the books' racism against most nonwhite characters, and particularly their atrocious depictions of Black Africans. Would it be better that he not see these images, or is it better that he does?

Robert DesJarlait offers a different take on stereotypes of Native Americans on p. 728.

I err on the side of the latter and try to model what I think our libraries and 18 schools should be doing. I make sure he has access to many other stories of the peoples that Hergé misrepresented, and I offer context with our discussions. These are not always easy conversations. And perhaps that's the real reason some people want to ban books that raise complicated issues: They implicate and discomfort the adults, not the children. By banning books, we also ban difficult dialogues and disagreements, which children are perfectly capable of having and which are crucial to a democracy. I have told him that he was born in the United States because of a complicated history of French colonialism and American warfare that brought his grandparents and parents to this country. Perhaps we will eventually have less war, less racism, less exploitation if our children can learn how to talk about these things.

For these conversations to be robust, children have to be interested enough to 19 want to pick up the book in the first place. Children's literature is increasingly diverse and many books now raise these issues, but some of them are hopelessly ruined by good intentions. I don't find piousness and pedagogy interesting in art, and neither do children. Hergé's work is deeply flawed, and yet riveting narratively and aesthetically. I have forgotten all the well-intentioned, moralistic children's literature that I have read, but I haven't forgotten Hergé.

Books should not be consumed as good for us, like the spinach and cabbage my   20
son pushes to the side of his plate. "I like reading short stories," a reader once said to
me. "They're like potato chips. I can't stop with one." That's the attitude to have. I
want readers to crave books as if they were a delicious, unhealthy treat, like the
chili-lime chips my son gets after he eats his carrots and cucumbers.

Read *Fahrenheit 451* because its gripping story will keep you up late, even if you   21
have an early morning. Read *Beloved*, *The Adventures of Huckleberry Finn*, *Close
Quarters* and *The Adventures of Tintin* because they are indelible, sometimes uncomfortable and always compelling.

We should value that magnetic quality. To compete with video games, streaming   22
video and social media, books must be thrilling, addictive, thorny and dangerous. If
those qualities sometimes get books banned, it's worth noting that sometimes banning a book can increase its sales.

I know my parents would have been shocked if they knew the content of the   23
books I was reading: Philip Roth's *Portnoy's Complaint*, for instance, which was
banned in Australia from 1969 to 1971. I didn't pick up this quintessential American novel, or any other, because I thought reading it would be good for me. I was
looking for stories that would thrill me and confuse me, as *Portnoy's Complaint* did.
For decades afterward, all I remembered of the novel was how the young Alexan-
der Portnoy masturbated with anything he could get his hands on, including a slab
of liver. After consummating his affair with said liver, Alex returned it to the
fridge. Blissfully ignorant, the Portnoy family dined on the violated liver later that
night. Gross!

Who eats liver for dinner?   24

As it turns out, my family. Roth's book was a bridge across cultures for   25
me. Even though Vietnamese refugees differ from Jewish Americans, I recognized some of our obsessions in Roth's Jewish American world, with its
ambitions for upward mobility and assimilation, its pronounced "ethnic"
features and its sense of a horrifying history not far behind. I empathized.
And I could see some of myself in the erotically obsessed Portnoy—so much so that
I paid tribute to Roth by having the narrator of *The Sympathizer* abuse a squid in a
masturbatory frenzy and then eat it later with his mother. (*The Sympathizer* has
not been banned outright in Vietnam, but I've faced enormous hurdles while trying to have it published there. It's clear to me that this is because of its depiction of
the war and its aftermath, not the sexy squid.)

Banning is an act of fear—the fear of dangerous and contagious ideas. The best,   26
and perhaps most dangerous, books deliver these ideas in something just as troubling and infectious: a good story.

So it was with somewhat mixed feelings that I learned some American high   27
school teachers assign *The Sympathizer* as required reading in their classes. For the

> Or insects?
> Grace Silva
> uses a rhetori-
> cal question to
> argue for a
> change in diet
> on p. 608.

most part, I'm delighted. But then I worry: I don't want to be anyone's homework. I don't want my book to be broccoli.

I was reassured, however, when a first-year college student approached me at an   28
event to tell me she had read my novel in high school.

"Honestly," she said, "all I remember is when the sympathizer has sex with a   29
squid."

Mission accomplished. ◆   30

FOR CLOSE READING

1. As a teenager reading Larry Heinemann's novel *Close Quarters* (1977), why did Viet Thanh Nguyen find the book so disturbing?

2. What does Nguyen mean when he says of his own novel *The Sympathizer*, "I don't want my book to be broccoli" (27)?

3. Why isn't Nguyen disappointed when a first-year college student tells him that the only thing she remembers from reading his Pulitzer Prize–winning novel is "when the sympathizer has sex with a squid" (29)?

4. According to Nguyen, what attitude should people bring to reading in general? Do you agree? Why or why not?

5. When his young son reads graphic novels with racist or colonialist implications, Nguyen asks, "Would it be better that he not see these images, or is it better that he does" (17)? How would you answer this RHETORICAL QUESTION?

STRATEGIES AND STRUCTURES

1. Nguyen's essay has elements of a LITERACY NARRATIVE. What are some of them, and how well do they support his argument against book banning?

2. What is the role of Nguyen's young son in his essay? Why is Nguyen so careful to include the views of children?

3. "Those seeking to ban books argue that these stories and ideas can be dangerous to young minds" (7). Is this a fair and accurate statement of the opposition's point of view? Why or why not?

4. Nguyen argues that by banning books we also ban ideas—and that free access to ideas and the opportunity for "difficult dialogues" about them are "crucial to a democracy" (18). Does he give sufficient EVIDENCE to support this CLAIM? Point to specific passages in the text that you find particularly convincing (or not).

5. *Other Methods.* How and how well does Nguyen's COMPARISON of his own novel with Philip Roth's *Portnoy's Complaint* (1969) and the work of other writers support his claim that books provide "a bridge across cultures" (25)? Explain.

THINKING ABOUT LANGUAGE

1. When Nguyen speaks of America's "heart of darkness" (6), he is referring to the novel of that name by Joseph Conrad, published in 1899. Research the background of that novel, and then decide if Nguyen's ALLUSION is fitting. Explain.

2. In geometry, "circumscribe" means "to draw a circle around." What does Nguyen mean by the word when he applies it to "empathy" (16)? Given the context of Nguyen's discussion, is this language effective? Explain.

3. According to Nguyen, books "should not be consumed as good for us," like "spinach and cabbage" (20). In his view, how should they be consumed, and what are the implications of this food METAPHOR?

4. Books, says Nguyen, should be "thrilling, addictive, thorny and dangerous" (22). Piling up words like this, particularly descriptive adjectives, is the rhetorical device of *synathroesmus*. Why might Nguyen use it when pitting books against video games, streaming video, and social media?

5. Derived from medieval science and philosophy, the word "quintessential" (23) refers to a "fifth essence." Look up more about the word's origins, identify the nature of this essence as well as the other four, and then explain why Nguyen would choose this word to describe Roth's novel.

FOR WRITING

1. "If we oppose banning some books," says Nguyen, "we should oppose banning any book" (11). In a paragraph or two, lay out the main points you would make in an argument supporting (or contesting) this claim.

2. Write a four-to-six-paragraph CRITICAL ANALYSIS of one of Nguyen's short stories—for example, "War Years," about a boy who works in his parents' convenience store in San Jose. Be sure to evaluate its form (how it is organized) as well as its function (how it accomplishes its purpose).

3. In a 500-to-700-word CRITICAL ANALYSIS of one of Hergé's graphic novels about Tintin's adventures with his dog, Snowy, focus on the author's depiction of non-White characters and make the case for whether or not they're "dangerous to young minds." Open with a clearly stated THESIS and support your claim with convincing EVIDENCE.

SHANNON PALUS

Trigger Warnings

Shannon Palus (b. 1990) is a science and technology writer and a senior editor at *Slate*. She is a graduate of McGill University in Montreal, Quebec, Canada, where she majored in physics with a minor in anthropology. As a freelance writer, Palus has contributed articles and essays to *Popular Science*, *Scientific American*, *Discover*, *Wirecutter*, and other publications. She also has been a frequent host on *The Waves*, a *Slate* podcast about gender, relationships, and feminism.

Before composing the following selection (from *Slate*, July 2019), Palus believed that "trigger warnings" on college assignments, outside of theaters, and elsewhere were "a good way to help people with mental injuries such as post-traumatic stress disorder stay safer as they move around the world." Recent research on the subject, however, has convinced Palus that trigger warnings don't work and may even cause harm, sometimes in the form of self-censorship.

"**T**RIGGER WARNINGS JUST DON'T HELP," Payton Jones, a clinical psychology doctoral student at Harvard, tweeted alongside a preprint of his new paper. He further explained that the paper actually suggests that trigger warnings might even be *harmful*.

When I saw the tweet, my gut reaction was that Jones was wrong. I have been for trigger warnings even before the Year of the Trigger Warning, which according to *Slate*, was 2013. Opponents of trigger warnings tend to argue that they are an unnecessary concession that only serves to further coddle already sheltered college students. I figure they might be a good way to help people with

> One good way to introduce an argument is by anticipating counterarguments (p. 604).

MLA CITATION: Palus, Shannon. "Trigger Warnings." *Back to the Lake: A Reader and Guide for Writers*, edited by Thomas Cooley, 5th ed., W.W. Norton, 2024, pp. 717-20.

mental injuries such as post-traumatic stress disorder stay safer as they move around the world, the same way that a person with a broken leg uses crutches. But after considering Jones' paper, and chatting with him, I've been convinced that we'd do better to save the minimal effort it takes to affix trigger warnings to college reading assignments or put up signs outside of theater productions and apply it to more effective efforts to care for one another.

Research that trigger warnings might not be all that helpful has been mounting 3 over a few studies, including the one that Jones and his colleagues published last year titled "Trigger Warning: Empirical Evidence Ahead." Yes, that title is trollish, but here is what they did: They had a few hundred participants read several passages, some of which were potentially disturbing. Half received no heads up before the passages, and half got a label ahead of the iffy ones that read: "TRIGGER WARNING: The passage you are about to read contains disturbing content and may trigger an anxiety response, especially in those who have a history of trauma." The results suggested that trigger warnings could actually help *generate* anxiety, thus making them counterproductive. But there was a major limitation in that study: It didn't focus on people who had experienced trauma. Two studies written up in the *New York Times* in March had similar limitations (those both concluded that trigger warnings didn't do anything, good or bad).

So what about people who actually might be, you know, triggered by the material? 4 Jones' latest paper addresses just that question. The methods are the same as the 2018 paper, but with a pool of 451 participants who had experienced trauma. (A consent form required for ethical purposes did require that participants acknowledge that they would be reading emotional material, Jones told me, which is sort of a trigger warning all on its own but a required step of the process.) In this population, trigger warnings still failed to lessen the emotional distress from reading a passage. The authors also found evidence, they wrote, that trigger warnings "countertherapeutically reinforce survivors' view of their trauma as central to their identity." Though more evidence is needed to say for sure, their research suggests that trigger warnings could be actively harmful to the very people for whom they are meant.

> Citing statistics is particularly useful when you're arguing about trends (p. 591).

I then wondered if trigger warnings might help folks simply avoid the triggering 5 material, a sort of opt-out system for people who aren't up for dealing with it. But the evidence on whether people actually avoid material based on trigger warnings is mixed, Jones outlines in the paper. It could be that most people who have been through trauma see trigger warnings and plow ahead regardless. If they do end up avoiding the material and the associated adverse reaction, that's not a good thing, either. "Cognitive avoidance is really counterproductive," psychologist Darby Saxbe told Katy Waldman for a 2016 *Slate* story on the then-current science of trigger warnings, a point Jones also made to me. I know this extremely well from my days avoiding public speaking: Having an anxious reaction, and living to tell the tale, is actually an important part of learning to live with one's brain.

That's not to say that people who have experienced trauma should be left on their own to have that panicked response and just get over it. "Rather than issuing trigger warnings, universities can best serve students by facilitating access to effective and proven treatments for P.T.S.D. and other mental health problems," Richard McNally, a Harvard psychologist and co-author on the paper with Jones, wrote in the *New York Times* in 2016. He argued that emotional reactions to assigned readings were "a signal that students need to prioritize their mental health and obtain evidence-based, cognitive-behavioral therapies that will help them overcome P.T.S.D." In other words, if you feel you need a trigger warning, maybe what you really need is better medical care.

My last justification: Could trigger warnings simply be important because they signal that you are in a space where your feelings and mental health needs are going to be respected and taken seriously? "I don't think trigger warnings are the best way to do that," Jones told me. "Making a statement to that effect sends the same signal." It could also help build more broadly inclusive spaces. Teachers and professors could make a general announcement about the atmosphere they are hoping to cultivate at the beginning of a class. Colleges could take requests for trigger warnings as a sign that they need to bolster access to mental health professionals. Theaters could find a way to offer people the explicit option to gracefully step out and reenter, no questions asked, for any kind of medical need.

There are other problems with trigger warnings. Even if they did work, how would we go about issuing them for all possible triggers? Different people have different triggers, which are based on personal experiences and may or may not be connected to what the average person considers disturbing or explicit. "My experience is that the audience can do a better job than I can at figuring out what kind of content will upset them by reading the headline than I ever could randomly guessing what blog posts count as triggering," Amanda Marcotte wrote in *Slate* in 2013. If you're still wondering if a polite heads up might be in order—one that doesn't invoke the language about anxiety that the explicit warning in Jones' study does—then consider that we do live in a world with headlines, and book jackets, and movie previews, and graphic content advisories. The world naturally comprises signals about what we are about to experience.

Trigger warnings may have been developed under incredibly well-meaning pretenses, but they have now failed to prove useful in study after study. Like many a random supplement, trigger warnings are probably useless for most people and potentially, though not definitively, a little harmful to some. So, with no clear upside, why risk it? Perhaps because it is certainly easy to issue one and feel like you're doing something helpful. Just remember that this might come at the expense of doing something that would actually help. ◆

FOR CLOSE READING

1. Before she read a forthcoming paper by a psychology grad student at Harvard, Shannon Palus thought trigger warnings might be helpful for some people. What kinds of people was she thinking of?

2. What assumptions are opponents making when they say that trigger warnings "further coddle already sheltered college students" (2)? Are those assumptions valid? Why or why not?

3. Where do trigger warnings generally appear?

4. What caused Palus to change her mind about the value of trigger warnings?

5. To what use does Palus now think we should put the "minimal effort" (2) that goes into affixing trigger warnings?

STRATEGIES AND STRUCTURES

1. Palus cites numerous articles and studies on the topic of trigger warnings and their effectiveness or lack thereof. Point to the paragraphs where these appear, and explain whether this strategy for supporting her argument is or is not effective.

2. Why does Palus mention the "limitation" of the evidence she cites in paragraph 3? Is she justified in using it to support her case anyway? Explain.

3. What is the main difference, according to Palus, between the 2018 study she cites and the "latest paper" (4) coauthored by Jones? How significant is that difference? Does she explain it adequately?

4. Palus says she's now "convinced" that trigger warnings don't work and may even do harm but that "more evidence is needed to say for sure" (2, 4). Point out places in her argument where Palus resolves (or fails to resolve) this contradiction.

5. Palus goes one by one through the usual "justifications" (7) that people give for providing trigger warnings. Why does she do this if she is arguing *against* such warnings?

6. *Other Methods.* Palus never actually says what trigger warnings are. What does this omission suggest about her intended audience? Should she have DEFINED this key term anyway? Why or why not?

THINKING ABOUT LANGUAGE

1. Palus used to think that trigger warnings might help traumatized people in "the same way that a person with a broken leg uses crutches" (2). What does this ANAL-OGY imply about "people with mental injuries" (2)?

2. The title of a 2018 study on her subject, says Palus, seems "trollish" (3). Is it? Why or why not?

3. Palus cites two psychologists on the subject of "cognitive avoidance" (5). What behavior does this term refer to? Why might the psychologists think it's "counter-productive" (5)?

4. Trigger warnings, says Palus, are based on "well-meaning pretenses" (9). What does "pretenses" imply in this context? Should Palus have said "intentions" instead? Why or why not?

FOR WRITING

1. Along with several of your classmates, make individual lists of the trigger warnings you see in the course of a week. At the end of that period, compare notes with the others and draw up a master list of the most common warnings you found and where you found them.

2. In a paragraph or two, outline the main points you would make in support of (or opposition to) the proposition that trigger warnings are a form of censorship, including self-censorship.

3. The new paper by Payton Jones and others, to which Palus refers, can be found on the internet under the title "A Meta-Analysis of the Efficacy of Trigger Warnings, Content Warnings, and Content Notes." Read the abstract and concluding paragraphs of the paper, and write a SUMMARY of the main evidence the authors cite to make their case against the efficacy of trigger warnings.

4. "If you feel you need a trigger warning," writes Palus, "maybe what you really need is better medical care" (6). In a well-supported ARGUMENT of five to eight paragraphs, evaluate the quality of medical care available to you, including mental health care, and outline what changes in the system (if any) you would advocate. Consider including EXAMPLES of personal experience (your own or that of someone you know) as supporting evidence.

DAVID FRENCH

The Dangerous Lesson of Book Bans
in Public School Libraries

David French (b. 1969) is a former attorney and a regular political commentator for the *New York Times* and the *Atlantic*. He is a former senior editor of *The Dispatch,* an online magazine intended, according to its website, "for a conservative audience." Born in Opelika, Alabama, French graduated from Lipscomb University and Harvard Law School. Much of his career has been devoted to issues of religious liberty. He is the author of *Divided We Fall* (2020), among other works.

"The Dangerous Lesson of Book Bans in Public School Libraries" appeared in the libertarian magazine *Reason* in August 2022. "There are easy ways of looking at this issue," French writes about book banning in public schools, "and there are hard ways. The easy ways are wrong. The hardest way is right."

A SMALL GROUP OF PARENTS attends a conference where they're educated about the threats to American morality embedded in modern education. There they obtain a list of books believed to present a clear and present danger to young people. They bring that list to a meeting of the local school board. It turns out that 11 of the titles are found in school district libraries or curricula.

Alarmed, school board members direct the superintendent to remove the books and to put out a press statement declaring the tomes "anti-American, anti-Christian, anti-Sem[i]tic, and just plain filthy." The board says, "It is our duty, our moral obligation, to protect the children in our schools from this moral danger as surely as from physical and medical dangers."

MLA CITATION: French, David. "The Dangerous Lesson of Book Bans in Public School Libraries." *Back to the Lake: A Reader and Guide for Writers*, edited by Thomas Cooley, 5th ed., W.W. Norton, 2024, pp. 722–26.

A book review committee is formed, and it recommends retaining most of the 3
books. But the school board disagrees. Nine of the books are removed: *Slaughterhouse-Five,* by Kurt Vonnegut; *The Naked Ape,* by Desmond Morris; *Down These Mean Streets,* by Piri Thomas; *Best Short Stories of Negro Writers,* edited by Langston Hughes; *Go Ask Alice,* of anonymous authorship; *A Hero Ain't Nothin' but a Sandwich,* by Alice Childress; *A Reader for Writers,* edited by Jerome Archer; *The Fixer,* by Bernard Malamud; and *Soul On Ice,* by Eldridge Cleaver.

Did this happen in Texas in 2022? No: The year is 1976, and the place is the 4
Island Trees Union Free School District on Long Island, New York. These events formed the core of *Island Trees School District v. Pico,* a quirky and mostly forgotten Supreme Court case that is suddenly relevant once again. That relevance is related less to legal precedent than to a powerful moral argument that a plurality of the court made in its dicta. That moral argument should guide our disputes about books in schools today.

Those disputes have been metastasizing. In April, the free speech advocacy 5
group PEN America issued a report detailing 1,586 instances of individual books being "banned" between July 1, 2021, and March 31, 2022, affecting 1,145 unique book titles. By *bans,* they mean "removals of books from school libraries, prohibitions in classrooms, or both, as well as books banned from circulation during investigations resulting from challenges from parents, educators, administrators, board members, or responses to laws passed by legislatures."

There are easy ways of looking at this issue, and there are hard ways. The easy 6
ways are wrong. The hardest way is right. Let's take each in turn.

The easy ways take a look at the complex and often competing interests at play 7
and simply declare a winner. In one view, parents have an unquestioned interest in governing their child's education, so the parents' desires should triumph. This is, increasingly, the position of the Republican Party. It's repositioning itself as a "parent's party," and when push comes to shove, parents win.

In another view, educators ask: *Which* parents should win? Is a majoritarian edu- 8
cation a quality education? Is parent-driven public education truly even majoritarian? Isn't the sad reality that school board politics is mainly activist politics, driven more by anger and reaction than by calm and thoughtful reflection? We train educators for a reason, they say. Let teachers teach.

A third line of thinking takes a pox-on-both-your-houses approach. Don't choose 9
between public school parents and public school educators. Blow up the system. Pass backpack funding. Expand school choice. That way, parents win *and* teachers win. Parents can find the school that meets their standards of excellence and/or teaches their values. Educators can build institutions centered around their expertise. Families will then choose from a menu, and that menu will cover almost every educational meal.

> To construct win-win arguments, try using Rogerian logic (p. 602).

I'm drawn to the third way. School choice de-escalates curricular culture battles 10 and enhances the autonomy and responsibility of every individual in the system. Both parents and teachers have the ability to vote with their feet, to seek schools and jobs that match their philosophy and priorities. Moreover, it builds a sense of constructive cultural purpose. An explosion of school choice could revitalize the lost art of institution-building and community formation.

But even the third way—the better way—isn't enough. It is both contingent and 11 distant.

Don't get me wrong: The school choice movement (including homeschoolers and 12 charter schools) has made immense progress. Homeschooling barely existed 50 years ago, but by the 2020–2021 school year roughly 3.7 million students were educated at home. Charter schools educate more than 3 million students a year, and in 2018 a half-million students were enrolled in private school choice programs. But that still leaves roughly 50 million students in conventional public schools. Until most families actually *have* backpack funding, we must deal with the world as it is, and that world is going to educate the vast majority of American students in conventional public schools for the indefinite future. What do we owe them as long as they're there?

That brings us back to *Pico.* A collection of students sued the Island Trees school 13 district, arguing that the board's book removal order violated the *students'* First Amendment rights to receive information. In other words, in the fight between parents and teachers, the students should have a constitutional say too.

The Supreme Court agreed, but its plurality opinion created almost as many 14 questions as answers. It left intact broad state authority over school curricula, and it excluded from the scope of the decision the acquisition of library books. It merely tried to answer whether, sometimes, *removing* a book from a school library could violate the First Amendment.

The answer was *yes.* The justices argued that the First Amendment includes a 15 "right to receive ideas" that is "a necessary predicate to the *recipient's* meaningful exercise of his own rights of speech, press, and political freedom." This right meant that schools did not have "unfettered discretion" to remove books from shelves. At the same time, the plurality held that "we do not deny that local school boards have a substantial legitimate role to play in the determination of school library content."

How does a school board square that circle? What are the limits of its "legitimate 16 role"? Here was the essential holding: "Petitioners rightly possess significant discretion to determine the content of their school libraries. But that discretion may not be exercised in a narrowly partisan or political manner. If a Democratic school board, motivated by party affiliation, ordered the removal of all books written by or in favor of Republicans, few would doubt that the order violated the constitutional rights of the students denied access to those books. The same conclusion would surely apply if an all-white school board, motivated by racial animus, decided to remove all books authored by blacks or advocating racial equality and integration. Our Constitution does not permit the official suppression of *ideas*."

Is that a clear standard? Well, no. It's the judicial equivalent of declaring, "Just 17 don't go too far." And how far is too far? Defining the extremes (no books by Republicans, no books by black authors) doesn't define the line. Indeed, the case was ultimately so unhelpful in drawing meaningful lines that there's real doubt the plurality opinion would hold in the current Court.

As a statement of legal principle, *Pico* is unhelpful. But as a statement of educa- 18 tional philosophy, *Pico* shines. It provides a prudential standard that should help school boards navigate the complexities of parent complaints and students' educational interests. That standard is rooted in the Court's description of the nature of students' rights and the purposes of American education itself.

In the *Pico* ruling, the Court quoted its earlier judgment in *Tinker v. Des Moines* 19 (1969): "In our system, students may not be regarded as closed-circuit recipients of only that which the State chooses to communicate. . . . School officials cannot suppress 'expressions of feeling with which they do not wish to contend.'" The Court added in *Pico*: "In sum, just as access to ideas makes it possible for citizens generally to exercise their rights of free speech and press in a meaningful manner, such access prepares students for active and effective participation in the pluralistic, often contentious society in which they will soon be adult members."

In those sentences, Justice William J. Brennan Jr. perfectly captured the problem 20 with book bans. No, it's not that any given book should be on the shelves. There are, for example, books that are either too explicit for young children or explicit enough that they should be viewed and checked out only with parental permission. It's that book bans inhibit a core function of public education. They teach students that they should be protected from offensive ideas rather than how to engage and grapple with concepts they may not like.

To borrow a phrase from Greg Lukianoff, president of the Foundation for Indi- 21 vidual Rights and Expression, book bans are part of unlearning liberty. The process of American education is inseparable from the process of building American citizens, whether those citizens are educated in private schools, home schools, or public schools. It's sometimes tempting to try to avoid cultural conflicts by asking schools to stick to the basics, such as reading, writing, and arithmetic. But one of those "basics" is preparing young people for "active and effective participation" in American pluralism.

As a practical matter, that means that book removal should be a last resort, both 22 because limiting access to content can implicate students' ability to receive ideas and because of the message of the removal itself. It teaches a lesson—that the response to a challenging thought is to challenge the expression itself rather than the idea.

That does not mean that anything goes. As a matter of common sense, elemen- 23
tary school libraries should have different standards from high schools. And some
books are so graphic that parents should have a say in whether even their older child
can check them out.

But the bottom line remains. When school boards and principals hear challenges 24
to books or consider restrictions on curriculum, they need to understand
the very purpose of their educational project. It is not, as the Island Trees
district declared back in 1976, to protect children from "moral danger." It is
to prepare citizens for pluralism. Our nation's schools must not suppress
"expressions of feeling with which they do not wish to contend."

> Citing a doubt-
> ful authority in
> an argument is
> a common
> logical fallacy
> (p. 600).

American students are being taught that speech is dangerous. They are learning 25
that the proper response to an offensive idea is to ban the idea and punish the
speaker. And who taught them these lessons? Both the parents who sought to protect their children and the educators who forgot their central purpose. ◆

FOR CLOSE READING

1. More students now attend private schools or are schooled at home than ever
   before. So why, according to David French, isn't "school choice" (9) the answer to
   questions about which books should be taught in school? Explain.

2. If *Island Trees School District v. Pico* is "unhelpful" as a statement of legal principle,
   as French says, why is he citing this 1976 US Supreme Court case as "relevant once
   again" (17, 4)?

3. What group brought *Pico* to the Supreme Court? On what basis did this group
   claim to have a say in the matter of banning books versus allowing open access?

4. Besides reading, writing, and arithmetic, what other "basics" (21) should schools
   teach, in French's view? Do you agree? Why or why not?

5. French claims that "American students are being taught that speech is dangerous"
   (25). Who is doing this to them, according to French?

STRATEGIES AND STRUCTURES

1. French was trained as a lawyer. Is his ARGUMENT about the dangers of arbitrarily
   removing books from public school libraries primarily a legal or a moral one?
   Explain.

2. What exactly is the "lesson" that French mentions in his title? Does he provide sufficient EVIDENCE to suggest that it is "dangerous"? Explain.

3. French does not spell out the dangerous lesson, as he sees it, of book bans in
   public schools until the end of his essay. Should he have done so earlier? Why or
   why not?

4. "That brings us back to *Pico*" (13), French writes after asking what public schools "owe" (12) their students. Point to other places in the essay where French uses clear and direct TRANSITIONS like this between major sections of his argument.

5. *Other Methods.* French opens his argument with a NARRATIVE about "a small group of parents" in 1976. Why doesn't he return to their story at the end of his essay? Reread his concluding paragraphs (24, 25), and decide whether they do or do not provide a stronger conclusion than a return to the story about the parents would have done.

THINKING ABOUT LANGUAGE

1. The "*v.*" in *Island Trees School District v. Pico* (4) is, of course, an abbreviation for "versus." What does the universal use of this term in the titles of legal cases suggest about the nature of most cases?

2. What are the CONNOTATIONS of "metastasizing" in paragraph 5? Explain the METAPHOR and whether you think French uses it effectively to convey his attitude about disputes over books in schools today.

3. When French mentions a "pox-on-both-your-houses approach" (9), the ALLUSION is to *Romeo and Juliet*. Look up Shakespeare's play to see what Mercutio actually says, and then explain whether French's allusion is or is not fitting here.

4. What is "backpack funding" (9), and why is it called that?

5. French says he is "drawn to" school choice as a solution to the problem of book banning (10). How is this different from saying that he is "in favor of" or "convinced by" it?

FOR WRITING

1. One of the most frequently banned (or threatened-to-be-banned) books in American literature is Mark Twain's *Adventures of Huckleberry Finn*. Do some research on the history of the book's reception, and then write a six-to-eight-paragraph REPORT on the various reasons that have been given over the years for removing it from school bookshelves.

2. Banning books from school libraries, French argues, is a violation of the First Amendment to the US Constitution. Read the First Amendment and then, based on your interpretation of the text, write a persuasive ARGUMENT of 500 to 700 words agreeing with or dissenting from this position. Be sure to address the CLAIM that the "right to receive ideas" is "a necessary predicate to the *recipient's* meaningful exercise of his own rights of speech, press, and political freedom" (15).

3. Write a brief PROFILE of former Supreme Court justice William J. Brennan Jr. Include an assessment of his contribution to freedom-of-speech issues, including the ruling in *Pico* that free access to ideas "prepares students for active and effective participation in the pluralistic, often contentious society in which they will soon be adult members" (19).

ROBERT DESJARLAIT

They Got Rid of the Indian and Kept the Land

Robert DesJarlait (b. 1946) is a writer, artist, historian, and educator who is a member of the Red Lake Ojibwe Nation of northern Minnesota. Among other activities, he has illustrated curriculum materials for Native American educational programs in Minnesota and has served as a cultural adviser on many public art projects. Born in Red Lake, he grew up in Minneapolis, where his father, Patrick DesJarlait, worked as a commercial artist. As a boy, DesJarlait remembers seeing his father at work on a portrait of "Mia," the Native American woman featured for many years on the packaging of Land O'Lakes dairy products. In 2020, the company, having earlier reduced Mia's image to a headshot, removed it altogether. Did Land O'Lakes yield to public pressure and remove its long-term trademark because she was considered by some to be a stereotype of Native American culture?

In "They Got Rid of the Indian and Kept the Land" (editor's title; from the *Washington Post*, April 2020), DesJarlait argues that the redesigned Mia was not a stereotype but a representation with direct connections to Ojibwe art and places. Banishing her, says DesJarlait, was an act of censorship that is "all too familiar" to Native Americans.

> It's never a bad idea to begin an argument with a clear and direct statement of your claim (p. 593).

S HE WAS NEVER A STEREOTYPE. 1

    That was my thought earlier this month when I heard that "Mia," as 2 the Land O'Lakes Native American maiden was known, had been taken off the butter box. She was gone, vanished, missing. I knew Mia had devolved into a stereotype in many people's minds. But it was the stereotype some saw that bothered me.

MLA CITATION: DesJarlait, Robert. "They Got Rid of the Indian and Kept the Land." *Back to the Lake: A Reader and Guide for Writers*, edited by Thomas Cooley, 5th ed., W. W. Norton, 2024, pp. 728–30.

North Dakota state Rep. Ruth Buffalo (D), for instance, told the *Pioneer Press* in 3
St. Paul, Minn., that the Land O'Lakes image of Mia went "hand-in-hand with
human and sex trafficking of our women and girls . . . by depicting Native women
as sex objects." Others similarly welcomed the company's removal of the "butter
maiden" as long overdue.

How did Mia go from being a demure Native American woman on a lakeshore to 4
a sex object tied to the trafficking of native women?

I know the meaning of stereotypes. I participated in protests against 5
mascots and logos using American Indian images in the early 1990s, including outside the Metrodome in Minneapolis when Washington's team played
the Buffalo Bills in the 1992 Super Bowl. In 1993, I wrote a booklet for the
Anoka-Hennepin Indian Education Program about these stereotypes.

> To establish your credibility in an argument, cite any special knowledge or experience you might have (p. 602).

Mia was originally created for Land O'Lakes packaging in 1928. In 1939, 6
she was redesigned as a native maiden kneeling in a farm field holding a
butter box. In 1954, my father, Patrick DesJarlait, redesigned the image again.

My father had been interested in art since boyhood, when he drew images related 7
to his Ojibwe culture. After leaving Pipestone boarding school in Minnesota in
1942, he joined the Navy and was assigned to San Diego, where he worked alongside animation artists from MGM and Walt Disney producing brochures and films
for the war effort. In 1946, he established himself as one of the first modernists in
American Indian fine art.

After I was born in 1946, my family moved from Red Lake, Minn., to Minneapo- 8
lis, where my father broke racial barriers by establishing himself as an American
Indian commercial artist in an art world dominated by white executives and artists.
In addition to the Mia redesign, his many projects included creating the Hamm's
Beer bear. By often working with Native American imagery, he maintained a con-
nection to his identity.

I was 8 years old when I met Mia. My father often brought his work home, and 9
Mia was one of many commercial-art images I saw him work on in his studio.

With the redesign, my father made Mia's Native American connections more spe- 10
cific. He changed the beadwork designs on her dress by adding floral motifs that are
common in Ojibwe art. He added two points of wooded shoreline to the lake that had
often been depicted in the image's background. It was a place any Red Lake tribal citizen
would recognize as the Narrows, where Lower Red Lake and Upper Red Lake meet.

In my education booklet, *Rethinking Stereotypes*, I noted that communicating 11
misinformation is an underlying function of stereotypes, including through visual
images. One way that these images convey misinformation is in a passive, sublimi-
nal way that uses inaccurate depictions of tribal symbols, motifs, clothing and historical references. The other kind of stereotypical, misinforming imagery is more
overt, with physical features caricatured and customs demeaned. "Through dominant

language and art," I wrote, "stereotypic imagery allows one to see, and believe in, an invented image, an invented race, based on generalizations."

I provided a number of examples. Mia wasn't one of them. Not because she was 12 part of my father's legacy as a commercial artist and I didn't want to offend him. Mia simply didn't fit the parameters of a stereotype. Maybe that's why many Native American women on social media have made it clear that they didn't agree with those who viewed her as a romanticized and/or sexually objectified stereotype. Instead, Mia seems to have stirred a sense of remembrance and place, one that they found reassuring about their existence as Native American women.

I don't know why Land O'Lakes dropped Mia. In 2018, the company 13 changed the image by cropping it to a head shot. That adjustment didn't seem like a bow to culturally correct pressure. Perhaps her disappearance this year is about nothing more than chief executive Beth Ford's explanation that Land O'Lakes is focusing on the company's heritage as a farmer-owned cooperative founded in 1921. But questions remain.

> The company's new graphics are analyzed in detail in Chapter 10, pp. 305–8.

Mia's vanishing has prompted a social media meme: "They Got Rid of the Indian 14 and Kept the Land." That isn't too far from the truth. Mia, the stereotype that wasn't, leaves behind a landscape voided of identity and history. For those of us who are American Indian, it's a history that is all too familiar. ◆

FOR CLOSE READING

1. When and how did "Mia" become the Land O'Lakes "butter maiden" (3)?

2. What changes and adjustments did Robert DesJarlait's father make to the original Land O'Lakes depiction of a young Native American woman on the brand's packaging?

3. Why does DesJarlait think the redesigned version of the Land O'Lakes maiden is not a stereotype? What do you think?

4. According to DesJarlait, why do some Native American women miss Mia? What did she remind them of?

5. DesJarlait says he doesn't know why Land O'Lakes removed the butter maiden from its packaging. What do you suppose the reasons were?

STRATEGIES AND STRUCTURES

1. Where and how does DesJarlait use a RHETORICAL QUESTION to set up the rest of his essay? Explain whether or not you think this is an effective strategy.

2. How and how well does DesJarlait establish his CREDIBILITY as someone who can say whether or not a particular depiction of a Native American woman or other figure is a stereotype?

3. What **EVIDENCE** does DesJarlait give to support his **CLAIM** about the authenticity of Mia's portrait? Is it sufficient to prove his point? Why or why not?

4. *Other Methods.* In his booklet on stereotypes, DesJarlait says that their "underlying function" (11) is to convey misinformation. How and how well does he use this **DEFINITION** to support his argument that Mia is not a stereotype?

THINKING ABOUT LANGUAGE

1. "She was gone, vanished, missing" (2). What is the effect of DesJarlait's piling up **SYNONYMS** like this to describe Mia's disappearance?

2. Devolution is the reverse of evolution. What are the implications of DesJarlait's use of "devolved" to refer to what "many people" think about stereotypes (2)?

3. According to *Merriam-Webster's* online dictionary, the first meaning of the noun "stereotype" is "a plate cast from a printing surface"—that is, the product of an early, often crude means of reproducing images in print. Do some research on the word's subsequent **ETYMOLOGY**, and then explain how and how well it applies to the visual aspects of the Land O'Lakes butter packaging that DesJarlait discusses.

4. What are the **CONNOTATIONS** of "maiden" and "demure" (2, 4) as DesJarlait uses them to describe the image of a Native American woman conceived in part by his father?

5. The root meaning of "meme" (14) is "mime" or "mimic." What do memes typically mime or mimic? What are the specific and broader meanings of the meme "They Got Rid of the Indian and Kept the Land"?

FOR WRITING

1. The British scientist Richard Dawkins is credited with inventing the word "meme" in *The Selfish Gene* (1976). Do some research on Dawkins's coinage, and write a paragraph or two explaining how it came about.

2. Outline the argument you would make in an essay on the effect of memes on social media and other internet discourse. Be sure to define what the term "meme" has come to mean.

3. Write an essay of 600 to 800 words in which you **ARGUE** that accounts of Pocahontas—or some other Native American figure, historical or fictional—should or should not be removed from school curricula because they invite harmful stereotypes or repeat "a history that is all too familiar" (14). Support your position with facts and examples.

4. Look up various versions of the Land O'Lakes butter box on the web. Then write a four-to-six-paragraph **CRITICAL ANALYSIS** of DesJarlait's essay that defends or challenges his **CLAIM** that these images, especially those designed by his father, represent authentic Native American culture.

Debating the Ethics of Banning Books and Canceling People and Ideas

The following questions refer to the arguments on pp. 710-30.

EVALUATING ARGUMENTS

1. Among the four arguments in this cluster, which one best explains, in your view, why people ban books or ideas or cancel other people? Why do you think so?

2. Which of the arguments in this cluster do you find least persuasive? Why?

3. Among the four authors of this cluster of essays, which one seems the most *objective*? the most *subjective*? Explain your assessment.

4. According to David French (and the US Supreme Court justices he quotes), the "right to receive ideas" (15) is a key aspect of the freedom of speech guaranteed by the First Amendment. Thinking about the other writers in this cluster, point to places in their arguments where they appear to agree or disagree with this presumption.

FOR WRITING

1. In a paragraph or two, explain why you disagree with the writer's position in one (or more) of the arguments in this cluster.

2. Write an argument of five to seven paragraphs in which you take a position on the subject of book banning or other forms of cancelation or censorship that is fundamentally different from the point of view expressed by Nguyen, Palus, French, or DesJarlait. Give lots of EVIDENCE to support your CLAIM.

3. Among the books banned most often in recent years were *Gender Queer* by Maia Kobabe; *Flamer* by Mike Curato; *Tricks* by Ellen Hopkins; a graphic novel edition of *The Handmaid's Tale* by Margaret Atwood; and *Milk and Honey*, a poetry collection by Rupi Kaur. Read a review of one of these books—or better, the book itself—and write a brief REPORT explaining why you think some readers found it offensive or inappropriate for certain audiences.

16 Combining the Methods

The web of our life is of a mingled yarn . . .
—WILLIAM SHAKESPEARE, *All's Well That Ends Well*

When you have a single, clear purpose in mind, you may be able to write a well-organized essay by using a single method of development. The yarns of life, however, are often mingled, as Shakespeare notes, and when you're writing on a complex topic, you will likely end up combining a number of different methods in the same essay. Professional writers do this all the time—as we'll see in the first five pages of best-selling author Michael Lewis's book *Liar's Poker* (p. 737).

Trained in business and finance (as well as in literature), Lewis began his career as a bond salesman on Wall Street—the financial district of New York City—where he spent much of his time on the telephone. After a few years, Lewis decided he wanted to try his hand at a different kind of verbal communication and became a professional writer. In *Liar's Poker*, Lewis compares the economic climate of Wall Street to a high-stakes game.

Lewis isn't simply telling an amusing story about Wall Street and its pastimes, however. Like an anthropologist studying a strange tribe, he's giving an expert's view of an entire culture. To this more complicated end, Lewis draws on *all* the methods of development discussed in this book. He begins to develop his topic with a **NARRATIVE** of the day the head of the firm challenged one of the traders to play an office gambling game for a million dollars:

> It was sometime early in 1986, the first year of the decline of my firm, Salomon Brothers. Our chairman, John Gutfreund, left his desk at the head of the trading floor and went for a walk. . . . This day in 1986, however, Gutfreund did something strange. Instead of terrifying us all, he walked a straight line to the trading desk of John Meriwether, a member of the board of Salomon Inc. and also one of Salomon's finest bond traders. He whispered a few words. The traders in the vicinity eavesdropped. What Gutfreund said has become a legend at Salomon Brothers and a visceral part of its corporate identity. He said: "One hand, one million dollars, no tears."

Throughout his narrative, Lewis also weaves in a detailed **DESCRIPTION** of the field of play ("like an epileptic ward"), the spectators ("nerve-racked"), and the key players. First there is the challenger, John Gutfreund:

> Gutfreund took the pulse of the place by simply wandering around it and asking questions of the traders. An eerie sixth sense guided him to wherever a crisis was unfolding. Gutfreund seemed able to smell money being lost.

Then there is the champ himself, as Lewis describes him:

> John Meriwether had, in the course of his career, made hundreds of millions of dollars for Salomon Brothers. He had an ability, rare among people and treasured by traders, to hide his state of mind. . . . He wore the same blank half-tense expression when he won as he did when he lost. . . . People would

say, "He's the best businessman in the place," or "the best risk taker I have ever seen," or "a very dangerous Liar's Poker player."

And what is Liar's Poker? To explain this, Lewis must include a **PROCESS ANALYSIS:**

In Liar's Poker a group of people—as few as two, as many as ten—form a circle. Each player holds a dollar bill close to his chest. The game is similar in spirit to the card game known as I Doubt It. Each player attempts to fool the others about the serial numbers printed on the face of his dollar bill. . . . The bidding escalates until all the other players agree to challenge a single player's bid. Then, and only then, do the players reveal their serial numbers and determine who is bluffing whom.

Why are Gutfreund, Meriwether, and the other grown men in the office of Salomon Brothers playing what looks, on the surface, like a child's game? Because a good Liar's Poker player was also likely to be a good bond trader. Lewis, it would seem, is using the game as an **EXAMPLE** of how the trader's mind works:

The questions a Liar's Poker player asks himself are, up to a point, the same questions a bond trader asks himself. Is this a smart risk? Do I feel lucky? How cunning is my opponent? Does he have any idea what he's doing, and if not, how do I exploit his ignorance?

Now we know how Liar's Poker is played and, in general, why the traders played it. We don't, however, know why, on this particular day, Gutfreund challenged Meriwether to play for the unheard-of sum of a million dollars.

To provide this information, Lewis must do a **CAUSE-AND-EFFECT** analysis, in which he adds a **COMPARISON AND CONTRAST** of the two men; that comparison, in turn, is based on a **CLASSIFICATION** of the men according to their functions as managers or traders within the firm:

Gutfreund was the King of Wall Street, but Meriwether was King of the Game. . . . Gutfreund had once been a trader, but that was as relevant as an old woman's claim that she was once quite a dish. . . . Compared with managing, trading was admirably direct. You made your bets and either you won or you lost. When you won, people—all the way up to the top of the firm—admired you, envied you, and feared you, and with reason: You controlled the loot. When you managed a firm, well, sure you received your quota of envy, fear, and admiration. But for all the wrong reasons. *You did not make the money for Salomon. You did not take the risk.*

Why (the causes) Gutfreund challenged Meriwether (the effect) on this particular day is now clear: "[T]he single rash act of challenging the arbitrage boss to one hand for a million dollars was Gutfreund's way of showing he was a player, too." But it is not yet clear why Meriwether felt obliged to accept the challenge. To explain *this*, Lewis adds a **DEFINITION** of the player's "code" of conduct:

> The code of the Liar's Poker player was something like the code of the gun-slinger. It required a trader to accept all challenges. Because of the code—which was *his* code—John Meriwether felt obliged to play. But he knew it was stupid.

Okay. So now we know how the game is played and why the chief manager of Salomon Brothers challenged the chief bond trader to play a hand of Liar's Poker for a million dollars. We also know why the arbitrage boss felt obliged to accept the challenge. (To see how Meriwether actually met the challenge, you'll have to read the rest of the story.)

But what's the point? The story of the great Liar's Poker challenge may be interesting if you just want to know what happened one day in a big Wall Street firm when people were playing when they should have been working. But what's the significance of these people and their actions? Why should you as a reader want to know about them?

Lewis has already told us the significance of the game for the players. In order to tie all the threads together, however, he must also explain what it might mean to us, his readers and audience. Here's his explanation:

> The game has some of the feel of trading, just as jousting has some of the feel of war. . . . Each player seeks weakness, predictability, and pattern in the others and seeks to avoid it in himself. The bond traders of Goldman, Sachs, First Boston, Morgan Stanley, Merrill Lynch, and other Wall Street firms all play some version of Liar's Poker.

Now we understand the point of Lewis's essay and, indeed, of the entire book it introduces. He is **ARGUING** that the nation's financial markets amount to one big game of Liar's Poker. The purpose of all the other methods of narration, description, and exposition that he uses is to support this claim, which is similar to the claim Lewis made in his book *The Big Short* (2010) and that some economists still make today about risky loans to companies with bad credit.

You won't always use every method of developing a topic in every piece of writing you do, however. Depending on your main purpose in writing, one or two will usually dominate, as in most of the model essays in this book. Your purpose—whether to **REPORT** on some research you've done, take a **POSITION** on an issue, **PROFILE** a person or group, **PROPOSE** a new project or idea, **ANALYZE** a text—will likewise determine the overall type of writing you choose, as well as the methods you use to construct it.

MICHAEL LEWIS

Liar's Poker

IT WAS SOMETIME EARLY IN 1986, the first year of the decline of my firm, Salomon Brothers. Our chairman, John Gutfreund, left his desk at the head of the trading floor and went for a walk. At any given moment on the trading floor billions of dollars were being risked by bond traders.[1] Gutfreund took the pulse of the place by simply wandering around it and asking questions of the traders. An eerie sixth sense guided him to wherever a crisis was unfolding. Gutfreund seemed able to smell money being lost.

He was the last person a nerve-racked trader wanted to see. Gutfreund (pronounced *Good friend*) liked to sneak up from behind and surprise you. This was fun for him but not for you. Busy on two phones at once trying to stem disaster, you had no time to turn and look. You didn't need to. You felt him. The area around you began to convulse like an epileptic ward. People were pretending to be frantically busy and at the same time staring intently at a spot directly above your head. You felt a chill in your bones that I imagine belongs to the same class of intelligence as the nervous twitch of a small furry animal at the silent approach of a grizzly bear. An alarm shrieked in your head: Gutfreund! Gutfreund! Gutfreund!

Often as not, our chairman just hovered quietly for a bit, then left. You might never have seen him. The only trace I found of him on two of these occasions was a turdlike ash on the floor beside my chair, left, I suppose, as a calling card. Gutfreund's cigar droppings were longer and better formed than those of the average Salomon boss. I always assumed that he smoked a more expensive blend than the rest, purchased with a few of the $40 million he had cleared on the sale of Salomon Brothers in 1981 (or a few of the $3.1 million he paid himself in 1986, more than any other Wall Street CEO).

This day in 1986, however, Gutfreund did something strange. Instead of terrifying us all, he walked a straight line to the trading desk of John Meriwether, a member of the board of Salomon Inc. and also one

Marginal notes:

> Begins with a NARRATIVE: the King of Wall Street goes for a walk.

> DESCRIBES the trading floor and the traders' response to the king's presence.

> Leaving his "droppings" is an EXAMPLE of the king's need to establish his territory.

1. *Bond traders*: Salespeople who specialize in promissory notes (IOUs) that pay interest.

MLA CITATION: Lewis, Michael. "Liar's Poker." *Back to the Lake: A Reader and Guide for Writers*, edited by Thomas Cooley, 5th ed., W. W. Norton, 2024, pp. 737–41.

of Salomon's finest bond traders. He whispered a few words. The traders in the vicinity eavesdropped. What Gutfreund said has become a legend at Salomon Brothers and a visceral part of its corporate identity. He said: "One hand, one million dollars, no tears."

One hand, one million dollars, no tears. Meriwether grabbed the 5 meaning instantly. The King of Wall Street, as *Business Week* had dubbed Gutfreund, wanted to play a single hand of a game called Liar's Poker for a million dollars. He played the game most afternoons with Meriwether and the six young bond arbitrage[2] traders who worked for Meriwether and was usually skinned alive. Some traders said Gutfreund was heavily outmatched. Others who couldn't imagine John Gutfreund as anything but omnipotent—and there were many—said that losing suited his purpose, though exactly what that might be was a mystery.

The peculiar feature of Gutfreund's challenge this time was the 6 size of the stake. Normally his bets didn't exceed a few hundred dollars. A million was unheard of. The final two words of his challenge, "no tears," meant that the loser was expected to suffer a great deal of pain but wasn't entitled to whine, bitch, or moan about it. He'd just have to hunker down and keep his poverty to himself. But why? You might ask if you were anyone other than the King of Wall Street. Why do it in the first place? Why, in particular, challenge Meriwether instead of some lesser managing director? It seemed an act of sheer lunacy. Meriwether was the King of the Game, the Liar's Poker champion of the Salomon Brothers trading floor.

On the other hand, one thing you learn on a trading floor is that winners like Gutfreund *always* have some reason for what they do; it might not be the best of reasons, but at least they have a concept in mind. I was not privy to Gutfreund's innermost thoughts, but I do know that all the boys on the trading floor gambled and that he wanted badly to be one of the boys. What I think Gutfreund had in mind in this instance was a desire to show his courage, like the boy who leaps from the high dive. Who better than Meriwether for the purpose? Besides, Meriwether was probably the only trader with both the cash and the nerve to play.

The whole absurd situation needs putting into context. John Meriwether had, in the course of his career, made hundreds of millions of dollars for Salomon Brothers. He had an ability, rare among people and

Margin notes:
- Introduces DIALOGUE and TENSION into the PLOT as the king challenges an adversary.
- Begins Lewis's ANALYSIS of the king's motives.
- Explains the CONTEXT of the game and characterizes the other main player as a rival king (or magician).

2. *Arbitrage*: The buying of stocks, bonds, and other securities for immediate resale to profit from price differences in different markets.

treasured by traders, to hide his state of mind. Most traders divulge whether they are making or losing money by the way they speak or move. They are either overly easy or overly tense. With Meriwether you could never, ever tell. He wore the same blank half-tense expression when he won as he did when he lost. He had, I think, a profound ability to control the two emotions that commonly destroy traders—fear and greed—and it made him as noble as a man who pursues his self-interest so fiercely can be. He was thought by many within Salomon to be the best bond trader on Wall Street. Around Salomon no tone but awe was used when he was discussed. People would say, "He's the best business-man in the place," or "the best risk taker I have ever seen," or "a very dangerous Liar's Poker player."

Meriwether cast a spell over the young traders who worked for him. His boys ranged in age from twenty-five to thirty-two (he was about forty). Most of them had Ph.D.'s in math, economics, and/or physics. Once they got onto Meriwether's trading desk, however, they forgot they were supposed to be detached intellectuals. They became disciples. They became obsessed by the game of Liar's Poker. They regarded it as *their* game. And they took it to a new level of seriousness.

John Gutfreund was always the outsider in their game. That *Business Week* put his picture on the cover and called him the King of Wall Street held little significance for them. I mean, that was, in a way, the whole point. Gutfreund was the King of Wall Street, but Meriwether was King of the Game. When Gutfreund had been crowned by the gentlemen of the press, you could almost hear traders thinking: *Foolish names and foolish faces often appear in public places.* Fair enough, Gutfreund had once been a trader, but that was as relevant as an old woman's claim that she was once quite a dish.

At times Gutfreund himself seemed to agree. He loved to trade. Compared with managing, trading was admirably direct. You made your bets and either you won or you lost. When you won, people—all the way up to the top of the firm—admired you, envied you, and feared you, and with reason: You controlled the loot. When you managed a firm, well, sure you received your quota of envy, fear, and admiration. But for all the wrong reasons. *You did not make the money for Salomon. You did not take risk.* You were hostage to your producers. They took risk. They proved their superiority every day by handling risk better than the rest of the risk-taking world. The money came from risk takers such as

ANALYZES the EFFECT that the King of the Game (Meriwether) has on the younger traders.

ANALYZES the EFFECT that Gutfreund has on the others: the old king's powers are failing.

COMPARES AND CONTRASTS managing vs. trading, Gutfreund vs. Meriwether.

Continues Lewis's ANALYSIS of the players' motives.

Meriwether, and whether it came or not was really beyond Gutfreund's control. That's why many people thought that the single rash act of challenging the arbitrage boss to one hand for a million dollars was Gutfreund's way of showing he was a player, too. And if you wanted to show off, Liar's Poker was the only way to go. The game had a powerful meaning for traders. People like John Meriwether believed that Liar's Poker had a lot in common with bond trading. It tested a trader's character. It honed a trader's instincts. A good player made a good trader, and vice versa. We all understood it.

The next three paragraphs ANALYZE the PROCESS of playing Liar's Poker.

The Game: In Liar's Poker a group of people—as few as two, as 12 many as ten—form a circle. Each player holds a dollar bill close to his chest. The game is similar in spirit to the card game known as I Doubt It. Each player attempts to fool the others about the serial numbers printed on the face of his dollar bill. One trader begins by making "a bid." He says, for example, "Three sixes." He means that all told the serial numbers of the dollar bills held by every player, including himself, contain at least three sixes.

Once the first bid has been made, the game moves clockwise in the 13 circle. Let's say the bid is three sixes. The player to the left of the bidder can do one of two things. He can bid higher (there are two sorts of higher bids: the same quantity of a higher number [three sevens, eights, or nines] and more of any number [four fives, for instance]). Or he can "challenge"—that is like saying, "I doubt it."

The bidding escalates until all the other players agree to challenge a 14 single player's bid. Then, and only then, do the players reveal their serial numbers and determine who is bluffing whom. In the midst of all this, the mind of a good player spins with probabilities. What is the statistical likelihood of there being three sixes within a batch of, say, forty randomly generated serial numbers? For a great player, however, the math is the easy part of the game. The hard part is reading the faces of the other players. The complexity arises when all players know how to bluff and double-bluff.

The game has some of the feel of trading, just as jousting has some 15 of the feel of war. The questions a Liar's Poker player asks himself are, up to a point, the same questions a bond trader asks himself. Is this a smart risk? Do I feel lucky? How cunning is my opponent? Does he have any idea what he's doing, and if not, how do I exploit his ignorance? If he bids high, is he bluffing, or does he actually hold a strong hand? Is he trying to induce me to make a foolish bid, or does he actually have four of a kind himself? Each player seeks weakness, predictability, and pattern in the others and seeks to avoid it in himself. The bond traders of Goldman, Sachs, First Boston, Morgan Stanley, Merrill Lynch, and other Wall Street firms all play some version of Liar's Poker. But the place where the stakes run highest, thanks to John Meriwether, is the New York bond trading floor of Salomon Brothers.

> ARGUES that the traders on Wall Street see the financial system as some kind of game.

The code of the Liar's Poker player was something like the code of the gunslinger.[3] It required a trader to accept all challenges. Because of the code—which was *his* code—John Meriwether felt obliged to play. But he knew it was stupid. For him, there was no upside. If he won, he upset Gutfreund. No good came of this. But if he lost, he was out of pocket a million bucks. This was worse than upsetting the boss. Although Meriwether was by far the better player of the game, in a single hand anything could happen. Luck could very well determine the outcome. Meriwether spent his entire day avoiding dumb bets, and he wasn't about to accept this one.

16

"No, John," he said, "if we're going to play for those kind of numbers, I'd rather play for real money. Ten million dollars. No tears."

17

> The plot reaches a CLIMAX as Meriwether issues a counter-challenge to Gutfreund.

Ten million dollars. It was a moment for all players to savor. Meriwether was playing Liar's Poker before the game even started. He was bluffing. Gutfreund considered the counterproposal. It would have been just like him to accept. Merely to entertain the thought was a luxury that must have pleased him well. (It *was* good to be rich.)

18

On the other hand, ten million dollars was, and is, a lot of money. If Gutfreund lost, he'd have only thirty million or so left. His wife, Susan, was busy spending the better part of fifteen million dollars redecorating their Manhattan apartment (Meriwether knew this). And as Gutfreund *was* the boss, he clearly wasn't bound by the Meriwether code. Who knows? Maybe he didn't even know the Meriwether code. Maybe the whole point of his challenge was to judge Meriwether's response. (Even Gutfreund had to marvel at the king in action.) So Gutfreund declined. In fact, he smiled his own brand of forced smile and said, "You're crazy."

19

> The CONFLICT is resolved as Gutfreund refuses the challenge.

No, thought Meriwether, just very, very good.

20

> Meriwether reigns as King of the Game.

---

3. *Code of the gunslinger:* Code of conduct rooted in the legendary Wild West of the eighteenth- and nineteenth-century United States. The phrase refers to a stoic, warrior-like way of life that required a gunfighter to accept all challenges.

A Book Cover

The basic methods that good writers draw on every day are sometimes used in combination with one another. This cover for a book about human cadavers, for example, employs a number of them all at once. The title, *Stiff*, is a DESCRIPTION of the physical condition of the human body after death; "stiff" is also a slang term for a dead person. Going beyond physical description, Roach's title is a name or label identifying an important aspect of her subject—the sometimes conflicting legal, moral, and medical DEFINITIONS of death itself. Good writers often kill even more than two birds with one stone, however. As you describe and define a subject, you may also tell a story about it, as this book cover does by adding a NARRATIVE element. We see just enough of the person pictured on the cover of Roach's book to know that they ended up in the morgue with a tag attached to the big toe. End of story—usually. For the human cadavers in Roach's book, however, death is only the beginning. Simultaneously grim and humorous, the image on the cover captures the first stages of this narrative. The later stages are implied in Roach's subtitle, *The Curious Lives of Human Cadavers*, which tells us that *Stiff* is a book about what happens to our bodies after we die.

[FOR WRITING]...

With its oversize footnote, so to speak, the cover of Mary Roach's *Stiff* is both informative and humorous. Write a brief RHETORICAL ANALYSIS of the words and images on the cover of Roach's book and the "mixed" impression they are likely intended to leave on the reader.

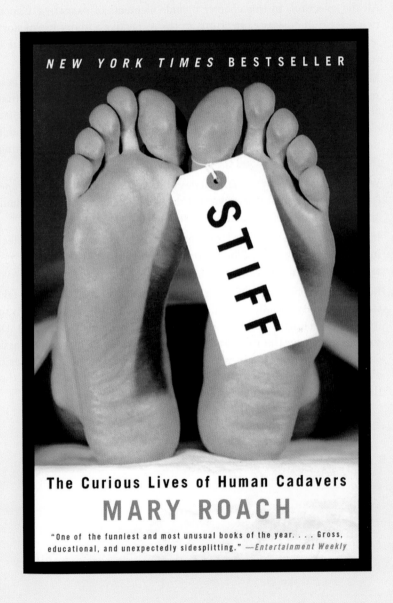

SUGGESTIONS FOR WRITING

1. All the selections in this chapter include elements of **NARRATIVE**. Choose two titles, and **COMPARE AND CONTRAST** the respective authors' use of story-telling to explain and support the key points they are making. Be sure to refer to particular issues and to specific passages in the two texts.

2. Michael Lewis's "Liar's Poker" (p. 737) is the introduction to his best-selling book of that title about the gamblers and gambling culture he finds characteristic of Wall Street. Are the financial markets of New York and elsewhere driven largely by a gambling mentality? Using Lewis's introduction as a starting point, write a **POSITION PAPER** supporting (or contesting) this view of Wall Street and the world of finance.

3. Write a 300-word **RHETORICAL ANALYSIS** of Joan Didion's "On Going Home" (p. 745) as a personal **NARRATIVE** that deals with universal issues of home and family. Give lots of specific **EXAMPLES** to support your reading.

4. In approximately 400 words, **COMPARE AND CONTRAST** Linda Hogan's "Hearing Voices" (p. 749) with Gloria Anzaldúa's "Linguistic Terrorism" (p. 755) as essays about the uses and power of language.

5. Recent biographers and critics have questioned whether Eric Blair (aka George Orwell) actually shot an elephant in colonial Burma (now Myanmar) as he claims to have done in "Shooting an Elephant" (p. 759). Do some research on the issue and write a **CRITICAL ANALYSIS** of this classic essay in which you explain why—for the author's rhetorical purposes of exposing the evils of colonialism—it matters (or does not matter) whether the events of the story are literally true.

JOAN DIDION

On Going Home

Joan Didion (1934–2021) was a native of Sacramento, California. She graduated from the University of California, Berkeley, and worked on the staff of *Vogue* magazine before becoming a full-time writer. A novelist and screenwriter, Didion is perhaps best known for her essays, collected in *Slouching towards Bethlehem* (1968), *The White Album* (1979), *Where I Was From* (2003), and *Let Me Tell You What I Mean* (2021). *The Year of Magical Thinking* (2005), a reflection on the sudden death in 2003 of her husband, the writer John Gregory Dunne, won the National Book Award for nonfiction; it was adapted into a one-woman play staged on Broadway with Vanessa Redgrave. Didion's *Blue Nights* (2011) is a memoir about aging and her relationship with her only child, an adopted daughter who died not long after Didion's husband did. In 2017, Didion was the subject of a *Netflix* documentary, *The Center Will Not Hold*, directed by her nephew Griffin Dunne.

That Didion is a master of the memoir form—which combines narration and description into reflection on the past, intertwined with commentary on life in the present—is immediately apparent in "On Going Home," first published in 1967 in the *Saturday Evening Post*. Although Didion lived for years in New York City and later Los Angeles, home for her was "the place where my family is, in the Central Valley of California." "On Going Home" captures that place in fine detail, but it also raises the question of whether the idea of going home has been lost.

MLA CITATION: Didion, Joan. "On Going Home." *Back to the Lake: A Reader and Guide for Writers*, edited by Thomas Cooley, 5th ed., W. W. Norton, 2024, pp. 746–48.

I AM HOME FOR MY DAUGHTER'S FIRST BIRTHDAY. By "home" I do not mean the
house in Los Angeles where my husband and I and the baby live, but the place
where my family is, in the Central Valley of California. It is a vital although trouble-
some distinction. My husband likes my family but is uneasy in their house,
because once there I fall into their ways, which are difficult, oblique, deliberately inarticulate, not my husband's ways. We live in dusty houses ("D-U-
S-T," he once wrote with his finger on surfaces all over the house, but no
one noticed it) filled with mementos quite without value to him (what could
the Canton dessert plates mean to him? how could he have known about
the assay scales, why should he care if he did know?), and we appear to talk
exclusively about people we know who have been committed to mental hospitals,
about people we know who have been booked on drunk-driving charges, and about
property, particularly about property, land, price per acre and C-2 zoning and
assessments and freeway access. My brother does not understand my husband's
inability to perceive the advantage in the rather common real-estate transaction
known as "sale-leaseback," and my husband in turn does not understand why so
many of the people he hears about in my father's house have recently been committed to mental hospitals or booked on drunk-driving charges. Nor does he understand that when we talk about sale-leasebacks and right-of-way condemnations we
are talking in code about the things we like best, the yellow fields and the cotton-
woods and the rivers rising and falling and the mountain roads closing when the
heavy snow comes in. We miss each other's points, have another drink and regard
the fire. My brother refers to my husband, in his presence, as "Joan's husband." Marriage is the classic betrayal.

Or perhaps it is not anymore. Sometimes I think that those of us who are now
in our thirties were born into the last generation to carry the burden of "home," to
find in family life the source of all tension and drama. I had by all objective
accounts a "normal" and a "happy" family situation, and yet I was almost thirty
years old before I could talk to my family on the telephone without crying after I
had hung up. We did not fight. Nothing was wrong. And yet some nameless anxiety colored the emotional charges between me and the place that I came from. The
question of whether or not you could go home again was a very real part of the
sentimental and largely literary baggage with which we left home in the fifties; I
suspect that it is irrelevant to the children born of the fragmentation after World
War II. A few weeks ago in a San Francisco bar I saw a pretty young girl on crystal
take off her clothes and dance for the cash prize in an "amateur-topless" contest.
There was no particular sense of moment about this, none of the effect of romantic
degradation, of "dark journey" for which my generation strived so assiduously.
What sense could that girl possibly make of, say, *Long Day's Journey into Night*?
Who is beside the point?

<aside>
While telling about going home, Didion also DEFINES the idea (p. 736) of going home.
</aside>

1

2

That I am trapped in this particular irrelevancy is never more apparent to me than when I am home. Paralyzed by the neurotic lassitude engendered by meeting one's past at every turn, around every corner, inside every cupboard, I go aimlessly from room to room. I decide to meet it head-on and clean out a drawer, and I spread the contents on the bed. A bathing suit I wore the summer I was seventeen. A letter of rejection from *The Nation*, an aerial photograph of the site for a shopping center my father did not build in 1954. Three teacups hand-painted with cabbage roses and signed "E.M.," my grandmother's initials. There is no final solution for letters of rejection from *The Nation* and teacups hand-painted in 1900. Nor is there any answer to snapshots of one's grandfather as a young man on skis, surveying around Donner Pass in the year 1910. I smooth out the snapshot and look into his face, and do and do not see my own. I close the drawer, and have another cup of coffee with my mother. We get along very well, veterans of a guerrilla war we never understood.

Days pass. I see no one. I come to dread my husband's evening call, not only because he is full of news of what by now seems to me our remote life in Los Angeles, people he has seen, letters which require attention, but because he asks what I have been doing, suggests uneasily that I get out, drive to San Francisco or Berkeley. Instead I drive across the river to a family graveyard. It has been vandalized since my last visit and the monuments are broken, overturned in the dry grass. Because I once saw a rattlesnake in the grass I stay in the car and listen to a country-and-western station. Later I drive with my father to a ranch he has in the foothills. The man who runs his cattle on it asks us to the roundup, a week from Sunday, and although I know that I will be in Los Angeles I say, in the oblique way my family talks, that I will come. Once home I mention the broken monuments in the graveyard. My mother shrugs.

I go to visit my great-aunts. A few of them think now that I am my cousin, or their daughter who died young. We recall an anecdote about a relative last seen in 1948, and they ask if I still like living in New York City. I have lived in Los Angeles for three years, but I say that I do. The baby is offered a horehound drop, and I am slipped a dollar bill "to buy a treat." Questions trail off, answers are abandoned, the baby plays with the dust motes in a shaft of afternoon sun.

It is time for the baby's birthday party: a white cake, strawberry-marshmallow ice cream, a bottle of champagne saved from another party. In the evening, after she has gone to sleep, I kneel beside the crib and touch her face, where it is pressed against the slats, with mine. She is an open and trusting child, unprepared for and unaccustomed to the ambushes of family life, and perhaps it is just as well that I can offer her little of that life. I would like to give her more. I would like to promise her that she will grow up with a sense of her cousins and of rivers and of her great-grandmother's teacups, would like to pledge her a picnic on a river with fried chicken and her hair uncombed, would like to give her *home* for her birthday, but we live differently now and I can promise her nothing like that. I give her a xylophone and a sundress from Madeira, and promise to tell her a funny story. ◆

READING WITH AN EYE FOR THE METHODS

1. "On Going Home" is an intimate DESCRIPTION of family life long rooted in a particular place and its ways. Point out specific details in Didion's description that you find most evocative of this place and the people in it. What makes those details so effective?

2. Didion's essay combines rich descriptive detail with a NARRATIVE of going back home to celebrate her daughter's first birthday. What happens on this occasion? What doesn't happen? How does Didion's husband figure into telling the story of people who can be "deliberately inarticulate" (1)?

3. Combining NARRATION and DESCRIPTION as in a short story, Didion's essay is also a commentary on the idea of home. How does Didion define home, and what position does she take on the issue of "going home"?

USING THE METHODS

1. Write an essay-length MEMOIR of going home. Describe the place and people in detail; tell what they typically do and say; and link your recollection to your present life, perhaps showing how it is different now from what it was in former times.

2. "The question of whether or not you could go home again," says Didion, "was a very real part of the sentimental and largely literary baggage with which we left home in the fifties" (2). Using Didion's essay as a starting point, do some research on the "can't-go-home-again" theme in American literature, and write a REPORT of 500 to 700 words explaining what it was and how it came about.

3. In your journal, keep notes of your visits home during the coming months. Include incidents and vivid details as Didion does, but also reflect in your journal on home as a conception—literary, sentimental, or otherwise.

4. Collect going-home stories from several of your classmates, and compile them into a collaborative essay with commentary on the nature of home and going back to it.

LINDA HOGAN

Hearing Voices

Linda Hogan (b. 1947) is a Chickasaw poet, novelist, and short-story writer. Born in Denver, she and her extended family are members of the Chickasaw Nation, for which she has served as writer in residence. After graduating from the University of Colorado, Colorado Springs, Hogan earned a master's degree in English and creative writing from the University of Colorado, Boulder, where she later taught creative writing and ethnic studies. Hogan has also been a professor at the University of Oklahoma. Her collections of poetry include the award-winning *Seeing through the Sun* (1985) and *Rounding the Human Corners* (2008). Like her poetry and essays, Hogan's fiction, including *People of the Whale* (2008), deals with environmental issues and Indigenous traditions. Her latest collection of poems is *Dark, Sweet* (2014).

In "Hearing Voices," an essay from the collection *The Writer on Her Work*, vol. 2, *New Essays in New Territory* (1991), Hogan defines writing (particularly poetry) and analyzes its causes and effects, both practical and mystical, in a personal narrative of her experience with the power of language. In Hogan's version of the literacy narrative genre, however, oral tradition and the spoken word are as important as the written language in its more traditional forms.

W HEN BARBARA MCCLINTOCK WAS AWARDED A NOBEL PRIZE for her work on [1] gene transposition in corn plants, the most striking thing about her was that she made her discoveries by listening to what the corn spoke to her, by respecting the life of the corn and "letting it come."

MLA CITATION: Hogan, Linda. "Hearing Voices." *Back to the Lake: A Reader and Guide for Writers*, edited by Thomas Cooley, 5th ed., W. W. Norton, 2024, pp. 749–54.

"As an Indian woman, I come from a long history of people who have listened to the language of this continent, people who know that corn grows with the songs and prayers of the people, that it has a story to tell, that the world is alive."

McClintock says she learned "the stories" of the plants. She "heard" them. She watched the daily green journeys of growth from earth toward sky and sun. She knew her plants in the way a healer or mystic would have known them, from the inside, the inner voices of corn and woman speaking to one another.

As an Indian woman, I come from a long history of people who have listened to the language of this continent, people who have known that corn grows with the songs and prayers of the people, that it has a story to tell, that the world is alive. Both in oral traditions and in mythology—the true language of inner life—account after account tells of the stones giving guidance, the trees singing, the corn telling of inner earth, the dragonfly offering up a tongue. This is true in the European traditions as well: Psyche received direction from the reeds and the ants, Orpheus knew the languages of earth, animals, and birds.[1]

This intuitive and common language is what I seek for my writing, work in touch with the mystery and force of life, work that speaks a few of the many voices around us, and it is important to me that McClintock listened to the voices of corn. It is important to the continuance of life that she told the truth of her method and that it reminded us all of where our strength, our knowing, and our sustenance come from.

It is also poetry, this science, and I note how often scientific theories lead to the world of poetry and vision, theories telling us how atoms that were stars have been transformed into our living, breathing bodies. And in these theories, or maybe they should be called stories, we begin to understand how we are each many people, including the stars we once were, and how we are in essence the earth and the universe, how what we do travels clear around the earth and returns. In a single moment of our living, there is our ancestral and personal history, our future, even our deaths planted in us and already growing toward their fulfillment. The corn plants are there, and like all the rest we are forever merging our borders with theirs in the world collective.

Our very lives might depend on this listening. In the Chernobyl nuclear accident,[2] the wind told the story that was being suppressed by the people. It gave away the truth. It carried the story of danger to other countries. It was a poet, a prophet, a scientist.

Sometimes, like the wind, poetry has its own laws speaking for the life of the planet. It is a language that wants to bring back together what the other words have torn apart. It is the language of life speaking through us about the sacredness of life.

---

1. *Orpheus, Psyche:* In Greek mythology, Orpheus was said to be able to charm animals, trees, and even rocks into dancing with the power of his beautiful voice. Psyche overcame a series of difficult tasks set by the goddess Aphrodite with the help of a reed, an eagle, and a group of ants.

2. *Chernobyl accident:* On April 26, 1986, an accident at the Chernobyl nuclear power plant resulted in radioactive contamination over large areas of what are now Belarus, Ukraine, and Russia.

This life speaking life is what I find so compelling about the work of poets such 8
as Ernesto Cardenal, who is also a priest and was the Nicaraguan Minister of Culture. He writes: "The armadilloes are very happy with this government. . . . Not only humans desired liberation / the whole ecology wanted it." Cardenal has also written "The Parrots," a poem about caged birds who were being sent to the United States as pets for the wealthy, how the cages were opened, the parrots allowed back into the mountains and jungles, freed like the people, "and sent back to the land we were pulled from."

How we have been pulled from the land! And how poetry has worked hard to set 9
us free, uncage us, keep us from split tongues that mimic the voices of our captors. It returns us to our land. Poetry is a string of words that parades without a permit. It is a lockbox of words to put an ear to as we try to crack the safe of language, listening for the right combination, the treasure inside. It is life resonating. It is sometimes called Prayer, Soothsaying, Complaint, Invocation, Proclamation, Testimony, Witness. Writing is and does all these things. And like that parade, it is illegitimately insistent on going its own way, on being part of the miracle of life, telling the story about what happened when we were cosmic dust, what it means to be stars listening to our human atoms.

But don't misunderstand me. I am not just a dreamer. I am also the practical 10
type. A friend's father, watching the United States stage another revolution in another Third World country, said, "Why doesn't the government just feed people and then let the political chips fall where they may?" He was right. It was easy, obvious, even financially more reasonable to do that, to let democracy be chosen because it feeds hunger. I want my writing to be that simple, that clear and direct. Likewise, I feel it is not enough for me just to write, but I need to live it, to be informed by it. I have found over the years that my work has more courage than I do. It has more wisdom. It teaches me, leads me places I never knew I was heading. And it is about a new way of living, of being in the world.

Combining NARRATIVE and ARGUMENT is discussed on p. 736.

I was on a panel recently where the question was raised whether we thought 11
literature could save lives. The audience, book people, smiled expectantly with the thought. I wanted to say, Yes, it saves lives. But I couldn't speak those words. It saves spirits maybe, hearts. It changes minds, but for me writing is an incredible privilege. When I sit down at the desk, there are other women who are hungry, homeless. I don't want to forget that, that the world of matter is still there to be reckoned with. This writing is a form of freedom most other people do not have. So, when I write, I feel a responsibility, a commitment to other humans and to the animal and plant communities as well.

Still, writing has changed me. And there is the powerful need we all have to tell 12
a story, each of us with a piece of the whole pattern to complete. As Alice Walker

says, We are all telling part of the same story, and as Sharon Olds has said, Every writer is a cell on the body politic of America.[3]

Another Nobel Prize laureate is Betty William, a Northern Ireland co-winner 13 of the 1977 Peace Prize. I heard her speak about how, after witnessing the death of children, she stepped outside in the middle of the night and began knocking on doors and yelling, behaviors that would have earned her a diagnosis of hysteria in our own medical circles. She knocked on doors that might have opened with weapons pointing in her face, and she cried out, "What kind of people have we become that we would allow children to be killed on our streets?" Within four hours the city was awake, and there were sixteen thousand names on petitions for peace. Now, that woman's work is a lesson to those of us who deal with language, and to those of us who are dealt into silence. She used language to begin the process of peace. This is the living, breathing power of the word. It is poetry. So are the names of those who signed the petitions. Maybe it is this kind of language that saves lives.

Writing begins for me with survival, with life and with freeing life, saving life, 14 speaking life. It is work that speaks what can't be easily said. It originates from a compelling desire to live and be alive. For me, it is sometimes the need to speak for other forms of life, to take the side of human life, even our sometimes frivolous living, and our grief-filled living, our joyous living, our violent living, busy living, our peaceful living. It is about possibility. It is based in the world of matter. I am interested in how something small turns into an image that is large and strong with resonance, where the ordinary becomes beautiful. I believe the divine, the magic, is here in the weeds at our feet, unacknowledged. What a world this is. Where else could water rise up to the sky, turn into snow crystals, magnificently brought together, fall from the sky all around us, pile up billions deep, and catch the small sparks of sunlight as they return again to water?

These acts of magic happen all the time; in Chaco Canyon,[4] my sister has seen 15 a kiva, a ceremonial room in the earth, that is in the center of the canyon. This place has been uninhabited for what seems like forever. It has been without water. In fact, there are theories that the ancient people disappeared when they journeyed after water. In the center of it a corn plant was growing. It was all alone and it had been there since the ancient ones, the old ones who came before us all, those people who wove dog hair into belts, who witnessed the painting of flute players on the seeping canyon walls, who knew the stories of corn. And there was one corn plant growing out of the holy place. It planted itself yearly. With no water, no

---

3. *Sharon Olds* (b. 1942): American poet. *Alice Walker* (b. 1944): American writer best known for her novel *The Color Purple.*

4. *Chaco Canyon*: A US National Historical Park, located in northwestern New Mexico, which was once home to an ancient pueblo people.

person to care for it, no overturning of the soil, this corn plant rises up to tell its story, and that's what this poetry is. ◆

READING WITH AN EYE FOR THE METHODS

1. Hogan explicitly **DEFINES** writing, particularly poetry, in paragraph 9. In what ways, according to her definition, is writing "a string of words that parades without a permit"? Where else in the narrative does Hogan define writing? Point to specific passages in the text, and explain what they add to her definition.

2. What **EFFECTS**, in Hogan's view, can language have upon the world? In her analysis, what gives language its power? What are some of the **CAUSES** of its coming into being?

3. As a **LITERACY NARRATIVE**, how and where does "Hearing Voices" tell about Hogan's coming to understand and use the power of language? According to this near-mythic story, why does she write?

USING THE METHODS

1. According to Hogan, mythology is "the true language of inner life" (3). In a paragraph or two, speculate on what she might mean by this definition as evidenced by her comments on nature and the origins of language.

2. Referring to the work of Barbara McClintock, who won a Nobel Prize in 1983 for her discovery of genetic transposition in corn, Hogan notes "how often scientific theories lead to the world of poetry and vision" (5). Write a **POSITION PAPER** of approximately 450 words supporting (or contesting) this view by referring to a specific scientific theory.

3. Hogan says she is "interested in how something small turns into an image that is large and strong with resonance" (14). Write a **RHETORICAL ANALYSIS** of a poem or short story that illustrates this principle, as does, for example, the stalk of corn at the end of Hogan's essay.

4. Take your journal into the woods or a field or park, and listen to the "voices" around you. Make notes describing what you hear, and record in your journal the words and images they call to mind.

GLORIA ANZALDÚA

Linguistic Terrorism

Gloria Anzaldúa (1942–2004) was known for her contributions to Chicana, feminist, postcolonial, and gender studies, which grew out of her sense of being "on the margins" in terms of sexuality, nationality, language, and skin color. Anzaldúa was born in the Rio Grande Valley along the Mexican border in southern Texas, where her ancestors, the descendants of early Spanish settlers in Mexico and of Indigenous Americans, had long been ranchers. After graduating from the University of Texas, Pan American (now the University of Texas Rio Grande Valley), she earned a master's degree from the University of Texas at Austin and taught in preschools and special education classes before moving to California. An editor of *This Bridge Called My Back: Writings by Radical Women of Color* (1981), Anzaldúa wrote fiction and poetry as well as several books for children.

"Linguistic Terrorism" is from Anzaldúa's semiautobiographical *Borderlands / La Frontera: The New Mestiza* (1987), a "mixed" form of writing that combines prose and poetry, two varieties of English, and six varieties of Spanish. Anzaldúa used this mixture deliberately to make the text frustrating for most readers to follow and thereby evoke the author's sense of herself as an outsider with multiple identities.

MLA CITATION: Anzaldúa, Gloria. "Linguistic Terrorism." *Back to the Lake: A Reader and Guide for Writers*, edited by Thomas Cooley, 5th ed., W. W. Norton, 2024, pp. 756–57.

> Deslenguadas. Somos los del español deficiente. *We are your linguistic nightmare, your linguistic aberration, your linguistic* mestizaje, *the subject of your* burla. *Because we speak with tongues of fire we are culturally crucified. Racially, culturally and linguistically* somos huérfanos—*we speak an orphan tongue.*

CHICANAS WHO GREW UP SPEAKING CHICANO SPANISH have internalized the belief that we speak poor Spanish. It is illegitimate, a bastard language. And because we internalize how our language has been used against us by the dominant culture, we use our language differences against each other.

Chicana feminists often skirt around each other with suspicion and hesitation. For the longest time I couldn't figure it out. Then it dawned on me. To be close to another Chicana is like looking into the mirror. We are afraid of what we'll see there. *Pena.* Shame. Low estimation of self. In childhood we are told that our language is wrong. Repeated attacks on our native tongue diminish our sense of self. The attacks continue throughout our lives.

Chicanas feel uncomfortable talking in Spanish to Latinas, afraid of their censure. Their language was not outlawed in their countries. They had a whole lifetime of being immersed in their native tongue; generations, centuries in which Spanish was a first language, taught in school, heard on radio and TV, and read in the newspaper.

If a person, Chicana or Latina, has a low estimation of my native tongue, she also has a low estimation of me. Often with *mexicanas y latinas* we'll speak English as a neutral language. Even among Chicanas we tend to speak English at parties or conferences. Yet, at the same time, we're afraid the other will think we're *agringadas* because we don't speak Chicano Spanish. We oppress each other trying to out-Chicano each other, vying to be the "real" Chicanas, to speak like Chicanos. There is no one Chicano language just as there is no one Chicano experience. A monolingual Chicana whose first language is English or Spanish is just as much a Chicana as one who speaks several variants of Spanish. A Chicana from Michigan or Chicago or Detroit is just as much a Chicana as one from the Southwest. Chicano Spanish is as diverse linguistically as it is regionally.

See p. 735 for tips on introducing CLASSIFICATION into your text.

By the end of this century, Spanish speakers will comprise the biggest minority group in the United States, a country where students in high schools and colleges are encouraged to take French classes because French is considered more "cultured." But for a language to remain alive it must be used.* By the end of this

---

*Irena Klepfisz, "Secular Jewish Identity: Yidishkayt in America," in *The Tribe of Dina*, Kaye/Kantrowitz and Klepfisz, eds., 43. [Author's note]

century English, and not Spanish, will be the mother tongue of most Chicanos and Latinos.

So, if you want to really hurt me, talk badly about my language. Ethnic identity is   6
twin skin to linguistic identity—I am my language. Until I can take pride in my language, I cannot take pride in myself. Until I can accept as legitimate Chicano Texas Spanish, Tex-Mex and all the other languages I speak, I cannot accept the legitimacy of myself. Until I am free to write bilingually and to switch codes without having always to translate, while I still have to speak English or Spanish when I would rather speak Spanglish, and as long as I have to accommodate the English speakers rather than having them accommodate me, my tongue will be illegitimate.

I will no longer be made to feel ashamed of existing. I will have my voice: Indian,   7
Spanish, white. I will have my serpent's tongue—my woman's voice, my sexual voice, my poet's voice. I will overcome the tradition of silence.

> *My fingers*
> *move sly against your palm.*
> *Like women everywhere, we speak in code. . . .*
> —MELANIE KAYE/KANTROWITZ* ◆

READING WITH AN EYE FOR THE METHODS

1. In "Linguistic Terrorism," Anzaldúa CLASSIFIES Spanish-speaking Americans into different types. Which type (or types) does she belong to? Why does it matter, according to her?

2. In addition to identifying different types of language and speakers, Anzaldúa analyzes the CAUSES of her own linguistic diversity. What are some of them? What specific EFFECTS do they have on her identity, both linguistic and personal?

3. Who are the linguistic terrorists in Anzaldúa's account? What POSITION does she take to oppose them? How and where does she use the different languages she speaks to support that position?

USING THE METHODS

1. Before explaining how and why she speaks and writes as she does, Anzaldúa gives a demonstration of her use of mixed languages. Taking Anzaldúa's opening paragraph as a model, write a "mixed" paragraph of your own using the different languages you know, including different varieties of English.

---

*Melanie Kaye/Kantrowitz, "Sign," in *We Speak in Code: Poems and Other Writings* (Pittsburgh, PA: Motheroot Publications, Inc., 1980), 85. [Author's note]

2. "By the end of this century," Anzaldúa wrote in 1987, "Spanish speakers will comprise the biggest minority group in the United States" (5). Did her prophecy come to pass? Do some research on the composition of minority groups in the United States today, and write a **REPORT** on how they are **DEFINED** and **CLASSIFIED**, both ethnically and linguistically.

3. "Ethnic identity," says Anzaldúa, "is twin skin to linguistic identity—I am my language" (6). Write a 400-to-600-word **POSITION PAPER** supporting (or contesting) this proposition. Be sure to identify the linguistic type (or types) you belong to and to **ANALYZE** the causes and effects of that identity.

4. In your journal, take note of the different varieties of English and other languages that you use in speaking and writing over a period of time. Include specific words and phrases, and consider the different levels of usage (formal, slang, technical) that they fall into.

GEORGE ORWELL

Shooting an Elephant

George Orwell (1903–50) was the pen name of Eric Arthur Blair, a British novelist and essayist who is perhaps best known for *Animal Farm* (1945) and *Nineteen Eighty-Four* (1949), his political satires on collectivism and dictatorship. Although Orwell was educated at Eton College in Berkshire, England, he was born in Bengal, India, and served in the Indian Imperial Police in Myanmar (then called Burma) from 1922 to 1927. Wounded in the Spanish Civil War, Orwell returned to England and settled in Hertfordshire to raise hens and vegetables and to write.

"Shooting an Elephant" (1936) captures Orwell's time as an official agent of British colonialism in Southeast Asia. The essay combines startlingly vivid description and narration with disturbing observations on the role of colonial administrators and their attitudes toward local inhabitants. These were to be Orwell's final days of doing "the dirty work of Empire," he tells us. "For at that time I had already made up my mind that imperialism was an evil thing and the sooner I chucked up my job and got out of it the better."

I N MOULMEIN, IN LOWER BURMA, I was hated by large numbers of people—the only time in my life that I have been important enough for this to happen to me. I was sub-divisional police officer of the town, and in an aimless, petty kind of way anti-European feeling was very bitter. No one had the guts to raise a riot, but if a European woman went through the bazaars alone somebody would probably spit betel juice over her dress. As a police officer I was an obvious target and was baited whenever it seemed safe to do so. When a nimble Burman tripped me up on the

MLA CITATION: Orwell, George. "Shooting an Elephant." *Back to the Lake: A Reader and Guide for Writers*, edited by Thomas Cooley, 5th ed., W. W. Norton, 2024, pp. 759–65.

football field and the referee (another Burman) looked the other way, the crowd yelled with hideous laughter. This happened more than once. In the end the sneering yellow faces of young men that met me everywhere, the insults hooted after me when I was at a safe distance, got badly on my nerves. The young Buddhist priests were the worst of all. There were several thousands of them in the town and none of them seemed to have anything to do except stand on street corners and jeer at Europeans.

All this was perplexing and upsetting. For at that time I had already made up my mind that imperialism was an evil thing and the sooner I chucked up my job and got out of it the better. Theoretically—and secretly, of course—I was all for the Burmese and all against their oppressors, the British.[1] As for the job I was doing, I hated it more bitterly than I can perhaps make clear. In a job like that you see the dirty work of Empire at close quarters. The wretched prisoners huddling in the stinking cages of the lock-ups, the grey, cowed faces of the long-term convicts, the scarred buttocks of the men who had been Bogged with bamboos—all these oppressed me with an intolerable sense of guilt. But I could get nothing into perspective. I was young and ill-educated and I had had to think out my problems in the utter silence that is imposed on every Englishman in the East. I did not even know that the British Empire is dying, still less did I know that it is a great deal better than the younger empires that are going to supplant it. All I knew was that I was stuck between my hatred of the empire I served and my rage against the evil-spirited little beasts who tried to make my job impossible. With one part of my mind I thought of the British Raj as an unbreakable tyranny, as something clamped down, in saecula saeculorum,[2] upon the will of prostrate peoples; with another part I thought that the greatest joy in the world would be to drive a bayonet into a Buddhist priest's guts. Feelings like these are the normal by-products of imperialism; ask any Anglo-Indian official, if you can catch him off duty.

> A NARRATIVE should maintain a consistent POINT OF VIEW (p. 119) even when the writer is of two minds.

One day something happened which in a roundabout way was enlightening. It was a tiny incident in itself, but it gave me a better glimpse than I had had before of the real nature of imperialism—the real motives for which despotic governments act. Early one morning the sub-inspector at a police station the other end of the town rang me up on the phone and said that an elephant was ravaging the bazaar. Would I please come and do something about it? I did not know what I could do, but I wanted to see what was happening and I got on to a pony and started out. I took my rifle, an old 44 Winchester and much too small to kill an elephant, but I thought the noise might be useful in terrorem.[3] Various Burmans stopped me on the way

---

1. Myanmar declared independence from Britain on July 4, 1948.
2. "Forever and ever," traditional ending of many of the Latin prayers in the Catholic liturgy.
3. A mere threat (Latin for "in fear").

and told me about the elephant's doings. It was not, of course, a wild elephant, but a tame one which had gone "must." It had been chained up, as tame elephants always are when their attack of "must" is due, but on the previous night it had broken its chain and escaped. Its mahout, the only person who could manage it when it was in that state, had set out in pursuit, but had taken the wrong direction and was now twelve hours' journey away, and in the morning the elephant had suddenly reappeared in the town. The Burmese population had no weapons and were quite helpless against it. It had already destroyed somebody's bamboo hut, killed a cow and raided some fruit-stalls and devoured the stock; also it had met the municipal rubbish van and, when the driver jumped out and took to his heels, had turned the van over and inflicted violences upon it.

The Burmese sub-inspector and some Indian constables were waiting for me in 4 the quarter where the elephant had been seen. It was a very poor quarter, a labyrinth of squalid bamboo huts, thatched with palmleaf, winding all over a steep hillside. I remember that it was a cloudy, stuffy morning at the beginning of the rains. We began questioning the people as to where the elephant had gone and, as usual, failed to get any definite information. That is invariably the case in the East; a story always sounds clear enough at a distance, but the nearer you get to the scene of events the vaguer it becomes. Some of the people said that the elephant had gone in one direction, some said that he had gone in another, some professed not even to have heard of any elephant. I had almost made up my mind that the whole story was a pack of lies, when we heard yells a little distance away. There was a loud, scandalized cry of "Go away, child! Go away this instant!" and an old woman with a switch in her hand came round the corner of a hut, violently shooing away a crowd of naked children. Some more women followed, clicking their tongues and exclaiming; evidently there was something that the children ought not to have seen. I rounded the hut and saw a man's dead body sprawling in the mud. He was an Indian, a black Dravidian coolie,[4] almost naked, and he could not have been dead many minutes. The people said that the elephant had come suddenly upon him round the corner of the hut, caught him with its trunk, put its foot on his back and ground him into the earth. This was the rainy season and the ground was soft, and his face had scored a trench a foot deep and a couple of yards long. He was lying on his belly with arms crucified and head sharply twisted to one side. His face was coated with mud, the eyes wide open, the teeth bared and grinning with an expression of unendurable agony. (Never tell me, by the way, that the dead look peaceful. Most of the corpses I have seen looked devilish.) The friction of the great beast's

---

4. Originating in India as a term for a day laborer, the now pejorative term "coolie" is roughly equivalent to "peasant" in English. The word may have derived from the word for "wages" in Dravidian, a language group spoken mainly in southern India where the dead man apparently came from.

foot had stripped the skin from his back as neatly as one skins a rabbit. As soon as I saw the dead man I sent an orderly to a friend's house nearby to borrow an elephant rifle. I had already sent back the pony, not wanting it to go mad with fright and throw me if it smelt the elephant.

The orderly came back in a few minutes with a rifle and five cartridges, and meanwhile some Burmans had arrived and told us that the elephant was in the paddy fields below, only a few hundred yards away. As I started forward practically the whole population of the quarter flocked out of the houses and followed me. They had seen the rifle and were all shouting excitedly that I was going to shoot the elephant. They had not shown much interest in the elephant when he was merely ravaging their homes, but it was different now that he was going to be shot. It was a bit of fun to them, as it would be to an English crowd; besides they wanted the meat. It made me vaguely uneasy. I had no intention of shooting the elephant—I had merely sent for the rifle to defend myself if necessary—and it is always unnerving to have a crowd following you. I marched down the hill, looking and feeling a fool, with the rifle over my shoulder and an ever-growing army of people jostling at my heels. At the bottom, when you got away from the huts, there was a metalled road and beyond that a miry waste of paddy fields a thousand yards across, not yet ploughed but soggy from the first rains and dotted with coarse grass. The elephant was standing eight yards from the road, his left side towards us. He took not the slightest notice of the crowd's approach. He was tearing up bunches of grass, beating them against his knees to clean them and stuffing them into his mouth.

I had halted on the road. As soon as I saw the elephant I knew with perfect certainty that I ought not to shoot him. It is a serious matter to shoot a working elephant—it is comparable to destroying a huge and costly piece of machinery—and obviously one ought not to do it if it can possibly be avoided. And at that distance, peacefully eating, the elephant looked no more dangerous than a cow. I thought then and I think now that his attack of "must" was already passing off; in which case he would merely wander harmlessly about until the mahout came back and caught him. Moreover, I did not in the least want to shoot him. I decided that I would watch him for a little while to make sure that he did not turn savage again, and then go home.

But at that moment I glanced round at the crowd that had followed me. It was an immense crowd, two thousand at the least and growing every minute. It blocked the road for a long distance on either side. I looked at the sea of yellow faces above the garish clothes—faces all happy and excited over this bit of fun, all certain that the elephant was going to be shot. They were watching me as they would watch a conjurer about to perform a trick. They did not like me, but with the magical rifle in my hands I was momentarily worth watching. And suddenly I realized that I should have to shoot the elephant after all. The people expected it of me and I had got to do it; I could feel their two thousand wills pressing me forward, irresistibly. And it was at this moment, as I stood there with the rifle in my hands, that I first grasped the hollowness, the futility of the white man's dominion in the East. Here was I, the white man with his gun, standing in front of the unarmed native crowd—seemingly the leading actor of the piece; but in reality I was only an absurd puppet pushed to and fro by the will of those yellow faces behind. I perceived in this moment that when the white man turns tyrant it is his own freedom that he destroys. He becomes a sort of hollow, posing dummy, the conventionalized figure of a sahib.[5] For it is the condition of his rule that he shall spend his life in trying to impress the "natives," and so in every crisis he has got to do what the "natives" expect of him. He wears a mask, and his face grows to fit it. I had got to shoot the elephant. I had committed myself to doing it when I sent for the rifle. A sahib has got to act like a sahib; he has got to appear resolute, to know his own mind and do definite things. To come all that way, rifle in hand, with two thousand people marching at my heels, and then to trail feebly away, having done nothing—no, that was impossible. The crowd would laugh at me. And my whole life, every white man's life in the East, was one long struggle not to be laughed at.

> Detaching himself from the scene here, Orwell constructs a CRITICAL ANALYSIS (p. 300) of it.

But I did not want to shoot the elephant. I watched him beating his bunch of grass against his knees, with that preoccupied grandmotherly air that elephants have. It seemed to me that it would be murder to shoot him. At that age I was not squeamish about killing animals, but I had never shot an elephant and never wanted to. (Somehow it always seems worse to kill a large animal.) Besides, there was the beast's owner to be considered. Alive, the elephant was worth at least a hundred pounds; dead, he would only be worth the value of his tusks, five pounds, possibly. But I had got to act quickly. I turned to some experienced-looking Burmans who had been there when we arrived, and asked them how the elephant had been behaving. They all said the same thing: he took no notice of you if you left him alone, but he might charge if you went too close to him.

It was perfectly clear to me what I ought to do. I ought to walk up to within, say, twenty-five yards of the elephant and test his behavior. If he charged, I could shoot; if he took no notice of me, it would be safe to leave him until the mahout came back. But also I knew that I was going to do no such thing. I was a poor shot with a rifle and the ground was soft mud into which one would sink at every step. If the elephant charged and I missed him, I should have about as much chance as a toad under a steam-roller. But even then I was not thinking particularly of my own skin, only of the watchful yellow faces behind. For at that moment, with the crowd watching me, I was not afraid in the ordinary sense, as I would have been if I had been alone. A white man mustn't be frightened in front of "natives"; and so, in

8

9

---

5. A term of address, like sir or mister, for a government official during the British "raj" (or "rule").

general, he isn't frightened. The sole thought in my mind was that if anything went wrong those two thousand Burmans would see me pursued, caught, trampled on and reduced to a grinning corpse like that Indian up the hill. And if that happened it was quite probable that some of them would laugh. That would never do.

There was only one alternative. I shoved the cartridges into the magazine and lay   10 down on the road to get a better aim. The crowd grew very still, and a deep, low, happy sigh, as of people who see the theatre curtain go up at last, breathed from innumerable throats. They were going to have their bit of fun after all. The rifle was a beautiful German thing with cross-hair sights. I did not then know that in shooting an elephant one would shoot to cut an imaginary bar running from ear-hole to ear-hole. I ought, therefore, as the elephant was sideways on, to have aimed straight at his ear-hole, actually I aimed several inches in front of this, thinking the brain would be further forward.

When I pulled the trigger I did not hear the bang or feel the kick—one never   11 does when a shot goes home—but I heard the devilish roar of glee that went up from the crowd. In that instant, in too short a time, one would have thought, even for the bullet to get there, a mysterious, terrible change had come over the elephant. He neither stirred nor fell, but every line of his body had altered. He looked suddenly stricken, shrunken, immensely old, as though the frightful impact of the bullet had paralysed him without knocking him down. At last, after what seemed a long time—it might have been five seconds, I dare say—he sagged flabbily to his knees. His mouth slobbered. An enormous senility seemed to have settled upon him. One could have imagined him thousands of years old. I fired again into the same spot. At the second shot he did not collapse but climbed with desperate slowness to his feet and stood weakly upright, with legs sagging and head drooping. I fired a third time. That was the shot that did for him. You could see the agony of it jolt his whole body and knock the last remnant of strength from his legs. But in falling he seemed for a moment to rise, for as his hind legs collapsed beneath him he seemed to tower upward like a huge rock toppling, his trunk reaching skyward like a tree. He trumpeted, for the first and only time. And then down he came, his belly towards me, with a crash that seemed to shake the ground even where I lay.

I got up. The Burmans were already racing past me across the mud. It was obvi-   12 ous that the elephant would never rise again, but he was not dead. He was breathing very rhythmically with long rattling gasps, his great mound of a side painfully rising and falling. His mouth was wide open—I could see far down into caverns of pale pink throat. I waited a long time for him to die, but his breathing did not weaken. Finally I fired my two remaining shots into the spot where I thought his heart must be. The thick blood welled out of him like red velvet, but still he did not die. His body did not even jerk when the shots hit him, the tortured breathing continued without a pause. He was dying, very slowly and in great agony, but in some world remote from me where not even a bullet could damage him further. I felt that I had got to put an end to that dreadful noise. It seemed dreadful to see the great beast Lying there, powerless to move and yet powerless to die, and not even to be able to finish him. I sent back for my small rifle and poured shot after shot into his heart and down his throat. They seemed to make no impression. The tortured gasps continued as steadily as the ticking of a clock.

In the end I could not stand it any longer and went away. I heard later that it took 13 him half an hour to die. Burmans were bringing dash and baskets even before I left, and I was told they had stripped his body almost to the bones by the afternoon.

Afterwards, of course, there were endless discussions about the shooting of the 14 elephant. The owner was furious, but he was only an Indian and could do nothing. Besides, legally I had done the right thing, for a mad elephant has to be killed, like a mad dog, if its owner fails to control it. Among the Europeans opinion was divided. The older men said I was right, the younger men said it was a damn shame to shoot an elephant for killing a coolie, because an elephant was worth more than any damn Coringhee[6] coolie. And afterwards I was very glad that the coolie had been killed; it put me legally in the right and it gave me a sufficient pretext for shooting the elephant. I often wondered whether any of the others grasped that I had done it solely to avoid looking a fool. ◆

READING WITH AN EYE FOR THE METHODS

1. Why did George Orwell shoot the elephant if he didn't want to and "had no intention" of doing it (5)? How do his motives as a character in a public drama reinforce his **ARGUMENT** about the evils of "imperialism"?

2. In Orwell's **NARRATIVE**, why does the death of the man (4) lead inevitably to the death of the elephant (11–13)? Why does Orwell mention the dead man again in the last paragraph of his essay? Is there a **CAUSE-AND-EFFECT** relationship here? Explain.

3. Point out specific details in Orwell's **DESCRIPTION** of the crowd that dehumanize them—and him. Where and why does Orwell's description of the dying elephant sometimes have the opposite effect?

USING THE METHODS

1. "Afterwards, of course, there were endless discussions about the shooting of the elephant" (14). In a paragraph or two, outline the position you would take in these "discussions."

---

6. Another group, like "Dravidians," of migrant workers from southern India.

2. The British ruled Burma (present-day Myanmar) from 1824 to 1948. Do some research on the end of the British Raj, and then write a brief **REPORT** explaining the context of Orwell's essay—particularly the role of a "sahib" like himself.

3. "And afterwards I was very glad that the coolie had been killed" (14). This is a shocking statement coming from a man who "was all for the Burmese and all against their oppressors, the British" (2). In a 400-to-600-word **CRITICAL ANALYSIS** of Orwell's essay, discuss this **IRONY** and explain how it confirms (or does not confirm) Orwell's claim that "when the white man turns tyrant it is his own freedom he destroys" (7).

ANNIE DILLARD

The Death of a Moth

Annie Dillard (b. 1945) is a poet, essayist, and novelist. Born in Pittsburgh, she attended Hollins College in Roanoke, Virginia, where she earned a master's degree in English literature in 1968. In 1975, Dillard moved to an island in Puget Sound in Washington State near the Canadian border. Living alone "in full flight from success," Dillard remembered a vivid moment from a camping trip that she had taken two years before in the Blue Ridge Mountains. "Perhaps I'd try to write a short narrative about it," she recalls in "How I Wrote the Moth Essay—and Why" (p. 328).

With a title echoing that of Virginia Woolf's classic essay, the piece that Dillard composed on that November day on a lonely island in Puget Sound was "The Death of a Moth," first published in *Harper's Magazine* and later incorporated in a longer prose narrative, *Holy the Firm* (1977). A personal account of living alone and the demands of writing and the writer's life, Dillard's moth essay is also a little masterpiece of description that captures the illuminating essence (or "moth-essence") of the natural scene.

I LIVE ON NORTHERN PUGET SOUND, in Washington State, alone. I have a gold cat,   1 who sleeps on my legs, named Small. In the morning I joke to her blank face, Do you remember last night? Do you remember? I throw her out before breakfast, so I can eat.

There is a spider, too, in the bathroom, with whom I keep a sort of company. Her little outfit always reminds me of a certain moth I helped to kill. The spider herself is of uncertain lineage, bulbous at the abdomen and drab. Her six-inch mess of a web works, works somehow, works miraculously, to

Why keep company with spiders when plotting a narrative? See Miss Muffet's adventures on p. 117.

MLA CITATION: Dillard, Annie. "The Death of a Moth." *Back to the Lake: A Reader and Guide for Writers*, edited by Thomas Cooley, 5th ed., W. W. Norton, 2024, pp. 767–70.

keep her alive and me amazed. The web itself is in a corner behind the toilet, connecting tile wall to tile wall and floor, in a place where there is, I would have thought, scant traffic. Yet under the web are sixteen or so corpses she has tossed to the floor.

The corpses appear to be mostly sow bugs, those little armadillo creatures who 3 live to travel flat out in houses, and die round. There is also a new shred of earwig, three old spider skins crinkled and clenched, and two moth bodies, wingless and huge and empty, moth bodies I drop to my knees to see.

Today the earwig shines darkly and gleams, what there is of him: a dorsal curve 4 of thorax and abdomen, and a smooth pair of cerci[1] by which I knew his name. Next week, if the other bodies are any indication, he will be shrunken and gray, webbed to the floor with dust. The sow bugs beside him are hollow and empty of color, fragile, a breath away from brittle fluff. The spider skins lie on their sides, translucent and ragged, their legs drying in knots. And the moths, the empty moths, stagger against each other, headless, in a confusion of arching strips of chitin like peeling varnish, like a jumble of buttresses for cathedral domes, like nothing resembling moths, so that I should hesitate to call them moths, except that I have had some experience with the figure Moth reduced to a nub.

Two summers ago I was camping alone in the Blue Ridge Mountains in Virginia. I 5 had hauled myself and gear up there to read, among other things, James Ramsey Ullman's *The Day on Fire*, a novel about Rimbaud that had made me want to be a writer when I was sixteen;[2] I was hoping it would do it again. So I read, lost, every day sitting under a tree by my tent, while warblers swung in the leaves overhead and bristle worms trailed their inches over the twiggy dirt at my feet; and I read every night by candlelight, while barred owls called in the forest and pale moths massed round my head in the clearing, where my light made a ring.

Moths kept flying into the candle. They would hiss and recoil, lost upside down 6 in the shadows among my cooking pans. Or they would singe their wings and fall, and their hot wings, as if melted, would stick to the first thing they touched—a pan, a lid, a spoon—so that the snagged moths could flutter only in tiny arcs, unable to struggle free. These I could release by a quick flip with a stick; in the morning I would find my cooking stuff gilded with torn flecks of moth wings, triangles of shiny dust here and there on the aluminum. So I read, and boiled water, and replenished candles, and read on.

One night a moth flew into the candle, was caught, burnt dry, and held. I must 7 have been staring at the candle, or maybe I looked up when a shadow crossed my

1. *Cerci*: Plural of cercus, posterior "feeler" of an insect.
2. French poet Arthur Rimbaud (1854-91) himself began writing at age sixteen and produced his major work before he was twenty. Ullman's novel was published in 1958.

page; at any rate, I saw it all. A golden female moth, a biggish one with a two-inch wingspan, flapped into the fire, dropped her abdomen into the wet wax, stuck, flamed, frazzled and fried in a second. Her moving wings ignited like tissue paper, enlarging the circle of light in the clearing and creating out of the darkness the sudden blue sleeves of my sweater, the green leaves of jewelweed by my side, the ragged red trunk of a pine. At once the light contracted again and the moth's wings vanished in a fine, foul smoke. At the same time her six legs clawed, curled, blackened, and ceased, disappearing utterly. And her head jerked in spasms, making a spattering noise; her antennae crisped and burned away and her heaving mouth parts crackled like pistol fire. When it was all over, her head was, so far as I could determine, gone, gone the long way of her wings and legs. Had she been new, or old? Had she mated and laid her eggs, had she done her work? All that was left was the glowing horn shell of her abdomen and thorax—a fraying, partially collapsed gold tube jammed upright in the candle's round pool.

And then this moth-essence, this spectacular skeleton, began to act as a wick. She kept burning. The wax rose in the moth's body from her soaking abdomen to her thorax to the jagged hole where her head should be, and widened into flame, a saffron-yellow flame that robed her to the ground like any immolating monk. That candle had two wicks, two flames of identical height, side by side. The moth's head was fire. She burned for two hours, until I blew her out.

> When DESCRIBING an essence, use CONCRETE and SPECIFIC details (p. 185).

She burned for two hours without changing, without bending or leaning—only 9 glowing within, like a building fire glimpsed through silhouetted walls, like a hollow saint, like a flame-faced virgin gone to God, while I read by her light, kindled, while Rimbaud in Paris burnt out his brains in a thousand poems, while night pooled wetly at my feet.

And that is why I believe those hollow crisps on the bathroom floor are moths. I 10 think I know moths, and fragments of moths, and chips and tatters of utterly empty moths, in any state. How many of you, I asked the people in my class, which of you want to give your lives and be writers? I was trembling from coffee, or cigarettes, or the closeness of faces all around me. (Is this what we live for? I thought; is this the only final beauty: the color of any skin in any light, and living, human eyes?) All hands rose to the question. (You, Nick? Will you? Margaret? Randy? Why do I want them to mean it?) And then I tried to tell them what the choice must mean: you can't be anything else. You must go at your life with a broadax. . . . They had no idea what I was saying. (I have two hands, don't I? And all this energy, for as long as I can remember. I'll do it in the evenings, after skiing, or on the way home from the bank, or after the children are asleep. . . .) They thought I was raving again. It's just as well.

I have three candles here on the table which I disentangle from the plants and 11 light when visitors come. Small usually avoids them, although once she came too close and her tail caught fire; I rubbed it out before she noticed. The flames move light over everyone's skin, draw light to the surface of the faces of my friends. When the people leave I never blow the candles out, and after I'm asleep they flame and burn. ◆

READING WITH AN EYE FOR THE METHODS

1. Annie Dillard's essay is made up of three interlocking NARRATIVES, beginning with an account of what she finds "today" on the bathroom floor of her home (4). Where do the other two parts of her story begin and end, and what happens in them? When does she return to the present?

2. What is the purpose of Dillard's detailed DESCRIPTION of the "corpses" on her bathroom floor, including "two moth bodies, wingless and huge and empty" (3)? How do the physical details of this little scene anticipate her account of the camping trip in the Blue Ridge Mountains?

3. In paragraph 10 of her narrative, Dillard is talking to her students about writing. What aspect of the process is she trying to explain? What does this discussion have to do with her account of the burning moth?

USING THE METHODS

1. Write a paragraph DESCRIBING a spider in its web—and any other objects you find in and around that little scene.

2. In a brief NARRATIVE, tell the story of how you were inspired to engage in some creative activity (for example, writing, painting, singing, dancing) by observing nature. Try to capture the place in sufficient detail for the reader to visualize it— and perhaps hear, feel, smell, or taste certain elements of the composition.

3. In a five-to-seven-paragraph CRITICAL ANALYSIS of "The Death of a Moth" as an essay about writing and the life of the writer, COMPARE AND CONTRAST Dillard's narrative with Virginia Woolf's classic "The Death of the Moth" (1942), which is readily accessible online.

17

Doing Research, Using Sources

Quiet
Area

Research is formalized curiosity. It is poking and prying with a purpose.

—ZORA NEALE HURSTON

Doing research requires "poking and prying" into sources of information that go well beyond your own immediate knowledge of a subject. In this chapter, we'll discuss where to look for sources that are relevant to your topic, how to test the reliability and accuracy of those sources—particularly if you find them online—and how to cite and document what you learn from your research (or "formalized curiosity") in your own writing.

Finding Primary and Secondary Sources

As you begin your research, you will encounter a wide range of potential sources—print and online, general and specialized, published and firsthand, primary and secondary. *Primary sources*, incidentally, are original works, such as historical documents, literary works, eyewitness accounts, diaries, letters, and lab studies, as well as any original field research you do. *Secondary sources* include books and articles, reviews, biographies, and other works that interpret or discuss primary sources.

Whether a work is considered primary or secondary often depends on your topic and purpose. If you're analyzing a poem, a critic's article about it is a secondary source—but if you're investigating the critic's work, the article would be a primary source. The topic and purpose of your research will determine not only the kinds of sources you look for but also where you look for them. If you're doing research on a literary or historical topic, for instance, you might consult scholarly books and articles and standard reference works such as the *Dictionary of American Biography* or the *Literary History of the United States*. If your research is aimed at a current issue, you would likely consult newspapers, magazines, and other periodicals, as well as websites and recent books. These sources can all be found in your school library.

LIBRARY SOURCES

When you conduct academic research, it's often more efficient to begin with your library's website rather than with a *Google* search, because looking for sources on the internet can require extra time and effort to ensure that what you find is accurate and reliable. Library websites provide access to a range of well-organized and trustworthy resources, including scholarly databases through which you can access authoritative articles that have been screened by librarians or specialists in a particular field. In general, there are three kinds of sources you'll want to consult: reference works, books, and periodicals.

Reference works. These are standard collections of information, such as encyclopedias, dictionaries, atlases, almanacs, and bibliographies—many of which now exist only in electronic form. Although they're only a starting point, general reference works such as *Oxford Reference* and *CQ Press Library* can often lead you to more specific sources. For instance, the *Encyclopedia of Native American Shamanism* includes entries on basic topics such as "Animism" and "Divination," but it also identifies individual shamans and specific practices.

Books. The library catalog is your main source for finding books. Most catalogs are digitized and can be accessed through the library's website. You can search by author, title, subject, or keyword. When you click on a specific source, you'll find more bibliographic data about author, title, and publication; the call number (which identifies the book's location on the library's shelves); related subject headings (which may lead to other useful materials in the library)—and more.

Periodicals. To find journal and magazine articles, you'll need to search periodical indexes and databases. Indexes (such as the *New York Times Index*) provide listings of articles organized by topics; databases (such as *LexisNexis*) provide the full texts. Although some databases are available for free, many may be accessible at no cost through your library.

ONLINE SOURCES

The internet is your passport to a vast virtual library with sites sponsored by countless governments, educational institutions, organizations, businesses, and individuals. It is so vast and dynamic, in fact, that navigating the web safely and efficiently can be a challenge. (We'll discuss how to meet that challenge in a moment.) To get started with an online search, however, try one of the following methods:

- *Keyword searches. Google, DuckDuckGo, Microsoft Edge,* and many other search sites scan the web looking for the keywords you specify.

- *Nonlibrary, academic searches.* In addition to *Google Scholar*, search *RefSeek* or *BASE* for peer-reviewed academic writing in many disciplines. *Science.gov* offers results from more than fifteen US federal agencies, and *CORE* collects open-access research papers.

Although many websites provide authoritative information, keep in mind that online content varies greatly in its stability and reliability: what you see on a site today may be different (or gone) tomorrow. So save or make copies of pages you plan to use, and carefully evaluate what you find. Here are just a few of the many resources available on the web.

Indexes, databases, and directories. Information put together by specialists and grouped by topics can be especially helpful. You may want to consult multidisciplinary databases such as *Academic Search Complete* or *JSTOR*, but there are also many databases dedicated to single subjects.

News sites. Many newspapers, magazines, and radio and TV stations have websites that provide both up-to-the-minute information and also archives of older news articles. Through *Google News*, for example, you can access current news worldwide, whereas *Google News Archive Search* has files going back to the 1700s. Check out the source of news to make sure you're reading facts and not MISINFORMATION.

Government sites. Many government agencies and departments maintain websites where you can find government reports, statistics, legislative information, and other resources. *USA.gov* offers information, services, and other resources from the US government.

Digital archives. These sites collect and organize materials from the past—including drawings, maps, recordings, speeches, and historic documents—often focusing on a particular subject or country. For example, the National Archives and Records Administration and the Library of Congress both archive items relevant to the culture and history of the United States.

Discussion lists and forums. Online mailing lists, newsgroups, discussion groups, and forums let members post and receive messages from other members. To join a discussion with people who are knowledgeable about your topic, try searching for a forum specifically on your topic—for example, "E. B. White discussion forum." Don't take what you read at face value, though; be sure to check out claims and statements of fact to be sure they're accurate.

SEARCHING ELECTRONICALLY

When you search for subjects online or in library catalogs, indexes, or databases, you'll want to come up with keywords that will lead to the information you need. Specific commands vary among search engines and databases, but most search engines offer "Advanced Search" options that allow you to narrow your search by typing keywords into text boxes labeled as follows:

- all these words
- the exact phrase
- any of these words
- none of these words

In addition, you may filter the results to include only full-text articles (articles that are available in full online); only certain domains (such as ".edu," for educational sites; ".gov," for government sites; or ".org," for nonprofit sites); and, in library databases, only scholarly, peer-reviewed sites. Type quotation marks around words to search for an exact phrase: "Twitter revolution" or "Neil Gaiman."

Some databases may require you to limit searches through the use of various symbols or Boolean operators (AND, OR, NOT). See the Advanced Search instructions for help with such symbols, which may be called "field tags."

If a search turns up too many sources, be more specific ("homeopathy" instead of "medicine"). If your original keywords don't generate good results, try synonyms ("home remedy" instead of "folk medicine"). Keep in mind that searching requires flexibility, both in the words you use and in the methods you try.

Evaluating Sources

Searching the database of the American College Health Association for information on the incidence of meningitis among college students, you find about a dozen articles. An "exact words" *Google* search on "meningitis among college students" yields more than a thousand. Which sources are reliable and worth reading? The following questions can help you decide.

Is the source relevant? Look at the title and at any introductory material to see what it covers. Does the source appear to relate directly to your purpose? What will it add to your work?

What are the author's credentials? Has the author written other works on this subject? Is the author known for taking a particular position on it? Do an internet search to see what others say about the author. Do other reliable sources confirm the author's credentials? Do you learn anything else important about the author?

What is the stance? Does the source cover various points of view or advocate only one perspective? Does its title suggest a certain slant? If you're evaluating a website, check to see whether it includes links to sites expressing other perspectives, and visit those links to see that they're trustworthy too.

Who is the publisher? Books published by university presses and articles in scholarly journals are peer-reviewed by experts in the field before being published. Those produced for a general audience don't always undergo such rigorous review and fact-checking. At well-established publishing houses, however, submissions are usually vetted by experienced editors or even editorial boards.

If the source is a website, who is the sponsor? Is the site maintained by an organization, interest group, government agency, or individual? If the site doesn't give this information on its homepage, look for clues in the URL domain: ".edu" is used mostly by colleges and universities, ".gov" by government agencies, ".org" by nonprofit organizations, ".mil" by the military, and ".com" by commercial organizations. Be aware that the sponsor may have an agenda—to argue a position, present biased information, or sell a product—and that text on the site may not necessarily undergo rigorous review or fact-checking. Also, don't trust what the site says about itself—do an internet search to see what other reliable sources reveal about the site and its sponsor.

What is the level of the material? Texts written for a general audience might be easier to understand but may not be authoritative enough for academic work. Scholarly texts will be more authoritative but may be harder to comprehend. Don't assume a source is scholarly just because it sounds academic, especially if you turned up the source online.

How current is the source? Check to see when books and articles were published and when websites were last updated. (If a site lists no date, see if links to other sites still work; if not, the site is probably too dated to use.) A recent publication date or updating, however, doesn't necessarily mean the source is better—some topics require current information, whereas others call for older sources.

Does the source include other useful information? Is there a bibliography that might lead you to additional materials? How current or authoritative are the sources it cites? Are the cited sources trustworthy?

Verifying Facts

One of the great benefits of the internet is the power it gives you to verify facts quickly and reliably. Fact-checking websites like *Snopes, Washington Post Fact Checker, PolitiFact*, and *FactCheck.org* are especially useful for finding information to help debunk (or verify) wild claims. Did a recent scientific study actually conclude that "drinking young people's blood could help you live longer and prevent age-related diseases"? A quick search on *Snopes* reveals that this sensational claim is based on a study of transfusions in mice and is, therefore, bloody false.

For verifying simple facts and figures, however, you don't need a specialized fact-checker. Just type the information you want to verify into your preferred search engine. For example, a news article published in *USA Today* at the end of 2016 carried the following disturbing headline: "Ambush-Style Killings of Police Up 167% This Year." Is this alarming figure accurate? Googling "police killed in ambush in 2016" turns up several reliable sources with confirming information like this:

> Ambush-style attacks of police officers rose dramatically in 2016. Nationwide, 21 law enforcement officers were killed in such attacks. . . . Only eight officers were killed in ambushes in 2015.
>
> —Tasha Tsiaperas, *Dallas News*

So the grim figure reported in *USA Today* wasn't fake news. It was, unfortunately, correct. As a rule, facts reported as facts by reliable sources—such as a major national newspaper or an academic journal—can be taken as accurate.

Known facts and figures are verifiable; they're either accurate or inaccurate. Evaluating the accuracy of general statements based on the facts, however, is a bit more difficult. One reason—to put it proverbially—is that "figures don't lie, but liars figure." Consider the following statement by Mark Zuckerberg, CEO of Meta (then Facebook) in testimony before Congress:

> All the data that you put in, all the content that you share on *Facebook*, is yours.

How accurate is this statement? Unlike most of the wild rumors debunked on *Snopes*, Zuckerberg's claim about the personal data you enter on *Facebook* isn't totally false. But it's not absolutely true either. According to fact-checkers at the *Washington Post*, by accepting *Facebook*'s terms of use, you grant the company "a non-exclusive, transferable, sub-licensable, royalty-free, worldwide license to use any IP content that you post on or in connection with Facebook." In other words, you own it, but they can use it. So Zuckerberg's claim, as the *Post* points out, is "not the whole story."

Mark Zuckerberg testifying before Congress.

Applying "Information Literacy" to the Web

Simple facts are either accurate or inaccurate. More complex statements based on the facts can be accurate, inaccurate, or—like the Zuckerberg testimony—somewhere in between. When you evaluate the accuracy of a statement that presents itself as factual or true, one of the first steps to take is to examine the evidence the writer offers within the text. Is that evidence factually correct? Is it sufficient to prove the writer's claim? You will also need to look beyond the text itself—at the writer's credentials or sources, or at what others have to say about the source—to determine if what you're reading is accurate and the source is reliable. If you find that source online, determining its accuracy and authenticity will take more than your best skills at critical reading; it will also require a measure of what has come to be called "information literacy."

Considering the Source

As an example of how to master the web-like properties of the internet instead of being snared by them, let's suppose you were conducting research for an essay on a particularly troubling research topic—bullying at school. Searching for information to get started, you come upon the following headline on the website for the American College of Pediatricians: "Bullying at School: Never Acceptable."

On the face of it, this looks like an important source—one that might inform your research and that you might want to cite in your own work on the topic. Before dipping further into the information this source has to offer, however, you need to evaluate it.

THE CRAAP TEST

Many authorities on web literacy would advise you to check out potential sources by running down a checklist, such as the CRAAP test. The acronym stands for Currency, Relevance, Authority, Accuracy, and Purpose. Here are some typical CRAAP test questions:

Who is the author / source / publisher / sponsor?

What does the URL reveal about the author or source?

Are there spelling, grammar, or typographical errors?

What is the purpose of the information? Is it to inform, sell, entertain, persuade?

Does the point of view appear to be objective and impartial?

Let's apply this checklist approach to "Bullying at School: Never Acceptable." The "author / source / publisher / sponsor" of this online article has an imposing name, the American College of Pediatricians; the ".org" in the URL of the website suggests it's a legitimate organization; the site is free of grammar, spelling, and typographical errors; the purpose of this information seems to be "to inform, teach"; and, yes, the point of view appears to be "objective."

Judging from its favorable results on a CRAAP test, "Bullying at School: Never Acceptable" would seem to be a reliable source for beginning your academic research. The only potential red flag on the site comes in the fine print: "no group should be singled out for special treatment." What about groups who are frequent victims of school bullying, such as students who are LGBTQ? Should they be given specialized advice?

Many of the CRAAP test questions are good ones to ask when your objective is to analyze how a piece of writing works—how it's organized; the rhetorical strategies and language it uses; the author's tone and style. In fact, you'll see questions like these applied to texts throughout this book. However, when your objective is to evaluate a source's *trustworthiness*, the CRAAP test doesn't go far enough. Any checklist is limited if it asks you to evaluate the accuracy of a source by reading only the source itself.

Recent research in information and web literacy suggests that most people go about checking internet sources in the wrong way at first. "When confronted with a new site," writes Michael A. Caulfield in *Web Literacy for Student Fact-Checkers*, "they poke around the site and try to find out what the site says about itself by going to the 'about page' . . . or scrolling up and down the page." Reading "vertically" like this to verify a text's authenticity from within the text itself is a faulty approach because, as Caulfield says, "if the site is untrustworthy, then what the site says about itself is most likely untrustworthy, as well." Instead of trying to authenticate a source by reading "vertically" within the source, Caulfield advises, we should read "laterally" outside the source.

READING LATERALLY

"When reading laterally," say the researchers at Stanford who coined the term, "one leaves a website and opens new tabs along a horizontal axis in order to use the resources of the Internet to learn more about a site and its claims." Let's reevaluate "Bullying at School: Never Acceptable," this time by reading laterally about—rather than vertically within—the website on which it appears. When you google "American College of Pediatricians," the website we're investigating is one of the first items that's likely to come up in your search results, along with links to *Wikipedia* and the websites, among others, of the Southern Poverty Law Center and the American Civil Liberties Union.

If you click on any one of these results, you find yourself in a new window on the site you've opened; and the list of search results is no longer visible.

A better strategy is to open relevant items in your search results, each in a new tab, by right-clicking on the link. "Although knowing how to right-click to open a new tab might seem purely technical," write the Stanford researchers, "for our participants it proved anything but. Indeed, the failure to right-click thwarts lateral reading, piling new windows on top each other and making it impossible to quickly scan multiple sources."

So right-click on any link in the results that appear when you search, and you'll see a menu like the one below. (On most laptops, hold down the Control key before clicking or tapping on the link; on a smartphone or tablet, hold your finger on the link for a few seconds.)

Open link in new tab
Open link in new window
Open link in incognito window
Save link as...
Copy link address
Inspect   Ctrl+Shift+I

Choose "Open link in new tab," and the page will do just that, usually to the right of any tabs already open at the top of your browser. This time, however, the original list of search results won't disappear because you've opened a tab inside the window you're working on.

Repeat the process with each source you choose to read: open it in a new tab by right-clicking on the link in the list of results. All the tabs you open will stay in place at the top of the browser, along "a horizontal axis." You can now read "laterally" back and forth among different websites—comparing, with relative ease, what they have to say about the source you're investigating.

Checking What Others Say about the Source

Let's go back to the source of "Bullying at School: Never Acceptable." The website for the American College of Pediatricians, where the article first appeared, has this to say about itself:

> The American College of Pediatricians (ACPeds) is a national organization of pediatricians and other healthcare professionals dedicated to the health and well-being of children.

Now, if you go back to the list of search results and open the *Wikipedia* result in a new tab, however, you will find something like this:

> The American College of Pediatricians (ACPeds) is a <u>socially conservative</u> advocacy group of <u>pediatricians</u> and other healthcare professionals in the United States. . . . ACPeds has been listed as a hate group by the Southern Poverty Law Center for pushing "anti-LGBTQ junk science."

As you open more tabs across the top of your screen, you uncover more and more information suggesting that this source is not the mainstream organization it might appear to be at first click.

Following Clues in Citations and Footnotes

Let's take a closer look at the *Wikipedia* entry. From it, you learn that the American College of Pediatricians was founded in 2002 in opposition to the American Academy of Pediatrics (AAP) and has an estimated maximum membership of "700 active." (The AAP, by contrast, was founded in 1930 and has approximately 67,000 members, according to *Wikipedia*.) *Wikipedia* is the go-to site for many people when they want basic information about a topic or when they're beginning academic research. Just how reliable is *Wikipedia*?

Pretty reliable, according to the experts. "While *Wikipedia* must be approached with caution, especially with . . . contentious subjects or evolving events," writes Michael Caulfield in *Web Literacy for Student Fact-Checkers*, ". . . its articles are often the best available introduction to a subject on the web." Notice the word "introduction" in this endorsement. The main problem with using *Wikipedia* as a research tool is stopping there.

Wikipedia is, nevertheless, a decent starting place for gathering information online. One reason, according to Caulfield, is that *Wikipedia* "has strict rules about sourcing facts to reliable sources." *Wikipedia* articles are full of footnotes, so users can, in Caulfield's words, "follow the footnote on the claim to a reliable source."

One of *Wikipedia*'s most useful features is that its footnotes are usually active links. For example, the wiki entry on the American College of Pediatricians not only identifies the source of the claim that ACPeds is pushing "junk science," but it also links directly to the site where the claim is made.

Showing "Click Restraint"

To avoid wasting time on potentially unreliable sources as you search the internet, look—and look again—before you leap. Let's say you type this claim from *Wikipedia* into your search engine:

LGBTQ students five times more likely to miss school because of bullying

One of the first results to turn up is "StopBullying.gov." The ".gov" in this URL indicates an official US government website. You right-click on the link and open the website in a new tab. You do not, however, click on the tab and begin reading.

Instead you keep looking until you've opened several new tabs across the top of your browser, all with URLs that look promising. Once you've gathered a number of new tabs at the top of your screen, you then click tab-by-tab and compare the contents of each tab. (The keyboard commands Control + 1–9 will open tabs in numerical order, left to right.)

What you discover is that all of the more authoritative sources you've located say virtually the same thing: LGBTQ students are about five times more likely than other students to skip school because of bullying. You can be relatively confident now that this information is correct. (Remember that the web is dynamic, and search engines use algorithms to "learn" what you're looking for. So each time you do a web search, you may get somewhat different results—or even the same results but in a different order.)

No matter how diligently you look when doing an internet search, one of the most valuable sources of information will largely elude you: printed books. So you might want to try a *Google* book search. Instead of entering your search criteria directly into *Google* (or some other search engine), go to *Google Books* ("the world's most comprehensive index of full-text books") and enter your search criteria there:

LGBTQ students five times more likely to miss school because of bullying

What comes up is an array of images depicting the covers of books, accompanied by descriptive snippets that often refer to particular pages inside. Click on a link, and often it opens at the page in the printed text where the information you're looking for is located. *Google* meets Gutenberg.

Taking Notes

When you find relevant, reliable, and accurate material that is pertinent to your research project, you'll want to take careful notes on it by following these guidelines:

- *Use index cards, a digital file, or a notebook,* labeling each entry with information that will enable you to keep track of where it comes from—author, title, the pages or the URL, and (for online sources) the date of access.

- *Take notes in your own words, and use your own sentence patterns.* If you make a note that is a detailed paraphrase, label it as such so that you'll know to provide appropriate documentation if you use it.

- *If you find wording that you'd like to quote,* be sure to enclose the exact words in quotation marks to distinguish your source's words from your own.

- *Label each note with a subject heading* so you can organize your notes easily when constructing an outline for your paper.

TIPS FOR EVALUATING WHAT YOU READ

Be suspicious. The internet is a tangled web; don't get caught in it. Learn to use the web's web-like properties to verify the accuracy of the information you find there.

Check the facts. If a site or source gets the facts wrong, everything else it says is suspect. Fact-checking sites like *Snopes* and *FactCheck.org* can help you verify facts; or do a web search using the facts and figures you want to check to see if other reputable sources confirm their accuracy.

Don't look to the site or source you're evaluating to verify itself. Most people try to verify the authenticity of a site or source by reading "vertically"—up and down within it. Professional fact-checkers don't trust what a source says about itself; they check it by leaving it—reading "laterally" across other sources instead.

Compare what others say about the site or source. "When reading laterally," say the Stanford researchers who coined the term, "one leaves a website and opens new tabs along a horizontal axis in order to use the resources of the Internet to learn more about a site and its claims."

Check out sources of citations. Follow the footnotes and other documentation for citations to see where the information came from. *Wikipedia* entries, for example, are full of footnotes that link to original sources. Check out the source you're led to in order to ensure it's valid.

Show a little "click restraint." Professional fact-checkers don't just click on the first results that come up. Look at the source, URL, and snippet of preview text before choosing which links to open.

Incorporating Source Materials into Your Text

There are many ways to incorporate source materials into your own text. Three of the most common are quoting, paraphrasing, or summarizing. Let's look at the differences among these three forms of reference, and then consider when to use each one and how to work these references into your text.

Quoting

When you quote someone else's words, you reproduce their language exactly, in quotation marks—though you can add your own words in brackets or omit unnecessary words in the original by using ellipsis marks (. . .). This example from Mary Roach's "How to Know If You're Dead" uses all these conventions:

> In her analysis of the life-saving role of human cadavers, Mary Roach notes that "a gurney with a [newly deceased] cadaver commands no urgency. It is wheeled by a single person, . . . like a shopping cart" (167).

Paraphrasing

When you paraphrase, you restate information from a source in your own words, using your own sentence structures. Because a paraphrase includes all the main points of the source, it is usually about the same length as the original.

Here is a paragraph from Diane Ackerman's essay "Why Leaves Turn Color in the Fall," followed by two sample paraphrases. The first demonstrates some of the challenges of paraphrasing.

ORIGINAL SOURCE

Where do the colors come from? Sunlight rules most living things with its golden edicts. When the days begin to shorten, soon after the summer solstice on June 21, a tree reconsiders its leaves. All summer it feeds them so they can process sunlight, but in the dog days of summer the tree begins pulling nutrients back into its trunk and roots, pares down, and gradually chokes off its leaves. A corky layer of cells forms at the leaves' slender petioles, then scars over. Undernourished, the leaves stop producing the pigment chlorophyll, and photosynthesis ceases. Animals can migrate, hibernate, or store food to prepare for winter. But where can a tree go? It survives by dropping its leaves, and by the end of autumn only a few fragile threads of fluid-carrying xylem hold leaves to their stems.

UNACCEPTABLE PARAPHRASE

Ackerman tells us where the colors of leaves come from. The amount of sunlight is the trigger, as is true for most living things. At the end of June, as daylight lessens, a tree begins to treat its leaves differently. It feeds them all summer so they can turn sunlight into food, but in August a tree begins to redirect its food into its trunk and roots, gradually choking the leaves. A corky group of cells develops at the petioles, and a scar forms. By autumn, the leaves don't have enough food, so they stop producing chlorophyll, and photosynthesis also stops. Although animals are able to migrate, hibernate, or stow food for the winter, a tree cannot go anywhere. It survives only by dropping its leaves, and by the time winter comes only a few leaves remain on their stems.

This first paraphrase borrows too much of the language of the original or changes it only slightly. It also follows the original sentence structure too closely. The following paraphrase avoids both of these pitfalls and also—importantly—provides a page reference to the source.

ACCEPTABLE PARAPHRASE

Ackerman explains why leaves change color. Diminishing sunlight is the main instigator. A tree nourishes its leaves—and encourages photosynthesis—for most of the summer. By August, however, as daylight continues to lessen, a tree starts to reroute its food to the roots and trunk, a process that saves the tree but eventually kills the leaves. In autumn, because the leaves are almost starving, they can neither manufacture chlorophyll to stay green nor carry out photosynthesis. By this time, the base of the petiole, or leaf's stem, has hardened, in preparation for the final drop. Unlike animals, who have many ways to get ready for winter—hiding food ahead of time, moving to a warm climate, sleeping through winter—a tree is immobile. It can make it through the winter only by losing its leaves (257).

Summarizing

Unlike a paraphrase, a SUMMARY doesn't present all the details in the original source, so it is generally as brief as possible. Summaries may boil down an entire book or essay into a single sentence, or they may take a paragraph or more to present the main ideas. Here, for example, is a summary of the Ackerman paragraph:

In late summer and fall, Ackerman explains, trees put most of their food into their roots and trunk, which causes leaves to change color and die but enables trees to live through the winter (257).

Deciding Whether to Quote, Paraphrase, or Summarize

Follow these rules of thumb to determine whether you should quote a source directly, paraphrase it in detail, or merely summarize the main points.

- *Quote* a text when the exact wording is critical to making your point (or that of an authority you wish to cite) or when the wording itself is part of what you're analyzing.

- *Paraphrase* when the meaning of a text is important to your argument but the original language isn't essential, or when you're clarifying or interpreting the ideas (not the words) in the text.

- *Summarize* when the main points of the text are important to your argument but the details can be left out in the interest of conciseness.

Using Signal Phrases

When you quote, paraphrase, or summarize a source, identify your source clearly and use a signal phrase ("she says," "he thinks") to distinguish the words and ideas of your source from your own. Consider this example:

> Professor and textbook author Elaine Tyler May claims that many high school history textbooks are too bland to interest young readers (531).

This sentence summarizes a general position about the effectiveness of certain textbooks ("too bland"), and it attributes that view to a particular authority (Elaine Tyler May), citing her credentials (professor, textbook author) for speaking as an authority on the subject. By using the phrase "claims that," the sentence also distinguishes the words and ideas of the source from those of the writer.

The verb you use in a signal phrase can be neutral ("says" or "thinks"), or it can indicate your (or your source's) stance toward the subject. In this case, the use of the verb "claims" suggests that what the source says is arguable (or that the writer of the sentence believes it is). The signal verb you choose can influence your reader's understanding of the sentence and of your attitude toward what it says.

Acknowledging Sources and Avoiding Plagiarism

As a writer, you must acknowledge any words and ideas that come from others. There are numerous reasons for doing so: to give credit where credit is due, to recognize the various authorities and many perspectives you have considered, to show readers where they can find your sources, and to situate your own arguments in the ongoing academic conversation. Using other people's words and ideas without acknowledgment is plagiarism, a serious academic and ethical offense.

MATERIAL THAT REQUIRES ACKNOWLEDGMENT
- direct quotations, paraphrases, and summaries
- arguable statements and any information that is not commonly known (statistics and other data)

- the personal or professional opinions and assertions of others
- visuals that you did not create yourself (charts, photographs, and so on)
- collaborative help you received from others

MATERIAL THAT DOESN'T HAVE TO BE ACKNOWLEDGED

- facts that are common knowledge, such as the name of the current president of the United States
- well-known statements accompanied by a signal phrase: "As John F. Kennedy said, 'Ask not what your country can do for you; ask what you can do for your country.'"

Plagiarism is (1) using another writer's exact words without quotation marks, (2) using another writer's words or ideas without in-text citation or other documentation, (3) paraphrasing or summarizing someone else's ideas using language or sentence structure that is close to the original. The following practices will help you avoid plagiarizing.

Take careful notes, clearly labeling quotations and using your own phrasing and sentence structure in paraphrases and summaries.

Check all paraphrases and summaries to be sure they're stated in *your* words and sentence structures—and that you put quotation marks around any of the source's original phrasing.

Know what sources you must document, and identify them both in the text and in a works-cited list.

Check to see that all quotations are documented; it isn't enough just to include quotation marks or indent a block quotation.

Be especially careful with online material—copying source material directly into a document you're writing invites plagiarism. Like other sources, information from the web must be acknowledged.

Recognize that plagiarism has consequences. A scholar's work will be discredited if it too closely resembles the work of another scholar. Journalists who plagiarize lose their jobs, and students routinely fail courses or are dismissed from school when they're caught cheating—all too often by submitting essays that they have purchased from online "research" sites.

So don't take the chance. If you're having trouble with an assignment, ask your instructor for assistance. Or visit your school's writing center. Writing centers can help with advice on all aspects of your writing, including acknowledging sources and avoiding plagiarism. And, for immediate help, turn to the tips on documentation you'll find in the rest of this chapter.

Documentation

Taken collectively, all the information you provide about sources is your *documentation*. Many organizations and publishers—for example, the American Psychological Association (APA), the University of Chicago Press, and the Council of Science Editors (CSE)—have their own documentation styles. The focus here is on the documentation system of the Modern Language Association (MLA) because it is one of the most common systems used in college courses, especially in the liberal arts.

Need to document sources using APA, CSE, or Chicago style? Visit **digital.wwnorton.com/backtothelake5**, and open *The Little Seagull Handbook* ebook to find complete documentation guides for these styles.

MLA style calls for (1) brief in-text documentation and (2) complete bibliographic information in a list of works cited at the end of your text. The models and examples in this chapter draw on the ninth edition of the *MLA Handbook*, published by the Modern Language Association of America in 2021. For additional information, or if you're citing a source that isn't covered in this guide, visit **style.mla.org**.

MLA In-Text Documentation

Whenever you quote, paraphrase, or summarize a source in your writing, you need to provide brief documentation that tells readers what you took from the

author   title   publication

source and where in the source you found that information. This brief documentation also refers readers to the full entry in your works-cited list, so begin with whatever comes first there: the author, the title, or a description of the source.

You can mention the author or title either in a signal phrase—"Toni Morrison writes," "In *Beowulf*," "According to the article 'Every Patient's Nightmare'"—or in parentheses—(Morrison). If relevant, include pages or other details about where you found the information in the parenthetical reference: (Morrison 67).

Shorten any lengthy titles or descriptions in parentheses by including the first noun with any preceding adjectives and omitting any initial articles (*Norton Field Guide* for *The Norton Field Guide to Writing*). If the title doesn't start with a noun, use the first phrase or clause (*How to Be* for *How to Be an Antiracist*). Use the full title if it's short.

The first two examples below show basic in-text documentation of a work by one author. Variations on those examples follow. The examples illustrate the MLA style of using quotation marks around titles of short works and italicizing titles of long works.

1. AUTHOR NAMED IN A SIGNAL PHRASE

If you mention the author in a signal phrase, put only the page number(s) in parentheses. Do not write "page" or "p." The first time you mention the author, use their first and last names. You can usually omit any middle initials.

> David McCullough describes John Adams's hands as those of someone used to manual labor (18).

2. AUTHOR NAMED IN PARENTHESES

If you do not mention the author in a signal phrase, put their last name in parentheses along with any page numbers. Do not use punctuation between the name and the page number(s).

> Adams is said to have had "the hands of a man accustomed to pruning his own trees, cutting his own hay, and splitting his own firewood" (McCullough 18).

Whether you use a signal phrase and parentheses or parentheses only, try to put the parenthetical documentation at the end of the sentence or as close as possible to the material you've cited—without awkwardly interrupting the sentence. When the parenthetical reference comes at the end of the sentence, the period follows it.

3. AFTER A BLOCK QUOTATION

When quoting more than three lines of poetry, more than four lines of prose, or dialogue between two or more characters from a drama, set off the quotation from the rest of your text, indenting it half an inch (or five spaces) from the left margin. Do not use quotation marks, and place any parenthetical documentation *after* the final punctuation.

> In *Eastward to Tartary,* Robert Kaplan captures ancient and contemporary Antioch:
>
>> At the height of its glory in the Roman-Byzantine age, when it had an amphitheater, public baths, aqueducts, and sewage pipes, half a million people lived in Antioch. Today the population is only 125,000. With sour relations between Turkey and Syria, and unstable politics throughout the Middle East, Antioch is now a backwater—seedy and tumbledown, with relatively few tourists. I found it altogether charming. (123)

4. TWO OR MORE WORKS BY THE SAME AUTHOR

If you cite multiple works by one author, include the title of the work you are citing either in the signal phrase or in parentheses.

> Robert Kaplan insists that understanding power in the Near East requires "Western leaders who know when to intervene, and do so without illusions" (*Eastward to Tartary* 330).

Put a comma between author and title if both are in the parentheses.

> Understanding power in the Near East requires "Western leaders who know when to intervene, and do so without illusions" (Kaplan, *Eastward to Tartary* 330).

5. AUTHORS WITH THE SAME LAST NAME

Give each author's first and last names in any signal phrase, or add the author's first initial in the parenthetical reference.

> "Imaginative" applies not only to modern literature but also to writing of all periods, whereas "magical" is often used in writing about Arthurian romances (A. Wilson 25).

6. TWO OR MORE AUTHORS

For a work with two authors, name both. If you first mention them in a signal phrase, give their first and last names.

Lori Carlson and Cynthia Ventura's stated goal is to introduce Julio Cortázar, Marjorie Agosín, and other Latin American writers to an audience of English-speaking adolescents (v).

For a work by three or more authors that you mention in a signal phrase, you can either name them all or name the first author followed by "and others" or "and colleagues." If you mention them in a parenthetical reference, name the first author followed by "et al."

Phyllis Anderson and colleagues describe British literature thematically (A54–A67).

One survey of British literature breaks the contents into thematic groupings (Anderson et al. A54–A67).

7. ORGANIZATION OR GOVERNMENT AS AUTHOR

In a signal phrase, use the full name of the organization: American Academy of Arts and Sciences. In parentheses, use the shortest noun phrase, omitting any initial articles: American Academy.

8. AUTHOR UNKNOWN

If you don't know the author, use the work's title in a signal phrase or in a parenthetical reference.

A powerful editorial in the *New York Times* asserts that healthy liver donor Mike Hurewitz died because of "frightening" faulty postoperative care ("Every Patient's Nightmare").

9. LITERARY WORKS

When referring to common literary works that are available in many different editions, give the page numbers from the edition you are using, followed by information that will let readers of any edition locate the text you are citing.

Novels and Prose Plays. Give the page number followed by a semicolon and any chapter, section, or act numbers, separated by commas.

In *Pride and Prejudice,* Mrs. Bennet shows no warmth toward Jane when she returns from Netherfield (Austen 105; ch. 12).

Verse Plays. Give act, scene, and line numbers, separated with periods.

Shakespeare continues the vision theme when Macbeth says, "Thou hast no speculation in those eyes / Which thou dost glare with" (*Macbeth* 3.3.96–97).

Poems. Give the part and the line numbers (separated by periods). If a poem has only line numbers, use the word "line" or "lines" only in the first reference; after that, give only numbers.

> Walt Whitman sets up not only opposing adjectives but also opposing nouns in "Song of Myself" when he says, "I am of old and young, of the foolish as much as the wise, / . . . a child as well as a man" (16.330–32).

> One description of the mere in *Beowulf* is "not a pleasant place" (line 1372). Later, it is labeled "the awful place" (1378).

10. WORK IN AN ANTHOLOGY

Name the author(s) of the work, not the editor of the anthology.

> "It is the teapots that truly shock," according to Cynthia Ozick in her essay on teapots as metaphor (70).

> In *In Short: A Collection of Creative Nonfiction,* readers will find both an essay on Scottish tea (Hiestand) and a piece on teapots as metaphors (Ozick).

11. ENCYCLOPEDIA OR DICTIONARY

Acknowledge an entry in an encyclopedia or dictionary by giving the author's name, if available. For an entry without an author, give the entry's title.

> According to *Funk and Wagnall's New World Encyclopedia,* early in his career, most of Kubrick's income came from "hustling chess games in Washington Square Park" ("Kubrick, Stanley").

12. LEGAL DOCUMENTS

For legal cases, give whatever comes first in the works-cited entry. If you are citing a government document in parentheses and multiple entries in your works-cited list, start with the same government author, give as much of the name as you need to differentiate the sources.

> In 2015, for the first time, all states were required to license and recognize the marriages of same-sex couples (United States, Supreme Court).

13. SACRED TEXT

When citing a sacred text such as the Bible or the Qur'an for the first time, give the title of the edition as well as the book, chapter, and verse (or their equivalent), separated by periods. MLA recommends abbreviating the names of the books of the Bible in parenthetical references. Later citations from the same edition do not have to repeat its title.

author   title   publication

The wording from *The New English Bible* follows: "In the beginning of creation, when God made heaven and earth, the earth was without form and void . . ." (Gen. 1.1–2).

14. MULTIVOLUME WORK

If you cite more than one volume of a multivolume work, each time you cite one of the volumes, give the volume *and* the page number(s) in parentheses, separated by a colon and a space.

Carl Sandburg concludes with the following sentence about those paying last respects to Lincoln: "All day long and through the night the unbroken line moved, the home town having its farewell" (4: 413).

If you cite an entire volume of a multivolume work in parentheses, give the author's last name followed by a comma and "vol." before the volume number: (Sandburg, vol. 4). If your works-cited list includes only a single volume of a multivolume work, give just the page number in parentheses: (413).

15. WORKS CITED TOGETHER

If you're citing two or more works closely together, you will sometimes need to provide a parenthetical reference for each one.

Dennis Baron describes singular "they" as "the missing word that's been hiding in plain sight" (182), while Benjamin Dreyer believes that "singular 'they' is not the wave of the future; it's the wave of the present" (93).

If you are citing multiple sources for the same idea in parentheses, separate the references with a semicolon.

Many critics have examined great works of literature from a cultural perspective (Tanner 7; Smith viii).

16. SOURCE QUOTED IN ANOTHER SOURCE

When you are quoting text that you found quoted in another source, use the abbreviation "qtd. in" in the parenthetical reference.

Charlotte Brontë wrote to G. H. Lewes, "Why do you like Miss Austen so very much? I am puzzled on that point" (qtd. in Tanner 7).

17. WORK WITHOUT PAGE NUMBERS

For works without page or part numbers, including many online sources, no number is needed in a parenthetical reference.

> Studies show that music training helps children to be better at multitasking later in life ("Hearing the Music").

If you mention the author in a signal phrase, or if you mention the title of a work with no author, no parenthetical reference is needed.

> Arthur Brooks argues that a switch to fully remote work would have a negative effect on mental and physical health.

If the source has chapter, paragraph, or section numbers, use them with the abbreviations "ch.," "par.," or "sec.": ("Hearing the Music," par. 2). Don't count lines or paragraphs on your own if they aren't numbered in the source. For an ebook, use chapter numbers. For an audio or video recording, give the hours, minutes, and seconds (separated by colons) as shown on the player: (00:05:21–31).

18. AN ENTIRE WORK OR A ONE-PAGE ARTICLE

If you cite an entire work rather than a part of it, or if you cite a single-page article, there's no need to include page numbers.

> Throughout life, John Adams strove to succeed (McCullough).

MLA Notes

Sometimes you may need to give information that doesn't fit into the text itself—to thank people who helped you, to provide additional details, to refer readers to other sources, or to add comments about sources. Such information can be given in a footnote (at the bottom of the page) or an endnote (on a separate page with the heading "Notes" or "Endnotes" just before your works-cited list). Put a superscript number at the appropriate point in your text, signaling to readers to look for the note with the corresponding number. If you have multiple notes, number them consecutively throughout your paper.

TEXT

> This essay will argue that giving student athletes preferential treatment undermines educational goals.[1]

NOTE

> [1] I want to thank those who contributed to my thinking on this topic, especially my teacher Vincent Yu.

author   title   publication

MLA List of Works Cited

A works-cited list provides full bibliographic information for every source cited in your text. See p. 825 for a sample works-cited list.

Core Elements

MLA style provides a list of core elements for documenting sources in a works-cited list. Not all sources will include each of these elements; include as much information as is available for any title you cite.

For guidance about specific sources you need to document, see the templates and examples on pp. 801–13, but here are some general guidelines for how to treat each of the core elements.

CORE ELEMENTS FOR ENTRIES IN A WORKS-CITED LIST
- author
- title of the source
- title of any "container," a larger work in which the source is found—an anthology, a website, a journal or magazine, a database, a streaming service like *Netflix*, or a learning management system, among others
- editor, translator, director, or other contributors
- version
- number of volume and issue, episode and season
- publisher
- date of publication
- location of the source: page numbers, DOI, permalink, URL, etc.

author   title   publication

The above order is the general order MLA recommends, but there will be exceptions. To document a translated essay that you found in an anthology, for instance, you'd identify the translator after the title of the essay rather than after that of the anthology. You may sometimes need additional elements as well, either at the end of an entry or in the middle—for instance, a label to indicate that your source is a map, or an original year of publication. Remember that your goal is to tell readers what sources you've consulted and where they can find them. Providing this information is one way you can engage with readers—and enable them to join in the conversation with you and your sources.

AUTHORS AND CONTRIBUTORS

- An author can be any kind of creator—a writer, a musician, an artist, and so on.
- If there is one author, put the last name first, followed by a comma and the first name: Morrison, Toni.
- If there are two authors, list the first author last name first and the second one first name first: Lunsford, Andrea, and Lisa Ede. Put their names in the order given in the work. For three or more authors, give the first author's name followed by "et al.": Greenblatt, Stephen, et al.
- Include any middle names or initials: Toklas, Alice B.
- If the author is a group or organization, use the full name, omitting any initial article: United Nations.
- If an author uses a handle that is significantly different from their name, include the handle in square brackets after the name: Ocasio-Cortez, Alexandria [@AOC].
- If there's no known author, start the entry with the title.
- If there's an editor but no author, put the editor's name in the author position and specify their role: Lunsford, Andrea, editor.
- If you're citing someone in addition to an author—an editor, translator, director, or other contributors—specify their role. If there are multiple contributors, put the one whose work you wish to highlight before the title, and list any others you want to mention after the title. If you don't want to highlight one particular contributor, start with the title and include any contributors after the title. For contributors named before the title, specify their role after the name: Fincher, David, director. For those named after the title, specify their role first: Directed by David Fincher.

TITLES

- Include any subtitles and capitalize all the words except for articles ("a," "an," "the"), prepositions ("to," "at," "from," and so on), and coordinating conjunctions ("and," "but," "for," "or," "nor," "so," "yet")—unless they are the first or last word of a title or subtitle.
- Italicize the titles of books, periodicals, websites, and other long works: *Pride and Prejudice, Wired.*
- Put quotation marks around the titles of articles and other short works: "Letter from Birmingham Jail."
- To document a source that has no title, describe it without italics or quotation marks: Letter to the author, Photograph of a tree. For a short, untitled email, text message, tweet, or poem, you may want to include the text itself instead: Dickinson, Emily. "Immortal is an ample word." *American Poems*, www.americanpoems.com/poets/emilydickinson/immortal-is-an-ample-word.

VERSIONS

- If you cite a source that's available in more than one version, specify the one you consulted in your works-cited entry. Write ordinal numbers with numerals, and abbreviate "edition": 2nd ed. Write out names of specific versions, and capitalize following a period or if the name is a proper noun: King James Version, unabridged version, director's cut.

NUMBERS

- If you cite a book that's published in multiple volumes, indicate the volume number. Abbreviate "volume," and write the number as a numeral: vol. 2.
- Indicate volume and issue numbers (if any) of journals, abbreviating both "volume" and "number": vol. 123, no. 4.
- If you cite a TV show or podcast episode, indicate the season and episode numbers: season 1, episode 4.

PUBLISHERS

- Write publishers', studios', and networks' names in full, but omit initial articles and business words like "Inc." or "Company."
- For academic presses, use "U" for "University" and "P" for "Press": Princeton UP, U of California P. Spell out "Press" if the name doesn't include "University": MIT Press.

author   title   publication

- Many publishers use "&" in their name: Simon & Schuster. MLA says to use "and" instead: Simon and Schuster.
- If the publisher is a division of an organization, list the organization and any divisions from largest to smallest: Stanford U, Center for the Study of Language and Information, Metaphysics Research Lab.

DATES

- Whether to give just the year or to include the month and day depends on the source. In general, give the full date that you find there. If the date is unknown, simply omit it.
- Abbreviate the months except for May, June, and July: Jan., Feb., Mar., Apr., Aug., Sept., Oct., Nov., Dec.
- For books, give the publication date on the copyright page: 1948. If a book lists more than one date, use the most recent one.
- Periodicals may be published annually, monthly, seasonally, weekly, or daily. Give the full date that you find there: 2019, Apr. 2019, 16 Apr. 2019. Do not capitalize the names of seasons: spring 2021.
- For online sources, use the copyright date or the full publication date that you find there, or a date of revision. If the source does not give a date, use the date of access: Accessed 6 June 2020. Give a date of access as well for online sources you think are likely to change and for websites that have disappeared.

LOCATION

- For most print articles and other short works, give a page number or range of pages: p. 24, pp. 24–35. For articles that are not on consecutive pages, give the first page number with a plus sign: pp. 24+.
- If it's necessary to specify a section of a source, give the section name before the page numbers: Sunday Review sec., p. 3.
- Indicate the location of an online source by giving a DOI if one is available; if not, give a URL—and use a permalink if one is available. MLA notes that URLs are not always reliable, so ask your instructor if you should include them. DOIs should start with "https://doi.org/"—but no need to include "https://" for a URL, unless you want the URL to be a hyperlink.
- For a geographical location, give enough information to identify it: a city (Houston), a city and state (Portland, Maine), or a city and country (Manaus, Brazil).

- For something seen in a museum, archive, or elsewhere, name the institution and its location: Maine Jewish Museum, Portland, Maine.
- For performances or other live presentations, name the venue and its location: Mark Taper Forum, Los Angeles.

PUNCTUATION

- Use a period after the author name(s) that start an entry (Morrison, Toni.) and the title of the source you're documenting (*Beloved.*).
- Use a comma between the author's last and first names: Ede, Lisa.
- Some URLs will not fit on one line. MLA does not specify where to break a URL, but we recommend breaking it before a punctuation mark. Do *not* add a hyphen or a space.
- Sometimes you'll need to provide information about more than one work for a single source—for instance, when you cite an article from a periodical that you access through a database. MLA refers to the periodical and database (or any other entity that holds a source) as "containers" and specifies certain punctuation. Use commas between elements within each container, and put a period at the end of each container. For example:

> Semuels, Alana. "The Future Will Be Quiet." *The Atlantic*, Apr. 2016, pp. 19–20. *ProQuest*, search.proquest.com/docview/1777443553?accountid+42654.

The guidelines that follow will help you document the kinds of sources you're likely to use. The first section shows how to acknowledge authors and other contributors and applies to all kinds of sources—print, online, or others. Later sections show how to treat titles, publication information, location, and access information for many specific kinds of sources. In general, provide as much information as possible for each source—enough to tell readers how to find a source if they wish to access it themselves.

SOURCES NOT COVERED

These guidelines will help you cite a variety of sources, but there may be sources you want to use that aren't mentioned here. If you're citing a source that isn't covered, consult the MLA style blog at **style.mla.org**, or ask them a question at **style.mla.org/ask-a-question.**

author　　　title　　　publication

Authors and Contributors

When you name authors and other contributors in your citations, you are crediting them for their work and letting readers know who's in on the conversation. The following guidelines for citing authors and contributors apply to all sources you cite: in print, online, or in some other media.

1. ONE AUTHOR

Anderson, Chris. *The Long Tail: Why the Future of Business Is Selling Less of More.* Hyperion, 2006.

2. TWO AUTHORS

Lunsford, Andrea, and Lisa Ede. *Singular Texts/Plural Authors: Perspectives on Collaborative Writing.* Southern Illinois UP, 1990.

3. THREE OR MORE AUTHORS

Sebranek, Patrick, et al. *Writers INC: A Guide to Writing, Thinking, and Learning.* Write Source, 1990.

4. TWO OR MORE WORKS BY THE SAME AUTHOR

Give the author's name in the first entry, and then use a three-em dash (or three hyphens) in the author slot for each of the subsequent works, listing them alphabetically by the first word of each title and ignoring any initial articles.

Kaplan, Robert D. *The Coming Anarchy: Shattering the Dreams of the Post Cold War.* Random House, 2000.

———. *Eastward to Tartary: Travels in the Balkans, the Middle East, and the Caucasus.* Random House, 2000.

5. AUTHOR AND EDITOR OR TRANSLATOR

Austen, Jane. *Emma.* Edited by Stephen M. Parrish, W. W. Norton, 2000.

Dostoevsky, Fyodor. *Crime and Punishment.* Translated by Richard Pevear and Larissa Volokhonsky, Vintage Books, 1993.

Start with the editor or translator, followed by their role, if you are focusing on that contribution rather than the author's. If there is a translator but no author, start with the title.

Pevear, Richard, and Larissa Volokhonsky, translators. *Crime and Punishment.* By Fyodor Dostoevsky, Vintage Books, 1993.

>   *Beowulf.* Translated by Kevin Crossley-Holland, Macmillan, 1968.

6. NO AUTHOR OR EDITOR

When there's no known author or editor, start with the title.

>   *The Turner Collection in the Clore Gallery.* Tate Publications, 1987.

>   "Being Invisible Closer to Reality." *The Atlanta Journal-Constitution,* 11 Aug. 2008,
>   p. A3.

7. ORGANIZATION OR GOVERNMENT AS AUTHOR

>   Diagram Group. *The Macmillan Visual Desk Reference.* Macmillan, 1993.

For a government publication, give the name that is shown in the source.

>   United States, Department of Health and Human Services, National Institute
>   of Mental Health. *Autism Spectrum Disorders.* Government Printing
>   Office, 2004.

When a nongovernment organization is both author and publisher, start with
the title, and list the organization only as the publisher.

>   *Stylebook on Religion 2000: A Reference Guide and Usage Manual.* Catholic
>   News Service, 2002.

If a division of an organization is listed as the author, give the division as the
author and the organization as the publisher.

>   Center for Workforce Studies. *2005–13: Demographics of the U.S. Psychology
>   Workforce.* American Psychological Association, July 2015.

Articles and Other Short Works

Articles, essays, reviews, and other short works are found in journals, magazines, newspapers, other periodicals, and books—all of which you may find in
print, online, or in a database. For most short works, you'll need to provide
information about the author, the titles of both the short work and the longer
work, any page numbers, and various kinds of publication information.

8. ARTICLE IN A JOURNAL

PRINT

>   Cooney, Brian C. "Considering *Robinson Crusoe's* 'Liberty of Conscience' in an
>   Age of Terror." *College English,* vol. 69, no. 3, Jan. 2007, pp. 197–215.

author   title   publication

ONLINE

> Schmidt, Desmond. "A Model of Versions and Layers." *Digital Humanities Quarterly,* vol. 13, no. 3, 2019, www.digitalhumanities.org/dhq/vol/13/3 /000430/000430.html.

9. ARTICLE IN A MAGAZINE

PRINT

> Burt, Tequia. "Legacy of Activism: Concerned Black Students' 50-Year History at Grinnell College." *Grinnell Magazine,* vol. 48, no. 4, summer 2016, pp. 32–38.

ONLINE

> Brooks, Arthur C. "The Hidden Toll of Remote Work." *The Atlantic,* 1 Apr. 2021, www.theatlantic.com/family/archive/2021/04/zoom -remote-work-loneliness-happiness/618473.

10. ARTICLE IN A NEWS PUBLICATION

PRINT

> Saulny, Susan, and Jacques Steinberg. "On College Forms, a Question of Race Can Perplex." *The New York Times,* 14 June 2011, p. A1.

To document a particular edition of a newspaper, list the edition before the date. If a section name or number is needed to locate the article, put that detail after the date.

> Burns, John F., and Miguel Helft. "Under Pressure, YouTube Withdraws Muslim Cleric's Videos." *The New York Times,* late ed., 4 Nov. 2010, sec. 1, p. 13.

ONLINE

> Banerjee, Neela. "Proposed Religion-Based Program for Federal Inmates Is Canceled." *The New York Times,* 28 Oct. 2006, www.nytimes.com/2006 /10/28/us/28prison.html.

11. ARTICLE ACCESSED THROUGH A DATABASE

> Stalter, Sunny. "Subway Ride and Subway System in Hart Crane's 'The Tunnel.'" *Journal of Modern Literature,* vol. 33, no. 2, Jan. 2010, pp. 70–91. *JSTOR,* https://doi.org/10.2979/jml.2010.33.2.70.

12. ENTRY IN A REFERENCE WORK

PRINT

Fritz, Jan Marie. "Clinical Sociology." *Encyclopedia of Sociology,* edited by Edgar F. Borgatta and Rhonda J. V. Montgomery, 2nd ed., vol. 1, Macmillan Reference USA, 2000, pp. 323–29.

"California." *The New Columbia Encyclopedia,* edited by William H. Harris and Judith S. Levey, 4th ed., Columbia UP, 1975, pp. 423–24.

ONLINE

Document online reference works the same as print ones, adding the URL after the date of publication.

"Baseball." *The Columbia Electronic Encyclopedia,* edited by Paul Lagassé, 6th ed., Columbia UP, 2012, www.infoplease.com/encyclopedia.

13. EDITORIAL OR OP-ED

EDITORIAL

Editorial Board. "A New Look for Local News Coverage." *The Lakeville Journal,* 13 Feb. 2020, p. A8.

Editorial Board. "Editorial: Protect Reporters at Protest Scenes." *Los Angeles Times,* 11 Mar. 2021, www.latimes.com/opinion/story/2021-03-11 /reporters-protest-scenes.

OP-ED

Okafor, Kingsley. "Opinion: The First Step to COVID Vaccine Equity Is Overall Health Equity." *The Denver Post,* 15 Apr. 2021, www.denverpost.com /2021/04/15/covid-vaccine-equity-kaiser.

If it's not clear that it's an op-ed, add a label at the end.

Balf, Todd. "Falling in Love with Swimming." *The New York Times,* 17 Apr. 2021, p. A21. Op-ed.

14. LETTER TO THE EDITOR

Pinker, Steven. "Language Arts." *The New Yorker,* 4 June 2012, p. 10.

If the letter has no title, include "Letter" after the author's name.

Fleischmann, W. B. Letter. *The New York Review of Books,* 1 June 1963, www .nybooks.com/articles/1963/06/01/letter-21.

author   title   publication

15. REVIEW

PRINT

Frank, Jeffrey. "Body Count." *The New Yorker,* 30 July 2007, pp. 86–87.

ONLINE

Donadio, Rachel. "Italy's Great, Mysterious Storyteller." *The New York Review of Books,* 18 Dec. 2014, www.nybooks.com/articles/2014/12/18/italys -great-mysterious-storyteller.

If a review has no title, include the title and author of the work being reviewed after the reviewer's name.

Lohier, Patrick. Review of *Exhalation,* by Ted Chiang. *Harvard Review Online,* 4 Oct. 2019, www.harvardreview.org/book-review/exhalation.

16. COMMENT ON AN ONLINE ARTICLE

ZeikJT. Comment on "The Post-Disaster Artist." *Polygon,* 6 May 2020, 4:33 a.m., www.polygon.com/2020/5/5/21246679/josh-trank-capone -interview-fantastic-four-chronicle.

Books and Parts of Books

For most books, you'll need to provide information about the author, the title, the publisher, and the year of publication. If you found the book inside a larger volume, a database, or some other work, be sure to specify that as well.

17. BASIC ENTRIES FOR A BOOK

PRINT

Watson, Brad. *Miss Jane.* W. W. Norton, 2016.

EBOOK

Watson, Brad. *Miss Jane.* Ebook ed., W. W. Norton, 2016.

ON A WEBSITE

Ball, Cheryl E., and Drew M. Loewe, editors. *Bad Ideas about Writing.* West Virginia U Libraries, 2017, textbooks.lib.wvu.edu/badideas/badideas aboutwriting-book.pdf.

WHEN THE PUBLISHER IS THE AUTHOR

MLA Handbook. 9th ed., Modern Language Association of America, 2021.

18. ANTHOLOGY OR EDITED COLLECTION

Kitchen, Judith, and Mary Paumier Jones, editors. *In Short: A Collection of Brief Nonfiction.* W. W. Norton, 1996.

19. WORK IN AN ANTHOLOGY

Achebe, Chinua. "Uncle Ben's Choice." *The Seagull Reader: Literature,* edited by Joseph Kelly, W. W. Norton, 2005, pp. 23–27.

TWO OR MORE WORKS FROM ONE ANTHOLOGY

Prepare an entry for each selection by author and title, followed by the anthology editors' last names and the pages of the selection. Then include an entry for the anthology itself (see no. 18).

Hiestand, Emily. "Afternoon Tea." Kitchen and Jones, pp. 65–67.

Ozick, Cynthia. "The Shock of Teapots." Kitchen and Jones, pp. 68–71.

20. MULTIVOLUME WORK

ALL VOLUMES

Churchill, Winston. *The Second World War.* Houghton Mifflin, 1948–53. 6 vols.

SINGLE VOLUME

Sandburg, Carl. *Abraham Lincoln: The War Years.* Vol. 2, Harcourt, Brace and World, 1939.

If the volume has its own title, include it after the author's name, and indicate the volume number and series title after the year.

Caro, Robert A. *Means of Ascent.* Vintage Books, 1990. Vol. 2 of *The Years of Lyndon Johnson.*

21. BOOK IN A SERIES

Walker, Alice. *Everyday Use.* Edited by Barbara T. Christian, Rutgers UP, 1994. Women Writers: Texts and Contexts.

22. GRAPHIC NARRATIVE OR COMIC BOOK

Barry, Lynda. *One! Hundred! Demons!* Drawn and Quarterly, 2005.

If the work has both an author and an illustrator, start with the one you want to highlight, and label the role of anyone who's not an author.

Pekar, Harvey. *Bob and Harv's Comics.* Illustrated by R. Crumb, Running Press, 1996.

author   title   publication

Crumb, R., illustrator. *Bob and Harv's Comics.* By Harvey Pekar, Running
 Press, 1996.

To cite several contributors, you can also start with the title.

Secret Invasion. By Brian Michael Bendis, illustrated by Leinil Yu, inked by Mark
 Morales, Marvel, 2009.

23. SACRED TEXT

If you cite a specific edition of a religious text, you need to include it in your
works-cited list.

The New English Bible with the Apocrypha. Oxford UP, 1971.

The Torah: A Modern Commentary. W. Gunther Plaut, general editor, Union of
 American Hebrew Congregations, 1981.

24. EDITION OTHER THAN THE FIRST

Smart, Ninian. *The World's Religions.* 2nd ed., Cambridge UP, 1998.

25. REPUBLISHED WORK

Bierce, Ambrose. *Civil War Stories.* 1909. Dover, 1994.

26. FOREWORD, INTRODUCTION, PREFACE, OR AFTERWORD

Tanner, Tony. Introduction. *Pride and Prejudice,* by Jane Austen, Penguin,
 1972, pp. 7–46.

27. PUBLISHED LETTER

White, E. B. "To Carol Angell." 28 May 1970. *Letters of E. B. White,* edited
 by Dorothy Lobrano Guth, Harper and Row, 1976, p. 600.

28. PAPER HEARD AT A CONFERENCE

Hern, Katie. "Inside an Accelerated Reading and Writing Classroom."
 Conference on Acceleration in Developmental Education, 15 June 2016,
 Sheraton Inner Harbor Hotel, Baltimore.

29. DISSERTATION

Simington, Maire Orav. *Chasing the American Dream Post World War II: Perspectives from Literature and Advertising.* 2003. Arizona State U, PhD dissertation. *ProQuest,* search.proquest.com/docview/305340098.

For an unpublished dissertation, end with the institution and a description of
the work.

Kim, Loel. *Students Respond to Teacher Comments: A Comparison of Online Written and Voice Modalities.* 1998. Carnegie Mellon U, PhD dissertation.

Websites

Many sources are available in multiple media (for example, a print periodical that is also on the web and contained in digital databases), but some are published only on websites. A website can have an author, an editor, or neither. Some sites have a publisher, and some do not. Include whatever information is available. If the publisher and title of the site are essentially the same, omit the name of the publisher.

30. ENTIRE WEBSITE

Proffitt, Michael, chief editor. *The Oxford English Dictionary.* Oxford UP, 2021, www.oed.com.

PERSONAL WEBSITE

Park, Linda Sue. *Linda Sue Park: Author and Educator.* 2021, lindasuepark.com.

If the site is likely to change, if it has no date, or if it no longer exists, include a date of access.

Archive of Our Own. Organization for Transformative Works, archiveofourown .org. Accessed 23 Apr. 2021.

31. WORK ON A WEBSITE

Cesareo, Kerry. "Moving Closer to Tackling Deforestation at Scale." *World Wildlife Fund,* 20 Oct. 2020, www.worldwildlife.org/blogs/sustainability -works/posts/moving-closer-to-tackling-deforestation-at-scale.

32. BLOG ENTRY

Hollmichel, Stefanie. "Bring Up the Bodies." *So Many Books,* 10 Feb. 2014, somanybooksblog.com/2014/02/10/bring-up-the-bodies.

Document a whole blog as you would an entire website (no. 30) and a comment on a blog as you would a comment on an online article (no. 16).

33. WIKI

"Pi." *Wikipedia,* Wikimedia Foundation, 28 Aug. 2013, en.wikipedia.org /wiki/Pi.

author　　　　title　　　　publication

Personal Communication and Social Media

34. PERSONAL LETTER

Quindlen, Anna. Letter to the author. 11 Apr. 2013.

35. EMAIL OR TEXT MESSAGE

Smith, William. Email to Richard Bullock. 19 Nov. 2013.

Rombes, Maddy. Text message to Isaac Cohen. 4 May 2021.

O'Malley, Kit. Text message to the author. 2 June 2020.

You can also include the text of a short email or text message, with a label at the end.

Rust, Max. "Trip to see the cows tomorrow?" 27 Apr. 2021. Email.

36. SOCIAL MEDIA POST

Oregon Zoo. "Winter Wildlife Wonderland." *Facebook*, 8 Feb. 2019, www
.facebook.com/80229441108/videos/2399570506799549.

If there's no title, you can use a concise description or the text of a short post.

Millman, Debbie. Photos of Roxane Gay. *Instagram*, 18 Feb. 2021, www
.instagram.com/p/CLcT_EnhnWT.

Obama, Barack [@POTUS44]. "It's been the honor of my life to serve you.
You made me a better leader and a better man." *Twitter*, 20 Jan. 2017,
twitter.com/POTUS44/status/822445882247413761.

Audio, Visual, and Other Sources

37. ADVERTISEMENT

PRINT

Advertisement for Grey Goose. *Wine Spectator*, 18 Dec. 2020, p. 22.

VIDEO

"First Visitors." *YouTube*, uploaded by Snickers, 20 Aug. 2020, www.youtube
.com/watch?v=negeco0bIL0.

38. ART

ORIGINAL

> Van Gogh, Vincent. *The Potato Eaters.* 1885, Van Gogh Museum, Amsterdam.

IN A BOOK

> Van Gogh, Vincent. *The Potato Eaters.* 1885, Scottish National Gallery. *History of Art: A Survey of the Major Visual Arts from the Dawn of History to the Present Day,* by H. W. Janson, Prentice Hall / Harry N. Abrams, 1969, p. 508.

ONLINE

> Warhol, Andy. *Self-portrait.* 1979. *J. Paul Getty Museum,* www.getty.edu/art/collection/objects/106971/andy-warhol-self-portrait-american-1979.

39. CARTOON

PRINT

> Mankoff, Robert. Cartoon. *The New Yorker,* 3 May 1993, p. 50.

ONLINE

> Munroe, Randall. "Up Goer Five." *xkcd,* 12 Nov. 2012, xkcd.com/1133.

40. SUPREME COURT CASE

> United States, Supreme Court. *District of Columbia v. Heller.* 26 June 2008. *Legal Information Institute,* Cornell Law School, www.law.cornell.edu/supremecourt/text/07-290.

41. FILM

Name individuals based on the focus of your project—the director, the screenwriter, or someone else.

> *Breakfast at Tiffany's.* Directed by Blake Edwards, Paramount, 1961.

ONLINE

> *Interstellar.* Directed by Christopher Nolan, Paramount, 2014. *Amazon Prime Video,* www.amazon.com/Interstellar-Matthew-McConaughey/dp/B00TU9UFTS.

If your essay focuses on one contributor, you may put their name before the title.

> Edwards, Blake, director. *Breakfast at Tiffany's.* Paramount, 1961.

author   title   publication

42. TV SHOW EPISODE

Name contributors based on the focus of your project—director, creator, actors, or others. If you don't want to highlight anyone in particular, don't include any contributors.

BROADCAST

"The Storm." *Avatar: The Last Airbender,* created by Michael Dante DiMartino and Bryan Konietzko, season 1, episode 12, Nickelodeon Animation Studios, 3 June 2005.

DVD

"The Storm." 2005. *Avatar: The Last Airbender: The Complete Book 1 Collection,* created by Michael Dante DiMartino and Bryan Konietzko, episode 12, Nickelodeon Animation Studios, 2006, disc 3. DVD.

STREAMING ONLINE

"The Storm." *Avatar: The Last Airbender,* season 1, episode 12, Nickelodeon Animation Studios, 2005. *Netflix,* www.netflix.com.

STREAMING ON AN APP

"The Storm." *Avatar: The Last Airbender,* season 1, episode 12, Nickelodeon Animation Studios, 2005. *Netflix* app.

If you're focusing on a contributor who's relevant specifically to the episode you're citing, include their name after the episode title.

"The Storm." Directed by Lauren MacMullan. *Avatar: The Last Airbender,* season 1, episode 12, Nickelodeon Animation Studios, 3 June 2005.

43. ONLINE VIDEO

"Everything Wrong with *National Treasure* in 13 Minutes or Less." *YouTube,* uploaded by CinemaSins, 21 Aug. 2014, www.youtube.com/watch?v=1ul-_ZWvXTs.

44. PRESENTATION ON *ZOOM* OR OTHER VIRTUAL PLATFORM

Budhathoki, Thir. "Cross-Cultural Perceptions of Literacies in Student Writing." Conference on College Composition and Communication, 9 Apr. 2021, online.

45. INTERVIEW

If it's not clear that it's an interview, add a label at the end. If you are citing a transcript of an interview, indicate that at the end as well.

PUBLISHED

> Whitehead, Colson. "Colson Whitehead: By the Book." *The New York Times*, 15 May 2014, www.nytimes.com/2014/05/18/books/review/colson -whitehead-by-the-book.html. Interview.

PERSONAL

> Bazelon, L. S. Telephone interview with the author. 4 Oct. 2020.

46. MAP

If the title doesn't make clear it's a map, add a label at the end.

> *Brooklyn.* J. B. Beers, 1874. Map.

47. MUSICAL SCORE

> Frank, Gabriela Lena. *Compadrazgo.* G. Schirmer, 2007.

48. ORAL PRESENTATION

> Cassin, Michael. "Nature in the Raw—The Art of Landscape Painting." Berkshire Institute for Lifelong Learning, 24 Mar. 2005, Clark Art Institute, Williamstown, Massachusetts.

49. PODCAST

If you accessed a podcast on the web, give the URL; if you accessed it through an app, indicate that instead.

> "DUSTWUN." *Serial,* hosted by Sarah Koenig, season 2, episode 1, WBEZ / Serial Productions, 10 Dec. 2015, serialpodcast.org/season-two/1 /dustwun.

> "DUSTWUN." *Serial,* hosted by Sarah Koenig, season 2, episode 1, WBEZ / Serial Productions, 10 Dec. 2015. *Spotify* app.

50. RADIO PROGRAM

> "In Defense of Ignorance." *This American Life,* hosted by Ira Glass, WBEZ, 22 Apr. 2016.

51. SOUND RECORDING

If you accessed a recording on the web, give the URL; if you accessed it through an app, indicate that instead.

author   title   publication

Beyoncé. "Pray You Catch Me." *Lemonade,* Parkwood Entertainment /
Columbia Records, 2016, www.beyonce.com/album/lemonade-visual
-album/songs.

Simone, Nina. "To Be Young, Gifted and Black." *Black Gold,* RCA Records,
1969. *Spotify* app.

ON A CD

Brown, Greg. "Canned Goods." *The Live One,* Red House, 1995. CD.

52. VIDEO GAME

Animal Crossing: New Horizons. Version 1.1.4, Nintendo, 6 Apr. 2020.

53. GENERATIVE AI CONTENT

At the time of this printing, the *MLA Style Center* website gives brief initial
advice on how to cite content generated by AI tools such as ChatGPT. See
style.mla.org for more information.

"Explain how a lightbulb works" prompt. *ChatGPT,* 23 Mar. version, OpenAI,
14 Apr. 2023, chat.openai.com.

If you're citing a creative work, you can use the title and a concise description
instead of including the prompt. If there's no title, you can use the first few
words of the text.

"New sneakers, so fresh . . ." haiku about sneakers. *ChatGPT,* 23 Mar. version,
OpenAI, 24 Apr. 2023, chat.openai.com.

Sample Research Paper

The following report was written by Jackson Parell for a first-year writing
course. It's formatted according to the guidelines of the *MLA Handbook,*
9th edition (2021).

Jackson Parell

Professor Hammann

Writing and Rhetoric 1

21 May 2018

Free at Last, Free at Last:

Civil War Memory and Civil Rights Rhetoric

When Martin Luther King, Jr., addressed the huge crowd in Washington, DC, on August 28, 1963, he did so on the steps of the Lincoln Memorial, in Lincoln's symbolic shadow (Sundquist 146). Using the words and legacy of the Great Emancipator, King intended to make an appeal to the moral conscience of America to rid itself of the vestiges of slavery and to realize Lincoln's new birth of freedom one hundred years after it was first proposed. On this day, and throughout the Civil War Centennial years (1961–65), African American leaders, including King, successfully accessed the language of the Civil War's promise of racial justice to shape a compelling message for future progress. As historian Robert Cook writes, "The advent of the Centennial furnished [African Americans] with powerful leverage in their intensifying efforts to close the gap between the promise and the reality of American community life" (96).

However, the rhetoric of the Civil War could only serve as an appeal for racial equality if Americans commonly understood its history in the context of social justice and equal rights.

Annotations (margin labels):

- 1" margin
- 1/2"
- Title centered
- Double-spaced throughout
- 1" margin
- Author named in signal phrase; page number in parentheses
- 1" margin
- 1" margin

Unfortunately, for many Americans in the 1960s, this was not the case (Blight 3). Northerners and Southerners alike, looking to mend sectional strife after the war, were willing to adopt a memory of reconciliation that focused on the shared honor of battle as opposed to the racial issues over which those battles were fought. Civil War valor, bravery, and brotherhood shaped American wartime memory into a "shared experience"—one that would remain a potent source of nationalism well into the civil rights era (Cook 4). "For the majority, especially of white Americans," as historian David Blight writes, "emancipation in Civil War memory was still an awkward kind of politeness at best and heresy at worst. . . . In 1963, the national temper and mythology still preferred a story of the mutual valor of the Blue and Gray to the disruptive problem of black and white" (3). Therefore, civil rights leaders, including King, attempted to remind Americans of the war's cause and enduring racial legacies. Through pen and podium, he leveraged that history in a powerful appeal for racial justice one hundred years after Lee's surrender at Appomattox.

> In October 1961, President John F. Kennedy invited King to the White House for lunch. The meeting was unofficial—it was not recorded in the secretary's docket, nor was there any official business set to be discussed (Branch 27). After lunch, Kennedy led King on a tour of the residence. Hung outside the door of Lincoln's bedroom was a copy of the original Emancipation Proclamation. It

No signal phrase; author and page number in parentheses

Embeds signal phrase in the middle of the quotation

gave King the opportunity to bring up, ever so gently, the issue of civil rights (27). Already, the Montgomery bus boycotts, the Greensboro sit-ins, and the Freedom Rides had brought racial tensions to the forefront of American culture. King believed he had a solution. "Mr. President," he said, "I would like to see you stand in

this room and sign a [second] Emancipation Proclamation outlawing segregation 100 years after Lincoln's. You could base it on the Fourteenth Amendment" (qtd. in Sundquist 34). In the summer of 1962, King and his associates delivered the first copy of this second Proclamation to the White House, bound in leather. This document serves as an important example of the ways in which King reshaped the memory of the Civil War and leveraged its rhetoric to advance claims for equality in civil rights. The proclamation directly engages in the battle between white reconciliationist memory and the memory of racial justice. In it, King pushes back on traditional narratives of mutual valor and bravery by instead placing emphasis on the guarantees of equality embodied in Civil War documents. But before King could make the revisions to Civil War history necessary to frame his plea for racial justice, he needed to provide Kennedy with a compelling reason for doing so. By 1962, racial tensions in the United States had come to a head. Politicians, including Kennedy, wished to deescalate the

problem as fast as possible (Branch 52), so in his preamble, King cites increasing racial tensions as well as the Centennial of the

Civil War as impetus to dive into the "wellsprings of history" from which the civil rights movement began ("Appeal" 3):

> Mr. President, sometimes there occur moments in the history of our nation when it becomes necessary to pause and reflect upon the heritage of the past in order to determine the most meaningful course for the present and the future. America today in the field of race relations is such a moment. We believe the Centennial of the Emancipation Proclamation is a particularly important time for all our citizens to rededicate themselves to those early precepts and principles of equality before the law. ("Appeal" 1)

With his first words, therefore, King encourages the president to think about Civil War history as a tool for addressing modern issues.

After establishing the importance of looking to the past to resolve the racial tensions of the present, King proposes the version of Civil War history upon which he believes Kennedy should reflect. It is a version that promotes the war's promises of racial equality over the valor and bravery of its veterans. He references the Gettysburg Address and the Emancipation Proclamation as the war's defining documents, both of which place the issue of slavery as the central cause of the Civil War

Two works cited within the same sentence

Uses block format for quotation longer than 4 lines. Indents ½ inch or 5 spaces

Parenthetical documentation follows punctuation in a block quotation

Includes short title because there's more than one source from that author

and uphold concepts of equal justice for all ("Appeal" 1–2). King engages here with a larger historical movement to remind Americans of the documents and narratives from their past that support claims for racial equality. In the 1960s, historians and researchers alike looked to rewrite Civil War memory in a way that neither disregarded the importance of slavery as the agent of conflict in the Civil War nor portrayed African Americans as naturally inferior—a people without agency in the struggle for their own freedom (Snyder 1–2, 36). By reshaping the narratives of the past to reflect a nuanced version of the Civil War, these historians attempted to break down the justifications for the racial hierarchy that structured the white status quo.

Paragraphs indent ¹/₂ inch or 5 spaces

By reshaping Civil War memory to focus on its promises of equality, King develops a strong appeal for change on the grounds that those promises had not yet been fulfilled. King draws compelling parallels between the past and present, which framed the Civil War as a battle unfinished, one fought today by the civil rights movement:

> The struggle for freedom, Mr. President, of which our Civil War was but a bloody chapter, continues throughout our land today. The courage and heroism of Negro citizens . . . is only further effort to affirm the democratic heritage so painfully won, in part, upon the grassy battlefields of Antietam, Lookout Mountain, and Gettysburg. ("Appeal" 3)

The metaphor of a modern Civil War presents Kennedy with the moral imperative to follow in the footsteps of Lincoln, his forebearer, and to help finally end the battle for equality begun one hundred years before. "The time has come, Mr. President," King says, "to let those dawn-like rays of freedom, first glimpsed in 1863, fill the heavens with noonday sunlight of complete human decency" ("Appeal" 4). King believed that the present situation demanded more than legislative action—it demanded from Kennedy an executive order that appealed to the "moral conscience of America" ("Appeal" 4).

But Kennedy never responded, and King found his ambivalence very disheartening. Without Kennedy, King felt that the civil rights movement would stall. He needed to re-create the conditions under which a document like the first Emancipation Proclamation came about—to foster the same tensions that brought to light the deep moral flaws of racism and propelled them to a national stage (Ward and Badger 141). Time was running out. The eyes of the world were focused on the civil rights movement, and King intended to capitalize. At midnight on June 1, he called his aides with an urgent message: in August, the civil rights movement would descend on the capital (Branch 53).

Names both authors in a work with two authors

If King could not convince the president to change the moral conscience of America, he would attempt to do it himself. Two months later, King began to outline the speech that would conclude the ceremonies of the March on Washington. In essence, it reflected the same historical appeal he had made to the president in the Second Emancipation Proclamation. He intended to shift predominant public memory from one that highlighted the mutual sacrifice of the Blue and Gray to one that focused on the Civil War's guarantees of equality. These guarantees served as the grounds on which King would build his argument for modern civil rights progress. Evoking the language of past Republican leaders, including Lincoln, he appealed to the American public to adopt a policy of inclusion, one with a vision for the future that was, in many ways, shaped in stark contrast to America's oppressive past.

On the morning of August 28, the turnout was slim, estimated at 25,000. Soon, however, protesters began arriving in swarms. At Union Station, trains pulled in first from Baltimore, then Georgia, the Carolinas, Maryland, and further north (Hansen 33–35). By the time King took the podium, he spoke before a crowd of nearly 250,000. "Five score years ago," King began, "a great American in whose symbolic shadow we stand today signed the Emancipation Proclamation" ("Dream" 1). This first sentence of King's "Dream" speech refers both to Lincoln's Gettysburg Address and to the Emancipation Proclamation, placing both documents at the forefront of America's Civil War consciousness (Sundquist 145). As in the Second Emancipation Proclamation, King intended to divert the predominant reconciliationist

Includes page range because the information cited spans multiple pages

Uses past tense ("began") to describe the scene — and present tense ("refers") to describe the text

memory of the Civil War to one that memorialized the guarantees of racial justice embodied in the war's documents. Although his remarks on those documents were brief, the broader, more inclusive historical narratives toward which they gesture—those in which slavery is accepted as the cause of the Civil War and African Americans are acknowledged for their strategic contributions to military efforts—gave further justification to uphold the guarantees of equality memorialized in the documents themselves.

These guarantees served as the moral structure of King's national appeal for racial justice. If, as King argues, equality was a right ensured by the course of American history, then segregation was simply a breach of contract between the American government and its African American constituents. King employs the metaphor of a "bad check" to explain the chasm between historical promises of racial equality and the realities faced in 1960s culture:

> In a sense we've come to our nation's capital to cash a check. . . . This note was a promise that all men—yes, black men as well as white men—would be guaranteed the unalienable rights of life, liberty and the pursuit of happiness. It is obvious today that America has defaulted on this promissory note insofar as her citizens of color are concerned. ("Dream" 1)

Ellipses indicate that some words are left out

For a nation that claimed to uphold basic precepts of justice, the "bad check" metaphor was particularly compelling. Americans were posed with a moral imperative to rid themselves of the modern vestiges of slavery or else risk contradicting the principles of equality upon which the nation was founded.

King's powerful appeal to the moral conscience of America was only made possible by shaping a new narrative in Civil War memory that upheld equality as a basic right for all: "Many of our white brothers . . . have come to realize that their freedom is inextricably bound to our freedom" ("Dream" 3). King begins here the process of linking the fulfillment of the civil rights cause to the betterment of the nation as a whole, a process necessary to garner the support of white moderates, partial to their own self-interest and thus indifferent to historical appeals for racial justice.

The incentive for civil rights progress was only strengthened by King's final moments at the podium, from which his speech gains its name. The appeal of King's utopian dream serves as a powerful motive to pursue civil rights equality. King dreams that "sons of former slaves and the sons of former slave-owners will be able to sit down together at the table of brotherhood" ("Dream" 4). He dreams that freedom will ring from "Stone Mountains of Georgia"—where the faces of

Confederate generals are etched in rock—to "Lookout Mountain of Tennessee," the site of one of the Civil War's most famous battles (6). In essence, King's dream is that America will finally live up to the principles of freedom espoused at the time of its origin and live out "the true meaning of its creed" (4). Only then, King believes, will the battle for freedom begun at Fort Sumter finally reach its conclusion. King's direct references to the issue of slavery and to the battlegrounds on which the Civil War was fought serve as anchors in history that shape a clearer vision of future progress for all Americans. The moral imperative that King presents to white individuals in order to tender the check of racial justice is thus only made more pressing by the collective will to realize King's dream—a dream rooted in the rhetoric of the Civil War.

Ultimately, therefore, King's "Dream" speech promoted a memory that prioritized the war's promises of equality as opposed to the honor of its many battles. Historian David Blight explains:

> As Lincoln implied in that brief address at Gettysburg, the Civil War necessitated a redefinition of the United States, rooted somehow in the destruction of slavery and the . . . principle of human equality. In the "Dream" speech, King argued the same for his own era: the civil rights movement

heralded yet another re-founding in the same principle, one hundred . . . years after Lincoln's promise. (2)

Throughout the Centennial years, civil rights leaders, including King, waged war not only over modern policies and ideals, but over historical truth as well. African American activists pushed back on the predominant Civil War memory of the 1960s, promoting the war's guarantees of equality over those of reconciliation. Such guarantees became the grounds on which King and others shaped a compelling appeal for civil rights progress in the modern era. "Just as abolitionists had sought to exploit the promises enshrined in the Declaration of Independence," historian Robert Cook writes, "their intellectual successors had used the events of the Centennial to raise the conscience of the American public in the 1960s" (qtd. in Ward and Badger 144). Ultimately, therefore, civil rights leaders molded the rhetoric of the Civil War to inspire a nation to throw off its shackles of oppression and to breathe new life into the old slave hymn: "Free at last, Free at last, Great God a-mighty, We are free at last" (King, "Dream" 6).

Source quoted in another source

Works Cited

Blight, David W. *American Oracle: The Civil War in the Civil Rights Era.* Belknap Press of Harvard UP, 2013.

Branch, Taylor. "A Second Emancipation." *Washington Monthly,* Jan.– Feb. 2013, pp. 27–52.

Cook, Robert. *Troubled Commemoration: The American Civil War Centennial, 1961–1965.* Louisiana State UP, 2011.

Hansen, Drew. *The Dream: Martin Luther King, Jr., and the Speech That Inspired a Nation.* HarperCollins, 2003.

King, Martin Luther, Jr. "An Appeal to the Honorable John F. Kennedy President of the United States." 17 May 1962. *Civil Rights Movement Archive,* www.crmvet.org/info/emancip2.pdf.

———. "I Have a Dream . . . Speech by the Rev. Martin Luther King Jr. at the 'March on Washington.'" 28 Aug. 1963. *National Archives,* www.archives.gov/files/press/exhibits /dream-speech.pdf. Accessed 14 May 2019.

Snyder, Jeffrey Aaron. *Making Black History: The Color Line, Culture, and Race in the Age of Jim Crow.* U of Georgia P, 2018.

Sundquist, Eric. *King's Dream.* Yale UP, 2009.

Ward, Brian, and Tony Badger. *The Making of Martin Luther King and the Civil Rights Movement.* Macmillan, 1996.

1"

Heading centered

The list is alphabetized by authors' last names

Double-spaced

Each entry begins at the left margin; subsequent lines are indented ½ inch or 5 spaces

Multiple works by a single author are listed alphabetically by title. After first entry, the author's name is replaced with a 3-em dash (or 3 hyphens)

Every source used is in the works-cited list

Credits

ILLUSTRATIONS

CHAPTER 1: **p. 1**: Oksana Bratanova/Alamy Stock Photo.

CHAPTER 2: **p. 19**: ChaiyonS021/Shutterstock.

CHAPTER 3: **p. 33**: binik/Shutterstock.

CHAPTER 4: **p. 47**: daltonoo/iStockphoto/Getty Images; **p. 65**: Doug Steley B/Alamy Stock Photo.

CHAPTER 5: **p. 79**: Kane Reinholdsten.

CHAPTER 6: **p. 89**: Ruth Jenkinson/Dorling Kindersley ltd/Alamy Stock Photo.

CHAPTER 7: **p. 107**: Markik/Shutterstock; **p. 109**: The Granger Collection; **p. 133**: Photo by Barbara Joy Cooley; **p. 135**: Caroll Taveras/eyevine/Redux; **p. 142**: Merlijn Doomernik/Hollandse Hoogte/Redux; **p. 154**: Drew Hansen; **p. 156**: Bob Parent/Hulton Archive/Getty Images; **p. 160**: Paul Grover/Shutterstock; **p. 165**: Ryan Enn Hughes/The New York Times/Redux; **p. 170** T.J. Kirkpatrick/Redux.

CHAPTER 8: **p. 179**: BenThomasPhoto/iStockphoto; **p. 184**: Curt Teich Postcard Archives Collection, Newberry Library; **p. 185**: Courtesy of belgradelakesmaine.com; **p. 199**: Cephas Picture Library/Alamy Stock Photo; **p. 207** top and bottom: Courtesy of Tony Mendoza; **p. 208**: Reproduced from R. C. Cross and M. S. Wheatland; From Modeling a falling slinky. Am. J. Phys. 80, 1051 (2012); doi: 10.1119/1.4750489, with the permission of the American Association of Physics Teachers; **p. 209**: Emily Schoone; **p. 215**: New York Times Co./Archive Photos/Getty Images; **p. 223**: Photo by Nancy L. Ford; **p. 226**: T.J. Kirkpatrick/Redux; **p. 231**: Philippe Matsas/Agence Opale/Alamy Stock Photo; **p. 237**: Shutterstock; **p. 242**: Kristina Bumphrey/Shutterstock.

CHAPTER 9: **p. 249**: Nina Firsova/Alamy Stock Photo; **p. 265**: Natan Dvir/Polaris; **p. 269**: WildSnap/Shutterstock; **p. 273**: Amelia Martin/Shutterstock; **p. 275**: Geraint Lewis/Alamy Stock Photo; **p. 281**: AP Photo/Matt Rourke; **p. 286**: Maggie Shannon/The New York Times/Redux.

CHAPTER 10: **p. 291**: Eugene Sergeev/Shutterstock; **p. 293**: AP Photo/Steve Dykes; **p. 305**: Richard Levine/Alamy Stock Photo; **p. 308**: Carlos Yudica/Shutterstock; **p. 319**: Robert W. Ginn/Alamy Stock Photo; **p. 328**: Photograph by Phyllis Rose; **p. 330**: Anne Dillard; **p. 337**: Magdalena Ostas; **p. 343**: Dan Redding; **p. 344**: DenisMArt/Shutterstock.

CHAPTER 11: **p. 349**: Maksym Fesenko/Shutterstock; **p. 373**: Courtesy of John St.; **p. 375**: Photo by David Archer; **p. 377**: Heather Ainsworth/The New York Times/Redux; **p. 383**: Stephanie Sowl; **p. 387**: Tony Cenicola/The New York Times/Redux; **p. 392**: Jacquelyn Tierney.

CHAPTER 12: **p. 399**: richVintage/iStockphoto/Getty Images; **p. 401**: Sabine Dowek; **p. 419**: ©WeRide Australia www.weride.org.au; **p. 421**: Lars Niki/Getty Images for Hickey Freeman; **p. 426**: Joe Mabel; **p. 429**: Photos 12/Alamy Stock Photo; **p. 430**: AF archive/Alamy; **p. 433**: Basso Cannarsa/Agence Opale/ Alamy Stock Photo; **p. 435**: Jo-Anne McArthur/Redux; **p. 436**: Andrew F. Kazmierski/Shutterstock; **p. 441**: Library of Congress, Prints & Photographs Division, Courtesy Katherine Young LOT 13309-1, no. 30 [P&P]; **p. 443**: Library of Congress Prints and Photographs Division, LC-DIG-pga-05039; **p. 448**: Jesse Winter; **p. 454**: ©Alexander Lumans.

CHAPTER 13: **p. 459**: Alex Eggermont/age fotostock; **p. 461**: Photo by Barbara Joy Cooley; **p. 479**: ©Universal Pictures/Courtesy: Everett Collection; **p. 481**: Gary Gershoff/Getty Images; **p. 482**: ©1989 Jim McHugh; **p. 489**: Matt Doyle/Contour by Getty Images; **p. 495**: Carol T. Powers/The New York Times/Redux; **p. 503**: Ian Cook/Getty Images; **p. 506**: Stewart Slater; **p. 512**: Xavier Collin/Image Press Agency/Alamy Live News; **p. 518**: Ringo Chiu/ZUMA Wire/Alamy Live News.

CHAPTER 14: **p. 525**: Kostenko Maxim/Shutterstock; **p. 547**: Roz Chast/The New Yorker Collection/ The Cartoon Bank; **pp. 549, 551, 553**: Naohiro Matsumura; **p. 557**: Chris Hardy Photography; **p. 565**: Frazer Harrison/Getty Images; **pp. 569, 570, 573**: Courtesy of Mike Rose; **p. 579**: Drew Altizer Photography/Shutterstock.

CHAPTER 15: **p. 587**: Elena Elisseeva/Alamy Stock Photo; **p. 590**: 'The Influencing Machines' from The Influencing Machine: Brooke Gladstone on the Media by Brooke Gladstone. Illustrated by Josh Neufeld. Copyright ©2011 by Brooke Gladstone and Josh Neufeld. Used by permission of W.W. Norton & Company, Inc.; **p. 613**: The Advertising Archives; **p. 616**: IanDagnall Computing/Alamy Stock Photo; **p. 623**: Library of Congress Manuscript Division, Sojourner Truth Collection (MMC) LC-USZ62-119343; **p. 626**: Markus Kirchgessner/laif/Redux; **p. 627**: Poznyakov/Shutterstock; **p. 632**: Chuck Kennedy - White House via CNP/Newscom; **p. 640** left: Courtesy of CATO Institute, right: Photo Courtesy of Pacific Legal Foundation; **p. 646**: Michaela Oteri; **p. 653**: Billy Bennight/AdMedia via ZUMA Press Wire/Alamy Stock Photo; **p. 658**: courtesy of Angela Duckworth; **p. 663**: courtesy of Carol Dweck; **p. 670**: Stephen Lovekin/REX/Shutterstock; **p. 676**: Photo by Ibl/Shutterstock; **p. 683**: Jennifer Silverberg/eyevine/Redux; **p. 688**: Erik Jacobs/The New York Times/Redux; **p. 696** left: Jayne Riew, right: Sandy Huffaker/The New York Times/Redux; **p. 702**: Photo by Ron Bolander; **p. 710**: Matteo Nardone/Pacific Press/Alamy Live News; **p. 717**: Earl Wilson/Redux; **p. 722**: Tony Cenicola/The New York Times/Redux; **p. 728**: TJ Turner Pictures.

CHAPTER 16: **p. 733**: Africa Studio/Shutterstock; **p. 743**: Mary Roach, Stiff. New York: Norton. Photo by Mark Atkins/Panoptika.net; **p. 745**: AP Photo/Kathy Willens; **p. 749**: Chris Felver/Getty Images; **p. 750**: Chuck Place/Alamy Stock Photo; **p. 755**: Katherine Kendall; **p. 759**: CPA Media Pte Ltd/Alamy Stock Photo; **p. 767**: Photograph by Phyllis Rose.

CHAPTER 17: **p. 771**: **ScantyNebula/iStock/Getty Images**; **p. 777**: AP Photo/Andrew Harnik; **p. 780**: Google.

Glossary / Index

This glossary / index defines key terms and concepts and directs you to pages in the book where they are used or discussed. Terms set in SMALL CAPITAL LETTERS are defined elsewhere in the glossary / index.

Adichie, Chimamanda Ngozi, "Dear Ijeawele," 256, 275–80
adjectives, 75, 193, 470
Adler, Shawn, "Iron Man vs. Batman," 400, 402
advertisements, citing MLA style, 809
"affect," 363
agreement, 25
AI content, citing MLA style, 813
"Ain't I a Woman?" (Truth), 622–25
Alexie, Sherman, "Superman and Me," 102
Alice in Wonderland (Carroll), 403
"All Seven Deadly Sins Committed at Church Bake Sale" (*The Onion*), 253, 271–74

ALLUSION A passing reference, especially to a work of literature. For example, the title of Barack Obama's speech "A More Perfect Union" is an allusion to a phrase in the preamble to the US Constitution.

"although," 84
American Academy of Pediatrics (AAP), 781
American College of Pediatricians (ACPeds), 778–82
American Psychological Association (APA), 788
"among," 411

ANALOGY, 600 A COMPARISON that points out similarities between otherwise dissimilar things, or ones not usually compared. Analogies can help you to DESCRIBE, EXEMPLIFY, DEFINE, or ANALYZE an unfamiliar subject (the flow of electrons along a wire) by likening it to a more familiar one (the flow of water through a pipe). Drawing analogies is also a useful strategy in ARGUMENT, where you claim that what is true in one, usually simpler case (family finances) is true in another, more complicated case (national fiscal policy).

ANALYSIS, 4, 16, 96, 291–347, 736 The mental act of taking something apart to understand and explain how the pieces fit together,

such as the steps in a PROCESS or the chain of events leading from a CAUSE to a particular EFFECT.

argument and, 606
audience and, 294–95, 300–301, 310
breaking a subject into parts, 292, 302
cause-and-effect analysis and, 296, 310, 353, 359, 361, 365
chronological order in, 294, 302
classification, 311
common errors in, 309
comparison and contrast and, 308
composing a, 294–305
concluding a, 299–300, 311
considering context for, 307–8
considering how the parts make up the whole, 303
critical analysis of a text, 300–304
defining, 292
definition and, 536
description and, 305
drafting a, 296–304
evaluating and explaining results, 303–4
example and, 310
generating ideas and, 295–96, 301
identifying how the parts are organized, 302–3
narration and, 302–3
organization and, 296–304, 310
with other methods, 310, 735
process analysis, 294–300
pronouns and, 296–97, 309, 310
purpose and, 294–95, 300–301, 310
putting the steps in order, 296
readings
  "Emily Dickinson and the Space Within" (Ostas), 337–42
  "How I Wrote the Moth Essay—and Why" (Dillard), 328–36
  "How to Get Out of a Locked Trunk" (Weiss), 321–27
  "What Does the Nike Logo Mean?" (Redding), 343–47
reading with a critical eye, 310–11

ANECDOTE, 10, 100, 110, 592 A brief NARRATIVE, often told for the purpose of attracting a reader's interest or leading into a larger point.

ANNOTATE, 9-11 To make notations about a text by writing questions and comments in the margins and by highlighting, underlining, circling, or otherwise marking specific words and phrases.

ANTONYM A word whose meaning is opposite to that of another word, as "weak" is the antonym of "strong." Antonyms and SYNONYMS are especially useful in establishing and extending a DEFINITION.

APPEAL TO DOUBTFUL AUTHORITY, 600 A FALLACY of citing as expert testimony the opinions of people who do not necessarily have special knowledge of the issue.

ARGUMENT, 4, 16, 26, 63, 67, 99, 134, 587-732 Writing that takes a position on an issue and seeks to convince its AUDIENCE to act in a certain way, to believe in the truth or validity of a statement, or simply to listen with an open mind.

drafting a, 353–62
example and, 258
generating ideas and, 352–53
narration and, 353, 361, 364
organizing a, 353–62, 364
with other methods, 361–62, 364–65,
    735
punctuation and, 605
purpose and, 352, 364
reading a with a critical eye, 364–65
readings
    "Three Reasons College Graduates
        Return to Rural Areas" (Sowl),
        383–86
    "Why Are Textbooks So Expensive?"
        (Roediger), 375–82
    "Why Don't Young People Vote?"
        (Bouie), 387–91
    "Yale Will Not Save You" (Wang),
        392–98
reverse chronological order and, 355, 364
stating the point in, 354, 364
student example, "Family History" (Gon-
    zalez), 365–70
templates for drafting, 356
thesis in, 354, 364
transitional words and phrases, 93
types of causes, 364
usage errors in, 363
verbs and, 363
visuals and, 359–61, 364
why analyze?, 350–51

"caused," 362

CAUSES, 364 Conditions or events necessary to produce an EFFECT. The *immediate
cause* of an effect is the one closest to it in time
and most directly responsible for producing
the effect. *Remote causes* are further in time
from an effect and less direct in producing it.
The *main cause* of an effect is the most important cause; it is not only necessary to produce
the effect but sufficient to do so. *Contributing*

causes are less important but still contribute
to the effect; they are not, however, sufficient
to produce it on their own. *See also* CAUSE-
AND-EFFECT ANALYSIS

Cawley, Stephanie, "The Veil in *Persepolis*,"
    311–17
"Chameleon" (Noah), 512–17
Chandler, Raymond, 191
Chandrasekaran, Priya, "Cutting Our
    Grandmothers' Saris," 186, 223–25
"A Change in the Menu" (Silva), 595,
    608–11
Chapman, Elwood, *Working Woman*, 406–7
Chast, Roz, "An Epitaph," 546–47
"Chemistry 101 for Pound Cakes" (McDaniel),
    295

CHRONOLOGICAL ORDER, 94–95, 115
The sequence of events in time, particu-
larly important in a NARRATIVE or PROCESS
ANALYSIS.
    in analysis, 294, 302
    in cause-and-effect analysis, 354, 364
    in narration, 115

citations, following, 781. *See also* MLA-STYLE
    DOCUMENTATION

CLAIM, 4, 9, 60, 115, 588, 593–94, 598
The main point you make or position you
take on an issue in an ARGUMENT.
    analysis and, 301
    argument and, 607
    stating, 593–94

**CLASSIFICATION, 16, 26, 63, 98, 459–
523** Writing that assigns individuals to
groups, and divides groups into subgroups.
Strictly speaking, classification sorts individuals into categories ("Red is an Irish setter");
and division separates a category into subcategories ("The dogs at the pound included pit
bulls, greyhounds, and Boston terriers"). In
this book, the general term "classification" is
used for both sorting and dividing.

adjectives and, 470

analysis and, 311

argument and, 470

audience and, 462–63, 471

breaking categories into subcategories, 469, 471

cause-and-effect analysis and, 469–70, 472

choosing inclusive categories that don't overlap, 468–69, 471

choosing significant characteristics, 467, 471

common errors in, 470, 472

comparison and contrast and, 408, 412

composing a classification essay, 462–70

defining, 460

definition and, 463, 467, 469–70, 472

description and, 469–70, 472

drafting a classification essay, 464–70

generating ideas and, 463–64

organizing a classification essay, 464–70

with other methods, 469–70, 472, 735

parallelism and, 470

principle of, 462, 471

purpose and, 462–63, 471

reading a classification essay with a critical eye, 471–72

readings

"Ancient Archetypes and Modern Superheroes" (Slater), 506–11

"But What Do You Mean?" (Tannen), 495–502

"Chameleon" (Noah), 512–17

"Her Kind" (Sexton), 503–5

"Mother Tongue" (Tan), 481–88

"Types of Women in Romantic Comedies Who Are Not Real" (Kaling), 489–94

"What If They Bury Me When I'm Just in a Coma?" (Doughty), 518–23

stating the point of, 466–67, 471

student example, "Shades of Character" (Watson), 472–77

templates for drafting, 465

thesis and, 466–67, 471

using visuals, 468, 471

why classify?, 460, 462

classification and division. *See* CLASSIFICATION

clauses, 605

CLICHÉ A tired expression that has lost its original power to surprise because of overuse: "cut to the chase," "let the cat out of the bag," "last but not least."

"click restraint," 781–82

Climate Change Impacts in the United States: Highlights (US Global Change Research Program), 105

CLIMAX, 14, 117 The moment when the action in the PLOT of a NARRATIVE is most intense—the culmination, after which the dramatic tension is released.

"Climbing the Golden Arches" (Nuñez), 91, 92

CLUSTERING, 58, 254, 352–53, 463–64, 531–32 A way of GENERATING IDEAS by using circles and connecting lines to group ideas visually into related clusters or topics.

Cohen, Roger, "The Meaning of Life," 97–98

coherence, 38–40

COLLABORATING, 52–54 Working with other people on a research and writing project, either by face-to-face contact or by the online exchange of ideas, comments, and drafts.

colons, outside quotation marks, 122

comic books, citing MLA style, 806–7

commas

after introductory elements, 76

before conjunctions in compound sentences, 76

with connectors, 605

inside quotation marks, 76, 121

in a series, 76

CONCRETE, 56, 86, 181, 193, 251, 260
Definite, particular, capable of being perceived directly. "Rose," "Mississippi," "pinch" are more concrete words than "flower," "river," "touch." "Five miles per hour" is a more concrete idea than "slowness." When you begin a piece of writing with an ABSTRACT idea, try BRAINSTORMING for more concrete particulars about it, and then flesh out those concrete details by using DESCRIPTION, EXEMPLIFICATION, DEFINITION, and other methods of development.

CONNOTATION, 530 The implied meaning of a word; its overtones and associations over and above its literal meaning. The strict meaning of "heart," for example, is "the organ that pumps blood through the body," but the word connotes warmth, affection, and love. *See also* DENOTATION

CONTEXT, 4, 307-8 The circumstances in which a text is written and published, thereby affecting a reader's understanding of it. These include time and place of writing, identity of author, author's stated or unstated purpose, and location of publication (e.g., academic journal, newspaper, magazine, blog).

COORDINATING WORDS, 83-85 One of these words—"and," "but," "or," "nor," "so," "for," or "yet"—used to join two elements in a way that gives equal weight to each one ("bacon and eggs"; "pay up or get out").

COUNTERARGUMENT An objection that might be raised against a CLAIM you're making in an ARGUMENT. As you construct an argument, try to think of the strongest possible reasons not to agree with your position, and address them in advance. It's always better to put out a fire before it gets started.

CREDIBILITY The power (or lack thereof) of a writer to inspire trust and belief in the mind of the reader. A writer is likely to seem more trustworthy—and thus more credible to the reader—if they cite reliable sources, report facts clearly and accurately, and use solid evidence to support their claims.

CRITICAL ANALYSIS, 134, 300-304, 309 A type of writing that closely examines a text, idea, or object with an eye to understanding and explaining how it is put together (form) and how it works (function). Typical methods: CAUSE AND EFFECT, DESCRIPTION, EXAMPLE, PROCESS ANALYSIS. *See also* EVALUATION; RHETORICAL ANALYSIS; TEXTUAL ANALYSIS

DEDUCTION, 594, 596–99 A form of logical reasoning that proceeds from general principles to a particular conclusion, useful in persuading others that an ARGUMENT is valid. *See also* INDUCTION

DEFINITION, 16, 26, 63, 98–99, 525–85 Writing that explains what something is— and is not—by identifying the characteristics that set it apart from all others like it. *Extended definitions* enlarge on that basic meaning by analyzing the qualities, recalling the history, explaining the purpose, or giving SYNONYMS of whatever is being defined.

DENOTATION The literal meaning of a word; its dictionary definition. *See also* CONNOTATION

DEPENDENT CLAUSE, 84 A clause that begins with a subordinating word and therefore cannot stand alone as a sentence: "She feels good when she exercises." "My roommate, who was a physics major, tutors students in science."

DESCRIPTION, 10, 16, 26, 39, 59, 62, 63, 67, 71, 95, 110, 123, 179–248 Writing that appeals to the senses: it tells how something looks, feels, sounds, smells, or tastes. An *objective description* describes the subject factually, without the intrusion of the writer's own feelings, whereas a *subjective description* includes the writer's feelings about the subject.

DIALOGUE, 101, 119–20, 123 Direct speech, especially between two or more speakers in a NARRATIVE, quoted word for word. Dialogue is an effective way of introducing the views of others into a FIRST-PERSON narrative.

EXPOSITION, 13, 15 Writing that explains a subject by using EXEMPLIFICATION, ANALYSIS, COMPARISON, CLASSIFICATION, DEFINITION, and other methods of development. *See also* MODE

F

FALLACY, 10, 599–600 An error in logical reasoning to be avoided when constructing an ARGUMENT. Common fallacies include reasoning POST HOC, ERGO PROPTER HOC; NON SEQUITURS; BEGGING THE QUESTION; arguing AD HOMINEM; and FALSE ANALOGIES.

FALSE ANALOGY, 600 A FALLACY committed when an ARGUMENT is based on a faulty comparison.

FIGURE OF SPEECH, 10, 191–92, 195 Words and phrases used in symbolic, nonliteral ways to enhance all kinds of writing, particularly NARRATION and DESCRIPTION. Examples are HYPERBOLE, METAPHORS, PERSONIFICATION, PUNS, and SIMILES.

FIRST PERSON, 119 A grammatical and NARRATIVE point of view—expressed by the personal pronouns "I" or "we"—that allows a narrator to be both an observer of the scene and a participant in the action, but is limited by what the speaker knows or imagines. *See also* THIRD PERSON

FLASHBACK, 118 A scene that interrupts the CHRONOLOGICAL ORDER of a NARRATIVE to show what happened in the past, before the events of the main plot.

FLASH-FORWARD, 118 A scene that interrupts the CHRONOLOGICAL ORDER of a NARRATIVE to show what happens in the future, after the events of the main plot.

Fleming, David, "Sports' Perfect 0.4 Seconds," 293, 300, 303–4

focus, 66, 88

footnotes, 781, 794

"for," 84

"for example," 258

"for instance," 258

formatting essays, 77–78

Franklin, Benjamin, 353, 355, 530
    Autobiography, 108–12, 117–18

"Free at Last, Free at Last" (Parell), 814–25

FREEWRITING, 55-56 A means of GENER-ATING IDEAS by writing down, without stopping, whatever thoughts come to mind over a set period of time.

French, David, "The Dangerous Lesson of Book Bans in Public School Libraries," 722–27

FUSED SENTENCE, 83 Two or more INDEPENDENT CLAUSES with no punctuation between them: "I came I saw I conquered."

future tense, 118

G

Ganteaume, Cécile R., "Major New Exhibition Asks, Why Do Images of American Indians Permeate American Life?," 306

Garza, Alicia, "The Meaning of Movement," 579–85

Gay, Roxane, "Why People Are So Awful Online," 35–36, 683–87

generalizations, hasty, 600

GENERATING IDEAS, 55-60 A stage of the writing process that deals with the discovery of ideas, topics, points to consider, examples, and other raw materials for a text. Methods include BRAINSTORMING, CLUSTERING, FREEWRITING, JOURNALING, LOOPING, and LISTING.

analysis and, 295–96, 301

argument, 591–92

asking "who," "what," "where," "when," "why," and "how," 58–59, 113–14, 301

brainstorming, 57, 254, 295–96, 352–53, 404–5, 531–32, 591

cause-and-effect analysis and, 352–53

classification and, 463–64

clustering, 58, 254, 352–53, 463–64, 531–32

comparison and contrast and, 404–5

definition and, 531–32

description and, 185–86

differences, 404–5

freewriting, 55–56

journaling, 59–60

listing, 57, 254, 295–96, 404–5, 463–64, 531–32, 591

looping, 56–57, 463–64

similarities, 404–5

generative AI content, citing MLA style, 813

GENRE, 463 A kind of writing or other form of expression; in academic writing, these include REPORTS, POSITION PAPERS, RHETORICAL and TEXTUAL ANALYSES, and EVALUATIONS.

George III (king of England), 100

gerund ("-ing") forms, 118–19

Gladstone, Brooke, and Josh Neufeld, "The Influencing Machines," 590

Gladwell, Malcolm
    Blink, 250
    "David and Goliath," 76, 676–80

Gonzalez, Elisa, "Family History," 365–70

"good," 411

Google Books, 782

Gould, Jonathan R. Jr., "The People Next Door," 466–67

government websites, 774

Graff, Gerald, and Cathy Birkenstein, *"They Say / I Say"*, 22

Grant, Ulysses S., 97

"Grant and Lee" (Catton), 97, 409, 441–47

HASTY GENERALIZATION, 600 A FAL-
LACY that draws a conclusion based on far
too little evidence.

HYPERBOLE, 141, 675 A FIGURE OF SPEECH
that uses intentional exaggeration, often in a
DESCRIPTION or to make a point: "The professor explained it to us for two weeks one afternoon." See also UNDERSTATEMENT

LITERACY NARRATIVE, 134 A kind of writing that tells a personal story about learning to read and write—or about otherwise dealing with written language, or such related forms of symbolic representation as painting or musical notation. Typical methods: CAUSE AND EFFECT, DESCRIPTION, EXAMPLE, NARRATION.

LOOPING, 56–57, 463–64 A directed form of FREEWRITING in which you GENERATE IDEAS by narrowing your focus—and summarizing what you have just written—each time you freewrite.

M

MEMOIR A personal recollection of people and past events from the standpoint of the present. Typical methods: NARRATION, DESCRIPTION, EXAMPLE.

METAPHOR, 15, 192 A FIGURE OF SPEECH—often used in DESCRIPTIVE writing—that compares one thing with another, without the use of a stated connecting word: *Throughout the battle, Sergeant Phillips was a rock.*

methods of development, 16–17, 26, 62–63, 67
   analysis, 26, 63, 291–347
   argument, 26, 63, 67, 587–732
   cause-and-effect analysis, 26, 63, 67, 120, 349–98
   choosing, 102–3
   classification, 26, 63, 98, 459–523
   combining, 733–70
   comparison and contrast, 26, 63, 120, 399–458
   definition, 26, 63, 525–85
   description, 26, 62–63, 67, 71, 95, 179–248
   example, 26, 63, 95–96, 249–89
   narration, 26, 63, 67, 94, 107–77
   readings, mixing methods
     "The Death of a Moth" (Dillard), 114, 119, 767–70
     "Hearing Voices" (Hogan), 749–54
     Liar's Poker (Lewis), 63, 734–41
     "Linguistic Terrorism" (Anzaldúa), 755–58
     "On Going Home" (Didion), 745–48
     "Shooting an Elephant" (Orwell), 759–66
     Stiff (Roach), 402–3, 408, 742–43
metonymy, 225
Minard, Charles, 360
"Mind over Mass Media" (Pinker), 23
"Mirror" (Plath), 192

MISINFORMATION, 774 False or inaccurate information that may or may not be intended to deceive (lies, on the other hand, are always told deliberately).

MLA-STYLE DOCUMENTATION, 77–78, 788–825 A two-part DOCUMENTATION system created by the Modern Language Association that consists of brief in-text parenthetical citations and a list of sources at the end of the text. This documentation style, explained fully in chapter 17, is often used in literature and writing classes.

   footnotes and endnotes, 794
   in-text documentation, 788–94
     after a block quotation, 790
     an entire work, 794
     author named in a signal phrase, 789
     author named in parentheses, 789
     authors with the same last name, 790
     author unknown, 791
     dictionaries, 792
     encyclopedias, 792
     legal documents, 792
     literary works, 791–92
     multivolume works, 793
     novels, 791
     one-page article, 794
     organization or government as author, 791
     poems, 792
     prose plays, 791
     sacred texts, 792–93
     source quoted in another source, 793
     two or more authors, 790–91
     two or more works by the same author(s), 790
     verse plays, 791
     works cited together, 793
     work(s) in an anthology, 792
     work without page numbers, 793–94
   list of works cited, 795–813
     advertisements, 809
     art, 810
     articles/short works, 802–5
     books, 797–802, 805–8
     cartoons, 810
     citing sources not covered by MLA, 800
     comments on online articles, 805
     core elements, 796–800

MODE A form or manner of discourse. In classical rhetoric, the four basic modes of speaking or writing are NARRATION, DESCRIPTION, EXPOSITION, and ARGUMENT.

MODIFIER, 80-81 A word, phrase, or clause that describes or specifies something about another word, phrase, or clause ("a long, informative speech"; "the actors spoke in unison"; "the man who would be king").

N

NARRATION, 14, 16, 26, 39, 59, 63, 67, 94, 107-77 An account of actions and events that happen to someone or something in a particular place and time. Because narration is essentially storytelling, it is often used in fiction; however, it is also an important element in almost all writing and speaking. The opening of Lincoln's Gettysburg Address, for example, is in the narrative mode: "Four-score and seven years ago our fathers bought forth on this continent a new nation."

NARRATOR, 118-19 The person (or thing) telling a story. A FIRST-PERSON narrator ("I," "we") is both an observer of the scene and a participant in the action, but is limited by what they know or imagine. A THIRD-PERSON narrator ("he," "she," "it," "they") is limited to the role of observer, though sometimes an all-knowing one. *See also* POINT OF VIEW

NAYSAYER, 24 A potential opponent, especially in an academic argument. "Planting a naysayer" in a piece of academic writing is a rhetorical move that allows you to anticipate and disarm possible arguments against your THESIS.

NON SEQUITUR, 599-600 Latin for "does not follow"; a FALLACY of using a statement that has little or no logical connection to the preceding statement.

NOUN A word that names a person, place, thing, or idea (teacher, Zadie Smith, forest, surgeon general, Amazon River, notebook, democracy).

O

OBJECT, 80 A word or phrase that follows a preposition or that receives the action of a VERB. In the sentence "I handed him the mail that was on the table," "him" is an indirect object and "mail" is a direct object of the verb "handed"; "table" is an object of the preposition "on."

ONOMATOPOEIA A FIGURE OF SPEECH that uses words that sound like what they refer to: "buzz," "purr," "bark," "tick-tock."

P

PARADOX A FIGURE OF SPEECH in which a statement appears to contradict itself but, on closer examination, makes sense: "They have ears but hear not."

RÉSUMÉ, 252 A kind of writing that summarizes a person's accomplishments in a short form that can be readily reviewed by the intended audience. The conventional way of doing this is by breaking your academic and employment history into categories and giving specific examples, in each category, of your education, skills, experience, and other attributes. Typical methods: CLASSIFICATION, DESCRIPTION, EXEMPLIFICATION.

RHETORIC, 24, 26, 39–40, 129, 203, 266, 315, 369, 415, 476, 543, 610 The art of using language effectively in speech and in writing. The term originally belonged to oratory, and it implies the presence of both a speaker (or a writer) and a listener (or reader).

RHETORICAL ANALYSIS, 134 An examination of what a piece of writing (or photograph, painting, work of architecture, or other form of expression) says or means—and how that meaning is conveyed to an audience. Typical methods: NARRATION, DESCRIPTION, EXAMPLE, PROCESS ANALYSIS, COMPARISON, CAUSE AND EFFECT, ARGUMENT.

RHETORICAL QUESTION, 10, 258, 595 A question for which the speaker already has an answer in mind; often used in ARGUMENT.

ROGERIAN ARGUMENT, 602–3 A strategy of ARGUMENT developed by the psychologist Carl Rogers that seeks common ground among opposing points of view and that treats the participants on all sides as colleagues rather than adversaries.

S

SUBJECT, 80 The NOUN or pronoun plus any MODIFIERS that tell who or what a sentence or clause is about. A simple subject is a single NOUN or pronoun. A complete subject is the simple subject plus any modifiers. In the sentence "Ten commuters waited for the late bus," the complete subject is "Ten commuters" and the simple subject is "commuters."

SUBJECT-BY-SUBJECT COMPARISON, 406–7, 412 A way of organizing a comparison (or contrast) in which two or more subjects are discussed individually, making a number of points about one subject and then covering more or less the same points about the other subject. A subject-by-subject comparison of London and New York would address first London, examining its nightlife, museums, theater, and history, and then look at New York in all these aspects. *See also* POINT-BY-POINT COMPARISON

SUBORDINATING WORDS, 83, 84 A word such as a relative pronoun or a subordinating conjunction that introduces a subordinate clause: "The ice sculpture melted because the ballroom was too hot." Common subordinating words include "although," "as," "because," "if," "since," "that," "which," and "why."

SUMMARY, 23, 53, 93, 785–87 A restatement, in your own words, of the main substance and most important points of a text—useful for reading critically, GENERATING IDEAS by LOOPING, serving as a transition between ideas in your writing, and (when DOCUMENTED) incorporating ideas from other sources.

SYLLOGISM, 596–97 A basic form of DEDUCTIVE reasoning, in which a conclusion to an ARGUMENT is drawn from a major premise or assumption and a minor (or narrower) premise. For example, *Major premise:* All men are mortal. *Minor premise:* Socrates is a man. *Conclusion:* Socrates is mortal.

SYNONYM, 527, 533, 539 A word or phrase that has essentially the same meaning as that of another word or phrase, such as "cope," "carry on," "get by," "make do," "manage," "survive." Synonyms and ANTONYMS are particularly useful in establishing and extending a DEFINITION.

TEXTUAL ANALYSIS An examination of a piece of writing or other text that focuses on what the text says—and how it says it.

THESIS, 6, 35–38, 60–61, 66, 122 The main point of a text. A *thesis statement* is a direct statement of that point.

THIRD PERSON, 119 The grammatical and NARRATIVE point of view—expressed by the personal pronouns "he," "she," "it," and "they"—that limits the narrator to the role of observer, though sometimes an all-knowing one. *See also* FIRST PERSON

The Norton Writer's Prize

I have something to say to the world, and I have taken English 12 in order to say it well.

—W. E. B. DU BOIS

The Norton Writer's Prize recognizes outstanding original nonfiction by undergraduates. All entries are considered for possible publication in Norton texts—in fact, several of the essays that appear in this book were nominated for the prize.

The contest is open to students age 17 and above who are enrolled in an accredited 2- or 4-year college or university. Three cash prizes of $1,000 apiece are awarded annually for coursework submitted during the academic year, one in each of the following three categories:

- writing by a first-year student in a 2- or 4-year college or university
- writing by a student in a 2-year college or university
- writing by a student in a 4-year college or university

Submissions must be between 1,000 and 3,000 words in length. Arguments, analyses, narratives, description essays, reports, memoirs, multimodal pieces, and other forms of original nonfiction will be considered if written by a student age 17 or above in fulfillment of an undergraduate course requirement at an eligible institution. Entries submitted in accordance with the Official Contest Rules will be considered for all applicable prizes, but no more than one prize will be awarded to any single entry.

For full contest rules, eligibility, and instructions on how to enter or nominate students, please visit **wwnorton.com/norton-writers-prize**. For questions, please email us at **composition@wwnorton.com**.

Index of Templates for Drafting

PREVIEWING A TEXT 5

- My ultimate purpose in reading X is _____.

- Judging from the context and title, I would say the main subject of X is _____.

- Skimming the headings and other design elements in X, I see that it is organized by / as / into _____, perhaps indicating _____.

- About the general subject of X, the introductory and concluding paragraphs suggest that the writer is saying, specifically, _____ and/but _____.

- This reading is supported by the overall form and method of the text, which appears to be basically a _____ developed largely by _____.

QUESTIONING A TEXT 7

- On the general subject of _____, the main point of this text seems to be that _____.

- The text supports this thesis mainly through _____ and _____.

- As further evidence for this view, the text also offers _____.

- The ultimate purpose of the text would seem to be _____.

- The overall tone of the text can be described as _____.

- The intended audience for the text is apparently _____.

RESPONDING TO OTHERS 25

Agree

- One of the most respected experts in the field is X, who says essentially that _____.

- Advocates of this view are Y and Z, who also argue that _____.

- Persuaded by these arguments, I agree with those who say _____.

Disagree

- In my view, these objections do not hold up because _____.

- Like some critics of these ideas, particularly X and Y, I would argue instead that _____.

◆ Z's focus on _____ obscures the underlying issue of _____.

Both agree and disagree

◆ Although I concede that _____, I still maintain that _____.

◆ Whereas X and Y make good points about _____, I have to agree with Z that _____.

◆ X may be wrong about _____, but the rest of their argument is persuasive.

STATING A THESIS   61

◆ The main point of this paper is that _____, which is significant because _____.

◆ As this paper will show, recent studies in the field demonstrate not only _____ but also, and more important, _____.

◆ According to the latest evidence, it no longer seems to be the case that _____.

INTRODUCTORY PARAGRAPHS   103

◆ The key points of this paper can be illustrated by a brief story about _____. The story goes like this: _____.

◆ The usual definition of X is _____. The problem with such a definition, however, is that it ignores _____, _____, and _____.

◆ What led up to X, historically, was _____. Recently, however, it has become evident that _____ and _____.

CONCLUDING PARAGRAPHS   106

◆ The takeaway here is clearly _____; however, it is also important to remember that _____.

◆ Why did X have these effects on Y? The ultimate cause seems to have been _____.

◆ Given this state of affairs, the way forward would seem to be _____.

NARRATION   116

◆ This is a story about _____.

◆ The time and place of my story are _____ and _____.

◆ As the narrative opens, X is in the act of _____.

◆ What happened next was _____, followed by _____ and _____.

◆ At this point, _____.

◆ The climax of these events was _____.

◆ When X understood what had happened, he / she / they said, "_____."

- The last thing that happened to X was _____.
- My point in telling this story is to show that _____.

DESCRIPTION   189

- X is like a _____; it has _____, _____, and _____.
- He / She / They looked a lot like _____, except for _____, which _____.
- From the perspective of _____, however, X could be described as _____.
- In some ways, namely _____, X resembles _____; but in other ways, X is more like _____.
- X is not at all like _____ because _____.
- Mainly because of _____ and _____, X gives the impression of being _____.
- From this description of X, you can see that _____.

EXAMPLE   256

- About X, it can generally be said that _____; a good example would be _____.
- The main characteristics of X are _____ and _____, as exemplified by _____, _____, and _____.
- For the best example(s) of X, we can turn to _____.
- _____ is a particularly representative example of X because _____.
- Additional examples of X include _____, _____, and _____.
- From these examples of X, we can conclude that _____.

PROCESS ANALYSIS   298

- The process of X can be divided into the following steps: _____, _____, _____, and _____.
- The steps that make up X usually occur (or can be arranged) in the following order: _____, _____, _____, _____, and _____.
- The end result of X is _____.
- To repeat X and achieve this result, the following tools and materials are needed: _____, _____, and _____.
- The main reasons for understanding / repeating X are _____, _____, and _____.

CRITICAL ANALYSIS   304

- The text itself can be broken down into the following basic components: _____, _____, and _____.

- Presented in _____ order, these components take the general form of a / an _____ on the subject of _____.

- The writer's ideas on this subject are most clearly stated (or implied) when they say _____ and _____.

- In support of these views, the writer offers the following evidence: _____, _____, and _____; that evidence is (is not) sufficient because _____ and _____.

- The accuracy of the writer's conclusions and the significance of this text can be summed up as follows: _____, _____, and _____.

CAUSE AND EFFECT 356

- The main cause/effect of X is _____.

- X would also seem to have a number of contributing causes, including _____, _____, and _____.

- Some additional effects of X are _____, _____, and _____.

- Among the most important remote causes/effects of X are _____, _____, and _____.

- Although the causes of X are not known, we can speculate that a key factor is _____.

- X cannot be attributed to mere chance or coincidence because _____.

- Once we know what causes X, we are in a position to say that _____.

COMPARISON AND CONTRAST 409

- X and Y can be compared on the grounds that both are _____.

- Like X, Y is also _____, _____, and _____.

- Although X and Y are both _____, the differences between them far outweigh the similarities. For example, X is _____, _____, and _____, while Y is _____, _____, and _____.

- Unlike X, Y is _____.

- Despite their differences, X and Y are basically alike in that _____.

- At first glance, X and Y seem _____; however, a closer look reveals _____.

- In comparing X and Y, we can see that _____.

CLASSIFICATION 465

- X can be classified on the basis of _____.

- Classified on the basis of _____, some of the most common types of X are _____, _____, and _____.

- X can be divided into two basic types, _____ and _____.

- Experts in the field typically divide X into _____, _____, and _____.
- This particular X clearly belongs in the _____ category, since it is _____, _____, and _____.
- _____, _____, and _____ are examples of this type of X.
- By classifying X in this way, we can see that _____.

DEFINITION   534

- In general, X can be defined as a kind of _____.
- What specifically distinguishes X from others in this category is _____.
- Other important distinguishing characteristics of X are _____, _____, and _____.
- X is often used to mean _____, but a better synonym would be _____ or _____.
- One way to define X is as the opposite of _____, the distinguishing characteristics of which are _____, _____, and _____.
- If we define X as _____, we can then define Y as _____.
- By defining X in this way, we can see that _____.

ARGUMENT   595

- In this argument about X, the main point I want to make is _____.
- Others may say _____, but I would argue that _____.
- My contention about X is supported by the fact that _____.
- Additional facts that support this view of X are _____, _____, and _____.
- My own experience with X shows that _____ because _____.
- My view of X is supported by _____, who says that X is _____.
- What you should do about X is _____.

BRIEF MENU OF READINGS

+Annotated student writing   *New to the 5e

READ AND CHECK YOUR UNDERSTANDING
The Norton Illumine Ebook includes Check Your Understanding questions for every chapter and reading in the text, helping you gauge your understanding as you read, with personalized feedback along the way.

PRACTICE WRITING, RESEARCHING, AND SENTENCE EDITING
InQuizitive for Writers' self-paced activities and animated videos help you become a more confident and prepared writer and researcher. Students agree! "I loved using InQuizitive. I was able to practice, and it helped me grow." —Jena G., student at Pearl River Community College

FIND MORE HELP FOR DOCUMENTING SOURCES AND EDITING
Visit *The Little Seagull Handbook* ebook, a brief, easy-to-use reference for editing your writing and documenting sources using MLA, APA, CSE, or Chicago style.

Access all these resources, included for
free with new copies of this book, at
digital.wwnorton.com/backtothelake5

Cover design: Georgia Feldman Design
Cover images: Book: Javier Zayas Photography/Getty Images;
dragonfly: Darkdiamond67/Shutterstock

WWNORTON.COM/EDUCATOR

ISBN 978-1-324-06025-3

90000

9 781324 060253